b14134883

YO-BKD-463

WITHDRAWN

Center for Basque Studies
Conference Papers Series, No. 15

IGOR AHEDO GURRUTXAGA

The Transformation of National Identity in the Basque Country of France, 1789–2006

Translated by

Cameron J. Watson

Center for Basque Studies
University of Nevada, Reno
Reno, Nevada

The Center for Basque Studies wishes to gratefully acknowledge the generous financial support of the Bizkaiko Foru Aldundia / Provincial Government of Bizkaia for the publication of this book.

This book was published with generous financial support from the Basque Government.

Center for Basque Studies
Occasional Papers Series, No. 15
Series Editor: Joseba Zulaika

Center for Basque Studies
University of Nevada, Reno
Reno, Nevada 89557
http://basque.unr.edu

Copyright © 2008 by the Center for Basque Studies
All rights reserved. Printed in the United States of America.

Cover and Series design © 2008 Jose Luis Agote.
Cover photograph: Gaizka Iroz, 2005.
 Ximun Haran, speaking in Itsasu on the anniversary of the 1963 declaration that marked the foundational document of Basque nationalism in Iparralde.

Library of Congress Cataloging-in-Publication Data

Ahedo Gurrutxaga, Igor.
 The transformation of national identity in the Basque country of France, 1789-2006 / Igor Ahedo Gurrutxaga ; translated by Cameron J. Watson.
   p. cm. -- (Conference papers series ; no. 15) (Occasional papers series ; no. 15)
 Includes bibliographical references and index.
 Summary: "This work traces the meaning of identity in the Basque Country of France between the late eighteenth century and the present, including French state-building efforts in promoting a French national identity, attempts to encourage French and Basque sentiment, and the emergence of Basque nationalism with its emphasis on a Basque national identity"--Provided by publisher.
 ISBN 978-1-877802-78-2 (hardcover) -- ISBN 978-1-877802-79-9 (pbk.)
 1. Basques--France--Ethnic identity. 2. Pays Basque (France)--History--Autonomy and independence movements. 3. Minorities--Government policy--France. 4. France--Politics and government. 5. Pays Basque (France)--Politics and government. I. Title. II. Series.

DC611.B318A44 2008
944'.716--dc22

2008040429

IGOR AHEDO GURRUTXAGA

The Transformation of National Identity in the Basque Country of France, 1789–2006

TABLE OF CONTENTS

List of Abbreviations	11
Introduction	15
Chapter One – A "Living Museum"	21
Chapter Two – Basque Identity and the Spread of Nationalism in Iparralde	45
Chapter Three – Dominique-Joseph Garat and the "New Phoenicia"	53
Chapter Four – Chaho: Father of the "People of Light"	73
Chapter Five – Sabino Arana and the "Two Brothers"	89
Chapter Six – Lafitte and the Death and Resurrection of Basque Identity: The Eskualerriste Movement	97
Chapter Seven – Legasse: At the Vanguard of the Rear Guard of the Basque Nation	113
Chapter Eight – Between the Calm and the Storm	127
Chapter Nine – Enbata: The Wind Before the Storm	147
Chapter Ten – The Storm	179
Chapter Eleven – The Decade of Change	207
Chapter Twelve – The Strength of Basque Nationalism in Local Political Dynamics	239
Chapter Thirteen – The Emergence of the Territory	267
Chapter Fourteen – Toward a New Horizon	281
Conclusion	305
Afterword	311
Notes	315
Bibliography	361
Index	383

List of Abbreviations

AB: Abertzaleen Batasuna; Nationalist Unity, a Basque nationalist party in Iparralde

ADPB: Association pour le Département Pays Basque; the Association for a *Département* of the Basque Country

AED: Association des Élus pour un Département Pays Basque; the Association of Elected Officials for a *Département* of the Basque Country

AEK: Alfabetatze eta Euskalduntze Koordinakundea; Coordination of Education and Literacy in Euskara

AND: Association pour un Nouveau Département; the Association in Favor of a New *Département*

ANV: Acción Nacionalista Vasca; Basque Nationalist Action, a Basque nationalist party in Hegoalde

BAB: the Baiona-Angelu-Biarritz conurbation

BVE: Batallón Vasco-Español; the Spanish Basque Battalion

CAA: Comandos Autónomos Anticapitalistas; the Anticapitalist Autonomous Commandos in Hegoalde

CCI: Chambre de Commerce et d'Industrie; the Baiona Chamber of Commerce and Industry

CD: Centre Démocratique; the Democratic Center, a French centrist party

CDPB: Conseil du Développement du Pays Basque; the Development Council of the Basque Country

CEPB: Conseil des Élus du Pays Basque; the Counsil of Elected Officials of the Basque Country

CFDT: Confédération Française Démocratique du Travail, the French Democratic Confederation of Labor

Demo: Demokrazia Euskal Herriarentzat; Democracy for the Basque Country, a Basque nationalist civil disobedience group

DL: Démocratie Libéral; Liberal Democracy

EA: Eusko Alkartasuna; Basque Solidarity, a social democratic Basque nationalist party

EAS: Euskal Alderdi Sozialista, the Basque Socialist Party in Hegoalde

EB: Euskal Batasuna; Basque Unity

EE: Euskadiko Ezkerra, the Basque Left, a party later integrated into the PSE

EGB: Eskualdun Gazteen Biltzarra; the Association of Basque Youth

EGI: Eusko Gaztedi del Interior; Basque Youth of the Interior, the PNV youth wing

EH: Euskal Herritarrok; Basque Compatriots, a later incarnation of HB in Hegoalde

EHAS: Euskal Herriko Alderdi Sozialista, the Socialist Party of the Basque Country

EHBai: Euskal Herria Bai; the Basque Country, Yes, a coalition of Basque nationalist parties

EIA: Euskal Iraultzarako Alderdia, the Basque Revolutionary Party, a creation of ETA (pm) in Hegoalde

EKE: Euskal Kultur Erakundea; the Basque Cultural Institute

ELA-STV: Eusko Langileen Alkartasuna-Solidaridad de Trabajadores Vascos; the Basque Workers' Union

ELB: Euskal Laborien Batasuna; the Basque Workers' Union, a union of agricultural workers in Iparralde; ; later renamed Euskal Herriko Laborarien Batasuna, United Workers of the Basque Country

EMA: Ezkerreko Mugimendu Abertzalea; the Basque Patriotic Movement of the Left

ETA: Euskadi ta Askatasuna; Basque Country and Freedom

ETA (m): The "military" faction of ETA

ETA (pm): The "political" faction of ETA

ETA-V: A faction of ETA defined by its adherence to the primacy of nationalist struggle

ETA-VI: A faction of ETA defined by its emphasis on Marxist-Leninist class struggle

ETB: Euskal Telebista, the public television service of the Basque Autonomous Community

FDSEA: Fédérations Départementales des Syndicats d'Exploitants Agricoles; Departmental Federations of Agricultural Producers' Unions

FLNC: Fronte di Liberazione Naziunale di a Corsica; the Front for the National Liberation of Corsica

- FRAP: Frente Revolucionario Antifascista y Patriota; the Revolutionary Anti-Fascist and Patriotic Front
- GAL: Grupos Antiterroristas de Liberación, Antiterrorist Liberation Groups
- HAS: Herriko Alderdi Sozialista, the Popular Socialist Party
- HASI: Herriko Alderdi Sozialista Iraultzailea; the Popular Revolutionary Socialist Party
- HB: Herri Batasuna; the Popular Unity party, in Hegoalde, radical left-wing Basque nationalist party
- HA: Herriaren Alde; On the Side of the People
- HT: Herri Taldeak; Popular Groups
- IK: Iparetarrak, "those of ETA from the North" in Euskara, a group dedicated to using violence to achieve national liberation in Iparralde
- IU: Izquierda Unida, the United Left, a Spanish Communist political party
- KAS: Koordinadora Abertzale Sozialista; the Socialist Nationalist Coordinating Council in Hegoalde
- MDB: Mouvement Démocratique Basque; the Basque Democratic Movement
- MLNV: Movimiento de Liberación Nacional Vasco; the Basque National Liberation Movement in Hegoalde, also known as the Izquierda Abertzale, or Left-Wing Basque Nationalism
- MoDem: Mouvement Démocratique; the Democratic Movement
- MOP: Maîtrise d'Ouvrage Publique; Master of Public Works
- MRC : Mouvement Républicain et Citoyen ; the Citizen and Republican Movement
- MRP: Mouvement Républicain Populaire; the Popular Republican Movement, a Christian Democratic party in France
- PCF: Parti Communiste Français; the French Communist Party
- PSU: Parti Socialiste Unifié; the Unified Socialist Party, a splinter of the French Socialist Party
- PNB: Parti Nationaliste Basque, the Basque Nationalist party, the PNV in Iparralde
- PNV: Partido Nacionalista Vasco; the Basque Nationalist Party
- PP: Partido Popular; the Popular Party, the Spanish conservative party
- PS: Parti Socialiste; the French Socialist Party
- PSE: Partido Socialista de Euskadi, the Socialist Party of the Basque Country, affiliated with the PSOE
- PSOE: Partido Socialista Obrero de España, the Spanish Socialist Party

RPF: Rassemblement du Peuple Français, Rally of the French People, a Gaullist party in France

RPR: Rassemblement pour la République; Rally for the Republic, a Gaullist party in France

SFIO: Section Française de l'Internationale Ouvrière, the French Section of the Workers' International, the French Socialist Party

SNCF: Société Nationale Chemins de Fer, the French national railroad service

UDF: Union pour la Démocratie Française; the Union for French Democracy

UDR: Union des Démocrates pour la République; the Union of Democrats for the Republic

UMP: Union pour un Mouvement Populaire; Union for a Popular Movement

UNR: Union pour la Nouvelle République; Union for the New Republic, the successor party to the RPF

Introduction

Before setting out to trace the eventual development of a sense of Basque identity and Basque nationalism in Iparralde, the northern or French Basque Country,[1] it is first necessary to trace briefly the theories of nationalism (and identity) on which the following work is based.[2] I understand by the term "peripheral nationalism" those political movements whose discourse rests on the articulation of a clearly differential identity, a minimum level of internal organization, and a stable external projection within their own community, which they define as a nation. As a result, such movements clearly and explicitly seek to wrest political power from the center (the state) on which the territory in question—which the movement claims as its own—depends. Such demands for political power may be adapted by these nationalist movements in light of their strength in relation to the central authority. That is, they might, for tactical or strategic reasons, adopt (in most cases) any of the following goals: regionalism, autonomy, federalism, sovereignty, or independence.

These ideas underpin several important perspectives that govern this exploration of the issues of identity and nationalism in Iparralde. For example, cultural claims alone, however well organized, are not enough for a movement to be considered nationalist, because peripheral nationalism implies the specific goal of seeking political power for the periphery based on its self-definition as a nation. Moreover, it is crucial that such a demand is directed toward a center (or centers) on which the differentiated community depends. In turn, the same demand implies a differential and differentiating strategy in the political activity of the movement or its adherents, compared with other, nonnationalist groups. Furthermore, the fact that there are certain people who define themselves as nationalists within a given historical era does not necessarily mean that nationalism exists as a sociologically meaningful political reality. Rather, as mentioned above, for nationalism to exist in meaningful terms, there must be a clearly articulated discourse, a degree of internal organization, and an external program designed to seek political power. Finally, while its adherents may possess a dual identity (that of the periphery and that of the center), the feeling of belonging that underscores the movement must ultimately rest on the territory in which it aspires to achieve political power.

In other words, in the example under consideration here, one cannot speak about Basque nationalism in Iparralde until 1963, when the Enbata movement presented its objectives in the Itsasu Charter. Prior to this, there were individual Basque nationalists, such as Marc Legasse in the 1940s, but one cannot properly speak in terms of an organized nationalist movement. Similarly, further back in history, there were individuals (such as Dominique-Joseph Garat in the late eighteenth century or Agosti Chaho in the early and mid-nineteenth century) and political movements (such as Aintzina in the 1930s) that contained elements that later came to characterize Basque nationalism. For the purposes of this work, however, I will not discuss these individuals and movements as nationalists. At most, one might speak of them as protonationalists, having noted that—through their discourse and practice—they foreshadowed the development of Basque nationalism in Iparralde.

In fact, the politico-cultural demands and the territorial recognition demanded of the center by Garat, Chaho, and Aintzina remained subordinate to an uneven sense of identity. That is, they all felt a dual sense of belonging that gave rise to a logic of the (political) *grande patrie*, or France, thereby abrogating any need for a peripheral political agenda, and the (cultural) *petite patrie* (the Basque Country), which was relegated to the realm of cultural socialization. From this perspective, one can understand the emergence of Basque nationalism in Iparralde only when this uneven sense of identity was inverted as a result of the politicization of cultural activity. When this took place, a new logic emerged whereby the former *petite patrie* became the sole nation for the movement, despite the continued adherence of some individuals to a dual sense of identity. Only from this moment on can one properly speak of a Basque national idea in Iparralde, an idea whose political and organizational projection was based on the definition of nationalism that I will follow in this work.

I understand nationalism as "a political (collective behavior organized around a nationalist ideology directed at obtaining thus defined objectives) and ideological (doctrinal) movement related to political power." Nationalism is thus a "type of political behavior that implicitly carries with it proposals of a normative character" with the goal of "preserving the nation and defending its special interests."[3] To expand on this general notion, Pedro Ibarra notes,

> nationalism asserts the necessity of political power for the nation, because it understands that this people, this *demos*, who shape the nation are and can be the only authentic people insofar that they do not depend on any other. Every people, every nation, considers itself different from the other nations and believes it can be different, believes it can sustain as a credible fact that notion of "singularity" (which gives it internal cohesion and loyalty) only if it is not governed by another nation and its corresponding state.[4]

As a result, "the demand for political power by the nation is the essential feature of nationalism," that is, a political exigency "above all, from the position of a single, different and autonomous people."[5] Consequently, it is hardly surprising that Anthony D. Smith differentiates between "an organized ideological movement of nationalism, on the one hand, and a more diffuse feeling of national belonging, on the other." Such a distinction, he continues, is "sufficiently clear to allow us to treat the concept of national consciousness or sentiment separately from that of nationalism, even if in practice there is often some degree of overlap between them."[6] In other words, one can see in the discourses of Garat and Chaho, for example, a protonational or even national consciousness without this implying that Basque nationalism existed during the time in which they lived.

When I refer to nationalism in these terms, I base my analysis on two key concepts: the nation and a differential consciousness or sense of belonging or identity. However, in this work, I do not adopt a conventional approach. That is, I get around the eternal debate about the authenticity of both notions as applied to the Basque case–the existence of *one* single Basque nation or of *one* single Basque national identity–by proposing an inverse perspective.

As Benjamín Tejerina contends,[7] "the configuration of collective identity . . . is based on common attributes or participation in symbolic common acts," elements "that are converted by actors into categories of attachment or identification" with a special emphasis on "generating difference with other social groups, that is, they establish limits or boundaries between groups." Despite all this, however, the importance of such attributes does not stem from their precise or scientifically demonstrable reality. Nor does it even seem possible, for Tejerina, "to determine the cultural content, and symbolic common attributes and acts" that are supposed to configure a collective identity, given that from a purely scientific point of view, "it is impossible to form a definition" of such an identity. Instead, the importance of common attributes and common symbolic acts stems from their "social meaning." In fact, although one cannot frame a specific definition of collective identity, "the same is not true of the discourse maintained by the actors about the consciousness of group belonging."[8] This is a question that ultimately refers to the main goal of the present work: that is, an analysis not only of the existence of a nation, but of the form in which this is understood as a "reality" or as "social evidence," in that it is shared collectively by "its" members.

In similar fashion, for Walker Connor, nationalist behavior stems "not from *what is*, but [from] what people *believe is*,"[9] to the extent that (citing Walter Sulzbach) "a history of national consciousness should not, like a history of philosophy, simply describe the thought of a limited number of eminent men without regard to the extent of their following. As in the histories of religion, we need to know what response the masses have given to different doctrines."[10] However, the response of the masses to nationalist discourse– whether true or not–is not created out of nothing, but rather is influenced by the relationship or conflict between these proposals and those of the objectified state community in which the peripheral community is located.

I will examine in circular fashion (although not necessarily in a circle of the ever-decreasing variety)[11] the form in which the French-Basque identity conflict was resolved in Iparralde through a zero-sum game in which the creation of the French state was followed by a crisis of Basque identity, together with both an objective and subjective blurring of the Basque territory. However, the very complexity of this process highlights the key role played by two important figures–Garat and Chaho–who, despite assuming a centralized logic (both were fervent republicans), through their discourse also began to foment those "common attributes" described by Tejerina and to convert them into differentiating boundaries.

To outline the concepts involved in the development of Basque nationalism in France, I should add to this initial (objectifying) sketch with a subjective premise that is also an important influence on the general analysis to follow: my attempt to capture the form in which these common attributes were developed (or not, and why) among the population in Iparralde. In effect, the very impossibility of any such development during the initial period under study here leads one again into the terrain of French-Basque identity conflict and the concomitant zero-sum game. In other words, there are only three possible explanations for the impossibility of such a development: the differentiating attributes initially developed by Garat and Chaho were unacceptable to the populace as a whole, or there was insufficient willpower among elites at that time to encourage them, or both factors were at play, thereby denying any possibility that Basque nationalism could have emerged during this period. Forcing the argument somewhat, one might speak, at most, of the emergence of a diffuse feeling of national belonging within the discourses of Garat and Chaho. I say "forcing the argument" because, of course, both individuals felt an unproblematic connection to France, and at no moment did they ever envisage an organized ideological Basque nationalist movement.

Much later, in the 1930s, the Aintzina movement drew on the work of these earlier figures and gave their ideas a political twist. Does this, then, mean that it became a nationalist movement? I do not think so, because, although a minimum degree of political organization did exist within Aintzina, the diffuse feeling of national belonging of which Smith speaks[12] never managed to overcome the logic of two *patries* established by Garat and Chaho in Iparralde and driven still further into the zero-sum game by the effects of World War I. As a result, the preeminence of the *grande patrie* (France) over the *petite patrie* (the Basque Country) prevented any movement from emerging that developed an ideology around one nation, fundamentally, I would argue, because, even despite the wishes of some of its leaders, in practice, Aintzina still recognized two nations.

However, a few years later, a form of Basque nationalism did emerge in Iparralde, although not as a movement, but rather as a consummate personal expression of national consciousness. This individual expression, in both the discourse of Legasse and, slightly earlier (from within Aintzina) in that Eugène Goyheneche, together with that of some of their followers, however, was unable to develop into an organized movement. Here, once again, I will highlight the public response to these ideas, based on a rational analysis not of the (nationalist) "idea," but of the form in which the public responded to it (or not).

Ultimately, I will examine how and why an expressly political Basque nationalist movement, Enbata, emerged in the early 1960s. Yet it is impossible to understand this development without first considering the notions of identity that were developed previously by Garat, Chaho, Aintzina, and Legasse, to which one should add the seductive effects of a more rooted nationalism in the Basque-Navarrese territories to the south.

That said, nationalism in Iparralde was and is not just a question of the past and the present, but also of the future. As such, I will closely examine the arguments of the early nationalists (Enbata), together with those of the forerunners (Garat, Chaho, and so on) and the broader influences from the southern Basque Country or Hegoalde (from Arturo Campión, Sabino Arana, and so on), in order to understand the uncertain nature that the future held for the movement, a future that was strongly influenced in France and Europe by the growth of progressive ideologies in the 1960s. Finally, I note that all of this was, moreover, framed by the extension of political violence to Iparralde in the 1970s and 1980s, with clear consequences for both the population as a whole and its feeling of belonging.

As a result of these developments, Basque nationalism in Iparralde went gradually down a kind of blind alley. Once its political proposals were explicitly stated, it realized the limits of socially diffusing its central idea. It thus entered a new (and the current) stage of its historical development, a time in which Basque nationalism went back to its origins: that is, in a strategy in which the zero-sum game based on the subordination of its differentiating attributes to the centralizing efforts of the French state was broken open when Basque nationalists positioned themselves at the core of these same attributes, a positioning that was based on making the notion of territory a central feature of the dynamic.

From this moment on, territory thus became a more flexible attribute than earlier characteristics such as language, history, or traditions. As such, it has come to serve Basque nationalists more fruitfully, within the dynamic of economic development and local recognition, as a base from which to overcome previously established breakwaters. Ever since the development of Basque nationalism in France entered its present stage of "necessary differentiation" based on the notion of a territory taken back by the citizenry, it would seem nationalism has been in a better position to develop wider support through the use of other differentiating elements, such as language, tradition, and history, a strategy previously unthinkable for many people in Iparralde, given the need of the Basque populace to become "uniform" French citizens.

This, however, is a process that has just begun in the twenty-first century, and we still have a good way to go before arriving at this most recent state of affairs. Let us first, then, start from the beginning.

CHAPTER ONE

A "Living Museum"

At the close of the nineteenth century, Louis de Fourcaud, the French minister of public instruction and fine arts, pronounced the following words on the occasion of the opening of a conference on Basque traditions in Donibane Lohizune (Saint-Jean-de-Luz):

> There is a culture that enlivens: it is the tradition of spontaneous thoughts handed down from generation to generation. There is a tradition that drains and kills: the tradition of formulas. Things of the past, in some ways, persevere among those today . . . How much wisdom is often clarified by consulting a people on their customs, habits and language! Without this contradicting the fact that, from an advanced perspective, some of us do, and will, rely on others. Yet it is not true that an advanced point of view requires useless sacrifices. No, however many Basques you are, you will be better as Frenchmen. You will work with all your strength for the progress of your province. And you will provide France—sweet France, as the poets used to say—with original attributes.[1]

He was right. Even though previously there had been some proponents of Basque unity—such as Dominique-Joseph Garat, Agosti Chaho, and Antoine d'Abbadie—whose writings seemed to echo a certain protonationalism, at the time that Fourcaud spoke, there was no organized nationalist movement in Iparralde. The "original attributes" of which the minister spoke—that is, objective facts such as the existence of a different language—were not politicized. *Fin-de-siècle* Iparralde had not witnessed a progression from cultural or linguistic difference to political mobilization, as had occurred, for example, a few years earlier in Bizkaia, to the south.

On the other hand, Fourcaud's notion that however many Basques there were, they would be better off being French must have sounded profoundly important to the inhabitants of Iparralde at century's end. At the time, most northern Basques had begun to take for granted the notions—presented with a certain urgency in the face of Sabino Arana's cultural and political wake-up call for Basque identity[2] in the southern Basque Country—presented by the French minister:

> I compare the provinces to different families, equal in rights and duties, sharing things among themselves, inseparably united by common bonds. In the same way that family

has its name and traditions, its heritage . . . each province has its personality, its means, its inheritance. Each one its particularism and together they are absorbed into the indivisible nation. Not one nation to the exclusion of others, but a nation that, at the same time, is in one and all. Thus an indissoluble organism is strengthened.[3]

This is the point of departure for considering the question of identity in Iparralde at the end of the nineteenth century: the belief that particular identities should be absorbed by the French nation, with the nation understood as an indissoluble organism. The truth of the matter is that it makes little difference whether Minister Fourcaud's observations were correct or not. It is not my aim here to judge their veracity, just as it is not the task of the sociologist of religion to judge whether God exists or not.[4] What is important is that both God and the French nation exist as indissoluble entities in the eyes of many people, and France existed for the population of Iparralde at the end of the nineteenth century. However, it is equally important to note that these words would have been questioned by important numbers of people in Hegoalde who had discovered Basque nationalism at the end of the nineteenth century, a movement that, by the time of the Spanish Civil War (1936–39), had evolved into a significant social and political force.

Why such a contradiction between the North and the South? Why were such "original attributes" such as Euskara (the Basque language) abandoned to their fate in Iparralde, while in Hegoalde, they formed the platform from which a dynamic of cultural and linguistic renaissance took off? Why such an inverse reflection? The answers to these questions lie in the different patterns of state building on each side of the border, as well as in the way that the national idea (scarcely of any "real" importance, given that it was imagined) was accepted (or not) in Iparralde and Hegoalde.

This leads me to the starting point in examining the development of notions of Basque identity in Iparralde, a process that has possessed both subjective and objective dimensions: an "external" dynamic (managed from Paris), expressed in objective, real, and concrete action by a French state whose aim was to cover up the differential elements that might have generated a distinct (Basque) identity to compete with that of France, and an "internal" dynamic (integrated by the population of Iparralde) that was based on the subjective assumption of belonging to the French nation.

I will thus veer between different state strategies and the way in which these were accepted by the population as a whole to reach this starting point: the Basque linguistic and identity crisis that emerged after World War I, an event that made French identity omnipresent and omnipotent over its Basque counterpart, but that also led to the bases by which a sense of Basque identity emerged, grew, and was transformed so that it might be reborn in phoenixlike fashion.[5] First though, some discussion is required of the territorial arrangements that delimited the French and Spanish states, the root cause dividing the Basque community and the basic circumstance that conditioned its integration into two distinct national projects.

Territory as a Condition of Plausibility

Objectively, territory is the basic condition on which a given state exists. Territory configures the framework by which the state is qualified to exercise the legitimate monopoly of violence over its citizens. For that reason, for its very existence, the state needs to be obeyed, and such obedience is forthcoming when its citizens perceive themselves as members of a specific community and no other.[6]

This, in turn, requires at least two complimentary processes: As we will see, the state must construct a national society to sustain its existence, resulting in the creation of a unified market and an efficient administrative structure, the political socialization of the masses through mandatory universal education, and/or their integration through political mechanisms such as universal suffrage. However, this objectification is insufficient without also anchoring the idea of the state within the consciousnesses of the people. Thus, it is essential that both the state and national society also construct a national community from a base of a political culture that nourishes the loyalty of the citizenry to the state and that generates a feeling of belonging to the nation.[7] Delimitation and difference are, then, determining factors in the establishment of modern states.

Language, communication networks, the administrative structure, the press and publishing, health and social security policies, and so on allow people to feel tied in some way to the rest of the community, sharing the same destiny and same day-to-day experiences. In other words, this is an "imagined community" that generates loyalty and similarities between people who will never know one another personally or interact directly.[8] These are all factors that reinforce a communal subjectivity. However, one of them, due to its delimiting character, is more sensitive (to put it one way) than all the others: A border, by its very nature, makes a periphery part of a state. As Hastings Donnan and Thomas M. Wilson put it, "borders are political membranes through which people, goods, wealth, and information must pass in order to be deemed acceptable or unacceptable by the state. Thus borders are agents of a state's security and sovereignty, and a physical record of a state's past and present relations with its neighbours."[9] Consequently, the border excludes because it becomes the limit to which state-based nationalism extends, and further, because this same nationalism must prevent any expansion of the vectors that legitimate the neighboring state or states.

In their processes of consolidation, states need, respectively, "areas of contact" to be also "areas of exclusion" for their citizens. This has been even truer in the Basque case, for in the eighteenth century, it became a meeting point for the construction of two different state models, whose clash led to the definitive fragmentation of a community united by a common language and culture. Since 1789, (the point at which the French Revolution broke out), the Basque border has marked the line between two models of state construction: that of a liberal revolutionary nation-state to the north and a conservative *ancien régime* state to the south—in other words, a buffer zone between heresy (for some) and reaction (for others). That border originated for several political and economic reasons.[10] The 1679 Treaty of the Pyrenees delimited the border for the first time in a charter designed to "seal peace between the two monarchies, at odds through continual confrontations." However, beside politico-diplomatic considerations, there were also economic issues between the peoples who lived on either side of the Bidasoa River (the principal "natural" dividing line between Iparralde and Hegoalde) when it came to drawing up the border. Thus, for example, agreements made over common land between communities on different sides of the *muga* (border), but within the same valley, to avoid confrontation over use of such terrain for livestock, came to explain the flexible nature of a later settlement drawn up during the mid-eighteenth century.[11]

Although the political and administrative boundary between France and Spain was agreed to on the premise of taking account of previous economic relations between the border communities, at root, it represented the logic of creating two states that needed a clear demarcation of the territories in which they exercised their sovereignty. However, for any lasting success, this process of politico-administrative objectification also needed the clear demarcation of difference between the peoples of the two states, and above all between those most sensitive to the changes: the border people.

The history of confrontation between France and Spain was crucial to the process of creating both states. Spanish incursions into Lapurdi in the seventeenth century and the concomitant French occupation of Gipuzkoa in the long run gave rise to a growing connection of Basques to either France or Spain. Txomin Peillen has shown that such attachments were unknown at the beginning of that same century. Furthermore, as the seventeenth century wore on, a feeling of loyalty to and protection from their respective states led Basques to an irreversible process of division.[12]

Linguistic unification during the early years of the French Revolution played a crucial role in this process. Specifically, new elites "tried to establish a linguistic barrier in the Franco-Spanish demarcation, in order to halt cross-border contacts in the same language."[13] Similarly, the French revolutionaries found, in these cross-border tongues, an obstacle to creating a unified market—that is, the founding of a national society. As a result, Euskara became a doubly threatening enemy for the process of state construction. It defied the necessary imposition of one unified state language and, as a cross-border language, it recognized no political limits, only human ones.

Eventually, the differentiating nature of two obligatory national educational systems, two communication systems, two "national" languages and literatures, and the pro-European vocation of France throughout the twentieth century and the isolationism of Spain during the Franco years (1939–75) resulted in the creation among Basques of the most important of all boundaries: a mental one. Consequently, for many decades, a Basque dividing line was marked out by using elements identified with the respective states—from traffic signals to urban architecture. As Zoe Bray has noted, it is "starkly evident for the person crossing [the border] that he or she is going from one particular space to another. Just as in ritual passages, this change in context obliges the individual to reflect on his or her position in relation to the changing environment."[14]

With the French and Spanish having thus established (agreed on, for some—imposed, for others) the border between the two states, the process of creating nation-states began. As observed earlier, this process required two developments: the founding of a national society that would be *created* deliberately by an apparatus of political control on behalf of a class, political party, and so on and the emergence of a national community that would be *formed* in a conflictual, involuntary, and largely unconscious process, steered in the disorder of confrontation and commitment by a mass of anonymous citizens.[15] Below, I will explore more fully the factors that objectified (or constructed) the state for its citizenry (territory, language, education, the military, a unified administration, and so on). For now, in order to understand how effective this process was, we should examine the formulas that allowed (or formed) individual loyalty to the new project, formulas that gradually emerged by means of the media of communication, that were taught in school, that were spoken in French, and that, ultimately, reclaimed their debt in blood and honor.

The Objective and Subjective Integration of the Nation

Ludger Mees, Santiago de Pablo, and José Antonio Rodríguez highlight a key difference in the contradictory evolution of identity on both sides of the border: the two different ways in which the process of state construction took place and the effects of this for the development of Basque identity:

> While in France, postrevolutionary elites, especially those of the Third Republic [1870–1940], faced creating the nation and all the problems that this entailed with an active, aggressive and even "colonialist" attitude, thereby making this objective the principal feature of its public budget of the new nationalist discourse, in nineteenth-century Spain, passivity, inefficiency, and incapacity prevailed. The weakness of the liberal state and its precarious financial situation resulted in its lowest point of nation building and enormous difficulties in the problem of dissemination, participation in identity, and legitimacy. The nation was only half-constructed, which, in many ways, was hardly surprising, given that, according to the dominant moderate discourse of the time, there was nothing to create, for this Spanish nation was already a historical phenomenon with a long trajectory whose roots were lost in the mists of time. Within the frame of this setting of loose and incomplete nation building, local and regional loyalties and distinctions never integrated into the Spanish nation. By contrast to what happened in the French state, sufficient space remained for their survival and, in some cases, for their evolution toward alternative national projects. In sum, peripheral nationalisms did not destroy a supposed Spanish national unity, but rather the failure of Spanish nationalism in the nineteenth century, or the crisis of its social diffusion, facilitated as a response the political success of alternative nationalisms.[16]

These authors underscore the contrast between the processes of state construction in France and Spain, making special note of the respective elites' discourses and practices and their effectiveness in convincing the rest of the population. In this sense, the role of centrist elites in both Paris and Madrid was crucial, because they bore, elaborated, and translated the discourse that sought to question, mobilize, and integrate the peripheral peoples into the new national project. Ultimately, they achieved this in France, but only partially in Spain. Yet discourse alone was not enough. It was also necessary to present a structure of plausibility and possibility that would allow such discourse to be incorporated or accepted by the people. In other words, the idea of belonging to the French nation, beyond being based merely on some kind of objective truth, had to be made credible to the people. Let us now examine the elements that made up this structure of plausibility and that made French citizenship seem credible to the inhabitants of the French Basque Country.

Modernization and Periphery in Iparralde

This dual process of state building, by creating a national society and national community, discriminates against other groups that differ from the dominant centrist one. The groups that suffer such discrimination do not, as a result, have full, equal access to the cultural, political, and occasionally economic benefits distributed by the state. Such groups may remain passive or even resist, initially, in defense of their language, religion, or culture. Later, they might even demand some kind of political institutionalization for their territory.[17] Whatever the case, the emergence and consistency of such peripheral nationalist movements will depend on how strong the dual construction of a national community and national society is by the center. In turn, this depends on the center's capacity to create a cohesive market. Thus, while in the French case there was no contradiction between the localization of the political and economic centers (both emanating from Paris), in the Spanish case, the political periphery (the Basque Country and Catalonia) actually formed the driving economic force of the state. In part, this explains the different levels of development achieved by peripheral movements in the two states.

In this way, the basic conditions for the objective and subjective integration of the state were optimum in the French case. That is, there were scarcely any impediments to state consolidation, especially at the end of the nineteenth century. In Hegoalde, however, a structure of plausibility existed that allowed for an economic elite to successfully demand the right for the Basque periphery to develop as both an economic and a political center. These centers, in turn, thus possessed practical and differential qualities that were politically useful for advocating Basque differential attributes such as language, traditions, and history. By contrast, due to its peripheral political and economic nature, the conditions did not exist in Iparralde for an economic elite to elaborate (either successfully or not) a discourse that reclaimed Basque political difference based on linguistic (or historical, or cultural, or tradition-based) particularity.

For a nationalist discourse to develop as a response to the modernization process, the role of local intelligentsia is crucial. Specifically, they try to give political form to their respective cultures or differentiating attributes.[18] Clearly, then, in this way, the emergence of nationalism in Bizkaia might be partially explained as a response to the effects of modernity, specifically, the effects of the industrialization process, with the resulting arrival of tens of thousands of immigrants from other parts of Spain. This was a transformation interpreted by some of the resident population as the beginning of a new era that would undermine the cement of traditional society.[19] It is generally accepted that this process, conceived of by some as destroying the Basque soul, generated a sense of urgency that facilitated the development of a nationalist discourse from a member of the Bizkaian elite, Sabino Arana. Likewise, it facilitated the filtering of this discourse among other elites and, finally, to wider sections of society.

However, the fact that such modernization was "external"[20] or industrialization "exogenous"[21] made a similar transformation in Iparralde impossible, to the extent that the driving force in creating new identities there remained in the hands of external actors. These actors, members of the state administrative structure, imposed one educational system, one language, one official history, and homogenizing media that took the leading role in the process of consolidating the national community throughout France, including Iparralde. Cultural differences that were common to both sides of the border constituted preexisting conditions that *might* have led to the growth of a peripheral nationalist consciousness on the French side, as well as on the Spanish,[22] but here I underscore only the potential nature of these elements.[23] That is, at the time, a nationalist discourse did not develop on the basis of such conditions. As Walker Connor argues, "in the final analysis, the coincidence of the customary tangible attributes of nationality, such as common language or religion, is not determinative. The prime requisite is subjective and consists of self-identification of people with a group—its past, its present, and, what is most important, its destiny."[24]

However, revolutionary France nevertheless encountered problems in extending its project to Iparralde. Clearly, there were no elites there capable of elaborating a peripheral nationalist discourse in the French Basque Country. Yet, paradoxically, the very exogenous nature of modernization in there explains the specific relationship that emerged there between the clergy and Basque culture, at least during one specific time period.

Religious Instrumentalization

The continued importance of religion in Iparralde after the French Revolution was based on the increasingly close connection between religious elites and the culture of their parishioners. Put simply, to remain legitimate, the clergy had little choice but to accept and endorse Basque culture. As a result, from the French Revolution on, there was a growing alliance between a religious elite trying to preserve its privileges and those sectors in Iparralde that were trying to maintain Basque traditions and the Basque language. Both came into confrontation with the secular, centralist spirit that underscored the new state.[25] At the same time, and in mirrorlike fashion, the anticlerical policies of Paris embraced the total denial of a local culture and identity that identified with faith and antirepublican principles.

A first glance at this emerging game of alliances and divisions involves understanding that the process of French state construction may be characterized as the best example of the dissemination of secular nationalism,[26] that is, a secular and occasionally antireligious perspective expressed (since the French Revolution) in French nationalism. In the final analysis, as well as being based on Enlightenment principles, the secular foundation on which the French state was constructed should also be understood in terms of the previous support for and influence on the *ancien régime* by the clergy,[27] as well in terms of as a deeper historical antirepublican tradition within the Catholic Church. For the above reasons, secular French nationalism soon came into conflict with the sociocommunitarian reality of Iparralde.

In effect, the clergy came to use Euskara as an obstacle to purge republican values, once the population in Iparralde had overcome its initial republican fervor and had begun to feel somewhat dissatisfied with the state. As we will see, this came about as the result of the combined effects of the border conflict, Jacobin repression, the elimination of foral institutions, and the territorial integration of Iparralde into an unwanted *département* together with the Occitanian province of Béarn. In this context, "in their [the clergy's] hands, the Basque language became an instrument of clerical reaction which politicized the Basque population behind a phalanx of local notables and the clerical elite . . . The church, through the manipulation of ethnic symbols, achieved a predominance in the Basque country that surpassed the level of religiosity of nearly every other region of France."[28]

The Basque clergy enjoyed a strong position in relation to the state administrative structure during this period. The French administration knew only French, a language that was still little used in the rural environment of Iparralde, while bilingual priests became the only mediators between the local reality, expressed in Euskara, and centrist aspirations, articulated in French.

Furthermore, the Basque system of inheritance guaranteed the unity of the *etxe* (home) by granting succession to the eldest-born male, thereby establishing a static system of social hierarchy, encouraging Basque emigration and serving as a source of successive generations that swelled the ranks of the clergy with the younger sons of families in Iparralde. Consequently, it should come as no surprise that these religious elites became the (subjective) champions of maintaining the Basque tradition of inheritance and teaching in Euskara: in sum, of preserving Basque customs politically asserted by an organizational model that existed prior to the French Revolution, set down in the *Biltzarrak*, or foral assemblies (in Zuberoa, this institution was known as the *Silviet*).[29]

This alliance, which was maintained throughout the nineteenth century, unquestionably explains why the authority of the French state in Iparralde remained incomplete until the coming of the Third Republic in 1870.[30] As James E. Jacob, paraphrasing Count Massimo d'Azeglio on the Italian *risorgimento*, puts it, the state authorities must have concluded that "we have created France. Now we must create the French."[31] It was therefore necessary to establish an efficient policy based on the multiple pillars of education, transportation, and the military, but more than anything else, on a transformation of church-state relations in order to make headway in a rural society that, when it was not outrightly hostile, just "ignored" republican France.[32]

It is hardly surprising, then, that the French state authorities became worried about this situation and took the first concrete steps to address it after the consolidation of the Third Republic. In 1901, for example, the first catechism in French was drawn up for Iparralde, licenses for congregations were refused, and the church was denied the right to control education. Similarly, on December 11, 1905, a law separating church and state was approved, and the following February, in 1906, an inventory was carried out of all church possessions. That same year, all students were expelled from the main seminary in Baiona (Bayonne), while that of Larresoro (Larressore) was confiscated by the state, with its members taking refuge in a similar institution in Belloc, a commune outside Iparralde. However, despite some angry initial reactions, the Basque church gradually came to terms with the new situation—to such an extent, in fact, that by 1903, only ten "recalcitrant" priests maintained an intransigent position against the new state policy. All told, the Basque clergy were resigned to accepting the new measures.[33]

According to Xipri Arbelbide, the principal ally of Basque culture since the French Revolution became—mainly during the Third Republic—an instrument of its decline.[34] And as Xabier Itçaina observes, "dissidence had been practical, but not ideological. If the majority of the clergy preached timidly in favor of French integration, it was just better to combat an anticlerical state from the inside. As such, this discourse evolved from an implicit call for rebellion into a celebration of French patriotism and even a defense of sacrifice in 1914."[35]

Thus, French patriotism began to appear in the catechisms, which, in turn, began to serve as the first point of contact with the state for young people educated by the church. Arbelbide, a priest himself, recalled: "Did you have a commitment to the people? Yes, I had to obey the leaders of the people, I had to obey the laws . . . The most important obligations to the people were: pay your taxes, defend your people if necessary with your blood, vote with your conscience."[36] As a result, Basques, for whom the church played a key role, found themselves faced with a new dilemma: "Not obeying the state was one thing, fine; the church had done the same thing up to that time. But now, should one disobey the church? This would be to deny your very self; they were difficult times."[37]

Ultimately, as Itçaina demonstrates, "once the republican ideal was accepted . . . it would not be questioned." However, as he also notes, "the clergy's political involvement during the Third Republic had the effect of encouraging acceptance of the principle of electoral participation as a civic duty. Voting developed into a moral obligation, and abstention a sin." Further still, the foundations were laid for the "communal vote" in which the "nature of the mandate became distanced from free representation: It was an aggregate of interests, masked by a discourse on the identity-based representation of Basque believers."[38] Thus were created the bases by which a religious patronage system emerged.

The "Notable" Model and Cultural Translation

It is widely known that the system of centralized organization in the French state generates a form of economic development and political control that flows from the state, regional, and departmental centers to the different electoral districts, regions, and municipalities. Thus, while church influence waned, a series of actors emerged to mediate between center and the periphery, and this, in turn, allowed for the local implementation of decisions made nationally. These elites—known as "notables," important local individuals—facilitated the dominant relationship and came to form the cornerstone of interaction and interdependence between the local and national spheres. In other words, they were mediators between the periphery and the center who became the coordinators of policies that were drawn up outside their territories, but that were implemented there directly, thanks to them.

According to this new system, however, the locally elected notable was also bound by electoral time limits: By necessity, therefore, he had to retain close contact with his electorate, achieve short-term results, and strongly embrace the political culture of his fellow citizens. This dual relationship between both the locally elected figure in his immediate environment and the more distant state forced him into a twofold discourse: realist within decision-making circles, but sympathetic to the electorate around him.[39] As such, the classic profile of the notable would be that of a conservative, Basque-speaking mediator controlled for decades by the church.

Beyond such temporal considerations, however, the spatial limits of his domain also conditioned his activity. Local notables were notable within their electoral districts alone, to the extent that their influence was limited to their own fiefdom or, at most, the territory over which they might exercise some influence, however limited. Therefore, while such people may have been Basques, they did not represent Iparralde. Rather, the extent of their influence at most might have been measured within the coastal or interior regions or within a particular canton or municipality—to such an extent that, given the waning recognition of local institutions after 1790, any notion of a Basque territory declined gradually in the eyes of the people. In other words, Iparralde fragmented into a puzzle whose pieces would not fit together for decades.

That said, the notable as elected representative, with his proximity to the local populace and culture, together with his prudence regarding and obedience to the center, became a key link in guaranteeing local development for his electorate, as well as control of the periphery by the center. And this all functioned through a system of client relations that allowed him a privileged position in local politics, sometimes for decades.

Due to the fact that this elected representative also mediated between two important social groups in France—those of tradition and modernity—it is important to remember that

> he continued to belong to traditional society and participated in the functioning of the local community. He understood its workings, beliefs and character from within. Yet at

the same time, he was fully integrated into modern society. He understood its obligations and rules . . . Thanks to the notables, the state adapted to local traditions and communities [and] . . . the notable was an intercultural translator: He adapted local demands to the rules of the national institutional system and translated the expectations of the state into clear terms for the traditional mentality.[40]

For this reason, as will be explained later, many such notables were initially quite open to Basque culture and traditions, especially after the introduction of universal suffrage.[41] However, this became less necessary once the crisis of Basque identity had taken root, and in most cases, the notables began to embrace outright Jacobinism originating in Paris.

Later still, it became even more problematic to adopt a stance in favor of Basque culture, because gradually, traditional power relations began to change. Previously, families of notables were able to base their power on a combination of conservative and pro-Basque identity policies. Yet, little by little, these families were replaced by organized parties that increasingly based their agendas on political and ideological concerns rooted in state issues, more than in local issues. In this way, developing out of its Catholic-conservative past, Iparralde became a prime site for the dominance of right-wing politics: principally, the Christian Democracy of the UDF (Union pour la Démocratie Française, the Union for French Democracy) and, to a lesser extent (at least until the Fifth Republic, constituted in 1958), the Gaullism of the RPR (Rassemblement pour la République, Rally for the Republic).[42]

In the final analysis, the French Revolution thus brought with it the foundations of an exogenous form of modernization in Iparralde. Until that moment, as Pierre Bidart reminds us, "the communitarian principle that governed Basque social units was centered on one fundamental mechanism that assured its reproduction: the [inheritance] rights of the first-born"—in other words, the continuation of the essential core of rural economic and community development, the Basque farmstead or house, *etxea*. Bidart continues:

> This [inheritance right] not only established an economic relationship—the maintenance of the indivisible nature of the birthright—but also more broadly created a power structure: the dominance of the first-born over their younger siblings, with the material and symbolic benefits that came with it. The transmission from generation to generation of the entire family inheritance . . . imprinted on the social and economic landscape of the community certain features of stability and inertia that might be disturbed only by the eventual protests of younger siblings.[43]

However, the abolition of these first-born rights after the French Revolution led to conflict and social change in Iparralde. A prospect of social mobility emerged that went to "the heart of domestic educational strategies, transforming traditional social relations and encouraging access to the rural environment by new elites possessing cultural capital [the notables] who were desirous of converting this into economic capital." This was a process that "corresponded to a transformation in the mechanisms of identity reproduction (with de-Basquization one of its most significant indices)."[44] Ultimately, with the removal of the traditional bases of Basque domestic and social stability, the floodgates of a new economic mobility, whose principal point of reference was Paris and the culture emanating from the capital, opened up. As a result, a sea change in identity took place in which parents in Iparralde began to transmit to their children one single feeling of belonging (to France) in one language (French), while at the same time, the rural Basque world began to assume an inferiority complex about its language and culture.

Modernity in Iparralde thus was imported. It did not spring from the reality of local conditions, but rather emerged in and emanated from Paris to the periphery.[45] Throughout the nineteenth century, Basque identity in Iparralde was conditioned by a number of key factors: the lack of an elite capable of defining a differential political discourse based on the peripheral nature of Iparralde, a crisis among religious elites that had manipulated Basque culture for their own interests, the consolidation of a patronage system based in Paris and extending to the Basque periphery through mediators (the notables) between tradition and modernity, and the emergence of a system of social mobility that removed differentiating cultural and linguistic features from the Basque population for their "inefficiency." The foundations had been laid for the machinery of state to make a credible case in the minds of people in Iparralde that they belonged to a nation that spoke French, and, as regarded Basque culture, that at most that they maintained something of their "particularism."

The Machinery of State

The twin processes of constructing a national community and a national society—both necessary for the emergence of a nation-state—clearly were fortified in France by the practical and ideological consequences of the French Revolution. Yet before addressing the form in which revolutionary France set about territorially configuring its power, a brief overview is necessary of the ideological basis on which it was founded.

States can be analyzed by classifying the way in which the political control of power is exercised over a territory. The state does not monopolize all social and economic life in Western societies, for there remains one sphere of independent activity: that of individuals and private groups (civil society). Despite everything, the border between the state and civil society is extensive, which means that one should distinguish between two societal models: that of a strong state, in which the state is conceived of as being above civil society and therefore creates a structure to reflect this, and that of a weak state, in which such a structure is more simply constructed as the boundary between the state and civil society.[46] Both state models reflect the causes and consequences of their theoretical foundations. In the former case, Jean-Jacques Rousseau, basing his argument on the "popular will" that emerged to regenerate a society corrupted by inequalities, emphasized strong state centralization. In the latter, John Locke argued that a state should protect society and defend it from external danger, reflecting the "weak" British model.[47] France is the best example of the former—that is, strong state construction and centralization as the defining principle of the nation and its unity.

In France, membership in the national community was open to anyone who lived within its borders, and all were to be equal before the law. Individual liberties were therefore tied to the center, and because of the doctrine of popular sovereignty, forms of collective action that were not in some way connected to the nation-state were considered illegitimate. The Rousseauean tradition bequeathed to French nationalism an important civic dimension in that it emphasized constructing the nation from the individual upward. Yet at the same time, it fostered a conception of the state that allowed little intermediary space for these two realities—that is, there was no place for an intermediate authority between the state and the individual, given that both were grounded in the notion of the "people," the "nation," or the "universality of French citizens."[48] In France, democracy came to mean national unity, centralization, and uniformity,[49] all articulated in one language, as exemplified by the 1784 Grégoire Report—based on a survey of language use in France during the initial revolutionary period—which called for the need to destroy patois tongues and spread the use of French.

As Cécile Laborde points out, this issue was tied intimately to the identity-shaping ideals of *liberté, égalité, fraternité,* and *laïcité* on which the state was built after the French Revolution. *Liberté* implied "rational self-determination through the exercise of individual autonomy . . . [in which] particular cultural attachments are contingent . . . attributes of individual identity, and human dignity lies in the ever-possible emancipation of the human mind from its cultural limitations."[50] From this point of view, Laborde continues (following Katherine Kintzler), "the function of state schools is not to respect the ethnic, social, or cultural particularities of individual children but rather to treat children as autonomous human beings, potentially capable of distancing themselves from their original affiliations."[51] As a result, "this 'bracketing off' of cultural difference [that is, difference from the culture of the state] in the public sphere is fundamental because it guarantees that individuals will be treated equally,"[52] or uniformly.

The term *égalité*, as Laborde (citing Dominique Schnapper) notes, refers to a conception whereby "cultural differences are unimportant in the face of the essential unity of mankind."[53] Therefore, "state policies should aim at the reduction of structural inequalities . . . rather than contribute to the entrenchment of cultural difference through policies of affirmative action and the attribution of special rights to particular communities." Similarly, from the notion of *fraternité*, "republican community is a community of 'public similars' as much as of 'private others'; it requires that citizens be able to leave behind their private interests and identities to promote the common good."

Finally, Laborde contends, "these three pillars of universalist republicanism are subsumed by . . . *laïcité*." Although this originally referred to the separation between church and state, it subsequently came to imply a separation between the public and private spheres. In sum, within contemporary republican thought, "the public sphere, in the name of autonomy, equal respect, and civic solidarity, should remain neutral toward ascribed identities, as well as toward a number of private social practices that, typically, include religions.

These ideals of the French Revolution took root in the new democracy that emerged. One of the principal theorists of the revolution, Abbé Sieyès, following Rousseau's *Social Contract* (1762), equated the nation with the French people from a social, rather than an ethnic point of view. This universalist conception of the people required the rejection of distinct local and religious characteristics in order to achieve equality.

This notion of democracy underscored the work of the state's new administrators to such an extent that the elimination of all such distinct local characteristics gradually became the foundation on which the new territorial structure of power was conceived, a power for which there was no space between the individual citizen and national sovereignty, itself seen as emanating from the citizenry as a whole and represented in the National Assembly.

The construction of the French state thus combined a mathematical rationalism with the elimination of existing "intermediary bodies" between the center (possessor of "legitimate power") and the people. It was ultimately a question of replacing earlier political and administrative structures in France, and, in the Basque case, several specific provincial bodies.[54] For these reasons, the new state was organized around *départements* and followed a clearly instrumental logic that not only disrespected the cultural boundaries of historic communities, but consciously sought to avoid any similarities with the previous territorial organization. The principal goal, without any doubt, was to "destroy the spirit of the province, which for the state was just an individual spirit."[55]

This restructuring was carried out in two stages in Iparralde. On the night of August 4, 1789, the provincial institutions of Lapurdi, Zuberoa, and Nafarroa Beherea were abolished. Thereafter, the three Basque provinces were amalgamated with the western part of Béarn to form a new *département*: the Basses-Pyrénées. This, in turn, was divided into five *arrondissements* (districts), two of which included the former Basque historic territories. One of these included most of the municipalities in Lapurdi, while the other included those of Nafarroa Beherea and Zuberoa. However, this structure was later changed, in 1926, into three decentralized structures: the Baiona region (in Lapurdi) was extended into the interior to include the Nafarroa Beherea cantons of Baigorri (Saint-Étienne-de-Baïgorry), Donibane Garazi (Saint-Jean-Pied-de-Port), Iholdi (Iholdy), and Donapaleu (Saint-Palais), while the Maule (Mauléon) and Atharratze (Tardets) regions in Zuberoa—which had previously been in the Maule *arrondissement*—became, together with several others in Béarn, part of a new division with its capital in the Béarnais town of Oloron.

Thus, in the twentieth century, Iparralde came to be controlled administratively by the subprefectures of Baiona and Oloron. And, until 1997,[56] there was no specifically Basque administrative structure or organ, given that the historic Basque territories had been grouped into one *département* with Béarn and were internally divided by the aforementioned two decentralized structures. Consequently, the process of state building in France blurred or gradually erased notions of Basque territorial unity in a twofold manner: first, because Iparralde was inserted into an unwanted *département* together with the western part of Béarn, and second, because this process further divided up the Basque historic territories. This ocurred by, for example, encouraging close ties between Zuberoa and the bordering Bearnais cantons, or breaking up links between the rural interior and the coast—a coast that, moreover, where economic growth began to develop, built around the development of the port of Baiona.

This lack of local identity structures and the divisions within Iparralde led to a growing identity crisis among the population there through the first half of the nineteenth century. To this were added other factors grouped around the state-building process: A common language and educational system, military conscription, and the pattern of economic development were all tools used by the state to integrate the Basque population into republican discourse and practice.

So was linguistic unification. As Jean Marie Izquierdo argues, "through the nineteenth and the beginning of the twentieth centuries, France attempted to guarantee its domination through the development of republican ideology."[57] Within this policy, the most adequate instrument for the creation of a national community was the imposition of the French language. The reports of Abbé Grégoire on the need to eliminate patois and universalize French reflected the voluntary nature with which republican ideology adopted the ideal of uniformity. And in 1794, Bertrand Barère de Vieuzac concluded before the Committee of Public Safety that "federalism and superstition speak low Breton; emigration and hate for the Revolution speak German; the counterrevolution speaks Italian; and fanaticism speaks Basque. Let us break these instruments of control and error."[58]

"While the encyclopedists saw French as the 'language of the capital' and the languages of rural areas as patois," Bidart claims, "the Revolution considered French the 'national language' and other languages as feudal products. The substitution of the capital/rural dichotomy (a geographical perspective) by the national/feudal dichotomy (a historical dimension) highlighted a transformation of the linguistic question: the foundation of language as a political institution."[59] However, it would appear that, initially, at least, the French authorities did not directly link the use of Euskara with feudalism in Iparralde. Indeed, quite the contrary, for as the Barère Report also demonstrated, there was a high degree of republican public spirit in Iparralde, even if it was accompanied by an equally high degree of ideological activism by the clergy against the Republic.[60] Thus, once again initially, at least, there was an attempt to instrumentalize Euskara to disseminate republican values through the translation of legal and revolutionary texts into the Basque language.

However, this situation soon changed with a new policy of systematic persecution of France's regional languages, especially after 1793 (with the rise of Jacobin power), when leaders and representatives of this quasi-apostolic mission decided that such languages formed not only an obstacle to the transmission of republican propaganda, but also fomented counterrevolutionary resistance.[61] Thus, the process of imposing linguistic uniformity was set in motion once more, this time with even more force, a process whereby, concomitantly, the vernacular or patois languages were devalued while French was prized.

Yet this pressure on the regional languages was not confined to the ideological level, for it also appeared in a series of repressive measures from which not even the famous Dominique-Joseph Garat could save Basque. The names of towns and districts in Iparralde were changed in an attempt to erase any religious or Basque-language connections.[62] Nevertheless, until the coming of the Third Republic, most of these efforts by central elites fell on deaf ears,[63] to the extent that 65 percent of the people in Iparralde were still Basque speakers in 1868.[64]

However, at precisely this moment, a more concrete policy came into being that targeted the objective of universal education in French and the complete elimination of Basque from the private education system. Between the 1860s and the 1880s, the French authorities came to the belief that there were areas in the state with important numbers of citizens who had not been "civilized." As a result, it was necessary to teach manners, morals, and the alphabet, while at the same time imparting both French and the nation's history. "The peasant had to be integrated into the national society, economy, and culture," as Eugen Weber puts it, "the culture of the city and of the City par excellence, Paris."[65] Consequently, the large-scale introduction of French by the enlightened authorities, coupled with the definitive crisis of traditional society, led to the breakdown of a model of social relations that had remained unchanged for decades and that been noteworthy for the stability of the local system.

At the same time, industrial and administrative development opened up Iparralde to social mobility. Thus, speaking French gradually became a means of climbing the social ladder. This, in turn, marked the beginning of a decline in the fortunes of Basque and a blossoming of French, a moment that reflected the growing crisis in Basque identity and traditional social and cultural relations, as well as the consolidation of state power over the Basque periphery.

Linguistic relations were a key part of this process. Pierre Bourdieu contends that there is a linguistic market in society where linguistic competence functions as a kind of capital and where the variable "laws of price formation characteristic of a given market offer to holders of a given linguistic capital" symbolic profit.[66] All linguistic practices are measured against "legitimate practices" or "the practices of those who are dominant,"[67] meaning that it is they who attribute value to language. In other words, linguistic value is socially constructed within a hierarchy of power relations. It was by accumulating this capital and the benefits that accrued to it that individuals in Iparralde during the nineteenth century could climb the social ladder, abandoning the negative value of Basque.

Furthermore, the state did not just formulate the policy of linguistic unification with regard to the technical necessities of joining diverse parts of its territory (that is, between Paris and the regions). The centralist premise meant that the state also had to eliminate all specific local features: "The conflict between the French of the revolutionary intelligentsia, and the dialects or patois was [also] a struggle in which what was at stake was the formation and reformation of mental structures. In short, it was not only a question of communicating but of gaining recognition for a new language of authority."[68] This new language, in turn, included a whole new vocabulary of terms and references designed to give it specific authority. Moreover, Bourdieu notes:

> The recognition of the legitimacy of the official language has nothing in common with an explicitly professed, deliberate and revocable belief, or with an intentional act of accepting a "norm." It is inscribed, in a practical state, in dispositions which are impalpably inculcated, through a long and slow process of acquisition, by the sanctions of the linguistic marketplace, and which are, therefore, adjusted without any cynical calculation or consciously expressed constraints to the chances of material and symbolic profit, which the laws of price formation characteristic of a given market objectively offer to the holders of a given linguistic capital.[69]

Such unconscious encoding is evident in apparently insignificant practices (ways of looking at people, remaining silent, and so on) charged with imperatives that are difficult to revoke, owing to the power of suggestion imbued with the symbolic power of a given official language. In this sense, it is interesting to note the significant discursive transformation that Basque pastorals (a form of rural theater that will be discussed in more detail later, in Chapter 11) went through in the nineteenth century: specifically, from ending each pastoral with a religious song, "Te Deum," to chanting, instead, "Long Live the Republic!"[70] However, there were other real, significant, and institutionalized dimensions to this transformation, especially in the educational sphere.

The School Model

As Bourdieu notes, "by devaluing popular modes of expression and imposing recognition of the legitimate language," an educational system "fashions the similarities from which derives the community of consciousness, the cement of the nation."[71] Moreover, "the educational system . . . contributes significantly to constituting the dominated uses of language as such by consecrating the dominant use as the only legitimate one, by the mere fact of inculcating it."[72] As a result, parents, increasingly aware of the fact that language choice was crucial to their children's "value" in the "educational market" (to borrow expressions from Bourdieu), began to demand that French be spoken at home. In fact, in the absence of industrialization, or amid a weaker process of industrialization, the school became the principal conduit—through its direct connection to administrative positions—to social advancement.

Beyond the individual and subjective roles played by the republican school in social mobility, this institution also became a specific objectifying instrument to advance the social construction of the French nation. Anthony D. Smith observes that the function of national mass education in liberal and democratic states has been "to unify [the population] around certain shared values, symbols, myths and memories, allowing minorities among them to retain their own symbols, memories, myths and values, and seeking to accommodate or incorporate them within the broad public culture and its national mythology."[73] One should recall, in this sense, the words of the French minister of public instruction and fine arts that opened this chapter, an easy-going yet firmly national attitude that had evolved from the attitude of, for example, the subprefect for Maule who, in 1802, greeted the opening of a high school in the capital of Zuberoa as a means of "ending this ignorance of a people who know only their own language, [which is why] they can't make any contact with the rest of the nation." This center, he declared, would be "a great way of Frenchifying the Basques."[74]

Thus would appear then that the educational model on which the French state was built after the French Revolution, and especially during the Third Republic, reflected Ernest Gellner's contention that the primary purpose of schooling is to educate the masses into a passionate loyalty to the nation.[75] Consequently, the 1882 and 1886 Education Laws established compulsory education (in French), with schooling at the forefront of conquering the minds of children throughout the state. This attempt at constructing French national identity was part of a broad attempt to magnify the glory of France and to gloss over its shortcomings, especially in the context of a humiliating defeat for the country during the Franco-Prussian War of 1870–71. As Eric Savarèse puts it, "At the heart of this 'republicanization' of consciousnesses, national education occupied a privileged role: its goal was to favor, especially through the teaching of history and morality, the creation of a national citizen dedicated to the cause of the new republic. As such, the role assigned history was extremely political, given that it was a question of aiding the emergence of a national consciousness to serve republican integration."[76]

From this point of view, Ernest Lavisse, director of historical studies at the Sorbonne during the late nineteenth century, stands out. He edited twenty-seven volumes of French history that "established, for a long time, the dominant historiographical and pedagogical model in the discipline, in that they served as a basis from which all textbooks for primary and secondary schools were written."[77] This model, in turn, came to represent the state within these textbooks as a vital element in the lives of French schoolchildren through the idea that, "you must love France because nature made her beautiful and history made her great."[78] Phrases such as this, which had to be learned by heart by all French schoolchildren, were part of a wider national socialization. And the study of history was not intended to develop critical minds or a deep sense of the past,

> but to inculcate among the pupils a certain number of moral precepts and civic duties—especially their debt to the Republic. [In the words of Lavisse]: "Children, you will be the citizens of a free and glorious country ... Never, before yours, has a generation been obliged to recognize itself in its elders. In order to pay your sacred debt, in body and soul you must restore France, weakened by the ruin of her wealth and the blood she has shed. You must work as hard as you can."[79]

Ultimately, the model established by Lavisse and in place until the 1960s was based on a clear simplification of history in which "the burden of proof was abolished ... [and] methodological reflection eliminated."[80] As a result, he recast French history out of a few short sentences and several carefully chosen foundational dates in a clearly pedagogical, republican, and patriotic model. For example, as he saw it:

> On September 4, 1870, the Republic was reestablished. The Republic imbues us with all our liberties ... She protects work and the workers. The Republic is peaceful, but she must ensure that our rights and honor are respected. So she demonstrated by successfully defending France, attacked by Germany in August 1914. The Great War ended with the return to the motherland of the annexed territories, Alsace and Lorraine.[81]

The main goal behind this vision of teaching history was to visualize the unity of the nation.[82] Such unity was supposed to be free of social or divisive conflicts and was framed, especially within the pages of the *Petit Lavisse*—or the republican Gospel, as it was called—in a clear context of revenge against Germany, to such an extent, in fact, that his pedagogical work was not aimed just at making good citizens, but also good soldiers.

Thus we arrive at the final stage in the effort to forge a new identity among the people of Iparralde. By the early twentieth century, they had come to view Euskara as an archaic tongue, while at the same time participating in an educational system that invited them to become part of a grand national project. Finally, by fire and sword, war would mold the identity of the Basques. As I will explain shortly, the initial reaction of Basques to France's postrevolutionary wars was, to say the least, indifferent.[83] Initially, the effects of the revolutionary war with Spain in a strategic border area such as Iparralde were harmful to the local population. This, coupled with the beginning of religious persecution and the abolition of local Basque institutions, distanced local people from the French Revolution. It thus meant that war and conflict—so essential to cementing national identity in modern European history—actually worked against such a process, at least initially, in Iparralde.

It was only later, once the presence of the state was more tangible, that this dynamic functioned in Iparralde—specifically, with later conflicts in the nineteenth and especially the twentieth centuries, such as the World Wars and the Algerian War (1954–62). Only then did young men from Iparralde voluntarily leave their everyday surroundings to enter these global conflicts. For example, during World War I, they were uprooted from their homeland and thrown together in the trenches (and beyond) with eight million other French citizens from all corners of the country, all obliged to communicate in one language. At the same time, the existence of a foreign enemy or "other" served to fuel the feelings of common bonds, of an "us" as opposed to "them," among the people of Iparralde. Such bonds filtered into the collective memory of the people and were expressed in each and every monument erected in remembrance of those who fell during these conflicts—in the carved name of each and every Etcheverry[84] who died for France.

There is, then, a clear link between state nationalism and war, to such an extent that Rogers Brubaker believes that "if the French nation-state was invented in 1789, French nationalism was a product of war."[85] Likewise, Francisco Letamendia underscores the significance of the role of war and the army in creation nation-states, but he also points out that state nationalism and democratization are the basic conditions for generating citizen participation in the armed forces.[86] Thus, the relationship between democratization and the incorporation of the working class into modern political systems of which Letamendia speaks and the consolidation of a national consciousness through war could well have the same effect on other cultural minorities. In fact, whereas significant numbers of Basques attempted to avoid fighting in World War I through desertion, emigration, or absenteeism,[87] this was not the case either in the interwar period or during World War II. From 1914 on, whether they had participated in the Great War or not, people in Iparralde mourned their neighbors, brothers, or friends who had died for France and for those who would die in future conflicts. Thus, external conflict came to shore up the French state.

However, beyond the dramatic effects of World War I, an ex-combatant mentality emerged that consolidated a deeper sense of French identity.[88] As Arbelbide puts it, after paying their blood tribute, peasants could enter the pantheon of national heroes: "After spending four years of pain and suffering, the rewards were there. These men, farmers from small villages, dined with the prefect, the general, and the important figures, even at the same table. They shook hands with one another, while this was not the case for those who were not ex-combatants . . . They were honored as Frenchmen of the last war."[89] Arbelbide continues his analysis of the post-1914 period by citing the words of Jean Paul Malherbe: "The Basque Country was engrossed in the 'ex-combatant' ideology, which their political leader, Jean Ybarnégaray, a volunteer in 1914, fiercely stirred up. He spoke of an eternal France, of a greatness that should be preserved and advanced." Ybarnégaray, together with other elected officials, managed to instill a "surprising mystical, nationalist atmosphere"[90] in Iparralde, and the ex-combatant ideal definitively triumphed after World War II and the Algerian War.

As Michael Billig demonstrates, even the most "civic" nationalisms attempt to transcend the differences between the public and private spheres.[91] This was especially true during the interwar period, when the nationalist states made a concerted effort to enter the private sphere of their citizens' lives. Meanwhile, nationalism became banal, and consequently, latent—that is, it became a routine, internalized habit. French state nationalism—the "civic" model par excellence, according to many observers—also followed this pattern. In other words, when the French state was not "obliged" to exercise force, French nationalism was as banal as it was constant. Every year, in every commemoration to those *morts pour la patrie*, "in every village there were three flags, because every soldier from every war had their own . . . When an ex-combatant died, the three flags were there, in the church, in front of everyone, in the first row. They were there in every celebration, on every anniversary of the end of each war."[92]

Peripherality as "Living Museum"

As a result of all these policies and developments, Iparralde became a political and economic periphery for the Parisian center—not by chance, but, rather as a result of the state-building process. Basque culture was preserved within the French Republic, but its role became that of a "living museum." The elements that differentiated the French Basque country from the centralized French state lost any political dimension. In the words of Minister Fourcaud in 1897, "Your language is not for you, and has it not harmed, will it not ever harm development of the great national language?"[93] Basque culture was no longer understood as existing for Basques, but for others, as an isolated curiosity—a curiosity that, indeed, had been carefully isolated.

At the close of the 1960s, Robert Lafont published a detailed, extensive work in which he attempted to show that the nature of this French state-building process had created within the periphery a vicious circle of economic underdevelopment.[94] Indeed, his analysis proved that the dependant economic situation of Brittany and Occitania (and of Iparralde) was rooted in a system whereby such regions were mere links, like tentacles emanating from a centrally based economy.

One can highlight a dual sociological process at work in what we have seen: the cultural alienation of ethnic groups, on the one hand, and the economic alienation of regions, on the other. This process emerged quite early among the French haute bourgeoisie—the first class to abandon regional languages—then among the middle class, and finally (late, although also more definitively and radically) among the lower classes.[95]

From this perspective, any regional feeling was often considered to be a folkloric residue in which tourism played a key role in the process of "internal" colonialism. Lafont, who understood the reality of the Basque Country (among other regions in France), declared that "one should understand what I am denouncing: One encounters countries in the act of representing themselves."[96] What Lafont means here, that is, this notion of countries "representing" themselves—of displacing their sense of identity from something unreflectingly lived into something staged for an audience of others—evokes one of Pierre Loti's revealing late nineteenth-century tales:

> Then the old man who played the pan flute could be seen going toward the center of the square, and the dancers—some thirty of them—formed a narrow circle around him without holding hands. At the sound of a small, mysterious, and seemingly far away shrill noise, which came from the enormous old flute, the men began to move, solemnly, in time to the music . . . [yet] one could not help but note, here and there, some hearty laughs stemming from under those elegant hats.[97]

Jon Juaristi, too, has observed that "Basques were thus transformed . . . into a living museum":

> Ethnic identity and folklore furnished visitors [to Iparralde] complementary attractions to sea bathing . . . [but, unlike the case of the Béarnais], Basques were interesting for their language. It was Basque that gave them an aura and transubstantiated their folkloric customs in unfathomable mysteries . . . In all this, they saw a combination of enigmatic atavisms that necessarily had to come from a civilization already lost in the mists of time.[98]

However, what Lafont sees as internal colonialism is, for Juaristi, "patriotic" obligation. "The ethnic stereotype," contends the former head of the Instituto Cervantes (the official Spanish-government-sponsored organization to promote Spanish culture throughout the world), "was created for tourist consumption, but it soon became a patriotic task for any Basque to fit, as much as possible, that designer image, which even imposed a pedagogy of ethnicity."[99] However, the Basque patriotism to which Juaristi sophistically refers was, in reality, no more than a representation created for others, reflected in dances for tourists and expressed in French, for Basque had already been abandoned. It had no explicit political dimension. As Bourdieu reminds us, speaking *the* language "is tacitly to accept the *official* definition of the *official* language of a political unit," and of course, "the official language is bound up with the state, both in its genesis and its social uses." This imposition of one official language at the expense of all others (the argument might well equally apply to cultures) is grounded in political domination, because "promotion of official languages to the status of national languages gave them that *de facto* monopoly of politics."[100]

The Zero-Sum Game

As I have noted, the border dividing Basques allowed for a process of state development that encouraged the emergence and growth of Basque nationalism in certain parts of Hegoalde while limiting such possibilities in Iparralde. As a result, neither the first (royalist or reactionary) nor the second (populist) waves of peripheral nationalist movements to shake Europe at the end of the nineteenth century had any effect in Iparralde,[101] whereas in Hegoalde, they were both represented: first by Carlism and then by Basque nationalism.[102] In fact, Iparralde would have to wait for a third (progressive) wave of such movements in the twentieth century before it witnessed the emergence of a Basque nationalist movement, a fact that imbued that movement, from its beginnings there, with a decidedly leftist nature.

Furthermore, for a number of reasons, in Iparralde, the sense of urgency that characterized peripheral reactions elsewhere was not apparent. First, as opposed to the still-burning issue of foral abolition that marked the development of Basque nationalism in Hegoalde by Sabino Arana, the *fors* of Lapurdi, Nafarroa Beherea, and Zuberoa had been eliminated one hundred years previously, together with the rejection of Garat's proposals for some form of official recognition of Iparralde and (despite their initial radical stance) the decline of the Basque assemblies. Also, as opposed to the cultural clash that had marked the rapid emergence of a modern economy in Hegoalde as the result of widespread non-Basque immigration, in Iparralde, economic modernity was introduced only gradually, from the center to the periphery, and its introduction was marked by an exodus of people to other parts of France, as well as abroad. In addition, while a sense of rupture accompanied the changes in Hegoalde, interpreted by some as attacks on the Basque identity via attacks on Basque culture and language there, the cultural crisis in Iparralde was more gradual, although still regarded as an inescapable, and the crisis transformed identity there. In other words, while on one side of the border, the changes took place in a short space of time, on the other, they were marked by a *longue durée* decline. Finally, Basque nationalists in Hegoalde were able to construct (or invent—it amounts to the same thing) a history of struggle for Basque sovereignty, a history that connected the ninth-century Battle of Arrigorriaga with the two nineteenth-century Carlist Wars (1833–39 and 1873–76), while the population of Iparralde was more accustomed to hearing words such as those of the minister of public instruction and fine arts in 1897: "Tell me, in which French battle has Basque blood been spared, on land or at sea?"[103]

Thus, at precisely the same time that Basque nationalism emerged and grew in some parts of Hegoalde, Iparralde was undergoing a crisis among the politico-religious elite linked to Basque culture, suffering the consequences of an industrialization process that destabilized a predominantly rural society, dealing with the aftermath of the introduction of obligatory education in French, and coping with the psychological effects of young men's participation in two world wars in which they killed and were killed in the name of a nation they were just beginning to know. These combined to shape a new feeling of French identity that was increasingly assimilated in tandem with the values of modernity. This new sense of identity, in turn, came into confrontation with an older sense of Basque belonging based on language and culture, with the latter being dismissed by the former, negatively, as being a part of the past and of traditional lifestyles.

For this reason, the incorporation of Basques into modernity carried with it a critical understanding of their dual sense of belonging, something that, in many cases, led to the internalization of a feeling that the Basque language and culture were inferior compared with their French counterparts.[104] Ultimately, the French Republic converted the old Basque traditions into "a relic of the past anachronous to modern society," and with them, the Basque language, as well.[105] This view of Basque identity confirms the appearance of modernity in one, single form: that of efficiency, rational instrumentalism, and profitability.

One might, then, sum up the period between the French Revolution and the end of World War II in Iparralde as regards the question of identity as one of a "pathological" step from "field" to "apparatus." For Bourdieu,

> In a field, agents and institutions constantly struggle, according to the rules constitutive of this space of game, with various degrees of strength and therefore diverse possibilities of success, to appropriate the specific products at stake in the game. Those who dominate in a given field are in a position to make it function to their advantage, but they must always contend with the resistance, "political" or not, of the dominated."

In "fields," negotiations and compromises are ongoing, and there are no ultimate winners or losers. "The school system, the State, the church, political parties or unions are not apparatuses but fields." By contrast, the apparatus "is an infernal machine, programmed to accomplish certain purposes no matter what, when, or where."[106] As such, they aim at total victory: Theirs is a zero-sum game. In the conditions that prevailed in Iparralde, a zero-sum game began.

CHAPTER TWO

Basque Identity and the Spread of Nationalism in Iparralde

I do not know whether any French Basques present during the speech of Louis de Fourcaud at the conference on Basque traditions replied to his words. However, two prominent figures from Hegoalde certainly did: one, among the principal figures behind the Navarrese cultural and foral renaissance of the late nineteenth century, the other regarded as the "father" of Basque nationalism.

The first of these, Arturo Campión, participated in the conference, giving an extensive presentation on the Basque language and pointing out its unique quality, in opposition to certain intellectuals who identified it as a language of barbarians.[1] He began his presentation by surveying the existing dialects of the language, its phonology, orthography, word composition, and so on. And after examining its origins and links with the distinctive qualities of the Basque people, he concluded with some harsh words about the linguistic situation in Iparralde. In so doing, he openly disagreed with the optimism of the French government's view that, at the time, acknowledged no inherent conflict between the hegemony of the French state and the existence of the country's different cultures—the view, as Fourcaud expressed it, that "however many Basques you are, you will be better as Frenchmen. You will work with all your strength for the progress of your province. And you will provide France—sweet France, as the poets used to say—with original attributes." According to Campión, "Physically, the children of those who spoke Basque and no longer use it belong to the same race, yet one thing has changed: They are missing something! Immediately, they lost their soul! . . . They have lost the name 'Basques.' They have forsaken their race, their roots, their lineage. Poor wretches! They have forsaken their mother."[2]

Elsewhere, the founder of Basque nationalism, Sabino Arana, responded to Fourcaud's words with force and irony through the pages of a Bilbao newspaper:

> Behold the most curious case in the world: a people, a race, that has one small homeland and several larger ones: Spaniards and the pro-Spanish tell us that our large homeland is Spain; Frenchmen and the pro-French tell us that our large homeland is France . . . Behold

a son who has two fathers . . . that is as if he had none . . . Behold two brothers that have different fathers . . . Behold France and Spain assuring yet deceiving us that they are the mothers of the Basque people.[3]

Arana captured the notion (and dilemma) of two homelands that, as we will see, served as a distraction in the zero-sum game of identity in Iparralde.

As I have noted, borders serve as temporal and spatial markers of the relations between local communities and states. In the previous chapter, I observed that this is the condition, the sine qua non, by which state sovereignty is measured, that is, by which the limits of its nationalism—both internally and externally speaking—are drawn. Yet in the case of local communities divided by borders, the ambiguity of these frontiers becomes apparent: Just as they divide people, as we will see, they also generate new opportunities for contact.

In light of Max Weber's definition of the state in *Politics as a Vocation* as the only institution that can legitimately use violence, one can understand borders as the privileged domain of response to this ambiguity, spaces where local, national, and international groups negotiate relations of subordination and control. As a result, although borders form the basic structure of states,[4] they do not necessarily guarantee absolute security from external influences within such boundaries. In fact, border people frequently take part in informal networks and political institutions that compete with the state. Thus, in the example under consideration here, an analysis of the work of, for example, the writer Pierre Loti demonstrates the extent to which the modern history of the border is a tale of deep and stable exchange between the towns on both sides—in this case, on both sides of the river Bidasoa.

In *Ramuntcho* (1897), Loti recalls the smugglers who plied their trade between Hendaia (Hendaye, in Iparralde) and Hondarribia (Fuenterrabía, in Hegoalde):

> Several hours later, at the first uncertain flush of dawn, at the instant when shepherds and fisherman awake, they were returning joyously, the smugglers, having finished their undertaking . . . in a bark [small boat] of Fontarabia [Hondarribia], hired under the eyes of Spain's custom house officers, through the Bidassoa river . . . The boatman who was bringing the smugglers back to France pushed the bottom of the river with his long pole, and the bark dragged, half stranded. At this moment, that Bidassoa by which the two countries are separated, seemed drained, and its antique bed, excessively large, had the flat extent of a small desert . . . They talk in their mysterious language, the origin of which is unknown and which seems to the men of the other countries in Europe more distant than Mongolian or Sanskrit. They tell stories of the night and of the frontier, stratagems newly invented and astonishing deceptions of Spanish carbineers [carabineers].[5]

According to Loti's field notes, at this time, a constant stream of people crossed the border: young women from Hegoalde going to Hendaia to observe visiting tourists, people smuggling goods in order to avoid paying import dues, and dancers from Zuberoa who were taking part in festivals in Irun.[6] For Loti, all this pointed to the continued sense of belonging among a millenarian people. This was a romanticized vision, to be sure, but evidently the sharing of some common cultural traits facilitated the ease by which people traversed the border, to the extent that these border people understood the frontier as a history of exchange that "went back to the twilight of time."[7]

As Carlos Fernández de Casavedante Romani observes, "according to the data, it would seem that there have always been contacts between the people on both sides of the border, thereby demonstrating the clear fact that the border has never constituted a barrier."[8] Furthermore, as Fermín Rubiralta adds, because of the layout of the Pyrenean massif, cooperation is not only important, but necessary,[9] an argument confirmed by Javier Fernández and Paloma Miranda's contention that "in the reduced Basque-Navarrese area, certain minorities moved between Baiona and Donostia, Bilbao or Navarrese and Gipuzkoan border towns . . . from one side to the other, as if it formed a scarcely differentiated continuous territory. For these groups of merchants, politicians, smugglers and adventurers, on horseback between two states, the Bidasoa would be much more a link between two complementary settings than a dividing line."[10]

The border has not even been capable of serving to prevent the flow of ideas from one side of the Bidasoa to the other, as the noteworthy example of the influence of French revolutionary thought in the Iberian peninsula demonstrated, an influence in which "the ancient city of the Adour [Atturi river, Baiona] served as the main center from which this campaign [of revolutionary propaganda] was diffused throughout the western Pyrenees, while Perpignan served a similar role in the Catalan region."[11] Conversely, later (as I will discuss shortly), the seductive discourse of Basque nationalism traveled in the other direction, gaining adherents among religious and student sectors in Iparralde from the mid-1930s on.[12] That said, this flow of ideas in relation to Basque identity was not only from the South to the North. There also emerged in Iparralde a series of ideas about the constitutive elements of this identity, seeds, however, that were forced to seek a terrain and context more inclined to aid their development in the South.

What will emerge in the following chapters is a threefold argument: First, despite the reality of the border, we will see how it was transcended by political and intellectual elites in Iparralde from the French Revolution on. As a result, the discourse of individuals such as Dominique-Joseph Garat or Agosti Chaho concerning the institutional division of the Basque territories became the strongest expression of the feeling of cross-border belonging during the first half of the nineteenth century. Moreover, within their discourse one finds an analysis of Basque difference that heralds a kind of protonationalism, the emergence of which would ultimately lead to the appearance of a powerful Basque nationalist movement in Bizkaia several decades later. Thus, the first stage of my exploration of Basque identity—an examination of the work of Garat and Chaho—concerns the degree to which the seed planted by Sabino Arana in creating Basque nationalism in Hegoalde was already present among intellectual and political elites in Iparralde.

Second, I wish to emphasize that this was, indeed, a protonationalist, rather than a nationalist discourse. It was based on a vision of Basque identity that lacked any form of political expression. Further, one might say that the attitudes of Garat and Chaho constituted clear examples of the way in which elites in Iparralde configured a more or less complete vision of the cross-border Basque identity that was also republican and French. Following the work of Chaho, especially after World War I, there emerged a crisis of Basque identity and the consolidation of the French state in Iparralde and in the minds of its inhabitants. The reality of these local conditions made it impossible for a Basque nationalist to emerge successfully, albeit in an area where there were cultural, linguistic, and shared features in common with its neighbor to the south, where, by contrast, they had taken political shape. The arbitrariness of collective identities thus came to reflect their most paradoxical qualities in the Basque Country. The analysis of such individuals (Garat, Chaho, Arana and, later, Pierre Lafitte), together with the recognition that the border served as both a buffer and a conduit for the flow of ideas, leads me to observe that there emerged among Basque elites a cross-border discourse between 1789 and 1945. This discourse took shape in a more or less explicit common program and the spread of ideas in both directions: from the North to the South through to 1890 and, thereafter, from the beginning of the twentieth century on, in the opposite direction.[13]

Third, from a methodological perspective, I focus on several key issues. I am not interested in analyzing the scientific value of Garat's or Chaho's (and to a lesser extent, Arana's) arguments about the cross-border nature of the Basque community or about its essential unity and its consequent differential character in relation to Spain and France. Instead, what interests me is why some ideas (those emerging in Iparralde) did not take root, while others (those emerging in Hegoalde from Arana) did. As Alfonso Pérez-Agote has put it, "the social effectiveness of an idea, that is, its capacity to influence behavior, does not depend on its scientific veracity, but rather on the degree of certainty it achieves, on its capacity to assert itself as true, which, in turn, depends on the mechanisms of social gestation and reproduction of the idea."[14] .

Also, I am interested in examining the ideas of Garat, Chaho, and others as expressions of a certain degree of common belonging that existed among the inhabitants of Iparralde. In the same way, I am interested in exploring the extent to which Arana's discourse was taken up in Iparralde, even though it was only among a small group in the Eskualerriste movement, and I want to find out the extent to which his ideas survived in the collective memory of Iparralde's inhabitants. I am interested, too, in examining the extent to which these figures were instrumentalized by contemporary Basque nationalists to legitimize their own discourse, thereby reconstructing history and local memory. Once again to invoke Pérez-Agote, "Social reality is very conventional, and when social actors define a collective or group reality, their behavior is predicative in that they configure something. But it is also performative in the sense that they do something, since they generate the same reality that they define."[15]

Finally, through an examination of the work of these figures, I will seek an explanation for why civic values, once they had been (re)elaborated in the discourse of Garat, Chaho, Arana, and others and returned to the inhabitants of Iparralde, did not take root. At the same time, I will address the question of how the discursive suitability of the

Basque self-identifications[16] of the Aintzina group from 1933 on was able to gain some ground among a population ridden with the French ex-combatant mentality. To cite Pérez-Agote once more, "for a group to succeed, it requires social, rather than logical or scientific, plausibility. In other words, it needs a social milieu in which the definition makes sense for the actors; it depends more on their perceptions than on the objective reality of the defining feature itself."[17] How, then, did Basque self-identification eventually come to make sense for social actors in Iparralde?

Traces of Basque Nationalism in Iparralde

From the mid-nineteenth century on, the ambiguous nature of the French-Spanish border as both an exclusionary barrier and a contact zone between communities that are divided administratively and politically was exploited by some individuals interested in maintaining cross-border links: Chaho and Antoine d'Abbadie from Iparralde, together with Campión and Arana from Hegoalde.

However, one of the first voices to question the division of the Basque Country was Dominique-Joseph Garat, who served as representative for Lapurdi at the meeting of the Estates General, as well as the French minister of both justice and the interior in the 1790s. Prior to this political activity, he had already demonstrated a certain cultural affinity toward the land of his birth when, after the abolition of the *fors* and after the French government turned down a request to create a single Basque *département* in 1790, he protested in the name of his province before the French National Constituent Assembly. Later, after Napoleon's rise to power, he presented the emperor with a plan to unite all the Basque provinces (of both Iparralde and Hegoalde) in an autonomous political unit—to be known as New Phoenicia—integrated into the Napoleonic empire.

Shortly after Garat's death in 1833, Agosti Chaho published the novel *Voyage en Navarre pendant l'insurrection des Basques* (Journey to Navarre during the Basque Insurrection), a work that condensed its author's views on the original universal nobility and freedom of the Basque people. Thus, for Chaho, the Basque Carlist general Tomás Zumalacárregui—at the time leading his troops in the First Carlist War—was fighting for Basque freedom and independence. Years later, the maverick Chaho, who had been part of the esoteric movement in nineteenth-century France and an avid believer in clairvoyance, led the 1848 French Revolution in Baiona and went down in history as the first Basque (allegedly) to be buried in a civil, rather than religious service after his death in 1858.[18]

Finally, after a personal "revelation" (a recurring theme for Chaho), Sabino Arana elaborated an ideology that, initially, called for the independence of Bizkaia, a call that he later extended to the whole Basque Country. Basing his ideas on a fervent Catholicism and on racial interpretations of Basque identity, thereby distancing himself from Campión's (as well as Garat's and Chaho's) basically linguistic vision of Basque difference, he created the foundations of a Basque nationalist movement that, by the 1930s, became a significant political factor in Hegoalde.[19]

Garat, Chaho, and Arana were ultimately the three most important individuals in this initial (re)configuring of Basque identity, as well as the consequent emergence of first a protonationalism and then a full-fledged nationalism. Through their personal development, intellectual formation, and political influence, they could be considered a kind of elite that both directed and translated a certain reality to others. And as with any elite, they might have been capable of organizing a new worldview, that is, of "objectively" constructing a reality that *might* one day become "subjectively" assimilated by an entire or part of a people.

The role of elites is a recurring theme in the study of nationalism. Indeed, modernists—that is, those who view nationalism as a product of the modern age—tend to grant such elites a decisive role in the emergence and spread of nationalism.[20] Thus, from instrumentalist positions inspired by Mancur Olson's rational choice theory,[21] the emergence of nationalism is seen as connected to elite strategies for mobilizing a people, coordinating its interests, and legitimizing elite activities with the ultimate goal of attaining power.[22] Beginning from similar interpretations, some authors have attempted to link nationalism to the importance of certain rootless intellectuals. The principal exponent of this theory, Elie Kedourie,[23] makes a connection between the millenarian dimensions of this elite discourse and the emotional (or even fanatical) adherence of the people to it. In similar fashion, from a militant Spanish nationalist perspective, Jon Juaristi would seem to advocate a similar role to the elite framers of Basque nationalist discourse, for he constantly refers to their pasts as humble office workers or notaries,[24] as if they were searching dreamily for a mystical cure for their most human frustrations. These interpretations see the nation as converted, in alchemist fashion, into a representation of the elite self—or rather, these elites come to represent the nation.

I would not deny that such rational, instrumentalist psychological approaches do have some merit in understanding nationalism. However, they tend to mask, if not to ignore altogether, a crucial feature of the phenomenon: As Walker Connor points out, one cannot reduce nationalism to the simple quest for power—whether, I would add, by an individual or a group—for it is also a nonrational or emotional bond. While many academics have failed to acknowledge this, however,[25] through history, political leaders have understood perfectly well that "at the core of ethnopsychology is the sense of shared blood, and they have not hesitated to appeal to it."[26] Therefore, the important thing is not *what is*, but what *one says is*. Furthermore, "The question is not the sincerity of the propagandist, but the nature of the mass instinct to which the propagandist appeals. Napoleon was unquestionably more a manipulator of than a believer in nationalism, but his armies were certainly filled with soldiers fired up by nationalism."[27]

Here, it is of less interest to me whether, for example, Garat should be analyzed in his role as the French minister of justice and the interior,[28] and therefore as an exemplary French Jacobin, or as a founding thinker on Basque territorial unity or nationalism.[29] Similarly, I am not concerned in this work whether Chaho should be considered an enlightened opportunist,[30] as a sui genesis precursor of Nietzsche from Zuberoa (as his work would seem to indicate, although that is not the focus of the present study), as a genius,[31] or as the first Basque separatist.[32] By the same token, it is of little importance here whether Arana should be considered an ultra-Catholic,[33] the father of Basque nationalism,[34] or merely the Tartarin of Bizkaia.[35] Instead, what interests me here is the popular response to their ideas—both at the time they were first disseminated and during more recent eras.

For this reason, a methodological approach to the following question is required: How were the ideas that nationalists used, controlled, constructed, and/or recovered to mobilize a particular population—so that these ideas resonated among the people to whom they were directed? Anthony D. Smith highlights three basic goals of nationalism: national autonomy, national unity, and national identity. In other words, all nationalist movements seek to achieve and maintain the "autonomy, unity and identity for a population which some of its members deem to constitute an actual or potential nation."[36]

The concept of autonomy is based on the notion of "self-regulation, having one's own internal laws or rhythms, listening only to one's own inner voice, free of every external constraint."[37] This, in turn, is linked to the concept of collective unity: territorial unification that must be expressed internally, a fact highlighted in the Basque case—being divided between two states—as well as externally. This territorial unity is the basic condition for a later social and cultural unification of the members of the nation: that "they should *feel* an intense bond of solidarity, therefore *act* in unison on all matters of national importance."[38] Finally, national identity is characterized by "its concern for collective character and its historical-cultural basis," with "the implication that to each nation there corresponds a distinct historical culture, a singular way of thinking, acting and communicating, which all the members share (at least potentially)." From this, "It follows that, [even] where such a distinct culture has been 'lost', 'forgotten' or 'submerged', it can and must be found, remembered and brought to light. The task of nationalists is to rediscover the unique cultural genius of the nation and restore to a people its authentic cultural identity." As such, one can comprehend the role of intellectuals or the intelligentsia in their attempts to discover the national essence through archeology, anthropology, sociology, and folklore, trying to answer the questions, Who are we? When did our history begin? How did we develop? Where are we going? And so on. However, Smith continues, these abstract ideals require concrete political and cultural programs, hence the need to elaborate discourses of authenticity, continuity, dignity, destiny, attachment, and homeland.[39]

Authenticity obliges nationalists to seek out the original elements of their people's existence, eliminating everything that was subsequently added on, in order "to be 'truly' ourselves." "Here," then Smith argues, "authenticity translates into correspondence with 'truth', opposing the genuine to the fake." Further,

> This leads on imperceptibly to the notion of authenticity as originality and . . . to a myth of origins and descent: 'who we are' is a function of 'whence we came' in time and space; character is determined by origin. But this overlaps with yet another meaning: the idea of being originary and indigenous, that is, not only the first of its kind but also autochthonous,

sprung from the soil. That in turn leads on to another sense of the authentic as pure and unmixed.[40]

Continuity implies that the nation has not changed with the passage of time and is merely "awaiting its moment of regeneration."[41] Meanwhile, the notion of dignity is opposed to a situation of humiliation, prostration, and oppression that nationalism is attempting to overcome. Yet at the same time, dignity "must be 'rediscovered' within." As a result, it supposes "'true worth', concealed by external disfigurements." This stance, then, "promises a status reversal in which the oppressed and peripheralized will be restored to their former greatness," although "dignity can also come from noble pedigree and antiquity." As regards destiny, it speaks "of transcendence, perhaps immortality . . . always glorious, like its distant past." As such, "the destiny of each nation is not to return to the glorious past, but to recreate its spirit in modern terms."[42]

Attachment implies that the supreme virtue should be love of the nation, amplified, according to Letamendia's argument, by the game of mirrors that all nationalisms specify, trying to subsume at their core the state they seek.[43] As a result, on numerous occasions, a nationalist movement becomes a projection of the national society, and the nationalist community that of the national community. Finally, this love must find shape, and the preferred setting is that of a homeland, to the extent that "'attachment' and the '*homeland*' reinforce each other in a quest to return to roots. Even nations that reside in their homelands need 're-rooting', reattaching themselves to their pristine origins, their authentic self."[44] This, in turn, explains nationalism's fascination with the rural world or its ties with the peasantry.[45] Similarly, the homeland acquires a sacred character as the land in which one's ancestors lie. At the same time, it is also the setting of epic deeds—whether real or invented—all this in the context of a landscape that one takes to have a personality of its own.

With this in mind, let us begin by tracing all these ideas in the discourses of Garat and Chaho, the two individuals chiefly responsible for the first stage of the articulation of a Basque identity in Iparralde. Yet this initial articulation was also a reconstruction, grounded in a certain reality, for their ideas must have expressed, to a greater or lesser degree, the values of certain sectors of the population at these moments. As we will also see, more recently, these values have been refined further still, in the twentieth century, to link the present with the past, thereby legitimizing contemporary Basque nationalism and connecting it with its predecessors.

CHAPTER THREE

Dominique-Joseph Garat and the "New Phoenicia"

Dominique-Joseph Garat was born in Baiona in 1749, although he spent his childhood in Uztaritze (Ustaritz). After studying law in Bordeaux, in 1777, he began work as a journalist in Paris, where, among other events, he covered the American Revolution. In 1789, he was elected representative of the Third Estate for Lapurdi to attend the meeting of the Estates General, which had been called by King Louis XVI. Later, in 1792, despite his own personal opposition to the decision, as minister of justice in Revolutionary France, he was charged with communicating to the king the death sentence that had been passed on him. Garat resigned after this decision and was arrested twice by the Jacobin authorities. However, with the Jacobin fall from power, from 1794 to 1795 he led the commission charged with implementing the new educational system and in 1798 was named French ambassador to Naples. That same year, he was elected president of the Council of Elders (the upper house of the French Directory) and later became a senator in Napoleonic France. Furthermore, Napoleon appointed him to head a study of the French-occupied Netherlands, and in the subsequent report, Garat recommended to the emperor that it should remain an autonomous region within the empire. After opposing Napoleon during the events associated with the arrival of Louis XVIII on the French throne and Napoleon's subsequent (although brief) return to power in 1814–15, he retired from his post in the senate. He abandoned politics altogether and settled once more in Iparralde, where, in Basusarri (Bassussary), on December 9, 1833, he died.

Garat is a key figure in the political history of Iparralde for his role after the abolition of the Basque institutions with the triumph of the French Revolution. Furthermore, he is also important for the plans he drew up to unite the Basque provinces of both Iparralde and Hegoalde in one political unity: New Phoenicia, a confederation that would have formed a part of the Napoleonic French empire. Before examining these events, however, let us first trace the impact of the Revolution in Iparralde.

The French Revolution

The French Revolution initiated a new stage in the history of Lapurdi, Zuberoa, and Nafarroa Beherea. However, how that new stage began has been the subject of much contestation. Three contradictory interpretations of the reception of the French Revolution appear in the historiography of the development of Iparralde. In one, Basques saluted enthusiastically the triumph of the Revolution, or at least the growth of the new state, as if by magic they had become, overnight, more French than the Marseillaise. On the contrary, another interpretation insists, both the population as a whole and the elites of Iparralde were from the outset dedicated counterrevolutionaries and reactionaries. No, a third insists, while certain elements in the ideas of Garat and Chaho might be taken to reveal a hostility to the Revolution, that hostility was not counterrevolutionary or reactionary, but instead was based on identity-related criteria, almost as if, already, during the revolutionary period, the people of Iparralde resisted integration into France from national or nationalist premises.

These interpretations clearly reflect the interests of the authors that wrote them. As Jean Goyhenetche observes, "The French Revolution in the Basque Country and other areas has been invoked in the context of struggles, controversies, [and] political and ideological debates, giving rise to a stimulating and intense historiography, but [one that] does not always respect the rules of academic scrutiny."[1] For example, unconditional attachment to the Revolution has been frequently portrayed by both historians and sociologists aiming to underscore the fact that Iparralde differed little from other areas in France. Elsewhere, the importance of religion in French and Basque historiography has influenced observers who, like Father Pierre Haristoy, attempt to include in their analyses the almost perpetual conflict between church and state in France, invoking martyrology to explain certain forms of hostility toward the Revolution in Iparralde.[2] Thus, for Jean Goyhenetche, "Fr. Haristoy's work . . . was marked by the turbulent interventions of the Basque clergy, coming from a conservative monarchist tradition [and] opposed to the strengthening and stabilizing of the republican system."[3] Moreover,

> The role of history was extremely ideological and apologetic, in an attempt to legitimize the ideology, politics, system, or church that Haristoy said he defended in the face of a [new] system—a state to oppose. His program was [therefore] part of wider plan followed by an important part of the church in the Basque Country in the late nineteenth century. History became a field of conflict between two social groups linked [on the one hand] to the republican state and the Third Republic, and [on the other] to the church or a part of it that opposed any relations with [the state]. At the center of the controversy lay the Revolution.[4]

We also should bear in mind how, from a Basque nationalist perspective, authors such as Eugène Goyheneche[5] and Jean-Louis Davant[6] explain the conflict associated with the development of the Revolution in Iparralde as a struggle over national identity, judging the local response to these events in a language that would be later employed by Arana's (re)interpretation of the Basque Country following the abolition of the *fueros* in Hegoalde. For example:

> The result of the emergence of Basque identity and its political claims, the historiography of the last thirty years has been marked by the consciousness of (Basque) national belonging transformed into an object of history that opposes the traditional institutional history, that of the state. We are witnessing what Marc Ferrer terms "institutional antihistory," that of the "defeated," the intellectual milieu of a society searching for its identity and collective memory.[7]

The reality of the historical situation in Iparralde during the French Revolution, however, was more complex, and might possibly be defined as a kind of aggregate of all of these three positions. In other words, already at the outset of the Revolution, there were widespread liberal sympathies in Iparralde among both elites and the regular population in urban and coastal communities, and they, in turn, found some common ground with the lower classes and peasantry of the interior who had grievances against the aristocracy. Therefore, one can conclude that the Revolution was greeted enthusiastically among certain sectors of the population in Iparralde. However, elite sectors soon focused their concerns on the maintenance of the Basque institutional system. These elites argued for their place in the new France within a context of the "national regeneration" they hoped would follow the Revolution. That said, and in the face of irreversible facts such as the abolition of provincial institutions, they attempted, as a last resort, to safeguard their differential status by demanding their own *département*. The disillusionment resulting from the loss of their administrative traditions and being forced into a *département* with Béarn, together with a growing apathy among the inhabitants of Iparralde (especially in Lapurdi) toward the Revolution as a result of being forced to participate in the war against Spain, led, in turn, to a repressive response on the part of the revolutionary authorities, and this alienated even further large sections of the lower classes from the revolutionary fervor sweeping the country. Moreover, this, one should recall, was a population suffering the worst effects of the war. And when the state began to implement a series of measures against church interests, the clergy in Iparralde managed to foment this social disillusionment by essentializing the Basque language and customs, thanks to its still significant social power and prestige. Thus, it managed to sustain a reactionary position in Iparralde through to the beginning of the twentieth century.

It is necessary, then, to look more closely at the impact of the French Revolution in Iparralde, for only by unraveling this complex series of events can we understand better the nuances of Garat's and Chaho's thought, and only from such a perspective can we judge whether or not they were, indeed, Basque or French nationalists, revolutionaries or counterrevolutionaries.

Republican Fervor

Thanks to the diligent research of people such as Xipri Arbelbide and, above all, Manex Goyhenetche, it is now possible to examine the effects of the French Revolution in Iparralde. Only by basing my observations on their findings—especially regarding the sense of belonging in Iparralde at this time—can I hope to understand better the discourse of Garat and Chaho.[8]

The dispute between Baiona and Uztaritze over which town should send representation to Paris in the name of Lapurdi appears to have been the first expression of a process that began with the convocation of the Estates General by the King Louis XVI of France and Navarre.[9] This dispute reflected the urgency to become part of something new that was beginning to stir and, as Goyhenetche observes, that was evident in the participation of 152 delegates in the provincial assembly of Lapurdi on April 19, 1789—after official recognition of the representational rights of the province's *Biltzar* at the expense of the seneschal authority of Baiona, proof of the interest that participation in the Estates General had raised in Iparralde.[10]

Beyond this level of interest, however, it does not seem that there were any differences between the nature of the debates that took place in Baiona and in towns in the rest of the country. For example, one can see in records of these meetings in Baiona clear references to the sacred nature of property as connected to the concept of citizenship, an interpretation that preceded Emmanuel Joseph Sieyès' later distinction between "active" and "passive" citizens. At the same time, the report drawn up for Baiona's participation in the Estates General also anticipated the perimeters around which the later republican discourse of the National Assembly was based: that all provinces should make up the composition of the assembly of the Estates General according to their wealth and population, that the first two orders should be counterbalanced by the third, that elections should be held freely, and that votes should not be assessed by orders, but by people.[11] In sum, what we see here are the principles of property, freedom, and equality based on Alexis de Tocqueville's basic criteria: the equality of political rights before the aristocracy and clergy and the equating of legal status with material conditions as long as a citizen possessed wealth.

In similar fashion, the *ahiers de doléances* (documents listing provincial grievances) presented by the Third Estate of Lapurdi displayed a modern, liberal tone and included, for example, a demand for the abolition of slavery. They also called for a clear and conclusive defense of individual rights, together with freedom of conscience and the press.[12] Goyhenetche describes the general attitude of the Lapurdi nobility as "liberal, eager to participate in the government of the monarchy within the framework of regular meetings of the Estates General." Therefore, and from a Physiocratic perspective[13] pervading this outlook, "one sees in Lapurdi a nobility whose members feel called to play a new role through their own capabilities. Maintaining their privileges, and still supported by the monarchy and the forces of order, they became intermediaries between the king and the people in the exercise of duties associated with social and political order and within the framework of a structure proposed by Montesquieu."[14]

Similarly, the clergy in Lapurdi also tended to distance itself from absolutism and the concentration of powers. It is especially worth noting one document (which remained unpublished until 1922) cited by Goyhenetche where, under the title *Doléances du sexe de Saint-Jean-de-Luz et Ciboure* (Gender Grievances of Donibane Lohizune and Ziburu), a critique was published of "the ways in which the three Estates have been convened to address the question of the three social orders, but not that of the presence of women: Your majesty wanted to assemble the whole nation, but you forgot us in your call."[15]

Although the claims of Nafarroa Beherea centered on its insertion into France (or, as the province's texts put it, the "nation"), in some of its arguments, one also finds modern principles that have little to do with reactionary thought.[16] Finally, in some of the declarations of various communes in Zuberoa, there were calls for a free press and freedom of conscience, the equality of fiscal duties, and so on.

Consequently, it is hardly surprising that Baiona found itself in the revolutionary vanguard once events began to unfold. Indeed, as Goyhenetche points out, the Revolution was not just "imported" from Paris, but also began in Iparralde, and events there even to some extent anticipated later developments throughout France.[17] This explains the fact that Basques such as Garat, Pierre-Eustache D'Hiriart, and Daguerressar were important both *locally* in Iparralde and *nationally* in France.[18] Thus one can understand the initial response of Bertrand Barère de Vieuzac, the notorious Jacobin,[19] to events in the Basque Country, deliberately not identifying it with the counterrevolution and highlighting its clear support for the cause. However, he did add an important caveat: the resistance of the Basque clergy to outright pro-revolutionary sentiment. This probably explains, together with the position of Iparralde in the war with Spain, the revolutionary attitude toward the Basque provinces: an initial suspicion, hesitantly expressed by Barère de Vieuzac, followed by outright repression.

The Basque Arrangement

This reformist spirit clearly supported some kind of reform of the state. It lay behind the institutional demands of the Basque representatives and forms the context for the role that Garat played in his position as representative for Lapurdi.

That said, the initial position of the Estates General of Nafarroa Beherea was an angry rejection of any change and an attempt to defend the legal status quo. Meeting in Donibane Garazi on March 27, 1789, they thought that "the form of convocation by *bailliages* and *sénéchaussées* [*ancien régime* forms of assembly] is, as regards Navarre [Nafarroa Beherea], irregular, illegal, and anticonstitutional." Later, on April 4, they decreed that "the letters of convocation sent to Navarre [Nafarroa Beherea] infringe on the rights and constitution of this kingdom."[20] Within this kingdom, in their opinion, they were "the true and legitimate representatives of the Nation," although the convocation "classified Navarre [Nafarroa Beherea] as a province of the Kingdom of France, while Navarre

[Nafarroa Beherea] has never ceased to be a kingdom separate and distinct from that of France." In sum, as Goyhenetche observes, initially, the historic and legal rights of the Kingdom of Navarre–both in appearance and theory–were, indeed, respected.[21]

Later, on June 19, 1789, a document was produced that officially reflected the province's position. It was a thoroughly political text in which sixty-three of its seventy-one articles referred directly to provincial institutional organization. Here, Goyhenetche contends, the Estates of Nafarroa Beherea

> proposed to restore with all their power the historic and juridical reality of the institutions in the Navarrese kingdom. A National Assembly was contemplated, with powers of control over legislative affairs, administration, the application of justice, collecting taxes, [and] public order. It was an attempt to end the weakening of [its] representative institutions by reconfiguring the Estates of Navarre [Nafarroa Beherea] as a National Assembly "that had always represented the whole nation." . . . [Consequently] the Estates proposed a return to an original form of pact making embodied by a mutually guaranteed loyalty to a contractual monarchy.[22]

This, for Goyhenetche, was a kind of return to the pact making that underscored the medieval agreements of the *fors*, but that had not been put into practice since the sixteenth century. However, in his opinion, such an agreement would not sit well with absolutism. Further still, in advocating a distinct institutional framework, it amounted to a complete denial of the system of the *ancien régime*. Thus for Goyhenetche, "the ideal government" proposed by the Estates of Nafarroa Beherea was reflected "in the law associated with the Enlightenment movement, inspired at the same time by the ideas of Montesquieu and Rousseau. They interpreted in the historical and juridical past of Navarre [Nafarroa Beherea] the same foundations as those of the principle of individual liberty."[23] As the June 1789 document itself put it, "the Kings of Navarre swear to maintain their rights and their *fors*. This general promise is applied not only to the Nation *en Corps*, but also to those of the individuals that form it. The most important of all individual rights is that which affects individual liberty."[24] However, for Jean Goyhenetche, this pact-making policy did not stem from a questioning of the institutional unity of the state.[25] For that reason, he emphasizes the juridical nature of the June 1789 document without finding "any constitutive or foundational elements of a Navarrese nation-state." In fact, he continues,

> The nobility and the Third Estate had acquired social and political benefits that nobody wanted to lose in an eventual confrontation with the French monarchist state. Under the appearances of a "special administrative regime" . . . they were in favor of a system of power that had guaranteed them control of the institutions or government structures at the level of Basse-Navarre [Nafarroa Beherea]. It was about protecting the benefits gained from Navarrese foral law.[26]

The *cahiers* of Zuberoa also contained ample evidence of an attachment to local institutions. The "commune" is the lowest level of administrative division in the French state, roughly equivalent to a municipality. For the communes in Zuberoa, custom was associated with a constitution even at that level,[27] a fact—as we will see—later picked up by Chaho and, one hundred years after him, by Lafitte. Therefore, and in moderate terms, these *cahiers* called for the continuation of the privileges enjoyed by the province while at the same time accepting the need to reform some customs, especially in the realm of inheritance rights.

The *cahiers* of Lapurdi were the most widely known *cahiers* of the three provinces, thanks mainly to the role played by Garat. Paradoxically, the initial position of the Third Estate in Lapurdi—of which Garat was a member—was extremely compliant to the demands of Paris. It is true that it asked for the restoration of powers in the legislative and judicial affairs of provincial parliaments and local assemblies. Yet these demands of the *Biltzar* were not drawn up in any specific form that might respond to any future institutional, administrative, or social development in the province. Similarly, the directives of the *Biltzar* to its representatives did not evince any need for urgency, which, tied to Garat's likely wish to not seem out of place with the other representatives in the National Assembly, probably accounts for him not defending the maintenance of privileges in Lapurdi on the evening of August 4, 1789. In fact, it was only the abolition of these privileges that provoked a heated response from both the *Biltzar* and Garat.

In contrast, the clerical *cahiers* presented, from the first moment, an unambiguous stance, one in which, with Manex Goyhenetche, one can see a clear definition of the Basque nation, the term used in their texts. According to one clerical *cahier*, "our topographical situation, our particular character, our customs . . . the arrangements of our tradition, our language, our ways, everything, in one word, demands that we should govern ourselves and that we should have our own particular administration." Goyhenetche argues that such words seem to echo the spirit of the American Revolution or the theories of Rousseau, who "had defended the idea of a national character for every people or country." Indeed, the term "particular character" formed an entry in volumes 11 and 12 of the 1765 edition of that famous Enlightenment document, the *Encyclopédie*, and was connected to the concept of self-government.[28] In sum, the Basque clergy appeared to be thinking ahead by arguing in favor of a form of federalism—a fashionable theory at the time, yet one clearly distinct from both the *ancien régime* rulers of the time and the later Jacobin regime in France.

The Beginnings of Disillusionment

Within this context, the decision to abolish the *fors* came as a tremendous shock to the Basque representatives. Although they continued to express their loyalty to the Revolution, they tried with everything at their disposal to maintain the previous institutional system. For example, in November 1789, the town of Donapaleu drafted a letter in which, after expressing its support for the decrees of the National Assembly, it stated its loyalty to *its* laws and *its* monarchs; a curious declaration of royal vassalage (in plural terms), given that the king of France and Navarre (Nafarroa Beherea) had become (in October that year) merely the king of France.

In Lapurdi, the *Biltzar*, after severely reprimanding its representatives for their "voluntary" abandonment of the "orders" to defend their institutions, drafted a long document in which it presented its arguments to avoid implementation of the foral abolition law. Here, it contended that,

> The French Basques of Lapurdi have not ceased to repeat, constantly, to the government that their present constitution is the only one under which they can live ... A decree of the National Assembly has been passed that introduces the general abolition of provincial privileges, and as the consequence the destruction of the region. They regret deeply that they cannot state that the first law ... the law at the base of all others and the foundation of the National Assembly's decrees, prevents them from the sweet satisfaction of feeling, without any pain, the blessed regeneration of the state.[29]

As Goyhenetche contends, "after a time of hope, dreams, enthusiastic attachment, came the time of disillusion. Until that moment, the Third Estate of Lapurdi had drawn on many sources to justify its position: In the first instance, the historic and juridical foundations were based on custom," the tenets of which, about "the rights of inhabitants," had been developed out of a communitarian notion of local problems that shared with Enlightenment thought a vision of *regnum non est regis, sed comunitatis*—the kingdom does not belong to the king, but to the community As such, the revolutionary state should have emerged out of the community. Ultimately, the members of the *Biltzar* "did not consider themselves as mere individuals, subject to the law, without belonging or without attachment. Their conception of citizenship did not exclude ties with the group, society, the collectivity, [or their] hereditary legacy."[30]

This idea was likewise present in the creation of the United States, the provincial development of the Netherlands, and in the drafting of the French Declaration of the Rights of Man and the Citizen. "For the Third Estate of Lapurdi," Manex Goyhenetche continues, "the suppression of the *ancien régime*'s 'privileges' did not imply a rejection of intermediary bodies, such as the *Biltzar*, which for its members was still a social force and a social means of embodying the general interest. The political thought of the inhabitants of Lapurdi was [thus] inspired by an English model." That is, in England the evolution from *ancien régime* to social and political modernity took place through the gradual democratization of local structures.[31] Thus,

> On reading documents from the era, there is no doubt that the inhabitants of Lapurdi accepted the "national constitution" ... [while] also accepting "common law," a notion that did not contradict, from their perspective, the maintenance of the "constitution" of the "Basque nation," to use the terminology found in the preparatory texts of the *cahiers de doléances*. The citizenry was formed in plural and could have lived with the maintenance of the *Biltzar*. Its members understood the nation as a federation of provinces whose institutions would be "*regenerated*" thanks to the Revolution. As readers of Locke, Mably, Montesquieu

[and] Rousseau, [*Biltzar* members] understood the federal idea. Hopes of a nation were framed in Lapurdi in federal terms.[32]

In light of this conflict between centralization and federalism, one might begin to understand a certain deception in Iparralde, something that increased with the (unwanted) unification of the three Basque provinces with Béarn into one *département*. In similar fashion, the spirit of the *Biltzar* and the other Basque institutions was out of step with the idea of the Revolution and the Republic remade under Jacobin rule. Specifically, the Jacobins contrasted the two modes of sociopolitical organization in their charges of a lack of patriotism, in turn provoking a spiral in Iparralde of increasing popular apathy toward the Revolution, answered by a lack of confidence in the region on the part of the authorities and by official repression, leading to further civic apathy, lack of official confidence, and so on. This was a vicious circle that began with Barère de Vieuzac's notion that "fanaticism speaks Basque," which, in turn, forged an even deeper bond between the Basque clergy and Basque culture, eventually leading (especially during the Third Republic) to profoundly conservative positions in Iparralde.[33]

It is true that for certain revolutionaries such as Sieyès, it was extremely difficult to accept a distinct Basque perspective. However, "later, under Robespierre's leadership, the notion of a 'federal republic' was synonymous with an aristocratic conspiracy, with secession. However, on closely examining the archival texts dating from that time, there is no doubt that one could not confuse, as regards the *Biltzar*, feudalism with federalism, for if there was an assembly that maintained constantly antifeudal and antinoble positions, it was the *Biltzar*."[34] Whatever the case, the seed of antipatriotism had been planted, so that the *Biltzar* was forced to declare that "it is a quite strange misfortune not being able to exercise the first of all rights, the defense of one's existence, without being accused of pigheadedness or lack of patriotism." This was the reason its members refused to be considered "bad Frenchmen incapable of sacrificing anything for the great regeneration of France."[35]

The consolidation of the French state after the Revolution, beginning with the abolition of Basque institutions and the territorial blurring of Iparralde within the context of a new *département*, thus tempered the original Basque revolutionary fervor, so that, from this time on, there were clear differences in Iparralde between certain popular sectors of society attracted by the overtures of the Catholic Church (in need of support for its crusade against the secular state) and those who joined the new national project. This was perhaps most evident in Nafarroa Beherea, where from an originally radical position of hostility toward the Revolution, the authorities moved toward a policy of accommodation with it.[36]

The Effects of War

The outbreak of war with Spain in March 1793 had a direct effect on Iparralde, because it became the principal theater of operations. As a result, its population was submitted to a human and economic mobilization without precedent. This, in turn, "had a deep impact on the perception of the Revolution among the inhabitants of [Iparralde]. Specifically, under the pressure of military activity, the region assumed a new profile at a political, as well as economic level."[37]

One should first note that the state's *levée en masse* (the military call-up of all unmarried men between eighteen and twenty-five) was not well received in Iparralde. One might even say it was a disaster.[38] Indeed, so bad was the response that the revolutionary authorities—from the executive authority, the Directory, on down—were forced to take extreme measures and began to penalize economically the families of the men who deserted. However, it would appear that even the implementation of such harsh measures did not lead to significant change.[39]

Further, during the war against Spain, the resources of Iparralde were under pressure and its economy suffered as the result of having to host thousands of soldiers from across the country.[40] The economic strain resulted from a system whereby the military had the right to requisition goods from local households, in turn resulting in an extraordinary effort by the people of Iparralde to try to overcome the effects of such requisitions. Municipal documents from the time detail the hardship and in many cases describe a scenario where families could barely get by.[41] At the same time, grain, bread, and the entire production of the land were placed at the disposal of the military by official decree, while all artisans were required to offer their services to the armed forces.

It is hardly surprising that the situation for the local people deteriorated rapidly. At the end of December 1793, the General Council of Donibane Lohizune in Lapurdi pleaded to "seek the means to provide us with grain to guarantee the survival of the inhabitants of our town, in view of the fact that currently they are destitute . . . We must take care to prevent starvation, by all means."[42] This alarm was repeated throughout the early part of 1794 by several municipalities in the interior of Iparralde. In fact, they were forced to sell municipal land in order to be able to raise the revenue necessary to feed the local population. At the same time, prices rose sharply, including housing costs, which rose dramatically under the pressure of needing to house the soldiers stationed there. In such a situation, many local authorities in Iparralde—Baiona among them—began to yearn for a previous age when they enjoyed privileged commercial ties with Spain. Finally, the introduction of paper money led to a doubling of prices that depleted people's incomes, given that the real value of this new money was clearly less than that of its previous counterpart. Yet while the new notes were used by the soldiers stationed in Iparralde, and the business community was obliged to accept them, these same business people were forced to pay the difference when trying to use the money thereafter, because their fellow inhabitants would not accept them.

In light of these factors, one can better understand the dissatisfaction felt among the inhabitants of Iparralde with the institutional treatment they were receiving and even better understand their indifference toward the war with Spain. Within this context— and specifically in view of the effects of the war on the local population—one might also appreciate the reluctance of male inhabitants to enlist in the revolutionary forces. And there was yet another level of repression aimed at the population of Iparralde, an indiscriminate policy that targeted entire communities accused of being "reactionaries." Furthermore, this discrimination was used by the clergy to accord Basques a kind of martyr status in the face of the advance of the secular-revolutionary ideology.

This explains the desertion of forty-seven young men from Itsasu (Itxassou) in Lapurdi in 1794, later to enlist in royalist ranks. In reprisal, in February 1794, four people were executed for complicity with the insurrection.[43] Suspicion, however, had already fallen on Lapurdi at the beginning of the conflict, for the revolutionary authorities had sought some kind of explanation, over and above the military situation, for Spanish advances to the outskirts of Sara (Sare), one of the principal border towns in the province.

Initially, the suspicion that the inhabitants of these border communes were collaborating with the Spanish led the authorities to design a series of measures aimed at gaining their unconditional support, for example, through the use of Basque.[44] However, the subsequent arrival of new state representatives in Iparralde coincided with the beginnings of a cleansing strategy. This started with the drafting of a list of towns with populations that needed to be "evacuated," among which Sara stood out. As the Popular Society of Donibane Lohizune stated:

> The population of Sara has always demonstrated clear hatred toward the Revolution. This commune is inhabited only by aristocrats [the pejorative term for enemies of the Revolution] who, open to both sides, communicate with both the Republic and its enemies; desertions are common news; all the satellite spies of the Spanish despot pass through Sara . . . the antisocial behavior of the inhabitants of this commune reflects a clear animosity toward all patriots and [the desire for] revenge against the Republic; it is dangerous to allow in our environment corrupt individuals like this who, through their knowledge of the locality, might reinforce their criminal ties with Spain.[45]

In sum, then, after initial attempts to understand the local reality, "official" revolutionary positions soon became more radical, to the extent that the authorities attempted to build a *cordon sanitaire* on the border with Spain as a means of creating a no-man's land, thanks to the eviction of communes suspected of counterrevolutionary sympathies.[46] At the same time, taking into account the tensions and divisions throughout revolutionary France—including the revolts of certain regions, such as the Vendée between 1793 and 1796—the authorities attempted to cut out the source of what they saw as a potential rebellion in Lapurdi. Thus, in 1794, a decree was proclaimed that stated "the land known from here on as the Basque Country, in the area that skirts our borders, appears to be entirely sold to Spain; the priests of this nation have made of a great number of its inhabitants . . . fanatics and friends of the king."[47] As a result, it called for the deportation of all the inhabitants from the "infamous" communes of Sara, Itsasu, and Azkaine (Ascain), together with some of the people in Ezpeleta (Espelette), Ainhoa, Zuraide (Souraïde), Luhuso (Louhossoa), Makea (Macaye), Lekorne (Mendionde), Larresoro (Larressore), Biriatu (Biriatou) and Kanbo (Cambo-les-Bains).

Ultimately, this would be an easy decision for the revolutionary authorities to make, because it served as a good excuse to explain the military failure of the campaign against Spain, punishing the inhabitants of the borderland by accusing them of collaborating with the enemy under the influence of a recalcitrant clergy. Consequently, in simplistic and Manichean fashion, the inhabitants of these communes were accused of being "aristocrats" and counterrevolutionaries. Yet, on the contrary, as Manex Goyhenetche contends, the reality of Iparralde was that "in a region favorable to reforms in questions of justice and taxes, as observed in the *cahiers de doléances*, the people were not against the end of the *ancien régime*, but the form in which the new political and administrative model was being constructed." This question was tied, he adds, "to the more or less clandestine resistance to the civil constitution of the clergy or forced conscription," but not necessarily to "aristocratic" or counterrevolutionary sympathies.[48]

To be sure, the population of Iparralde was divided between those who followed those priests who acceded to the civil constitution of the clergy and those who resisted it.[49] Yet beyond the politicization of these differences, there was another, more personal or intimate dimension: the role of the church. As Arbelbide puts it,

> Seeing no other way out, [the people] had one means of escape: the church [and] their beliefs. Yet the churches were closed . . . There were no priests! . . . Nor funerals! Nor weddings! Even crosses themselves had been thrown to the ground in some places to make way for the planting of trees of liberty in their place. Think how believers must have felt at the time![50]

Thus a key divide began to take shape, a divide that helps us to comprehend the political evolution of Iparralde and France: that of the differences between religious and secular positions. As we will see, Basque culture fell trapped between the two, languishing insofar as both poles gradually came together in a consensus on one thing: French nationalism.

I must end this part of the discussion by returning to Manex Goyhenetche, a figure who, as will have been evident from the preceding pages, remains for me the most lucid and thorough observer of these events. For Goyhenetche,

> In a land that had largely agreed with the reforms of 1789 and that had complied with the decrees of the National Assembly, the disillusion provoked by the integration into one [non-Basque] *département* and [official] suspicion toward the greater part of the clergy was aggravated in the period from 1792 to 1794 by war, starvation, rising prices, [and] the burden of supplying requisitions for both men and goods. We have seen . . . the hope represented for the peasants and popular rural classes by the new fiscal system and equality of taxes. This was the peasants' hope that they might . . . be able to recover at least some of their income from the land, confiscated prior to 1789 by different fiscal dues. Yet despite the institutional change, the peasantry continued . . . to respond, voluntarily or by being forced, to different requisition orders. It was easy for nostalgic supporters of the *ancien régime* to use the land issue to increase their influence in a rural society that was on its knees as a result of the burden of all these problems and the [consequent] disillusion . . . [Yet] we have also seen that the attitude of young people, their discontent with military conscription

and even the revolutionary mythology . . . was a natural, spontaneous outlook. Blaming such behavior on "aristocrats" or rebel priests and emigrants accused of "fanaticism" misses the nuance of the situation . . . The answer to this was a multiple form of repression (political, linguistic, religious) that became a political instrument with which to stamp out any danger that might threaten the interests of state [the basic reason behind the deportation of people from the communes in and around Sara]. It was neither the excesses nor the errors . . . of the revolutionary government, but rather the social and political behavior of Basques that made them into the scapegoats for all the problems. This justified the internment of Basques for [Jacques] Pinet [organizer of a revolutionary tribunal in Baiona]: "[by] removing these men from the border and therefore the Spanish, dispersing them, mixing them with other people, one could hope for a change in their habits . . . a still more justified hope given that, belonging to the *sans-culottes* [poorer] class, their crimes must be explained by ignorance in which their priests have kept them." What logic! They were not, then, "aristocrats," these victims of Jacobin politics, but *sans-culottes*, that is, people from the popular classes.[51]

I quote Goyhenetche at some length to demonstrate that it is not surprising, as a consequence, to observe that a dark memory of this time persisted among the inhabitants of Iparralde, beyond even any capitalization on these events by the church.[52]

Garat and Basque Difference

Initially, only Baiona was called on by the king to participate in the meeting of the Estates General. This, in turn, resulted in a protest by the *Biltzar* of Lapurdi, which stated that it did not recognize Baiona as the capital of the province and, as a result, did not feel represented by the city. Finally, after a period of arduous negotiation, the royal order of March 28, 1789, recognized the right of Lapurdi to send representation while at the same time denying Baiona this authority. At the same time, Nafarroa Beherea, appealing on "historic and juridical doctrinal grounds as a distinct kingdom separate from France,"[53] refused to take its place among the delegates to the meeting.[54] And Zuberoa, likewise, was not represented at the convocation.

Before attending the meeting of the Estates General, the *Biltzar* of Lapurdi drew up its *cahier de doléances*. As mentioned, it was designed to maintain provincial "privileges" within the coming new system, based on its specific vision of what the "regeneration" of the state should imply. However, Garat did not speak during the night of August 4, when Lapurdi's traditional institutions were abolished, an issue that earned him the reprobation of the *Biltzar*. In his own defense, Dominique-Joseph Garat recalled:

> The motion [abolishing the privileges] was not only received with applause, but a wave of enthusiasm and generosity swiftly being passed on from one person to another. They interrupted one another [only] to offer, promise, [and] confirm sacrifices. One motion did not wait for another; they were all passed as soon as they were presented. Yesterday's adversaries embraced one another with tears in their eyes. The most unlucky ones were, without doubt, those who possessed no advantage that they might have been able to give up.[55]

However, the *Biltzar* responded angrily to the abolition of the privileges and on November 18, 1789, (the last date it would meet) published a document that listed the reasons why the maintenance of its customs was crucial to the survival of the province. Among these points, its limited agricultural resources and the costs associated with maintaining the border stood out. At the same time, the document noted that abolishing certain levies, as decreed by the Assembly, did not help the reality of the region at all, given that they had never previously been sufficient. Finally, it pointed out that Lapurdi would oppose any integration with Baiona and Béarn in the event of any administrative reorganization. Yet it also mentioned that "if against our wishes it were impossible to leave Lapurdi as it was, it would be with the Basques of Navarre [Nafarroa Beherea] and Zuberoa with whom it would fraternize best, for between them, there is an identity of customs and laws."[56]

Subsequently, the mandate of the *Biltzar* and Garat's later discourse before the National Assembly during the debate on the creation of new *départements* would center on linguistic differences with Béarn and were based on the fact that such differences would lead to an insurmountable barrier between the two. Therefore, for Garat, the plan to unite the Basque provinces with Béarn within the proposed *département* of the Basses-Pyrénées would be "psychologically and morally impossible."[57] However, despite such protests, the debate ended with approval for the project, and Iparralde was joined to Béarn in a single *département*. After asking for the right to respond, Garat turned to the president of the National Assembly:

> I have just one more thing I must do: I am not dictated to by reason or by personal conscience. My personal opinion is that all French people must obey the decrees of the National Assembly. Yet I do have an express order from my electors, passed in a unanimous vote, that obliges me to protest in their name against any decree that joins them with Béarn. I ask for the minutes to acknowledge my compliance with this order.[57]

The protest was meaningless. On January 12, 1790, it was formally agreed that the Basque provinces be joined with Béarn in a single *département*. On February 8, it was decided that this *département* would be divided into six districts, three of which corresponded to the historic Basque provinces. Despite the initial protest, however, as Joseba Agirreazkuenaga argues, the new administrative structure was gradually put in place without any explicit objection of the part of the municipalities.[59] Yet as we have seen, this decree also put an end to support for state reform that Basque elites had initially shown.

Basque Unification

Years after these events, on the several occasions between 1803 and 1811 when Garat presented the Emperor Napoleon with an ambitious project that envisaged uniting Basques on both sides of the border in one administrative unit, named "New Phoenicia," to be governed by France, it was the first explicitly political project for uniting the entire Basque Country. Yet it should not be considered a Basque nationalist initiative. For even if it did anchor its claims in linguistic, cultural, and historical terms (tradition and the *fors*), its autonomy was designed to fit squarely within the Napoleonic empire. Thus, Garat attempted to convince the emperor on purely rational or instrumental grounds.

Moreover, it seems clear that, beyond such rational claims (a theme I will return to below), this proposal signaled an attempt to alleviate in Iparralde the harsh reality it had been submitted to as a result of the war with Spain. In this way, Garat's plan attempted to improve the living conditions of his neighbors. Trade with Spain, a traditional source of wealth for Lapurdi, had all but dried up; the fishing industry was in a precarious situation, given the English blockade (another consequence of the Napoleonic wars); and the previous commercial exceptions enjoyed by Baiona had been abolished in 1789.[60] As a result, Garat did not fail to mention the potential economic benefits that such a plan might have for Iparralde.

Similarly, his plan found support among sectors of the Spanish Basque population, whose elites had tentatively welcomed the occupation of Napoleon's troops in return for respecting their laws and religion. For that reason, the head of these forces, General Bon Adrien Jeannot de Moncey, had already alluded to the idea of cultivating Basque neutrality in the conflict. Specifically, in 1795, he sent a report to the Committee of Public Safety (the de facto executive authority of Revolutionary France at the time) explaining his plan: "You know that the people of this land exercise their sovereignty . . . everything is democratic among them. For that reason, it would be like paying homage to the people of Gipuzkoa, who have always exercised it, restoring their old government: so that the people meet again as they did in the past . . . the inhabitants of these places clutch onto their laws."[61] Moncey's view was based on a reflection that did not hide the risk of a possible uprising that, taking the form of guerrilla warfare, would make any occupation difficult to maintain, something that, in fact, occurred a decade later. To avoid any local hostility, Moncey proposed joining the provinces of Araba, Bizkaia, and Gipuzkoa into an independent, autonomous unit under French protection, with France promising to respect the customs, freedoms, and religion of its inhabitants. Ultimately, this plan was rejected, yet later Garat picked up the idea once more, extending its application to Iparralde and Navarre.

It is possible that Moncey's initiative was based on a French strategic change of attitude at the time to allow for a potential tactical alliance with the local authorities of Hegoalde that might facilitate the neutrality of Bilbao (and therefore its port) in July 1795. However, just at that time, the war with Spain came to an end, and the subsequent Peace of Basle reestablished the border at its prewar position. In Hegoalde, the "ambiguous" reaction of Gipuzkoa toward the French occupation was greeted by the Spanish authorities with the increasingly bitter suspicion that certain local elites there were sympathetic to the French Republic.[62] Indeed, some commentators have speculated whether these events lead, as a consequence, to calls to abolish the *fueros* in Hegoalde.[63] Without doubt, the ambiguous position of the authorities in Gipuzkoa encouraged Garat to devise a form of Basque unification that, despite its grounding in a cultural argument, also served the interests of the Republic.

Therefore, following Moncey's ideas, Garat based his proposal on the Basques' popular belief in their secular nobility, on local laws and customs, and on the existence of a shared language—in sum, on entirely cultural elements in which more than likely the emperor had little interest. Consequently, Garat had to make the idea more attractive for Napoleon by seeking a more practical dimension, and this he aimed to do through the title of his report: "A Succinct Statement on a Project to Merge Some Cantons in France and Spain and the Creation of a Powerful Fleet." In other words, he highlighted the strategic possibilities of such a proposal. Specifically, grounding his argument in the potential creation of a large naval fleet with which to gain control of the ocean for what, when he first proposed the project in 1803 under the Consulate, with Napoleon as First Consul, were still the revolutionary forces, he contended that New Phoenicia would serve as the buffer zone between France and "reactionary" Spain and that losing this part of their territory would entail significant costs for the Spanish authorities.[64] However, in the long run, this proposal was never seriously considered, because, in the opinion of Iñaki Aguirre, it came too late:

> In 1811, when he [Garat] finalized his task, the first cracks appeared in what would subsequently turn into the collapse of the Napoleonic edifice. The imperial dream of a "United States of Europe" . . . was being threatened by the resistance of Spain and Portugal against the French armies and the threat on their eastern front from the war preparations of the huge Russian Empire. The "corner of Europe" from which Garat wrote in 1803—the date of his first letter to Napoleon—once more became [for the Emperor] . . . a miniscule canton.[65]

On the basis of the New Phoenicia project, Michel Duhart suggests that Garat should be "considered among the precursors of Basque nationalism, given that he was the first to make an effort to join the seven provinces in one unit."[66] However, if Garat was a precursor of Basque nationalism, it was not so much for his politics—which I believe to have been more instrumental than ideological in their application to Basque issues—but rather for his general writings. These, in effect, prefigured the contours around which the discursive components of Basque nationalism—authenticity, continuity, dignity, antiquity, a sense of attachment to the homeland, and, of course, a homeland that claims ones feelings and allegiances—would later be drawn.

In Garat's work, the three principal elements associated with the recovery (or production) of an authentic cultural identity— purity, originality, and a myth of origins—were closely connected to the most advanced thought of the age.[67] Indeed, Garat "reproached those learned men who, wishing to test Rousseau's theories of the 'noble savage,' journeyed to the far corners of the world to observe the tribes that inhabited them, when, right next to them, there were in the Basque Country men who lived 'under the influence [Garat's words] of primitive institutions, in which natural instinct alone ruled in the villages.'"[68] Garat's thought here is understandable if one recalls his ideas about the mythical origins of Euskara: "As regards Phoenician, all that remains is the Hebrew of the Old Testament; they were probably two dialects of the same language, and I have more than one reason and more than one source for speculating that Hebrew and Basque, [despite] the distance of so many centuries and lands, have a great deal in common."[69]

Thus, as that claim suggests, the recovery of an authentic Basque identity would constitute the reappearance of an enduring continuity that had been only superficially affected by extraneous forces and events. As Garat put it,

> Allow me, citizen First Consul [Napoleon] to speak for a moment about my Basques: They continue to be what they were four or five thousand years ago. While everything around them has changed so much through conquest, laws [and] arts, they have stayed the same as ever. The Christian religion itself, which is very important for them, gave them a new faith without giving them a new personality ... While the progress of civilization has corrupted or improved peoples, Basques have not taken part [in it], neither for better nor for worse. They have lost little and acquired nothing. The French Revolution has passed them by as a great phenomenon about which they have not understood much, and that has left them as before.[70]

This was because the Basques had preserved their dignity in the face of adversaries and their attempts at conquest. Garat recalled that

> the Romans changed everything ... but their rule over Spain was neither long nor complete ... If the Cantabrians had been conquered, they would have become Roman, but they continued to be Cantabrians. At the beginning of the fifth century, Vandals, Suevi, [and] Goths, after wreaking havoc on the shores of the Rhine and in Gaul [and] seeking to take Spain, found in the Pyrenees, where the Cantabrians lived, steps through, but no place to stay; they crossed the Pyrenees, [but] did not defeat them.[71]

As for the antiquity of Basque origins, "the Basque tambourine and the flute that accompanies it are clearly very ancient instruments ... Here, dances are still solemn public ceremonies, as in Boeotia and Attica, and the first magistrates head them, as did Plutarch leading the dances of Chaeronea."[72] And from time immemorial, they had preserved their concept of universal nobility: "they do not aspire to the nobility of families ... between them they retain a feeling of equality, and the distinctions [derived from] the privileges of fortunes do not destroy this feeling between those who own and those who do not."[73]

About Basque attachment to such a homeland, Garat was equally forthright. In one of his works, dating from 1785, he spoke of a "friend" who Michel Duhart[74] believes to be Garat himself:

> He was going to spend his vacation in the Basque Country, his homeland. He traveled alone, on horseback. On entering Landes [the *département* to the north of the Basque Country], those bleak lands of nearly forty leagues that travelers did not cross in those days without risk, a Basque sailor approached him and asked whether he might accompany him on his journey. The sailor had not made his fortune on the high seas; he was dressed in rags and looked like he had survived a shipwreck. One felt pity for him, but he might equally have appeared frightening.

However, my friend agreed to travel with him through those desolate lands, but only if he walked in front of his horse, thereby being able to keep an eye on him. On arriving at the place from where one could see [for the first time] the Pyrenees, the Basque sailor, spotting the bluish peaks of the Sierra, stopped; overcome by joy, all of a sudden he stood motionless; he took off his hat in respect, and with tears in his eyes, shouted several times "I salute you, my land, my homeland I salute you." He got down on his knees, got up, did some cartwheels [and] several Basque jumps, screaming with joy. Moved by the spectacle, my friend, with tears in his eyes, called to him from the horse: "Now you may walk as you wish, in front, by the side, or behind. Now I do not fear you!"

What is that feeling so profound or heartfelt that unites man to poor countries [*pays*], where one does not find the pleasures one finds in other places? Wealth, taste, and the arts have brought together all those pleasures in Paris and London. I doubt whether those born in those cities, after being away for some time, can feel anything like the emotions expressed by the Basque sailor, on [re]discovering the towers of Notre Dame or the dome of St. Paul's [cathedral].[75]

Finally, as regards the importance of such a homeland, Garat frequently referred to his fascination with the Basque landscape and the sacred quality of the territory:

> Nature has produced here the different kinds of beauty that have been shared out between Switzerland and Italy, and without doubt, this stems from the fact that the Pyrenean sky resembles that of Italy and the land that of Switzerland. These two countries have suffered, in their customs, languages, laws, and traditions every mixture and change; when on the native soil that I see before me, there has been only one great revolution, the revolution that established the Christian religion. In every other way, everything has remained the same.[76]

These core values help form the basis on which nationalism is based: autonomy, a national identity, and territorial unity,[77] And indeed, as we have just seen, Garat emphasized all three in terms of Basque institutions, language, and geography: "They share between them practically all things that people can, and [have] almost nothing in common with the Spaniards with whom they are joined, nor with the French of whom they form a part. They understand one another very well among themselves, but they do not understand their respective compatriots. The Basque of Lapurdi understands the Euskara of Gipuzkoa with the same ease as that of Zuberoa."[78]

Having read this, one might naturally conclude that Garat was the first Basque nationalist. However, he was not. Garat's discourse lacks any reference to one of the most important core values of nationalist discursive formations: a sense of destiny for the autonomous national homeland and its people. For Garat, any such destiny lay instead in the grandeur of France:

> Sir, I believe I know quite well the cantons and people that you would want to unite under your empire and under the protection of your fleet, and my most profound conviction is that . . . your majesty will make of these people what you wish. No, Sir, among all the

subjects of your empire . . . there are none that might serve you as efficiently in achieving the voluntary submission of Spain and the later humiliation of England.[79]

Indeed, "It would be too absurd to give any importance to the noble and national pretensions of a race of men who do not, after centuries, possess more than the remnants of an ancient people . . . What occupies me . . . is making the Basques more useful, joining them all under the same power and in a service that is most appropriate to their talents and pride."[80]

However much he valorized Basques and the institutions and language of the Basque Country, Garat cannot be considered a Basque nationalist. Indeed, his later writings display a degree of scorn toward Basques. Such disdain was typical of the comfortable classes and their connection to the values of the "city" against those of rural peasants.[81] Yet if one looks at the passage just cited again, a question emerges: He spoke of the absurdity of Basques' "noble and national pretensions." Are we to infer, then, that such pretensions (however absurd) did exist?

The answer to this obliges one to consider the possibility that Garat was not just a social climber who invented a tradition and mythology in order to earn the emperor's approval through speculative fantasy. Undoubtedly, he reconstructed a series of national cross-border myths, customs, and heroic deeds. However, whether these were false or reformulated by him to make them more attractive to Napoleon, it is evident that they existed among the people. In this way, Garat was merely expressing certain demands and feelings associated with a notion of Basque difference for which there is documented evidence: for example, the plan for a single Basque *département* that, for one observer, demonstrated evidence of a notion of the Basque homeland defined in cultural terms or the emphasis on maintaining Basque institutions.[82] Garat's words reflected several demands made by the Basques of Iparralde and translated the customs and forms of self-identification that the Basques of Iparralde considered to define Basqueness. He was, then, was a revolutionary translator who did not deny belonging to a "small" people, but who tried to subordinate that people to the glory of the *grand patrie*. In effect, he tried to make the two compatible. More than the first Basque nationalist, Garat was the first Basque republican, the creator of a two-homeland logic.

Finally, it is also likely that Garat never intended to mobilize the people around the discourse that he elaborated. Ultimately, he was a Parisian politician who, despite this, never forgot his native land. As I stated, he appropriated already existing differential myths, customs, and feelings. And from this base, he reconstructed, reinterpreted and, naturally, invented traditions. Yet he neither communicated these to the people—for his ideas were aimed at Napoleon—nor, in the event that they might have reached Iparralde, did he show any interest in mobilizing them. For this reason, with the exception of his role during the early days of the Revolution, his political career as a revolutionary personality in Paris meant he had little connection with the people of Iparralde. Proof of this lies in the harsh verses dedicated to Garat by the rebel priest Salvat Moho when recalling Garat's role in the execution of Louis XVI: "What shame in making that choice/Oh!

How distressed am I/to have given the monster some sweet verses/asking the people of Lapurdi to vote for him."[83]

Such an explicit condemnation of Garat demonstrates the extent to which, despite appearing to be a defender of Basque traditions and laws, he was also an integral part of the development of the Revolution in Iparralde. This being the case, one should not underestimate the disaffection that emerged with the Revolution in Iparralde after the abolition of Basque institutions, integration with Béarn in a single *département*, the effects of war with Spain, the repression of Basques, and the attack on the clergy. Paradoxically, the individual initially chosen to defend Basque interests at the outbreak of the Revolution was the first major casualty of popular dissatisfaction with the regime he represented.

However, the new millennium has been kinder to the memory of Garat among the people of Iparralde. Two hundred years after his protest before the National Assembly, a group of young Basques–formed into a civil disobedience group–revived his name to demand the wishes of the last *Biltzar* in Lapurdi: a single Basque *département*. As if by magic, Garat was no longer a major figure of republicanism, but was reinterpreted as the link between Basque nationalism and history.[84]

CHAPTER FOUR

Chaho: Father of the "People of Light"

The complexity of Augustin (also known as Agosti) Chaho (or Xaho) is self-evident: a freemason, a fervent republican who played a leading role in Baiona during the 1848 Revolution, a journalist and esoteric writer in Paris, a keen and imaginative linguist, anti-Spanish, anti-clerical, and the first Basque to be buried in a civil ceremony. These are just a few aspects of a person considered by some to be the first Basque nationalist and even a separatist.[1]

The complex nature of Chaho stems from a particular vision of the world—judged from our own contemporary perspective—that framed his thought. In order to understand better (if not to believe) his vision of the origins and destiny of the Basque people, it is necessary to begin by exploring the esoteric foundations of his ideas.[2] Similarly, we must examine his political trajectory if we are to make any sense of his apparently contradictory nature. Only then might we begin to understand his notion of a Basque Country on both sides of the Pyrenees. In the words of Father Joseph Zabalo,

> It was 1834 and he was twenty-three. Agosti Xaho came down from the Sinai and proclaimed the good news that his angel had whispered into his ear. He announced that of the peoples that enjoyed their golden age during the initial millennia after the flood, only one had survived: the Basques, descendants of the ancient Iberians, maintaining the language of the first humans [and with] their regard for liberty. After thirty centuries of peace, civilization, and freedom came the invasions of the Hyperboreans, Scythians, and Celts, of their kings and priests, which spread terror and death. Of all the ancient Iberians, only the Basques saved, in a Pyrenean canton, their divine language and liberty. For nearly twenty centuries, humanity has been growing slowly. More than any other people, Cantabrians and Navarrese are ready to contribute to this [growth].[3]

This myth of a golden age—a recourse used, as Anthony D. Smith observes,[4] by almost all nationalists—was a recurring theme in Chaho's vision of the Basques and their history.

The Golden Age and Planetary Struggle

Chaho's intellectual starting point was a theory that claimed all human eras last sixty thousand years and that the passing of one era to another is always marked by a cataclysmic event, the last of which, in his opinion, had occurred with the Universal Flood. Similarly, each era is divided into five periods of twelve thousand years and each period into four ages of three thousand years. The first of these is always a golden age, which is always initially followed by a profound crisis and then by a kind of human pilgrimage as a means of the slow recovery toward a new golden age.[5]

Furthermore, this notion of an eternal return was complemented by another of Chaho's deeply held beliefs: the planetary confrontation between the forces of the North and the South. In his own words, "The North, the region of cold and darkness [is] where the race of giants came from . . . The Basque and the Celt share the same antiquity, but in the future, the two races will never be confused . . . The Celtic race has only ever invented warfare, only spread ruins, its works have been . . . killings, superstition, and evil."[6] According to Chaho, Basques are the antithesis of the invaders from the North: "How different are the men of our land! Their well-proportioned stature; the effect of a southern climate curled and darkened their long hair [and] gave copper tones to the complexion of their face. Our girls were filled with pride when the bards compared their beauty to that of a peach, whose golden sun-drenched skin, aroma, and pinkish hues announce its maturity."[7] Thus, as opposed to the people of darkness—warriors and hunters—the peaceful Basque gatherers would be, for Chaho, the people of light: seers, prophets, and clairvoyants.

In Chaho's opinion, the origins of these Basques, like the peoples of the North, had been lost in the mists of time. Unlike the Celtic warriors, "Basques, Iberians, inhabitants of the most fertile continents favored by nature, were the first shepherds, during the age of the Patriarchs."[8] What, then, was the origin of the Basques? What did they have in common with the Iberians? I cite Chaho at length in search of the answer to these questions in order to highlight important themes in his thought regarding Basque religion, Euskara, and the relationship between communities on both sides of the border. It is taken from an imaginary conversation between Chaho and a peasant who appears to know everything about visionaries.

> "You know as I do, man of Lapurdi, that Basques trace their origin back to the patriarch Aitor and that every Basque, every illustrious soldier of the race, every free man is considered among us to be noble and a son of Aitor, *Aitorren Semea*."
>
> "That's true," he replied.
>
> "I will say to you know that the name Aitor is allegorical and means grand, universal father [Aita], and it was thought up by our ancestors to recall the original nobility and great antiquity of the Basque race."
>
> "Our ancestors," said the old man, "were learned visionaries, with many seers and prophets."
>
> "Don't forget, man of Lapurdi, that our grandfathers repopulated Spain, Gaul, and Italy after the great flood, as [Wilhelm Friedrich von] Humboldt found out, and that the patriarchs, after creating their solar republic, through God's inspiration thought up our language, Euskara, in which every sound is harmony, every word truth, and that, ultimately, the Basques, standing out among the Western peoples for their knowledge of the

divine word, are known among themselves as Euskerians, Euskaldun [Basque speakers], at the same time as they give the name erdara, imperfect word, half language, to mixed dialects, the sinister gibberish of foreign peoples, without excluding the Spanish and French languages."

"This is all true," replied the old man, whose attention became more intense.

"Perhaps you will have heard of the invasion of the peoples of the North and the Tartars, who ended the golden age bringing about for humanity the age of blood and darkness and the kingdom of the evil spirit. The conquest of the Barbarians dispossessed our ancestors of their beautiful land and throughout Iberia uprooted the oaks of its federated republics. The country of the Euskerians, Eskual-Erria, that in primitive times included the whole Hispanic peninsula and a good part of Gaul, was restricted to the seven small regions that the Basques today occupy in the western Pyrenees.[9]

The Basque Country thus was, for Chaho, a nation predestined to regain its golden age, a chosen people, the descendants of primitive inhabitants and of a secret religion whose goal would be to reclaim the Republic of the Visionaries.[10]

The Original Religion

Given such bizarre conclusions, it is necessary to examine Chaho's political and religious thought in more detail. Chaho's religious outlook was conditioned principally by his esoteric beliefs. More than a believer, he was a seer, and not just any visionary, but the "father" of all clairvoyants. In his own words, "My religion is pure theism, that of the intellectualism of the Word."[11] Thus, as Joseph Zabalo notes, "he was a part of the theosophical tradition, declaring himself not a man of faith (he was not a 'believer'), but a man of evidence (he was a 'seer')."[12] Chaho believed that "pure theism is the philosophy of seers, because it is grounded in the evidence of principles and facts, the religion of primitive humanity, the revelation of natural science."[13] He divided humanity into Seers (those who see truth directly), Believers (those who accept the truth established by Christian authority), Sophists (those who doubt truth, such as the Spanish liberals described by Chaho in his *Voyage en Navarre pendant l'insurrection des Basques (1830–1835)* (1836)), and Atheists (those who deny truth). As Jon Juaristi contends, for Chaho, Basques, or at least Carlists, were Seers: They were a superior species, the remaining nucleus of former disciples who had possessed the secrets of the Seers.[14] For this reason, "the Western patriarchs, the Basques, children of the sun and the Lamb, practiced a theism without any sacrifice, without any prayer, and without any worship."[15]

In other words, he believed that Basques had possessed their own (and indeed, the "first") religion—that of "the sun and the Lamb"—as befitted a race that also had its own original language. Furthermore, the possession of this original religion allowed Chaho to point to the origins of God's name itself:

> Amid the shining rays of dawn and the shadows of night [the Basque] sung the eternal hymn. And then, overcome with happiness, carried away by delight, [and with] eyes filled with the brightness of the sky . . . declared himself the supreme being . . . the most

beautiful, the most expressive of all divine names: JAO—that summed up all the possibilities, all the harmonies of the word, a sacred name, resplendent, that is, for those of my race, a cry of joy, a national cry.[16]

The letters "JAO" thus reflected a primitive trinity composed of life, a god incarnate and a spirit.[17] As Juaristi observes, it is highly likely that such ideas were received enthusiastically by the most Catholic and traditionalist sectors of the Basque population: "For the defenders of primitive monotheism, the argument that Basques had maintained, since remote times, the worship of the Holy Trinity must have been pleasing. Moreover, Chaho considered Basques to be the people chosen by God to lead a new crusade that would restore the true religion, coinciding with the image of the Basque people as a new suffering Israel, [an idea] spread by foralism after 1876" in Hegoalde.[18]

Chaho, however, opposed this original primitive religion to the modern Catholic Church, claiming that Catholicism had ended the egalitarian way of life of the first peoples, among whom he naturally included the Basques. That said, Juaristi's reasoning that Chaho's religious beliefs found a kindred spirit among radical, ultrareligious, traditionalist sectors in Hegoalde still holds, for two reasons: On the one hand, he never criticized Christ directly,[19] and on the other, he remained lenient toward the Basque clergy in his writings as a result of his valorization of all things Basque, the consequence of the romantic nationalism of the era in which he lived,[20] as reflected in his notion that the "sins" of the local clergy were minor in comparison to their non-Basque counterparts.[21]

Liberty, Hierarchy, and Fraternity?

Chaho's esoteric outlook was not just mystical or religious. Jean-Claude Drouin sees it as also political, in that Chaho sought the resurrection of the Basque people through the creation of a new republic: the Republic of the Seers.[22]

For Chaho, the origins of humanity—the essence of social relations—resided in fraternity and equality. However, this original reality was crushed by the invasions of those from the North, and consequently Christianity thereafter justified the emergence of inequality. One might draw from this the conclusion that Chaho was an advocate of social justice. Yet this was not the case. He argued from an evidently elitist position in favor of different political rights for different citizens, and he even modified the French revolutionary slogan into his own version: liberty, hierarchy, and fraternity.

Despite this, I do not believe he can be classified as "a counterrevolutionary provocateur infiltrating republican circles with the deliberate aim of spreading confusion among French progressives."[23] On the contrary, Eugène Goyheneche sees a justification of this apparent inconsistency in Chaho's own foral outlook: "Basque rights reflected an ideal for Chaho, brought together in three words: Liberty, Equality [and] Hierarchy. For this guaranteed true liberty opposed to liberalism, true equality opposed to capitalism, and hierarchy opposed to anarchy!"[24] Zabalo, meanwhile, explains the contradiction from two other perspectives. In part, Chaho's social elitism may be explained by his profound megalomania. If he tried to establish himself as father of the Basques, is it not understandable that he should try to reserve for those of similar powers the right to direct political policy in his country? At the same time, Chaho only reflected the thought of the time, which favored government by the "best" people —the most educated and wealthiest of the age.[25]

From still another perspective, Chaho has been defined as at the vanguard of the democratic socialist left in the Basque Country and Béarn,[26] because of his wholehearted support for universal suffrage free of any restrictions.[27] Such leftist positions would, therefore, explain the reaction of Prefect Jules Cambacérès, who in 1849 sent "a confidential [letter] to the minister of the interior [so that] his 'friends in [public] order' might avoid any contact with a man like Mr. Chaho, who seeks to stir up the poor against the rich."[28] Indeed, it was true that throughout his political career, Chaho stood out for the support he received from both the peasantry and the working classes.

Let me return, though, to a theme that might be thought to justify Juaristi's argument that Chaho was more counterrevolutionary than progressive: his support for Navarrese Carlism. The notion that Chaho's emphasis on hierarchy, together with his Carlist sympathies, made him a reactionary makes sense only if he viewed Carlism as a backward-looking movement that supported the restoration of the Basque *fueros* for only instrumental reasons. However, to characterize his politics in this way would be erroneous, because it would necessarily rely on misinterpreting his own views on Carlism, as well as on avoiding the role he played in the 1848 Revolution (leading to the short-lived Second Republic), factors that only highlight the complex worldview of this man.

Despite his hierarchical tendencies, Chaho assumed a leading role in Baiona during the 1848 uprising, literally taking to the streets at the forefront of the protesters, demanding the entrance of the working classes into the National Guard, and serving as one of six members of the executive commission that organized the revolt in Baiona on February 27, 1848. Prior to this, he had been elected a member of the Republican Committee for the district of Baiona. As a result, he came to lead a battalion of the National Guard and became a municipal councilman for the town in May 1848. In August of that same year, he beat the royalist candidate in the Atharratze cantonal elections. He then supported the progressive candidate, Alexandre Auguste Ledru-Rollin, in December's presidential elections and was 149 votes short of being elected to the French National Assembly on a Republican ticket.[29] In sum, Chaho's many contradictions must be understood within the context of the repressive climate and fluctuations of French political life in which he lived.[30]

While it is true that Chaho believed in a social hierarchy, he also, for example, supported common grazing rights for the Basque peasantry (echoing the priest, Bernard Goyheneche, known as "Matalas," who had led a peasant revolt in Zuberoa in the seventeenth century) and successfully lobbied on its behalf in Paris.[31] Furthermore, he argued for social policies that were popular among the urban lower classes: "He was in favor of secular, free, and obligatory education for everyone, freedom of conscience, assembly, association, demonstration, [and] the complete freedom of the press."[32] Moreover, his later writings leave little doubt about an ideology that has led some observers to classify him as the first Basque socialist:[33]

> Every reform I call for has as its goal the liberation of man and the citizen. Until now, minorities have oppressed majorities, which was a crime. I do not only wish that this crime is not repeated, but also that majorities should not oppress minorities. What I call for is the free exercise of all consciences, in a spirit of justice . . . The army is an instrument of oppression and violence . . . it places one class under the domination of another . . . the army will disappear in a democratic republic, with defense of the land entrusted to the citizens' patriotism . . . I would hope to leave anyone free to be judge of their own convictions: I want to build a new heaven, a new earth, based on satisfying necessities and on the independence of human destinies. The end of social and political revolutions is Liberty![34]

Another Precursor of Basque Nationalism?

According to Chaho, as we have seen, "The origin of the Basques is lost in the mysteries of primitive antiquity. It is linked to the social world destroyed in the West by the Celtic invasion." Moreover, he asks, "What were these aborigines during the primitive age really like, when patriarchal federations dotted the land of this beautiful peninsula and trees similar to that of Gernika gave shade to the senate of each republic?" These were

> free men, men that inhabited Iberia, men that spoke Basque. The invasion of Spain by Celts and Gauls after the flood . . . fixed the settlement of Euskaros-Basques in the western Pyrenees . . . After this primitive invasion, the European situation changed innumerable times, both in aspect and in features. Different generations of Barbarians came and went like large waves that brought with them to the shores, one after another, resounding turmoil and tempestuous murmurings, and within this perpetual movement, the small Basque people, steady as the rocks guarding their mountains, suffered no change or modification.[35]

As is evident, here Chaho confronts two issues that concern every nationalist movement: a response to the question of a people's origins, demonstrating their originality and a clear account of the continuity of this immemorial ethnic group. Indeed, Chaho's concept of the latter differed little from the ideas developed by Garat, although for Chaho, it took on a more metaphysical dimension. However, Chaho consistently relied on a supposed historicism, a theme that underpinned his *Voyage en Navarre*, in which he narrated the heroic deeds of Basques against numerous "invaders": "Different peoples, such as the Carthaginians, Romans, Goths, and Moors, in turn, conquered Spain, and through more than thirty centuries of combat, the Basque federation, fortified in its mountains, knew how to defend the original independence of its republics, its customs and patriarchic laws, the dialects of a primitive language, and the glory of its ancient nationality against hordes of Barbarians."[36]

The recalling of blood sacrificed by a people's ancestors, a symbol frequently referred to in order to understand the seductive power of nationalism, was a recurring theme for Chaho:

The effect of these last words [Chaho had spoken to a peasant about a possible "war of extermination against the freedom of our race"] was stimulating for the French Basque. Magic recollections of national independence and the magnificence of the homeland, mixed with a thousand confusing images of a dangerous and bloody future, suddenly filled his soul, awakening as if by a sudden shock the intense patriotism of the highlander.[37]

All these elements combined to shape for Chaho a discourse surrounding the national identity of the Basque people, one of Smith's "fundamental ideals" of nationalism, and closely related to the core concept of authenticity.[38] For Chaho, this identity was to be found in the original nobility of the Basques, their mobility, their name, their physiognomy, their healthy customs, their language, and their virtues.[39] *Voyage en Navarre* is filled with such discourse, but it is on the last page that another of the defining elements of nationalism is perhaps most apparent: a people's destiny. Here, it is the Carlist general Tomás Zumalacárregui who, in Chaho's imagination, remarks that,

> our blood, spilled in combat, will lead to a generation of heroes being born in the mountains. Witnesses to the tears of the homeland and our wounded, our sons, stirred up by warriors' songs, will develop in their hearts an inextinguishable hatred for oppression and will meet together as brothers around the oak tree of liberty, hoisting the flag of liberation, and when their invincible phalanx, guided by the shining star of Aitor, is cast down on the uproar of peoples, it will be seen like a beam of light cutting through the horizon.[40]

In similar fashion, the notion of homeland, for Chaho, was connected to national unity. In other words, the Basque homeland differed from its French and Spanish counterparts even in physical appearance: "The traveler has only to cross the river [Ebro], and nature has changed its appearance, man his physiognomy . . . From Castile to the Basque Country, the captivating contrast is complete. It is no less so, on the French side."[41] It thus comes as no surprise to find out that the border was an accidental feature of Basque life: "We found ourselves at some distance from Sara, the last village in Lapurdi touching peninsular Navarre. Its terrain is the same as that of Bera [Vera de Bidasoa, in Navarre], without any natural boundary in the Pyrenees marking the separation between the two kingdoms. A boundary stone placed on [Mount] Larrun divided politically what nature united."[42] Chaho asserted that this border should be abolished:

> Ancient Basques told the Romans that "the Pyrenees begin at the Ebro and end at the Atturi [Adour]." Anchored to their rocks . . . Basques believed they were part of them, not understanding that, apart from a perfect identity [stemming from] origins, language, customs, and laws, the fact of inhabiting the northern or southern side of a mountain was sufficient to separate politically peoples who bordered and mixed with one another in the valleys. Based on this principle and that of historical law, perhaps one day Basques will try and regain [their] national unity, if bad motivations do not contradict the voice of justice and political health. The interjection of a small people prevents conflicts that neighbors of large nations are capable of generating.[43]

Consequently, Chaho believed in achieving Basque national autonomy, a belief that even took the form of calling for independence in Hegoalde through the Carlist struggle and the figure of Zumalacárregui, basing this call on Basque difference, as evinced by racial and linguistic factors: "The distinction of race and language . . . establishes, in my view, the right of a people to political independence. When consecrated by a secular outlook, this right seems to me covered by an inviolable sanctity . . . The boundaries of the Basque Country will be reestablished through its patriarchal independence, protected by France and Spain, in the image of the Swiss cantons."[44] This argument was based on Chaho's specific interpretation of the First Carlist War, to the extent that, going against his republican convictions, during the war, he clearly sided with the Basque-Navarrese Carlists against the liberal ideas of the *Isabelinos* or *Cristinos*—clearly the more "orthodox" revolutionary position.

Thus, Chaho considered that the customs and laws of the Basques (Seers) that the Spanish liberals (Sophists) were trying to eradicate were the foundations of a democratic Basque way of life, and that these customs and laws had much in common with the republican values he espoused: "If it is true that the initiative of social progress belongs to more advanced peoples, Basques therefore must be at the forefront of the Spanish movement, because there is no people in that land, I repeat, not one, whose institutions are more democratic, more egalitarian, than the Basque highlanders."[45] Furthermore, "Spanish liberals will find it impossible to subjugate this free-born people or govern them with laws different from their own."[46] And of Spanish liberals, he remarked: "You want to Gallicize Castile; our Spanish neighbors can gain much through such change; [however] we Basques can only lose by it. Your progressive institutions will be a step backwards for us."[47]

Eugène Goyheneche believes that Chaho's Basque nationalism was based on four elements: the natural geographical unity of a land inhabited by Basques, their language, their history, and their laws.[48] This nationalism exalted Basque unity against both Castile and France. Chaho announced the liberation of Basques and called on them to win it.

Eugène Goyheneche, moreover, sees the support for Carlism by an "anticlerical revolutionary socialist"[49] as anachronistic, if one understands Carlist ideology as purely reactionary and based on absolutist monarchism. However, he also points out (as Chaho did) that "there was another dimension to Carlism: Basques had embraced Don Carlos's cause only in order to defend their *fueros*, threatened again and again by a Jacobin liberalism imported from Spain."[50] Despite this being a debatable interpretation, Goyheneche adds an 1834 text by Marx to support the idea: "Carlism . . . is not simply the dynastic, retrograde movement it has been described by . . . well-paid liberal historians; it is a free, popular movement in favor of defending more liberal and regionalist traditions than official predatory liberalism. The Carlist tradition possesses more authentically popular and national roots, in the peasantry, smallholders, and the clergy."[51]

Éric Dupré-Moretti supports Goyheneche's argument, considering Chaho a "prophet" and the "forerunner of Basque nationalism."[52] Further, as he sees it, "Chaho had one goal: preaching Basques their history, making them conscious of the fact they constituted a nation."[53] There was, therefore, a Basque nation and Chaho believed that Basques "had a history that was revealed in their events and heroic deeds, their songs, masquerades and pastorals, [and] in their language."[54] Consequently, in his messianic role, Chaho was "a true theoretician of Basque patriotism, for he defined the fact that the Basques' revolutionary struggle should be based on knowledge of their history."[55] Dupré-Moretti sees Chaho's Carlist sympathies as "just circumstantial in the context of the struggle for Basque independence. More than [support for] Don Carlos, Chaho was interested in the legitimacy represented by Zumalacárregui, a man he defined as 'the ultimate Basque.' He dared to hope that [Zumalacárregui] would take control of the vanguard, once the time arrived, of the struggle for Basque independence."[56]

More recently, Zabalo has contended that Chaho's "nationalism" was based on a series of principles: that Basques constituted a nation,[57] that this "Iberian" nation was that of a model people—the most advanced, democratic, and free, that the Carlist conflicts were not wars of independence, but struggles to uphold their freedom, that this national liberty was expressed in the *fueros*, that with this struggle to preserve their freedom, Basques would take a leading role in the cause of other peoples in their ascension from darkness to light, toward a new golden age, and that "Chaho's Carlism was neither dynastic nor religious, but strictly foralist. Don Carlos interested him only insofar as he defended the freedom of Basques and Navarrese."[58] In fact, despite initially considering Don Carlos to be the king of Navarre, Chaho gradually distanced himself from the pretender to the throne and gradually came to consider Zumalacárregui a more worthy inheritor of the title.[59]

The apparent contradiction between the defense of Carlism by a progressive republican thus was resolved, for Chaho, by his almost mythical interpretation of Basque social organization. Ultimately, this interpretation rested on an essentialist reading of history linking Basques to other original peoples—the people of light—who had suffered invasions from the North, with Spanish liberals representing the modern incarnation of the essence of evil in Chaho's esoteric worldview.

I do not believe, as Juaristi does, that Chaho's view of Carlism hid secret counter-revolutionary sympathies or an inability to recognize publicly such tendencies.[60] I do, however, share Juaristi's judgment of the consequences of Chaho's discourse: "Having thus converted the *fueros* into a constitution, Carlists into authentic liberals, and Don Carlos into the model of constitutional monarchs . . . Chaho did not hesitate in attributing Zumalacárregui his own interpretation of Carlism. This would not now be, against all evidence, a desperate defense of the *ancien régime*, but rather the tacit expression of a Basque separatist movement."[61]

What, then, is this contradiction on which Juaristi relies to discredit Chaho? Juaristi's identification between Chaho's interpretation of the Basques' fall into darkness with a cataclysm, understanding it as a metaphor for the nineteenth-century liberal revolutions, seems somewhat forced. According to Juaristi, "Aitor can be read as political allegory: The

Basques, who preserved unscathed their ancient liberties despite revolutionary attacks, were threatened once more by the awakening of revolution. They would therefore have to take refuge in their mountains and from there resist the tide of History. Aitor was an invitation to concealment."[62]

This is an attempt to reaffirm an isolationist, melancholic vision of Basque nationalism by Juaristi.

Yet there is an alternative explanation. As Drouin notes, Chaho's mysticism had nothing to do with the liberal revolutions as cataclysms, but with republican positions. Indeed, he points out that Chaho's religious thought—as embodied in the faith of his cult—had one clear goal: achieving a Republic of Seers. Thus, Chaho believed, from his faith in the notion of an eternal return, in the emergence of this republic through the agency of the chosen people: the Basques. In this way, he followed "the thought of contemporaries [such as Jean-Marie Robert] La Mennais and, later, Edgar Quinet, Pierre Leroux, and Jules Michelet," to the extent that Chaho "saw himself as the prophet of a great social and political revolution that would serve as the continuation of the Christian revolution. He thus prepared the spirit of 1848, where the religion of Humanity and the worship of the People were some of the most dynamic, driving myths."[63] In other words, republics, for individuals such as Chaho, were the goal of a true cult, that is, the political expression of a new religion that allowed for the return to a primitive past in the etymological sense of the term "revolution"—that is, as a "return." This new religion would thus, in turn, lead to two fundamental notions: universal suffrage and popular education —the foundations of the Second and Third Republics in France.

Chaho embraced the 1848 Revolution, in contrast to what critics of his secretly "reactionary" tendencies might imply, as the first step in the quest for a democratic republic. If he supported the 1848 revolt, would he have opposed the Spanish liberal revolution from purely "reactionary" motives? Or was his opposition to Spanish liberalism based more on interpreting it as a threat to the "republican" freedoms of Basques in Hegoalde? In effect, he considered Spanish liberalism to be the truly reactionary turn of events for Basques. Indeed, in 1848, he argued for the extension of the revolution to Hegoalde, commenting that "perhaps soon—it is possible—we will plant the February banner on the highest mount of the western Pyrenees."[64] At the same time, this view also explains his support for a single *département* for Iparralde—shackled as it was by the "decidedly over-reactionary" nature of Béarn.[65]

However, Chaho's separatism was limited to the Spanish side of the Pyrenees, a view derived from the fact that the French Revolution had abolished the *fors* generations earlier in Iparralde, while the *fueros* remained, in some form at least, in Hegoalde. As a result, when asked about the potential independence of Iparralde, Chaho responded ambiguously that "when France languished under the tyranny of Louis Philippe [1830-48]," he would have welcomed it, but that "at the moment [1848], it was out of the question," at least as long as there was no "counterrevolution, or France found itself invaded by foreign troops."[66]

Further still, Chaho saw the French Revolution as resulting in a "union freely accepted by the Basques" that brought them under "the empire of common law," although also "the retrograde oscillations of French renovation." Until that time, "it would not appear that the people of Lapurdi had any problems in enjoying their ancient privileges."[67] And while it is true that, in *Voyage en Navarre*, he proclaimed his opposition to the harmful effects of the Revolution in Lapurdi,[68] it is equally the case that he stated a clear admiration for Napoleon, "to whose glory France is indebted for subduing the spirit of Basque nationality."[69]

Evidently, then, this Basque "nationalist" did not accept the same remedy for Iparralde that he proposed for Hegoalde. In fact, regarding the former, Chaho later came to call for increased administrative decentralization that would not conflict with the executive power's authority as regarded the general interest and the use of force, as well as with the unity and indivisibility of the French republic. In his own words, "As a supporter of French unity, *Ariel* [Chaho's periodical] favors a federal state only for Spain, on the other side of the Pyrenees."[70] I would therefore contend that Chaho never conceived of politically mobilizing the Basques of Iparralde to the nationalist cause and that his entire political activity took place within the parameters of a French patriotism. I believe that Chaho distinguished between loyalty to the *patrie* and the importance of kinship bonds: "France is my homeland [*patrie*]; for me, Cantabria is a beloved family, of which I would be the first theosophist, the first novelist, and the first bard. I, the Seer!"[71]

Chaho, like Garat before him, opened the way to a dichotomy of identity that persists to this day in Iparralde, but that found its maximum expression between the 1930s and the 1960s: the logic that differentiated a *petite patrie* (the Basque Country) from a *grand patrie* (France), with the former nourished solely through the realm of socialization, as if it were a family,[72] and the latter regarded as the only vehicle of political activity for pro-Basque activists.

On occasion, Basque nationalism has been accused of confusing the national community with the nationalist community.[73] Chaho established the most complete of all identifications: He invented a people to fit his own interests, so that he might be transformed into the father of this people. And because he regarded this people as the source of all humanity, it is hardly surprising that he claimed a place among the great prophets of the age. Chaho thus elaborated a discourse of Basque difference that allowed him to give free reign to his own megalomania. That said, the fact that Chaho "invented" this people does not mean that his views were based entirely on rambling fantasies.

The Invention of Tradition?

Chaho's, and to a lesser extent Garat's, ideas led to the beginnings of a literary movement in Hegoalde that shortly after their time achieved its maximum popular exposure: the foralist literature that defended Basque-Navarrese historical rights and particularity. Chaho, for example, followed Esteban de Garibay in locating the Basque origins of the peoples of the Iberian Peninsula and in the resultant Basque-Cantabrianism that infused his writings.[74] Similarly, he peppered his novels with notions of a primitive Basque monotheism, of the Basques as descendants of Noah, and of their heroic medieval deeds. In fact, as regarded the standard features of nineteenth-century foralist literature, the only theme missing from his work was that of an original pact between the Basques and their lords. One might contend, then, that both Garat and especially Chaho contributed significantly to creating a legend-based historical Basque literature that found its greatest expression in Hegoalde and that ultimately served as breeding ground for the later development of Basque nationalism. It should come as no surprise, then, to learn that Arturo Campión was one of the principal translators of Chaho's work into Spanish.

As Antonio Elorza points out in his examination of the nineteenth-century Euskaro movement in Navarre, in its protonationalism (in reference to Campión's role, although one might extend the idea to both Garat and Chaho), literature was essential

> to link up with nationality, it was necessary to occasion a spiritual community [based on] culture, in turn the foundation of national consciousness . . . And this [national culture] affects [national consciousness], to the extent that the collective psychology and differential markers that a people acquires through time are shaped and updated. In this sense, history serves the members of a community to take on, through its glorious events, aspirations, and failures, a people's destiny. History is always national history. And when the lack (or scarcity) of evidence allows for great gaps to be seen in that historical tradition of the nation, literature covers the cracks by falling back on mythological stories and legends.[75]

Indeed, Elorza argues that the significant number of stories, ballads, and epics in nineteenth-century "parapolitical" Basque literature—established, in his opinion, by Chaho—shaped and determined the basic characteristics of Sabino Arana's first work, *Bizkaya por su independencia* (1892). Moreover, both Chaho and Juan Venancio de Araquistain sought the "creation of a Basque national consciousness. From this [stemmed] their insistence on certain themes and cycles with an epic treatment. From this also [stemmed] their early links with the cultural forms of Sabino [Arana]'s nationalism."[76]

Ultimately, the aesthetic form of these novels was secondary, because at root, they sought to "show through key historical conflicts [how] a nation's forces reacted, with the didactic goal of pointing out the correct behavior that placed above all else the maintenance of Navarre's [and the Basque Country's] political personality and the evils of foreigners, traitors, or the apathetic."[77] For these reasons, it is not surprising to see this design repeated in Chaho's *Voyage en Navarre* (1836), with Zumalacárregui as the exemplary model to follow, in Hermilio de Olóriz's *Fundamento y defensa de los Fueros* (1880), in which the call to patriotism is based on a Basque-Navarrese foral league that underpinned the Euskaro political project, and in Arana's *Bizkaya por su independencia* (1892), which is centered on four glorious historical battles —"all of them precise demonstrations of a millennial war between Bizkaians and Spaniards."[78]

Elorza argues that, as regards the Asociación Euskara (the group to which the Navarrese Euskaros belonged), in the literature it favored, "although the description of a historical moment or a specific figure was undertaken with a certain critical rigor or display of erudition [or not, I would add], the ultimate goal was to link, without exception, this reconstruction to a patriotic history aimed at strengthening that ambiguous national and regional consciousness."[79]

In other words, this was literature, Juaristi observes, that, "like all invented traditions, responded to the need to reinforce the cohesion of a society whose organic links had suffered a severe deterioration of legitimizing institutions and authority relations instilling in the masses value systems, beliefs, and behavioral conventions."[80]

While I agree in great part with these observations, I do not believe the invented nature of a tradition must necessarily be a falsification—that is, a means of deliberately misleading or lying to a collective. Nor do I think that such behavior is the sole preserve of peripheral nationalisms. To cite one contemporary instance, the former Spanish prime minister José María Aznar, in his 2004 inaugural lecture as a visiting professor at Georgetown University, equated the eighth-century conquest of the Iberian peninsula by the Moors with the terrorism of Al-Qaeda.[81] Often, although this was probably not the case with Aznar, the authors of such statements are perfectly aware of the instrumental nature of their inventions. For one such inventor of traditions, Araquistain, "the value of traditions did not depend on the accuracy of the sources used, but on their capacity to catch the popular imagination, creating a collective consciousness."[82] In Araquistain's own words, "history will develop scholars, but not heroes, above all among the masses. Only traditions, songs, in short, popular stories, like the echo they are to feelings, ideas, and even preoccupations, are powerful enough to inflame the imagination of peoples."[83]

The nation also needs an affective selection of such features—as well as feelings, ideas, and preoccupations—for its members who ultimately agree to share their differences with certain others. Consequently, as Pedro Ibarra notes, there is clearly a high degree of subjectivity—and of course, falsification—in constructing a feeling of national belonging. Yet that should not lead one to concluding that this is a superficial or artificial feeling per se or that "invention" (if it exists) should necessarily be "false" or "evil." As Ibarra observes, "All one can definitively say is that it is subjective, the same subjectivity as any other form of collective belief, of any other ideology that—grounding itself in the existence of a differentiated community—encourages feelings and proposes things about [the nature of] reality."[84] Further,

> One should not interpret in too subjective, too literal a fashion the now famous concept of an imagined community. In effect, the nation does not emerge only because individuals need to imagine that they belong to something and therefore imagine that there are other individuals thinking and experiencing the same narrative as they are. Nationalism, in the sense of national belonging, also emerges through real networks of interconnection, through a solidarity that is experienced, extolled, and incorporated into the widest symbolic community. A nationalist . . . not only imagines the community. In some ways, he or she lives it.[85]

Chaho imagined "his" Basque nation, and this remains perhaps one of the clearest examples of invention in the history of Basque political thought. However, if all his ideas were merely the rambling thoughts or fantasies of one individual, how is it that there were so many coincidences between the ideas of Garat in the period from 1789 to 1808 and those of Chaho in the period from 1835 to 1849? In the discourse of both men, both noted the same differences between France and Spain, together with the same notion of linguistic purity and the same views on Basque nobility and the importance of historical rights.

One can only conclude that Chaho's fantasizing was rooted in some degree of collective feeling—regardless of whether this was subjectively true or false—whose contours are difficult to trace today, but that would appear to indicate that some notion of difference, some feeling of cross-border Basque communal belonging, existed in Iparralde, even if not among the majority of the population. This would substantiate Eugen Weber's argument that the French state found its influence limited in the rural peripheries of the country, at least until the implementation of the Third Republic after 1870.[86] Neither, I would contend, did French identity or nationalism have an especially strong influence among the peripheral rural masses—that is, among the majority of the population in Iparralde at the time.

However, I do not believe that there was a widespread feeling of absolute disconnection from France. More accurately, I would characterize the feeling in Iparralde as one of apathetic accommodation with the French Revolution and the new state that it ushered in, an apathy driven by the deception felt by many people after initially supporting revolutionary change. As a result, the population of Iparralde slowly came to embrace a notion of French citizenship during the nineteenth century and, initially at least, regarded doing so as perfectly compatible with the maintenance of a distinct Basque identity. Only later—as I will address below—did this sense of Basque identity lose ground to its French counterpart.

For these reasons, both Garat and Chaho assumed that a certain feeling of difference existed among the general population of Iparralde and even among its elite sectors—at least until it became obvious that the French Revolution would indeed lead to definitive change. However, in both cases, this assumption did not lead them to them develop a form of Basque nationalism. Garàt's proposal to Napoleon had little to do with the everyday concerns of his fellow Basques, and Chaho was elected not for any support for Basque independence, but for his passionate defense of communal rural and working-class rights, or perhaps for the power of his complex discourse: his ability to attract Catholics because of his religious mysticism, republicans because of his anti-Catholicism, those who felt themselves to be Basque because of his gloss on the past and future of his people, and those who felt themselves to be French because of his impassioned republican discourse.

Garat and Chaho tapped into something—some differential quality based on mythical precepts. However, there was little popular reception for and no widespread mobilization based on their ideas. Therefore, I can only conclude that the conditions were not ideal for developing a protonationalist discourse during their lifetimes. While the same differential substratum existed that was paving the way for the development of Basque nationalism in Hegoalde, in Iparralde, there was no plausibility structure to make such a development viable.[87] Thus, the arbitrary nature of collective identities becomes apparent on both sides of the border.

Furthermore, it seems that while there was little nationalist feeling (whether French or Basque) among the popular classes in Iparralde, it was a different story among the elite. Like Garat, Chaho was a French nationalist, albeit with a particular Basque twist. In fact, Garat's and Chaho's praise of Basques and the Basque Country was instrumental: Although sincere, Garat's emphasis on things Basque served him well in alleviating the strain produced by letting down his province in the early moments of the Revolution, while at the same time, it did not impede his service to the grandeur of the Republic. Equally sincere, Chaho's declarations about the character of Basques, their legal heritage, and their language also allowed him to satisfy his megalomaniacal desire to become someone's new Zoroaster—in the case, the Basques'.

Yet it was these same topics—whether articulated sincerely or not—above all the mysticism, religiosity, and the convincing nature of Garat's and Chaho's inventions that served as a springboard from which, in Hegoalde, through a traditionalist reading, both foralism and Basque nationalism emerged. It is hardly surprising, then, that Chaho's ideas enjoyed widespread circulation among traditionalist sectors in Hegoalde, despite his republican sympathies. Nor should it come as a surprise that today, he has been recovered and reinterpreted by the Basque nationalist left as the missing link who connected the "Basque idea" to the political activity of left-wing nationalism. Ultimately, Chaho was everything: Carlist, Basque nationalist, French nationalist, socialist—the list goes on.

I am not interested in reaching one single definition of Chaho—or of Garat, for that matter. Instead, what interests me in the life and work of these two figures is tracing the meaning of identity for the population of Iparralde between 1789 and 1848 through their ideas, their role in transforming that sense of identity, and their legacy today. As regards the first of these issues, I believe a study of Garat and Chaho reveals them to have been central to shaping a Basque feeling of belonging in the period prior to the effective consolidation of the French state after 1870. In other words, their discourse is comprehensible only if one accepts that there existed such an identity during this time. Second, their efforts to reformulate this feeling of belonging in (however limited) a form of protonationalism demonstrate the limited reception for such ideas in Iparralde during the same era. That is, once some kind of content (Basque unity in the case of Garat, independence in the case of Chaho) was applied to the form of their ideas, it was obvious that the material conditions did not exist for extending this cultural discourse into political action. Finally, as regards their legacy today, as we will see, they are key figures for understanding the reconstruction of collective memory in Iparralde. Both have been portrayed in recent pastorals in Zuberoa, while Garat has also been reclaimed by the civil-disobedience Demo movement to demand a single Basque *département* and protest the lack of specific institutions for Iparralde.

I could have addressed the paradoxical features of Garat and Chaho by simply referring to them as "cultural" nationalists. However, this would be misleading, because, as Ibarra argues, "there is no cultural nationalism, in the strictest sense of the term (although one might speak in terms of cultural patriotism). In nationalism, there is always a demand for political power."[88] Garat called for autonomy and Basque unity, while Chaho argued in favor of Basque foral independence. However, their political ideas were based on legend and theory and lacked any mobilizing capacity. Furthermore, Chaho's demand applied to only one part of the Basque Country, the same Basque Country that, for him, not even nature could divide. In sum, I repeat, for Chaho, like Garat before him and Pierre Lafitte afterward, France was his *patrie* and the Basques his family.

CHAPTER FIVE

Sabino Arana and the "Two Brothers"

The border dividing Iparralde from Hegoalde was often quite porous, allowing for the free flow of ideas between the two. Basque nationalism was invented by Sabino Arana within a specific geographical and temporal context: in Bilbao at the end of the nineteenth century. However, this new discourse was quickly disseminated throughout the Basque Country. When these ideas reached Iparralde, the Basque nationalist movement in Hegoalde seemed vigorous and dynamic, to the extent that it seduced a number of individuals, such as Pierre Lafitte. Yet whether these people in Iparralde agreed wholly or only partially with the tenets of Basque nationalism, in practice, if they were to undertake any political activity of their own, they would have to mold it to the reality of life there. As a result, the first such movement to emerge in Iparralde embraced a regionalism grounded in the logic of the two *patries* that had also pervaded the work of Garat and Chaho.

In the following, I examine the emergence of Basque nationalism in Hegoalde, together with its ideological application in and proposals for Iparralde. Then, more specifically, I explore the figure of Lafitte and the first organized pro-Basque political movement in Iparralde: the Aintzina or Eskualerriste movement. The analysis also highlights the fact that the cross-border flow of ideas did not just run from south to north, but in fact, went in both directions.

As Javier Corcuera notes, "with Chaho . . . an ideological current was born that interpreted the Carlist conflicts as national wars," and in Zumalacárregui, Chaho found "a national leader whose motive was the independence of the Basque Country."[1] Chaho was extremely important to the development of Sabino de Arana's ideas—not directly, for Arana never cited him (whether through ignorance of his work or disagreement with his "liberal" and "anticlerical" tendencies), but rather due to "the links he established between traditional myths and a clear anti-Spanish Basque nationalism that prefigured some of Arana's ideological elements."[2]

Regardless of whether one considers Chaho a fully fledged Basque nationalist or just a precursor, his ideas must have had some degree of resonance in Hegoalde. At the same time, the same events around which Chaho first began to develop his ideas—a Carlist war and the threat of foral abolition—also came to underpin the beginnings of Basque nationalism in the South, serving ultimately as the cementing force in politicizing already existing Basque ethnic and cultural differentiating elements. As a result, while in Iparralde both Garat and Chaho conceived a vague politico-cultural notion of Basque difference that ultimately lacked any practical application, in Hegoalde, first Arturo Campión and later Arana, too, developed politico-cultural demands, and this time, they were linked more closely to an effective mobilization.

Space precludes a detailed examination of the implications of Arana's theorizing and political trajectory. I will therefore limit myself to underscoring two elements of the emergence of Basque nationalism in Hegoalde through his efforts as a means, ultimately, of understanding more fully the different course of events in Iparralde. The first is the context that allowed Arana not only to create Basque nationalism, but also to attract adherents—that is, the structure of plausibility that facilitated some degree of acceptance for his particular historical vision and political program. The second is the way in which Arana transcended (or tried to transcend) the political and administrative boundaries that divided the Basques of Hegoalde from those of Iparralde. This second point is crucial, for by examining these attempts, one sees the emergence of the first (although limited number of) Basque nationalists in Iparralde, the dissemination of Basque nationalist ideas there (to be adapted later to local conditions), and, ultimately, the first tentative declarations of the slogan "Zazpiak Bat" (The Seven Are One)—an allusion to the unity of Iparralde and Hegoalde. The relevance of this latter idea is that the slogan appeared just at the moment when an identity crisis took hold of Iparralde, leading, eventually, to its subordinate role within Basque nationalist ideology. Early Basque nationalism then came to look on Iparralde as the "little brother" that the older sibling of Hegoalde was obliged to teach or lead or as constituting the Basque Country's geographical rear guard that would have to be sacrificed in the struggle for identity—a haven for exiles from the South, but a place where Basque nationalism would have to tone down its activity for fear of upsetting the French authorities. Only by taking account of this context can we begin to understand the different structures of plausibility that allowed for the consolidation of Basque nationalism in Hegoalde, together with its dissemination in Iparralde, as an integral part of the Basque nation in nationalist ideology, but with a difficult implantation there.

Basque Unity

Arana's belief in the unity of the Basque Country was based on two basic features that differentiated an "us" from "them": language and race. Language, as we have seen, was equally important for both Garat and Chaho, as it would be later for Antoine d'Abbadie in Iparralde and Campión in Hegoalde. In the latter two cases (and especially that of Campión), defense of Euskara was inextricably linked to the modernization of Basque society. They saw the decline of the Basque language as beginning with the destruction of traditional society brought about by industrialization,[3] a trend that emerged not just among the bourgeoisie, but that was also widespread among sections of the lower classes. This decline alerted a group of Navarrese intellectuals to the potential disappearance of Euskara. After 1876 and the conclusion of the Second Carlist War, they began to define and implement a program of cultural regeneration that soon extended throughout the Basque Country. This project specifically identified "language as the most significant factor in the Basque collective consciousness, uniting the destiny of one to the transformations of the other."[4]

Campión was important not just for raising the issue of the declining use of Basque, but also for theorizing about the everyday reality of the Basque Country around him. By attempting to impart to Euskara a degree of social value so as to make it compatible with modernization, he encouraged a form of activism that challenged the dominant tendency to abandon the language. Thus, following the model of the Basque-language and culture festivals organized by d'Abbadie in Lapurdi in 1853, the Asociación Euskara in Navarre (of which Campión was a leading member) organized several similar events in Hegoalde through the 1880s and 1890s.[5]

The Euskaros (members of the Asociación Euskara) played an important role in the development of Basque nationalism in that, in their political goals, they focused on a notion of Basque unity that found specific direction in their call for a Basque-Navarrese foral movement. At the same time, they pursued a cultural policy (as expressed in the festivals) that affirmed the concept of Basque unity based on sharing a common language. As an example of how this political idea found cultural expression, the following verse by the popular bard from Bizkaia, Felipe Arrese Beitia (a frequent participant in the aforementioned festivals),[6] is telling:

Bizkaya, Gipuzkoa, orobat Araba,	Bizkaia, Gipuzkoa, also Araba,
Nafarroakin emen lau anaya gara;	together with Navarre, here we are four brothers;
Frantziko irurak ta gu biltzen garela,	the three in France and us when we unite,
zazpirok bear dugu salbatu Euskara	the seven of us must save Euskara.[7]

In fact, Arrese became famous for his poem "Ama Euskeriari azken agurrak" (Final Farewell to Our Mother Euskara),[8] presented at the 1879 festival in Elizondo (Navarre), an event organized jointly by d'Abbadie and the Euskaros and therefore one of the first cross-border cultural initiatives of this kind.

Antoine d'Abbadie's father was from Zuberoa. After the Revolution, he fled France, first to Seville, then to London, and finally to Dublin, where his son was born.[9] Thanks to a generous inheritance, d'Abbadie finally settled in Urruña (Urrugne) in Lapurdi. There, besides undertaking major scientific research as a physicist, astronomer, philologist,[10] and explorer, he came to be interested in Basque issues as a result of contact with Chaho.[11] Following this early research, d'Abbadie organized an initial festival in 1851 and later came to settle on the model of a combined literary competition/festival. As Joseba Agirreazkuenaga notes, in the announcement for this competition, published in the

Memorial des Pyrénées, in which the conditions for participation were listed, the invitation was extended to Basques from both sides of the border.[12]

However, this clear acknowledgement of Basque unity based on a common culture lacked in practice any significant degree of political orientation. In fact, the affinity of d'Abbadie's thought with Carlist positions above all else demonstrated his obviously conservative tendencies. He was responsible for spreading some of Iparralde's most important Catholic myths throughout the Basque Country: for example, that a young girl from Iparralde, Madeleine Larralde, had been executed by French revolutionaries for taking Communion in Elizondo, in Hegoalde, during the Franco-Spanish War. As Manex Goyhenetche has demonstrated, Larralde was neither a young girl nor was she executed on the basis of her religious beliefs. Rather, she had been found guilty of smuggling.[13] Despite this, as a link to his cultural activities, d'Abbadie tried to create a Basque martyr, emphasizing the importance of religion through the mythical figure of someone who did not recognize the border, even in times of war. Therefore, one might conclude that he evinced the clearest connection between nineteenth-century intransigent Catholicism and the pro-Basque sympathies of the *xuriak* (literally "whites," a Catholic conservative faction in Iparralde that attempted to ground its support in traditional culture by appealing to Basque cultural elements). Yet while the pro-Basque elements of this traditionalism gradually disappeared, for d'Abbadie, they were increasingly important, to such an extent that, in the festival he organized in Donibane Lohizune in 1892, "in his closing speech, he called for a unanimous cheer in favor of the unity of the seven Basque territories."[14]

As a result of his extensive research, d'Abbadie had been admitted to the French Academy of Sciences in 1867 and was elected its president in 1892. In 1895, he bequeathed his estate to the academy on the condition that it would continue to finance the literary competitions/festivals, as well as to promote the Basque language. However, the academy reneged on the agreement after his death in 1897.[15] It was not d'Abbadie, however, but Sabino Arana (cousin of the organizer of the first Bizkaian festival) who ultimately came to create Basque nationalism.

Arana's discourse, grounded in intransigent Catholicism, was based on race, the historical laws or *fueros*, the historico-cultural dimension of Basque difference, and language, all elements used to justify his argument in favor of separatism.[16] Within this list, however, some elements were more important than others. And only one—race—was "objectively" differential (with the one exception, naturally, of religion, which transcended everything). Thus, for Arana, it was on the basis of race alone and the need to preserve the Basque race that he understood the need to preserve the particular linguistic, cultural, and juridical characteristics of the Basque Country. Consequently, for Arana, in contrast to the other individuals examined thus far, language was only one instrument used to justify preserving the Basque race. For him, racial differences marked the boundaries of the Basque Country and also underscored his notion of Basque unity.

Paradoxically, however, although race was more important for Arana than language, most important of all was the concept of territory itself. Thus, breaking with the tradition established by Garat and Chaho (among others), Arana opened a discursive space that transcended merely speaking of "the Basque people." For him, the Basque nation was a single territory, termed by his own neologism "Euzkadi." Yet if the Basque race disappeared, then Basques would lose their sociological foundation. Even if everything else survived, they would disappear: "If our race disappears from these mountains . . . if a confederation of six partial states were to come into being and each of these were to be established on the respective traditions of our race, our language . . . this Basque Country would not be our homeland, but another, different Basque Country; family members would have disappeared, the entire family would have disappeared."[17]

However, Arana's racial notions did fit the instrumental dimension that links nationalism with modernity. Much has been written on the racist current within Basque nationalism,[18] but there is, I think, an intermediary point that most observers share: that Arana's racism or xenophobia was the result of a crisis in traditional society at a time when it was being transformed by modernity. This was most evident in the widespread industrialization of Bizkaia and the consequent large-scale (and non-Basque) immigration from Spain. According to Juan J. Linz, "this racism has been described as defensive and obviously presented [Basque nationalism], in practice, with numerous difficulties for its creation and growth. It was a logical, although extreme, response to the problem of growing immigration in Bilbao and the [high] proportion of immigrants in working-class neighborhoods." In effect, "ruralism opposed industrialism, [and was] linked to a hostility toward the nascent capitalist bourgeoisie and its ties with Spain and, increasingly, the monarchy."[19] Basque nationalism was therefore born with a number of primordialist ideas rejecting modernity, but, with time, the Partido Nacionalista Vasco (PNV, the Basque Nationalist Party) gradually modified or mostly abandoned these early notions, especially after it began to gain power and came to control these very same forces of modernity.[20]

Sabino Arana and the Notion of Zazpiak Bat

Arana created a Basque nationalist discourse and an organizational framework that grew (after his death in 1903) thanks to its increasing appeal to widespread sectors of the population in Hegoalde and a growing belief among these sectors that some degree of mobilization was necessary in the emerging age of mass ideologies during the early decades of the twentieth century. Yet at the same time, Basque nationalism was also the product of a specific local setting and context. Its territorial growth was complex,[21] and as we will see, Iparralde was soon relegated to the margins of the PNV's priorities.

Arana's views on Iparralde were based on a theoretical starting point drawn from the slogan "Zazpiak Bat," "The Seven Are One," most likely taken from the 1891 Basque literary and cultural festival. However, his conception of Iparralde lacked any specific political focus,[22] instead falling back on the cultural outlook that had predominated up to that time. A cross-border conception of the Basque nation was present, then, from the inception of Basque nationalism. This was reflected in Article 8 of the statute for the Euskeldun Batzokija (known later as the Batzoki), the first organizational apparatus of Basque nationalism. Here, the brotherhood of the Basque provinces was recorded, together with a plan to confederate Bizkaia with the other six provinces, forming a unit to be known as Euskelerria: "Bizkaia being, by its race, its language, its faith, its character, and its customs, sister of Araba, Nafarroa Beherea, Gipuzkoa, Lapurdi, Navarre, and Zuberoa, will join or confederate with these six peoples to form a whole called Euskelerria (Euskeria) [the Basque Country], but without detriment to its distinguishing autonomy. This doctrine is expressed in the following principle: *Free Bizkaia in a Free Basque Country*."[23] Six months after the Euskeldun Batzokija was created in Bizkaia, it was opened up to Basques from the other provinces.[24]

Arana's thought came to prioritize the whole Basque Country over Bizkaia, his initial focus.[25] Although the united Basque model was more specifically defined only after 1901, Arana's conception of a Basque Country incorporating Iparralde dates from prior to this. As a demonstration of this, Iñaki Aguirre cites various articles by Arana from 1894 on. According to one such document, from 1897, Arana confirmed that

> nationalism, aspires, as is known, to the complete independence of the Basque people, restoring to them the essential traits of their politico-religious tradition and establishing there in that part of the Pyrenees and the Bidasoa the Confederation of all the old states of the [Basque] race. It is well-known that there are six of these: Lapurdi and Zuberoa, to the north of the Pyrenees and the Bidasoa; Bizkaia, Gipuzkoa and Araba in the south; [and] Navarre on both sides of the aforementioned frontier.[26]

There is a contradictory idea here, though. In part, the passage would seem to mean that Arana had assumed a cross-border conception of the Basque Country prior to the post-1901 turn. Yet at the same time, the words also seem to denote a certain lack of confidence in achieving this goal in Iparralde, which, at the time, was being subjected to the full forces of French state building during the Third Republic. It would appear, then, as Aguirre suggests, that Arana had already come to the realization that a different dynamic existed on the two sides of the Bidasoa River, possibly as a result of the complete closure of the border during this period.

By contrast, Corcuera takes a different approach to the position of Iparralde within the transformation of Arana's thought from Bizkaian to Basque nationalism. For him, Arana was from the outset a Bizkaian nationalist, the result of an ideology initially based on foral demands typical of the era that could be only provincial. "There were no Basque *fueros*," contends Corcuera, "but different arrangements in each of the Basque territories. They were different, despite the structural similarity of the political institutions in each of them." However, as he also points out, "Despite these differentiating elements . . . they also shared certain ethnic, linguistic, and cultural traits. And when their different *fueros* were threatened at the same time and for the same reasons, the feeling of community among the inhabitants of the four Spanish provinces of the Basque Country increased."[27]

Consequently, the racial (as well as cultural, linguistic, and historical) argument on which Arana initially based his Bizkaian nationalism obliged him to extend his thesis to those territories that shared these differential qualities. As Corcuera notes, this forced him to consider similar political alternatives for the "other" Basque nations. Consequently, Arana's historical interpretation that justified Bizkaian independence "created a kinship among all the Basque territories . . . which were related also because of their race . . . and using, all of them, different dialects of the same language."[28] This would explain the confederative nature of the Euskeldun Batzokija's statute, which also included Iparralde. Finally, the extension of Arana's ideas to Iparralde itself, while limited,[29] also facilitated its territorial incorporation into his discourse. Thus in 1901, when Arana invented the term "Euzkadi" to denote the entire Basque Country (deriving from his word for the Basque race, *euzko*), he added a political dimension to the slogan "Zazpiak Bat."

Arana's confederative project was—as regarded its internal proposals—fundamentally democratic, in that it was based on the "absolute respect of the confederation towards the *foral* constitutions of each of its territories, endowing the confederated states full sovereignty, even to the extent of allowing them to decide whether or not to participate in the confederation and reducing to a minimum the extent of confederal powers."[30] Moreover, in his *El Partido Carlista y los Fueros Vasko-Nabarros* (The Carlist Party and the Basque-Navarrese *Fueros*) (1897), Arana clearly outlined the foundations on which the Basque Confederation would be built:

> 1st. That this confederation would be formed only by the freely expressed will of each and every one of the Basque states and all of them with the same rights in the formation of their bases; 2nd . . . once it [the confederation] was established, within it, all of the states would have the same rights and identical obligations; 3rd . . . the confederation would not join them only other than on the social order and on that of foreign relations, remaining on the others with the same absolute traditional independence.[31]

However, as Corcuera details, as Basque nationalism spread in Hegoalde, limits were placed on the original conception of the confederation, to the extent that Luis Arana (Sabino's brother) introduced a clause restricting the right of separation from the new polity, should it ever be achieved.[32] Thus, a tension emerged within Basque nationalism between two competing visions: one based on territorial criteria and grounded in provincial sovereignty, and the other, a pan-Basque notion that conferred sovereignty only on the Basque Country as a whole—a tension, in fact, that remains unresolved to this day within Basque nationalism.

What would be the fundamental nature of this confederation? In the first instance, there is no evidence that Arana used historical precedent as an argument in favor of the proposal,[33] which is interesting, because such justification is prevalent in later Basque nationalist ideology and doctrine. "To construct the bases of the national confederation," remarked Arana, "tradition is of no use to us, for it never existed before in history."[34] As a result, lacking the historical justification used by both Garat and Chaho, Arana had to focus his cross-border national project on race and (even more importantly for him) on religion, with the former constituting the primary material and the latter its guiding spirit: "Here I have, then, the two fundamental bases of the union of the Basque states to constitute themselves as a national confederation: unity of the race wherever possible [and] Catholic unity."[35]

Whatever the specific nature of Arana's thought, his proposals envisaged a common political project for the seven (or six) provinces based on the fraternity of Basques on both sides of the border. However, as we will see, and as is the case in many families, this Basque nationalist fraternity developed in unequal fashion, to the extent that the inequality came to condition the relationship. The resultant late development of Basque nationalism in Iparralde had numerous repercussions, among which was the increasing belief of nationalists in Hegoalde that they had the right to lecture their counterparts in Iparralde. In a similar fashion, the nationalist crises in Iparralde in both the 1930s and the 1970s made it seem, for Basque nationalists in Hegoalde, as if nationalists in Iparralde were merely bringing up the rear guard of the movement as a whole. One practical consequence of this was that Basque nationalists in Iparralde were expected, from the point of view of their southern counterparts, to concentrate their efforts on providing support and refuge to those from Hegoalde at the expense of developing policies more suited to their own conditions and needs. Paradoxically, however, the arrival of Basque nationalist refugees (especially those of ETA) came, ultimately, to reinforce Basque nationalism in the North, for they became both a point of common reference and an important nationalist socializing element.

In sum, then, the original Basque nationalism conceived in Bizkaia at the end of the nineteenth century had little difficulty in crossing the border, well before the first refugees arrived as a consequence of the Spanish Civil War (1936–39), so that a small nucleus of Basque nationalists emerged in Iparralde, demonstrating the porous nature of the state boundary dividing the Basque Country. As a result, Pierre Lafitte's Eskualerriste movement attempted, between 1933 and 1936, to find its own path, taking on board the basic doctrinal foundations of Basque nationalism, yet transforming them into a form of regionalism in the face of the impossibility of overcoming the contradiction created by Garat and Chaho—that is, the contradiction between the small Basque *patrie* and the greater French *patrie*, a greater homeland from which they still could not part.

CHAPTER SIX

Lafitte and the Death and Resurrection of Basque Identity: The Eskualerriste Movement

Nearly four decades after the emergence of the PNV in Hegoalde, the first organized political expression of Basque identity took place in Iparralde. This was not an expression of Basque nationalism, for this initial movement emphasized its regionalist credentials by downplaying any desire for significantly devolved political power in Iparralde. In order to understand why this was the case, one must look to the period from about the 1870s on, in which the development of a Basque identity took opposite directions on the two sides of the border. In Hegoalde, a sense of urgency deriving from the loss of the *fueros* and the effects of industrialization precipitated the rise of Basque nationalism. In contrast, in Iparralde, this period coincided with the consolidation of the French nation-state under the Third Republic and the definitive integration of the Basque population into the French nation, especially through the effects of World War I.

The emergence of a political Basque consciousness in Iparralde took place—under the guidance of Pierre Lafitte—in the 1930s, toward the end of the period of French national consolidation and coinciding with a boom decade for Basque nationalism in Hegoalde. Before examining the emergence of Lafitte's Eskualerriste movement in detail, I will consider the complex evolution of Iparralde between the 1870s and the 1930s, a period characterized by tensions between the rural and urban worlds, between republicanism and conservatism, and between secularism and religion—all within the framework of a French state attempting to consolidate its power by creating a statist nationalist model that challenged (in both ideas and practice) its German counterpart. These competing visions of the nation eventually culminated in a violent clash that not only led thousands of young Basques to the trenches of World War I, but that also significantly reduced what had until this time been a certain sense of "provincial" identity.

Iparralde between the 1870s and 1930s became the scene of political differences that characterized the development of modern Europe itself. That is, one sees the origins of the principal European political parties today in the crises that marked late nineteenth-century Europe. For example, debate raged over the political cleavage between church and state that differentiated clerical from secular parties, with the former arguing in favor of reinforcing the social and political influence of the church and the latter demanding a separation of church and state, together with a general secularization of social life. At the same time, the center-periphery divide, deriving, like the previous issue, ostensibly from cultural differences, pitted centralist parties against their regionalist, autonomist, federalist, and separatist counterparts. Then there were the tensions between the primary and secondary/tertiary sectors that differentiated urban, industrial, and commercial interests from those of the peasantry and that led to the emergence of agrarian parties to defend the rural world. Finally, there was the divide between owners and workers, or capital and labor, the friction that led to the emergence of Europe's two most important political blocs. For the owners, there emerged parties controlled by industrial, financial, and commercial interests and favoring a nineteenth-century liberalism that became a fundamental ideological pillar. Opposing them were the workers' parties whose strength derived from the support of the industrial workforce and especially the labor union movement.[1]

As we will see, these four basic divides that characterized *fin-de-siècle* European society would be translated in Iparralde into the factional differences between the so-called *xuriak* (whites) and the *gorriak* (reds). The *xuriak* were Catholic conservatives who initially tried to appropriate Basque ethnic symbols in order to gain support in more traditional areas and who reacted to the modernization of rural areas from a traditional political perspective. The *gorriak* were secular republicans who, to differing degrees, aligned themselves with the cultural homogenization of the Third Republic and who favored the modernization that was underway in coastal metropolitan areas and certain industrial enclaves in the interior.

Xuri, Gorri–and *Orlegi?*

Until comparatively recently, the struggle between proponents of a traditional, rural, conservative, and Catholic vision of society and adversaries who supported urban, industrial, secular, and progressive development was a central feature of political life in Iparralde. One variable, however, fell by the wayside: the identity divide that, subject to the zero-sum game of the French state after World War I, made adhesion to the French nation almost indisputable–almost, that is, but not quite. The *ikurriña*, the Basque nationalist flag, is tricolored: white (*xuri*), red (*gorri*), and green (*orlegi*). In the factional rifts between the *xuriak* (whites) and the *gorriak* (reds), what space was there for such a tricolored flag to be raised? Could they ever be brought together in the nationalist cause?

During this time, the exogenous economic development of Iparralde led to the emergence of an industrial proletariat in north Baiona, in Hazparne (Hasparren), on the coast of Lapurdi, and in certain industrial enclaves in Zuberoa. The new industrial middle class soon allied itself with the state's administrative functionaries and members of the liberal professions (doctors, lawyers, and so on) to form an initially small, but socially prestigious group that quickly adhered to the new ethos of the French nation.[2] At the same time, tourism was being developed along the Lapurdi coast,[3] to the extent that towns such as Biarritz quickly became part of an international cosmopolitan network while also attempting to retain a degree of attractive local "flavor" within the internationally renowned culture of France. And this led to a parallel identification of "international" (that is, French) culture with high culture in general, relegating the "local" (or Basque) variety to the folkloric level. In more practical terms, the development of tourism also led to the extension of the French railroad network to Iparralde, integrating the Basque Country into the new dynamic of the French state's modernization.[4] More important still, the arrival of the railroad created the foundations from which the national community of France became more plausible in Iparralde—that is, it could be more readily "imagined" by Basques.

Among the key divisions of *fin-de-siècle* European political life, the debate over the church's role in the modern state was perhaps felt most keenly in Iparralde. Despite the fact that the church initially attempted to appropriate the Basque language and culture to secure people's loyalty, ultimately, it yielded to the state's power and influence in linguistic and educational policies.[5] This resulted in a large part of the Basque population falling back on a kind of "apolitical Catholicism" that was difficult to break free of and that reduced the need for any kind of ethnic or peripheral political mobilization at all.[6] At the same time, as Xabier Itçaina notes, a logic emerged among the Catholic classes that viewed electoral participation as a kind of "civic rite" that "consecrated" the power of local notables.[7] Ultimately, without the explicit support of the clergy and faced with the ignorance or apathy of the industrial bourgeoisie, the Basque language and culture were not supported by any elite capable of endowing them with political content.

However, conservative political candidates in Iparralde continued to make use of their cultural and linguistic connections with the rural populace to maintain their political hegemony. That said, they also gradually adopted French statist positions that, in some cases, ultimately resulted in an adherence to extreme French nationalism. Meanwhile, moderate republicans became the champions of the centralized, uniform, and secular state that attempted to run the country from Paris. And finally, communism (which also, in principle, assumed the principle of state centralization) took root in the industrial areas of north Baiona and parts of Zuberoa. Indeed, communist ideology reinforced the centralized statist vision, viewing peripheral nationalism as an expression of bourgeois thought.

This was the context in which the Third Republic began the consolidation of the French state in rural areas of the country. The foundational moment of this new regime came with French imperial humiliation during the Franco-Prussian War of 1870–71 and the loss of Alsace and Lorraine. The defeat reinforced a sense of urgency toward the potential danger faced by French national unity, and as a result, the National Assembly, beyond its ideological differences, took on the imperative role of restructuring the state. After the consolidation of the new republic in 1877, all the political forces agreed on a deliberate strategy to create a series of symbols for the country that would cement a notion of French identity, with one of the best examples being the designation of the Marseillaise as the national anthem.

Later, after 1890, when the monarchist parties had definitively lost widespread support at a national or state level, successive republican governments attempted to eliminate the extensive network of political patronage that the church had established throughout the periphery of France, thanks to the importance it accorded regional languages, for these governments saw such networks and church support for linguistic and cultural differences as explaining the weak sense of French identity and values in rural areas. As a result, instruction in and the translation of the catechism into French became the central elements of a strategy designed to limit the social influence of the clergy. In this way, successive governments hoped to replace these church networks with a powerful state administrative system based on principles emanating from the center. French, then, gradually came to be seen as the language of modernity and civilization, as opposed to the "barbarism" and "tribalism" of regional tongues.[8] Moreover, this notion was increasingly adopted by women—the primary transmitters of language—who enthusiastically chose French over their own maternal tongues when raising their children.[9] At the same time, the new possibilities of social ascension offered by modernization were associated with knowledge of French, a "modern" language, as opposed to Basque, a "traditional" one. Together, these strategies formed a model of linguistic homogenization that had already been defined by the revolutionaries of 1789, but that now assumed a more ambitious French nationalist project that really came into focus only during the Third Republic.[10]

This same period also coincided with the emergence of intellectuals and theorists dedicated to defining the French nation and its nationalism. For example, Ernest Renan gave his famous lecture, "Qu'est-ce qu'une nation?" (What Is a Nation?) at the Sorbonne in 1882. And a more virulent and ethnic strand of French national consciousness was developed by Charles Maurras as a result of the debate surrounding the Dreyfus Affair in the late 1890s. Maurras led Action Française (French Action), a group that maintained an authoritarian nationalist vision based on deeply Catholic, conservative, and racist ideas that "imagined France was unchanging. Regimes might come and go, but the essential *pays* would persist."[11]

As I have already noted, the educational system would also play a key role in configuring the French nation.[12] Worth special mention, beyond the actual content of the system, are the social origins of the teachers themselves. As Eric Savarèse points out,

> under the Third Republic, teachers came from a group at the core of which many were [socially] modest in origin ... [A]mong the former students of the École Normale Supérieure, many were the offspring of modest social origins who had managed to gain a growing social mobility. However ... it was the Republic—a regime that made equal opportunities one of its most fundamental values—to which they owed this social improvement. For these children of the popular classes, the Republic was clearly the regime [responsible for] erasing the weight of their origins ... For the[se] teachers ... criticizing the Republic not only made no sense, but it was unthinkable ... Socialized in republican institutions and

with [both] a pedagogical and patriotic mission, these educators were clearly among the best "publicists" of the new regime.[13]

Rogers Brubaker underscores the importance of war in also shaping the French nation to that extent that, in his opinion, French nationalism was basically the result of military struggle—whether in 1792–93 or as a result of World War I.[14] Eugen Weber likewise points to the importance of European conflict in shaping the French nation, especially in rural areas of the country. In fact, for him, it was only after World War I that most people in France actually began to think of themselves as French.[15]

World War I indeed brought a profound change to the political map of Iparralde. With the outbreak of hostilities, much as in earlier conflicts, many young Basques actually sought to avoid military conscription,[16] following a migratory route to the Americas that had already been established in the nineteenth century for economic reasons.[17] This would seem to denote a lack of national belonging among at least some rural sectors and explains the pro-Basque positions of the *xuriak*, demonstrating the extent to which models of local socialization were still—although less and less—based on Basque cultural and linguistic parameters.[18] However, the course of events eventually drew the male Basque population into the French armed forces, with important consequences. First of all, one must note the loss of population that "for many Basque rural villages . . . severely reduced two generations of males and, with them, the reproductive capacity of the village."[19] The effect of this for Basque identity was, in turn, devastating: As we will see shortly, the French Army became during the war "the school of the nation" or a primary "instrument of socialization."[20]

Although after the war, there was a surge in French nationalism, centered on the cultivation of an ex-combatant mentality, that nationalist feeling had existed prior to the conflict, when it had, on occasion, shown clear signs of anti-Semitism.[21] In fact, during the course of the Third Republic, French nationalism was transformed into a populist ideology by those attempting to connect with the "regular" people by blaming France's ills on Jewish interests, with the most spectacular example being the Dreyfus Affair.[22] However, with the turn of the century, French nationalism—as expressed most obviously by Action Française—increasingly focused more on external, rather than internal enemies. Indeed, in 1907, the French nationalist Ligue de Patriotes (Patriots' League) opened its doors to Jewish members for the first time. Action Française—to which the Basque notable Jean Ybarnégaray remained close—focused its policies on what it classified as the defense and survival of the French nation. And its leader, Maurras, even questioned the democratic system when it interfered with the military threat posed by Germany. Ultimately, this growing French nationalism also took root in Iparralde, where the sense of a distinct Basque identity had been reduced by the educational policies of the Third Republic.

Furthermore, plans were initiated to socialize and nationalize the peasantry, thereby incorporating rural society into the state's general modernization.[23] The Third Republic also introduced schemes to place symbols of the French nation throughout the country: Statues of Marianne, the personification of Liberty and Reason that had become a symbol of the French Republic, thus were erected in town squares throughout France, and her likeness also adorned the country's city halls. The result of this was that republican and secular symbols gradually came to replace their religious counterparts, and the church progressively lost ground to the new rising force of local political power in France: the mayorship.

For the above reasons, there was a noteworthy decline in a distinct sense of Basque identity during the Third Republic. Most observers agree that the catalyst for this decline came in 1918 with the close of World War I. "In many ways," Cameron Watson concludes (following Eugen Weber's general thesis), "a specifically Basque identity in Iparralde began to slip into hibernation in the decade before World War I. The full effect of the war would soon speed up this decline."[24] Suzanne Citron notes that "the construction of [French] national identity was the result of an act of will on the part of the founding fathers of the Third Republic." Moreover, this sense of national identity that cemented a specifically French sense of belonging did not allow for the existence of other forms of belonging.

> Like all liberal republican elites of the nineteenth century, they maintained a proud and messianic image of France: "France as Superior as Any Dogma or Religion" was the title of a chapter from a short book by [Jules] Michelet, *Le peuple* [The People] in 1847. Urban men, bearers of a secondary educational and university-level culture, they believed sincerely that this culture was superior; [that] it was necessary to civilize the "barbarians" by nationalizing them.

Accordingly, history was reinterpreted ideologically to legitimize French historical conquests: "It was the history of 'winners,' of a triumphant force, a history in which the annexed, the vanquished, the opponents, the 'others' were not historical Subjects."[25] In sum, this integration

> was more Gallicization than civic conscience. The children of peasants, migrant laborers, Jewish refugees from Central and Eastern Europe, [and] the descendants of colonial peoples were sure they would discover a new homeland, an ancient and prestigious homeland. They were instructed to believe this, even though they were Jews or from the colonies, as if they were the adopted children of the Gauls, subject to the good king Saint Louis, brilliant subjects of the court of Louis XIV, younger siblings of the heroic child Barat, escorts in the strong heroic deeds of Napoleon's soldiers . . . and to bury silently their own ancestral cultures.[26]

In Search of a Basque Identity: Lafitte's Aintzina Movement

Despite these developments, prior to the outbreak of war in 1914, a new dynamic of cultural generation had emerged in Iparralde that connected with the foralist and later nationalist movements in Hegoalde. As we have seen, in the nineteenth century, d'Abbadie was central in promoting these cultural initiatives and even in extending them to Hegoalde. However, these initial elite contacts continued beyond both the nineteenth century and the particular role of d'Abbadie.

The First Steps

In 1901, sponsored by Martin Guilbeau (the republican mayor of Donibane Lohizune), a meeting was held in Iparralde between various forces of all political colors and from both sides of the border at which it was agreed that a conference on Basque orthography would take place. And in November of that same year, this conference was held in Hondarribia, Gipuzkoa, with the attendance of numerous figures, including Arana, Campión, Resurrección María de Azkue (one of the most prominent modern scholars of the Basque language), and Guilbeau.

Despite their evident differences, the various representatives from Iparralde decided thereafter to continue with the initiative, creating the first widespread cross-border cultural association, Eskualzaleen Biltzarra (Association of Basque Studies), in 1902. Although principally composed of people from Lapurdi, well-known individuals from Hegoalde, such as Campión and Telesforo de Aranzadi, were also members,[27] and Article 5 of its constitution stated that its goal was "to aid, by all the means at its disposal, the preservation, diffusion, and development of the Basque language."[28] This group was important because it allowed for the cross-border contact of pro-Basque elites, with a noteworthy presence of PNV activists from Hegoalde.[29] Such contacts allowed, in turn, for the gradual development of Basque nationalist ideas by some figures in Iparralde, among whom was Father Pierre Lafitte, founder of the future Eskualerriste movement.

In 1933, the Paris chapter of another group, Euskal Ikasleen Biltzarra (the Association of Basque Students) was formed by Jean Etcheverry-Ainchart (later an elected deputy as a "Basque" candidate) and Eugène Goyheneche (one of the few PNV members from Iparralde at that time). As James E. Jacob observes, the origins of this latter group resided in the desperate search by activists such as Goyheneche to mobilize Basque youth from what they considered its "defeatism."[30] This group based its strategies on an elitist conception of the need for a kind of cultural regeneration and assumed in straightforward fashion the connection between Basque nationality and religion, race, and language, following the original ideological line of Sabino Arana. However, beyond any practical headway this student group was able to make, its real importance lies in the creation of a core of individuals who—while their work was obviously more cultural than political—later came under the organizational wing of Lafitte. He created the Eskualerriste movement in 1933 and the journal *Aintzina* (meaning both "ancient" and "forward" in different dialects of Basque) a year later; both employing a markedly more political discourse. Thanks to the original informal cross-border contacts that emerged in the late nineteenth century, the later (and admittedly modest) influence of the Basque nationalist press in Hegoalde, the resultant reflections of certain individuals from Iparralde in their own local media, and, above all, the role of a small number of priests in the North responding to Arana's ideas, a form of Basque nationalism quietly emerged in Lapurdi, Nafarroa Beherea, and Zuberoa.

The Eskualerriste program was designed to respond to the local context in which it was created. Therefore I would not classify *Aintzina*, for example, as an unequivocally Basque nationalist publication. That is, although it supported the Basque nationalist cause in Hegoalde, its proposals for Iparralde were more obviously regionalist in tone. In fact, the Eskualerriste movement rested on three basic principles: regionalism, social conservatism, and the tension between a necessary pragmatism and the desire to diffuse more openly nationalist ideas.

The Regionalism of the Eskualerriste Movement

Despite the pragmatic necessities of initially pursuing regionalist demands, members of the Eskualerriste movement served as the forerunners of later, more obviously nationalist movements. For this reason, I would contend that it served as a transition, a kind of "toll" that the Basque movement had to pay before transforming into Basque nationalism and a means by which it could free itself of overtly Catholic content to become secular. In other words, this was a bridge between the past and the future, between the pro-Basque sentiments of certain religious elites and the Basque nationalism of what would ultimately be Enbata.[31]

The movement was important for three reasons: It represented the first attempt to overcome (however timidly) the conservative clericalism that had dominated Basque politics for generations, even though it died in the act; it established links with other regional movements in France, thereby creating the bases for a common federal political strategy; and it played an important role after political refugees began to arrive from Hegoalde as a result of the Spanish Civil War (1936–39), when it began to assume a more political notion of cross-border, national unity or Basque fraternity.

One should remember, however, that the Eskualerriste movement remained resolutely regionalist. In 1933, for example, Lafitte outlined the basic points of his strategy. These included following the slogan "God and the Ancient Law," working for political decentralization against the modern unitary state, a call for the co-official status of Basque alongside French, the general defense of Basque culture, the defense of women's rights and a call for their involvement in the movement, a foreign policy with regard to Basques in Hegoalde, and support for other regionalist and federalist movements in France.[32] Thus, although as Jean-Claude Larronde points out, certain members of the group held Basque nationalist views, in practice, they were forced to tone down any public expression of such ideas, faced with the dominant ex-combatant French nationalism of the era.[33] And consequently, the Eskualerriste movement rejected all charges of separatism by clearly stating its regionalist aims, given that the reality of local conditions in Iparralde meant that the region was (above all, economically) tied to France.[34] In *Aintzina*'s words, it was "GEOGRAFICALLY IMPOSSIBLE today to form a Basque nation with the Spanish-Basque and French-Basque territories . . . We do not seek the creation of a

Basque state that could not survive in current conditions and that might lead to the death of our people."[35]

Lafitte–like Garat and Chaho before him–never publicly renounced his French nationality and considered the Basque Country his *petite patrie*. For him, "the nation, far from seeing its unity compromised, will be exalted from many points of view: love for the small homeland will increase that for the larger one."[36] Thus, the regionalism of the Eskualerriste movement became part of a federal conception of France that saw as the movement's primary objective a statute of autonomy for Iparralde. What Lafitte defined as "a Basque Statute that might join our two *arrondissements* in a federal French state could be desirable from a cultural, linguistic, educational, and religious point of view."[37] Taken together with the support of the Eskualerriste movement for other minority or regional groups in France, their program favored a widespread administrative as well as cultural decentralization of the state. As Juan Carlos Jiménez de Aberásturi puts it, their "ideology, more than nationalist–as it has been described on occasion–was of a typically *pétainiste* [from Marshal Pétain] regionalist form that . . . preached a return to the land, in other words the countryside, and 'taking root' in traditions, overvaluing the model of rural life as an ideological reference, seeing it as a universal cure for all ills, especially the biggest and most dangerous one: Communism."[38]

Despite all this, although the movement explicitly rejected separatism, some of its members did favor stronger ties between Basques on both sides of the border.[39] For example, beyond the fiery discourse and epistolary exchanges of Goyheneche at this time, in 1933, another member, Dr. Jean de Jaureguiberry, publicly wrote in the journal, *Gure Herria*: "At a time when the great Western ship is adrift under a starless sky . . . the time has come, perhaps, to glance at the lifeboats. For we Basques, there is just one, one alone. Let's quickly get in it . . . let's not get in the wrong lifeboat. Ours has a name, Euzkadi."[40] Yet such statements were ultimately restricted to certain individuals. As a group, the Eskualerriste movement maintained a regionalist position in its attempts to regenerate Basque society. This, as Lafitte clearly argued in *Aintzina*, would be promoted as a "purifying" objective, a goal that had to allow for the promotion and consolidation of values linked to Basque culture. In other words, the individual, family, and religion were the central tenets on which the Eskualerriste movement based its strategies, and around these it constructed a conservative framework that was at odds with the developing modern world.

The Ideology of the Eskualerriste Movement

Most observers have seen the regionalism espoused in the pages of *Aintzina* as reflecting several currents of French philosophical and political thought in the 1930s,[41] for example, the nonconformist movement and, more specifically, the doctrines of Ordre Nouveau (New Order), which promoted individual considerations over those of society as a counterpoint to liberal individualism and Communism–that is, a notion of *personnalisme* as an antidote to the all-powerful statism of French society.

Larronde points out that Lafitte designed several concrete ways in which the Basque individual could achieve this personal liberation: educational freedom; religious freedom, as opposed to the secular policies of the state; a specific role for women in accordance with their esteemed position in Basque culture; a strategy to promote bilingualism and to halt the decline of Euskara; and, in a more general sense, the defense of traditions, centered on the importance of family.[42] The promotion of family values as an extension of Basque traditions rested on a number of principles: a condemnation of divorce, the importance and stability of the family inheritance, and familial rights as expressed through a defense of the so-called "family vote," which gave the family a vote for each child, and of salaries paid to parents to subsidize maternal care in the home.[43] The family unit thus was seen as connected with Basque origins. In Lafitte's words, "We are Basques, and, by consequence, of a race where the rights of the family are sacred."[44]

Finally, the economic position of the Eskualerriste movement rested on three basic principles: first, a defense of agricultural interests; then, a defense of a unionist corporatism, as opposed to the polarization of solely class-based union activity; and finally, the clear recognition of the self-regulating capacity of the Basque nationalist labor union in Hegoalde, ELA-STV (Eusko Langileen Alkartasuna-Solidaridad de Trabajadores Vascos; the Basque Workers' Union) as an example to follow. However, given the weak position from which the Eskualerriste movement was forced to work in Iparralde, it had to be content with initially favoring some form of cooperation with French Christian union activity.[45]

It would appear, then, that the Eskualerriste movement oscillated between certain progressive doctrinal elements (the importance of women in society, labor-union activity, and so on) and more conservative tendencies (opposition to divorce, support for the family, and so on), the latter the result of its defense of traditional (Basque) values and the strength of the French right at the local level in Iparralde. To be sure, such conservatism was only the result of the context in which the movement emerged. Just as the movement's latent nationalist tendencies were transformed into regionalism by the crisis of Basque identity, its progressive outlook was tempered by an overwhelmingly recalcitrant right-wing discourse that dominated Basque society. Within such a context, it was difficult for *Aintzina* to blend a pro-Basque orientation, progressive ideas, and Catholicism, especially when the conservative society in which it emerged also claimed such Basque values as its own. In fact, the journal could not escape such conservative positions.[46]

In other words, when forced to choose, the Eskualerriste movement opted for the conservative option, a choice that also explained its ambiguous position on the Spanish Civil War. As a result of this positioning within the local conservative political reality, although it was still critical of the centralism of Ordre Nouveau, *Aintzina* called for its readers to support the French right in the 1936 legislative elections, elections that famously gave the left-wing Popular Front coalition victory in France, but that the right won convincingly in Iparralde.[47]

Lafitte himself urged people to vote for Jean Ybarnégaray, René Delzangles, and Bernard de Coral, the three right-wing candidates, in the same elections. And although *Aintzina* also encouraged its readers to spread the regionalist message, in Larronde's opinion, victory for the right in Iparralde in 1936 was not the result of support from the Eskualerriste movement.[48] In fact, the conservative victors considered this support a blank check for which they owed the regionalist group nothing. Indeed, shortly afterward, Ybarnégaray savagely criticized the Eskualerriste movement and Basque exiles from Hegoalde fleeing the Spanish Civil War.

The tensions between the progressive and conservative tendencies in *Aintzina* also explain the journal's ambiguous position as regards the civil conflict in Spain.[49] This ambiguity probably resulted from Lafitte's attempts to maintain some harmony between the group's two factions. As a result, members of the group confronted the issue of the Spanish Civil War "without wishing to take part on any side of the conflict, trying to maintain a balanced position between Navarrese Carlists," who supported the military uprising ultimately led by General Francisco Franco, "and Basque, Bizkaian, and Gipuzkoan nationalists," allies of the progressive forces making up the democratically elected Spanish government.[50] At the same time, however, it would appear that if forced to choose between one side or the other, it was clear for *Aintzina* on which side it would fall: Put simply, the Communist threat outweighed that of a right-wing dictatorship, for "if the dictatorship, that is, a right-wing statism, triumphs, it will mean the end for the Statute [of Autonomy in Hegoalde]. If Communism, that is left-wing statism, triumphs, it will be worse. May God create an intermediary solution to bring an end to this ignoble killing."[51]

Alternatively, the reasons for *Aintzina*'s ambiguous position regarding the Spanish Civil War can be traced, according to Jacob, to the hostility of the church and elites in Iparralde to both the refugee problem and the instrumental alliance of Basque nationalists in Hegoalde with the Spanish Popular Front.[52] The strategic decision of the PNV to ally itself with the Spanish center-left as a means of gaining Basque autonomy in Hegoalde had serious political repercussions in Iparralde, most obviously, the loss of the support it might have enjoyed among notables there. Indeed, until this time, Ybarnégaray himself had been close to the PNV, but broke off relations after the latter's instrumental alliance to defend the Second Spanish Republic.[53]

Support for Franco was the result of a dominant mentality of the time in Iparralde and the submission of the populace to the continuing influence of notables and the most reactionary part of the clergy.[54] One clear example of this was the support of the local press in Iparralde for Franco's rebels, classifying the Basque government's alliance with the Second Spanish Republic as a monstrous error or just plain madness. In May 1937, for example, the newspaper *Presse du Sud-Ouest* stated that "Catholics should choose between the pope and President Aguirre," the head of the Basque government, and later published a statement aping the "official" Francoist view of the destruction of Gernika (Guernica), denying any rebel involvement in the atrocity.[55] Similarly, the influential weekly *Eskualduna* congratulated "Mola's Basques" for saving the "sacred tree" of the town.[56]

Ultimately, such positions were, for the Eskualerriste movement, its own political downfall.[57] One might say, then, that the Eskualerriste failure stemmed from an inability to find its own political or ideological space in a society that, at the time, enthusiastically belonged to the French nation and maintained a deep religiosity. In the face of the Eskualerriste ambiguous blend of traditionalism with a timid progressivism, the majority of people in Iparralde opted for "real" traditionalist, conservative options. It would be another generation before a qualitative ideological leap would be made among pro-Basque circles.

Between a Desire to Spread Ideas and Pragmatism

The tension between the pragmatic needs of the local context in which the Eskualerriste movement was formed and the desire to diffuse more openly nationalist ideas had been expressed earlier, in the pages of *Gure Herria*: "The position of our brothers in Spain can provide us with wonderful guidelines that, adapted, directed, and, if necessary, modified according to the needs of Basques in France to fit the environment in which they live, to the reality that surrounds them, should lead to marvelous results."[58] To be sure, the reality of local conditions—but also basic doctrinal principles—forced the Eskualerriste movement to adapt the Basque nationalism of the South to the North.

The first modification that stands out is that of the basic central thesis of Sabino Arana. Lafitte adopted as his own Arana's (and the PNV's) slogan "Jaungoikua eta Legizarra" (God and the Old Law), but he also adapted it to mean either "God and the Old Constitution" or "God and Law"—phrases resembling some of Chaho's ideas a century earlier.[59] At the same time, while the Eskualerriste movement accepted to some degree the racial dimension of Arana's original doctrine, it was also based on less exclusive precepts, thereby foreshadowing a generally more open form of Basque nationalism in Iparralde. For example, the statutes of Gure Etchea, local groups involved in the Begiraleak women's movement close to *Aintzina*,[60] stated that to be a member of the group, one only need live in Iparralde or sympathize with the Basque cause. Similarly, when drawing up conditions under which sympathizers might be involved in the Eskualerriste movement, Lafitte proposed that the group be formed by native Basques, the descendants of Basques, or anyone who had lived ten years or more in Iparralde and could be nominated by two current members.[61] Moreover, it was clear that this project involved attempts to reinforce Basque culture in Iparralde. As such, the Basque language would play an inclusive role, recalling, for example, the nineteenth-century Navarrese Euskaro movement more than the exclusive doctrines of Arana.[62]

That said, those involved in *Aintzina* were, ultimately, seduced by many Basque nationalist ideas originating in Hegoalde. In Lafitte's own words, "That youth, that enthusiasm, were truly amazing. I traveled the country from *batzoki* [PNV center] to *batzoki*. The birth of Euskadi appeared imminent... Without any doubt, what I saw in my experience in the South filled me with enthusiasm. I formed a team."[63] And the Eskualerriste movement did not hesitate to copy the socializing strategies of the PNV, by establishing hiking groups and women's sections, for example.

Thanks to these initial contacts, and especially the role of Eugène Goyheneche, the youth section of the PNV made several trips to Iparralde. Larronde notes that these visits went beyond "exchanges, contacts, or ties of friendship that might be established across the border, [for] the inhabitants of the northern Basque Country were able to see directly the number and enthusiastic patriotism of the Bizkaians."[64] As a result, at least among some people in Iparralde, a sense of belonging to a common nation emerged, and for them, the appropriation of symbols such as the *ikurriña*, the Basque flag designed by Arana, or the slogan "Jaungoikua eta Legizarra" became tangible ways in which to participate in a common national project.

In this way, a certain mimesis was evident among those who influenced or who might favor the consolidation of such a project in Iparralde: that is, among those sectors that could influence social mobilization and the integration of individuals into the (Basque) national community. Initially, the Eskualerriste movement attempted to imitate the PNV in constructing a community with the ultimate aim of mobilizing potential pro-Basque sentiment among the population there.

The Eskualerristes considered it necessary to break the power of the local notables. For this reason, they attempted to attract important local figures such as Dr. Jean de Jaureguiberry to their ranks. They also established contact with other groups, such as the Eskualzaleen Biltzarra, the journal *Gure Herria*, and Euskal Ikasleen Biltzarra.[65] At the same time, it was necessary to construct an apparatus of mobilization that would encourage new adherents.

Thus, for example, in 1935, the movement created the group Menditarrak, a hiking group that followed the PNV model, the Mendigoizaleak.[66] The Menditarrak group described itself as "a force to protect [the Basque Country] and help those who wish to maintain its traditions."[67] Beyond its basic organizational structure, however, what appears odd about the Menditarrak group is the paradoxical contrast between the supposedly pragmatic line that the Eskualerristes sought to follow and the quasi-military dimension that the group seemed to adopt,[68] a dimension similar to that of the Mendigoizaleak in Hegoalde and characterized by a similar aesthetic,[69] symbolism,[70] and role.[71] In many ways, the Menditarrak thus came to resemble their counterparts in Hegoalde who, through the 1930s and as a result of the worsening political situation in Spain, had increasingly come to adopt militaristic postures: uniforms, national anthems, and a call to action through the mystical and romanticized pastime of mountaineering, an endeavor where mind and body would remain pure through contact with nature and thus a product of the homeland.[72]

However, at most, the Menditarrak only had twelve members and undertook only two excursions. Clearly more successful among the associated groups within the Eskualerriste movement was the Begiraleak women's organization, created in the exact image of the PNV's Emakume Abertzale Batzar (Women's Patriotic Section). For Larronde, these Begiraleak groups were (according to their own definition) the "guardians of the faith and tradition" and formed thirty-seven chapters alone by 1937.[73] Formed and led by Madeleine de Jaureguiberry (sister of Jean),[74] their internal statutes left little doubt as to their objectives:

> Art. 1–A Basque regionalist women's group has been formed, under the name Begiraleak, whose goal is to defend the spiritual legacy left us by our ancestors: faith, language and traditions.
> Art. 2–To form part of this one must be Basque or a sympathizer.
> Art. 3–The relations between members must be based on the equality and solidarity of our race.[75]

This mirrored the Eskualerriste discourse of women as privileged defenders of Basque values and of the family unit in which they were considered to play the key role. Moreover, following the cross-class doctrine of the PNV in Hegoalde, the Begiraleak statute also identified equality and solidarity as important features of the Basque race, thereby avoiding any potential social differences by emphasizing the right to belong to the group on equal terms. Still further, and in contrast with the stricter interpretations of national belonging in the Basque nationalist movement in the South, the Begiraleak movement would admit sympathizers to the Basque cause from whatever background.

The generally more open notion of membership of these groups, as we will see, would be embraced later by the first truly Basque nationalist organization in Iparralde, Enbata. However, the general perception within society continued to associate Basque identity with traditions and the language, a cultural perception that existed until recent times, making for a contradiction that limited the development of Basque identity in the North. Indeed, this dynamic was broken (as we will also see) only when Basque nationalists in Iparralde began to base their positions and activity on more porous or malleable notions of identity, such as territory, for example.

Despite the attempts of the Eskualerriste movement and its satellite groups to forge a new political path in Iparralde, it was disbanded in 1937. This was due in part to its ambiguous stance on the 1936 French general elections and on the Spanish Civil War, but also in part to the ideological discourse and activity of *Aintzina*. That is, when the time came to make a decision one way or the other, it opted for the profoundly conservative alternative, thereby giving a blank check to the aforementioned notables, who felt no obligation to give the Eskualerristes anything in return. Moreover, *Aintzina* itself also went through a period of deep crisis as a result of its emphasis on focusing on the issue of Basque identity, a strategy taken from directly Basque nationalism in Hegoalde, and on justifying the instrumental alliance by this same nationalist movement with leftist forces in Spain, a crisis that not even the progressive element of the Eskualerriste movement's membership could resolve. That said, this was a nearly impossible situation for *Aintzina* when those rural sectors most likely to favor the Basque cause in Iparralde were also those that remained embedded in profoundly conservative and even occasionally extreme right-wing, positions. Finally, one should also point out that the Eskualerriste movement, which had gained so much through the involvement of young activists, gradually lost momentum as these young people were forced to leave Iparralde to continue their studies or in search of work, a recurring problem for the founding of Basque nationalism in the North.

The Eskualerristes were not just caught between tradition and modernity, as the Janus-faced name of their journal, *Aintzina*, suggested, but also marked a new stage in the quest to establish a specific Basque identity. This stage began with a crisis in Basque identity and ended with the first real political (and on this occasion, regionalist) expression of Basque identity in Iparralde. Although it ended in failure, it laid the foundation for later attempts to establish more explicitly nationalist movements. The experience of the Eskualerriste movement also demonstrates the importance of Basque nationalism in Hegoalde for developments in Iparralde, while at the same time demonstrating the need for those in the North to adapt their ideology to the local context there. The tension between these two facts would soon be raised by the first explicit and public expression of Basque nationalism in Iparralde, in the work of Marc Legasse. The Eskualerristes demonstrated that any successful expression of Basque nationalism in the North would have to be necessarily more instrumental, political, and civic—that is, that ethnic or ethnicist policies would have less success than in the South. Although it failed in the attempt, *Aintzina* did indeed promote such a strategy, thereby initiating the beginning of the end of the logic of two homelands: on the one hand, because the success of Ybarnégaray (and others) seemed to indicate that the people of Iparralde made a firm choice in favor of one *patrie*, France, and on the other, because any truly pro-Basque political strategy, be regionalist or nationalist, could not really embrace this logic.

CHAPTER SEVEN

Legasse: At the Vanguard of the Rear Guard of the Basque Nation

The 1940s marked a kind of transitory phase in Iparralde, characterized by the culmination of the crisis in Basque identity that began in the nineteenth century and the definitive consolidation of French identity through state measures. Yet within this context, one key figure emerged who would suddenly become the vanguard of Basque nationalism in the North, and despite his ultimate failure—somewhat predictable, given the almost impossible conditions he found in which to diffuse his ideas—he left a legacy that would be later adopted and adapted in the formation of the first true Basque nationalist movement there. Marc Legasse may plausibly be considered the pioneer of Basque nationalism in Iparralde. He was the first to underscore the importance of civil disobedience as a tactic to publicize the Basque cause; he was the first to criticize an overly touristy or folkloric conception of Basque identity that had been a strong component of Basque circles; he was the first to stand openly as a Basque nationalist candidate in elections; and he was the first to argue for full, institutional recognition of Iparralde. Moreover, Legasse was at the vanguard of those regarded by Basque nationalists fleeing Franco's Spain as their rear guard, for he began to organize an anti-Franco resistance in French territory. As a result, Legasse became a key critic of the hegemonic and pretentious views of Basque nationalism in Hegoalde that viewed Iparralde as a necessary "sacrifice" to the cause so that they might find refuge there.

On the Periphery of the Periphery

Another dividing line, beyond the center-periphery dynamic that has mostly characterized the present work, helps us locate and analyze the tension between separatist and centralist impulses in Iparralde: the notion of a "periphery of the periphery." As Juan J. Linz puts it, "nationalist peripheries, through their efforts to create an autonomous state, and even further in their separatist dreams, find the same problem as the central state: they also have peripheries that are difficult to integrate and dominate from their own center."[1]

This perspective allows us to consider two major paradoxes of Basque nationalism: If the Basque Country is, for Basque nationalists, a nation made up of seven provinces, then why is Basque nationalism so weak in Iparralde and Navarre? And further, if the Basque people are one, according to nationalist doctrine, then why has there been such mistrust on the part of significant numbers in Iparralde and Navarre of efforts to create more stable institutional relations between all the provinces? In the preceding pages, I have attempted to answer these questions as regards Iparralde, focusing my argument on the process of French state building and its consequences for Basque identity. However, the notion of a periphery of the periphery further illuminates the question of the crisis of Basque identity. Like the center-periphery dynamic itself, this notion is based on an understanding of the importance of borders, but it helps us understand conceptions of the provinces of Bizkaia and Gipuzkoa as the symbolic center of Basque space, with a periphery formed by Araba, Navarre, and Iparralde.[2]

Beyond the important state acculturation process that took place in Iparralde, the late and weak emergence of Basque nationalism there was based on the strategic focus accorded it by the nationalist movement in Hegoalde. In an instrumental interpretation of the area, the northern Basque Country was understood as an instrument at the service of the South. This logic was assumed by many Basque nationalists in Iparralde itself—despite the criticism of Legasse in the 1940s—because of the crisis situation that the provinces of Hegoalde experienced under both Franco's dictatorship and the Spanish transition to democracy, but also, crucially, as a result of the acceptance by people in Iparralde of the priority within the Basque nationalist movement to focus its efforts on Hegoalde. In short, Basque nationalism has operated from a logic more appropriate to sovereign states, conceiving Iparralde as a periphery that has, on occasion, been considered merely as home of an instrumental rear guard (as we will shortly see in more detail) or that at other times (principally during the past decade) has been seen as an inalienable element of Basque territoriality, reduced to being just one part of the meteorological map for weather forecasts on Euskal Telebista—ETB, the public television service of the Basque Autonomous Community.

From the end of World War II in 1945 on, the Basque government in exile (controlled by the PNV) maintained a clear position regarding Iparralde: Basques there would constitute no more than a rear guard of the Basque nation, a decision that was made as a result of the role of Iparralde as a safe haven for Basque refugees from Franco's Spain, the lack of any organized nationalist movement there, and, most importantly, the state of emergency that Hegoalde was at the time experiencing as a result of the Spanish dictatorship. Thus, Iparralde became a place where the Basque nationalist struggle would be put to one side. Indeed, the logic ran that any potential "freedom" of Iparralde could only follow the independence of Hegoalde.

In this regard, as James E. Jacob maintains, the Basque government in exile established a strategy that would soon come to define the price paid for creating a "sanctuary" in Iparralde during the Spanish Civil War and after the conclusion of World War II: put simply, its nonintervention in the affairs of Iparralde.[3] As Paul Sérant has observed, if the PNV had pressed for any other strategy, the French government would have withdrawn its support for the Basque government in exile's creation of a sanctuary in Iparralde. In other words, it would not have tolerated the existence of a Basque problem within its borders.[4] As Juan Carlos Jiménez de Aberásturi notes,

> The margin for maneuver for the nationalists was not very wide ... Given refuge in France and residing in large numbers in the continental [northern] Basque Country, they could not clearly express nationalist beliefs that implied attaining an independent Basque Country that, logically, following doctrinal coherency would have to include the Basque part of the French state. That would have implied taking advantage of their forced stay there to develop a campaign of agitation and propaganda with the goal of persuading the local population to the nationalist cause. The social structure of the [northern] provinces, their conservatism, and the profound influence of a Catholic Church actively opposed to any left-wing or even just liberal tendencies presented, in theory, a favorable field of expansion ... Yet it was clear that this direction, [which was not] even attempted or contemplated, could never be taken. The French reaction would have been terrible and would have provoked a closer collaboration with Franco's government, as well as the end of all nationalist plans.[5]

Given such circumstances, the Basque government in exile quickly clarified its position: "The best of relations exist between the Basque and French Governments. The Basque regions in France are directly under the French Government and do not play any politically important part in the affairs of the Autonomous Basque Country."[6]

This position was clarified further still in 1940 by the PNV (through Manuel de Irujo) when it eliminated Iparralde altogether from what it delimited as Euzkadi, the name invented by Sabino Arana to denote the Basque Country.[7] While Irujo opted to omit the provinces of Iparralde from his map, he also included non-Basque provinces such as Cantabria, La Rioja, Burgos, and Aragón,[8] perhaps explaining why he also favored only a bilingual constitution—that is, in Basque and Spanish—for Euzkadi. In regard to this question, Irujo "was a sufficiently realist politician to seek the aid of de Gaulle for a future Basque republic that would not take any land away from France. If Irujo, at the very least, wanted his project considered at international meetings, it was clear that he could never demonstrate any territorial interests beyond those of Spain."[9]

Pierre Letamendia also acknowledges the notion that the PNV avoided any political activity in Iparralde so as not to upset the French authorities, and that refugees from Hegoalde were tolerated only on the condition they did not engage in any such activity.[10] One should add to this that the PNV had no organizational structure in Iparralde at the time, so it is hardly surprising to see party policy in 1939 delimited thus: "The Basque Nationalist Party, regarding the regime and parties of Franco, fundamentally proclaims its freedom of action. The PNV will attempt to influence the political life of peninsular Euzkadi."[11]

Emilio Lopez Adan, however, takes another view: Compared with previous years, during the late 1940s, the PNV enjoyed excellent relations with the French authorities. This was due in part to the fall from grace of Jean Ybarnégaray as a result of his participation in the Vichy government during the war, the regime that was established in 1940 in the part of France not occupied by the Nazis but that collaborated with Nazi Germany. It was also due to the importance of Christian Democracy—with the PNV declaring itself part of this movement—among local elites in Iparralde at a time when the Basque government in exile was seeking external alliances that might help to bring down the Franco regime. Consequently, many of these local notables "thought the fall of Franco would be soon and saw in the PNV a conservative guarantee within the Spanish Republic."[12]

However, ultimately, the PNV strategy of nonintervention in French affairs did the party little good. In 1950, the French authorities expelled foreign Communists from the country, and a year later, they evicted the PNV from its headquarters in Paris, later giving it to Franco's government, which installed the Spanish embassy there. Furthermore, in 1954, the then French minister of the interior, François Mitterand, shut down the station from which Radio Euzkadi-Euzkadi Irratia was emitted in Mugerre (Mouguerre), Lapurdi. Yet perhaps surprisingly, these policies did not stop the PNV from "continuing with its conciliatory position toward France, to such an extent that it halted any political intervention by 'French Basques' in the 1956 World Basque Congress in order to avoid any unpleasantness with the French government."[13]

Whatever the true position of the PNV, the presence of refugees from the Spanish Civil War and the creation of delegations in Baiona, Biarritz, and Donibane Lohizune (which later disappeared in 1965) had a contradictory effect. On the one hand, it was clear that Basque activists concentrated their efforts on organizing shelter and accommodation for the refugees from Hegoalde, abandoning the political activity associated with the by now ailing *Aintzina*. Yet it is also true, as Jacob points out, that the influence of cultural groups established by members of the PNV and the ANV (Acción Nacionalista Vasca; Basque Nationalist Action) encouraged the dissemination of Basque culture from an obviously political perspective.[14] At the same time, the presence of socialist, Communist, and anarchist refugees from Spain, together with their Basque nationalist counterparts, opened Basque nationalism in general to new ideas. It was therefore no coincidence that, with the conclusion of World War II and the Nazi occupation in France, progressive Basque nationalist ideas began to emerge in Iparralde for the first time. Specifically, these views originated with one individual who did not hide his criticism of the PNV for its attitude toward his native Iparralde: Marc Legasse.

The First Expression of Basque Nationalism in Iparralde

Jacob uses the metaphor of the phoenix to describe the rebirth of *Aintzina* (after closing down in 1937) under the guiding hand of Marc Legasse in 1942. *Aintzina* was forced to close because activists in Iparralde devoted their energies to helping refugees from Hegoalde and because of financial problems and an increasingly hostile environment—promoted by the establishment of Iparralde, that is, the religious elites, notables, and the local press—for any form of Basque nationalist (and by association pro-Basque) expression.

Yet this picture would change during the Nazi occupation. First, Lafitte's experience with *Aintzina*, alongside his prodigious list of publications in *Eskualduna* (two hundred articles between 1915 and 1925) and *Gure Herria* (seventy articles between 1921 and 1939) accorded him an important position within local media circles.[15] This was even more so as the fortunes of the weekly *Eskualduna* (a journal of the local establishment) declined. Increasingly discredited for its role during the Nazi occupation, it was eventually shut down after the war for publishing excerpts from speeches by Hitler.[16] And a renewed Lafitte became editor of a new publication, *Herria*, that would continue in circulation for the next sixty years.

In this new context, Legasse began a series of conversations with several priests who stood out from others interested in the Basque cause for their more openly nationalist sympathies. As a result, with the money Legasse could put up, together with Piarres (Pierre) Charritton (a seminary student in Baiona) and Father Jean Diharce (the abbot of the Belloc Monastery), he went to Lafitte to ask his permission to use the name *Gure Herria* (the journal had been suspended in 1939) to "take this opportunity they had under Vichy to publish diverse kinds of material."[17] However, Lafitte preferred to maintain the name *Gure Herria* for his own projects and proposed they reform *Aintzina* instead.

Consequently, and after a series of ups and downs, the effective editorship of a newly implemented *Aintzina* went first to Charritton and then to Piarres (Pierre) Larzabal (another ordained priest), while Legasse took control of the financial arrangements. Despite this apparent agreement, differences within this new group soon emerged. Legasse, supported by Eugène Goyheneche, wanted to make the journal, as Jacob puts it, "the only proof of the existence of the Basque people under the occupation."[18] However, it seemed as if Larzabal wanted to continue an editorial line similar to that of Lafitte, which ruled out any talk of separatism. The result of this increasingly bitter dispute was that Larzabal left the group, and Legasse, at the request of Charritton, took over as editor. While Legasse was not altogether in agreement with the strictly cultural tone that Charritton had imparted the new *Aintzina*, he accepted it and published a series of articles that displayed a slightly more radical nationalist character than previously seen.[19] It would still be a couple of years, however, before more explicitly Basque nationalist ideas were published in Iparralde.

The friction between Legasse and Larzabal may be partly explained by the "acquiescent" attitude of many pro-Basque sectors in Iparralde during the Nazi occupation, which contrasted with the resistance activities of Basque nationalists from Hegoalde.[20] This acquiescence was more than evident among the members of Eskualdun Gazteen Biltzarra (EGB; the Association of Basque Youth), for example, who, after a meeting on April 27, 1943, published a manifesto that saw an opportunity to make the most of the decrees by Vichy government ministers of education Georges Ripert (1940) and Jérôme Carcopino (1943). The Ripert decree recognized that "local dialects" (including Basque, but not Occitan) might be useful additions to the school curriculum, whereas the Carcopino decree authorized the gradual introduction into the educational system of Basque, Flemish and Occitan as an optional choice during the school holidays.[21] As a result, these young Basques called on the authorities to promote Euskara in local schools and, further, appealed to elected officials, priests, the journal *Eskualduna*, and the Eskualzaleen Biltzarra association to support the Basque language. This was a political proposal, connected to a collective memory that already existed among certain sectors in Iparralde, the focus of which was centered on three aspects that continue to be important for Basque nationalism to this day: local institutional representation, the unity of the three provinces of Iparralde, and a wider sense of Basque territoriality grounded in the slogan "Zazpiak Bat." According to the manifesto:

> 2. Recovering the vote for the Biltzar of Lapurdi, [we] Basque Youth demand that, taking account of the provincial reorganization that is being passed around as one of the French government's preoccupations, the unity of the Basque Country [Iparralde] is reestablished in one distinct administrative region different from all others.
>
> 3 ... [We] Basque Youth proclaim our adherence to the traditional motto "Zazpiak Bat," symbol of the ethnic and moral solidarity of the Basques.[22]

The Basque Nationalist Candidates

That the third point of this manifesto centered on a concept of territoriality derived from the "Zazpiak Bat" notion led to severe criticism from many sectors of the local press in Iparralde. Behind this controversial point, as one would have expected, was Legasse. Later that same year, in the final edition of *Aintzina*'s second incarnation, Legasse penned an ironic article criticizing the outraged reaction of various commentators to a symbolic act by the EGB: the group (including Legasse himself) had replaced a symbol of the three northern Basque provinces on the Basque Museum of Baiona with another displaying the motto "Zazpiak Bat"—in fact, one that had previously adorned the museum since 1897. As the controversy continued, Legasse accused the director of the museum (who was ultimately responsible for replacing the original symbol) of separatism, in that he had been guilty of fomenting a notion that divided Basques of the North from those of the South. Interestingly, this example of nonviolent civil disobedience—manifested by symbolic activity—would be a strategy that Basque nationalists in Iparralde returned to in the 1990s,[23] following an unproductive flirtation with the use of political violence in the 1970s and 1980s. Legasse was therefore behind the first act of Basque nationalist disruptive protest in Iparralde,[24] a tactic that later came to form an important part of nationalist strategy there.

Legasse believed that the 1945 legislative elections in France, the first to be held after the liberation of the country the previous year, presented an opportunity for Basque nationalism in Iparralde. He felt that nationalist proposals there shared some common ground with more general and increasingly federalist notions in Europe at the time: for example, the proclamations of Pope Pius XII in favor of minorities, some declarations made by both Roosevelt and Churchill discussing the notion of "good government," Stalin's support for the principle of self-determination, and even some profederalist comments by de Gaulle.[25] Such optimism on Legasse's part was further encouraged by a general euphoria in Iparralde after the fall of the Nazi occupation and the feeling that the demise of Franco was imminent.

Consequently, he took part in the elections as a "Basque Nationalist" candidate for the canton of Donibane Lohizune with a specific proposal for a statute of autonomy for Iparralde. The proposal included creating a Basque *département*, official bilingualism, a series of reforms for the agricultural and fishing sectors (including the official expropriation of land and boats unused by their owners), the substitution of Basque civil servants for French ones, and a more prudent policy toward tourist development. Finally, within the realm of foreign-policy proposals, Legasse called on the "federal government of the French Republic" to recognize the establishment of a Basque republic in Hegoalde.

Together with his candidacy in the local cantonal elections, he was joined in these proposals by two independents—André Ospital for Northwest Baiona and Pierre Landaburu for Biarritz—as well as a "Basque Democrat," Joseph Darmendrail, for Northeast Baiona.[26] Darmendrail was by far the most successful, gaining 549 votes, compared with 57 for Ospital, 56 for Landaburu, and 95 for Legasse. The results demonstrated that there was little support for Basque nationalism in Iparralde in 1945.[27] Yet despite its failure at the polls, it was also clear that the French authorities were especially keen to discredit any form of nationalist sentiment, however much of a minority position it might be. And following the elections, a repressive strategy was developed to clamp down on Legasse, in particular, a tactic demonstrating the incapacity of French nationalism to accept any other form of nationalist expression. Consequently, Legasse was arrested in 1946 after putting up posters calling for the public to abstain "from interfering in the internal affairs of a people to which we don't belong and that doesn't recognize us"[28] in the forthcoming referendum called by de Gaulle to ratify the new constitution of the Fourth French Republic.[29]

His arrest provoked an angry response from Lafitte in the pages of *Herria*, where he contrasted the "heroic" activity of Legasse during the war with that of Maurice Thorez, leader of the French Communist Party, "a deserter before the enemy,"[30] concluding that while the latter was now a member of the French government, the former remained in prison, although his brother had been killed fighting for France in the war. Lafitte's litany recalled the ambiguity of his time at the helm of *Aintzina*: the sacrifice of pro-Basque interests on the alter of the *grand patrie*.

However, beyond this identity syncretism, there were now two discourses. A skewed binary logic of identities based on the zero-sum game began to emerge in Iparralde, a logic divided between the discourse of a French nationalism that began to feel itself somewhat aggrieved and that duly acted with unusual virulence and the beginnings of a clearly Basque nationalist discourse that sketched out not only an overall orientation, but strategies and a language that would be later be employed more widely.

French nationalism reacted so fiercely to the first appearance of Basque nationalism in Iparralde because the French authorities viewed Basque nationalism as a sign of complete moral collapse—as a form of anomie, "an absence, breakdown, confusion, or conflict in the norms of society."[31] From such a perspective, Basque nationalism was seen as deviant behavior that could be cured only through psychiatric treatment. Consequently, on his arrest, Legasse was obliged to undergo a full psychiatric examination, with the doctor examining him concluding that "the patient is convinced that Basques are a people and that Basque is a language . . . Consequently, Dr. R. B., an expert in mental illness, requests his immediate confinement in St. Luc [the Pau asylum], Ste. Anne [in Paris], in the Palais Bourbon [Paris Assembly], or in any other asylums for the insane."[32] Legasse was arrested and charged with "attempting to remove a territory from the authority of the Republic and an attack on the foreign security of the state," charges for which the prosecution called for a forty-year jail sentence. While in prison awaiting the trial, however, he began a hunger strike that lasted eighteen days. He was subsequently released on the condition that he undergo a full medical examination, the fruit of which was the above-cited request. Ultimately, the problem was resolved when the authorities, believing the prosecution's demand to be excessive, fell back on a law dating from the rule of Napoleon III to fine Legasse 1500 francs "for advocating [electoral] abstention."[33]

However, the sentence was not really based on the original offence for which Legasse was arrested—putting up posters—but rather had more to do with a previous idea: the drawing up by Legasse of an autonomy statute for Iparralde, an idea ultimately presented before the French National Assembly in 1945 by Jean Etcheverry-Ainchart.[34]

The Statute of Autonomy

Legasse was indeed a pioneer of Basque nationalism in Iparralde, not just for his role in first publicly demanding a statute of autonomy, but also more generally for the tactics and the discourse he employed. As regards tactics, his use of civil disobedience was copied later by both the Enbata and Abertzaleen Batasuna (AB, Nationalist Unity) movements, among others. Yet he was also an important figure for designing a modern discourse of Basque nationalism in Iparralde, calling for distinct Basque institutions, the defense of Euskara, stronger relations with Hegoalde, and a more cautious approach to tourist development—all key elements of later nationalist discourse between the 1960s and the 1990s.

After the election of Etcheverry-Ainchart (as a "Basque Independent") to the postwar Constituent Assembly in 1945, Legasse, Ospital, Landaburu, and others met with the newly elected representative, the notary of Baigorri in Nafarroa Beherea, to seek his support for presenting their proposal for a statute of autonomy during deliberations over the new constitution for the Fourth Republic. Article 1 of the draft text of this proposal stated:

> The Basque Country, formed by the *arrondissement* of Baiona and the cantons of Maule and Atharratze (the old provinces of Lapurdi, Nafarroa Beherea, and Zuberoa) make up a

natural and legal entity with its own political personality and as such has the right to form its own *département* in the French Republic, with which it will exist side by side according to the rules agreed in the present statute. The goal of the present statute is to establish, in common agreement with the French parliament, the juridical means that will confirm in law that natural personality and assure prosperity for the Basque Country, [together with] freedom for and the material and spiritual wellbeing of its inhabitants.[35]

Further, in Section 3, Article 12, Legasse set out the powers that an autonomous Iparralde would enjoy, among which were included local control of administration, justice, penal institutions, the tax and fiscal systems, economic development, education, social rights, the public-health system, and tourism. Article 13, in turn, declared that, "the national language of Basques is Euskara. It will be recognized equally with French." In Section 4, Article 20, Legasse demanded that "the Basque people be recognized as sovereign in all questions that have not been limited or ceded to the French state." Finally, Section 4 of the proposal stated that it would transfer the right to represent the French Republic in Iparralde to the current president of the Regional Council, a figure to whom the state would delegate all its powers, including that of public order. And there would also be mechanisms both to reform the statute, if needed, and to resolve any potential problems between Iparralde and the state.

The two points that subsequently became cornerstones of Basque nationalist demands in Iparralde—linguistic and institutional recognition—were key themes running through this document. Furthermore, Legasse also pursued another policy that would later become an important feature of Basque nationalism: a critique of development models based solely on tourism. As Amaia Ereñaga notes, in the magazine that Legasse started to replace *Aintzina*, titled *Hordago* (All or Nothing),[36] "the main target of its new items were, basically, tourists—portrayed as the Tourist Troops of Occupation," together with the director of the Basque Museum in Baiona.[37]

> Yet the proposal for a statute of autonomy was not even debated in the deliberations over the new constitution. Instead, it was vetoed by a leading member of the MRP party (Mouvement Républicain Populaire, the Popular Republican Movement), and Etcheverry-Ainchart's recollection of the events surrounding this decision is quite informative:
>
>> One day I decided to send a letter about our initiative to the commission studying the projected constitution, with certain accompanying explanations. If I had presented it [the statute initiative] to the General Assembly, it would only have been greeted by shouts and whistles. Every member opposed my project; some, horrified . . . responded harshly; others just smiled, objecting that there were other things to discuss; finally, [still] others showed no interest at all and didn't respond.[38]

Without being even presented or debated, the project was laid to rest for the next fifty years, when once again a text was drawn up (this time by the Eraikitzen collective) that recalled the original language of Legasse.

The Letter to Aguirre

Legasse had a lot of contact with the principal leaders of Basque nationalism from Hegoalde. He even married Verónica de la Sota y MacMahon, a member of the Sota family that had dominated the PNV alter the death of Sabino Arana in 1903. This led Legasse's meeting the principal figures of Basque nationalism, among them, Luis Arana, Sabino's brother. Some years later, he also got to know the influential priest and folklorist José Miguel Barandiaran, who actually took charge of his daughters' Communion.[39] Together with these figures, Telesforo de Monzón, the former minister of government in the autonomous Basque government, often visited the Legasse home: "It was he," recalled Legasse, "who, during the long . . . era of complete confusion and disorientation, with his mystical compass in his hand, knew how to point to a perfectly oriented north: the complete independence of a unified, Basque-speaking and communitarian Euskadi."[40] The Legasse family, moreover, socialized with other figures of the Basque cultural and political world, such as the writer and priest Piarres Larzabal and the exiled anarchist from Hegoalde, Félix Likiniano. Finally, in 1946, this lively group was joined by the *lehendakari* (president) of the Basque government in exile, José Antonio Aguirre.

Legasse met Aguirre through a public letter that the former sent the latter, a letter that was severe in its criticism of both the general strategy of the PNV and the leadership of the *lehendakari* with regard to the policy of Hegoalde nationalists toward Iparralde:

> Mr. President,
>
> I have the regret to protest to you by this present letter the attitude adopted by diverse influential members of the Basque Nationalist Party, certain ministers and functionaries of the Basque Government, and yourself toward the Basque nationalist movement in continental EUZKADI.[41]

Thereafter, Legasse attempted to contextualize the strategy adopted by the small group of nationalists he led, justifying his candidacy in the French elections because of the transition being experienced by the country after the period of occupation during the war. Thus, after recalling the anticolonial movements that had emerged to challenge French power outside of Europe, he pointed out how "for the first time in its history, France has been obliged to abandon its Jacobin policy of centralization and Gallicization practiced by its various administrations and has had to resign itself to satisfying certain demands of the peoples that it dominates."[42] Legasse thus considered that moment—with discussions taking place in France over a new constitution—an opportune one for Basque nationalists to stake a claim to certain historical demands.

In the early part of the letter, Legasse maintained a degree of optimism, yet this waned as he continued his missive. Indeed, it was apparent that he, too, was aware of the limitations of Basque nationalism in Iparralde, despite previously declaring that "a poll of people that have approached us [indicate] that they come from a wide range of political sensibilities, from moderate sectors to Socialists."[43] Moreover,

> one can say without exaggeration that the Basque Nationalist idea, whether of the autonomous form like the project for a statute or of the separatist form as conceived by the small group to which I belong, is an idea that counts at the present time in the Basque Country... This audience for nationalism—I would not say support for nationalism—has been a pleasant surprise. It would seem like the conditions exist to impart our movement with an official nature, to the extent that it might join openly and legally Basque political life.[44]

These were prophetic words. That is, he recognized that there was an "audience," rather than "support" for Basque nationalism in Iparralde—the same dilemma facing nationalists in the 1960s when, as we will see later, the first definably political movement emerged, only to lose impetus in the 1970s.

Therefore, one might say that Legasse anticipated this situation twenty years before it actually took place. And it explains the severity of his criticism of Aguirre: "It is thus that we have noticed that while we resist the pressure of the French administration, and we defend and specify our positions against the attacks and insults of our opponents, certain influential members of the Basque Nationalist Party are carrying out a work of sabotage behind our back that, strangely, seems to coincide with the maneuvers of the subprefecture in Baiona."[45] Furthermore, Legasse named individuals—members of the PNV's governing council and "different functionaries of the Basque Government," as well as Aguirre himself, who were guilty of attacking Basque nationalism in Iparralde. "In the refugee milieu," he continued, "has been created slowly but surely a psychology of fear and dread about the possible consequences of our action," but, he asked, "were there any rational reasons—that is, not based on panic—behind this lamentable attitude of the Basque Nationalist Party and the Delegation [government] of Euzkadi?" He went on:

> They first told us, in fact, that our work risked compromising your diplomatic activities and in particular your relations with the French Government. This assertion might have made some sense if your personal policies as President of EUZKADI required the particular or special support of the French Government... As many among us believed, if, on the strength of the prestige you earned for your attitude and adventures during the period 1936-1942, together with the sympathy gained, according to your own testimony, among important international figures, you had taken a step forward calling for the independence of the Basque people and if then the French Government had promised its support... then, yes, we would in all conscience be obliged to put to one side our demands faced with a government that would recognize and assure the independence of the peninsular Basque Country.
>
> Yet unfortunately, this was not the case.[46]

In France, according to Legasse, Aguirre was viewed as "a Spaniard, a republican Spaniard, a Basque political leader who is at the same time a Spanish functionary."[47] This, in turn, meant that (in Legasse's opinion) the Spanish republican cause would not be harmed by his political activity in favor of Basque nationalism in Iparralde, just as the activity of the Spanish republican *maquis* did not harm their own popularity in France.

For this reason, any "measures against Spanish refugees [were] impossible," especially from an electoral perspective in a country "where the Spanish republican cause is very popular."[48] Finally, Legasse apologized to Aguirre for "this letter so long, so violent, and so little respectful,"[49] for "I am Basque, I am young, and I am a disciple of Arana Goiri: three reasons to be a little crazy."[50]

The Oedipal Complex and a Parricidal Strategy

With this letter, Legasse initiated his political activity and a career that would span the history of Basque nationalism in Iparralde. He also introduced a parricidal strategy that was even more evident in the later Enbata movement, when generation after generation of young Basque nationalists attempted to wrest control of the movement in Iparralde from their "elders."[51] Legasse thus questioned the leadership of the principal Basque nationalist figures at the time, ridiculing a strategy that apparently was leading nationalism to a comfortable position within the Spanish republican political orbit. Moreover, he believed, nationalism was being sacrificed in Iparralde in order to maintain the region as a rear guard safe haven while nationalists from Hegoalde awaited the fall of Franco through international pressure. Of course, this never happened.[52]

This ever-present parricide in the development of Basque nationalism in Iparralde existed through a kind of Oedipal collective mimesis. The notion of any "complex" rests on a variety of emotional situations and relationships with other people. The Oedipal framework involves what Sigmund Freud described as a complexity of feelings in children between three and five years old about their parents and their more general family relations when they reach a certain age. Children experience this complexity of feelings—love, hate, jealousy and rivalry, for example—toward both parents in the search for their own identity and to assure themselves of their own individuality in regard to others. Consequently, the Oedipal complex plays a crucial role in structuring the personality of children. In its most negative sense, however (an allusion to the infamous Oedipal tale of a son's love for his mother and desire to kill his father), it can lead to feelings of tremendous guilt and the displacement of this guilt into practical and attainable goals by carrying out specific deeds.

Here, it would seem that the child, Basque nationalism in Iparralde, was born of a concept—Euskal Herria, the entire Basque Country extending across the border—as its mother, with Arana's vision of nationalism in Hegoalde (more specifically, Bizkaia and Gipuzkoa) as its father. Thus, with Legasse's letter, Basque nationalism in Iparralde began a process of trying to sever the link with its parents, blaming its father (Basque nationalism in Hegoalde) for failing to adhere completely to its mother (the concept of Euskal Herria)—a mother from whom, in turn, it was debarred, not just because of its own childlike fragility, but also because the father controlled any such access with paternal promises (a statute of autonomy, self-determination, and so on) of a future meeting: "One day, when you are old enough, you will be able to see her." This maternal love of the child would soon turn into contempt, and at the same time, it would have to experience the distance of the father, an experience that would lead it to challenge paternal authority ferociously. In Iparralde, the clearest exponent of that challenge was Legasse. Indeed, his letter to Aguirre—the venerated and respected father figure of Basque nationalism at the time—resonated with Oedipal overtones.

However, this parricidal attitude diverged with the nationalism of Enbata, so that the father figure was represented by two sources: Basque nationalism in Hegoalde and the immediate precursors of the movement in Iparralde. Thus, for example, and as we will see, two of Enbata's founders, Michel Labéguerie and Ximun Haran, abandoned the movement as a result of the "intrusion" of ETA—a new paternal figure in the 1960s. Then, in the 1970s, Iparretarrak (perhaps born out of ETA) challenged the policy of the armed organization from Hegoalde of denying their "northern brothers" the right to use violent methods in Iparralde. Finally, one must also view more contemporary developments, such as the tension between Abertzaleen Batasuna (AB, Nationalist Unity, a Basque nationalist party in Iparralde) and the northern "branches" of nationalist parties from Hegoalde as part of the same dynamic.

As noted, however, together with this external parricidal tendency there was also an internal and generational conflict. For example, Haran left the movement in the face of pressure from a new generation of more radical left-wing activists who joined Enbata in the late 1960s, and Manex Goyhenetche, when he led the EHAS (Euskal Herriko Alderdi Sozialista, the Socialist Party of the Basque Country), experienced first-hand the pressure of Iparretarrak, leading to the disbanding of this group.[53] Similarly, the radical nationalist youth of Iparralde that had been socialized in the 1980s in an environment of the so-called Basque radical rock were highly critical of their own "elders," EB (Euskal Batasuna, Basque Unity) and EMA (Ezkerreko Mugimendu Abertzalea, the Basque Patriotic Movement of the Left), in the 1990s. Finally, one should add to these internal tensions the conflict in the new millennium between AB and Batasuna, the radical nationalist party sustained by an important youth movement.

One recent example, though, of an attempt to overcome this parricidal dynamic is the support of AB for the predominantly youth-led Demo movement. Indeed, the success of the peaceful civil obedience favored by the Demo movement has once more shifted the political focus to relations between the younger and elder siblings, that is, between Basque nationalism in Iparralde and in Hegoalde, because the very success of the Demo protest has challenged the supposed conventional wisdom of the nationalist movement in Hegoalde. In other words, while the shadow of violence hangs over Basque nationalism in Hegoalde, in Iparralde, a nonviolent direct-action protest movement has apparently reawakened its northern counterpart. However, I will address the issue of how Basque nationalism in Iparralde now has much to teach its older sibling in more detail later.

For the moment, I would conclude that Basque nationalists in Iparralde in the 1940s had many reasons to disagree with the strategy of their counterparts from Hegoalde, not the least of which was because the latter appeared to have sacrificed the former in order to seek their own "freedom" in the South. Legasse came to the fore as a leader of the avant-garde of this rear guard cadre. He was the first to refute explicitly, in Oedipal fashion, the nationalism of Hegoalde, while at the same time being conscious of the fact that the corresponding movement in Iparralde depended on its southern sibling.

Despite his many eccentricities, Legasse foreshadowed what would eventually become the first true Basque nationalist movement in Iparralde: Enbata in the 1960s. At the time that he began to conceive this nationalism, however, in the 1940s, there was not sufficient opportunity to extend his ideas, with the result that there was little significant shift from the kind of individually driven dynamic that had characterized the efforts of Lafitte and the Eskualerriste movement. Legasse's legacy did, however, yield one important change: He broke the ties that the Basque movement had maintained with the church, ties that had retarded, although not impeded, the crisis of this movement in the interwar period. He thus imparted to any future development of nationalism in Iparralde the possibility of following a secular course, and when a third wave of peripheral nationalisms emerged throughout the world in the 1950s and 1960s,[54] Basque nationalism as a political movement finally took root there.

Moreover, Legasse's contribution to the development of nationalism in Iparralde should be remembered in other important ways: He consistently emphasized separatism over regionalism as the only way to challenge the nation-states that divided the Basque Country. He criticized a model of economic development centered solely on tourism, a model that condemned Basques to dancing to the tune of a song in which the people were forced to represent themselves, to become a "living museum" for the consumption of summer visitors. Finally, Legasse was also paramount in advocating a strategy that, with time, would come to serve Basque nationalists in Iparralde well: nonviolent civil disobedience in defense of Basque values, demonstrating a "nouvelle Basque cuisine" that would successfully leapfrog the bitter aftertaste of political violence and the often insipid options of institutional politics.[55] It comes as no surprise to learn that this character constantly passed himself off as the son of corsairs and enthusiastically embraced the pirate flag during his final years.

CHAPTER EIGHT

Between the Calm and the Storm

Jean-Louis Davant describes Legasse as someone frozen by circumstances: "the Chaho of our era: a prophet who railed against the times and often was a voice crying out in the wilderness in the hope of better times to come."[1] By contrast, the political, social, and cultural activity of Michel Labéguerie was clearly a manifestation of a major transformation in Iparralde: the decline of a religious, conservative-humanist, and cultural Basque movement and the emergence of secular, progressive, and politicized Basque nationalism. As a result, although he was an individual who remained "loyal to his [nationalist] ideas,"[2] he was also a contradictory figure.

Labéguerie began his long public life by taking part in many of the numerous Basque social and cultural activities in Iparralde during the "wilderness" years for Basque nationalism between 1945 and 1960.[3] Yet Basque cultural activity during the era was important because it paralleled the construction of the foundations that would ultimately lead to the political turn of Basque nationalism in the 1960s. At the inception of this political turn, Labéguerie was elected to public office on a nationalist ticket, but, as we will see, his premature withdrawal from the movement because of internal tensions after 1968 explains much about the period through which he lived. Specifically, the increasingly close relationship between Enbata and ETA was the pretext on which Labéguerie left the nationalist movement. He chose instead to explore different political options outside of Basque nationalism, such as a Basque-oriented Christian Democracy, a movement that, despite repeatedly failing to gain a significant foothold in the political landscape of Iparralde, surfaced once again in 2002 with the creation of Elgar-Ensemble (a nonnationalist pro-Basque group) led by his son, Peyo Labéguerie.

Furthermore, an examination of Labéguerie senior's public life, and especially his early withdrawal from Enbata, reveals much about the central points of debate within the Basque nationalist movement in Iparralde: the struggle between different generations, the friction between religious and secular visions, as well as those between federalism and separatism, between the ethical condemnation of or tactical support for violence in Hegoalde, the ever-present debate over the question of a *petit* or *grand patrie*, and so on.

The Cultural Struggle

The period between 1945 and 1960 might be considered one of the most productive moments in the development of Basque culture in Iparralde, when many of the initiatives undertaken served to alleviate the asphyxiating Francoist repression in Hegoalde, as well as to encourage nationalist sympathies in Iparralde. Among these labors, that of defending the Basque language was central. Before examining this point, which, together with debates over the economic situation in Iparralde and the consequences of the Algerian War, was pivotal in leading to the political context in which Enbata emerged, I would first like to address the broader cultural milieu of pro-Basque circles in the same period.

Eskualdun Gazteen Biltzarra

Labéguerie was a contributor to the second incarnation of *Aintzina* and represented Basque students on its editorial committee. In 1943, he also founded the cultural group Irrintzi in Bordeaux—a group that included in its repertoire dances not only from Iparralde, but also from Bizkaia and Gipuzkoa.[4] This group was important, however, not just because of its relative strength, but also because it was a key organization in promoting the creation of a new federation, the Eskualdun Gazteen Biltzarra (EGB), also in 1943 (see Chapter 7). Importantly, the EGB included in its foundational charter two clearly political demands, calling for the teaching of Euskara in the educational system and a separate institutional body for Iparralde.

During 1943 and 1944, the EGB held seven meetings and organized a series of cultural events in Uztaritze and Milafranga (Villefranque).[5] Furthermore, it also took part in one of the principal debates of the era among members of the Basque movement: whether or not to pursue a clearly political program once the war was concluded. Legasse, as the representative of *Aintzina* to the federation, was in favor of this option, while Eugène Goyheneche was against it. Ultimately, the EGB voted not to pursue a politicized strategy, which, in turn, led to the abandonment of the federation by *Aintzina*.

As Jean-Claude Larronde notes,

> More than a federation of folkloric groups, the EGB was—during the bleak moments of the occupation—a meeting place for Basque cultural leaders. It was not a question of folkloric activity (dances and songs) alone, but also of work in favor of the language, history, theater, [as well as] organizing lectures about culture . . . in sum, to use an expression of Eugène Goyheneche, it was the "soul of nationalism."[6]

The EGB combined cultural, social, and political demands, framed in a regionalist language.[7] As such, it devoted most of its energy to organizing specifically Basque cultural expressions at a time when, as Arbelbide recalls, French tunes dominated popular festivals in Iparralde.[8]

The Seventh Basque Studies Conference

In September 1948, Eusko Ikaskuntza (the Society of Basque Studies) organized the Seventh Basque Studies Conference in Biarritz—one of the most important Basque cultural expressions in Iparralde during the twentieth century to that date. Here, space precludes a detailed summary of the 260 presentations by experts from around the world.[9] Instead, I will highlight three reasons why this conference was so important: because it was the fruit of a joint effort by a number of different people (many of them nationalists) from both sides of the border,[10] because it was intrinsically academic and cultural in nature, leaving aside any politicization that may have led to friction between the participants, and because of the range of activities that took place alongside the academic presentations—helping to raise Basque cultural awareness in Iparralde.[11]

The idea for the conference came from Manu de la Sota, a close confidant of the Basque president Aguirre, through a slogan that revealed much about how worried those people dedicated to studying Basque culture were at the time: "Do not let the Basque soul die!" This was an attempt to gather together all pro-Basque cultural sectors, especially those from the Eskualzaleen Biltzarra.[12] The use of this slogan also revealed the wish of the conference organizers to avoid any controversy—that is, not to politicize the event. For example, Aguirre attended the meetings as just one among many Basques, rather than in any official capacity. And although Spain's Francoist authorities pressured France to ban the proceedings on the grounds of their being an excuse for separatism, the French Ministry of Foreign Affairs found no legal reasons to prohibit the event.

That said, the Basque government in exile played a central role in supporting the conference. For example, it bankrolled the proceedings, and people close to Aguirre were central participants: together with the *lehendakari*, those present included Telesforo de Monzón and José María Lasarte (both of them ministers of the Basque government in exile), the eminent scholar, Jose Miguel Barandiaran, representing the Society for Basque Studies, Louis Dassance, head of the Eskualzaleen Biltzarra, and Léon-Albert Terrier, the bishop of Baiona, plus the director of the Basque Museum, and the principal of the Biarritz Lycée. Moreover, to emphasize the lack of any political connotations with Basque nationalism, at the close of the proceedings, letters of greeting and congratulations from illustrious members of the French establishment were read out. These included Vincent Auriol, the first president of the French Fourth Republic, Édouard Herriot, the president of the National Assembly, Yvon Delbos, the minister of education, and Jean Sarrailh, rector of the University of Paris.

Among the 260 lectures presented in fifteen sessions before three hundred participants at the conference, the conclusions of Session 13, the discussion of education, stand out, because although they were not explicitly political, a decade later, they were embraced by the Ikas movement—an educational lobby advocating the teaching of Euskara and Basque culture in the school system. The participants in Session 13 agreed to both the creation of a commission to study the potential for a Basque university in Iparralde and another "charged with contacting the diocesan authorities in order to guarantee the application of certain decrees . . . on the teaching of regional languages and history at the secondary-school level."[13] Meanwhile, the conclusions of Session 14 on the arts called for radios to broadcast Basque music and for schools to create Basque choirs and *txistulari*, or flute-playing groups. Paradoxically, Session 11, devoted to the law, concluded with a series of harsh criticisms of Franco's measures against the Basque foral institutions and called for a common legal system for Araba, Bizkaia, and Gipuzkoa. In this session, there would appear to have been no references to Iparralde whatsoever.[14]

The conference closed with a rendition of "Gernikako Arbola," "The Tree of Gernika," and went down in history for the quality of its lectures. However, all participants were careful not to leave the strict confines of culturalist perspectives. It was, in the words of Lafitte, "a cultural apotheosis."[15] Thus, the wilderness years between 1945 and 1960 were not quite so barren, especially in the cultural realm. In fact, during this period, defenders of Basque culture managed to attract certain notables to their ranks who imparted to their discourse a degree of social legitimacy. In other words, Eugène Goyheneche's preoccupation with winning over important local figures to his ideals appeared to be working. Yet all this was carried out from decidedly nonnationalist positions. Instead, the strategy relied on the established logic of two *patries*, with Iparralde relegated to its customary secondary, cultural level. Indeed, for Basque nationalism to emerge in the region, this logic would have to be challenged. In fact, as we will see, the rupture between Labéguerie and Enbata signaled the moment when the necessary politicization of the pro-Basque movement became a reality.

Eskualzaleen Biltzarra

Formed in 1901 and originally intended to unite Basques from both sides of the border, Eskualzaleen Biltzarra gradually came to concentrate its labor in Iparralde, initially by organizing a series of Basque-language-related competitions.[16] Interestingly, it was at one such competition that Pierre Lafitte first came to public prominence, and figures such as Arturo Campión and Julio de Urquijo presided over successive meetings of the association in its initial years. In 1923, Jean Elissalde, known as "Zerbitzari," replaced Abbé Martin Landarretche as secretary of the Eskualzaleen Biltzarra, remaining in the post for the next forty years.[17]

From this moment on, the association continued in uninterrupted fashion to promote Euskara contests, for example among the school-age population of Iparralde. At the same time, it paved the way for the development of a pro-Basque political conservatism:

> The most important elements of the Eskualzaleen Biltzarra were members of the bourgeoisie. Their goal was to stay in power as local leaders, opposing the reforms brought about by the onset of modernity, understanding that [such reforms] might lead to harmful change within the organization of Basque society. Thus, with the help of the clergy . . . the bourgeoisie used traditional Basque customs to promote the conservative ideas of the old regime. They began, in sentimental fashion, by working in defense of Euskara and converted Basque culture into [a kind of] myth, a witness to the past, as it were. With this

gloss on the past, a conservative political thought emerged among the members of the Eskualzaleen Biltzarra, [something that was] also the political expression of what was happening at the Basque social and political level.[18]

In short, the association held political beliefs that embraced both France and the church, employing the traditional motto, "Euskaldun fededun"—"To be Basque is to be a believer."

As Manex Goyhenetche puts it, "the discourse of the Eskualzaleen Biltzarra was the juxtaposition, if not the synthesis, of complex opinions that attempted, at the same time, to defend French politics and Basque thought. It was simultaneously influenced by reactionary moralism and a French republicanism that was still Jacobin and centralizing, while the French right fell into provincialism."[19] Between 1924 and 1960, the association was led by Louis Dassance, and, thereafter, by Labéguerie. Curiously, and somewhat contradicting the above statements of Hernández and Goyhenetche, on assuming the presidency of the association, Labéguerie eulogized the recently deceased *Lehendakari* Aguirre.[20] This was the result, most likely, of an evolution of pro-Basque sentiment in Iparralde toward a greater politicization of the organization's discourse. Yet as Labéguerie himself recognized at the group's 1963 annual meeting, it had not met its own demands, having failed to publish anything or to organize any event. Larronde therefore is more generous than others in observing that "it is ridiculous not to recognize the merits of this veritable institution, which, through the course of the twentieth century, has kept the flame of Euskara alight."[21]

The fact of the matter is that, beyond the socializing function of this institution and beyond the criticism that might be leveled at it, it was a key actor in diffusing a sense of Basque identity (and its politicization) among a whole generation of leaders in Iparralde. Despite the fact it did not make significant practical gains, it was "one of the driving forces of a Basque consciousness. And that is not insignificant."[22] Indeed, its significance should be measured against a society in Iparralde where using Basque was associated with the past, the rural world, and an antiquated way of life that one was expected to reject, but that, despite all this, was a world and a culture to which that the Eskualzaleen Biltzarra attempted to give dignity.

Similarly, this organization's role was extremely important for Basque culture from various perspectives: It was the first cross-border pro-Basque group, anticipating the later development of Euskaltzaindia (the Academy of the Basque Language) and Eusko Ikaskuntza (the Society of Basque Studies). It also served as an organizational model for other groups in Iparralde, such as Euskal Esnalea before World War I or Euskeraren Laguntzaileak in the 1930s. It reduced the harsh effects of laws and proposals against Euskara among religious sectors who oversaw the education of large numbers of people in Iparralde. It allowed for the socialization of certain Basque identity symbols, although without breaking the large-small homeland model, and it guaranteed the involvement of local political leaders in promoting the Basque language and culture.[23]

Later, as we will see, the Eskualzaleen Biltzarra led by Labéguerie could not escape a more politicized organizational model that emerged in the 1960s and 1970s. Specifically, it condemned Francoist Spain's persecution of Basques and actively supported ETA refugees in Iparralde. It became a meeting place for a new generation of activists more openly Basque nationalist in their sympathies. For these reasons, it also served as a site of contest between politicized and nonpoliticized versions of the Basque consciousness in Iparralde, witnessing a kind of intergenerational tension masked in ideological terms (or vice versa)—that is, the clash between some who supported mainly cultural positions together with modest political demands (the logic of the two *patries*) and others who favored more overtly political activity, supported by a degree of cultural work (the logic of one Basque homeland).

It should also be remembered that a more political turn within the Eskualzaleen Biltzarra came before the watershed era of the 1960s and 1970s. Indeed, as early as 1933, there was a markedly nationalist tone to its general assembly:

> At the end of the banquet, Louis Dassance (president of the EB), José de Eizaguirre [or] "Oxobi," Eugène Goyheneche, [and] Aitzol [José de Aristimuño] gave speeches... Most of these had an evidently nationalist tone, a completely new feature of the assemblies of the Eskualzaleen Biltzarra. National claims were now no longer the isolated demands of isolated individuals, [because] several speakers embraced them:
>
> José de Eizaguirre: "Zazpiak bat is no longer a vague memory, but a fact."
>
> Aitzol: "Th[is] prestigious speaker, starting from the basic principle that a Basque can have only one mother, sings Euzkadi as the only homeland of all the Basque brothers and sisters."

And even Eugène Goyheneche remarked that "they have written that we are a people 'that is going' [a reference to the work of Pierre Loti]. It is not true. Basques are a people that are 'returning'... that return like the swallow in spring, with both its wings; Jaungoikua eta Lege Zaharra [God and the Old Laws, a reference to the slogan of the PNV]."[24]

Herria

The Basque-language weekly journal *Herria* was founded in the fall of 1944, after the liberation of France during World War II. It replaced the weekly *Eskualduna* (founded in 1887), which had been banned for pro-Nazi sympathies during the war. *Herria* was the initiative of Jean Saint Pierre, Louis Dassance, José de Eizaguirre, Jean Elissalde, and, above all, Pierre Lafitte.

Overcoming a number of problems associated with its official authorization,[25] the first edition of *Herria* was published on October 19, 1944. Such problems were hardly unexpected, given the hostility toward such pro-Basque initiatives of the local prefect (the state's representative in a *département* or region) and the still-influential Ybarnégaray. Indeed, for the latter, Lafitte remained "a red fish swimming in a baptismal font."[26] Yet it was Lafitte's sheer obstinacy that enabled *Herria* to overcome the official obstacles put in its way and eventually be published that fall.

Although the maximum circulation of *Eskualduna* had reached the mark of 8,000 readers, the initial aim of *Herria* was to achieve a readership of around 1,700, which would guarantee its economic survival. That said, it was able to meet the publishing costs involved only through the generous financial aid of Telesforo de Monzón, a wealthy member of the Basque government in exile. Within ten years, however, *Herria* had 7,000 subscribers and counted on the prominent Basque cultural leaders of the time for its writers: Lafitte himself and the founding group, as well as Etienne Salaberry and Piarres Larzabal.[27]

Although some of its contributors added a touch of nationalism to the discourse of the journal in this initial period, the editorial line of *Herria* could not be described as Basque nationalist. Lafitte was probably more receptive to the notion of introducing some nationalist elements into the journal—as opposed to his thoroughly regionalist positions at the head of *Aintzina* in the 1930s—but at most, in political terms, he favored a federalist editorial line.[28] As Arbelbide observes, "Lafitte a nationalist and not *Herria*. How is that possible? The reality was the following: Basques in Iparralde were not nationalists, especially Basque speakers. No, because they were French! . . . The problem was [either] a nationalist weekly with few readers or a weekly with Basque-language readers. He chose the second option."[29] In reality, although most of the individuals during this period that I have mentioned thus far—such as Lafitte or Labéguerie—contributed to developing a certain form of Basque consciousness, it was still difficult for them to give any political definition to this notion. That is, as was the case with *Aintzina*, there remained within the pages of *Herria* the logic of dual homelands.[30]

Piarres Charritton is in no doubt as to the causes and consequences of this paradox:

> Moreover, if we see our people oppressed and threatened with death—this is, not among large nations but, rather, within small nations, the luck that they often have—we must demonstrate a special connection to our land . . . We already know how the well-known writer Milan Kundera defines "small nations": "The small nation is that whose existence may be questioned, that may disappear, at any moment . . . and this is accepted." . . . When a state has at its feet a small nation that its discriminates against . . . that is, strengthening the powerful cultures, customs, beliefs, and languages, [while] weakening the fragile ones, then problems arise. Indeed, following Milan Kundera, one might say "that the French, Russians [and] English had no reason to invent this problem . . . a Frenchman, Russian [or] Englishman is not accustomed to questioning the survival of his nation. Their national anthems speak only of their greatness and eternity."[31]

The paradox of Lafitte, Labéguerie, and many other cultural nationalists at this time was that when they did approach more political positions, they did so as Frenchmen.

Eskualdun Gazteria

Worth mentioning, finally, in this examination of the crossroads period of Basque identity between the end of World War II and the 1960s is the church youth movement, Eskualdun Gazteria (Basque Youth), led by Father Piarres Charritton from 1954 on.

During his leadership, the group made important advances in the rural interior of Iparralde, organizing hundreds of young people for trips to Switzerland, West Germany, and Brittany, as well as helping to coordinate local festivals and the like.[32] At the same time, Charritton was also editor of the church youth magazine, *Gazte*, between 1954 and 1960, a period that witnessed, within the pages of *Gazte*, some of the first, tentative criticisms of France's war in Algeria—the reflection of the slow transformation of cultural activity into more explicitly political Basque nationalist positions.

For example, in 1958, Eskualdun Gazteria organized an excursion for thirty young people from Iparralde to Hegoalde in order to understand the reality of everyday life there at the time. After the trip, two of the young people that went on the trip wrote in *Gazte*:

> In the name of Eskualdun Gazteria, and in the name of the young people of the Basque Country, we want to say a few words as the result of a trip we made to the Basque Country beyond the mountains. We now know the differences that exist in the lifestyles on both sides of the border. There, work for everyone, and employment, and the need to bring people in from other regions or anywhere. Here, there is no work; outside of agriculture there is nothing; we must emigrate far from our villages . . . We say to the notables and the leaders that it is not true that nothing can be done, as we have seen, and we challenge them to what [will be done] and how [it will be done] to face the future and this people.[33]

Here, then, is evidence of a new sensibility, a new awareness that would subsequently form a key feature of the social program of Basque nationalism in Iparralde and something that continues to the present day. Emigration, for example, became a central preoccupation for the members of Eskualdun Gazteria. In the words of one such member, Martzel Rekalde, during a 1959 meeting of the organization in Baigorri,

> in Itxuritz [Izturitze in Unified Basque, Isturits in French, a village in Nafarroa Beherea] there are thirty-five young people; twenty-seven of whom have gone to the capital. In Makea [Lapurdi], out of 110 farms, 40 lie empty. In Baigorri, of the hundred young people [there], eighty have gone to the Americas, and ten to the capital . . . in [the region of] Garazi [Cize, in Nafarroa Beherea], there are 620 young people in the villages [while] 440 . . . have left . . . For a long time now we have been shouting out that the Basque Country is being abandoned, that it's falling into the gutter. And you, town leaders? [You should] be the doctors addressing your people's loss of blood. Don't let the young people abandon their land, going to the city. They have left . . . because they want to live.[34]

From this emergent struggle against emigration, there also appeared a parallel disenchantment with what had to that time been the only alternative economic-development model besides agriculture in Iparralde: tourism. Together, these twin features of disillusionment formed a base on which a politicization of pro-Basque tendencies would take place, a development that would gradually begin to incorporate similarly emergent theories of internal colonialism and develop alongside stronger and stronger pro-Euskara initiatives and the bitter experience of many young Basque males in the Algerian War.

The Politicization of the Cultural Movement

In 1946, the general councils of the *départements* of Finistère (Penn-ar-Bed in Breton) and Côtes-du-Nord—both in the historic region of Brittany—began to call for official support for the Breton language. As a result, on January 11, 1951, the French National Assembly approved a law, introduced by Maurice Deixonne of the Radical-Socialist alliance, authorizing the teaching of regional languages and dialects in schools. The Deixonne Law heralded the first official recognition of minority ethnocultural aspirations in France, if only symbolically.[35]

Specifically, Article 1 of the new law established that "the High Council of National Education will be charged with . . . seeking the best means by which to favor the study of local languages and dialects in the regions where these are in use."[36] The law sought to allow the teaching of Breton, Basque, Catalan, and Occitan from elementary through secondary education levels in the public system. However, the state never supplied the necessary funding to train qualified teachers, nor did it ever put into practice any specific policy to encourage the practical application of the law.[37] In other words, the French government never really implemented the new law, prompting one observer to classify it as more of an attempt to reduce an emerging peripheral sentiment.[38] While this may be the case, as we will see shortly, these legal changes also led to significant changes that actually encouraged the politicization of formerly purely cultural demands.

From Euskal Ikasleen Biltzarra to Ikas

Through the encouragement of Lafitte, in 1947, the Euskal Ikasleen Biltzarra organized the first of what would become a series of celebrations, known as Basque Student Days. These gatherings were designed to gather students together in a Catholic and Basque spirit.[39] While such gatherings recalled a certain continuity with the original efforts of the association in the 1930s, a significant change soon took place in this new postwar climate. One of its subgroups soon began to go by the name of Embata (with an "m") and, after a decade of cultural activity, would subsequently evolve into Enbata, the first explicitly politicized Basque nationalist group in Iparralde.

As James E. Jacob notes, the members of the Euskal Ikasleen Biltzarra at this time were a "conservative, bourgeois generation of young educated Basques . . . still solidly within the embrace of the church and its Christian Democratic tradition."[40] It comes as no surprise, then, to learn that when Enbata began to transform into a secular, federalist/separatist, and progressive movement, many of its original members left: For example, Michel Inchauspé (of the banking family from Donibane Garazi) became a Gaullist, while as noted, Labéguerie would eventually create a nonnationalist, but pro-Basque form of Christian Democracy. Initially, the renewed activity of the Euskal Ikasleen Biltzarra centered its efforts on cultural and folkloric events, but such activity was increasingly imbued with a greater degree of politicization, as exemplified by the Ikas group.

Following a series of meetings organized by Eskualzaleen Biltzarra on the teaching of Euskara held in Baiona in 1959, and with the participation of French and departmental educational representatives, several teachers and cultural activists created the Ikas collective. Its principal objectives were to aid materially and morally any initiative whose goal was to promote the teaching of Basque in the school system and to furnish the practical means for the teaching of Basque to both public and private educational institutions—that is, to facilitate its use in the study of traditional subjects, as well as in the teaching of popular culture.

After the approval of the group's statutes, drawn up by Jean Etcheverry-Ainchart, Ikas established its headquarters in the Basque Museum of Baiona. Its administrative council was formed by a number of individuals, such as Dassance, Lafitte, Madeleine de Jaureguiberry, and Michel Labéguerie, together representing two generations—that of the 1930s, in main purely cultural activists, and that of the 1950s, who, while also principally cultural militants, had also made a few tentative steps toward a more politicized version of Basque nationalism. Still absent, however, from this group were individuals who ultimately would represent a third and definitive step toward the politicization of a solely Basque sense of belonging: people such as Jakes Abeberry, Jean-Louis Davant, Ximun Haran, and Charritton. In fact, among the initial Ikas group, the only representation of this third or later group was marked by the "sole presence" of Jean Haritschelhar.[41]

During their meetings on the teaching of Euskara, a unanimous motion was passed calling for the training of teachers to give classes in what was termed regional civilizations, specifically calling for the presence of Basque-speaking educators in Iparralde. The participants thus sought to extend the notion of teaching all French children about the different cultures within the borders of France, thereby sustaining the cultural links between these children and their local surroundings, history, and so on.

Although the practical results of the Deixonne Law were limited in the public-school and administrative system, the church authorities responded more favorably to the new edict. For example, the Diocese of Baiona introduced the teaching of Euskara in all religious primary and secondary schools under its jurisdiction, to be overseen by Eskualzaleen Biltzarra and Ikas. And a few years later, a number of parents themselves took the initiative in Iparralde, bypassing all public institutions and without any official support, to create Basque-language schools. The first such school—known as an *ikastola*—in Iparralde was opened in 1969 by Argitxu Noblia in Arrangoitze (Arcangues), Lapurdi.

In sum, then, from the mid-1950s on, principally through the efforts of Ikas (created in 1959), education became an increasingly political issue. Indeed, by the early 1970s, Ikas had become a kind of lobby that pronounced statements on political candidates according to their support (or lack thereof) for implementing laws and decrees relating to the use of Basque in the educational system. At the same time, a similar process of transformation from a purely cultural to a more overtly political stance could be seen in the pages of both Lafitte's *Herria* and Charritton's *Gazte*. Here, though, a new issue became important for young people in Iparralde: the war in Algeria.

The Algerian War

For a number of reasons, the Algerian War was important for awakening a more politicized consciousness among many people in Iparralde during the 1950s and 1960s. First, it created a certain sense of solidarity among young Basque conscripts sent to the war. The time spent away from home, in turn, generated a sense of longing for the people, landscape, and culture of Iparralde and above all a desire to return home (a longing also noted in Basque migrant communities in Paris and Bordeaux). Second, although the phenomenon was less widespread, some of these young conscripts began to compare France's colonial problems with issues closer to home, viewing Algeria's dependence on Paris and economic underdevelopment as relevant to their own local concerns. Finally, on witnessing first-hand the brutal war of attrition in Algeria, which had in effect led to a stalemate situation with great loss of life on both sides, many of these young people began to consider federalism to be the only possible political solution to the conflict, an idea that gained more and more ground among the generation that ultimately created and led Enbata.

In 1958, Mixel Itzaina, taking into account the successes as well as the limitations of *Herria* and *Gazte*, founded a new daily in an attempt to spread news about and among Basques serving in Algeria: *Eskual-Herria*, subtitled (in French) *An Occasional Bulletin of the Basques in Algeria*. Despite the suspicions of the French authorities, who ultimately suspended the publication, Itzaina managed to distribute 450 copies of the bulletin. Itzaina himself recalled three main results of his managing to circulate the publication: the pleasure that the soldiers derived from hearing news of other Basque conscripts ("I am so pleased about your project [the bulletin], because we will see where our Basque friends are and what they have to say"); the importance of knowing about and having other Basque conscripts nearby ("This is my regret. I've never had any Basques with me! Although I do have good friends [we've been together for twenty-two months!]. But it's not the same as being with Basques. Yesterday I went to Mass, but I couldn't enjoy any Basque hymns"); and, finally, the lack of any reflections on the meaning of the war, with one exception: that of Xipri Arbelbide.[42]

In a recent work, Arbelbide himself reflects on his experience of the war, commenting that even *Herria* published 260 articles about Algeria written by Lafitte, 96 by Basque soldiers serving there, 45 verses composed by serving conscripts, and 67 photos showing around five hundred of the twenty thousand Basques who fought in the war.[43] Similarly, in a previous work, Arbelbide examines in detail a number of articles published in *Herria* and *Gazte* during the Algerian War that demonstrate a widespread feeling of common belonging among Basque soldiers, a feeling, however, that did not extend to teaching their children Basque—the language in which they wrote letters to the aforementioned magazines. That said, some of their comments did evince a certain degree of pro-Basque feeling: "When we return, we would like to find a vibrant and especially Basque-speaking, people."[44] However, as Arbelbide, notes (and Mixel Itzaina would agree):

> It has been said that patriotism [*abertzaletasuna*] grew in Algeria. Maybe it was true for a few. But in most cases, most of those who went to Algeria did not teach their wonderful Basque to their children . . . Algeria had the same consequences as most wars. After fighting, suffering for someone, in most cases you become one with him. In Algeria, they fought for France. They returned home more connected to France than when they left. When Enbata was founded, they did not go for that option. Basque nationalists were considered the *fellagha* [the term used to describe those fighting for Algerian independence] of the Basque Country.[45]

Once again, a third generation of young men from Iparralde became more French as a result of their experiences fighting a war for France.

For others, however, the Algerian War marked a watershed moment. For example, Philippe Mayte describes and reproduces almost all of the fifty texts concerning the conflict that appeared in twenty-eight editions of *Gazte*, the magazine of the church youth movement, Eskualdun Gazteria. One can analyze these texts using the same methodological approach that the church itself proposed for integrating the young people into the group: observation, reflection, and then action. First, they employ observation in describing the differences between Basques and Algerians, but then proceed to reflection—on the part of young men from a predominantly rural background—on the social and economic similarities between Algeria and Iparralde. For example, the following:

> "But, aren't you unhappy here?" "I have my wife and children . . . and I remain subject to the will of Allah," he told us with an air of satisfaction. And us, with our civilization and our modernity? Are we happy? . . . The bosses complain because they have only problems, and the workers because they earn little . . . peasants first want a moped, then a tractor.[46]

Yet such critiques went further than mere ethnographic comparison to encompass direct criticism—from a Christian humanist perspective—of the war itself: "Lord, end this Algerian War. We have already seen what we are, to what levels of hate we can descend . . . We are all your children. Whether white or black, we have all been touched equally by your love."[47] Finally, after observation and reflection, these young Christians revealed, through the pages of *Gazte*, a desire for action—organizing for news of home and Christmas care packages to be sent to the soldiers in Algeria. One contributor to the magazine even linked such activity to traditional Basque values: "We must continue this work, both to maintain the morale of our comrades and to be of service to our beautiful Basque language."[48]

Perhaps the most significant event that took place in regard to the gradual appearance of Basque nationalism during this period was the complaint of Jean Garat, editor of *Côte Basque Soir*, against *Herria* for an article that the latter published by Piarres Larzabal under a pseudonym, Goratik. As part of a series of eight articles published between February and August 1957 in the open forum section of the weekly, Goratik argued in favor of a decentralization process in France that would, naturally, affect both Algeria (considered an integral part of the French state) and Iparralde. He thus argued against two extremes—either independence for Algeria or its disappearance as a separate polity—but Garat based his complaint on the final sentence of the following citation:

> With regard to the Algerian revolt, our government calls for unconditional surrender and, as compensation, proposes creating in Algeria a series of French *départements*, each equipped with a degree, still not specified, of administrative autonomy ... but we Basques, Bretons, and the inhabitants of other regions of France, reduced to the state of *départements*, understand very well the most moderate wishes of the *fellagha*... Unfortunately, in Indochina, in Madagascar, [and] in North Africa, it has been necessary for guns to do the talking for our leaders to stop remaining deaf to legitimate aspirations. Should the "colonies" of metropolitan France revert to rebellion to achieve decentralization?[49]

Even before the official complaint lodged by Garat, a number of contributors to *Herria* also recorded their disagreement with the suggestion. On June 20, 1957, however, legal proceedings began against Larzabal, forcing Lafitte in his capacity as editor of *Herria* to comment on the issue. After denouncing the official complaint as politically charged—Garat was close to the progressive Radical Party, while the more conservative Lafitte tended toward Christian Democracy—the editor of *Herria* wrote that Larzabal, "far from instigating a revolt against the state, asks of it a policy of decentralization, precisely with the objective of avoiding the misfortune of a guerrilla war that has seen so much bloodshed." Moreover, Lafitte rejected any accusation that his journal was anticolonialist. He declared that *Herria* had "never had a colonial editorial line against the presence of France in North Africa, having always criticized sharply the crimes of the *fellaghas*."[50]

Garat, however, maintained his charge against *Herria* and, through the pages of his own journal, *Côte Basque Soir*, attempted to link both Lafitte and Larzabal to the cause of Basque separatism: "It may be the case, it will be pointed out, that French Basque separatism is more ridiculous than dangerous. Beside a few intellectuals ... no one takes it seriously. Defense of the language and tradition is one thing. The rest is only words."[51] Here, one sees an accurate assessment of the dominant thought in Iparralde at the time: a degree of support for cultural initiatives, but the absolute refusal to entertain any politicization of such issues. With these words, however, Garat, through an irony that only masked a degree of fear, also recognized a certain awakening of a Basque nationalist consciousness in Iparralde. It is hardly surprising, as a result, to learn that his solution to the problem was, in his opinion, as necessary as it was efficient: that "not only the author of the article, but also the editor who dared to publish it, should undergo a psychological examination."[52] Once more, the solution to the problem of potential Basque separatism seems to have been the recourse to locking its proponents up in a mental asylum.

I would emphasize here that Garat's view of Basque nationalism as madness applied squarely to Iparralde. As regarded Hegoalde, although he was still against the slow politicization of the phenomenon in Iparralde, he declared that:

> Basque separatism in Spain is a historical, political, and economic reality. The four provinces [in Hegoalde] ... make up one of the most hard-working, richest parts of the peninsula.

They have ports, beautiful mines [and] prosperous industries ... Individual rights were recognized until quite recently in the Basque provinces. The Basques of Spain have shed their blood to defend their independence.

The French Basque Country—on the other hand—has no mines, no great industry, no important energy source. Take away the port of Baiona and the casino in Biarritz, [and] there would only be the factories of Maule and Hazparne, together with the cherries of Itsasu, left ... Basque separatism in France has no economic, political, or historical foundation.

While "Basque separatism" remains abstract, cultivated by some poets, some fantasies ... it deserves a little sympathy.

If French Basque separatism ... looks into practical solutions and speaks of "federalism," then, it becomes ridiculous. Could this region survive isolated? ... Is it trying to get close to Spanish wealth? ... Or, leaving France, does it seek to join Spain?

All of this deserves no more than five minutes of attention for any serious being.[53]

These telling words reveal a number of recurrent themes: Ironically, for example, his description of Iparralde fit perfectly with that of those who connected the social, political, and economic situation of the region with Algeria. At approximately the same time, two seminal texts by Federico Krutwig and Robert Lafont were being widely disseminated in Iparralde, arguing precisely that economic underdevelopment was more a feature of life away from the metropolitan center, the first with an openly Basque nationalist message. As we will see, thanks in part to the influence of these texts, the theme of economic underdevelopment would be increasingly important for fomenting nationalism in Iparralde. Second, for all that Garat advised that considering such issues deserved no more than five minutes of one's attention, his crusade against Lafitte and Larzabal lasted several months, and in it, he was joined by several other important local figures. How might one explain this connection of federalism to separatism, but for the importance (or danger) seen by many in raising this idea in Iparralde? Finally, what better evidence is there of the transformation of pro-Basque sentiment from purely cultural or folkloric labors to a politicization of identity markers than Garat's acceptance of its initial form, regionalism, and rejection of its later evolution toward federalism?

One also notes in his words a slight decline in the belief in the absolute grandeur of France and the consequent opening up of some space in which some peripheral movements might be able to breathe after decades, if not centuries, of the powerful actions by a state that created the model of (an always centralized) civilization and of rationality. Garat's dramatic words in January 1958 contrast sharply with his triumphal air of a few months previously: "If we were in other times that we have known, in which the French nation, when confronted by those it felt threatened it, was firmly united, then we could remove this carnivalesque separatism. But today, our country, its grandeur diminished, cut off from its far-flung territories, mistreated by its allies, threatened by its enemies, is profoundly divided."[54]

I will return shortly to this particular part of the narrative, but I would also point out that Larzabal was not the only wayward intellectual who proposed a federalist solution to the problem of Algeria (and by extension the Basque Country) in the pages of *Herria*. In the words of Canon Etienne Salaberry, for example, a fervent defender of the Christian Democratic Mouvement Républicain Populaire (MRP, Popular Republican Movement), who assumed an intermediary position on the Algerian question amid the tensions between the right and left in France at the time:[55]

> Colonialism is dead, let me repeat. It has been dying for ten years. It has not been recognized. Yet the far right seek, by all means, to keep it going, while the far left want to abandon it . . . The solution of the new era into which we have just entered is to be found in European federalism, shaped [in tandem] with an African federalism. The Algerian problem proves insoluble day by day, [only] to be resolved in terms of an anachronistic nationalism: that of the nineteenth century.[56]

However, Salaberry was not a Basque nationalist. Just before his death in 1981, he remarked that "I see that there are three flags, the Basque one, the French one, and the European one. And if one of them is missing, there are none."[57] In other words, he personified the traditional belief in two homelands.

Of course, the proposals of Larzabal and Salaberry had nothing to do with the kind of mental instability that Garat had implied in his criticism. They were, in fact, much more reflective of the idiosyncrasy of certain pro-Basque sectors that, after a period of crisis during the interwar years, were beginning to emerge once more. Yet this renewed pro-Basque sentiment only gradually overcame the deeply embedded notion of two homelands. This was because the Basque *petite patrie* had actually begun to receive political support for the essentially cultural and folkloric focus on which it had been reproduced through different generations up to that time. Thus, the federalist proposals of Larzabal and Salaberry for Algeria were rooted in a growing movement within France itself, a movement that was also gaining ground in Iparralde and that, there, served as a watchtower from which more openly separatist demands could be observed until it gradually succumbed to them in the 1970s. Or put another way, it was a movement before which federalism lost increasing ground, because for Salaberry and many others, federalism was linked to a profound belief in Europe, a belief that was also strong among Basque nationalist circles until the 1970s.

Beyond the short-term effects of the Algerian war, there were also, perhaps more importantly, longer-term consequences. As Eguzki Urteaga puts it, "in Iparralde, decolonization in general, and the Algerian War in particular, played a major role in the emergence and assertion of Basque nationalist demands."[58] Indeed, for one of the first of the new generation of Basque nationalists, Jakes Abeberry,

> The wars in Indochina and, especially, in Algeria forged links between young Basques and colonialism, forcing them to struggle in their own home, observing that, in extremis, the French government had agreed to self-determination for Algeria, [while] refusing it to the Basques . . . [Thus,] the influence of the War in Algeria, in which many Basques par-

ticipated . . . was considerable in raising our national awareness, faced with a people who fought for their independence.[59]

The identification with Algeria rested on various points: first, the independence of seven former French colonies during the early 1960s "demonstrated above all else the fragility and vulnerability of states that ceased to be untouchable or irrefutable." As a result, there emerged the idea that existing political structures were transient, and not as durable as they may previously have seemed. This, in turn, "had the effect of making it seem possible for different national minorities to achieve autonomy, if not independence. This would explain the simultaneous nationalist demands of Bretons, Corsicans, and Occitanians."[60] Moreover, the identification of Iparralde with Algeria was based on the common belonging of these nations to France and, more specifically, to "the similarity of a situation of weak economic development and political dependence on the metropolis."[61] Ultimately, such concerns would result in a further step in the development of a sense of Basque identity in Iparralde: the transformation of these ideas into organized political action.

Internal Colonialism and *Vasconia*

As mentioned in Chapter 1, in the mid-1960s, the work of Robert Lafont revolutionized the way people thought about the economic relations between center and periphery in France. At the beginning of his seminal work *La revolution regionaliste* (1967), he observed that:

> The French problems that the present book addresses have been the object of considerable debate for fifteen years. Nobody in France now ignores the fact that the economy and social life of numerous regions in the country are showing depressing features, generally understood in a framework understood as underdevelopment. At the same time, one of the causes of this bleakness has become evident: administrative centralization that is as old as France itself, but that in the last 150 years has become feverish.[62]

This French regional underdevelopment could also be explained by a new concept that appeared offensive to more traditional French sensibilities: internal colonialism, the "most apt expression that I have been able to identify for my current examination when it comes to defining a certain number of economic processes whose most evident external dimension is regional underdevelopment," according to Lafont.[63]

Within this context, a series of works published in Iparralde in the 1970s began to view the region's own problems as deriving from a form of internal colonialism.[64] However, the origins of this argument in the Basque case can be traced further back, to the book *Vasconia* (1962) by Federico Krutwig, published under the pseudonym Fernando Sarrailh de Ihartza.[65] In addition to providing the theoretical basis for a definitive break between the PNV and ETA in Hegoalde, Krutwig's work was a crucial text for the emerging generation of Basque nationalists in Iparralde.[66] As regarded Iparralde, it was most important for applying the thesis of internal colonialism to the history of the Basque Country, and the creators of Enbata enthusiastically embraced his argument.

They conceived of Iparralde as, in effect, a colony dating from the time of the French Revolution, an interpretation of Krutwig that challenged the notion of the region as an isolated area of deep Christian faith fighting to maintain its religion in the face of the secular revolutionary terror. For Krutwig,

> The French Revolution was a disaster for the whole Basque Country; it was a poisoned arrow that pierced the body of the Basque Country and that was going to paralyze it until killing it by asphyxiation ... The greatest enemy of the Basque Country north of the Pyrenees is called France. And separating from [France], separating that channel through which the deadly poison is contaminating it, is a vital necessity for the Basque Country.[67]

Thus, after analyzing the economic situation in Iparralde through the ages, Krutwig concluded that, at that time (the early 1960s), unification of all the Basque provinces would drastically improve the situation there.

Focusing on emigration, the only real economic alternative for the population given the existing conditions, he saw only dramatic consequences for the Basque national consciousness: "The region today called the S.W. [the French region previously termed Sud Ouest, Southwest, and, nowadays, Aquitaine] of France is a land that is gradually becoming depopulated, and this will only increase with the plans being currently prepared by the government in Paris. With the exodus, there has been a hemorrhage of national lifeblood, and the Basque Country has been reduced to the status of a colony."[68]

The second of Krutwig's ideas that had a tremendous impact on the new generation of Basque nationalists in Iparralde was the notion that the division of the Basque Country between two larger states impeded the natural flow of economic relations that would guarantee local development. Consequently, Enbata's federalist strategy was based on a model whereby relations with Hegoalde would be strengthened. In effect, this was a proposal for the creation of a Euroregion that, many years later, would be embraced not only by nationalists, but also by the leading business and political interests in Iparralde.[69] According to Krutwig:

> The existence of the border of shame and disgrace that, drawn across the Bidasoa and the Pyrenees, divides our homeland in two, has stopped one economy from developing on both sides of the country. The creation of a powerful industrial and banking center in Bilbao has allowed the forces of the western Basque Country (Bizkaia and Navarre) to unite and has created a sense of unity that must characterize any nationality. The border of the Bidasoa has greatly impeded this sentiment from reaching the other side, so that [Iparralde] might take part in a common industrial development.[70]

Krutwig saw the creation of a unified Basque state as the only remedy for this situation—the principal idea behind the 1963 declaration of Itsasu by Enbata (as we will see below).[71] Furthermore, noting that the main aim of colonialism was the acculturation of other peoples, Krutwig argued in favor of recovering the Basque national consciousness by fomenting a feeling of belonging:

> Having heard it said in schools that France is the center of the world and that the *Grande Nation* never lost a battle, they [the Basques of Iparralde] have ended up with such confusion in their heads about the order of things, that they have lost their own personality and have become fifth-degree Frenchmen. Through the fault of French schools, they have mentally belittled themselves so much that that they don't even know how to conceive of Europe. The fatuity of the schools has passed into their bones. They are convinced that the only important literature in the world is French.

Krutwig put forward a groundbreaking proposal that might serve to remedy this situation:

> In this part of the Basque Country, one must present the Basque problem in linguistic terms, given that this country has been subject to a strong denationalization for centuries... Addressing the Basque problem in this part of the Basque Country can be done only in a so-called "psychological" way that, for everyone else, is the valid approach for Europe. It would consist, then, in raising the consciousness of all those individuals who for one reason or another might be considered to belong to the Basque national community.
>
> One must respond to the question Who are the Basques? with [the reply]: Anyone who feels so. The Basque nation would, then, be that consciousness grounded in an infrastructure of national factors. These factors, as I have explained, are the language, race, culture, spiritual interests, economic interests, history, etc.[72]

Interestingly, Krutwig based his argument in favor of developing a Basque national consciousness on popular will, and this was embraced, too, by Enbata. Indeed, from its founding, the group was significantly more inclusive in its definition of Basque identity than the initial incarnation of nationalism in Hegoalde. However, this strategy was, of course, defined by the local reality of Iparralde, where solely ethnic-based nationalism had to give way to a more inclusive, instrumental vision.

Krutwig, moreover, argued that to recover this national consciousness, the political system based on patronage under which relations of power operated in Iparralde would have to be challenged. That is, any form of Basque nationalism would have to take on the notables. This, he noted, would not be easy and involved addressing French nationalism directly:

> The defeat suffered by French imperialism [during World War II] was so great that it left centralist French patriots in such a ridiculous position that they lost all prestige in front of the peoples they had subjected to colonialism... Internal disorder in French politics brought different governments to power... During these, the Algerian revolt broke out... The centralist state gave autonomy to French regions outside the hexagon [mainland France] that, in the process of splitting up [from France], ended up breaking completely away from the old metropolis. The remedy of a French Commonwealth that the new autocrat [Charles de Gaulle] created, together with a number of new state leaders who, as in the time of the court of Louis XIV, should have revolved around the Sun King

like planets revolving around the sun, could not defend itself against the sudden attack. The sun ended up without any planets... General de Gaulle lost the whole empire... And even the region of Algeria, which had been declared an integral part of the metropolis, broke away and became independent... In the metropolis, Bretons now no longer want to think of Paris as a spiritual center or focus of interest. They would like to break free of their labor camp. Their voice is still silent due to the brutal repression with which the laws endow the state security forces with. Consequently, both the northern Basques and the Bretons use a trick, which they call Europeanism, that consists of saying that they do not wish to separate from France, but seek only a satisfactory Basque or Breton solution. It is a solution within a future European framework that the French authorities, jealous guardians of what they conquered by stealing, cannot oppose.[73]

From this position, Krutwig raised the issue of a new and mostly unknown group that had just been created at about the same time he published the work:

Lately, a nationalist movement has emerged in the northern Basque Country around a student group that, initially, began its activities in Bordeaux. Its name is Enbata. They publish a monthly journal with the same title that apparently has been quite popular. Its stance is clearly nationalist, although it seems unclear on some points. Enbata's demands are primarily limited to asking for a degree of autonomy for Lapurdi, Nafarroa Beherea, and Zuberoa. Its specific goals are unknown. Nobody knows if it is a party or a secret society. In its psychology, it greatly resembles the mysterious activity of ETA, of which it is apparently a section. On the one hand, in its publication, it argues forcefully in favor of using the Basque language, but unfortunately, in this it follows the example of the PNV on the other side of the border, because its magazine is published entirely in French. In a meeting held recently in Itsasu, it decided to become a political movement.[74]

While many observers have pointed to the importance of Krutwig's *Vasconia* in influencing a tactical shift within ETA during the mid-1960s, it was also an important text for the young people who founded Enbata. The work presented the Basque question in Iparralde as the consequence of colonialism and argued in favor of displacing entrenched elites. Moreover, it alluded to the existing model of tourism in Iparralde as a cause of the economic and identity problems there, along with emigration. It broke with the conservative and clerical nationalist model favored by the PNV. It argued in favor of Basque unification for economic reasons, as well as for an open, inclusive notion of Basque national identification, and while it did not altogether relinquish a racial element to the idea of a Basque identity, it based its ideas on the notion of popular will. Finally, it emphasized the importance of the Basque language in any process of awakening national consciousness.

With *Vasconia*, then, in 1962, came the end of an era that began with the second incarnation of *Aintzina* in 1942, one that might be characterized as the progressive politicization of the Basque cultural movement. As a result, the logic of two homelands began to decline, even within movements that had come to define themselves by this notion. Consequently, as we have seen, by the 1950s, the Euskal Ikasleen Biltzarra possessed two important sections, in Bordeaux and in Paris. The former included Michel Burucoa, Ximun Haran, Jean Fagoaga, and Laurent Darraidou, while the latter was composed of Michel Inchauspé, Henri Mathieu, and Charles Arribillaga.[75] By1953, the Euskal Ikasleen Biltzarra changed its name to Embata (with an "m")—a Basque term for the wind that precedes a storm coming off the ocean.

The first president of Embata was Michel Burucoa, and the organization had twenty members,[76] rising to 171 by 1960.[77] In the late 1950s, this organization remained politically ambiguous, but at about the same time, Michel Labéguerie wrote an article entitled "Toward a New Era" for the group's journal that appeared to hint at a new direction. He wrote: "There are three stages that seem to have marked the consciousness of Basque students during the last fifteen years: folkloric expression, cultural-studies meetings, [and] the assumption of a political consciousness."[78] It was time for the wind that preceded the storm, a wind blowing from cultural to political action. Labéguerie's words lit the way for Basque nationalism to emerge into a new era that, nevertheless, might still be considered another period of transition waypoint in the development of a politicized sense of Basque identity in Iparralde.

CHAPTER NINE

Enbata: The Wind Before the Storm

Basque nationalism emerged late and developed slowly in Iparralde, compared with its counterpart in Hegoalde. This had much to do with the profound crisis of Basque identity there as a result of the strong consolidation of the French state. At the same time, the fact that both the political center and the economic center of the country were located in Paris, together with the peripheral and dependant nature of the Basque economy, prevented elites from emerging in Iparralde that might have been able to give some degree of political shape to ethnic, linguistic, and cultural features that one finds at the root of all nationalist movements. By contrast, while in Spain, the political center was located in Madrid, the principal areas of economic development were to be found in two important peripheries: the Basque Country and Catalonia, to such an extent, in fact, that in these regions, elites emerged through the process of modernization that were able to articulate and lead nationalist movements. Thus, while in Hegoalde modernity was an internal dynamic, as reflected by the rise of both Basque nationalism and socialism in Bilbao at the end of the nineteenth century, in Iparralde, it was an imported or external phenomenon that had to learn to speak French.

As a result, from the beginning of the twentieth century on, Basque nationalist circles were required to search long and hard for any kind of political dimension in their linguistic and cultural demands, a search marked, moreover, by a profound crisis of belonging in Iparralde. Indeed, before any such politicization could take place, these same Basque sectors first had to undertake a significant degree of cultural dissemination. Finally, by the 1950s, their cultural efforts had reached a sufficiently broad level to entertain initial thoughts of politicizing at least some of the issues that concerned them.

Added to this historical context, a whole new series of elements made the emergence of Basque nationalism in Iparralde more possible in the 1960s and 1970s.[1] In the first place, the founders of Basque nationalism in Iparralde were mainly students who had been forced to leave the region to pursue their studies elsewhere and who felt in some kind of debt to their homeland—that is, they felt the need to recover a lost and crisis-ridden social identity. This first political expression of Basque nationalism was, then, "the expression of experts and intellectuals who believed they had been called to form the cadres of a future society"[2] in a homeland that they had abandoned. Indeed, as Jean Marie Izquierdo contends,[3] these young people had to adjust this vision to the changes they themselves were experiencing: the transformation of a traditional, rural society into which they had been socialized into an urban society into which they had been forced in a kind of educational exile, with all the consequences that this implied.

Moreover, beyond just an expression of moral conflict, Basque nationalism was a reflection of another grave crisis enveloping French society as a whole: a wider process of decolonization that would imprint at least some of the society's key aspects. Thus, state elites were seeing how their notion of a *grande patrie* was succumbing, at least in part, to the power of those who dared to demand more autonomy from the center.

This process of decolonization, in turn, led to the creation of dozens of new states and, together with the new winds of federalism blowing through Europe at the same time, this resulted in a certain confidence on the part of Enbata's founders, a confidence in pursuing the notion of a "Europe of nations" as a way of advancing toward full Basque sovereignty. In fact, as we will see, this was a central idea of the Itsasu Charter, the basic and founding policy statement of Enbata.

At the same time, the traditionally powerful Christian Democrat notables of Iparralde were gradually losing their status in a new French society dominated by another form of conservatism: Gaullism. This had the effect of making these young Basque nationalists potential allies for the notables if they wanted to retain their influence in Iparralde.

Within this context, the modest industrial sector of Iparralde (principally in Zuberoa) went through its own crisis and added to this, there was a degree of resentment in Iparralde toward the neighboring province of Béarn.[4] Together with the effects of the watershed events of May 1968—student and worker revolts in the streets of Paris—these developments encouraged, to some degree at least, a shift in favor of Enbata's platform, an ideology that increasingly defined the movement as both nationalist and leftist.

Then, a crisis in the agricultural sector of Iparralde resulted in the emergence of a new generation of rural young people who embraced Basque nationalism. They questioned the traditional politics of their forebears and were imbued with a dynamism that allowed them to vent their frustrations at the unfolding crisis.[5]

These developments all coincided with the slow, but steady emergence of a politicized Basque consciousness that was characterized by several sequential developments. First, there was: the initial diffusion of Basque nationalist proposals, principally as a result of the presence and influence of nationalist refugees from Hegoalde in the 1930s and of the work of Pierre Lafitte in adapting these ideas to the conservative political reality of Iparralde by fomenting a sense of regionalism. Later, there followed the consequent, albeit isolated eruption of more openly nationalist ideas through the work of Marc Legasse in the 1940s, which, in turn, was followed by the intense period of cultural activity in the 1950s. All of these developments culminated in the 1960s, when an openly nationalist political movement emerged after an industrial and agricultural crisis, a sharp decline in the population of the rural interior, the dissemination of anticolonial theories, and the identification of Iparralde with former French colonies that had achieved independence. While the older guard then began to favor federalism,[6] a new, younger generation demanded an independent state in unification with Hegoalde.

These ideas emerged within Enbata, a group composed of a cross section of interests, including (in part) those of displaced and traditionally Christian Democratic notables seeking a political lifeline, industrial leaders from the interior searching for support as they gradually lost their political power, coastal business leaders looking to create a new kind of economic expansion, and young idealists attempting to change society by replacing traditional power blocs with new, more dynamic sectors.[7]

Genesis of the Movement: From Embata to Enbata

There were three founding figures of Enbata: Ximun Haran, Michel Labéguerie, and Piarres Larzabal.[8] Haran, a well-known *pelota* player, had brought out a record in 1957 (on the Embata label) that covered a number of traditional Basque songs of Iparralde. Feeling the need to undertake more obviously political activity, he asked Telesforo de Monzón for advice as to how he might go about this. Monzón put him in contact with Labéguerie, and ultimately the two of them met with Larzabal.

Curiously, the priest Larzabal was central in steering the emergent new movement toward secular positions. However, he was also keen to remain outside the spotlight. Indeed, in Enbata's own founding texts, reference was made to the creation of the group's founders as Haran, Labéguerie, and "a priest."[9] Larzabal was interested in imbuing Enbata with a secular course, because "if the movement were perceived as being in the hands of a priest, then other priests would join, the youth would depart, and the movement would either be stillborn or sink slowly into conservatism."[10] As a result, Larzabal left the movement "to ensure the development of a secular nationalism free from the stifling apolitical embrace of the church."[11]

Despite this, there remained a Christian Democratic tendency among the group of people that emerged in the founding of Enbata. Thus, Labéguerie, Larzabal, Jean Etcheverry-Ainchart, and Michel Burucoa provided a link between the Basque advocates of the 1940s and the new generation of young activists. And even many of the younger members, such as Haran, Jean-Louis Davant, and Ramuntxo Camblong, had moved in Christian Democratic circles. As Jakes Abeberry recalled, "to be a Christian Democrat was to be progressive in the conservative Basque Country of the era."[12] However, most of the younger members favored more radical positions and the group adopted a secular position that broke with earlier pro-Basque activities.

Those first three individuals were soon joined by four others: Michel Burucoa, Michel Eppherre, Jakes Abeberry, and Jean-Louis Davant. And in 1961, the Embata student group changed the spelling of its name to Enbata, thereby initiating a new phase and the birth of Basque nationalism proper in Iparralde. Moreover, one should also note the continuing influence of Basque nationalists from Hegoalde in the birth of this new movement.[13]

The first edition of the new movement's journal, published in the fall of 1960 and still at this time entitled *Embata*, resonated with Romantic and dramatic formulations of the crisis that Iparralde was experiencing: "Euzkadi . . . you, my mother, there you are transformed into a prostitute."[14] That same fall, the weekly published a map under the title "The Europe That We Propose," showing a unified Basque Country (composed of the seven provinces), together with separate entities for the other nationalities in France. Indeed, the famous hexagon that traces the borders of the French state was reduced so that France all but disappeared from the map, "a sacrilege for many who thought the Basque Country should be the small homeland and France the large one,"[15] that is, for most people in Iparralde, whether they were in favor of Basque cultural nationalism or not. Enbata thus began to break the spell that had enveloped advocates of culture alone, keeping them from undertaking any political activity that might challenge the logic of the French state. That said, during this initial phase, the group distanced itself from radical separatist positions.[16]

Instead, between 1960 and 1963, Enbata concentrated its first efforts on promoting the notion of a Europe of peoples—that is, of European unification along federal lines—as a solution to the problem of minority nations. At the same time, the group also demonstrated its sympathies for working-class issues and rural problems, as well as publicly criticizing the dominant model of tourist development in Iparralde. This initial period was also marked by an important and controversial debate between the group and the maverick Germanophile Basque nationalist poet from Zuberoa, Jon Mirande,[17] with the result that Enbata definitively distanced itself from racial conceptions of Basque identity. Mirande had published an article in *Enbata* titled "Race, People, and Nation" with clearly racist positions: "It would be ill-fated to be in favor of the arrival of races inferior to the pure white one on our continent . . . if we accept the inequality between the great human races, according to an ascendant hierarchy from black to yellow people, and from these to whites."[18] The response to this, written by Davant and Abeberry, was conclusive: "on the outside, what safeguards the Basque is the language . . . on the inside, what will save the Basque people is the feeling of being Basque and the will to keep on being so."[19]

During its first two years of existence, then, Enbata formulated the central features of its political thought: a secular outlook as an attempt to overcome the conservative stranglehold of the church, yet with subtly maintained ties to religion through the Christian Democratic tendencies of some of its members; a clear definition of the voluntary basis of Basque identity, despite the group's still-existing links with the culturalist and racial inheritance of Sabino Arana's early Basque nationalism; the reinterpretation of Basque history; and, as we will see, a clear fraternal compromise with the plight of Basques in Hegoalde, as reflected in the group's defense of Basque political refugees.

The Politicization of the Movement: The Itsasu Charter

In 1962, the members of Enbata decided to take another important step in their short history. With the Easter holiday approaching, they decided to celebrate the Aberri

Eguna—the Day of the Basque Fatherland—in Iparralde, a Basque nationalist celebration that had been started in Hegoalde in the 1930s to coincide with Easter Sunday. By chance,[20] they chose the town of Itsasu (Lapurdi) to celebrate the Aberri Eguna, the town that, one year later, would be the scene of the foundational document of Basque nationalism in Iparralde, the Itsasu Charter.

Enbata presented its ideas in a ceremony to coincide with the Aberri Eguna celebrations before a public composed of various local figures, young Basque activists, and a large number of Basque political refugees from the Spanish Civil War, headed by Telesforo de Monzón.[21] At the event, Haran, after offering a brief overview of the course of Basque nationalism in Iparralde, asked whether or not, besides working from an ideological perspective, it would also be worthwhile to create a specifically political movement.[22]

Encouraged by a generally positive response to the question, Enbata decided once more to celebrate the Aberri Eguna in Itsasu in 1963 and this time make a more explicit political statement of intent. As a result, on Easter Sunday, 1963, a large gathering met once more in Itsasu,[23] including representatives of Breton, Catalan, Flemish, Walloon, Occitanian, and Quebecois nationalist movements, together with Senator Jean Errecart, the by-now deputy Labéguerie, the *conseiller général* and former deputy René Delzangles, and a number of mayors, such as Jean Poulou from Ziburu, Vincent Pochelu from Makea, and Paul Dutournier from Sara. Before the assembled crowd, Haran read a statement saying that Enbata had decided to become a political movement and as such had drawn up three reports and a foundational statement, thereafter known as the Itsasu Charter.

The task of reading the cultural report was assigned to Martxalin Arbelbide. After commenting on the difficult situation in which Euskara found itself, she underscored the earlier work of Basque activists such as Etcheverry-Ainchart and Legasse, before going on to list the group's demands: bilingual schools, a bilingual administrative system, and priority to be given to Basque speakers when choosing people for public posts. Interestingly, this was the only report to be read entirely in Euskara. As Krutwig had pointed out, most of *Enbata*'s articles were published in French. The publication justified this policy as the most effective way to get its message across among when many of its potential readers would not have known Basque.[24] As James E. Jacob notes, "This strategy was justified in part by the extent of linguistic assimilation of most ethnic Basques in the urban, coastal cities where *Enbata*'s early militants were most concentrated."[25] Indeed, many of the group's early activists did not have especially good levels of Euskara,[26] although from its initial moments, Enbata was quite open to a flexible interpretation of who could claim to be Basque. In other words, a French-language discourse designed to defend Euskara and an openness to the meaning of Basque identity were two sides of the same coin: an inclusive strategy of mobilization demonstrating an instrumental political outlook.

In this context, it is easier to understand Abeberry's political report in Itsasu. In the report, two ideas stood out. The first was Enbata's understanding of what it meant to be Basque, a point on which Abeberry was quite clear: "A Basque, in the national sense of the term, is he who, accepting the Basque ethnic factors, decides to be one."[27] As Jacob remarks, "For a movement which spoke of 'race' as a distinct marker of Basque historical distinction, *Enbata*'s own political use of ethnic barriers was virtually nonexistent."[28] Moreover, elsewhere, Abeberry was clear in defining some objectives that, in the Itsasu Charter, were toned down: "The Basque nation must realize its right of self-determination . . . the total liberation of our people in its unity remains our final goal; only the constitution of a Basque state will permit the full realization of the aspirations of the Basque people and will permit free rein to its genius."[29]

In the economic report, Davant, following Krutwig, made an implicit connection between economic and national development. Prominent in this report, by way of an example, was a topic that was becoming more and more controversial at the time: tourism. For many, the dominant model of tourist development was converting Iparralde into a kind of Native American "reservation," forcing young people there into a vicious circle of seasonal employment/unemployment and converting the land into a sort of folkloric exhibition for foreigners for three months of every year.

This all added up to Enbata adopting clearly Basque nationalist positions, thereby explaining why, soon after the Itsasu Charter, it lost some members who could not overcome the logic of two homelands, including Labéguerie, one of those who actually drew up the charter in the first place.[30]

The brief text of the Itsasu Charter was as follows.

> Today, April 15, 1963, on this ABERRI Eguna, those off us meeting here at the foot of the tree [of Gernika] planted in Itsasu wish to state the following:
>
> We Basques
> SAY that, through our land, race, language, and customs, are a PEOPLE,
> SAY that, through our past and present will, are a NATION,
> SAY that, by nature and history, are a DEMOCRACY.
> As the PEOPLE, NATION, and DEMOCRACY we are, we have the right to act together and we demand our full sovereignty [*jabetasuna*], given that during this century, every people has the right to govern itself.
> WE LET IT BE KNOWN
> That we want to govern our NATION ourselves,
> That we encourage other peoples to accept the Basque Country AS A NATION,
> Thus, the Basque Country will be ONE, and we will give life and continuity to our HOMELAND.[31]

Following the outlining of this foundation, the charter went on to present a political motion that would go down in history as the first official demand of organized Basque nationalism in Iparralde.

> Seeing,
>
> > That Spain and France now divide the Basque Country in two,
> > That the Basque language is in a weak position,

That the three provinces of Iparralde have been abandoned, with young people forced to emigrate.

Seeing,

That every French political formation has put to one side the interests of Basques, in terms of both their lifestyle and culture,

ENBATA, meeting on April 15, 1963, in Itsasu, proposes to the Basques:

In a first stage, within French law, the creation of a département that joins Lapurdi, Nafarroa Beherea, and Zuberoa, together with a law to give official status to Basque.

In a second stage, and within the framework of European unity, a Region that joins the seven Basque provinces, with its own jurisdiction in politics, administration, and culture, as all the other peoples of Europe enjoy.[32]

As we can see, besides articulating a demand that continues to be the central focus of Basque nationalist strategy in Iparralde–the creation of specifically Basque institutions– there is no mention here of independence. Further, popular will as a democratic expression of Basque nationality is stressed, together with the historical, cultural, territorial, and racial features that came to make up the Basque people. Similarly, self-determination is emphasized only from a universal perspective.[33] In fact, the message here had much more in common with the then fashionable currents of federalism flowing through France at the time than with the separatist postures of Arana or ETA. Specifically, in the 1964 document "Pourquoi Enbata?" (Why Enbata?), a clearly federalist stance was preferred to any mention of separatism. Up to that point, then, there was some resemblance in the ideological evolution of Enbata with earlier Basque activists such as Lafitte, who gradually moved from regionalist to federalist positions. And Labéguerie, for example, after leaving Enbata and in repeated later ideological confrontations with the group, always emphasized that he had not changed his original federalist ideas.

According to another of those present in 1963 in Itsasu, Jean-Louis Davant, the context in which Enbata emerged was dominated by African decolonization in general and the inexorable move toward Algerian independence in particular. Yet the beginnings of European unity were also important for the movement's founders. Davant notes that the European ideal "was a very important feature of Enbata from its earliest times. It still is today, although in idyllic form. It was, mostly, the [preferred] option of the leaders."[34] Moreover, Davant refutes the charge that Enbata was an ideologically ill-defined group. Instead, he recalls, "the connection between the national struggle and the social struggle was never clearly established during those years," and if Enbata became more socialist with time, it was because of "its militant experience."[35]

This experience was measured most clearly in electoral politics. Labéguerie was elected a deputy in the 1962 legislative elections to the National Assembly, and from 1964 on, the group concentrated on electoral politics. However, this electoral activity was increasingly conditioned by two parallel developments: on the one hand, the growing influence of ETA on Enbata and a consequent move to more separatist positions, and on the other, the gradual decline in the influence of the Christian Democratic views that had characterized, at least in part, the group at its birth. This culminated in the key year of 1968, a year when events in France propelled Enbata to a more avowedly progressive political ideology.

At precisely the same time, however, the group's limits were increasingly evident. And when Enbata was banned by the French authorities in 1974, it only highlighted the organization's loss of activists to a host of other Basque nationalist and leftist groups. Once again, a generational conflict brought down a pro-Basque movement in Iparralde, and to the parricidal logic of Basque nationalism there—that is, its confrontation with the father figure of the nationalist movement in Hegoalde—was added another conflict: an internal dynamic that pitted new generations against those that had founded the movement.

Electoral Activity and the Labéguerie *Affaire*

During the Fourth Republic (1944–58), the results of legislative elections to the National Assembly were measured according to the electoral list of each *département*, which makes it difficult to be precise about voting habits for Iparralde alone. The Christian Democratic Mouvement Republican Populaire (Popular Republican Movement, MRP) was probably the single most important party in Iparralde, given the personal popularity of key local notables close to its general ideology linked to pro-Basque positions: Jean Errecart, founder of the Lur Berri cooperative, and Jean Etcheverry-Ainchart, the notary of Baigorri, for example. Both were politically in the center, and both were close to Enbata when it first emerged.

The Local Political System

The Gaullist Rassemblement du Peuple Français (Rally of the French People, RPF) was less important in Iparralde, given the lack of support from local notables.[36] During this era, we might estimate that the MRP obtained on average between 30 and 38 percent of the vote in Iparralde, achieving a high point of 52 percent in the 1945 legislative elections (the first postwar ballot to elect the provisional government), but gradually losing momentum after 1956. The traditional right, at the same time, received between 12 and 15 percent of the overall vote, while the Radical Party gained between 10 and 15 percent of the votes at a departmental level. The Socialist Party—then known by the acronym SFIO (Section Française de l'Internationale Ouvrière, the French Section of the Workers' International)—obtained similar results, although at a slightly lower percentage, to the PCF, the French Communist Party (Parti Communiste Français), at between 12 and 18 percent of the overall vote.

However, the Algerian War plunged France into an internal domestic crisis that precipitated the founding of the Fifth Republic, and after 1958, the political landscape began to change. First and foremost, Charles de Gaulle imprinted his personality on the new regime. Within the new system, a number of referenda were held to validate de Gaulle's authority,[37] and he received strong support in Iparralde. Yet this change also shook up the political reality of the region to such an extent that the traditional power of Christian

Democratic and pro-Basque local notables was severely curtailed by the new institutional regime.[38] For example, the first noteworthy casualty of this scenario was Jean Errecart, defeated by a Gaullist opponent, Alexandre Camino, in 1958.

The Fifth Republic in effect finished off a stable, but hierarchical system where, for decades, all contact between the Basque rural world and the exterior—especially concerning anything to do with political or administrative questions—had been filtered through the traditional notables. However, as Jean Paul Malherbe points out, from the middle of the twentieth century on, technological advances and industrial growth increasingly made the role of these mediators between the urban and rural worlds more and more anachronistic. Indeed, as a result of new means of communication, widespread economic integration, the spread of tourism, and a crisis of traditional communal relations, the ideologies and lifestyles of the rural and urban worlds began to overlap more and more. In Iparralde, for example, the traditionally powerful institution of the family home—the *etxe*—began to lose ground amid the rising force of the real-estate business and a new generation that increasingly refused to follow the traditional inheritance model. Added to this, class consciousness emerged in Iparralde to complicate the social, economic, and political map even further.[39] Within the space of a few years, the stability of Iparralde had been shaken, and the effect of several different transformations was slowly to erode traditional society there. This, of course, was perfect for fomenting a new political discourse—that is, it was an ideal breeding ground for Enbata—even more so because of the favorable reception for the group by the notable class in its own desperate search for new allies in the changing political climate.

This new regime was received well in Iparralde, as it was in Brittany and Alsace. Indeed, as Jacob points out, "Ethnic France was Gaullist France" to such an extent that, even after de Gaulle's disappearance from the political scene, the Basques of Iparralde continued to vote for his political party in large numbers.[40] From the implementation of the Fifth Republic in 1958 on, then, French politics and its full party structure embraced Iparralde, forcing centrist and pro-Basque sectors to redefine their own politics.

After a short period of rapprochement with Enbata, these sectors soon abandoned the Basque nationalists to try to forge a local alternative to the polarization between Gaullists and the Democratic Center party. The result was the creation of the Mouvement Démocratique Basque (Basque Democratic Movement, MDB), but its failure ultimately forced the former local notables into the mainstream French political parties.

Between 1960 and 1965, then, there were two contrary political developments in Iparralde: pro-Basque Christian Democrats first courted Enbata, then did a political U-turn and ended up integrating within the French political party system. While there was a degree of opportunism to this about turn, one should also note that the transformation of Enbata itself made any potential alliance more and more difficult, in particular, its increasingly close ties with the clandestine world of ETA, but also its clearly more progressive political agenda.

Labéguerie's First Steps in Politics

One of the most representative figures of this political turmoil and of the shifting ideological patterns of the 1960s was Michel Labéguerie. We should recall that it was Labéguerie who, in 1957, published an article highlighting the need for Basque nationalism to take a political turn from its more comfortable cultural base.[41]

He was one of the clearest-headed (and indeed most charismatic) leaders of his time, and helped to inspire a new generation of young activists to adopt more political postures.[42] His definitive step toward more formal political activity came in the 1962 legislative elections, when he was selected by Christian Democratic sympathizers (including Senator Jean Errecart) to challenge Alexandre Camino.[43] Soon, he received the support of five *conseillers généraux*: Etcheverry-Ainchart in Baigorri, Louis Madré in Hazparne, André Ospital in Bastida (Labastide), Léon Salagoïty in Bidaxune (Bidache), and Errecart in Donapaleu. Camino's response was to use Labéguerie's membership in Enbata to confuse the electorate. He had posters put up with slogans such as "Vote Basque, vote French, vote antiseparatist,"[44] provoking Labéguerie's patrons to respond with a public letter that read, in part, as follows: "In order to avoid any confusion, we state that our adherence to Euskara, to our traditions, together with our preoccupation about the future and the industrial development of our region, should not be interpreted as separatism, that, in our opinion, is an assault on the territorial integrity and internal security of the state."[45]

Labéguerie, too, protested the charge of separatism, taking it as a personal insult. So it was within this context that the notables of the region gradually aligned themselves with one of the two candidates. Labéguerie–twenty years younger than Camino–closed his campaign by promoting slogans such as "Gazte eta berri, bozka Labéguerie" (Young and new, vote Labéguerie) and "Eskuararen, eskualdunen eta Eskualherriaren zerbitzari izatea. Hori da nahikunde bakarra" (To serve Basque, Basque speakers, and the Basque Country. That is our only wish).

Moreover, Labéguerie was not affiliated officially with any one political party, but, rather ran on a ticket entitled the "Union of local interests in the Basque Country." Yet problems arose with Enbata; or, rather, problems arose after the election, when he beat Camino convincingly with 57.3 percent of the vote after the first round of voting–a result that made him the candidate with the largest winning margin in the whole of France.[46] Camino, who some years earlier had defeated the pro-Basque candidate Carricart, was, in turn, humiliated with a mere 25.4 percent of the vote.

The Split and the Shadow of ETA

Enbata had worked tirelessly in favor of Labéguerie's candidacy, but although his victory encouraged the group to present candidates at subsequent elections, it would seem that he was not elected because of his closeness to the new nationalist organization.[47] Indeed, as many observers at the time saw it, he won *despite* his connections to Enbata. Larronde claims that the wide margin of Labéguerie's victory can be put down to the disenchantment felt by a large number of Gaullist voters who had previously supported Camino while he was a member of the UNR (Union pour la Nouvelle République, Union for the New Republic)—the successor party to the RPF—prior to 1962,[48] but who turned against him when he switched to the anti-Gaullist Centre National des Indépendants et Paysans (National Center of Independents and Peasants) thereafter. For this betrayal, many Gaullists may have voted for Labéguerie.[49]

Although Labéguerie took part in the Aberri Eguna celebration in 1963, soon afterward, he began to distance himself from Enbata. Indeed, only a few days later, when asked if he would promote Enbata's goals as a deputy in the French Assembly, he replied that he would not.[50] And during the cantonal elections of March 1964, when Labéguerie presented his candidacy for Ezpeleta in Lapurdi, he refused to campaign on any platform connected to Enbata, winning the contest easily (against a Communist opponent) with 92.4 percent of the vote after the first round.[51]

The specific cause of Labéguerie's break with Enbata seems to lie in the creation, in February 1963, of Euskal Idazkaritza, an umbrella organization designed to "coordinate all Basque activity in favor of the Basque Country and its inhabitants in all their forms, to place at the disposition of all organizations, social groups, societies, corporations or individuals, material means: a premises, a secretariat [and so on]."[52] Labéguerie had been named the first president of this body, but at a meeting held in January 1964 at which he was not present, two members of ETA, refugees from Hegoalde, Jose Luis Alvarez Enparantza (known as Txillardegi) and José Mari Benito del Valle, were elected to its administrative council. A month later, *Zutik*, ETA's internal journal, published an advertisement saying that the organization could be contacted through the Euskal Idazkaritza.[53]

Labéguerie took issue with this news, contending that the Euskal Idazkaritza should not become a political instrument or the vehicle for any other group. Enbata responded by creating a committee to examine Labéguerie's complaint in July 1964. The committee was composed of two ETA members (Eneko Irigaray and the Benito del Valle) and two Enbata members (Abeberry and Burucoa). On September 14, however, Labéguerie sent Enbata a letter of resignation, stating his willingness to return whenever the group rejected the interference of any outside political interests in its activities. Ospital, too, resigned with Labéguerie,[54] and it was clear that "the break between a cultural nationalism tied to the defense of the Basque language and an extremist political nationalism was complete."[55] In sum, then, Labéguerie's own original prophecy—that Basque nationalism should develop a more political edge and that the logic of two homelands should be challenged—ultimately consumed him.

Two Homelands: The Petite Patrie *for Labéguerie*

It is true, as Larronde has claimed, that Labéguerie was a contradictory figure, but that was hardly exceptional at the time.[56] Lafitte had exercised considerable influence over Labéguerie,[57] to the extent that he inherited what might be termed a practical vision of

Basque nationalism while at the same time not completely relinquishing the notion of two homelands.

In effect, in the late 1950s, Labéguerie began to assert the importance of the *petite patrie* (the Basque Country) over the *grande patrie* (France). As such, for example, in 1965, he denounced Franco's repression of the Basques in Hegoalde and called on the inhabitants of Iparralde to protest their plight. In 1970, he praised the figure of Joseba Elosegi, who that year had carried out an act of self-immolation in front of Franco to denounce his repression of the Basques. He also organized a 1973 concert in which several noted singer-songwriters from Hegoalde appeared, and through the 1970s, he continued to protest the uneven pattern of development between the coast and the interior of Iparralde, as well as supporting a Basque cultural charter and the defending the political refugees from Hegoalde.[58]

Moreover, politically, he was still active in defense of Basque concerns: In 1971, he presided over the Union for the Defense of Basque Issues, a lobby that numbered 110 mayors and 150 local leaders among its members, the embryo of what today is the Conseil du Développement du Pays Basque (CDPB, the Development Council of the Basque Country). Indeed, in 1972, the Union for the Defense of Basque Issues played an important role in mediating with the French authorities over the plight of several refugees from Hegoalde who had taken refuge in the Baiona cathedral and had gone on hunger strike to reclaim asylum in France. And Labéguerie even attended the funeral of one member of Iparretarrak who had died when the bomb he was transporting exploded.[59] Finally, he never ceased to stress the importance of cross-border social, economic, and cultural initiatives.[60]

And in the cultural sphere, he was also a crucial figure, especially for his contribution to Basque music. According to Jean Haritschelhar, he was prominent in effecting the transformation from an earlier age, when Basque songs were basically long poems adapted to music, to a more modern song structure designed to be produced on records.[61] Moreover, many of his songs were clearly nationalist in tone.[62] Similarly, Labéguerie was also important in the realm of Basque dance, working in favor of the wider dissemination of dances from Hegoalde in Iparralde while at the same time laboring endlessly to promote local traditions "at a time when few people were interested."[63]

The result of all this was that the *petite patrie* played an exceedingly important role in the life of Labéguerie, and because of this, it is easy to see how he was involved in the emergence of Enbata. Yet, the *grande patrie* was also important.

The Grande Patrie: *Labéguerie's Role in French Politics*

Four years after leaving Enbata, Labéguerie was one of the figures behind the founding of the Mouvement Démocratique Basque (MDB, the Basque Democratic Movement). As mentioned earlier, with the advent of the Fourth Republic after World War II, the French electoral system changed, and the former power of local notables was transferred onto more formal political party structures. In Iparralde, the result was the hegemony of the MRP between 1945 and 1958. In a conservative society where, for centuries, the church had remained the dominant institution, one can see how the Christian Democracy of the MRP appealed to the electorate of Iparralde, and this was even more the case if we add the feeling of many of its members for Basque culture.

However, when the Fifth Republic was created in 1958, Gaullism became the central state ideology. In Iparralde, this led to a crisis within the MRP and the replacement of its leading figures there by supporters of the new populist state nationalism of de Gaulle. This, in turn, provoked an initial period of rapprochement between pro-Basque Christian Democrats and the early followers of Enbata. However, as relations between these two sectors cooled, a group composed of the Christian Democrats and led by Pierre Letamendia, Jean Mendiboure, and Bernard Mendisco—as well as by Labéguerie, as their principal inspiration—formed the MDB, the last attempt to create a specific political space for nonnationalist pro-Basque politics, outside the "national" (that is, French) framework of the centrist Centre Démocratique (CD, the Democratic Center) and the Gaullist UNR.[64] Thus, the MDB, or Indar Berri (New Force) as it was also known (after the name of its journal), was an attempt by some notables and members of traditional Basque elites to retain power by promoting a pro-Basque Christian Democratic discourse and by not ruling out the possibility of a potential future alliance with the nationalists of Enbata.[65]

However, one cannot separate the emergence of the MDB from that of Enbata. As Jean Paul Malherbe notes, Enbata had managed "to be innovative in the terrain of local politics. It translated a widespread Basque feeling into political terms closely tied to a politico-geographic image, so that, more and more, politicians defined themselves as regarded their position toward the Basque issue, and not just in the terms of French party politics."[66] Consequently, like Enbata, the MDB anchored its discourse in a federalism linked to the notion of a Europe of peoples.

However, as Izquierdo points out, there were differences between the two groups: the members of the MDB

> became defenders of traditional, rural Basque society. Defenders of smallholders in mountain areas, the city was, for them, the enemy to struggle against: [In the words of Bernard Mendisco,] "The Basque must be able to live in his country without having to leave or worry about destructive and contentious germs, whether Marxist or capitalist." Conservative in the timeless Basque [political] order, the MDB did no more than resist the political, economic, and social change sweeping the Basque Country and France.[67]

In effect, then, the MDB came to resemble Lafitte's Eskualerriste movement. In contrast, Enbata positioned itself at the heart of these changes, embracing more leftist ideas and forging a close relationship with ETA. Yet precisely because of this, it, too, was doomed to failure. And eventually it succumbed to the weight of an internal debate and crisis that led to its downfall.

Despite its specific characteristics, however, the MDB could not help being the "Basque section of the MRP."[68] Consequently, the ultimate failure of the MRP at a national or French level translated into the failure of this pro-Basque Christian Democratic formation in Iparralde. However, some members of the later centrist UDF (Union pour la Democratie Française, Union for French Democracy) in Iparralde retained their former Christian Democratic sensibility with regard to Basque culture, to the extent that, in the early 1990s, cordial relations were established between the UDF and the Parti Nationaliste Basque (PNB, the Basque Nationalist Party, the PNV in Iparralde)—affording the latter an importance beyond its scarce electoral presence and tardy entry into French-Basque politics. Similarly, this same politico-cultural sensibility was evident in the creation of a new nonnationalist pro-Basque political formation in Iparralde in 2002, Elgar-Ensemble, led by Labéguerie's son, Peyo.[69]

With the disappearance of the MDB, Labéguerie wandered around the margins of French politics. Although previously he had defined himself as a federalist, once he left Enbata, he publically began to proclaim his commitment to France—as in the 1967 conference of the Centre Démocratique. Despite his defection to the CD, though, that same year in the French legislative elections he lost to the Gaullist, Michel Inchauspé.[70] And while in the aftermath of this defeat he seemed to return once more to favoring the federal notion of a Europe of peoples,[71] following the events of May 1968, he shifted once more to supporting the basic structure of the French state. After failing to get elected to the National Assembly once again in 1973, he was chosen to be a senator the following year.[72] And from that time on, he served in the French senate as a defender of family values and the rural world. This, as Xabier Itzaina sees it, was a clear return to the original principles of Lafitte's Eskulaerriste movement.[73] In 1980, however, just prior to his death, Labéguerie attended the investiture of Carlos Garaikoetxea (of the PNV) as president of the Basque Autonomous Community, the first *lehendakari* to be named after the death of Franco in 1975 and during the Spanish transition to democracy.

Labéguerie was the first prominent political victim of the founding of Basque nationalism in Iparralde in the 1960s. Until that time, the pro-Basque spectrum was able to accommodate a variety of political tendencies, but with the founding of a clear nationalist alternative, the notion of two homelands was called into question. Unlike Lafitte, Dassance, Jaureguiberry, and Eugène Goyheneche, Labéguerie was forced to choose between these two clear identities—between France and the Basque Country. His original support for Enbata, a political option that these other figures did not have,[74] led him to a personal crisis that reflected the age in which he lived. That is, the emergence of a new generation challenged the cultural strategy of the previous Basque activists and, of course, the idea that one could have two homelands.

Within the rapidly evolving context marked by the activity of ETA and the events of May 1968 in Paris, this new generation almost had no time to absorb the profound ideological sea change that these new ideas implied. A storm was brewing that would eventually take with it not just Labéguerie, but also Enbata itself. Ultimately, Labéguerie opted for what he perhaps saw as the only viable path to take: a Basque cultural strategy within a French political context, the dominant choice of individuals from Garat to

Lafitte. In 1979, Labéguerie reflected on these choices in an interview with the Basque nationalist daily from Hegoalde, *Deia*:

> Why did you leave Enbata?
>
> If I left Enbata, it was not because I was against its goals, but over the question of methods.
>
> How do you see nationalism in Iparralde?
>
> In elections, few people vote for nationalism, 1 or 2 percent. However, ultimately, I think people feel nationalist deep down. Those who stand as nationalists are too young, for a start, and they have poor arguments afterward. And they only offer a leftist alternative. Yet here, people are not leftists; they might agree with these young people, but they don't like the way they go about things. We need here a nationalist party, as in Hegoalde, that is not completely left-wing. If we want to construct Europe, it is normal that the Basque Country should also want to save its identity . . . From what I know, of [all] the mayors in Iparralde, more than half, if not nationalists, are pro-Basque and love the Basque Country. But people are afraid . . . Basque people, those who might be nationalist, are rural, and this rural people say of these young people: yes, good kids. But . . . they vote in French.[75]

Was this an adequate response to the question posed twenty years earlier by the creation of Enbata? I think so, and it predicted the emergence in Iparralde of a moderate, centrist nationalist party—in effect, the appearance of the PNB to take part officially in the French Basque political process at the beginning of the 1990s.[76] Labéguerie is important for highlighting the change in thinking about Basque identity in Iparralde—that is, for revealing the transformation from purely cultural to cultural and political action and the demise of the notion of two homelands.

The Influence of ETA

The creation of Enbata had a profound effect on political life in Iparralde: Its journal was widely read, it had modest (although qualified) success with Labéguerie's election, it enjoyed a growth in membership, and it had high hopes for achieving strong municipal representation.[77]

Yet from 1963 on, a campaign to discredit Enbata emerged, based principally on the group's close relations with ETA. After the Aberri Eguna that year, for example, the monument to the fallen soldiers of the two world wars in Baiona was daubed with slogans such as "Gora Euskadi!" (Long live the Basque Country!)—the work, ultimately, of this antinationalist campaign. Enbata's response was swift and clear. It issued a statement published in the weekly, *Herria*: "This provocative act is the work of shameless party hacks who are attempting to ruin the name of Basque nationalism, trying to make [people] believe that those who love the Basque Country have no respect, even for the dead."[78] However, the notion of *Enbata zikiña* (dirty Enbata) had been planted, and it would be difficult for the newly created group to rid itself of the stigma.

Electoral Strategy

Some months later, probably because of the tensions that had emerged as a result of the problems with Labéguerie, Enbata decided to change its strategy. After an important internal debate over whether to participate in the French electoral process or not, the group decided it would. Christiane Etxalus and Ximun Haran were selected to stand for Enbata at the March 1967 legislative elections on a platform based on the Itsasu Charter and especially emphasizing the economic problems of the interior part of Iparralde. In general, the group's efforts were considerable. Arbelbide, for example, records that eighty thousand leaflets were printed with the aim of distributing them throughout all the homes of Iparralde.[79] Furthermore, fifteen thousand electoral posters were put up and over 150 meetings were organized, most of them in the rural interior. This demonstrated the group's intentions to go beyond their more obvious source of support on the coast.[80] In total, approximately fifty-six hundred people attended these meetings.

Interestingly, the results obtained were similar in the two *circonscriptions* where they stood for election:[81] Etxalus gained 1,879 votes (4.72 percent) and Haran 3,156 votes (4.57 percent). Compared with the perceived success of the campaign and the expectations that had been raised, these figures were disappointing. Various factors contributed to the disappointing returns.[82] First and foremost, a wave of Gaullist pride swept Iparralde during the campaign, marked most obviously by de Gaulle's personal endorsement of Inchauspé (a fact that his campaign did not hesitate to promote on its own election posters), but also by the visit of Georges Pompidou, the Gaullist prime minister, who arrived in Iparralde by helicopter to remind Basques of the blood they had shed in the service of France.[83] This surge in Gaullism led to Labéguerie losing his seat as deputy, although he was reelected a senator in 1976.

Then, one should also point out that the strong attendance at Enbata's meetings during the campaign did not necessarily reflect agreement with the group's ideas and was perhaps more the result of curiosity rather than of anything else. Further, many people with sympathies close to the Enbata program probably voted for other candidates during the first round to prevent an outright victory there and then.[84] It is also probably true that a female candidate, Etxalus, was not well received among the conservative population of Iparralde. Moreover, Etxalus had been recently released from a Spanish jail after serving several months for alleged collaboration with ETA, and most likely this association generated a certain fear among the electorate of Iparralde.[85]

To these reasons for the failure of Enbata at the polls, we might add a more general factor: the tendency of the electorate to vote for the political formation that promised most to guarantee local stability—that is, the same (party) notables who were so unappealing to the younger voters who favored Enbata. Finally, and unsurprisingly, the local press, the central authorities, and the other candidates also dedicated much time to raising the specter of separatism associated with Enbata, provoking fear among the population of Iparralde, who had not really had enough time to assimilate the implications of the new group's proposals.

The consequences of this electoral failure were soon apparent. Although Enbata itself publicly refused to acknowledge its defeat, an internal coup d'etat in January 1968 removed Haran from his leading position on the executive committee. Thereafter, the number of people on this committee was raised to incorporate the entrance of a younger set of activists—Etxalus, Jean-Louis Davant, and Andde Galant—and Burucoa was elected secretary general of the movement. Abeberry, the principal figure behind the removal of Haran, did not present his candidacy for the executive committee. As Etxalus later recalled, "what we did was to remove the leaders, condemning them for being political schemers and because we wanted more action. I think that explains it all."[86]

Arbelbide confirms this view and highlights the internal fratricide that led to a second political casualty (after Labéguerie), Haran.[87] He argues that two currents existed within the group. One was composed of urban, educated individuals who cared less about the political consequences of their actions and were noted for the severity of their published articles—raising ideas that distanced other, more moderate members who were less used to the politics of provocation. The central philosophy of this current was activism, designed, paradoxically, during the drawing up of Enbata's electoral strategy. The other current, principally made up of members from the interior, understood better the concerns of the rural populace. Moreover, their rural background made them more aware of the time necessary to cultivate something. As a result, and in contrast to their coastal comrades, they did not expect change to happen overnight, and through their base in Hazparne, they advocated patience. To highlight these two different currents further, there was a generational difference between them, with the younger coastal activists challenging the older leadership from the interior.[88]

As a result of these internal tensions, more and more people left Enbata, mostly explaining their decision by the group's increasing proximity to ETA. However, this did not deter those who remained from pursuing an electoral strategy. At the cantonal elections during the fall of 1967, Enbata fielded seven, predominantly young, candidates. Yet the results were even worse than the in the legislative elections, with its vote slipping from just under 5 percent to 2.56 percent of the overall vote. Following the disappointing results of the 1967, in the June 1968 legislative elections and following the French political crisis of May that year, Enbata once more presented several candidates, including Abeberry, Burucoa, Argitxu Noblia, and Manex Pagola. However, the results this time were unquestionably bad: the group received a total of 1,711 votes, or 1.58 percent of the overall poll in the districts in which it took part. In just a year, Enbata had lost two-thirds of its small electoral base.

Compared with the previous year, there was much greater hostility toward Enbata in the 1968 campaign, in great part based on a widespread fear among the inhabitants of Iparralde that this new form of Basque nationalism would bring violence to the region. Indeed, the level of hysteria was such that many people associated Enbata with being Spanish and wanting to "make Franco come here."[89] These lies and rumors even scandalized readers of Lafitte's Basque-language weekly *Herria*, who demonstrated their indignation about such accusations. However, the decreasing support for Enbata cannot be explained alone by the media campaign against it.

Rather, one should also look to the internal divisions within the group. And quite possibly the emergence of younger militants did not sit too well with the electorate. The voters of Iparralde likely did not value the combative nature of this new generation any more than what they may have interpreted as the calm astuteness of Enbata's founders. Moreover, Iparralde was once more engulfed by a wave of pro-Gaullist sympathy after the events of May 1968, a development that hardly helped the nascent Basque nationalist group. And crucially, many people were indeed extremely worried about the specter of violence, a preoccupation that was hardly allayed by the increasingly close and public relationship between Enbata and ETA.

It is impossible to judge whether this last point was the main reason for the electoral failure of Enbata. In fact, this relationship probably aided the long-term development of Basque nationalism in Iparralde. Nor is it possible to blame the failure on the group's leftist turn, because this was only really a feature of Enbata after the legislative elections of 1968. However, a combination of the above—internal differences, the relationship with ETA, the emergence of a new generation, a greater emphasis on activism, and a gradual shift to the left—probably does explain the disappointment provoked by the raised hopes generated by the group's formation and ultimately its inability to fulfill these hopes.

The Relationship with ETA

ETA did not create Enbata. In fact, Enbata was created before the first ETA refugees arrived in Iparralde. This is when the two groups started to meet. As Jakes Abeberry recalls, "ETA was born at more or less the same time as us; it was from our generation, belonged to the second wave of refugees after that of '36, and it's true that we had a lot in common. We were the godfathers of their children and vice versa."[90] Yet according to this founder of Enbata, "ETA members were never members of Enbata and vice versa. However, there were major interferences. For example, they attended our meetings. We also attended ETA's assemblies, especially Ximun Haran under a pseudonym. He took part in the second and third assemblies as an observer, while I only did so in the third . . . [So] it is true that there were strong bridges that made us friends."[91] Indeed, in February 1963, ETA and Enbata published a joint statement in Paris calling for the union of all nationalist parties in Europe, with these two groups representing the Basque Country.[92]

However, the principal "interference" of ETA was the problem with the Euskal Idazkaritza and the resignation of Labéguerie. Gradually thereafter, this organization was taken over by both Enbata and ETA, with one of ETA's founding members, Txillardegi, taking a leading role in it. Indeed, most of the money raised to underwrite the Euskal Idazkaritza came from Paco Miangolarra, a man "close to ETA's ideas."[93] The goal of this organization was clear: to use any demonstration of pro-Basque sentiment to promote Basque nationalism: "The service [offered by the Euskal Idazkaritza] was not innocent. They knew that on those festival committees [that came to the body for help] were the young people of the villages, so that by establishing relations with them, they thought they would get to know the bravest young people in the Basque Country in order to get their ideas across to them."[94]

Yet it also seems clear that there was a secret agreement between Enbata and ETA to instrumentalize the Euskal Idazkaritza for their own ends. Indeed, ETA approved a motion at its third assembly in 1964 agreeing to strengthen Enbata through seminars and the like and even proposed creating a joint "National Assembly for the Struggle." Although Abeberry agreed to this in principle and on the condition that the members of this new body would remain anonymous, most members of Enbata did not want to establish such formal links, in part because the very name proposed implied a degree of militancy for which Enbata was not yet ready. According to the official response of Enbata at the time, "the idea was favorably received, and everyone proposed another solution that would be less aggressive in nature: 'Coordinating Committee.'"[95]

Enbata, however, was worried about the increasing distance between ETA and the PNV, to the extent that it tried to maintain a series of bilateral contacts with both with the aim of underscoring its own autonomy in relation to the two other groups, and especially ETA. Yet the PNV was not happy with the increasing contacts between Enbata and ETA, leading to the withdrawal of the historic Basque nationalist party from the Aberri Eguna celebrations of 1965 and 1966.[96] However, this left Enbata with only one option as regarded establishing links with Hegoalde: ETA.

Throughout the next year, though, Enbata actually reinforced its autonomy. De Gaulle had visited Latin America in 1964 and at various places had been received by protesters displaying the insignia of both Enbata and ETA—something that Enbata had not sanctioned. As a result, in 1965, Enbata passed a motion reaffirming its independence from all other groups.[97] Thereafter, Enbata reinitiated contact with the PNV, as well as with its affiliate groups, EGI (the PNV youth wing), and ELA-STV (the PNV labor union).

While Enbata and ETA did not merge, they continued to maintain close relations. One of the key issues over which they converged was the support demonstrated by Enbata for ETA refugees in Iparralde. For example, in November 1964, the French authorities ordered the expulsion from the region of four prominent ETA members, Iulen de Madariaga, Txillardegi, Irigaray, and Benito del Valle. In turn, Enbata managed to mobilize important sectors of the population to their defense, including Errecart, Ospital, Laurent Darraidou, Jean Poulou, and Etcheverry-Ainchart. Opposing them, the prefecture (the capital of the *département*) capitalized on Enbata's role to link the group directly with ETA, with the *préfet* himself commenting that "Spaniards heat up the minds of the Frenchmen in Enbata . . . Txillardegi is the head of ETA, coauthor of the infamous book *Vasconia*, and principal editor of the weekly *Enbata*."[98] At the same time, the rising tension in Iparralde saw extra numbers of police drafted into the region and scenes never before witnessed by inhabitants there.

The tension escalated even further when, in 1965, the police entered the office of one refugee, and founder of ETA, Madariaga, finding there an old pistol that did not work.[99] This was sufficient evidence for the French authorities to charge Madariaga and his colleague Irigaray with participating in levying the so-called "revolutionary tax."[100] It seems that the two had, some days earlier, slashed the tires of a car belonging to a longtime member of the PNV, Manu de la Sota, also in exile in Iparralde, for refusing to finance ETA. The reaction of Sota (Marc Legasse's father-in-law) was to accuse the two of this act of vandalism, and they were tried and sentenced to a six-month jail sentence and a further five-year period in which they would be required to stay away from the area.

Over and above this, the discovery of Madariaga's pistol had serious consequences for Enbata, because the public in Iparralde reacted with alarm to the potential escalation of violence.[101] As a result, when Etxalus, a member of Enbata, was detained a few months later and charged with transporting explosives for ETA, the consequences for Basque nationalism in Iparralde were severe. As Arbelbide recalls: "'Explosives,' that word stayed in the heads of people . . . This damaged Enbata enormously, because it was criminalized once again before public opinion just a few weeks after Madariaga's pistol affair. As a consequence, the 700 subscribers to *Enbata* were reduced to 350. In one fell swoop, 350 subscribers were lost."[102]

Enbata remained silent over the affair for five months, and only through the efforts of its youngest members was a solidarity committee established to address the Etxalus case. When the group, through the pages of its journal, finally came out in public support of its activist, the French authorities banned two successive editions of the publication while at the same time arresting several members of the organization. Rumors even began to spread that the explosives were in fact being transported from Hegoalde to Iparralde. Finally, eight months after her original detention, Etxalus went to trial in Spain and received a four-month sentence (the prosecution had asked for twelve years). On August 13, 1966, Etxalus was finally released, by the Spanish authorities at the border.

The Etxalus issue had important consequences for Enbata:

> The first [was] good: a youth mobilization that resulted in the entrance of many young people into Enbata as reflected by [the journal], *Ekin*: "at present there is an Enbata network in almost all the junior high and high schools, especially in those in Baiona and Biarritz." In Malherbe's opinion, there were 120 young people, which would bring problems for Enbata, needing a balance between older and younger people—something that is not always possible in Iparralde.[103]

Yet there were negative consequences, too: "nationalism was criminalized . . . in the eyes of the people for being linked with the issue of guns, among other things . . . something that Paris made use of to block the road of nationalism, criminalizing it and reducing it to nothing."[104]

At the same time, the relations between Enbata and ETA alienated those pro-Basque notables who initially had taken some interest in the new nationalist group. Together with the growth through the 1960s of Gaullist French nationalism, the failure of the pro-Basque alternative, the MDB, and the need of such notables to embrace the French political system as a means of safeguarding their own power, this ended any possibility of collaboration.

Finally, Enbata imploded, with the loss of many of its early members. After the departure of Labéguerie and Haran, many more followed in the wake of the events of 1967. One of these explained this decision as resulting from Enbata's "electoral orientation," the "systematic refusal by some Enbata leaders to denounce the secret ETA-Enbata agreements on the management of the Euskal Idazkaritza," and the "harmful relations between certain leaders and ETA members, whose Marxist-Leninist ideology has been denounced by its leaders themselves and its delegates in the Americas."[105]

According to Abeberry, however,

> to say that the relationship between Enbata and ETA held back the movement, I don't believe it all ... ETA slowed down our growth, certainly, a little, because it brought the image of major repression to nationalism ... But, on the other hand, I think it helped us enormously, laying the ground for agreements between nationalists that would hold strong: [such as] a reinforcing of our belief in a unified Basque Country, and so on. If there had been no ETA, there was a strong possibility we would have turned into a kind of regionalist movement, like that of the Basque advocates in the Eskualzaleen Biltzarra, for example.[106]

Similarly, this connection did in fact encourage more young people to join Enbata:

> It gave a young eighteen-year-old another motive, to have something "secret" in Iparralde ... knowing they were taking part in a high-level struggle ... When they first passed through a PAF [Police de l'Air et des Frontières, the French border police] control, and then another by the [Spanish] Guardia Civil, they felt emotions unrivalled by [for example] the days and hours spent in the *Gau Eskola* [a night school for learning Basque]; even more, knowing that, thanks to this shipment, an act or two might be committed. Safeguarding an [ETA] cell at home, living with them, [young people] found an experience they didn't have paying the annual fee of the magazine.[107]

In this context, then, Enbata enjoyed a rising level of support among young people, but the very dynamic of this activism imbued the group with a frenetic pace that ultimately contributed much to its downfall, especially after the second major defeat in the 1968 legislative elections. Yet for all its internal weaknesses, the defining moment that marked the downfall of Enbata was May 1968 and all that this implied for France as a whole.

For several months after the June 1968 legislative elections, Enbata's eponymous weekly journal failed to appear. When it did reappear, in October of that same year, it recognized the group's own shortcomings while outlining what it saw as the necessity of following a new policy strategy. In defining this strategy, it fell back on severe criticism of those pro-Basque notables who had originally been close to the group: "As in all colonies, imperialism recruits its auxiliaries ... Our official elites, some of whom might, at heart, share our patriotism, nevertheless participate in the bourgeois society of the winner. And despite the example we have given them with an ambition and courage dedicated exclusively to the service of our people, our elites only dream of careers in Paris."[108] As we can see, the discourse had changed. Where previously the ideological debate in Enbata had shifted between federalism and separatism, the events of May 1968 had provoked another ideological turn—this time, in another direction, to the left.

May 1968: Internal Differences and a Leftist Turn

The public reappearance of Enbata through publication, once more, of its journal was marked by even closer ties to ETA than before. This was also reflective of ETA's strategy of forging as many links with other Basque nationalist groups as possible. Indeed, in many respects, the ideological debates within ETA in the period through to 1975 were translated almost directly into the context of Iparralde, as well. That is, the internal differences that marked ETA also came to haunt Enbata.[109] While leftist and progressive ideas existed in Hegoalde outside the nationalist tradition, in Iparralde, there had been no such movement. This left the young nationalists of Enbata having to make up this new socialist ideology as they went along. To a certain extent, they were aided in this by the student uprising in Paris in May 1968, but this was also a double-edged sword, because nationalists in Iparralde were thereafter forced to find some kind of ideological accommodation with the extreme French left, as well as with ETA. So while a progressive discourse marked Enbata's evolution, it could not match that of other, more ideologically defined competitors.

The Evolution of Enbata

Christiane Etxalus recalls the basic common denominator that unified Enbata's members: "Like anywhere else, there were several tendencies. Some were more or less leftists, others, Christian Democrats. And the fusion of all this was the small catechism that was European federalism."[110] Similarly, according to Davant, "the ideological justification for this whole dynamic was centered on federalism, a federalism that, in itself, was at the beginning anarchic, instinctive, [and] perhaps enriched by Proudhonian inspiration. And it was nourished by the industrial cooperative ideology of Mondragón."[111]

According to Jacob, however, Enbata's shift to the left was more the result of ETA's influence.[112] Citing a later article by Haran,[113] he states that by 1967, there were two tendencies within Enbata: one driven by those who were attempting to focus the group's efforts on issues relating to the local context of Iparralde and the other by the new, younger activists who eventually took control of the organization and who believed in supporting the struggle of ETA. Consequently, when Enbata resurfaced publicly in the fall of 1968, its new leadership was forced to define its ideological position clearly. In the issue of *Enbata* published in October 1968, an interview with ETA appeared that took on the appearance of a lecture directed at Basque nationalists in Iparralde, together with a proposal to create a common national liberation front.

From this moment on, Enbata became increasingly embroiled in an internal ideological debate that mirrored the internal discussion of ETA through the 1970s. Between the two poles—one focusing more on a general social revolution in which the national struggle would follow, the other giving primacy to the national struggle first and foremost—Enbata's stance was clear:

> If we can have both [an independent] Basque Country and socialism, it would be better. But if we play the game of "all or nothing," we risk achieving neither one nor the other. On the other hand, seeking as a first step the creation of a [distinct] Basque [political] power—without abandoning, however, the social struggle, quite the contrary, in fact, for the two are connected—we have every chance of installing a socialism adapted to our personality.[114]

This position was maintained at least through 1971, when it was stated that "for the whole Basque Country, Enbata suggests a Basque National Front that regroups all nationalist groups and the social classes that make it up: workers, peasants, intellectuals, [and] the national bourgeoisie."[115]

Thus, Enbata fixed the ideological points on which any technical alliance with the group would be based: national liberation and the unification of the seven provinces within the framework of a United States of Europe, the cultural unification of the Basque people, based on Euskara, freedom for all political parties and labor unions in a democratic Basque state, the socialization of the media, and democratic planning for the economy—in sum, a posture similar to that of ETA-V at the same time (discussed below), the sector that would evolve into ETA (m).

As Davant observes, this progressive evolution of Enbata was most evident in the practical ways that the group sought to get its message across,[116] including the distribution of tens of thousands of leaflets in 1971 outside factories, schools, and so on. At the same time, Enbata came out in support of the working-class struggle and publicly celebrated, for the first time, on May 1, the international day of solidarity with workers: "We, Basques, before being exploited by capitalism, were exploited by the French (and Spanish) state, something that predates capitalism."[117] A year later, in 1972, Enbata reaffirmed its priority of national liberation over social liberation in a long policy statement emphasizing the need to give priority to the safeguarding of "our culture, our language."[118] Furthermore, in the 1973 Aberri Eguna celebration, the text written for the event by the organizing committee (including representation by Enbata) reflected the ideological development of Basque nationalism in Iparralde. Drawn up in an immediate context that had witnessed the death of an ETA activist, Eustakio Mendizabal (Txikia), at the hands of the Spanish police, the text read, in part, as follows: "Aberri Eguna. A symbolic day. The day the Basque people have chosen to call attention to their existence, not just to produce or enrich those who exploit it, but to achieve power... This year, too, Easter Sunday, we fishermen and peasants, we school kids and students, meet [here] to have our say. Because they have tried to take this away from us."[119] After detailing specific problems and aspects of the struggle, the text concludes: "In Donibane Garazi...

we want to show the chains that bind our ankles and gain the force to break them . . . We reaffirm our status as Basque workers."[120]

The transformation was complete. By 1973—the year that the cell headed previously by Txikia had assassinated Admiral Carrero Blanco, Franco's right-hand man and chosen successor to lead the Spanish dictatorship after his own demise and the year that Iparretarrak, a group dedicated to using violence to achieve national liberation in Iparralde emerged—Enbata had become explicitly left wing. And the latter of these contextual events would, in particular, thereafter force Enbata to clarify its position over the use of arms in the struggle for national liberation.

Basque Nationalist Socialization in Iparralde: From Amaia to Ezker Berri

Some Basque nationalists themselves argue that the Basque nationalist right was born with the creation of Amaia (The End) in the summer of 1968. However, behind this accusation, Bixente Vrignon contends, there lies a difference of opinion over this new group's supposed objectives and methods.[121]

In fact, Amaia cultivated an apolitical approach that allowed it to enter Basque political and cultural life without being stigmatized, even given the fact that many of its members were actively participating in the major issues of the day, such as aid for the ETA refugees in Iparralde. Amaia reaffirmed a cultural basis for nationalist strategies in Iparralde that had been progressively lost through the 1960s. It created a subgroup, Lauburu (literally meaning 'four heads', the name of a traditional Basque symbol), to coordinate this cultural activity, and despite the wide spectrum of the organization's objectives, it remained sufficiently focused on its central goal: to corner the market on positions with decision-making authority over socio-economic questions and to work in society without losing its ideals but, equally, without succumbing to one political label. This latter point, in particular, marked out Amaia's difference from Enbata.[122] It also marked the group as susceptible to being charged with being right wing. However, there was no outright ideological orientation in Amaia (publicly, at least) along the parameters of right or left. According to one of its members, Mattin Larzabal, "there was no revolutionary Romanticism in Amaia; on the contrary, it was not a question of breaking with, but integrating into society."[123] For this very reason, many young people were suspicious of the new group, accusing it of rightist leanings.

However, Amaia, too, succumbed to the leftist currents sweeping Iparralde at the time.[124] As Mattin Larzabal recalls:

> The sections had already been created by the beginning of 1968. The objective—and only thanks to the passing of time do I remember it—was to have people, organized leaders to be ready, should one day the opportunity present itself to take power. It was necessary to instruct people about their history, the geography, culture, and economy of the Basque Country, but also in the sciences, mathematics, and all that. The second objective was the creation of an economic network for Iparralde. This might seem a little strange, but one should highlight the hemorrhage of young people [at that time] who were forced to leave

Iparralde in search of work. Amaia's discourse was clear: Enough of outside bosses coming in while young people here without qualifications had to leave! Let's create our own network![125]

This emphasis on constant activism—work and sacrifice, sometimes promoted from a less than democratic internal leadership base—resulted in some of the group's members challenging its leaders.[126] And this, together with similar problems that had blighted Enbata (internal and personal differences, for example) ultimately led to the group's downfall.

After the break-up of Amaia, many of its members joined extreme left-wing groups, while others joined yet another project, Mende Berri (New Century). Despite Amaia's ultimate organizational failure, its ideas—which were initially very successful in attracting people—thus survived: for example, the concept of ideas as themselves socializing and the tactic of organizing cultural festivals, lectures, and so on. Even Enbata confessed in 1971 that Amaia had opened up new options: "between Amaia and (still unorganized) leftist positions, there is a space for Enbata."[127]

Similarly, as Jacob (following Malherbe) notes, Amaia's internal discipline and logic of sacrifice were important in encouraging other groups to form. Increasingly, these splinter groups embraced the use of violence in their struggle, and Jacob observes that many of the internal tensions that characterized both ETA and Enbata during the same period were repeated once more, for example, between some activists who were fascinated by guerrilla logic and saw themselves as latter day Robin Hoods and others who saw this as pure elitism—once again, then, the seeds of a debate sprouted over the comparative merits of a struggle for national or social liberation.[128]

Mende Berri filled the space vacated by Amaia, and this successor was ultimately more successful in achieving some of the goals associated with its forebear. Indeed, prominent among the founders of Mende Berri were former members of Amaia, such as Gabi Ohiarzabal. His ideological position was in many ways defined by his critique of Enbata. Mende Berri believed of Enbata that "even if it managed to raise the Basque issue politically, it has not been credible. Its electoral failures and refusal to organize itself internally drove many young to abandon the movement, whether choosing to retire [from political activity altogether], or joining French leftist parties, or embracing a new strategy."[129] In other words, the founders of the new group were trying to overcome an impasse in the Basque nationalist movement in Iparralde and were searching for a more universal and direct way of disseminating their ideas. As a result, Mende Berri was created with a specific focus: Use cultural and other means to raise Basque nationalist consciousness among young people in Iparralde.

This led to a thorough socialization process on the part of Mende Berri. For example, the musical duo Pantxo Ospital and Peio Carrera (popularly known as "Pantxo ta Peio," Pantxo and Peio) brought out their first record on the Mende Berri label. And the organization also began a systematic campaign of encouraging the learning of Basque, organizing courses and initiatives that might reasonably be considered the embryo of the later AEK movement in Iparralde.[130] As one member of Mende Berri, Arnaud Duny

Pétré, characterized these efforts, "it was groundwork to create a new Basque nationalism: The urgency was there; go and find nationalists and convert them into leaders." In fact, it would appear that the vanguard dimension of Amaia was maintained in Mende Berri: "For us, the goal was clear: It was a question of using the foundation of culture to sensitize young people to Basque nationalism . . . The logic of Mende Berri was more or less: recruit, sensitize, shape."[131] Moreover, in this search to extend the means for socializing the youth of Iparralde, the role of the Clubes Pays Basque (Clubs of the Basque Country) was crucial. They were founded in every high school with the goal of extending knowledge about the Basque Country.[132]

However, tensions arising from the porous boundary between cultural and political work soon surfaced, resulting, perhaps unsurprisingly, in the creation of Euskal Gogoa (Basque Spirit), a more politicized splinter group dedicated to aiding refugees from the South, in 1972. Actually, for a while, both groups worked side by side and attempted to approximate their structures to the common space of the Clubes Pays Basque. In particular, Euskal Gogoa insisted on taking control of the formation of political ideas and tended to emphasize class struggle, but the differences between the two could not be resolved, and Mende Berri itself began a more politicized or ideological course from about 1973 on.[133]

At root, Mende Berri was important for raising Basque consciousness among the youth of Iparralde at that time.[134] The Clubes Pays Basque were ultimately important breeding grounds for future activists. This was the case, for example, of Jakes Bortairu:

> I entered the nationalist movement mainly because of the alarm bells of support for the refugees. I had taken part in the Clubes Pays Basque, but had gone no further. At the beginning, I joined because of specific struggles. There was a hunger strike that lasted a month or two, with a huge mobilization, protests, demonstrations, and then it disappeared and there was nothing. We lost all contact [and] didn't know where to go or what to do; there was the Mende Berri store in Bourgneuf street [in Baiona]; it was the only nationalist spot, with some bars. We wanted to get into the movement, but had no idea who to ask.[135]

Indeed, the repressive measures leveled at Basque political refugees from Hegoalde by the French authorities were in great part the most important single socializing factor among this new, younger generation of Basque nationalists. Yet precisely because of this, there was also a lack of local reference points on which to build the nationalist movement in Iparralde. In fact, the local or specific dimension of nationalist activism in Iparralde had been increasingly subdued, faced with the context of the drama in Hegoalde—the Franco regime, ETA—that such young people were witnessing. The result of this was that, increasingly, young people began to assume the struggle of Hegoalde as their own. And this found concrete expression in yet another splinter group emerging from Mende Berri: Ezker Berri (New Left), a group dedicated to a more political form of activism based on the symbolism created by ETA.[136] The wave of protest associated with the activity of both ETA-V and ETA-VI at this time would have the result of encouraging a greater militancy among the younger nationalists of Iparralde, a tendency that would evolve into the creation of Iparretarrak.[137]

Ezker Berri explored new social and political ground previously untouched by the nationalist movement in Iparralde: the struggle for the rights of homosexuals, feminism, environmentalism, the antinuclear movement, and so on. The transformation of old social movements split by societal change into new social challenges and struggles was evident in the labors of both Mendi Berri and Ezker Berri.[138] However, these movements were unable to break the dynamic of internal tensions and divisions provoked in large part by the transformation of youthful idealism into a more mature activism. To complicate matters, as Arnaud Duny Pétré recalls, "each time the nationalist movement enters a crisis, one finds the causes in issues from Iparralde itself, international issues, and those that come from the South [Hegoalde]."[139]

From May 1968 to the Executions of 1975: The Competition with the Extreme Left

Together with the dynamic of Basque nationalism from Hegoalde—and especially, in the period under discussion here, the role of ETA—Basque nationalism in Iparralde also had to contend with the rise of leftist ideas in the wake of the events of May 1968. Basque nationalism in Iparralde was initially influenced in a leftward shift by its contacts with ETA and specifically by the Marxist turn that accompanied the latter's fifth assembly, held during 1966 and 1967. While the ETA-V faction, which took its name from this assembly, stressed the primacy of the struggle for national liberation, ETA-VI, formed after the next assembly, insisted on defining that struggle in Marxist-Leninist, not nationalist terms.[140] This split was translated to Iparralde. In fact, this was the precise moment when activists from the North—from Enbata to Mende Berri—could join the struggle of those from the South in the wave of protest that began to emerge around 1970. Very soon, a leftist logic became ingrained within Basque nationalism in Iparralde, although, as Jean Lissar recalls, this logic was not entirely exempt from its own contradictions:[141]

> We went to the Aberri Eguna in Donibane Lohizune (in 1971) and shouted "Long live the Red Basque Country!" It was a fundamental difference for us. It's a little anecdotal, but a demonstration that we were there for the same reasons as the nationalists, something that was not always well understood. In fact, Monzón's wife approached us to ask us why we had done this. For us, just being there was a sufficient response.[142]

In fact, the leftist evolution apparent within Mende Berri and Ezker Berri was, for all intents and purposes, unstoppable. As noted, Basque nationalists from Iparralde took part, for the first time, in the 1972 May 1 celebration. A few weeks later, on the occasion of a visit by Spanish authorities to the border village of Urepele (Urepel) in Nafarroa Beherea, some young activists draped a Basque flag on the church steeple while at the same time handing out leaflets denouncing the forced migration of people from Iparralde. And all the while, articles in *Enbata* continued to criticize the dominant model of economic development in Iparralde: tourism. In 1972, a group of people created the Jazar association in Donibane Lohizune. Thereafter, it developed a campaign to protest against the model of tourist development and especially its role in deindustrializing Iparralde, a critique, moreover, aimed from a clearly progressive position: "Tourism is class tourism: It is designed for people with means, through the development of marinas and luxury residences beside the ocean. This tourism is forced on us by plans about which we have no democratic way of giving our opinion. This tourism, ultimately, is one factor in de-Basquization, both cultural and linguistic."[143]

Furthermore, in September 1975, the trial of two ETA members, Juan Paredes Manot ("Txiki") and Angel Otaegi, together with three members of the revolutionary leftist FRAP (Frente Revolucionario Antifascista y Patriota, Revolutionary Anti-Fascist and Patriotic Front) in Spain—all of them eventually sentenced to execution—provoked widespread disapproval in Iparralde, with Basque nationalists and leftists protesting together against the Spanish authorities. As part of this protest, minor incidents of violence were recorded: A Spanish train was derailed in Ziburu, and a small incendiary device was placed in the Spanish school in Biarritz.

The origins of this Basque nationalist and leftist protest can be found in what is termed "the Burgos Trial": the trial of several activists associated with ETA that began in late 1970 and that provoked widespread international condemnation when six of them were sentenced to death (although these were later commuted to life sentences in jail). Between the Burgos Trial and the executions of Txiki and Otaegi, Basque nationalism in Iparralde became clearly more leftist. As Enbata observed during the Burgos Trial:

> The occasion is favorable for parties of the left, as well as French and Spanish labor unions, to exploit these events of national importance to the Basque Country, to dress the struggle of Basque patriots as only an anti-imperialist and anti-Fascist [one]. *L'Humanité* [a left-wing French journal] . . . speaks of the trial of "16 Basque anti-Fascists" as if they had risked their lives to only defeat "Fascism." We proclaim loudly that these prisoners . . . fight, before anything else, for a unified Basque Country free of all colonialism.[144]

Before May 1968, there were few left-wing activists in Baiona, but thereafter, numerous groups began to emerge.[145] Within this context of developing left-wing organization, the events unfolding in Franco's Spain served as a pretext for generating more and more political mobilization—a situation that also led to rising tension between the different militant groups. For example, on December 10, 1970, fifteen hundred people marched in Baiona in a demonstration organized jointly by Basque nationalists and leftists, including Enbata, ETA, French Socialists, and Communists. Four days later, these same Basque nationalists attended a protest organized by leftists in Donibane Lohizune to which they had not been invited, waving Basque flags and shouting slogans in Euskara—a fact that did not go down well among the organizers, who saw them taking over what had been planned as an anti-Fascist rally.[146] On December 29, however, the biggest protest of its kind involved both Basque nationalists and leftists, with ten thousand people marching through the streets of Baiona, and fifteen hundred in Maule to protest the Burgos Trial. According to Vrignon,

> The weather conditions did not help at all, because the demonstration took place in the streets of Baiona under an intense rainfall and was broken up . . . by tear gas, used for the first time in Baiona, after a Spanish flag had been burned. For the nationalist organizers, the trial had important repercussions: It was the first proof that it was possible to mobilize the population of Iparralde around an issue and some precise goals and that it was possible to work with other nonnationalist groups, as well as get the attention of international public opinion, which was major publicity for the nationalist struggle. And although the media were principally interested in ETA, the northern organizations also tried to get their voice heard.[147]

Thereafter, as noted, nationalists and leftists continued to work together through to 1975. Subsequently, however, it was the former who retained the activist dynamic, while the latter gradually lost their wider appeal in Iparralde.

The period between 1970 and 1975—in large part characterized by the defense of Basque political refugees from Hegoalde—thus also had important results for the nationalist movement in Iparralde, beyond its own process of socialization. On the one hand, the internal tensions within ETA were increasingly repeated among the nationalist groups of Iparralde. On the other, the increasing influence of southern concerns weakened the ability of northern nationalism to address its own "local" issues. Finally, the increasing influence of ETA ultimately led to the emergence of a violent strand of nationalism in Iparralde, too.

In addition, with the violent turn of ETA in 1968, a new cycle of repression began in Hegoalde, resulting in an increasing number of political refugees fleeing Franco's Spain into Iparralde. Despite a tradition of offering political exile in France, the authorities there did not look favorably on these refugees. Even before ETA had initiated its violent campaign, four of its members were expelled in 1962, as was Krutwig in 1964. In 1965, Madariaga and Irigaray were sent to jail, while Txillardegi and Benito del Valle were expelled from France, and in 1967, still more ETA members were expelled from French territory. Despite an international wave of sympathy for the defendants in the Burgos Trial, France continued this policy into the early 1970s, with various arrests, imprisonments and expulsions. And on September 9, 1972, France officially banned ETA, resulting in the group going underground thereafter on French soil. In response, Basque nationalism in Iparralde became more radical, with widespread demonstrations, including hunger strikes in the Baiona cathedral and protests in front of the Spanish consulate in the same city.

In 1974, on the occasion of a forty-eight-hour hunger strike in the Baiona cathedral, Enbata had been called on to play a supporting role in the mobilization—a task it did not accept. At that point, and to the surprise of all, the French government decided to ban Enbata, together with three other leftist groups. According to Davant, a first-hand witness to these events, "in this uncertainty, amplified by the cynicism of the government and the indifference of other nationalists, the twenty or so members [of Enbata] that met every Monday stopped all activity for the moment."[148] In referring to the indifference of other nationalists, Davant means Euskal Gogoa (which had organized the hunger strike), Mende Berri, Ezker Berri, Jazar, and even IK (Iparretarrak)—in effect, all the groups that had emerged out of Enbata. That same year witnessed the violent turn of Basque nationalism. On February 22, 1974, there were arson attacks on two premises belonging to the daily *Sud-Ouest* by the group Abertzale Guzien Oldarra (United Nationalists' Revolt).

As Vrignon has said, "most actors in this period recognize having been politically shaped, in large or some part, by the refugees they met. The struggle in defense of the refugees, starting with the Burgos Trial, would be, for a long time, the central focus of the [nationalist] movement [in Iparralde]; it was around this that all the nationalists converged."[149]

Yet the presence of ETA refugees in Iparralde had contradictory implications for Basque nationalism there, not unlike the effect of refugees from the Spanish Civil War in the 1930s and 1940s. Once more, the border was shown to be porous, a symbol of the underlying unity of the Basque Country, with nationalist symbolism from Hegoalde playing an increasingly important role in Iparralde, a symbolism strengthened by the arrival, in person, of ETA refugees from the South. And while the presence of ETA militants could have made the development of nationalism in Iparralde more complicated (and probably did, to some extent), ultimately, it served to "fill up the nationalist car with gas." Thus, according to Jakes Bortairu,

> This was a very important route for us, to get involved in the nationalist movement. At the beginning, we saw in the support [for the refugees] and the hunger strikes a democratic struggle, the right of Basques to live here, the struggle against the control of their movements, and all that, but ultimately, we discovered the nationalist struggle. Yes, it allowed for an important process of consciousness raising that allowed us to see how the French government also used repressive methods here.[150]

However, although ETA kick-started nationalism in Iparralde, once underway, nationalism there could not follow its own course. It was prevented from developing a local strategy more suited to the needs of the environment out of which it emerged. Given the historical evolution of nationalism in Iparralde—with the early importation of debates and internal tensions from the South into an embryonic and confused movement in the North—this is, perhaps, understandable. Similarly, the repressive actions of the authorities actually encouraged Basque nationalism to take root in Iparralde, but at the same time also stunted its future growth for the same reasons as those alluded to above: Once more, it was forced to take a detour from the more logical path of its local context.

To take one specific example, the success of the protest against the Burgos Trial also demonstrated that, in specific issues, the population of Iparralde could be rallied to a single cause and that nationalists and progressive sectors could work together. It also demonstrated the key role that sympathy for persecuted ETA activists could have in fomenting nationalist socialization in the North. Yet it showed that nationalism in

Iparralde was to a great extent subject to developments in the South (and specifically to what happened to ETA), as well as to the repressive policies of the authorities—in this case, Spanish, but in other examples, French, too.

Arbelbide recalls that there was no option for activists in Iparralde at this time but to aid the refugees from Hegoalde, while at the same time recalling the fascination of young people in the North for what was happening in the South: "The nationalist world [here] has imitated ETA . . . [and] we take Hegoalde as an example. What is good there must be [good] here, too. What is not done there is not done here. If they shout "Gora ETA!" [Long live ETA!] in the streets of Hegoalde, the same shout [is heard] in Baiona, Donibane Lohizune, and [Donibane] Garazi. Yet Iparralde is not Hegoalde!"[151] In the next chapter I will explore yet another feature of this imitation: the recourse to violence.

CHAPTER TEN

The Storm

On December 20, 1973, an ETA cell (named Txikia after its former commander) assassinated the Spanish prime minister, Admiral Carrero Blanco, reputedly the man who had been chosen by Franco to succeed him as dictator of Spain.[1] A week later, the robbery of some financial records in Banka (Banca), Nafarroa Beherea, was claimed by a new clandestine group, Iparretarrak (IK). Just as one might translate the Basque word *enbata* into English as "a wind preceding a storm," *Ekaitza*, a newspaper associated with the EMA (Ezkerreko Mugimendu Abertzalea; the Basque Patriotic Movement of the Left), a group close to Iparretarrak (IK), took its name from the Basque for "storm" itself. The prophecy of Enbata thus was fulfilled by the creation of IK.

However, it was a further three years before IK began to carry out acts of sabotage against businesses associated with tourism and French administrative centers. In the intervening period, there had been a number of popular mobilizations in favor of political refugees from Hegoalde and, in some cases, acts of violence associated with the arrests of Basque nationalists in Iparralde. It was at this very moment that the French authorities outlawed Enbata, a movement that James E. Jacob regards as "one of the most coherent examples of Basque political mobilization since the French Revolution," mainly because of "its deliberate decision to transcend the conservative and clerical regionalism which had characterized Basque politics in France since the early Third Republic."[2] However, the group's suspension provoked little popular reaction in what Jacob terms the "artificial" calm that settled over Iparralde: "the calm before the growing storm to come."[3]

In fact, just two months later, a new organization was founded that attempted to unite all the different Basque nationalist and progressive sectors in Iparralde: the Herriko Alderdi Sozialista (Popular Socialist Party, HAS). However, it was unsuccessful in this objective, because most of the existing nationalist groups at that time remained locked into an activist, antisystem logic whose roots lay in May 1968 and were deeply suspicious of what they perceived to be the overly rigid structure and ideological dynamic of the party politics proposed by HAS. Moreover, HAS's rejection of violence also undermined its appeal at a time when many young Basque nationalist activists were beginning to sympathize with the tactics of IK.

As a consequence, HAS—which subsequently became EHAS (Euskal Herriko Alderdi Sozialista, the Socialist Party of the Basque Country)—failed to generate any significant level of support. Instead, the new protagonists of Basque nationalism in Iparralde appeared to be the so-called Xan Committees, named after Jean-Claude "Xan" Marguirault, the first person arrested for ties to IK. As a result of the arrest, a committee was created to coordinate his defense, and this organization subsequently developed into the Xan Committees, cells sympathetic with the strategy of IK that were later renamed Herri Taldeak (Popular Groups). Interestingly, however, at that same moment, political circles close to ETA in Hegoalde decided that the use of violence in Iparralde would be counterproductive to their own strategy in the South. Once again, a North-South split undermined the potential of a united Basque nationalist movement on both sides of the border.

In order to understand this complex situation and the interplay between IK and HAS/EHAS, I will first examine the debates that took place in nationalist circles through the 1970s in Iparralde over the use of violence. I will then explore in more detail the ideological foundations of HAS/EHAS, paying special attention to its attempts to forge a cross-border movement, as well as to its ultimate electoral failure and relations with other nationalist groups. Finally, I will trace the development of Basque nationalism in Iparralde from the ashes of HAS/EHAS through the role of the Xan Committees and the parallel emergence of IK, concluding with an evaluation of the differences between this latter organization and ETA.

Iparretarrak and the Question of Violence

Although there had been sporadic minor incidences of politically motivated violence in Iparralde since 1970, the first major incident of this kind occurred on September 16, 1972, when a bomb exploded in the subprefecture buildings (the administrative headquarters of central state authority) in Baiona. No group claimed responsibility for the bomb, although it served to introduce a debate about the use of violence within Basque nationalism in Iparralde.

The Debate over the Question of Violence: Between Ethics and Tactics

The potential use of violence had been rejected by most Basque nationalists in Iparralde during the 1960s for two reasons. From an ethical point of view, several members of Enbata had clearly stated their opposition to the use of the violence in the wake of the events of May 1968. However, violence had been even more clearly rejected for tactical reasons, on the grounds that such a turn would alienate support for nationalist positions. As a result, a nonviolent but activist strand of Basque nationalism, fully devoted to direct-action tactics, emerged that would later evolve into the activity of the agricultural labor union ELB (Euskal Laborarien Batasuna, the Basque Workers' Union, (later renamed

Euskal Herriko Laborarien Batasuna, the United Workers of the Basque Country) and the Demo movement. In January 1969, *Enbata* observed that

> when the heroism demanded by nonviolence disappears, [only] violence remains . . . Yet, as a result, the principles of intelligent action are rarely observed, to such an extent that . . . violence leads to an escalation and the victory of the strongest . . . Violence motivated by the desire for revenge and hatred is scarcely effective and often disastrous. It implies an added risk: incurring the condemnation of patriots themselves, as has been evident in the Manzanas incident.[4]

This was, in effect, the same position adopted by HAS/EHAS since its founding, a position taken after an internal debate provoked by the emergence of IK. This debate centered on the question of whether violence was the only means of achieving national liberation. The answer for HAS/EHAS was no, because there were obvious differences between Hegoalde and Iparralde:

> The northern Basque Country is different from the southern Basque Country . . . In the North . . . violence would lead to repression, but against whom? Against a minority that people there still understand only very little; or, to be a factor in consciousness raising, repression must affect all groups. Furthermore, it is an open invitation to activity by fascist or irresponsible collectives who might easily carry out any kind of assassination whose awful nature could be used to discredit the revolutionaries, even if they denied any part in it. In conclusion, considering everything objectively, the recourse to violence at present in the northern Basque Country would be simply a political mistake.[5]

HAS/EHAS, then, opposed the use of violence on the grounds that it would lead to greater state repression, but also because any reference to the "successful" strategy of ETA implied denying the different characteristics of Iparralde and Hegoalde. As Jacob observes, from a Marxist-Leninist viewpoint,[6] HAS/EHAS believed "that violence must emanate from the support of the working class and that a premature use of violence might turn the working classes against an isolated Basque movement."[7] Thus, for HAS/EHAS, "For the use of violence in Euskadi North any reference to Euskadi South is absurd," and the "great danger is that a 'politics of rupture' theoretically engaged against 'the system' may become, in practice, a rupture pure and simple with the people."[8]

"Opportunities" for Violence

IK began its activity in 1973, but it is worth underscoring that two other groups advocating the use of violence also emerged during the same period: Euskal Zuzentasuna (EZ, Basque Justice) and Hordago! (All or Nothing!).[9] Most experts on social movements agree in classifying France as one of those states that, in completely closing down any space to challenge the basis of the state itself, together with a frequent recourse to the use of repression, provoke periodically violent responses on the part of different groups, and indeed, such responses have been a feature of French political life since 1789.[10] This at least partly explains the emergence of IK in the 1970s.[11]

The emergence of Iparretarrak was also conditioned by the founding and growth of nationalism in Iparralde as a whole—that is, by the development of Basque nationalism there during the third wave of peripheral nationalist movements in Europe. This wave was characterized by a progressive dimension lacking in more populist movements born at the beginning of the twentieth century, as well as by certain other key differences: a more utopian, forward-looking outlook than previous movements that had anchored their ideologies in remote origins and the past, an antiauthoritarian dimension born as a result of the struggles of may 1968, and a complete rejection of racial elements as a consequence of the effects of Nazism in Europe.[12]

Together with these more general structural influences, the emergence of IK depended on a number of conditions stemming from the specific historical conjuncture of Iparralde at that time—some of which are listed by Jacob as "demonstrator influences."[13] One of these to which I have already alluded was the trauma of decolonization for France. In other words, during the mid-1960s, as a direct result of the process of decolonization, the chimera of an eternal *Grande France* was seriously under threat. This, in turn, resulted in an ideological transformation within the Parti Socialiste (PS, Socialist Party) during the mid-1970s advocating a more favorable policy toward minority or regionalist demands, one consequence of which was the support of HAS for François Mitterand, the PS candidate, in the 1974 presidential elections.

It is likely, moreover, that the theories about internal colonialism advocated more generally in France by Lafont and specifically in the Basque Country by Krutwig conditioned this new context. The notion of Iparralde as an internal colony was assimilated by Basque nationalists. Indeed, in light of the successful path to independence paved by national liberation movements in the former colonies, it should come as no surprise to learn that the notion of armed struggle gained more and more acceptance among nationalist sectors, not only in Iparralde, but also in Brittany, Occitania, and Corsica.

Yet another influence of the time that I have already mentioned was the effect of May 1968 on young nationalists in Iparralde. Indeed, the failure of a so-called conventional strategy to change center-periphery relations in Iparralde—the strategy represented by Enbata—could well explain why some young activists there became disposed toward methods associated with more direct action. Once this activist logic was assumed, the addition of an ideological turn incorporating the notion of suffering and a mythical recourse to clandestine activity led to the possibility of taking up arms in defense of their cause.

The Influence of ETA

The most obvious factor in encouraging the emergence of IK, however, was the seductive and mystical way in which the activity of ETA appealed increasingly to young people in Iparralde.[14] As Jakes Bortairu, a young activist and member of Hordago! at that time, recalls,

In 1975, there were important social struggles surrounding the fishing industry, the environment, and, later, the campaign in favor of Txiki and Otaegi and the FRAP members. I think it was that summer when we broke a taboo. Until then, demonstrations had to be peaceful ... [Later] we began to organize a few more violent things in the demos, having a go back at the police, and as a result, the barricades, [Molotov] cocktails and things like that came into being. We thought that we had to take up violence. IK was, at the time, inactive.[15]

IK members themselves also believe that they were mostly influenced by ETA—that is, that the conditions existed for the armed struggle to be extended to the North. As such, the important social network made up by various Basque nationalist cultural and antirepression groups acted as a kind of ideological framework within which to generate a community of legitimation that all armed organizations need to consolidate their cause.[16]

This leads us to one of the thorniest questions of this inquiry: the precise role of ETA in the creation of IK. The very name "Iparretarrak" would seem to indicate close ties to ETA, since it means "those of ETA from the North."[17] For many Basque nationalists, the links between the two went beyond mere semantic borrowings. Christiane Etxalus, for example, points out that

> the problem in Iparralde at the time was that the [ETA] refugees used all kinds of *laguntzaileak* [collaborators], especially a lot of smugglers ... There was a time when they weren't bothered who it was. Then they saw a need to coordinate all this, to coordinate all the people from Iparralde involved in this ... [T]o return to the subject of Iparretarrak, I think that if up to 1973 one didn't hear a lot about them, it's because they spent most of their time undertaking *laguntzaile* work, to help get across the border.[18]

Similarly, Andde Galant, questioned over how arms got into the hands of IK, indicates that some activists from Iparralde must have gone beyond the mere role of being *mugalariak* (guides to help cross the border)—that they must have been entrusted with guarding supplies of arms.[19] This would explain the clear fascination with ETA in the first edition of *Ildo*, an IK publication, in which several pages were devoted to a detailed analysis of Carrero Blanco's assassination and the note claiming responsibility for the act by the armed organization. Following the same line, declarations by ETA at the time seemed to indicate that, initially at least, it looked favorably on the creation of an armed group in Iparralde in the event that the more mainstream development of Basque nationalism there did not decide to pursue the cause of national liberation.

Despite these observations, the extent to which ETA was actively involved in the creation of IK remains unclear. As Bixente Vrignon points out,

> The evolution of ETA ... is public knowledge, at least from its creation until the beginning of the 1980s. Its founders, different influences, and ideological transformations are known; the texts of its assemblies are publicly known, and its different internal divisions have been commented on and analyzed ... There is nothing comparable with

Iparretarrak . . . Nor have Iparretarrak, or those close to it, or the Basque nationalist movement [in Iparralde] ever produced texts or interviews to explain the structure of the group. Its founding or evolution are recalled from time to time, as is the case with *Ildo*, but always in very general terms.[20]

As a result, we really do not know the answer to the question of why IK waited three years before carrying out its second attack. And for the moment, we must limit ourselves to speculating that the confluence of a series of different influences probably contributed to the creation of IK. Some of these were most likely quite informal, while others were more premeditated, and together, they probably resulted in a general acceptance of some degree of violence. Thus, for example, it seems plausible to suggest that within certain nationalist circles, the use of violence would have been considered an adequate response to the failure of the strategy favored by Enbata, as a further step beyond the social demands of groups such as Mendi Berri and Ezker Berri, as the result of being seduced by the role that violence was playing in Hegoalde at the very moment that ETA had assassinated Franco's chosen successor, as an obvious consequence of the increasing presence of ETA refugees in the public life of Iparralde, with a concomitant quotidian presence in areas of Basque nationalist social reproduction (for example, in the bars, cafes, and associations of Baiona Ttipia, a neighborhood of Baiona), and, finally, as a result of the gradual strategic and ideological radicalization of certain youth sectors socialized through the ideas associated with May 1968 and the mysticism surrounding the anticolonial movements of national liberation.

Taken together, these factors were more than sufficient to create favorable conditions for the tactical needs of an organization such as ETA, an organization that had to "purge" the existing support structure for refugees in Iparralde by getting rid of the traditional *mugalariak*, who shared their political labors with those of smuggling, thereby making such cross-border operations more vulnerable. Later, it would appear that, little by little, the networks established as a support basis for ETA began to assume a certain degree of autonomy, perhaps from the early 1970s on. And it seems likely that the people involved in these networks began to envisage another role for themselves beyond that of merely supporting a strategy in the South and more to do with advancing similar strategies in the North. This qualitative step—that is, acquiring the sufficient "maturity" necessary to establish a group of these characteristics in Iparralde—would seem to be the theft of financial records in Banka, and the subsequent announcement of the existence of Iparretarrak. From then on and for the next three years, IK embarked on a plan of disseminating its ideas through nonviolent means (daubing slogans on walls or putting up posters and flyers) throughout Iparralde, accumulating forces and reorganizing itself internally until, in 1976, it was ready to undertake more armed activity. By that time, of course, it had also created the necessary support network it needed through the Xan Committees: the kind of community of legitimation necessary in the solidification of any successful armed group.

However, even if we cannot be clear as to the origins of IK, its relationship with ETA in the 1970s is more evident. In the early 1980s, the new group began to distance itself from ETA, as was evident from the editorial line of *Ildo*:

> For our part, as an organization of armed struggle, we have decided to count only on our own forces and not to expect the aid of anyone ... We intend to keep our autonomy, our freedom of action, our independence. We aren't refusing as such to have relations with other organizations who are pursuing the same goal as us, but on the condition that they respect us and that they don't try to co-opt us and impose on us their point of view.[21]

Not for the first or the last time, a division was emerging within leftist Basque nationalist circles.[22] Before examining the nature of these divisions, however, I would first like to examine in more detail the discourse of IK—its ideological conception, its legitimization of the use of violence, its conception of the role that violence should play in relation to institutional and mass struggles, and its proposals for the creation of a united Basque nationalist front.

IK: Its Ideology, Justification of Violence, and Views on Other Forms of Struggle

At its founding, IK defined itself as a "Basque socialist organization for national liberation," as did ETA before it. Further, IK believed that "workers suffer a global situation of exploitation and oppression ... 1. Social and economic exploitation ... 2. Cultural and political oppression ... 3. Division of their community by a border and a submission to two states: one of a fascist variety, the other a bourgeois democracy." Thus, "present society is based on ... the capitalist system, whose motives are profit and power. For workers, for peoples, this system means oppression and exploitation."[23] Given these assumptions, IK's insistence on socialism and independence was clear: "Workers' liberation can only be total. Eliminating capitalist exploitation is insufficient if, in addition, the workers suffer cultural and political oppression ... For us, Basque workers, our true liberation implies being aware of our all our exploitation and all our oppression and its total elimination—in other words, the establishment of a democratic socialism that necessarily implies our own political expression".[24]

For IK, such change necessarily implied the use of violence, for revolutionary violence was seen as the only method with which to confront the original oppression of the state. However, between 1974 and 1978, the group also considered more legal means with which to achieve these goals:

> In response to the everyday "legal" violence of the bourgeoisie, revolutionary activity must use all means, the mass struggle, the struggle within the system, and illegal struggles.
>
> The illegal struggle, whether violent or not, is at present complementary to the mass struggle: if legal activity bears no results or as a factor of radicalization. It can never be considered an activism that excuses the inertia of the masses; on the contrary, [it should be] an activity composed of political action and its consequences. The mass struggle is indispensable, for it leads to a raising of awareness of the social reality.

> It is in this sense that one can affirm that the mass struggle, the struggle within the system, and the illegal struggle (whether armed or not) form a whole that allow the contemplation of not only the development of the current system, but also, on the contrary, its transformation and the construction of a society based on a different purpose or legal foundation.[25]

From 1978 on, IK based its strategy on three principles: information, so that no one single collective might impose its views on everyone else; political formation to overcome personality politics and make each militant capable of politically defending Basque nationalist positions; and the creation of labor unions as the embryos of autonomous forces, such as a Basque agricultural union or workers' and student groups to facilitate aid to all socialist Basque nationalists.[26] An integral part of this strategy was cultural activity. IK called for a dissemination of Basque culture through the organization of Basque-language classes, music festivals, and so on as a means of challenging the diffusion of French culture.

IK's general strategy thus combined the use of violence with all other possible means in an attempt to achieve the widest potential popular support and thereby guarantee its social foundations:

> The supposed creation of a vanguard distant from the wishes and realities of the Basque people [must be] avoided. Militants far removed from combat with the people risk developing unacceptable theories and actions for the Basque people. If we live with the people, in contact with all those who wish it so, who listen and think every day, our organization will be able to adjust its activity more precisely to what this people is willing to take on and support. And this necessity is especially true in the realm of popular violence.[27]

From its earliest incarnation, then, IK assumed this dual strategy of armed and political methods.[28] It was an organization geographically centered in the Nafarroa Beherea regions of Baigorri and Amikuze (Mixe) and in Zuberoa, together with one cell in the interior of Lapurdi and three more on the coast.

This dual strategy, designed to appeal to as broad a spectrum as possible, was moreover to be facilitated by local work undertaken by the Xan Committees. This work was not to be limited either to one geographic area or to one issue. And as we will see, the Xan Committees would soon evolve into the Herri Taldeak, the embryo of a future political party: EMA (Ezkerreko Mugimendu Abertzalea, the Basque Patriotic Movement of the Left). Thus, these events were doubly important, both for creating a wide social support base for IK and, ultimately, for opposing the political direction laid down by HAS/EHAS.

A New Frustrating Experience: HAS/EHAS

Two months after the banning of Enbata in 1974, HAS was created. Its founders, almost to a person, had been members of Enbata, and the new party quickly defined itself as a leftist Basque nationalist organization.

Its Ideological Position

Logically, HAS initially attempted to find its own political space by distancing itself from the discredited Enbata. HAS thus attacked Enbata for being overly "bourgeois" and "centrist" and clearly identified itself as socialist:

> We have demonstrated . . . a fundamental aspect of our engagement: the establishment of reunited Pays Basque [Basque Country] with a democratic and popular government in which the working classes will take power. This presupposes the necessity of the destruction of all capitalist and imperialist structures, the appropriation by the people of all means of production, of distribution, of credit.[29]

By the summer of 1974, HAS was making a clear call to create a widespread Basque socialist movement based on the equally evident refusal of violent means to achieve this and the establishment of relations with other minorities to emphasize its internationalist position.[30]

Its internal structure reflected the vanguardist logic of revolutionary Marxism, while its internal organization recalled the "democratic centralism" of Leninism. This contradiction between progressive and rigid tendencies would soon manifest itself in other ways. For example, although it embraced the antisystem logic of revolutionary Marxism, HAS ultimately saw the need to participate in the system, eventually taking part in the 1978 legislative elections. Similarly, its self-declared internationalism meant that, prior to naming its own electoral candidates, it felt obliged to give its support to French socialism as representing the quickest means of dismantling the capitalist system. Finally, HAS also came to the realization that before the working classes could take power, there would have to be some degree of unity among Basque nationalist forces, thereby privileging the national over the social struggle.

This logic, in turn, propelled HAS into establishing an agreement with a political party from Hegoalde, Euskal Alderdi Sozialista (the Basque Socialist Party, EAS), to form EHAS, the first cross-border organization of its kind in Basque history. Later, conscious of the dynamic unifying role played by the Koordinadora Abertzale Sozialista (KAS, the Socialist Nationalist Coordinating Council) in Hegoalde,[31] EHAS in Iparralde attempted to create a common Basque nationalist platform to which groups of different sensibilities might subscribe. This proposal, however, ultimately was unsuccessful, because other groups in Iparralde viewed EHAS's idea as an attempt to co-opt them, and, once more, this failure reflected intergenerational or personal differences, the extension of a southern dynamic to the North, and, above all, a new reason: the clash of clearly different Basque nationalist positions in Iparralde itself, centered on the use of violence. As a result of this failure, EHAS would disappear from the political map of Iparralde.

The Common Ground with Hegoalde: The Birth of EHAS

EHAS was created in November 1975.[32] According to Jean-Louis Davant, during the summer of 1974, HAS arrived at a post-Francoist strategy for the whole Basque Country (north and south). The old dictator was not immortal. It was necessary to anticipate his end and the evolution of the Spanish state toward bourgeois democracy, in which the armed struggle could play no greater role than one of support. The Basque movement had to prepare itself for this opportunity and especially for future electoral combat. HAS therefore considered its extension to the south to become the BSP [Basque Socialist Party] of the entire Basque Country.

However, at the same time, another party was being formed in the South, the so-called EAS (Euskal Alderdi Sozialista, Basque Socialist Party). Contacts were made. EAS initially appeared as a social-democratic formation. But it quickly turned to the left, first through the influence of HAS and then through that of its own bases.

In November 1975 both came to make up EHAS (the Socialist Party of the Basque People). It was a clearly Basque and left-wing socialist party.[33]

And in December of that same year, the new formation published a list of clear objectives: the reunification of Iparralde and Hegoalde, the constitution of an independent Basque socialist state, the implementation of the Basque language as an expression of Basque national culture, the solidarity of the working classes with the oppressed peoples of the world, especially in the French and Spanish states, and the creation of a Socialist Nationalist Coordinating Council as an indispensable instrument of national liberation.[34]

As Jacob observes, the creation of EHAS (unlike that of HAS) was greeted favorably by ETA (m), which saw in it the basis of creating a mass party to challenge the hegemony of the PNV in the Basque political space.[35] At the same time, it should be remembered, ETA (m) was attempting to create its own political organization as a means of challenging ETA (pm), with the latter group in the process of creating its own party, as well, a process that culminated with the appearance of Euskal Iraultzarako Alderdia (the Basque Revolutionary Party, EIA) in 1977. However, after an initial period in which the two wings of EHAS worked together, there followed a gradual split between the two, with the Hegoalde section gradually coming to share ETA (m)'s vision of creating a mass party, a vision given more focus by the growth in activism as a result of the mobilizations in favor of Txiki and Otaegi and the creation of KAS in 1975.

As a consequence, in March 1977, EHAS declared: "The national congress [in] Pamplona of March 13, 1977, marks a date in the evolution of our party. E.H.A.S.-[South] is in the process of becoming a mass party. For the moment, E.H.A.S.-[North] is a party of militants, even though it has always had the ambition of transforming itself into a mass party, but what is possible today in the South is not necessarily possible in the North."[36] Thereafter, in July 1977, EHAS-South, after meeting with the Euskal Sozialistak (Basque Socialists) and a series of independent groups, re-formed itself as Herriko Alderdi Sozialista Iraultzailea (the Popular Revolutionary Socialist Party, HASI).[37] Despite these differences, the two wings of EHAS maintained cordial relations for some time, until in 1979, they ceased to form one single party. Thereafter, the northern section of EHAS disappeared, and HASI, as noted, concentrated its strategy on Hegoalde.

Communal Strategies in Iparralde: Attempts at Cross-Border Initiatives

The general aim of the leftist Basque nationalists in Hegoalde just prior to the death of Franco included plans for greater cross-border initiatives. This policy was embraced by KAS, the coordinating body that ultimately came to form the legitimizing framework for ETA. At the same time, leftist Basque nationalism in Hegoalde came to configure a general outlook whereby the armed struggle would be separate from the struggle of the masses, although the two would complement one another. And with this policy in mind, left-wing Basque nationalism, from 1980 on, organized its internal structure in a series of concentric circles, at the center of which was ETA, then KAS (with its own components classified as sectorial vanguards), and, finally, Herri Batasuna (HB, Popular Unity) and the numerous other smaller social, political, and cultural groups.

The situation was, of course, completely different in Iparralde, where the widespread weakness of Basque nationalism in general was only compounded by the fragmentation of nationalist groups and collectives. As HAS itself observed at its very founding, "a Basque movement in which power is in the hands of the working class and serves efficiently its interests must find as fast as possible the road to unity." Indeed, "The revolution in the Basque Country will be activated on the day when all forces unite, especially at the level of working class and peasant struggles. To destroy fascism and bourgeois hegemony, the working class must take charge of the Basque movement, forming a network of alliances with the entire scope of popular forces."[38] Similarly, and despite the aforementioned differences, the northern section of EHAS also saw the possibility of forming a nucleus by which HASI could extend into Iparralde, thereby encouraging the unity of all progressive Basque nationalist forces on both sides of the border. However, this process ultimately failed, in large part because of the disunity apparent in Iparralde itself.

Between 1976 and 1977, there were several meetings between EHAS, Jazar, Ezker Berri, and the antiestablishment group Herriaren Alde (HA, On the Side of the People) as a means of seeking ways in which some degree of common consensus might be found.[39] However, these were unsuccessful,[40] and the meetings were suspended amid much mutual recrimination.[41]

As Jacob notes, "the irony was that the attention of several of these groups was already gravitating elsewhere."[42] Indeed, at that very moment, many of the groups involved were already beginning to consider the possibility of creating a legitimizing network for Iparretarrak, something that EHAS never favored. As a result, on December 17, 1977, a meeting was held in Baigorri attended by five hundred people. At the meeting, which Vrignon classifies as the foundational act of the movement supporting Iparretarrak,[43] a young activist named Filipe Bidart stepped up to speak, demanding a solution to the problems of the rural interior of Iparralde, especially those affecting young people and agricultural workers.

Just a few days later, on December 23, Xan Marguirault was arrested and charged with collaborating with IK. As mentioned, his arrest prompted the creation of the Xan Committees, a series of groups that began to explore in more detail the conditions surrounding the emergence of IK and that ultimately became the Herri Taldeak, a powerful support structure for the armed group. Thus, gradually, EHAS lost support among an important sector of Basque nationalists in Iparralde, thereby weakening any electoral presence it might have had and ultimately precipitating its dissolution. As is perhaps understandable, in this environment of mutual hostility and recalcitrance, EHAS saw little hope of forging a unified Basque nationalist platform in Iparralde and even less hope of success when it decided to take part in the 1978 legislative elections.

The Electoral Strategy

From the outset, HAS defined itself as a socialist political party. This implied two consequences: As a political party, it assumed the necessity of taking part in elections while recognizing that the solution to the Basque problem could not be solved exclusively at the polls, and as a leftist organization, it favored an internationalist program in tandem with the other nations of Europe, including France. However, paradoxically, shortly after its creation, HAS had to make a decision about the French presidential elections of 1974, choosing between the European federalist proposals of Guy Héraud and François Mitterand's French socialist program. Finally, HAS opted to support Mitterand as the lesser evil, considering him to be the most appropriate candidate to connect with its socialist foundations. HAS understood its choice as a tactical one, given that these elections "represent for the workers a very important step in the conquest of their demands and their rights."[44] The party believed that a socialist president could be "an important stage on the path toward a socialist society in France."[45]

While at first glance this positioning, may appear contradictory, due to the radical nature of HAS's proposals for a unity of progressive nationalist forces, it nevertheless should be understood within the context of the group's privileged relations with local members of the PS and the PSU (Parti Socialiste Unifié, the Unified Socialist Party).[46] Despite this, however, the support for Mitterand, who gained more votes in Iparralde during the first round of voting than any other single candidate, still fell far short of that gained by the two right-wing candidates (the Independent Republican, Valéry Giscard d'Estaing and Jacques Chaban-Delmas of the Union des Démocrates pour la République (UDR, the Union of Democrats for the Republic).[47] However, in the second round of voting, there were a number of surprises: Mitterand won a majority in the coastal districts of Iparralde, with important victories in Baiona and Biarritz, and made a good showing in Angelu (Anglet) and Hendaia; and the socialist vote in the more conservative interior, in places such as Garazi and Baigorri in Nafarroa Beherea and the whole of Zuberoa, was also encouraging for HAS. Indeed, this support encouraged HAS to compete at the subsequent elections.[48]

Although HAS maintained its privileged position as an intermediary between Basque nationalists and French socialists through 1977, it was soon challenged by the emergence of another group, Izan (Being). Led by the former Enbata member Jakes Abeberry, Izan began a round of contacts with the PS that year. The result of these developments was that the PS, led by Mitterand, sensed an opportunity to use such contacts to make electoral inroads in what traditionally had been hostile territory for the party. Thus, in the municipal elections of March 1977, two EHAS candidates were included on the united leftist list for Baiona, a coalition that gained 38 percent of the votes there. Similarly, for the first time in history, a leftist list appeared on the electoral register for Hazparne, gaining creditable results, while other EHAS candidates, such as Robert Hirigoyen and Manex Pagola, obtained equally commendable results (19 and 15 percent, respectively) in Larresoro and Urketa (Urcuit), both in Lapurdi. Moreover, two other EHAS members were elected on the same list as the victorious winning mayor in Sohüta (Chéraute), Zuberoa, and finally, a youthful list supported by EHAS was successful in Larraine (Larrau), Zuberoa, thanks in part to its campaign against tourist development and in favor of addressing rural issues.[49] Encouraged by the good showing, at its general assembly of April 1977 in Itsasu, EHAS decided to present a full list of its own candidates in the future.

With an eye to the forthcoming legislative elections of March 1978, EHAS decided to field two candidates: Battitta Larzabal for the third *circonscription* (district) and Manex Goyhenetche for the fourth. The electoral program of EHAS was based on the following points: a defense of the right to live and work in the Basque Country; a defense of rural interests, specifically a struggle against land speculation; the freezing of further plans for tourist development; the struggle in favor of the Basque language and culture; the protection of the environment; and the demand for a specifically Basque institutional framework by means of a statute of autonomy and a single *département*.

EHAS then began a round of contacts with other Basque nationalist groups to gain support for these electoral points, in tandem with its more general efforts to seek a common platform among the different groups. Yet EHAS achieved neither one nor the other. In fact, misunderstandings arising from discussions over electoral points actually interfered with the other aim of these contacts, precipitating a failure to create a common Basque nationalist front. Moreover, this electioneering by EHAS coincided with the creation of the Xan Committees and their own campaign both to free Xan Marguirault and to sensitize the public in Iparralde to the aims of IK. Without doubt, this other campaign affected negatively EHAS's own efforts.

The subsequent legislative elections in March 1978 were disappointing for EHAS, with the party unable to better the results achieved by Enbata ten years earlier. Larzabal achieved 4.7 percent (2,130 votes) in the interior, and Goyhenetche 3.02 percent (2,794 votes) on the coast—in other words, slightly less than the 5,035 votes for Enbata at the 1967 legislative elections. Although a Basque nationalist nucleus of the electorate in certain areas of interior Iparralde had been consolidated, EHAS had not expected such a disappointing result.

Despite the setback, EHAS once more fielded candidates at the March 1979 cantonal elections, yet, as Jacob notes, "the results indicated declining support for EHAS and its program in the rural interior, where EHAS fell from 6.43 percent in the canton of Tardets [Atharratze], from 5 percent to 2.5 percent in Labastide [Bastida], and from 6 percent to 5.5 percent in Iholdy [Iholdi]." Meanwhile, in the urban coastal cantons, "the total number of votes EHAS received in the cantonals [the cantonal elections] (1,361) was virtually identical to that received in the legislatives a year before (1,376).[50] From this time on, EHAS began a slow decline, which was alleviated only by the continuing faith the party put in Mitterand as a potential agent of change for French (and therefore Basque) politics. This faith was rewarded when the Socialist candidate finally won the presidential elections in 1981. However, by that time, "EHAS was essentially dead in the water."[51] Finally, In May 1981 (the same month that Mitterand was elected president), EHAS announced its dissolution:

> [W]e were obliged to navigate against the current within the Basque movements. Today . . . many of our analyses and our ideas are accepted and taken up [by others]. But for them to blossom and become concrete required without a doubt the death of the father or the big brother. Why do the Basques escape the laws of psychoanalysis? . . . EHAS constituted a target against which converged shots from *Enbata* to Jazar, Herriaren Alde, *Pindar*, Ezker Berri, without speaking of the Comités Xan then Herri Taldeak. In effect, the *abertzale* movement has turned on itself . . . it will be psychologically easier for many to join a new organization that they'll create themselves than to come to EHAS.[52]

New Fissures: From the "United Front" to the "Principal Front"

As EHAS declined between 1979 and 1981, the structure surrounding IK assumed the leading role within Basque nationalism in Iparralde, dominating this space until the creation of two new political parties in 1986: Euskal Batasuna (Basque Unity, EB) and Ezkerreko Mugimendu Abertzalea (the Basque Patriotic Movement of the Left, EMA). The division evident in the creation of these two parties reflected the differences on several issues that had plagued Basque nationalism in Iparralde: on the potential role of Europe in addressing the aspirations of the Basque people, from the cautious optimism of EB to EMA's anticapitalist rejection of the European ideal; on a basic ideological strategy, from the social democracy of EB to the radical leftist stance of certain militants in EMA; on the extent to which practical needs might override ideological convictions, from the tactical pragmatism of EB's support for the limited goal of a Basque *département* to EMA's more ambitious call for a statute of autonomy for Iparralde; and especially divergent opinions on the question of using political violence in the struggle.

Starting with the leadership assumed by the structure surrounding IK in the wake of EHAS's dissolution, I will trace its development from the Xan Committees, through the creation of the Herri Taldeak, and, ultimately, to EMA. This was a strand of Basque nationalism in Iparralde that was marked by the following characteristics: its clearly socialist credentials; its local bases, which allowed for the widespread implantation of the organization throughout Iparralde; its radical separatist stance, configured in the demand for a statute of autonomy; and its refusal to submit on the question of using violence in the North to the demands of its counterpart in Hegoalde, the Izquierda Abertzale (Left-Wing Basque Nationalism)—also known as the Movimiento de Liberación Nacional Vasco (MLNV, the Basque National Liberation Movement), the umbrella organization for all the social, political, and armed organizations orbiting around the ideas of ETA.

A New Nationalist Constellation: From the Xan Committees to the Herri Taldeak

The arrest of Xan Marguirault in December 1977 "created a widespread solidarity movement that would have several consequences and, in the short term, lead to the creation of the Herri Taldeak."[53] The original Xan Committees were composed of numerous individuals from various other groups that would soon disappear, such as Jazar and Herriaren Alde, and that found a new focus in the emergence of IK. Beyond forming mere support groups for Xan Marguirault, these new groups began to denounce publicly the structural reasons behind his detention: "It was a question of demonstrating that Xan was a political activist, and not a terrorist . . . The objective of the committee was to convince [people] that if Xan existed, it was because the Basque Country was in agony."[54]

The dynamic awakened by the creation and activism of the Xan Committees, aided by IK's call to widen the struggle, led to a series of meetings between the different committees and, eventually, the creation of the Herri Taldeak in 1980.[55] At its founding general assembly in 1980, the group defined itself thus: "Herri Taldeak is the name which is given the organization which regroups the whole of the Herri Talde. A Herri Talde is an organization of struggle which has the will to gather together the militants of a geographic sector desiring to participate in Basque Socialist struggles and causes such as culture, tourism, employment, land-ownership, repression, [and the anti-] nuclear [movement]."[56] A year later, at its second annual assembly, the group was even more explicit in its support for the goals of IK: "Herri Taldeak is a Basque Socialist Organization of the left which, in the political, social, and cultural struggles in Euskadi North, agitates for the national and social liberation of the Basque People, in order to arrive at a Socialist and reunited Euskadi. Our combat for the Basque People is inseparable from our combat for socialism. Our combat for socialism is inseparable from our combat for the Basque People."[57]

Clearly, by this time, the Herri Taldeak had also taken a position in favor of armed struggle, most likely the result of an escalation of physical conflict during the 1980s. As we will see, IK reactivated its use of arms in the new decade and, despite IK's promise not to take lives, it was impossible for the Herri Taldeak to not assume a position on the question. This was even more the case when lives were taken as the result of IK activity. Thus, while a certain distance was maintained between the two groups, Herri Taldeak found it difficult to hide its common ground with the armed organization, commenting in 1982:

> There is no official position, but we can give an indication of the dominant opinion. HT is a political movement having defined its objectives . . . whereas other organizations having the same objectives as us have chosen the armed struggle as a means of action. It is not

for us to judge the opportuneness of these means of action and of the use of the armed struggle. We have chosen to carry out our combat on a political terrain with other means, but with common motivations . . . we will support . . . the Basque militants who will be the victims of repression.[58]

By 1985, if there remained any doubt, the Herri Taldeak officially observed that the socialist struggle was necessary for the survival of the Basque people and that "the armed struggle is an integral part of this struggle. In this sense, Herri Taldeak refuses to condemn an organization whose practices subscribe to this struggle."[59] This, however, was not contradictory with other statements by leaders of the Herri Taldeak (and later EMA) denouncing specific examples of armed actions.

To put this issue in its wider context, one must also take account of the fact that IK was not the only group to advocate the use of violence in Iparralde during this time. In fact, several groups emerged in the 1970s, such as Euzkal Zuzentasuna and Hordago!, that also favored this strategy. Furthermore, from 1975 on—and especially during the period from 1984 to 1987—Spanish paramilitary groups also operated in Iparralde, targeting (sometimes wrongly) ETA refugees there. Understandably, this escalation of violence was received with fear and perplexity by most people in Iparralde, who were forced to witness, through the 1980s, a series of assassinations, the balance alone for IK being five dead activists and five victims (members of the French security forces). This climate of fear extended also to the collective of ETA refugees and their families, who increasingly saw themselves as the weakest link in the chain, only reinforcing ETA's mistrust of IK's strategy.

Numerous observers agree in stating that the eventual decrease and disappearance of such clandestine Spanish paramilitary activity in Iparralde from the late 1980s on coincided with a concomitant rise in cooperation between the French state and its Spanish counterpart in rounding up and expelling Basque refugees.[60] The disappearance of the GAL (Grupos Antiterroristas de Liberación, Antiterrorist Liberation Groups) coincided with one of the biggest round-ups by the French authorities of Basque refugees in Iparralde, resulting in the arrest of hundreds of people on the pretext of "absolute urgency." It thus became clear that Iparralde would no longer serve as a "safe haven" for ETA refugees.[61] From Hegoalde, the Izquierda Abertzale began to note through the 1980s a tougher approach to the presence of its refugees by the French authorities, and this supported its view that any activity by IK could only worsen the situation further, compounding its belief that IK's strategy should be relegated to a secondary level, below that of the greater good—in other words, the national liberation struggle directed from the South. Only once this was achieved, it believed, could efforts be concentrated on the situation in the North. The basis had been laid for the split between ETA and IK and the concomitant division between EB and EMA.

The Radical Turn of Iparretarrak

On March 26, 1980, two IK activists died when a bomb they were transporting (to be placed under the car of Subprefect Biacabe's wife) exploded. The reaction of the French press was to underscore the "criminal" evolution of IK. However, the armed group responded immediately by saying it was not their intention to take any lives: "This act, as with all the acts we have undertaken to this point, was not directed against people, as the central authorities allege [through] its lackeys and the mass media at its disposal. In no way was this directed against Mrs. Biacabe."[62] Nonetheless, although the incident might not necessarily have represented a qualitative change in IK's tactics, "it would affect, to a large degree, the movement. One might say that the 'peaceful existence' of the nationalist movement was over once and for all."[63] Yet the effects of this incident were also felt within the nationalist community. For the first time in history, the deaths were those of activists from the North, not ETA members. Together with the fact that the two militants were popular individuals, their deaths gave the movement in Iparralde its first martyrs and served to reinforce more radical nationalist circles. Indeed, Michel Labéguerie attended their funerals, and thereafter, support for IK from young activists became more evident. For these young militants, the issue was clear: Some spoke from a pulpit (EHAS), while others gave up their lives for the cause (IK).[64] The escalation of violence had begun.

Two years later, on March 19, 1982, two police officers were killed in Baigorri. While the general reaction to this in Iparralde was one of astonishment, and undoubtedly the incident marked a watershed moment for IK, there remains some doubt over the responsibility for these deaths. For example, Filipe Bidart, the individual accused by the French authorities of the murders, denied any IK responsibility in the act—even years after it had taken place. And while Patrick Cassan alleges that it could have been planned by extreme right-wing groups interested in a more hard-line response by the authorities against ETA refugees and IK, there is no doubt that the murders of the two police officers severely damaged the latter.[65] Jacob, however, has no doubt whatsoever that Bidart was responsible. Most likely it was on his own initiative, as a means of forcing IK into a more radical turn. If this was true, then it apparently worked, for thereafter, IK intensified its campaign with more spectacular attacks on emblems of tourism, the state authorities, and the police.[66]

Whether the assassinations in Baigorri were the work of IK or not, events were escalating. On August 7, 1983, there was a shootout between IK members and the French police, with one officer killed and another seriously injured. However, as the IK militants fled, one of their number, Jean-Louis "Popo" Larre, disappeared. To this day, his whereabouts or those of his remains are not known. Recently, in the ongoing trial concerning the original incident, several former IK members have pointed to the French authorities as responsible for Larre's disappearance, a charge that recalls the involvement of the GAL (and therefore the Spanish authorities) in the kidnapping, torture, and murder of two ETA refugees in Iparralde, José Antonio Lasa and José Ignacio Zabala.[67] Yet IK continued its activities and in 1985 perpetrated twelve attacks, the majority of them directed toward tourist interests.

Although in its own publication, *Ildo*, the group reaffirmed its commitment to not directly targeting people, on August 25, 1987, during yet another shootout between IK members and the French police, one officer was shot dead. This time, Bidart (still on the run from the previous charges against him) was identified as the perpetrator, captured in 1988, and sentenced to life imprisonment. As Cassan observes, "In total, there were four deaths and two injuries . . . and one thing was clear: Even when the organization had apparently not sought casualties, its secrecy, its deliberate choice of violence, dragged it fatally into a logic of confrontation with the security forces."[68]

Among all the acts carried out by IK, perhaps the most spectacular was that of breaking two of its members out of Pau prison in December 1986, an incident that demonstrated the "serious" nature of the organization before the eyes of both the French authorities and ETA. Moreover, it also served to attract a new following for IK, whether merely in terms of support (tacit or otherwise) or actual militancy in the group.[69] Through 1987, IK continued its attacks on various establishment symbolism but that year also saw the death of two more of its members in accidents.

In this context, the French security forces decided to increase the measures against any form of armed activity, creating a special antiterrorist unit based in Paris and sending the French secret service into Iparralde. At the same time, IK was legally dissolved by French law, facilitating the incarceration of any members arrested by the police. Consequently, hundreds of police officers and secret-service members began to observe and follow dozens of nationalist activists in Iparralde, creating an asphyxiating climate of fear and suspicion designed to uncover the support structure for IK and thereby dismantle the group from the inside.[70] On February 19, 1988, this increased police activity resulted in the capture of Bidart. He was imprisoned immediately and thereafter sentenced to solitary confinement for two straight years.[71] During the arrest, a fellow militant in IK, Ttotte Etxebeste, was paralyzed by a police bullet. Although he was likewise imprisoned, social pressure on the French authorities forced his release. However, Bidart's arrest did not halt IK's activity, and in 1991, it carried out fifty-seven attacks, the most it had ever undertaken in one calendar year.

It is not worth detailing here the armed activity of IK between 1991 and 2002. It is sufficient to note that from 1991 on, the group began to suffer organizational difficulties that impeded it from undertaking anything like the level of activity it had managed during the previous decade. Further, the arrest or death of its principal activists implied the de facto dismantling of its military apparatus, which, in turn, provoked a major internal reflection by the group on the negative effects of its previous organizational model.[72] This self-reflection involved reconsidering its entire support structure at a time when, we should not forget, much potential support had migrated to positions closer to those of Euskal Batasuna, EB, a party created in 1986 that was closer ideologically to the strategy of ETA and that by this time had come to represent an important dimension of radical nationalist thought in Iparralde with the concomitant decline in influence of the Herri Taldeak. Added to this, the theoretical successor to the Herri Taldeak, EMA, quickly merged with EB to form Abertzaleen Batasuna (Nationalist Unity, AB) in 1988, leaving a weakened support structure for IK. Finally, IK was incapable of responding to the new social and political context of the 1990s, to the extent that it missed an opportunity to follow up on its own call for institutional recognition in 1993 by not, for example, calling a ceasefire on its activities.[73]

Paradoxically, during this time, when IK was increasingly losing support and becoming weaker, it actually intensified some of its activities: Car bombs were used for the first time in 1993 (suggesting a possible unity of action with ETA), and it also undertook activity outside Iparralde—in Pau, Bordeaux, and even Paris. This was also interspersed with inactive periods and even temporary ceasefires. Finally, in 1998, IK assumed the same strategy as ETA and declared an official ceasefire, congratulating the southern organization for comprehending the new social and political context in which "civil confrontation" was now the best strategy.

The failure of this 1998 ceasefire by both ETA and IK had important results: IK officially announced its return to armed activity, but has disclaimed responsibility for a number of incidents carried out in Iparralde since the turn of the millennium. This leads one to speculate that should IK's disclaimers be true, either new armed groups have emerged in Iparralde or ETA itself has begun to operate there. Whatever the case, with the passage of time, IK practically disappeared from the political scene in Iparralde, despite calls in its name claiming responsibility for certain acts of violence.[74] Importantly, such acts continued into the new millennium, especially the emergence of the so-called *kale borroka* (street violence), a euphemism for low-level vandalism and attacks that became an integral part of the radical Basque nationalist strategy in Hegoalde at the close of the 1990s.

IK was important for the development of Basque nationalism in Iparralde in two key ways: First, its call for official institutional recognition of Iparralde, made in 1993, ultimately gained sufficiently widespread support to generate a significant movement while at the same time, situating Basque nationalists at the center of politics in the region from the late 1990s on. Yet it also demonstrated the different approaches of IK and AB—the latter a new force willing to accept the minimalist proposal of a single *département*, as opposed to IK's demand for a statute of autonomy.

The Autonomy Policy

On April 11, 1993, IK proposed creating a distinct institutional framework in Iparralde through a statute of autonomy "that would be the first step on the road to self-determination." In the group's own words, its

> commitment had always been to the social and national liberation of the Basque Country... We favor sovereignty for the entire Basque Country; our whole people have the

right of self-determination, to live as a free people and to own our own future . . . However, taking account of the fact that we are under the control of the French state, we clearly see the necessity of an intermediary step on the road to the unification of the Basque Country, and that step is a Statute of Autonomy.[75]

IK claimed that this statute needed the institutional recognition of the French state "in such a way that its legal basis be clearly defined through an organic law that recognizes the union of the historic territories of Lapurdi, Nafarroa Beherea, and Zuberoa."[76] Taking up IK's proposal on June 5, 1993, the Eraikitzen (Building) collective was formed with the goal of "studying in depth and debating the future of the northern Basque Country." Eraikitzen believed it was necessary to clarify the concepts that until that time had been used to defend a specific institutional framework for Iparralde, bearing in mind that "terms such as *département*, statute [and] the necessity of an institution . . . mean the same thing: that Iparralde needs the recognition of the French state, and so that this [recognition] is proper, it needs some instruments: specifically, an institution that has powers."[77]

After various months of debating the issue, led by EMA, but with the participation of representatives from EB, HA, and various other social, cultural, and economic collectives and groups, the Eraikitzen collective presented a document highlighting the central bases on which this institution should be founded. Eraikitzen believed that "autonomy does not mean decentralization, but rather something very different; it is a step toward sovereignty based on popular gains grounded in the achieving of our national identity."[78]

After specifying this proposal, Eraikitzen considered that the objectives with which it had been formed had been completed, and it ceded the initiative to the various political parties and other groups that had taken part in the process. EMA recognized the association's proposals immediately and in 1995 began a series of initiatives promoting the idea of an autonomy statute for Iparralde, rejecting the more limited goal of a single Basque *département* because "it would increase dependency on Paris."[79] However, EB was more critical of this document, viewing it as defined by IK strategy. Instead, EB favored the creation of a separate institutional framework for Iparralde that might assume the powers of a *département* or region, together with a degree of control over education more usually in the hands of a sovereign state. And in a crucial difference from the position of EMA, EB considered that by achieving a single Basque *département*, a significant stride could be made toward the subsequent acquisition of more powers.

Ultimately, however, the three principal Basque nationalist forces in Iparralde—EB, EMA, and Herriaren Alde—managed to come to some general agreement that was officially presented (with the support, too, of HB in Hegoalde) in 1996. This so-called future alternative proposal was founded on four bases: territorial recognition through a specific institution for the Basque Country; legislation guaranteeing the protection and development of the Basque language; the beginnings of work to shape a specific Basque economic, political, and social space through closer relations with the southern Basque Country; and an end to state repression.[80]

From a United Front to a Single Principal Front

The transition to democracy in Spain opened up new possibilities for Basque nationalism in Hegoalde. Most obviously, such opportunities were encouraged by the timid opening up of society in general and the consequent possibilities that it afforded different political groups for formulating new avenues of activity. As a result, a positive strategy of Basque nationalism emerged that reflected its strength in Hegoalde.

As noted, the Izquierda Abertzale in Hegoalde initially viewed the emergence of IK positively, given that it formed "the clearest conformation of the objective unity of the Basque Country, of the capitalist exploitation that is found in the national exploitation of two states, the Spanish and French ones, and that at the same time is challenged by one single people."[81] These initial close relations between the two Basque armed organizations were cemented by the material and logistical aid given by ETA to IK.

However, the ultimate failure of the relations between ETA and IK had severe consequences for Basque nationalism in Iparralde. In the 1980s, this relationship changed as the result of a strategic change within the MLNV: acceptance of the claim that the struggle in Hegoalde should take priority. For example, Article 3 of the conclusions drawn at the third congress of HASI in 1988 stated:

> The Basque Country is a nation and this is the specific framework for the development of the class struggle. However, during this phase of the process and as a consequence of the different political and economic rhythms imposed by the Spanish and French states on the southern Basque Country and the northern Basque Country respectively, and complying with the liberating strategy and its priorities, defined by the leadership council of the MLNV (KAS), HASI establishes as the territorial framework for its structure and activity the part of the Basque Country under the dominion of the Spanish state.[82]

These were the parameters within which the Izquierda Abertzale defined its activity through the 1980s, criticizing the armed actions of IK in Iparralde on the grounds that there were neither objective or subjective conditions for such a strategy. In short, the 1980s witnessed the abandonment of a united front in favor of policies defined by a principal or single front:[83] in other words, the temporary abandonment of violence until the necessary new conditions were created on the other side of the border.

Challenging these conclusions, IK responded: "How is it that these same armed activists are revolutionaries in Hegoalde and reactionaries in Iparralde? Do they want to control the struggle in Iparralde so that the activists [there] fight only for the acquisition of the status of political refugees? Do they want to reduce the struggle to the cultural sphere and impose on activists in Iparralde the priority of the struggle in Hegoalde?"[84]

Furthermore, in *Erne*, IK's internal newsletter for its members, the increasing distance between the two armed groups was more and more obvious.[85] IK contended that these differences were the result of the opposing visions of a united front versus a single front. For IK, the existence of two armed groups was not contradictory, given that the struggle was taking place against two states. However, when ETA proposed a single (or principal) front, problems arose. As Jacob puts it, "at first there was no contradiction between armed struggles in both North and South: if anything, it was the full application of the slogan *Zazpiak bat*: The Seven are one (Euskadi)."[86] Yet for IK, ETA's new proposal was "the famous strategy of the single front, the single front of course being the South, and the eternal sacrifice the North,"[87] and the Iparralde group reproached ETA for its "big brother" attitude in trying to condition strategy in the North. Consequently, when both ETA and the Izquierda Abertzale began to criticize the actions of IK openly—most famously when it attacked a Spanish train while it passed through Iparralde in 1984—the northern group responded that it was being made a scapegoat for the harsh treatment of ETA refugees:

> The armed struggle in Euskadi North has become the ideal scapegoat for the partisans of the strategy of a single front: If the refugees have problems, it's because of the armed struggle; if the French government refuses to take into consideration the legitimate demands of the Basque people, it's because of the armed struggle; if new jobs aren't created, it's because of the armed struggle; if the movement is marginalized, it's because of the armed struggle.[88]

Bearing in mind the weak presence of ETA on French soil, it was natural that it would see the evolution of an armed strategy by IK as worrying.[89] This exasperated IK, and as Jacob observes, whether ETA created IK or not, the former soon distanced itself from the activity of the latter: "The resulting intensification of French government measures against the refugee community, which led the Socialist government to rethink France's long-standing tradition of asylum and begin to extradite ETA militants to Spain in the 1980s, was linked in many minds to the French government's perception of the tie between ETA and IK."[90] However, this change in attitude by the French authorities and the criticisms of ETA and HASI did not make IK change its strategy, and it continued with its attacks. Politically, IK counted on the support of the Herri Taldeak and their later incarnation as EMA, but it was challenged by Basque nationalists close to the original Enbata group, as well as by radical Basque nationalists in Hegoalde and other organizations in the north, such as EB, that assumed (to some degree at least) the postulates of ETA and HASI regarding the "principal front."

The Split between EMA and EB

Although the creation of EMA was an attempt to fill the space left by the early demise of EHAS, according to EMA leader Richard Irazusta, EMA's radical positions, refusal to condemn IK's violence, and indeed IK's own radicalization resulted in the party being marginalized in a kind of political ghetto defined by IK.[91] As a result, and also influenced by the creation of new Basque nationalist formations such as EB, within the spectrum of opinion in the original Herri Taldeak, a critical wing emerged known as "Laguntza" (Aid). Thus, even after EMA was created, its members were far from being unanimous in their support for IK. For Irazusta, these differences mean that one cannot classify

EMA as the political wing of IK—that is, in his words at the time, "we do not criticize their actions, but we do not depend on them politically, either."[92] Thus, "EMA's creation clearly reflected an effort to become more inclusive and to overcome the stigma of association with IK and its violence."[93]

EMA's position as regards the use of violence was articulated in several points: the original violence was that of the state, the armed conflict was political in nature, EMA was an open and public organization, and more debate on the use of violence was necessary. The resultant position for EMA was that it came neither to defend nor to condemn the armed struggle of IK.[94] Yet the symbolic links between the two groups continued through the early 1990s.

EMA took part in the 1986 legislative and regional elections. In the coastal region, it managed to gain more than 5 percent of the vote only in Uztaritze, achieving 1.35 percent in Biarritz, 1.78 percent in Angelu, and 2.33 percent in Baiona. By contrast, results in the interior were much better. In Baigorri, the home of many early IK militants such as Bidart, EMA gained 11.58 percent of the vote. In total, it gained 5,111 votes, or 3.77 percent for the legislative elections and 4.21 percent for the regional elections. In other words, almost twenty years after Enbata first entered the French political scene, the electoral results for Basque nationalism in Iparralde were scarcely any better. Ultimately, EMA failed to distance itself sufficiently from its ambivalence over IK's use of violence. In the words of one Basque militant, "They think they've distanced themselves from IK, but not in the eyes of others."[95]

Furthermore, in the mid-1980s, EB was created as a counterpoint to the activity of IK (and the concomitant ambivalent stance of EMA), but also, in the words of an EB founder, Eñaut Etchemendi, it was an attempt to create a support base in Iparralde for the Hegoalde party Herri Batasuna and thereafter develop a common strategy that would exclude the Herri Taldeak.[96] Eventually, EB was officially presented in Makea, Lapurdi, in 1986, as a representative of the Izquierda Abertzale in Iparralde taking ETA's position on a single front. Yet as Jacob notes,

> Euskal Batasuna's creation reflected the desire of ETA-front Herri Batasuna to create an affiliated movement, if not satellite section, of Herri Batasuna in France. While this was proposed when the discussions over the creation of the new movement were taking place, the French Basque militants ultimately decided not to adopt the name Herri Batasuna, reasoning that to do so would be to deprive themselves of ultimate freedom of maneuver and oblige them to defend probably unpopular theses decided in the South.[97]

However, if at the outset there were clear ties between EB in the North and HB in the South, this connection was less obvious during the subsequent development of the Iparralde party. For example, EB was composed of a wider variety of opinion than HB, the latter being increasingly subject to the strict ideological control of HASI during this period. EB found support from significant individuals from different backgrounds: Jakes Abeberry of Enbata, Jean-Louis Davant of EHAS, as well as well-known people from Mende Berri, Jazar, Herri Taldeak, Amaia, ELB, and Seaska (the coordinating body of

Basque-language schools, *ikastolak*, in Iparralde). Moreover, EB's tactical and strategic proposals differed significantly from those of HB, and its ideological orientation shifted from the Marxism of its southern partner to a kind of social democracy reminiscent of the later evolution of Enbata. And from this ideological foundation, EB began to conceive (to a certain extent) the limited initial goal of a single Basque *département* as the most attainable policy goal, as opposed to the more radical postulates of EMA (a statute of autonomy for Iparralde) or HB (the KAS alternative, that is, self-determination for Hegoalde and the unification of the Basque Autonomous Community with the Foral Community of Navarre). Finally, alongside EB's criticism of IK's violence, the party also tacitly supported ETA's general strategy, although by the mid-1990s, it was also able to condemn specific acts by the Hegoalde organization.

At its inaugural act, on July 11, 1986, EB outlined its program in a series of points that recalled the basic founding principles presented by Enbata in Itsasu in 1962: territorial recognition for Iparralde, the recovery of Basque national identity, the establishment of a democratic society together with a specific project for the economic development of the region, greater ties with Hegoalde, and the participation of the northern Basque Country in the construction of a Europe of the peoples. Together with a renewed call for the defense of the Basque language, EB placed special emphasis on the territorial question, because, in its opinion, "we are members of the same people, separated by an artificial border, and we are optimistic about the political development of the Basque Country."[98]

As regarded an armed struggle, EB—following the line established by the Izquierda Abertzale in Hegoalde—commented that "it seems as if it does not favor the advance of nationalist ideals among the population of the northern Basque Country, pushing the undecided toward conservatism or inaction." Moreover, although certain nationalist circles had opted for "the armed struggle against the original violence of the state, we note that this strategy distances, nowadays, most people from mobilizations surrounding legitimate objectives." By contrast, EB's proposals, it believed, were centered on "the mass dynamic, prioritizing demands and means of action accessible to the majority, promoting unity in specific dynamics with other movements, especially Basque nationalist ones."[99]

By the end of the 1980s, then, there were three main nationalist organizations in Iparralde—EMA, EB, and Herriaren Alde—at a time of maximum electoral weakness for Basque nationalism there. And if these three options were not enough for the five thousand people who voted for Basque nationalism, soon, two more parties joined the spectrum in the late 1980s and 1990s, this time, directly from Hegoalde.

New Divisions: The Birth of Moderate Basque Nationalism in Iparralde

As we saw previously, the principal nationalist formation in Hegoalde, the Basque Nationalist Party (PNV), had maintained some presence in Iparralde since the 1930s, mainly as the result of the forced exile of many of its members and its leadership during and after the Spanish Civil War. Despite this presence, however, its activities remained external to the local political context. Indeed, this was one of the reasons why the French authorities tolerated its presence in Iparralde. However the PNV's strategy of lobbying the French government to put pressure on the Franco regime was not successful. For example, as noted previously, in the 1950s, the French authorities forcibly expelled the PNV from many premises that it owned, and these were subsequently occupied by representatives of the Franco dictatorship in Spain. And the French government, through the figure of the then minister of the interior, François Mitterand, banned the PNV-controlled Radio Euzkadi-Euzkadi Irratia in 1954. In many respects, these failures resulted in the PNV losing any potential widespread support it might have achieved in Iparralde, in stark contrast to what would be its subsequent hegemonic status in the Basque Autonomous Community after the Spanish transition to democracy.[100]

Consequently, other movements, such as Enbata (strongly influenced by the mysticism surrounding ETA's struggle against the Franco dictatorship) became the principal nationalist point of reference in Iparralde. And with the PNV voluntarily abandoning any political activity in the North, it was not until this formation suffered its own internal split—resulting in the creation of Eusko Alkartasuna (EA, Basque Solidarity) in 1986—that "moderate" Basque nationalism appeared in Iparralde, with EA introducing a northern section soon after its formation. However, there was a precedent to the emergence of this so-called moderate Basque nationalism: In 1981, the PNV-influenced weekly *Ager* first appeared to inform the population of Iparralde about the Basque question, an attempt by the PNV to extend its influence in the North, albeit indirectly and without any formal political organization, given the weak presence of nationalism there. The editorial line of *Ager* reflected the PNV's political strategy in Hegoalde, as well as its rejection of the use of violence.

It was not until the early 1990s, however, that the PNV formally established itself in Iparralde: On April 7, 1990, the Ipar Buru Batzar (Northern Governing Council) was established as the PNV's wing in Iparralde: It was now the PNB (Parti Nationaliste Basque, the Basque Nationalist Party) there. However, as opposed to all the other nationalist options in Iparralde, it was not initially PNB strategy to take part in elections. This was because, despite the support of individuals such as Jean Etcheverry-Ainchart (the former deputy for Baigorri) and Ximun Haran (formerly of Enbata), it lacked a social base that would have given it sufficient affiliates to be able to structure itself accordingly. Consequently, despite officially forming in 1990, it was not legally constituted as a political party in France until 1996.[101]

When it did enter the political arena proper, moreover, it did so from the outset independently of all other Basque nationalist formations. This was because, on the one hand, it wanted to be seen as an alternative to the leftist nationalism of most of the other parties in Iparralde, but also because it could not make an alliance with EA, which was, after all, a splinter group of the PNV originally.

When, soon after its formation in 1986, EA created a northern branch to become one of the few truly cross-border formations, the northern section was led by well-known nationalist figures such as Ramuntxo Camblong (future president of the Development Council of Iparralde between 1994 and 1998) and the historian Jean-Claude Larronde. The EA program in Iparralde was composed of the following points: a commitment to working within the system and a rejection of the use of violence, working toward the liberation of the Basque Country, and defining the first steps toward this goal: the creation of a single Basque *département* and the passing of a statute that would safeguard the Basque language and culture. After its constituent assembly in Hazparne on March 2, 1987, with the attendance of eighty people, the Iparralde section of EA was formally incorporated into the party structure as a whole, with representation on its national executive committee.[102]

Despite the efforts of both the PNB and EA, so-called moderate Basque nationalism never gained a significant foothold among the nationalist electorate (achieving at most a third of this particular vote). At the same time, their relative electoral strengths also wavered, with an initial support of moderate nationalists for EA gradually shifting to the PNB. Yet the PNB could never attract pro-Basque Christian Democrats to its fold, despite underscoring its clearly regionalist credentials in Iparralde. And while it maintained close ties with certain notables in the region, it never managed to exploit these for electoral gains, and ultimately another formation emerged to occupy the conservative pro-Basque political space in 2002: Elgar-Ensemble. Indeed, the emergence of this formation, temporarily at least, closed the door to any moderate nationalist consolidation in Iparralde, something to which the PNB was forced to respond by a more committed electoral strategy under the leadership of Ramuntxo Camblong, formerly of EA.

Toward a United Strategy

In 1987, at precisely the moment that Basque nationalism seemed most divided in Iparralde, the various nationalist formations began a period of self-reflection over their combined electoral weaknesses, and out of this realization, a new policy emphasizing the need for unity emerged.

As a result, prior to the Aberri Eguna celebrations of 1987, EB made a public call for some kind of united demonstration of Basque nationalism, a call seconded by both EMA and EA. Interestingly, the Iparralde section of EA, at this time at least, maintained closer ties with radical nationalists than its counterpart in the South, where any contact with HB was limited as long as HB did not condemn the violence of ETA. Indeed, through the early 1990s, EA in Iparralde maintained close relations with EB and EMA, to the extent of appearing on a joint ticket in the 1988 legislative elections. Although this joint slate did not break the 5 percent barrier obtained by Enbata, there were significant changes in voting patterns. For example, the total votes cast for the so-called Abertzaleen Batasuna coalition was around seven thousand, and within this figure, there were important results—Richard Irazusta of EMA (in alliance with EA in the sixth *circonscription*) achieved 13.78 percent of the vote in Azkaine and 12.34 percent in Biriatu, while Piarres Charritton (EA) achieved 21.36 percent in Ahierra (Ayherre) and 22.37 percent in Izturitze, Nafarroa Beherea, while Jacques Aurnague (EB) obtained 13.36 percent in Baigorri and 12.52 percent in Iholdi, also in Nafarroa Beherea. As a consequence of these election results, Basque nationalism became the third-largest political force in Iparralde, ahead of the extreme-right National Front and extreme-left Communist Party.

The success of these results led the same forces to present a joint ticket in the 1988 cantonal elections (with the exception of Uztaritze and Donibane Lohizune, where no common agreement could be reached). This time, the percentage of the total vote rose to 7.19 percent, and in the 1989 municipal elections, Abeberry was elected on a "plural" list for Biarritz, while Claude Harlouchet gained 6.5 percent of the total vote in Baiona, becoming a city councilmember, as was the case with Robert Arrambide in Hendaia. According to Jacob, "This electoral unity represented a clear maturation of the Basque nationalist camp in France, which presented itself as a responsible and electable electoral alternative."[103] A new era was beginning to unfold for Basque nationalism in Iparralde, one defined by an increasingly united nationalist front and an emphasis on competing through the institutional system. The long journey through the electoral wilderness was coming to a close.

CHAPTER ELEVEN

The Decade of Change

The 1990s was an era of great change in the fortunes of Basque nationalism in Iparralde, a transformation marked by a series of separate, but related elements that resulted in Basque nationalists occupying a position closer to the center of the stage in local political affairs. A central reason for this transformation was the changing sense of belonging in Iparralde, something that may be characterized as the replacement of the need for uniformity by the need for differentiation among the local population.

I will examine the development of Basque nationalism in the 1990s first through the prism of various fields, such as cultural work, the defense of the Basque language, and the youth question, together with economic, labor union, and institutional considerations. At the same time, I will return to the unifying dynamic established by Abertzaleen Batasuna (AB, Nationalist Unity), and the consequences of the self-criticism undertaken by the Izquierda Abertzale in Hegoalde during this era with regard to the struggle in Iparralde. Specifically, this period of self-reflection resulted in the temporary abandonment of "external" divisions (those deriving from the extension of the southern discourse to the North) and the consequent reinforcing of AB's position in Iparralde. I will then turn to the role of AB in the two most important questions during this time: the discussions that took place over the possibility of fielding a united Basque nationalist strategy and the movement in favor of a single Basque *département*, discussions in which AB took a leading role and in which leading figures from across the political and social spectrum in Iparralde took part. Prior to analyzing these developments, however, I must first return to the relationship between the Basque nationalist movement in Iparralde and IK. Only then can we understand the margin of maneuver that AB enjoyed in its attempts to center political discourse on the demand for a single *département*, as opposed to the more radical positions of IK.

After initial discussion of this political context, I will then proceed to explore the reasons for the important shift in people's feeling of belonging in Iparralde, a transformation explained in general terms by the strengthening of a sense of Basque identity that was articulated by Basque nationalists and by the rise of a new, hybrid identity articulated by pro-Basque activists that was based on a belonging to both the Pays Basque and

France. A significant change had taken place whereby, despite their allegiance to France, many also gradually came to support the call for a single Basque *département*, a reflection, no doubt, of a renewed sense of feeling Basque among large sections of the population in Iparralde. In short, the logic of two *patries*—with the smaller homeland relegated to familial and cultural spheres and the larger one reserved for political activity—had been replaced by a new dynamic: on the one hand, a strengthening of the single-homeland thesis of Basque nationalism, and on the other, the emergence of this new sense of feeling both Basque and French, which accommodated political activity in favor of the Basque nation. In effect, Basque identity enjoyed renewed vigor in a society facing widespread global cultural homogenization, as well as the longer process of state construction.

Strategies by Sector

One cannot understand the changes in Iparralde during the 1990s in both a general sense and in terms of the fortunes of Basque nationalism without first examining the work of Basque nationalists in certain key social sectors—in some cases, since the 1970s. During the 1990s, a series of dynamics culminated in propelling Basque nationalism to the forefront of politics in Iparralde: the demand for a single *département*; the cultural movement, in general, and more specifically, that part of the movement dedicated to defending the Basque language;[1] the economic context and the cooperative and labor union movements; and even the growing importance of festivals dedicated to renewing Basque identity in Iparralde, such as Euskal Herria Zuzenean (The Basque Country Live).

The Institutional Demand: From the Izan Collective to the 1980s

After Enbata was banned, some Basque nationalists in Iparralde, unconvinced by the positions of HAS/EHAS, founded the Izan (Being) Collective. For one of the founders, Jakes Abeberry, the goal of the new collective was not so much to create a political party, but rather to form a lobby that would attempt to extend Basque nationalist ideas throughout Iparralde. It was Abeberry's task in the collective to promote its most political objective, the idea of a single Basque *département*, and, he recalls, while Izan never denied its Basque nationalist credentials, at the same time, it was pragmatic enough to realize that, for example, a greater sympathy for regionalist demands by the opposition Socialists, the PS, in the late 1970s could be exploited.[2]

Interpretations of Territory

The demand for a single Basque *département* dates from the original creation of the Béarnais-Basque institutional framework during the French Revolution and currently rests on three fundamental bases.[3] First, the territorial base of the Basque Country is identified as the subject of a distinct culture and ethnic affiliation. Thus, the demand for a single Basque *département* is based on the reality of a particular identity stemming from the prior existence of customs and culture geographically located in the three historic

Basque territories of Iparralde, together with the symbolic unity forged by a distinct language: Euskara. I have already traced the political claims associated with this specific identity—from the proposals of Garat to those of Legasse and the subsequent emergence of Basque nationalism in Iparralde. This basic political demand—essentially rooted in ethnic or identity terms—is based on a temporal notion that attempts to regain a historical autonomy by means of contemporary institutional recognition. This is the first step in redefining power relations in Iparralde, one designed to root power in natural peoples and cultures, and not merely within the framework of states. Ultimately, that a territory can be the subject of a distinct identity is the claim of Basque nationalism, and this movement, in its maximum demands, underlies the notion of an independent nation made up of seven provinces on both sides of the border.

The second territorial interpretation views the local space as a principal actor in economic development. From this, a number of observers see the creation of a single Basque *département* as a means of redeveloping the region economically according to its specific needs. This view does not interpret the Basque geographical space ethnically, but rather uses as its point of departure the development possibilities afforded by the port of Baiona. Thus, for example, in 1836, the Chamber of Commerce and Industry in Baiona—strongly influenced by the new emergent bourgeoisie in the city—proposed the creation of a new *département* based on the necessity of establishing a compact economic and technological space within which to assist further development. And it was on similar bases that renewed calls for a distinct form of institutional organization once again emerged in the 1970s, demands that found organizational expression in two lobbies: the civil Association pour un Nouveau Département (AND, the Association in Favor of a New *Département*) and the Association des Élus pour un Département Pays Basque (AED, the Association of Elected Officials for a *Département* of the Basque Country).

The third and final fundamental factor in shaping this movement was its own inability to provoke a response by social means alone, resulting in a politicization of its positions. As a result, for example, the AED increasingly turned to using the demand for a new *département* to feed the political ambitions of some of its members—specifically, those in the rising PS, which used the issue of greater powers for the peripheries to cement its own growth in support throughout France. As a result, the call for institutional reorganization in Iparralde became a useful tool to extend PS influence there in the 1980s, to such an extent that the Socialists attempted to appeal to both moderate Basque nationalist sectors and those sections of society in Iparralde that favored a single *département* for economic reasons. However what was initially a pragmatic attempt to appropriate an issue for instrumental means actually became an integral part of Socialist policy—that is, a new emphasis on the decentralization or deconcentration of power.

In the context of these three tendencies, Izan fulfilled the role of a Basque nationalist lobby attempting to attract people from both the business or commercial sectors (centered on the Baiona Chamber of Commerce and Industry) and the French left to the notion of a single Basque institutional space. Yet this call for a new *département* only really began to find wider social support in Iparralde in the 1990s.

The Baiona Chamber of Commerce and Industry and Institutional Demands

The Baiona Chamber of Commerce and Industry (Chambre de Commerce et d'Industrie, CCI) has been a central agent in the call for a single Basque *département*. Its early founding in 1726 reveals the historical economic importance of Baiona, an importance tied to the development of the port facilities. As the port developed, a strong and vibrant bourgeoisie emerged that increasingly viewed its potential as restricted by a lack of political power with respect to the departmental capital in Pau (Béarn) and, of course, Paris. As a consequence, some voices began to criticize the centralist state model that took little interest in the specificities of regional conditions. And the CCI, too, began to argue that administrative boundaries should more accurately reflect their sphere of economic activity.

In 1836, the CCI proposed dividing the actual *département* of the Basses-Pyrénées in two, with Iparralde forming a new administrative unit—the *département* of the Adour (Atturi, the river running through Baiona and more or less forming the northern boundary of the Basque Country). This demand was not based on ethnocultural reasons. It did not ground its argument in the existence of a cultural community, but rather in the fact that there existed a community of interests. It was therefore a purely instrumental demand and economic in nature. Even the proposed name omitted any cultural connotations and was based purely and simply on the spatial boundaries that would have justified its creation, for the Atturi formed the natural economic route along which development took place in Iparralde. Despite receiving support from local political elites, however, the 1836 proposal was rejected by the central authorities.

A century later, in 1945, a formal division was created between the two Chambers of Commerce in Baiona and Pau, effectively recognizing two distinct economic spheres within the same *département*. This division between Iparralde and Béarn, however, was not so straightforward, for the cantons of Maule and Atharratze in Zuberoa remained under the jurisdiction of the subprefecture of Oloron in Béarn and therefore were dependant on the Pau Chamber of Commerce. In 1990, these two cantons were once more integrated into the Baiona CCI's sphere of influence. Indeed, from 1990 on, the newly reorganized institution became formally known as the Chamber of Commerce of Baiona-Basque Country.

In the mid-1970s, after a new economic class had emerged in Iparralde and taken control of the Baiona CCI, voices calling for a specific administrative space for the Basque Country were once again heard. These new business leaders, assuming a more modern strategy aimed at getting their plans across, formed a lobby whose ideas were also of interest to nationalists and Basque activists in the Izan collective. At the time, the Baiona CCI initially began to reclaim the term "Pays Basque" as a means of delimiting the region it envisaged as forming a distinct economic and administrative space, as opposed to the older plan's use of the concept of the Atturi. However, sensing the politicized implications of this term, the Baiona CCI gradually changed its discourse, first referring to a new "prefecture" for Baiona and then simply referring to the possible creation of a new *département*. In parallel fashion, growing public interest in the proposal meant that it gradually became a political issue, and within this context, an association was created by Izan members with the specific aim of convincing the population of Iparralde of the merits of the proposal: the Association pour un Nouveau Département (AND) mentioned above.

However, the very fact that there was a growing interest (for different reasons) in the demand forced its proponents to redefine the proposal in the late 1970s beyond the strict limits of economic benefit. And the call for a separate *département* subsequently became grounded in a number of central points: the greater proximity of decision-making authority, as a means of guaranteeing increased development and better organization within Iparralde, the potential economic benefits derived from such a change, as the only effective way to end the economic imbalance between coast and interior, and, therefore, as an attractive option to combat underdevelopment in Zuberoa.

As a result, a discreet alliance emerged between the Baiona CCI and other (most notably, Basque nationalist) sectors, with the latter assuming center stage in organizing initiatives in favor of a single Basque *département*. Central among these was the AND, an association that grouped people of various political and economic sensibilities in its ranks. As Jean Daniel Chaussier comments,[4] the AND based its strategy on attempting to convince people of the benefits of local decision-making authority while at the same time beginning to argue the case for some kind of popular consultation on the question. This strategy coincided with that of moderate Basque nationalists who, from a more political perspective, saw it as a means of shoring up their own somewhat weak position in the local political spectrum. Consequently, the proposals of the AND lost their neutral or technical, dimension and gradually assumed a more political nature. However, realizing the official difficulties that any such popular consultation would imply, in 1979, the AND decided to first carry out a consultation of mayors in Iparralde in order to judge their willingness to support the proposal.

This consultation revealed the apathy and lukewarm attitudes of the elected officials to the notion of a distinct Basque *département*. Of 159 mayors consulted, only 19 responded, 17 of whom were favorable to the proposal. As we will see, however, when a similar poll was conducted twenty years later, the results were quite different.[5] This original response, however, forced the AND to reflect critically on its own strategy for advancing the notion of a distinct institutional space, concluding that before any popular consultation, it should first seek to convince the elected officials of Iparralde of the viable nature of its proposal. The AND thus proposed the creation of a separate body composed of elected municipal officials who were in favor of the proposal, and, with the founding of the Association des Élus pour un Département Pays Basque (AED), one cycle came to a close. In other words, what began as an instrumental call for greater local control as a means of benefiting local economic development was transformed into a more politically charged movement by the time of the 1980s. As such, the movement in favor of a Basque *département* also began to demand greater citizen participation in the decision-making process and, in effect, the AED began to link political and identity-related arguments to economic ones.[6]

Despite these efforts, however, the AED was still ineffective in generating sufficient change. The outright rejection by the French authorities of these proposals forced the pro-*département* lobby to seek an alternative strategy: social pressure by more obvious electioneering. That is, the lobby envisaged putting the issue in as prominent a position as possible by getting it onto the local political agenda, making it a key issue at the center of any electoral contest in the region. Consequently, the French Socialists, the PS, gradually came to view this issue as a potential opening through which they might extend their own influence in Iparralde, and from the early 1980s on, the PS began to respond positively to the demands of the lobby, forming a tactical alliance with the AND and the AED.

However, after the victory of the PS candidate, François Mitterand, in the 1981 presidential elections, the new Socialist authorities embarked on a more ambiguous course. Although they did not reject out of hand the original proposals for a new *département*, they did put up a new series of obstacles to dilute the issue, thereby frustrating the efforts of both the AND and the AED. Finally, the 1983 municipal elections acted as a watershed moment, because many of the members of the AED were removed from office, and thereafter, the lobby found it difficult to restart its campaign. For almost a decade thereafter, an organized movement in favor of a separate Basque administrative space disappeared from the political map.

The PS and the Call for a Basque Département

As noted, the PS became, for a short time, admittedly, the principal legitimating agent of the call for a separate Basque *département*. Indeed, as we have also seen, Basque nationalists also realized this, and for a short time, as well, HAS/EHAS enjoyed close relations with the PS. Izan, too, saw the potential of close ties with the PS. As Abeberry puts it,

> always following this political goal [the creation of a separate *département*], in 1977–78 there was the leftist program . . . I had dozens of meetings with Louis Le Pensec, who was in charge of regional identities, and later with Maurice Laurissergue, a *député* for Agen. They helped the PS evolve from within by helping it approve [in the National Assembly] the propositions on a law for a *département* of the Basque Country and regional languages that were later incorporated into Mitterand's propositions number 54 and 55. All this was not by chance! I was there![7]

For a time, then, the French Socialist PS coincided with the economic interests of the AND and the AED, as well as with those of some Basque nationalists, in favoring the demand for a single Basque *département*. This PS policy found practical expression on

December 18, 1980, in the presentation before the National Assembly, by the Béarnais deputy André Labarrère, of a law to create a *département* of the Basque Country.[8] The Socialist support for the proposal, in turn, gained Mitterand the support of many nationalists and pro-Basque sympathizers in the 1981 presidential elections.

The wording itself of the PS proposal signaled that, "taking account of the need to return the dignity and culture to the Basque people of France, to give its young people the right to live and work in the country, recognizing the specificity of the problems of this territory, the Socialist Party thinks it necessary to create a new *département* that should take the name Basque Country."[9] As such, the PS integrated two key elements of earlier proposals for a single administrative unit in Iparralde: that it would be a key agent of economic development, a notion that would be attractive to the leaders of the Baiona CCI, and that it would form the subject of a certain culture and identity, an idea that moderate Basque nationalists would favor.

These two economic and cultural dimensions were thus incorporated into the electoral program of the PS candidate for the 1981 presidential elections, François Mitterand. In the program—his March 1981 "110 propositions pour la France"—he promised to create a separate Basque *département* and make minority languages co-official with French once he got into power.[10]

In short, then, during the late 1970s and early 1980s, several local and national interests combined to attract the PS to the idea of a Basque *département*. And together with recognizing Iparralde as possessing a distinct culture or identity and as a specific territorial space in which to concentrate economic development, this policy implied another dimension: Iparralde became a key player in the growth of the PS itself.[11] Further, this growth was aided not just by the issue of a *département* for Iparralde, but also by Basque nationalists themselves, and prominent moderate nationalists such as Abeberry (Enbata), Battitta Larzabal (EHAS), and Jean Haritschelhar (Euskaltzaindia—the Academy of the Basque Language) led the lobby to make sure Mitterand kept his promise on the issue.[12]

Yet as we have seen, it was not to be. After Mitterand's victory in the 1981 presidential elections, the PS discourse on the issue of a Basque *département*—up to that point so clear and forthright—began to change, and ultimately, the PS distanced itself from the idea altogether.[13] The reasons for this about-face were numerous: At bottom, the PS found stringent opposition to the plan from the main elected officials of the center and right in the *département*, including Basques. Moreover, despite PS gains in Iparralde, within the *département* as a whole, there were few. To some extent, the PS even lost some ground there. At the same time, the PS found out that there would be a number of legislative hurdles in pursuing its decentralization policy. Specifically, the idea of giving Corsica its own stature of autonomy, as well, was very controversial. To these factors, one might add that Spain did not favor the creation of a specific Basque *département* and, after considering the potential radicalizing effect such a measure might induce within Basque nationalist circles, the PS formally abandoned its policy.[14]

Consequently, in 1984, with Mitterand's laconic pronouncement in Baiona that he would "never allow the fabric of France to be broken," Socialist support for a single Basque *département* came to an end. This signaled the failure—to many Basque nationalists—of the moderate route in search of their demands.[15] Thereafter, the main nationalist groups began to redefine their aims. EB came round to the departmental-regional strategy of EHAS (although considering it as just the first step on the route to more autonomy), while EMA and Herriaren Alde pursued a clear autonomist strategy—that is, a policy that, by definition, challenged the structure of the French politico-administrative system.

Identity-Based Economic Strategies: The Cooperativist Movement

As noted, Izan proposed working for change in not just the politico-administrative sphere, but within the realm of economics, too. Under the leadership of Patxi Noblia and with the objective of "halting the exodus of young people,"[16] a series of steps were undertaken to facilitate local development strategies that ultimately led to the creation of Hemen (Here), an economic development association founded in 1979, which, in turn, in 1980 created Herrikoa (Of the people), a risk-based capital society whose aim was to bankroll the more fragile businesses within the Basque cooperative system. From moderate nationalist circles, a policy of local economic intervention thus emerged: the notion of economic development as a means of preserving and fomenting Basque identity.

The emergence of this identity-based economy (grounding economic practices in an awareness of territorially defined identity) in Iparralde was based on a foundation composed of four ideological and cultural cornerstones: participation, derived mainly from the experience of the Mondragón cooperative movement in Gipuzkoa, a Catholic corporatism that attempted to forge an alternative form of economic relations outside of the market and the state, a Basque nationalism that condemned the exodus of young people from and lack of industrial development in Iparralde—an ideology that found in the cooperative movement an instrument with which to act politically, and, finally, the continuing strength of local traditions within Iparralde.[17] Indeed, Xabier Itçaina claims, "the strength of agricultural union activity stems initially from the survival of references to the *etxe* [house, home] as the central social institution of rural society." The pioneers of the cooperative movement in Iparralde based their ideas such as "single-inheritance [primogeniture] transmission [and] collective work patterns [known as *auzolan*] . . . [that] were transferred into representations . . . of cooperatives and equal partnership in the workplace . . . The cooperative formula thus appeared to its supporters as a means of finding a fourth way via the triumvirate formed by the local community . . . the all-encompassing market, and the all-encompassing state."[18]

The practical application of these ideas, in turn, resulted in the creation of a few cooperatives in Iparralde that since the mid-1970s have distinguished the territory. As of 2001, the *département* of the Pyrénées Atlantiques led the region of Aquitaine in being home to twenty-seven cooperatives, seventeen of which were located in Iparralde. As

Itçaina points out, the goal of this cooperative surge in the 1970s was clear: to guarantee existing jobs in Iparralde, in contrast to the cooperative experience elsewhere in France, which was more the result of attempting to create new forms of employment for the unemployed. Consequently, between 1975 and 1985, these Basque cooperatives were gradually transformed into "openly militant" businesses that "attempted to apply the links between the economy and territorial development."[19]

However, as Itçaina recalls, with the coming of the 1990s or even before, within the cooperative movement territorial development came to imply "institutionalization." Thus the cooperative movement could not detach itself from the political trajectory of Iparralde, and cooperatives began to take an increasing role in development networks established by the government or other officially established networks.[20] Between 1994 and 1997, the Conseil de Développement du Pays Basque (CDPB)–a plural organization composed of political, administrative, economic, social, and cultural leaders of diverse identities and ideologies–was led by Ramuntxo Camblong, a well-known moderate Basque nationalist and head of the cooperative association of Aquitaine, evidence that Basque nationalism retained a degree of importance within the local economic framework and that different political ideologies were no barrier to achieving common ground on certain local economic issues. Indeed, by the 1990s, the ties between Basque nationalists and local business leaders meant that their common proposals began to gain increasing support among the population of Iparralde.[21] As local development plans entered a crisis toward the end of the 1990s, the cooperatives of Iparralde began to embrace the demand for a separate Basque *département*, and they were gradually joined by more and more local business leaders.[22]

Consequently, by the turn of the new millennium, Basque nationalists occupied a more central role in economic affairs than their political strength warranted. For example, according to Patxi Noblia, by the mid-1990s, at least 40 percent of the CDPB's members could be defined as nationalists or as harboring pro-Basque sympathies,[23] while Basque nationalism itself hovered politically around the 10 percent mark.

Thus, during this era, Basque identity was driven by a powerful cooperative movement that attempted to encourage young people to seek a different work model that was more suited to local conditions in Iparralde. At the same time, other factors came into play as regarded the changing nature of Basque identity: most notably, the continuing importance of both traditions and the church. As a result, by the 1990s, the CDPB and the Conseil des Élus du Pays Basque (CEPB, the Council of Elected Officials of the Basque Country) came to occupy a key position in local networks, and created a series of new strategies to aid local economic development.

Basque Agricultural Labor Union Activity: Euskal Herriko Laborarien Batasuna

In her analysis of the creation and growth of the agricultural labor union ELB, Martine Sistiague begins by examining the debates among certain nationalist sectors through the 1970s, principally over whether it was viable to leave the French agricultural labor union structure—Fédérations Départementales des Syndicats d'Exploitants Agricoles (FDSEA, Departmental Federations of Agricultural Producers' Unions) and create an openly nationalist group.[24] Gradually, certain groups began to leave the FDSEA structure and, from 1982 onward, to develop an alternative form of union organization. That year, four working groups were established to examine the conditions for creating a specifically Basque labor union. The findings of these groups were that favorable factors did exist—for example, the already established cooperative movement—and that if a new organization were to be created, it should emphasize its commitment to environmental protection and solidarity with the Third World.

In November 1982, a meeting was held among former members of the FDSEA in Iparralde, and the result of this was that the ELB was created. Very quickly thereafter, the ELB became the second most powerful labor union in Iparralde, behind Force Paysanne. As Sistiague notes, "the need to establish ELB had been verified in practice."[25] With this support, the ELB began a campaign to spread its ideas, and it soon came to favor the creation of specifically Basque institutions, not necessarily for political reasons, but rather because this would lead to the establishment of an agricultural chamber[26] to respond to the urgent needs of what it viewed as specifically Basque issues, as opposed to those of Béarn. Indeed, the pursuit of this chamber ultimately came to form the central demand of the ELB. At the same time, the ELB proclaimed its solidarity with Third World producers and argued against the exploitative Western production model. Furthermore, while the ELB was an independent organization, it was also federated within larger groups, such as the Confédération National des Syndicats de Travailleurs Paysannes (National Confederation of Rural Workers' Unions) and, later, José Bové's Confédération Paysanne.

Yet the ELB was also careful not to ally with those organizations, especially the Herri Taldeak, that it believed might try to co-opt it for their own purposes and maintained positions opposed to the tactics of other Basque nationalist groups—for example, the attacks against tourist interests. Indeed, the ELB challenged the notion that only IK represented a vanguard nationalist option in Iparralde. "The work of ELB," Sistiague observes, "like that of many other collectives and associations in Iparralde, wants to be an alternative to violent activity, with the goal of attracting as many people as possible."[27] And this clear policy, which unambiguously charted out a path differentiated from that of IK, served the ELB well. It was a high-profile strategy, made up of demonstrations and civil disobedience, that served to publicize quite effectively the group's demands, and its effects were obvious: In elections to the departmental agricultural chamber in 1995, for the first time, the ELB (just) beat the traditionally powerful FDSEA in Iparralde.

Encouraged by this success, in 1999, the ELB (together with other groups) embarked on a new strategy to demand specifically Basque institutions, a strategy that gained much publicity after 2002 with its adhesion to the cross-party platform of Batera (Together, discussed at length in Chapter 12), an association that made four clear demands: the creation of a Basque *département*, the founding of a full, working university in Iparralde, official administrative status for Euskara, and the establishment of a Basque agricultural chamber.

Transformations in Festive Expressions: From Folklore to Mobilization

Festivals, celebrations, and the like—especially those emphasizing community and social cohesion—are of major importance in mapping Basque identity in Iparralde. Specifically, popular and participative rural theater (the pastoral and charivari), carnival celebrations (the *maskarada*), and some aspects of dance are important elements of cultural expression.

Festivals

The pastoral, whose origins date to medieval mystery plays of the fifteenth or early sixteenth centuries,[28] is probably the only form of popular rural theater in France that survives to this day. Most observers agree that the pastoral can be divided generally into two types: one religious, the other historical.[29] The central element of the pastoral through time has been its Manichean representation of reality, on which one basic message rests—the struggle between good and evil, between faith and paganism. From this base, the pastoral is constructed through its costumes, the space in which it is represented, the form of interpretation, the music, its movements, and its acts.[30]

For the town in Zuberoa that organizes it, the pastoral thus becomes a cultural demonstration binding the local inhabitants together in an interpretation of the world based on traditional principles that have shaped and continue to shape the people of the province. Indeed, it has been one of the main agents of fomenting and maintaining community identity. It has also served to promote the interests of those in power, and as such, the central themes of the pastoral have changed over time, from evidently religious themes reflecting the power and influence of the church to narratives emphasizing French history as a way of substantiating the construction of the French state and extending the idea of France to the periphery. Parallel to the rise of the modern state, of course, the pastoral also lost its former importance, becoming more a show than a socializing agent. Indeed, this evolution led many observers to question whether the traditional pastoral would eventually disappear altogether.[31]

Following the same basic narrative of the pastoral, the *maskarada* (masquerade) is also a performance that divides the world in two: "reds," who, like the Christians of the pastoral, perform the best dances and wear the best clothes, and "blacks," who, somewhat unlike the devils or Turks in the pastoral, are disorganized, as well as being disorderly. Between the two groups a dialectic is established that some observers have defined as a duel between honor and dishonor, with honor interpreted as linked to tradition and dishonor linked to anything strange or foreign.[32] Interpretations differ,[33] but I am inclined to follow those of François Fourquet and Kepa Fernández de Larrinoa,[34] who see in the *maskarada* an opposition between the rural and urban worlds representing two kinds of opposing spaces—one, that of different communes, and the other a traditional and ideal Basque space against a developed, yet chaotic exterior.

From this perspective, the *maskarada* represents the importance of local tradition for social reality in Zuberoa. It also serves as a kind of intergenerational legitimating channel. Young people, having reached a certain age, can take part in the performance, thereby assuming a new social role through a kind of rite of passage and becoming members of a community led by elders—represented by the dance instructors—who have acquired the knowledge bequeathed by previous generations. This dance instruction by the elders becomes a form of communication and a way of transmitting social values and practices from parents to their children. And this serves to bind a particular community—those of the town that prepares the performance—in relation to other communities in which it will be performed.

The *maskarada* entered a period of crisis in the 1950s as a result of the widespread malaise felt in the postwar era. It was increasingly felt that the dynamic that sustained the *maskarada* performances was outdated. Fourquet argues that behind the more apparent causes for the demise of the *maskarada*—emigration and a declining birth rate—there lay another reason: a shame at feeling Basque.[35] If true, then this would point to the triumph of the French state model over its peripheral identities.

Yet another historically important Basque cultural manifestation were the *toberrak* or *astolasterrak*—forms of charivari. These were performances in which all the young people of a particular town would take part. They dealt not with the more serious themes, but instead, more everyday events. Although rooted in the quotidian experience, they also served to highlight a life that, as Patri Urkizu characterizes it, was "full of needs, fights, anger, and infidelity" in representations that were "cruder than those represented in the pastoral." Moreover, "nobody or nothing, including the clergy, was free of the harsh, acerbic, and sometimes blatant criticism."[36]

Both Urkizu and Hélène Etchecopar Etchart believe that these performances functioned as a kind of social punishment for behavior that local communities believed to be unacceptable.[37] As such, they attempted to ridicule conduct that, despite not being officially considered against the law, was frowned on by the local population. From initially serving as a means to sanction morally certain behavior, however, they subsequently served to criticize power relations in these communities. Yet ultimately, the performances gradually lost their social importance during the twentieth century.

One element that all these performances share is the importance of dance. Dance, both in Iparralde and Hegoalde, has an importance beyond mere entertainment or spectacle, for it reinforces a sense of solidarity among its performers, both within the group itself and toward the outside the world. As such, it is an important inclusive means by which social hierarchies are fostered, gender roles attributed, social status accorded to the best dancers, and local or communal identity celebrated. In certain areas of Iparralde, the ritual aspect of dance, associated with studying and initiation, also clearly excludes people until they have mastered an arduous process that really reveals a code by which one adheres to the community.[38]

At the same time, the dances of Iparralde differ from those in Hegoalde in two ways: Firstly, in Iparralde, dance is a more extroverted phenomenon in that there is more interaction between the performers and the public.[39] Second, the complicated structure of the dances in Iparralde requires a detailed knowledge and aptitude that, in turn, imparts a twin dimension to them as both a refined and a popular art.

As Itzaina and Ikardo state,[40] after the Spanish Civil War, the localized nature of Basque dance festivals, centered on a particular municipality or valley, began to change. In Iparralde, the arrival of refugees from Hegoalde meant that dance was appropriated as a way of maintaining and displaying a Basque national identity, a transformation influenced by the refugees' experience of war and exile. As a consequence, too, along the coast of Lapurdi (where most of the refugees settled), dance groups began to learn the dances of Bizkaia and Gipuzkoa—dances that were in effect more colorful and spectacular and that were more evidently charged with nationalist symbolism. All this took place to the detriment of local dances. And while this development served as a form of nationalist consciousness raising among young people, it also led to hostility on the part of traditionalists who did not have such a strong Basque feeling.

In the 1980s, this trend was halted somewhat by the activities of several cultural collectives that argued in favor of regaining the localized nature of these performances at the expense of preparing them as Basque cultural manifestations. Inspired in the main by Michel Labéguerie, groups such as Lapurtarrak (meaning 'those from Lapurdi', and closely tied to the Eusko Dantzarien Biltzarra, the Association of Basque Dancers) emerged to defend a more localized interpretation. Ironically, other, more national(ist) interpretations of the dances were assumed quite naturally into the pastoral, *maskarada*, and *toberrak*. A twin dynamic thus emerged whereby both the local nature of these performances was regained while at the same time they also evinced numerous national aspects.

The Politicization of Folklore

The recovery of certain lost traditions and the local dimension assumed by those that were not lost recalls a similar phenomenon that took place all over the world throughout the twentieth century. Many observers have pointed out that the revolution in information technology, coupled with the reshaping of capitalism, have combined to produce a new kind of society: a network society characterized by the globalization of economic activity and cultural models that has, in turn, led to the appearance of new forms of social organization—one example of which is the emergence of new suprastate structures such as the European Union—that are transforming culture and identity across the globe. However, this apparently all-conquering cultural globalization has encountered resistance in certain places, provoking the resurgence of local identities.[41]

Viewed from this perspective, it comes as less of a surprise to learn that in the late 1970s, young people in Zuberoa began to search for lost cultural references and attempted to organize themselves effectively so that they might regain these weakened traditions. In effect, they did not have to confront a crisis of identity, as their parents and grandparents had done. They knew that such traditions and practices existed, as well as their meaning and communal importance, yet they could not practice them. At the same time, the emergence and development of Basque nationalism served to spur them on. As a result, in 1977, the *maskarada* was performed once more, three decades after it had disappeared in Zuberoa. However, the social role of these performances had changed and when people once again began to perform the *maskarada*, they broke with some previous traditions. In some cases, the all-powerful role of the older generations—as represented by the dance instructors—was questioned by those learning the dances. Moreover, attempts were increasingly made to break free of the limits of one single municipality in which the *maskarada* would take place,[42] and, finally, women began to take part in the performances after 1982. Yet perhaps most importantly, the communal feeling generated by the *maskarada* was transformed from an emphasis on Zuberoa to underscoring a Basque national identity centered on Iparralde.

As regards the pastoral performances, while in origin they reflected religious topics, through the eighteenth century their subject matter was more historical in nature, and following the French Revolution, they increasingly came to promote revolutionary values in a society strongly influenced by the church. However, from the mid-nineteenth century on, a local dimension was introduced to the pastoral that embraced historical characters and themes associated with Zuberoa, then later Iparralde as a whole, and eventually the entire Basque Country.[43] Thus, the pastoral evolved from a localized celebration designed to reinforce village identity in Zuberoa to a kind of popular national theater that aimed to evoke the history of the entire Basque Country.[44]

To the reasons for such changes, I would add another salient factor in the reemergence of such customs in Zuberoa: the growth of Basque nationalism in Iparralde. For despite its poor showing in the corridors of political power, the Basque nationalist movement played a key role in the recovery and reshaping of certain cultural manifestations, in the main due to its successful organizational capacity.

As regards the *toberrak*, Basque nationalist groups actually came to use this cultural event as a means of expressing their political platform.[45] The power of these performances resides in their ability to convey a critical message. Therefore, when appropriated by Basque nationalist groups, they were able to publicize their own platform to a wider audience than they might usually have been able to reach.[46] At the same time, Basque nationalism played a central role in other endeavors, such as efforts to recover the study and use of Euskara, leading to a number of cultural initiatives such as Herri Urrats (the annual festival to celebrate and raise money for the *ikastola* movement—schools where Basque is the medium of instruction—in Iparralde), and Korrika, a sponsored run in favor of the Basque language instruction for adults that lasted various weeks and traversed the entire Basque Country.[47] Similarly, Basque nationalist groups were also important in the local organization of village festivals, guaranteeing the presence of activities emphasizing Basque identity. Finally, nationalists have also been central in articulating various activities in relation to other cultures in a twofold way: first by rejecting a uniform, global model inspired by Anglo-American trends and second by forging links between Basque culture and members of other non-European minority cultures who migrated to Iparralde. The practical effects of this dual strategy were, first, the establishment of the Euskal Herria Zuzenean (Basque Country Live) festival, an annual music festival that attracts thousands of young people from Iparralde, the Basque Country as a whole, and France, and second, the intercultural festivals held in the northern neighborhood of Baiona, or the Jazz au la Rue (Jazz in the Street) festival.

By the 1990s, then, the previous crisis of identity had been gradually overcome through the gradual normalization of a Basque nationalist dimension in cultural expressions, thanks in part to the localized response to the excesses of globalization, to the dynamics of the Basque nationalist movement itself, and, of course, to the evolution of society in Iparralde. With this transformation, Basque identity was no longer considered negative or archaic. Instead, it increasingly became a key part of the general identity and culture of Iparralde and, interestingly, one of the main modernizing influences on this general culture and identity.

The Cultural and Linguistic Movement: From Ikas to Linguistic Policy

From its founding in 1959, the Ikas collective operated as a kind of informational organization to promote Euskara within the educational system (See Chapter 8). In the 1973 legislative elections, it interviewed every candidate to determine the extent to which they supported legal initiatives to promote Euskara, and everyone with the exception of the Communists responded that they were in favor of such initiatives. Yet faced with a certain amount of ambivalence on the part of many school principals and teachers, Ikas organized campaigns to remind them that French law actually supported its proposals and that they could take the initiative to implement pro-Euskara measures if they so wished. Such campaigning, however, was in vain.

As a result, Ikas gradually transformed itself into a more dedicated lobby, eventually drawing up a report in 1976 entitled "The Teaching of Euskara—A Miserable Situation." In the words of the report, "Finally, after countless activities, hundreds of promises, motions, petitions, once more there is deception. Official promises, never fulfilled, are always delayed . . . the same policy of suffocating our language continues, sometimes in an insidious and camouflaged fashion, but also in the same cruel way as in the past. Meanwhile, the Basque language is gradually and inescapably disappearing."[48] Ikas concluded that the Deixonne Law was outdated and that it had not been and indeed could not be applied. The report continued: "Effectively, the teaching of Basque is authorized only within the range of activities always organized and undertaken outside the normal school timetable."[49]

After the election of Valéry Giscard d'Estaing as president of France in 1974, and through the influence of Ikas, the *Biltzar* (the local assembly composed of the mayors of Lapurdi) then took up the issue. It subsequently pointed to the "notorious lack of specific provisions, up to the present, favoring teaching in Basque, the national language of Basques, which constitutes part of France's artistic heritage." As a result, the *Biltzar* "called solemnly on the honorable president of the Republic that Basque be given a statute that might allow (1) its teaching, at the same level as that of French, at every level of public education [and] (2) its use in the mass media (radio and television) to be officially recognized, confirmed, and aided."[50]

In 1976, Giscard d'Estaing signed the first Regional Culture Charter for Alsace, followed by a similar agreement for Brittany in 1978. Subsequently, Renaud d'Elissagaray (a leading ally of Giscard d'Estaing in Iparralde), supported by sixteen associations and seventeen prominent figures, drew up a draft proposal for a Basque charter in 1979. This proposal, rejected by certain nationalist groups for its moderate tone, called for the use of Basque in education and suggested the creation of a cultural council for Iparralde to act as a consultative body in the promotion of the Basque language and culture. However, Paris did not reply to the proposal, and d'Elissagaray promptly resigned from Giscard d'Estaing's support committee in Iparralde.

Thus, Basque cultural initiatives began to emerge from sectors outside (politically weak) Basque nationalism, most notably those linked to Christian Democracy that attempted to link republican values to pro-Basque sentiments. However, when Paris ignored these attempts to achieve some limited aims through the official, state channels, the emphasis shifted solely to a local context marked by a number of different political sensibilities. For example, the first notions were mooted of a new kind of political allegiance: "Basque republicanism" or "republican *Basquism*."[51]

Statewide Movements

After 1981, when François Mitterand became president of France and the Socialist Party pursued a new regional policy that initially seemed favorable to the notion of a single Basque *département*, there was another dimension to Socialist regional policy. In 1980, the PS proposed a law that would redress the damage done to regional languages and cultures by the former national educational law.

In the preamble to this proposal, the PS spoke not only of the need to recognize the "dignity and worth of different autochthonous ethnic languages . . . that, with French, make up . . . an infinitely beautiful heritage in both its rich quality and diversity," but also that "the regions should be given all the indispensable legal, administrative, [and] financial means to guarantee the setting up of measures that allow the true promotion of their languages and cultures in the different areas of modern life." The proposal therefore included measures to guarantee the teaching of these languages within the public-education system, to help with the education of teachers in this regard, the safeguarding of the cultural heritage of the regions, aid in encouraging and using the different languages in various social spaces (such as radio and television), and their use in road signs, legal and commercial areas, as well as in all other public spaces.[52]

In 1982, a commission to study the proposals was established. Presided over by a civil servant from the Ministry of the Interior, Jean Ravail, the commission was composed of representatives from various other ministries. The goal of the so-called Ravail Mission was to study "the specific problems of the Basque Country and the precise measures that might facilitate the solution of pending questions in education, culture, and social and economic development."[53] One of its first proposals was the creation in Baiona of a subdelegation to the *conseil général* (the regional council) of the *département* of the Pyrénées-Atlantiques, based in Pau (Béarn). This revealed, to some extent at least, the willingness of the commission to consider a restructuring of regional power. Yet at the same time, the Ravail Mission was also an attempt to free the Mitterand administration of its former pledge to support a single Basque *département*. The definitive conclusions of this commission, presented in May 1982, offered two kinds of recommendations. Some proposals responded to specific questions to be treated by a corresponding ministry: for example, the plan to create a Basque cultural center and the approval of a statute for the Basque language and culture. Other more immediate measures, however, were designed to address economic development through the establishment of bodies made up of both elected officials and representatives of civil society.[54]

The Cultural Center of the Basque Country was ultimately created in June 1984 as the result of lobbying from various cultural organizations. It was made up of three representatives of the state, three of the region, three of the *département* and Baiona, and three people from the various Basque associations. However, internal differences stemming from the clash of local right-wing notables and left-wing government representatives, financial problems, and especially the lukewarm response by Basque cultural figures to a body that seemed interested only in promoting elitist and French initiatives resulted, by 1988, in limited activity and a severe crisis for the organization.[55]

In response, the various Basque cultural groups that were mainly federated in an umbrella organization known as Pizkundea (Renaissance)[56] redoubled their efforts to pressure the French government into creating a more effective institution, and in 1989, the Euskal Kultur Erakundea (EKE, the Basque Cultural Institute) was founded. Yet this, too, was far from unproblematic. Initially, many right-wing local notables did all they could to impede the EKE, and it was further hampered by being restricted to a consultative, rather than an active capacity.[57]

Ultimately, throughout the 1990s, the pro-Basque language and culture movement, after gaining adherents beyond the confines of the Basque nationalist world, began to make significant advances. Importantly, too, this movement began to occupy a prominent position within Iparralde in terms of the decision-making process.

Linguistic Policies

With the continued activity of IK and the ongoing refusal of Paris to consider any major territorial reforms, the dramatic cultural, but also economic, social, and institutional realities of Iparralde during the 1990s resulted in a new series of initiatives aimed at self-reflection on the advances being made (or not) by the Basque cause. One hundred well-known local people from all walks of life and all political sensibilities contributed to an initiative that became known as the "Basque Country 2010 Report." Chief among its conclusions was that knowledge and use of the Basque language was declining at an alarming rate.

After analyzing the reasons behind the crisis in Basque identity during the first half of the twentieth century, the report observed that the crisis had been overcome by the early 1990s. It even noted a slight rise in the number of children studying in bilingual education programs,[58] thereby indicating a potential new sensibility in the population, possibly as the result of the pro-Basque cultural campaign through the 1970s and 1980s. However, the report also concluded that despite this recent upturn, the general decline in Basque was so acute that it ran the risk of disappearing altogether by 2010.[59]

As a result of these findings, two new bodies were created: the CEPB and the CDPB. In 1997, they jointly published a development plan composed of a series of proposals that, they hoped, might help alleviate some of the problems. Although they had no power to implement such proposals, they hoped to influence the state, regional, and departmental authorities into taking some action.[60]

Using this plan as a guide, two development programs were drawn up, composed of thirteen specific measures in which the goals, methods of application, starting date, budget, and individuals taking part were all mentioned. Point 10.7, for example, called for a Council of the Basque Language to be established as a "device for aiding and promoting Euskara" and with the goals of "regrouping all those actors that work in the field of Euskara and coordinating their activity" and "creating a way of monitoring Euskara, formulating linguistic projects for the relevant authorities, and accompanying them in putting these projects into practice." Similarly, point 11 proposed setting up a French-Basque bilingual signposting project to complement the process of making bilingual road signs and public-service signs that had already been set in motion. Finally, point 11.5 proposed a viable method for making all public services bilingual in practice.[61]

As noted, one of the central points of this plan was the creation of a Council of the Basque Language—a persistent demand for some time. According to Michel Oronos, this demand dated from the 1994 "Manifesto for the Basque Language," according to which, "taking as a reference point the European Charter (art. 7b), a special political institution to administer the question in Iparralde should be created. This body would have the public responsibility of a policy of recuperation for the Basque language."[62]

Similarly, in 1996, the president of the EKE, Erramun Bachoc, presented another proposal, stating that, "in the political sphere, a Council of the Languages of the Country, or a general secretariat of the Basque Language, is also a necessity, similar to what exists in Navarre and the Basque Autonomous Community, in harmony with the rest of these official bodies."[63]

In this context, on March 3, 1996, the administrative council of the Euskal Konfederazioa (the Basque Confederation), a coordinating body composed of eighty cultural and linguistic associations in the Basque Country, presented a formal motion. It called for the creation of a council to oversee the development of Euskara that, "would group all the actors that work in favor of Basque and representatives of the different institutions. Its principal function would be to promote the use of this language and draw up a policy for its normalization. That is: understanding the sociolinguistic situation, defining both short-term and long-term goals, detailing measures to develop in all areas, and promoting collaboration between public bodies and social actors."[64]

On October 19, 1996, the president of the *conseil général* of the *département* of the Pyrénées-Atlantiques, François Bayrou, responding to these demands, stated: "I propose, to all those interested, the creation of a Council of the Basque Language charged with grouping together all the public, associative, scientific, [and] educational actors. I propose, for this, establishing a Council of the Language next month."[65]

The general plan for overseeing cultural and linguistic development in Iparralde thus received official approval, and the project to create a Council for the Language was set in motion between 1996 and 1997. This included a promise by a newly elected Socialist government to finance part of the scheme. However, official funding of the linguistic dimension of the various proposals failed to materialize. Seaska, the association of *ikastolak*, called for public protest to reclaim the promised funds, and on January 3, 1998, twenty-five hundred people attended a demonstration in Baiona. At the same time, the Euskal Konfederazioa began a campaign in favor of reclaiming the promised financial aid, and eventually a petition with fifteen thousand signatures and supported by thirty-five elected officials, 104 associations and labor unions, and three hundred people who worked in the field of Basque language and culture was handed to the Socialist (and Basque) minister in charge of this financial question, Nicole Péry. In April 1998, four thousand people once again demonstrated in Baiona to reclaim official support for the Basque language.

Together with this public mobilization, the EKE began to lobby public officials in Iparralde, and that same spring, the president of the CEPB stated that the official promise to set up a public service for regional languages in the *conseil général* did not go far enough to satisfy the government's own previous agreements or public demands on the issue. All the while, negotiations continued over more general questions of local development until, in March 2000, the official amount of aid for linguistic initiatives was announced: From the originally promised 103 million francs (approximately $17 million) in 1999, the figure had now been reduced to 43.5 million francs (approximately $7 million), out of which 5.6 million francs (approximately $930,000) were destined for the Council of the Language.[66]

Even though the agreement could be renegotiated in 2003, and despite the prefect's threats (who had remarked that it was this or nothing), the Euskal Konfederazioa publicly responded that this was unacceptable. Similarly, the president of the CEPB also publicly stated that the financial program was not suitable to create an effective development strategy.[67] Meanwhile, the Euskal Konfederazioa called for more protests, and in the summer of 2000, after a call by the political party AB to boycott the regional institutions, the prefect called a meeting with various cultural associations. Here, he proposed establishing an organization composed of representatives from different levels of public and civil bodies, the first of which, to cover linguistic policy, would be specifically composed of the Ministry of National Education, the *conseil régional*, the *conseil général*, and the intercommunal syndicate for Basque culture–a proposal that was greeted in lukewarm fashion by the Euskal Konfederazioa.[68]

Despite all this, the Council of the Language was officially inaugurated on July 3, 2001, with its headquarters in the Chamber of Commerce of Baiona. Its mission statement included promises to coordinate policy in developing the Basque language, to formulate proposals to the relevant authorities in linguistic matters, and continually to evaluate the plans put in practice, proposing any necessary changes and watching over their successful completion. Finally, an additional point suggested setting up an authority to assess linguistic development through, for example, sociolinguistic polls.[69]

Thereafter, the strategies of pro-Basque circles began to differ. For example, some people worked through the Batera platform to lobby for an official status for Basque. Others worked through public channels, such as the CDPB, participating in the definition of public policy as regards the language.[70] Finally, other (mostly young) people began to call for the official status of Basque in a campaign of peaceful civil disobedience promoted by the Demo movement.

Despite encouraging results for supporters of a single Basque *département* in the 2001 cantonal elections, the 2002 legislative election results were a disaster. While two of the three deputies elected in 1997 supported the initiative, in 2002, all three were against it. Similarly, while Lionel Jospin (the Socialist prime minister of France, from 1997 to 2002) actually supported the call for a single *département*, if that was the wish of the majority, his successor–the conservative Jean-Pierre Raffarin (prime minister from 2002 to 2005)–and President Jacques Chirac did not.

However, Raffarin's announcement of a new policy of decentralization at the close of 2002 opened up new opportunities for many advocates of Basque causes. As a result, both the CEPB and the pro-*département* lobby changed their strategies, concentrating on an issue that had become more and more focused over the years: the desire for some degree of institutional recognition for Iparralde. Indeed, as part of this changed strategy, the CEPB even came to adopt demands that had been historically associated with nationalist sectors.[71]

This "official" support on the part of the CEPB for many initiatives that had been previously considered only nationalist demands breathed new life into other sectors, and these quickly organized the Batera platform, a lobby clearly organized around four basic demands: a *département* of the Basque Country, official status for Euskara, an agricultural chamber for Iparralde, and a full university for the territory.[72] Thus, Batera used some of the bases established by the CEPB, but as a civil body was free to organize mobilization in favor of the same demands. And at this moment, the call for official status for Euskara assumed center stage in the general strategy.

The New Strategy

On November 21, 2002, as a result of Raffarin's proposals for greater decentralization, the French National Assembly debated the modification of various articles in the Constitution. During the debate, various members of the National Assembly presented potential amendments so that France's regional languages might receive some official recognition. Although the Basque deputy, Daniel Poulou, had planned to present a proposal that had been prepared by the *Biltzar* in response to a call by the CEPB, in the end, he did not raise the issue, preferring instead to support the motion by the Breton deputy, Marc Le Fur. Le Fur suggested an addition to the Article 1 of the Constitution that originally was to read that France would respect the regional languages and cultures of France. However, the amendment was rejected by a vote of 50 to 39, even though its sponsors publicly stated their opposition to any concessions that would lead to the break-up of France. During the process, one of the evident themes was the enduring strength of Jacobin beliefs within the French political classes.[73]

Ultimately, the expectations raised by the Raffarin administration for those in favor of more decentralization in France were dashed and thereafter unrest grew in Iparralde. This was heightened even more by the trial at the time of several young people involved in the civil-disobedience Demo and Zuzen movements. They had been arrested for replacing a monolingual French sign in the main railroad station of Baiona with one in both French and Basque.[74]

With such a negative response by the French authorities to any notion of reform and to the legal attempts by elected officials of the CEPB to effect some degree of change, Batera began to contemplate a more radical way of pursuing its goals. In October 2003, it called for what would be the last of its conventional mobilizations: a demonstration attended by seventy-five hundred people. And at the beginning of 2004, Batera presented a new program of action that would consist of disruptive actions more along the lines of what had been practiced by Demo to that point, the convocation of a referendum in 2005 on the question of a separate *département*, and the creation of several groups to coordinate efforts calling for departmental and agricultural recognition for Iparralde.[75] One of the first examples of this new strategy (as I will discuss in more detail below) was the establishment by the ELB of its own agricultural chamber in January 2005, an event that marked the adoption of a new set of tactics by those seeking greater institutional recognition for Iparralde, turning away from looking toward Paris to take matters into their own hands. And as I write, a campaign is underway to petition for the convocation of a referendum on the question of the *département*.

There has been a big gap between the words spoken and the deeds fulfilled with regard to linguistic policy in Iparralde. The official response to popular demands in this area was often marked by good intentions, but ultimately, that is all they were. It took a decade from the initial promise to implement the Basque Cultural Institute, seven years to establish a Council of the Language, and forty years to effect bilingual education. Most recently, it has taken three years to create a public office to oversee issues related to Basque. In November 2004, the French minister of the interior, Dominique de Villepin, arrived in Iparralde to announce that the state would fund the office to the tune of 520,000 euros, a figure deemed insufficient by all those involved in promoting Basque culture. During Villepin's visit, no mention was made of a Basque *département*, or of an agricultural chamber for Iparralde, or of the official use of Euskara in local signs. In effect, his stay, during which he was wined and dined on renowned local products, was more of a gastronomic and tourist exercise than anything else.[76]

Yet general and widespread support for Basque culture and identity had grown by the end of the twentieth century. Elected officials such as Alain Lamassoure, who had originally proposed Article 2 of the Constitution, stating that French is the only language of France, ultimately came to support its modification in 2003, so that Euskara would be accorded some official status. Elected officials such as Max Brisson, a self-defined supporter of the traditional order and no friend of Basque nationalism, ultimately blamed SNCF (Société Nationale Chemins de Fer, the French railroad service) for its part in the conflict with the young activists in Demo over the question of bilingual signs in Basque railroad stations. Elected officials such as Michel Inchauspé, who were opposed to Basque institutionalization in the 1980s, actually funded the movement in favor of a Basque *département* in the 1990s.

I have demonstrated in the preceding pages how Paris addressed the linguistic issue and how there was a great deal of difference between official words and deeds. Likewise, we have seen how various groups and associations had no choice but to fall back on popular mobilization and demonstration as a means of making manifest the strength of feeling regarding the issues. Despite these difficulties, however, all these efforts in favor of the Basque language and culture were not in vain. By the turn of the millennium, there was widespread sympathy for Basque nationalist demands, especially for measures dealing with the promotion of the language.

Ultimately, this reveals that a major transformation took place during the 1990s. Through to the 1980s, the responsibility for linguistic defense measures fell principally on the shoulders of Basque activists. However, in the 1990s, the same measures were increasingly supported by a wider social base. And importantly, the sense of the injustice of the attitude of the French authorities, originally felt only by nationalists, began to be felt as well by other people in Iparralde, to the extent that it was gradually tied to an increasing connection between territory and identity. The negative response to efforts to promote Basque was increasingly seen as something "external" to Iparralde or as emanating from Paris. And this, in turn, gradually required the reshaping of the legitimating community for the Basque language and culture to accommodate these new social and political sectors.

As a result, following other similar developments, people in Iparralde began to take matters into their own hands. The CEPB, for example, without waiting for the state authorities to give their blessing, set up its own public body charged with overseeing pro-Euskara strategies. Meanwhile, the ELB, tired of endless negotiations and empty promises, established its own agricultural chamber in 2005, while members of the Demo movement, too, in the face of the lack of efforts to promote bilingualism, have continued to put up their own street signs and to occupy ticket offices at railroad stations in order to offer a bilingual service to train users.

We are thus in the midst of a new era characterized by strategies that emerged as the result of the principal transformations of the 1990s: the consolidation of Basque nationalist unity around the political party, AB, and a majority rejection of violence, as well as the promotion of development strategies for Iparralde by Basque nationalists and their central role in the plural movement calling for more institutional recognition. In sum, Basque nationalism finally had achieved maturity.

Basque Nationalist Unity: Abertzaleen Batasuna

This growing identification with the territory took on increasing momentum. Yet, initially, at least, it occurred within the context of great disunity among competing Basque nationalist sectors. However, this would change with the emergence of a new political formation, Abertzaleen Batasuna (AB) that ultimately managed to define its own political course, freeing itself of control from Hegoalde, distancing itself from the autonomist strategy of IK, and charting a path within the specific context of Iparralde alone. This is an interesting development in itself, for AB is a left-wing nationalist party that, unlike its counterpart in Hegoalde, successfully distanced itself from violent strategies, although this was at a price—the defection of militants closer to the beliefs of radical nationalists in the South.

Self-Criticism within Radical Basque Nationalism in Hegoalde

The relationship between the Movimiento de Liberación Nacional Vasco (the Izquierda Abertzale) and IK began to deteriorate in the 1980s. That same decade, the radical Basque nationalist movement in Hegoalde began a period of self-criticism regarding its policy toward Iparralde, concluding with an agreement between HB in Hegoalde and EB, EMA, and HA in Iparralde.[77] Then, in the early 1990s, radical Basque nationalists in Iparralde also began a process of self-reflection that culminated in the formation of the new group AB—a kind of coalition of forces intended to have more of a presence within society. Thereafter, and through the 1990s, a twin process took place based on the convergence of nationalist forces in Iparralde as a whole and closer ties between AB in Iparralde and HB in Hegoalde.

In Hegoalde, at the fourth congress of HASI in 1989, it was observed that the MLNV strategy regarding Iparralde highlighted a "lack of analysis of the political reality of these territories . . . [and] had been one of the most constant and damaging deficiencies" within the movement. The justification for this error, it was recalled, was "the unconscious assimilation of the part of the MLNV of the geopolitical framework imposed on our people, assuming in practice the division of the Basque Country and falling back, in practice, on the conception of the nation in terms of Hegoalde, conceding only a token role to Iparralde in our emancipating process."[78] As a result, it was concluded that the unity of action among nationalist forces in both the North and the South "has led the MLNV to consider that, in the practical political reality, Iparralde cannot be disregarded, or relegated to the level of merely strategic advances in the North, but that is should advance according to its own rhythm."[79] As HASI saw it, moreover, a degree of sectarianism within radical Basque nationalism had impeded relations with both IK and EMA (the Basque Patriotic Movement of the Left in Iparralde), and as a result, it posited the notion of uniting radical nationalist forces on both sides of the border in search of a single liberation strategy that would at the same time respond to the necessarily different rhythms it might encounter.

Parallel to these developments, a new generation of young activists had emerged in Iparralde who were responsive to such overtures. And these overtures were aided, in turn, by several cultural and linguistic groups whose work traversed the border, as well as by other, more general activist groups—in the field of environmentalism, for example. Together, a series of contacts were initiated between EB, EMA, and HB. This new context then forced a critical rethinking of the KAS strategy, to the extent that KAS itself stated the necessity of "integrating Iparralde with full rights into our structure . . . Having said that, and without prejudice against an organization that might include all the historical territories of Iparralde, we ourselves understand that [KAS] must promote, in both conception and practice, the true recovery of territorial unity."[80]

In May 1995, the press agency Vasco Press reported that, on the basis of evidence gained from the Spanish state security forces, in March 1993, ETA and IK had met to discuss the possibilities of forming a joint strategy in questions ranging from armed struggle to participation in the electoral process.[81] Indeed, in early 1994, within the MLNV, rumors began to spread of a possible unity of action between ETA, IK, and Iraultza (Revolution), another group that practiced low-level violence through the 1980s. This idea was confirmed by an interview with IK and a recently published book, both in 1996.[82] These events, in turn, took place within the context of a new strategy promoted by KAS and HB after the 1994 European elections: the strategy of national construction.

As KAS saw it, this policy of national construction would take place outside the political context and any potential grouping together of forces. In its own words, "we cannot be always waiting on negotiation [with the state]; things will be settled then, but when that happens, the structure of the Basque Country must more or less be in place, or at least the mechanisms leading to its structuring must be in motion."[83] In this sense, the left-wing nationalist movement tasked itself "to start describing, from now on, what will be our national model, what internal articulation we are going to promote as a political movement, given that this debate cannot be postponed until we enter a new democratic era deriving from the recognition of the Basque Country and its territorial unity."[84]

As KAS saw it, this strategy would have to overcome two fundamental errors. On the one hand, the organization would have to overcome conceiving its strategy in terms of Hegoalde alone, and on the other, it would have to address the issue of violence in Iparralde. As regards the latter, the "Oldartzen" process (Basque for "attacking" or "confronting") within HB during 1994–95 addressed the subject. Departing from its previous clear and sharp criticism of IK, HB now opined that "while the French and Spanish states deny the possibility of a solution to the so-called 'Basque problem' through democratic means, its is legitimate for the Basque Country to defend its sovereignty using all forms of struggle, both institutional and in the street, like that of a political nature practiced by ETA and IK; in other words, armed struggle itself."[85]

As a result, left-wing nationalists in Iparralde gradually began to conceive of the possibility that a common front might be achieved with their counterparts in Hegoalde. For example, Jakes Sarraillet, a spokesperson for EMA, pointed out that "after the reflection of the Izquierda Abertzale in the southern Basque Country on its points of view, we find ourselves confronting a new position by HB regarding Iparralde and consequently regarding EMA." Therefore, "leaving to one side past differences and arguments, accepting the challenge of the future, we take on the responsibility of forming one single Izquierda Abertzale."[86]

In addition to this reflection, on March 23, 1994, a manifesto for common political action in the northern and southern Basque Country was signed allowing for the temporary unity of EB, EMA, Herriaren Alde, and HB, uniting for the first time radical nationalists on both sides of the border. The manifesto, while acknowledging the different realities in both the North and the South, called for a unity of objectives, given that "the common aspiration is achieving an independent and socialist Basque Country." It thus laid out the foundations on which this common political action would take place: "The political forces of Hegoalde and Iparralde will struggle together in favor of the independence denied us by the Spanish and French states . . . We will fight so that the Basque Country is recognized in Europe, and we will promote the road to political negotiation as the means by which to overcome the existing conflict between both states and the Basque Country." At the same time, and in line with the stated common goals, it was argued that "the Basque Country needs . . . a new development model, a leftist model based on the popular interests of the majority of the population." In conclusion,

> The Basque Country, north and south, is a nation. Therefore, despite its actual division in three politico-administrative parts, it must have the power to decide its future. The Basque Country, like any other people, has a right to self-determination and territorial

unity, together with the ability to decide what kind of relationship it wishes to establish with the Spanish and French states. For left-wing nationalists, national liberation and the construction of a society with no repression based on social justice are inseparable goals.[87]

However, despite underscoring the need for common action, the signatories of this document also pointed out the need to differentiate their strategies in the North and the South, to the extent that, while "the Spanish government must guarantee territoriality and self-determination to the four territories (Bizkaia, Araba, Gipuzkoa, and Navarre) through a new politico-juridical framework . . . the French government must recognize the northern Basque Country as a political community by means of an institution that defends, plans, and manages its political, economic, and cultural-linguistic interests."[88] Such an institution, based on calls for a statute of autonomy for Iparralde, would be based on the parameters devised by the Eraikitzen collective that, in turn, had been adapted from IK's proposals in 1993.

The Road to a United Front

After the push for more unity among the various nationalist groups of Iparralde resulted in the creation of AB as an electoral platform composed of, initially, EB, EMA, and EA (although later, EA would leave), support for AB steadily grew in both the cantonal and legislative elections through the first half of the 1990s. However, the most important factor in cementing the alliance between the two core parties, EB and EMA, was the local experience of cooperation before and during the municipal elections. What emerged, in particular, was a renewed sense of being able to overcome former ideological differences and to work together for common progressive nationalist goals, a level of cooperation that was facilitated by the possibility of working within AB at an "individual" level—that is, without necessarily having to represent any political party or faction.

At the same time, a new generation of young activists—members of the Patxa and Oldartzen groups,[89] on the one hand, and of the left-wing nationalist youth group Gazteriak (Youths), with its closer ties to similar collectives in the South, on the other—displayed a similar commitment to working together. Indeed, in 1994, Patxa and Oldartzen united to form a political group, and as a result, members of Herriaren Alde began to attend AB meetings as observers. Meanwhile, Gazteriak increasingly assumed a key role—due its strong internal cohesion—in the leftist nationalist youth movement, with its members having been socialized outside the traditional historical differences between the various left-wing nationalist groups in the North. Later, however, it would retreat from this increasingly united platform in the North and ally with the Izquierda Abertzale in the South.

In the mid-1990s, AB held two general assemblies, in December 1994 and January 1995, achieving a minimum degree of consensus over what the party's organization and objectives would be. By majority vote, AB would be defined as "a platform of convergence established by nationalists in Iparralde with the goal of uniting them in the most unified way possible, especially in regard to electoral consultations." As regarded organization, "membership of AB is voluntary, which means that its leadership vehicle is the National Assembly formed by all its members." And as regarded its goals, they were based on "the irrevocable recognition of the Basque Country, together with its legal existence, through the creation of a specific institution, and possessing a status for the Basque language and culture, and with its own powers in the *département*, region and state, especially in the field of training and education."[90]

With these resolutions, AB began its transformation from a short-term coalition platform that operated principally during elections into a fully fledged political party. The next step was a series of measures designed to reinforce its own internal cohesion: a structuring of the party around the temporary local groups that had formed to fight elections. At the same time, a unified strategy was approved, centered on the call for some degree of institutional recognition for Iparralde. Thereafter, at AB's general assembly in December 1996, the individual basis of involvement within the party was reaffirmed and its internal organization cemented further. At the same time, though, it began to take on more of a formal political party structure, to the obvious detriment of the two parties that had originally made up the electoral platform. At the assembly, it stated that it was "no longer a federation or confederation of political parties or organizations," despite the fact that it still allowed dual membership with other formations. At the same assembly, its members also resoundingly rejected a proposal to allow other political parties a say in the direction AB should take, for, it was concluded that AB was a "structure of union between nationalists, whatever their allegiances or beliefs," and as such, it considered itself "neither right-wing nor left-wing nationalist, given that ideological allegiances are part of political parties."[91]

By the mid-1990s, then, AB had consolidated its position as the principal nationalist political reference in Iparralde. And it gradually took shape as a political party at the same time as the parties out which it had emerged—EB, EMA, and HA—were progressively weakened. However, ideological, tactical, and strategic differences did not disappear within AB, and there were major differences of opinion over key questions, such as the role of violence, participation in the European Union, basic ideology, and the exact tactics to follow. For example, the sector within AB that had emerged out of EB began to criticize ETA's armed struggle,[92] to the extent that it even suggested publicly condemning ETA activity. At another level, members of AB remained divided over whether the general objective should be a *département* or a statute of autonomy, and between those in favor of or against the growing European Union. Given these differences of opinion, one sector within AB proposed establishing an official line (as existed within the MLNV) as regarded the steps necessary to achieve sovereignty and territoriality, while another sector argued in favor of gradually achieving sovereignty through the process of European unity and the progressive institutionalization of the already emerging Basque Euroregion.[93]

AB thus managed to consolidate its position as the principal nationalist force in Iparralde, thanks mainly to achieving a minimum level of consensus and a willingness to work on that basis among its members. That said, at its very birth, it was a fragile organization, to the extent that, despite repeated electoral success in the late 1990s, it existed under the constant threat of internal divisions and splits.

Two Models of Radical Nationalism

AB became the main nationalist party in the late 1990s at the expense of a decline in fortunes for older nationalist formations. Although it was identified with an organizational structure similar to that of the MLNV in Hegoalde, this comparison was not warranted. In fact, it differed from the MLNV both tactically and organizationally. On the one hand, it did not have the degree of antistate, clandestine organization present within the MLNV, or support organizations such as IK and ETA, or need to sustain a legitimating community of support. On the other, despite close links with HB during its formative years, from the mid-1990s on, AB gradually distanced itself from the more radical elements of MLNV strategy, especially those that included direct confrontation with the state and with other political parties and social agents. Instead, AB began to pursue a more pragmatic line through dialogue and aimed at achieving a Basque *département*.

It is worth exploring these two different approaches as a means of highlighting the emerging differences within the leftist nationalist world.[94] At the close of the 1960s and beginning of the 1970s, a series of internal and external conditions existed that favored the emergence of violence on both sides of the border. In the Spanish context, there was a "feeling of exclusion" derived from the Franco dictatorship, a "sense of danger" caused by sociopolitical transformations associated with industrial growth, and a sense of frustration as the result of greater economic, but not political freedoms.[95] At the same time, traditional Basque nationalism remained in its "French" exile, and the lack of any other means by which to confront the dictatorship meant that the conditions favored the emergence of an armed resistance.[96] As regarded the French context, the Algerian War of Independence and the events of May 1968 in Paris facilitated the belief in violence as a conduit to social and political change. This, coupled with an extensive network of anti-system and pro-Basque culture groups and the symbolic role played by ETA refugees led to a growing feeling among certain nationalist youth sectors in Iparralde that an armed struggle could be effective in achieving their aims.

Francisco Letamendia offers a general schematic approach for examining the creation and consolidation of all peripheral nationalist armed groups, an approach grounded in four phases:

> The first phase is the production of social violence with a defensive-aggressive "response." The second phase is the appearance of an armed group, the product of a double process of fusion and totalization. The third and fourth phases develop simultaneously; they are the transformation of an armed group into a group-state which imitates the state, and the formation of a nationalist socio-political community of an anti-repressive nature which legitimates the group-state, accepting it as such.[97]

Using this scheme as a guide, one can see parallels in the emergence of armed groups on both sides of the border in the first two phases, while in the latter two stages, they tend to differ.

The transformation of an armed group into antistate organization derives, basically, from how the group defines itself. The central role played by the armed struggle for ETA (m) meant that, for its legitimating community, the organization became the principal reference point for a future state, because a future state was the ultimate objective of the vanguard organizational structure of the MLNV, represented, symbolically, by ETA. This structure, in turn, was grounded in an analysis by ETA dating from the late 1960s, a reading of the situation according to which the basic contradiction in all political processes was what confronted the oligarchy with the proletariat, despite the fact that, in the Basque context, the fundamental contradiction was that between the Basque Country and the Spanish state. Consequently, ETA strategy was designed to achieve a Basque state from which socialism would then emerge, thereby eliminating the principal contradiction.[98]

Following the vanguard line of Marxist-Leninism definitively embraced by ETA after the Burgos Trial, the subject of this process would be the proletariat, and taking account of the fact that armed struggle was the principal expression of this class conflict, it was logical for ETA to emerge as the core unit of the MLNV for radical Basque nationalists. This kind of self-definition on the part of ETA allowed the group to conceive itself as an antistate organization in the symbolic universe of its legitimating community, and ultimately, it was articulated as a central component of the antirepressive movement in the wake of the Burgos Trial.[99] Later, in the 1980s, ETA was organized (again, symbolically) around a structure defined by KAS, thereby closing the organizational cycle.

By way of contrast, IK never achieved the same degree of internal development to become an antistate organization around which the radical nationalist world might organize. One of the main reasons for this was the amount of criticism levied at the armed struggle, not only from within the nationalist community as a whole, but also from within antisystem nationalist circles. Furthermore, IK's own self-definition impeded it from successfully completing the third and fourth stages of Letamendia's schematic progression. IK never became the vanguard organization that would have made it the "symbolic reference point" in Iparralde. Further, its activity never managed to overcome other strategies, such as mass struggle, or the tremendous internal divisions that marked radical nationalism as a whole, as in Hegoalde with ETA (pm). Finally, the threshold of violence was limited to a kind of "armed propaganda" similar to that theorized in the 1970s by the Corsican nationalist movements.

In this sense, IK appeared indebted to the anti-authoritarian legacy of May 1968 and the social movements that emerged in the 1960s. As such, its most immediate points of reference were not ETA, but similar armed groups emerging in Corsica and Brittany. At the end of the 1970s, this progressive influence, together with the example of ETA (pm)'s alternative, led IK into an intense campaign designed to structure the nationalist movement beyond the more established model of a merely antirepressive organization. As a result, IK tried to extend its influence in already existing cultural groups, as well as to aid in the creation of labor union organizations, agricultural and youth groups, and, later, political entities.[100] IK's prioritizing of such social and political work enables us to understand its basic differences from ETA (m). Ultimately, for IK, "violent activity is not the only means of liberation; it is a necessary means . . . that is subordinate to the struggle of the Basque people. The priority today is in reinforcing the popular struggle."[101]

Both armed groups coincided in their strategic goals, and both were influenced initially by socialist liberation movements and then by the new social movements. Consequently, both saw their ultimate objective as achieving independence and socialism. Yet they differed in their tactical goals. For ETA, this objective was to be reached via the official recognition of the Basque right to self-determination and territorial unity for Hegoalde,[102] while for IK, it was to be achieved by some kind of institutional recognition for Iparralde through gaining a statute of autonomy.[103] Moreover, IK failed to transform itself into an antistate body around which antisystem nationalism grouped, a fact underscored by the fact that while HB assumed ETA's positions in Hegoalde, AB distanced itself from IK in Iparralde by arguing for a single Basque *département* as its principal goal.

Another differentiating element between the two armed groups stemmed from their respective legitimating communities. In Hegoalde, the structural organization of the vanguard radical nationalist movement situated ETA at the top of a symbolic pyramidal structure whose base was composed of the "masses" and the HB coalition. However, given the impossibility for ETA of leading the political direction of the process because of its clandestine nature, an intermediate body emerged in the 1980s to undertake this work: KAS–itself composed of various composite organizations undertaking delegated work.[104]

In Iparralde, however, there was nothing like the same degree of organized legitimating community. For example, despite the fact that some radical antisystem nationalist organizations–such as EMA–evinced a level of sympathy for IK, others were quite open in their criticism of the armed group's activities. This basic division within the radical nationalist world over IK meant that it was much more difficult to create and sustain an effective legitimating community and, crucially, only reinforced what has been one of the key differences in the North: the prioritizing of "political" over "military" objectives.

Thus, once the different radical nationalist political organizations were able, first, to overcome tactical differences by consolidating a united front regarding electoral activity and then to create a coherent political movement (AB), radical nationalism in Iparralde could chart its own course away from any notion of armed struggle, and in 1997, this movement began to enact a twin strategy: On the one hand, it undertook a pragmatic tactical movement to argue for a Basque *département* by centering the demand on political debate, and on the other, it sought to help resolve the question of the armed conflict in Hegoalde by seeking to build bridges with all other nationalists on the other side of the border—in a context (after 2000) marked by the return to arms by ETA after the ceasefire of 1998–99 and by the resulting heightened political tension.

Another way of measuring the effectiveness of armed groups is their relative capacity to control exclusively any activity within their particular terrain. Both IK and ETA claimed exclusive legitimacy for armed activity in their respective terrains, Iparralde and Hegoalde. In the early 1970s, a number of small armed cells emerged in Iparralde (Hordago!, Euskal Zuzentasuna, and IK) that, through the decade, complemented one another's actions. However, by the end of the 1970s, only IK remained as an operative armed group. Initially, IK found support from ETA. However, when a tactical change occurred within the MLNV, abandoning the notion of a united front and endorsing the notion of a principal (or only) front, relations deteriorated between the two groups. Indeed, IK broke off all relations with ETA and sought new allies in similar movements in Corsica and New Caledonia, and even with Action Directe (Direct Action, a French libertarian communist armed group active in the 1980s).[105] And from this moment on, IK sought exclusive responsibility for its strategy and activity in Iparralde, refusing any symbolic or ideological intervention by ETA in the North.

However, the appearance of the tactic of *kale borroka* (street violence, or urban warfare) after 1994—low-level acts of violence, such as vandalism—as part of a new tactical strategy favored by the MLNV brought a new wave of direct action to Iparralde. This violence, although not comparable to the levels of Hegoalde,[106] provoked the reaction of IK that in Iparralde there was room for only one armed organization. Thus after a period of better relations with ETA in the early 1990s, suddenly, in mid decade, IK began to observe an increase in acts of this kind in Iparralde, in the main perpetrated by young, radical, antisystem nationalists who had been seduced by the message of the MLNV in the South.[107]

However, in Hegoalde, ETA's armed struggle and the *kale borroka* were, for the MLNV, complementary.[108] Specifically, this new kind of low-level violence was a way for ETA to seek alternative forms of struggle while it sought to declare a ceasefire.[109] Historically, ETA also denied the validity of other armed groups in Hegoalde, such as ETA (pm), CAA (Comandos Autónomos Anticapitalistas, the Anticapitalist Autonomous Commandos), and Iraultza, as well as in the Basque Country as a whole (IK). Indeed, as regards the first three groups, either their members ultimately joined ETA or they abandoned armed struggle altogether. Therefore only IK remained to challenge ETA's authority in this field, a challenge that was intensified after the MLNV's decision to abandon the strategy of a united front.

When addressing the existence and activity of IK and ETA, one thus is looking at two different models, which, in turn, explains the different strategies and tactics favored by the two leftist nationalist armed organizations. Moreover, on the political front, from the mid-1990s on, the left-wing Basque nationalist groups in Iparralde gradually began to distance themselves from HB in Hegoalde, especially after the tactical shift within ETA that saw it begin to target "civilians," principally in the shape of politicians.[110] Although there was a brief moment of respite from the violence (and even hope for a negotiated end to the conflict) during the ceasefire of 1998–99, the return to arms by ETA provoked a clear and definitive response by AB to the question: a demand for an immediate and definitive ceasefire on the part of ETA. Yet just at that same moment, AB suffered its first splintering, with a breakaway group among its ranks forming an Iparralde section of Batasuna (the successor party to HB in Hegoalde). Once more, then, left-wing nationalists in Iparralde severed relations with each other, and thereafter, for its part, AB continued to define itself as a left-wing nationalist organization, forging closer ties with breakaway groups from HB in Hegoalde such as Zutik and Aralar.[111]

CHAPTER TWELVE

The Strength of Basque Nationalism in Local Political Dynamics

The development of Basque nationalism in Iparralde was conditioned historically by its marginal political and electoral presence, its late consolidation, its progressive nature in a predominantly conservative society, and its profound internal divisions. As we have seen, such divisions were themselves the result of different tactical and strategic opinions deriving from other nationalist discourses in Hegoalde, as well as different responses—both social and internal—to the question of violence.[1] These conditions meant that radical Basque nationalism in the North assumed, in general, a different strategy from its southern counterpart. This strategy was based, fundamentally, on a tactical line conditioned by minimum objectives and designed to attract as wide a spectrum of people as possible, as well as by a gradual distancing from the use of violence that allowed it to gain legitimacy with society.

As we also have seen, because of the divisions of the 1980s, in the early 1990s, Basque nationalism in Iparralde began a period of self-reflection on the need for some degree of unity, a necessary step because divisions clearly had led to the electoral weakness of nationalism, an ideology that could barely exceed 5 percent of the vote in the various elections in which it took part. By contrast, when different nationalist forces did share the same slate, as was the case in some municipal elections in the late 1980s, their results improved dramatically. AB emerged in the 1990s as a coalition platform to capitalize on the success of this joint front strategy.

As AB took more shape as a political party through the 1990s, it began to play more of a role—together with the PNB and EA—in local development policies and territorial institutionalization in a united nationalist strategy that gave the ideology a certain importance in local political dynamics.[2] Indeed, this growing importance indicated that the crisis of Basque identity in Iparralde had been, or at least was being, overcome by this time.

The Role of Basque Nationalism in Development Policy

Local political officials play a key role in the French political system as mediators between central and peripheral authority. In turn, their power derives from an obviously highly localized context: the municipality, canton, or, at most, their *circonscription* (district or constituency).[3] Historically, because this power has been concentrated in a highly localized context, it has been a major impediment to developing intercommunal politics of cooperation, thereby preventing any noninstitutionalized territory—such as Iparralde—from developing a unified political identity.[4] As a result, a laissez-faire logic deriving from the French political system itself has historically constricted any such development.

Networks of Governance

In the 1990s, however, a change took place that gradually allowed the development of a specific public policy for Iparralde: the creation of policy networks—think tanks composed of local elected officials, together with important representatives from the social, economic, and cultural worlds.[5]

As mentioned in the previous chapter, in the early 1990s, a series of opportunities emerged to effect some change.[6] For example, under the direction of the prefect and subprefect of the *département* of the Pyrénées-Atlantiques, a process began by which local elected officials and representatives of civil society met to reflect on the social reality of Iparralde. The result of these meetings, held between September 1992 and December 1993, was the publication of the *Basque Country 2010 Report* (1993), a detailed analysis of Basque society at the time, presented in the Chamber of Commerce and Industry (CCI) in Baiona in December 1993 before the deputies for the three Basque *circonscriptions*: Michèle Alliot-Marie, Alain Lamassoure, and François Bayrou. The report was composed of three parts, corresponding to the three fields in which different working groups had researched Basque society.

One part dealt with the principal social, economic, cultural, and administrative questions in Basque society. It highlighted the fact that the Basque Country represents an important region of Europe, that the *département* of the Pyrénées-Atlantiques has exercised a bipolar influence between Baiona and Pau, and that the Basque Autonomous Community in Hegoalde has exercised a strong attraction for Basques in Iparralde. It also emphasized the lack of a coherent policy to govern Iparralde and the inequalities between an urban, coastal region enjoying most of the services and economic development and a rural interior increasingly left behind. Finally, it highlighted the importance of local identity as a unifying and mobilizing factor among the population of Iparralde.[7]

The second report concentrated on the most important structural features in Iparralde, both current features and those believed to be potentially important in the medium term. For example, it emphasized the increasing significance of cross-border cooperation, together with the importance of generating a feeling of belonging to the Basque Country, the potential for developing the Baiona-Angelu-Biarritz (BAB) urban conurbation, the need to create better communications for Nafarroa Beherea and Zuberoa, and especially the possibility of legally establishing a new body to serve as a collective organ to oversee territorial development and structuring.[8]

Finally, the investigation concluded with a series of observations about potential future developments, drawing on a variety of opinions, from a worst-case scenario to the most optimistic outlook. The first scenario, which sought to highlight tendencies, envisaged the period to 2000 from the starting date of 1990. The following three were contrasting scenarios and extended these tendencies, in the possible absence of widespread public agreement or a general policy for the whole of Iparralde, to 2010. Finally, two other possibilities, about which there was widespread agreement, were put forward as best-case scenarios and were based on the prior establishment of sound public policies to aid local development and the organization of the region. Consequently, the fifth scenario envisaged effective planning for Iparralde as a whole, together with a balanced and integrated development plan based on the importance of territorial solidarity and widely supported institutional policies, while the sixth scenario looked to the successful development of a Euroregion, open to strong long-term forms of development and productive innovation.[9]

After this diagnosis of the contemporary social reality and of the potential future alternatives, the general conclusions were that a stable network, allowing the continuation of this quasi-institutional territorial organization and macro policies to facilitate local development, was necessary for Iparralde.[10] Thus, and in response to the dramatic findings of the *Basque Country 2010 Report*,[11] the numerous figures who drew up the publication came to defend what had been, until that time, a series of propositions claimed only by Basque nationalists: recognition of the territorial unity and the distinct nature of the French Basque Country, despite the fact it was at that time divided into two sub-prefectures and incorporated into the *département* of the Pyrénées-Atlantiques with Béarn; the need for greater cooperation with the Basque Autonomous Community and the Foral Community of Navarre (that is, Hegoalde); recognition of the cohesive potential of fomenting local identity as a means of generating more solidarity and aiding local development, and as such, the promotion of Basque culture and Euskara; and, finally, a call to establish representative mechanisms for the Basque Country.[12]

Based on these findings, the principal actors in this process chose, from the various proposals aimed at creating a quasi-institutional structure,[13] to create two bodies in the period from 1994 to 1995: the Conseil du Développement du Pays Basque (CDPB) and the Conseil des Élus du Pays Basque (CEPB) discussed in the last chapter. The CDPB was a forum for practically all the main social, cultural, economic and political actors in Iparralde and focused on elaborating a series of planning strategies, while the latter, composed of elected officials in Iparralde, took on decision-making authority, although it was not given the power to implement public policy, a power that remained in the hands of the municipal, departmental, regional, and national authorities.[14]

This, in effect, was an exercise in political engineering, given that it emerged from a consensus between two sectors that had previously shown tremendous reticence in undertaking initiatives of this kind: Basque nationalists had traditionally been lukewarm toward proposals for parainstitutional structures such as this because, they believed, such initiatives were intended solely to absolve the French government of its promise to create a Basque *département* and because they lacked institutional authority. However, they ultimately accepted the creation of these bodies because they incorporated a clear and prominent place for Basque identity in their organization (to that time almost a forgotten factor among elected officials in Iparralde) and because, from the outset, nationalists—due to their importance in social and cultural circles—enjoyed prominent positions within these new organizations. For example, as noted, Ramuntxo Camblong served as president of the CDPB between 1994 and 1997. On the other hand, the political class of Iparralde had historically been opposed to any initiatives of this kind because, they believed, they detracted from the notion of popular will as expressed at the polls during the multiple elections associated with the French political system.[15] However, in the 1990s the elected officials of Iparralde changed their attitude on understanding the initiative as stemming from a consensus-based politics of (implicit, rather than explicit) cooperation, a consensus based on putting the demand for a separate *département* to one side and because the CEPB would, in effect, be able to control the CDPB.[16]

The first task of this two-headed policy network was, once again, to draw up a diagnosis to address the problems affecting the territories making up Iparralde. Titled *Blueprint for Territorial Planning*,[17] it was composed of ninety-six measures aimed at guaranteeing a coherent form of development and was to be put into effect from 1997 on. However, the very lack of the CDPB's or the CEPB's own mechanisms or powers to implement such proposals meant that they had to negotiate with the relevant authorities the means that would put the proposals into action. And despite the fact that this general development plan was agreed to in principle by the three institutional levels of *département*, region, and national government, it was not until the end of 2000 that a specific agreement was signed to designate public funds to finance the plan.

Given this delayed response by the authorities, it perhaps came as no surprise that those sectors within the CDPB and the CEPB most favorable to some degree of institutional recognition for Iparralde once again took up the issue, and as they did so, the original consensus that had formed the basis of the agreement to create these two new bodies was broken. Between mid-1997 and early 2001, the entire plan to encourage a new form of development in Iparralde consequently went through a profound crisis due to the breaking of this consensus and the failure of the authorities to finance the original blueprint. And gradually, the debate changed from how to guarantee an effective form of development (that is, from a debate over public policy), to who should be charged with implementing the policy (that is, to a debate over institutional demands).

A Renewed Conception of Territory and the Centrality of Basque Nationalism

The emergence of this new consensus-based politics can be looked at from different perspectives useful for judging development strategies. To the first of these, I would accord special importance: the importance of a distinct notion of territory among the inhabitants of Iparralde. In addition, it can be viewed in terms of the immediate implications of consensus-based politics for Basque nationalism, from the point of view of the political process in itself, and according to the actual content of these strategies employed in that process.

First of all, thanks to this new dynamic, Iparralde became a specific and privileged frame of reference for public policy.[18] Indeed, the whole blueprint for development clearly outlined Iparralde as a distinct territorial unit. This was something recognized by the French state when it signed both the 1997 development agreement and the 2000 agreement to finance the proposals. These were acknowledged by the *conseil général* of the *département* of the Pyrénées-Atlantiques, which voted on and approved the blueprint in October 1997, and were approved by the *conseil régional*, which endorsed the same plan in February 1998.

This general endorsement of the development plan by the three principal institutional levels of the French political system carried with it a number of important implications. Specifically, it acknowledged Basque singularity as justification for a specific strategy that differed from that followed in other areas within France, the demand for a strong public policy regarding territorial planning, the need to establish mechanisms for autonomous control and implementation of these proposals, the call for greater coordination of financial measures designed to address specifically Basque problems, the implicit recognition of a need for territorial institutionalization, a similar recognition of the importance of local identity (officially termed "Pays Basque") as a means of generating the solidarity necessary to implement the development proposals, and all this as the result of an unprecedented consensus among local actors (in the CDPB and CEPB), experts, representatives of the national administrative system, and government agencies.[19]

Widespread assumption of Iparralde as a specific territorial space in which to develop a coherent policy of planning and development indeed led to its designation in 1997 as the Pays Basque, an officially recognized territorial unit that lacked any political power, but that allowed for a symbolic (and partially administrative) form of unity among the Basque provinces of France for the first time in modern history. As a result, the *arrondissement* (*circonscription*) of Baiona, for example, now had an official connection to the cantons of Maule and Atharratze in Zuberoa, even though the latter two remained under the jurisdiction of the subprefecture in Oloron (Béarn). The French state, then, recognized that the Basque Country "was geographically, culturally, economically, and socially consistent" and "constituted a space [to generate specific] projects."[20]

From this moment on, a complex structure emerged, although it was based on the single premise of the existence of the Pays Basque, a particular designated space in which planning proposals were to be developed in order to help guarantee its continued existence. The CDPB and the CEPB would be coordinating bodies designed to assume and promote this territorial perspective in their own internal philosophies. For example, the CEPB "translates, through its activities, a common identity that encourages actors to think of the Basque Country as an indivisible possession."[21] Similarly, the Council of the Basque Language, as it name implies, would oversee development in the linguistic field. From now on, it was officially recognized that Euskara was spoken not just within the limits of the subprefecture of Baiona, but also in that part of the subprefecture of Oloron located in Zuberoa—in other words, within the *pays* of the Pays Basque. Linguistic planning would thus take place within this *pays*, and not the *département*. Finally, as regards the remaining areas of public policy, departmental strategies would be complemented by local Basque structures such as the *Biltzar* of mayors in Iparralde (a unified body since 1994); an agency for agricultural coordination in Iparralde known as the Service for Territorial Agricultural Use, whose remit extended, again, throughout the *pays* of the Pays Basque; a council to coordinate scientific and technological higher education in Iparralde; the CCI of Baiona-Pays Basque, which Zuberoa had joined in 1991; and the Txingudi Consortium, a joint body incorporating the coastal towns between Baiona and Donostia, aimed at fomenting cross-border cooperation.[22]

Thus, the various development strategies drawn up by the principal actors in Iparralde coincided in that they were all grounded in the same perspective: the centrality of the Basque territory to the formulation of public policy. Examples of this abounded in the cultural and linguistic realm, as well as in the field of the environment, or, more generally, of economic development. Yet perhaps the clearest cases occurred in the issue of cross-border cooperation or spatial organization, where the territorialization of public policy was, necessarily, more precise.[23]

We are currently witness to a paradoxical outcome of this planning. On the one hand, the policy of specific development strategies for Iparralde approved by the French authorities in the 1990s has gained its own momentum over the ensuing years, to the extent that Iparralde has become a privileged site for the implementation of public policies. As a consequence, Basque nationalist strategies for building and preserving Basque institutions that emphasize the existence and presence of Iparralde have coincided with public policies that, de facto, also recognize Basque unity and difference, leading to a slow, but inexorable growth in the "appropriation" of the territory (Iparralde) by its inhabitants, in effect marking the first stage that any identity under construction must go through: internal self-recognition.[24] Paradoxically, however, Iparralde still lacks any specific administrative or institutional power (the capacity both to make and to implement decisions), so any strategies designed by its leading actors are liable to being blocked or boycotted by other institutions—institutions that perhaps see in the increasingly "visible" presence of Iparralde as a distinct spatial unit a threat to their own power. This, in short, is the paradox of a territory that in practice exists, but that needs a degree of institutionalization to develop further.

All the development strategies that have been drawn up and disseminated have done so in tandem with a growing social base of Basque nationalist and pro-Basque *département* collectives. Or, to put it another way, the paradox is that anyone drawing up a plan or a proposal within the present context ultimately finds that it would be better if there were, indeed, some form of institutional recognition for Iparralde. In reality, any governing potential for these new bodies that emerged in the 1990s was in practice limited,[25] leading to a growing questioning of the value of the consensus originally achieved if it could not resolve the fundamental problem: the lack of institutional recognition.

As noted, however, there are other perspectives from which we can analyze these new development strategies. For example, the twin structure underpinning the CDPB and the CEPB allowed the widespread participation of actors from many different fields, together with elected officials and administrative figures, in drawing up numerous proposals. Thanks to this new structure, Basque nationalists realized they could now intervene directly in political debate within Iparralde, as well as seek alliances with nonnationalist sectors that were in favor of the institutionalization of Basque territorial and cultural difference to some degree. Indeed, this realization underscored the rise of AB as the key, central force in the wide social movement campaigning for a Basque *département* at the end of the 1990s and also strengthened the position of pro-Basque, but nonnationalist republicans, politically represented since 2002 by Elgar-Ensemble.

Examining the formation of public policy as a process, one clearly sees that the creation of these new networks parallels four of the five steps in the development of public policies described by both Charles O. Jones and Yves Mény and Jean-Claude Thoenig:[26] identification of the problem, represented here by the publishing of the *Basque Country 2010 Report* (1993); the proposal of alternatives, as manifested here in the *Blueprint for Territorial Planning* (1996); decision making, appearing here in the acceptance by the French authorities of this development plan; and an evaluation of the dynamic, as represented here in various publications by the CDPB. However, ultimately, both bodies lacked power in what is characterized as the fifth phase of this public-policy process: implementation—a key power that remained in the hands of the (national, departmental, and regional) French authorities, that is, in the hands of *maîtrises d'ouvrages publiques* (project directors) and certain private collectives or *maîtres d'oeuvres* (project managers). In other words, for the successful implementation of any plan, the authorities first had to agree to apply its proposals. However, the general feeling that these same authorities were not responding to the expectations raised by the new developments in the 1990s indirectly reinforced the inclination of the main actors who were taking positions calling for specific local institutions. Consequently, Basque nationalists attempted to forge alliances with these actors in order to assume center stage in the political debate and the growing movement for institutional representation.

Finally, in terms of the precise content of these strategies, the fourth perspective from which to assess such approaches, two main types of coalition emerge in these networks: one that links development within defined territories to the level of institutionalization they have, a linkage in the Basque case seen as essential by nationalists, and another that attempts to differentiate the debate over public policy from that over institutional representation.[27] In Iparralde, both kinds of coalition have operated in tandem with one another since 1994. Between 1992 and 1997, development policies were characterized broadly by negotiation between all the relevant actors, which explains the logic of consensus between Basque nationalists and local notables. Between 1997 and 2000, however, in response to the lack of any implementation of these proposals by the authorities, those in favor of a Basque *département* pursued a new logic of mobilization, most obviously expressed by a first wave of protest aimed at demanding institutional representation, a cycle that had actually begun already in 1994. Yet after the authorities had signed the specific agreement in 2000 promising to finance the agreed proposals, a new era of cultivating self-government began, during which the first serious attempts were made to implement the previously designed proposals at the same time as the movement in favor of a specific Basque *département* also gained momentum. In 2002, however, this pro-Basque institutionalization movement began to change its strategy, initiating an era of confrontation with the authorities through the Batera platform (discussed below) as a result, mainly, of the frustration felt after the breakdown of negotiations over decentralization with the Raffarin government that same year. The bases were in place, then, for a second (and the current) major wave of protest, now characterized by active measures, rather than the previous reactive strategy.

The development policies approved by the French authorities from 1992 on opened up policy windows that allowed the incorporation of a debate on the future of Iparralde into the discursive logic of the different actors involved. Basque nationalist sectors were central to this whole process, taking control of the first (and decisive) stage in the CDPB, the principal body representing civil society, and managing to introduce numerous elements of their own discourse into the local debate. As a result, in the late 1990s, by breaking free of the marginalization they had suffered since the 1960s and faced with a lack of will on the part of the French authorities to financially aid the proposals that had been made, these same nationalist sectors felt justified in adopting a more radical strategy to achieve their goals. At the same time, nationalists aided in the creation of an opportunity structure that situated them at the center of a historical call for a single Basque *département*, a development that, in turn, converted them into a sector capable of drawing together people of different political sensibilities who nevertheless shared the same institutional demands. Finally, and throughout this whole process, the idea of a specifically Basque space gradually took hold among both the central actors and the population as a whole, thanks mainly to the links between the public policies put forward and the territorial space in which they were conceived. And this was a development that ultimately served to generate a new Pays Basque identity—that is, the ability to feel Basque in France and French in Iparralde—but this new Basque identity (in many ways, a more politicized version of former pro-Basque positions) also became an important force in demands for a separate *département*. At the same time, this Pays Basque sense of belonging also emerged in tandem with the growth of a specifically Basque identity articulated by Basque nationalists—Iparralde as an integral part of Euskal Herria. Together the development of these two forms of identity encouraged a greater awareness of Iparralde as a distinct space with a right to have some say in its own development.

The Call for the Institutionalization of Basque Difference

The call for a single Basque *département* began as soon as the historic provinces of Lapurdi, Nafarroa Beherea, and Zuberoa were incorporated into a *département* with Béarn.[28] For two hundred years, these calls had been consistent and generally rested on three principles: the identity, economy, and political realities of the region, defended, respectively, by Basque nationalists, the modernizing bourgeoisie associated with the CCI of Baiona, and the French Socialist party (PS).[29]

As a result, the new movement in favor of a Basque *département* that took shape with the declaration of October 9, 1999, did so thanks to various actors from different social, political, and economic backgrounds: the AED (the Association des Élus pour un Département Pays Basque, the Association of Elected Officials for a *Département* of the Basque Country) serving as a pressure group, the PS functioning as a traditional political party, and AB as the political expression of a peripheral nationalist social movement. Together with these, there were other, more obviously pro-*département* collectives that, for reasons of space, I will not analyze here.[30] In short, there were three principal and different ideological foundations to the movement that gradually converged over the same issue.

The Convergence of Pro-Département Actors

Each of these three principal actors, the AED, PS, and AB, developed separate, yet parallel and therefore complementary strategies during the period from 1994 to 1997–98. To them, we may add a fourth. The new shift toward a call for a Basque *département* was implemented by one of the most important notables from the interior of Iparralde: Michel Inchauspé, a well-known member of the conservative Rassemblement pour la République (RPR, Rally for the Republic). Despite his antipathy to any form of Basque institutionalization in the 1980s, in 1994, he proposed the creation of a "3B" region (that is, Basque, Béarnais, and including Bigorre, a historic province located in the *département* of the Hautes-Pyrénées) that would incorporate Iparralde, Béarn, and Bigorre. The fact that an important conservative figure such as Inchauspé saw the need for some form of territorial reorganization encouraged others to consider the question. And soon, various ideas began to emerge that transcended the proposals of any one individual while at the same time awakening a collective action that had lain dormant for decades thanks to the apathy generated by the power and control of the major elected officials.

These attitudes, revealing a greater interest in the demand for a single Basque *département*, were the result of a transforming political scenario that witnessed a significant change from the 1980s to the 1990s. The territorial limits that defined the activity of elected officials in Iparralde began to change, from the highly localized context of canton and *arrondissement* to a wider and more "Basque" space,[31] mainly as the result of the new state-sponsored policy of territorial organization, one of whose basic references was the notion of a Pays Basque. Moreover, as this new policy was consolidated through the creation of the CDPB and the CEPB, these same elected officials were forced to take more account of other actors—people who for decades had been marginalized from the realm of local debate and decision making: indeed, civil society itself, led mainly by advocates for economic and cultural interests, many of whom were Basque nationalists.

This shifting context was most likely responsible for the changing attitude among the elected officials of Iparralde, represented most visibly by Inchauspé. For rational political reasons,[32] he realized that there were greater benefits to be obtained from encouraging the debate over a Basque *département*. However, this instrumental or rational logic,[33] despite resting on a plan to create a (not entirely Basque) region that would have made him into a kind of mini or Basque de Gaulle, wavered when it came to finding support for his proposal. Indeed, the plan was adamantly opposed by both the centrist Union pour la Democratie Française (UDF, Union for French Democracy) and even by the RPR. Thus, from a purely rational perspective, the negative balance between personal gain and cost should have made Inchauspé rethink his original proposal. Instead, however, despite his proposal falling on deaf ears in 1994, four years later, he repeated the plan, and once again found a negative response in the French National Assembly.

To be sure, Inchauspé, who personally financed a poll to be taken among all the homes of the "3B" region he proposed (the results of which demonstrated a majority in favor of the plan), was a singular individual.[34] Yet quite apart from any individual initiatives, a new correlation of forces was gradually emerging that demanded more action from those parties—such as the PS—interested in some form of change, as well as a reconsideration on the part of those elected officials still hostile to Basque institutional claims. In short, for the first time in decades, civil society in Iparralde was questioning the denizens of the corridors of power.

Within this slowly transforming picture, the AED once again surfaced (after a long dormant period) to take part in the *départmental* debate, thanks in the main to Inchauspé's promptings. As regards its internal organization, the AED might best be defined as a kind of rational pressure group that sought to protect the interests of certain elected officials across the political spectrum in Iparralde. This internal heterogeneity was reflected by the different interpretations of the existing demands among its members:[35] identity-based for Basque nationalists, political (linked to a belief in greater decentralization and "closer" democracy) for Socialists, and economic, especially for those elected officials of the center and the right. The diverse nature of such interpretations impeded strong internal cohesion and even more so a shared, common identity. Yet the AED's influential capacity in the political system was (almost casually) reinforced by the new correlation of these different sectors that followed in the wake of the favorable vote of the *Biltzar* of mayors on the question of a separate *département* in 1996.[36]

The success of this initiative encouraged various dynamics within the AED, and it gradually began to reorganize the way it operated. For example, it gradually abandoned several sluggish practices based on personal and individual contact between individual elected officials in favor of a wider dynamic of mobilization, as exemplified in the organization of the referendum in each of the Basque municipal councils or city halls.[37] This new mobilizing dynamic, moreover, was complemented by the publication of a document that served as an instrument for strengthening the two dimensions in which the AED operated: externally, leading to a process that seduced local representatives, and internally, allowing a greater cohesion of its members. The document, entitled "Pour quoi un département Pays Basque" (Why a *département* of the Basque Country?) attempted to socialize the arguments for the institution among the elected officials by highlighting the rational dimension of such a proposal: its potential economic benefits. In this way, it established the focus its members should adopt in looking to influence both other elected officials and, ultimately, the representatives of civil society. From this internal perspective, the document allowed a basic minimum consensus to be established among the group's members, an important step, considering its heterogeneous nature.[38] Thus, and without realizing it, the AED established a "master frame"[39] in terms of which the later social movement in favor of a *département* developed, one that incorporated elements of a more specific frame contributed by Basque nationalists.

Gradually, the AED began to lose the features that distinguished it as a pressure group, becoming more of a social movement—mainly as the result of the negative response by the French authorities to its efforts. Here, we see the reverse of the process that usually culminates in social movements becoming interest groups.[40] Rather, as a result of the activity of various pro-*département* (and mainly Basque nationalist) business leaders,[41] this pressure group (the AED) adopted more of the features of a social movement.

As noted, this "radical" turn of the AED came as the result of the ambivalence or hostility of the French state to any notion of change, the principal reason, too, behind the shift within the PS toward a stance more in favor of Basque institutions. In the mid-1990s, the PS also began to comment favorably on these new institutional proposals in an attempt to not lose ground on those centrist and right-wing sectors that had already embraced this discourse. Once again, as in the 1980s, this was a PS maneuver to retain its position within the local (Basque) political system. Consequently, initial PS strategy was aimed at gaining a majority in favor of a single *département* at the local level.[42] And therefore the PS looked favorably on the initial line developed by both the AED and the *Biltzar*, as well as on the ballot undertaken within the municipal councils. Similarly, the election of the Socialist Nicole Péry in the fifth *circonscription* in the 1997 legislative elections after her clear support for a single *département* and her later incorporation into Jospin's Socialist government raised many expectations—expectations that were gradually disappointed by Péry's more centralist colleagues within the PS. Clearly, some Basque members of the PS were involved in an internal struggle with the leadership of their own party, and this explains these local PS members' later participation in the emerging organized pro-*département* social movement and the declaration of October 9, 1999, on both occasions bringing them into direct conflict with Jospin's Socialist government.

Finally, the role of the dominant Basque nationalist party, AB, was ultimately conditioned by the traditional makeup of leftist peripheral nationalism in Iparralde. Clandestine armed groups existed on both sides of the border, and these groups had been extremely influential (symbolically) in the emergence and development of leftist Basque nationalism in Iparralde. However, as we have seen, left-wing nationalism in the North—as represented until 2001 exclusively by AB—was significantly different from its counterpart (the Izquierda Abertzale movement) in the South. In Hegoalde, ETA created a whole community of legitimation within which the Izquierda Abertzale had an important position. However, neither ETA nor IK could create the same extensive community in Iparralde, so that armed struggle never took on more importance than its political counterpart, and AB remained significantly more autonomous than, for example, HB in the South. Consequently, AB was free to follow the pragmatic goal of demanding a single Basque *département*, as opposed, for example, to IK's call for a statute of autonomy for Iparralde.

At the same time, AB gradually adopted a more rational approach in line with that of any political party while also increasingly playing down the original identity-centered discourse that had marked its creation. The strength of this leftist nationalism was in marked contrast with the traditional electoral weakness of nationalists in Iparralde, something that did not reflect their importance in these new politics of development. Therefore a more pragmatic or practical line served AB well in a political climate that was still in many ways hostile to Basque nationalism.[43] However, this growing campaign in favor of the institutionalization of Basque difference, a campaign that transformed AB from a coalition of different forces into one single party, and the pragmatic line that the party had decided to follow in it did not help overcome internal conflicts. Although AB dedicated all its efforts to the question of a *département* from 1997 on, at the same time, its internal unity began to break down, until, in 2001, it suffered a significant internal split.

The root of this split was AB's decision to prioritize demands for a *département* over those for a statute of autonomy, the position favored by IK and part of AB's militant wing. At root, as regards the question of identity, AB clearly favored spatial boundaries that related their group to an ethnic territory, temporal boundaries understood in a utopian way, and cultural boundaries rooted in the specificity of the Basque language, with all three dimensions orientated toward the strategic objective of independence and territorial unity for Iparralde and Hegoalde. However, externally, the party was forced to conform to more instrumental or rational demands.[44] This obliged AB to go beyond ethnic lines in its search for adherents to the demand for a *département* among the whole population of Iparralde and to seek an agreement based on minimum accords, given its weak electoral presence. Consequently, the party defined a pro-*département* strategy based on three stages or objectives: situating the party at the center of the pro-*département* movement, then generating a widespread movement to socialize the demand, thereby potentially achieving a majority favorable to the institutionalization of Basque difference, and finally spreading a dynamic of civil disobedience that would make any attempts to maintain the status quo impossible in case a Basque *département* was not forthcoming.[45]

My examination of these four actors participating in the pro-*département* movement—the AED, the PS, and AB, with Michel Inchauspé, the notable, as an instigator—demonstrates the movement's widespread ideological base. Consequently, it is difficult to speak of a clear consensus of action among the different interests and much less so of the various groups forming some kind of united social movement.[46] Yet despite the differences, and despite the alternative strategies adopted by each of these groups, each of their strategies reinforced the others: Michel Inchauspé provided the initial impetus that motivated others to start organizing. The AED envisaged the importance of bringing different forces together at the local level, which led ultimately to the PS supporting the initiative. Similarly, the tendency of the PS to foster support among its base members in order to pressure the party leadership, in turn, strengthened the position of the AED. Elsewhere, Basque nationalists saw in this growing movement the potential to enter mainstream politics and therefore a possibility to publicize their own agenda, particularly as regarded Euskara and sovereignty. Moreover, the nationalists also contributed a mobilizing element that was unknown among the other groups, guaranteeing a very public presence for pro-*département* demands.

As a result, AB (but also EA and the PNB), the PS, and the AED gradually began to recognize the internal conditions necessary to consolidate some form of unified approach, because all had something to contribute and to gain from such a strategy: the Socialists contributed a legitimacy derived from their access to the highest decision-making circles and would theoretically gain electorally in the eventuality of achieving a single Basque *département* as the symbolic political driving force behind the movement. The AED contributed its importance as a representative of local elected officials and would gain, in the same circumstances, the realization of its original objective. AB (and Basque nationalism in general) contributed its popular mobilizing capacity and would gain a greater centrality in everyday political life, thereby consolidating a tactical step toward its other strategic objectives.

Importantly, too, the negative response of the French authorities to the initial demands between 1997 and 1999 reinforced the need for a unified approach among these different collectives, and this—the need for collective action—was tied to the local political opportunities that emerged during the same period as a result of assorted factors: various possibilities of access, unstable alignments, division among the elites and influential allies,[47] together with the existence of several institutions and host settings that legitimize unified action such as that of the *Biltzar* of mayors.

Opportunities for the Movement

On January 30, 1999, AB organized a demonstration in Baiona—the first of its kind in history—calling for a Basque *département*. It was attended by six thousand people, thereby making a very public and social statement about the demand. At the same time, AB also began a round of contacts with the other groups interested in the demand with the aim of unifying their different strategies. Thereafter, one hundred individuals representing the different groups began a campaign to mobilize the population in favor of a Basque *département*.[48] The so-called call of the hundred (later renamed the call of October 9) culminated that same year on October 9 with a demonstration in Baiona attended by thirteen thousand people, the largest of its kind since World War II.[49] To complement this popular mobilization, polls published in both 1999 and 2000 suggested that as much as 66 percent of the population of Iparralde was in favor of creating a single Basque *département*.[50]

How does one account for the transformation of society in Iparralde, from widespread apathy to such institutional demands in the 1980s, to large-scale popular mobilization at the close of the 1990s? Further, how does one explain the confluence of such different forces—Basque nationalists, Socialists, the traditional conservatives of the center and the right, together with business leaders and labor unions—in creating a single, unified social movement? The answers to these questions lie in the political opportunity structure that opened up between 1997 and 1999.

During this time, an effective pressure-group strategy by these disparate forces encouraged the opening up of such possibilities and, consequently, the incorporation of new recruits to the cause. A key player in this dynamic was the *Biltzar* of mayors that, through its support for the creation of a *département*, acted as a central institution in legitimizing (from a political point of view) the activity of the other organizations, even publishing a seminal document calling for the institutionalization of Basque difference.[51] Thus, a host setting was created that began to feed the expectations of the principal actors involved in this demand. Crucially, however, this initial sustaining framework soon evolved into a more active one, and through 1999, a pressure-group dynamic emerged in tandem with the gradual creation of a unified social movement as expressed most obviously by the call of October 9, to the extent that the institutional demand was increasingly communicated to the French government directly.

At the same time, the support of a wide variety of other actors—for example, the moderate nationalists of the PNB and one of the largest and most important French labor unions, the Confédération Française Démocratique du Travail (the CFDT, the French Democratic Confederation of Labor)— served only to reinforce these institutional demands. Meanwhile, although it came later to the movement, AB quickly established itself—mainly as a result of its mobilizing capacity—as the central driving force, demanding a more active pressure-group philosophy, a strategy that was also quickly seconded by the political AED and the civil AND (the Association pour un Nouveau Département, the Association for a New *Département*). Indeed, these two collectives, because of their representative and therefore legitimizing nature, became the main public face of initial calls to unify the movement. On these foundations, and with the cautious and gradual adoption of more cultural elements in the originally (and predominantly) economic argument in favor of a single *département* supported by the AED, new doors opened to an even greater degree of cooperation between different actors.

The consequences of this dynamic were increasingly evident: Basque Socialists, for example, were ever more at odds with the central leadership of the PS—to such an extent that they were also forced to demonstrate to their new partners within the pro-*département* social movement that they really did believe in the demand. And ultimately, the frustrated attempts by Inchauspé to go through the official channels—specifically, his presentations before the French National Assembly in 1994 and 1998—demonstrated to all concerned the futility of relying on some kind of official reform of the system from above and that, by definition, the only possible route to such reform was by massive public mobilization from below to force the issue with the French authorities.[52]

However, an examination of the possibilities of maneuver for the pro-Basque institution movement at the national level demonstrates the limits of the demand. Indeed, the very nature of a strong national state with exclusive powers is always likely to reduce the effectiveness or drive of any movement that challenges state power.[53] Furthermore, in the particular case of the demand for a single Basque *département*, two more factors hindered the movement and reinforced the opposition of various elites: one derived from the nature of the dynamic driving the demand for a new *département* and the other conditioned by the international (cross-border) context of events in Hegoalde.

As regards the first of these, the actions and attitudes of the different groups involved in this demand were increasingly conditioned by their position on the center-periphery scale, a position interpreted in two ways: as a struggle between Basque and French identity and as whether one supported or was against the process of decentralization. Thus, the two groups that had a greater French identity—RPR and the PCF (the Communists)—completely denied the existence of any Basque element in the institutional demands. And although it made sense for other political formations—such as the PS, where the issue of French identity was not so important—to support institutional demands, they ultimately began to retreat from these positions at the close of 1998 as a result of an issue that went beyond the borders of France.[54]

Once more, events in Hegoalde came to influence those in Iparralde through the declaration and later breaking of the ETA ceasefire between 1998 and 1999. As a consequence of the ceasefire, a new Basque nationalist coalition emerged through the Lizarra-Garazi pact.[55] The signing of this pact distanced PS leaders from favoring greater institutional recognition for Iparralde, for, in effect, the confusion between the "process of pacification" and the "process of national construction" outlined by the Lizarra-Garazi agreement incorporated Iparralde into the nationalist vision of the future.[56] Therefore, the extension of the pact from Lizarra to Garazi and calls on the French state to help resolve the question on its territory,[57] together with pressure from the Spanish government on France to resist the initiative, definitively closed down any possibility of Basque institutional claims through the regular political process in France. At the local level, however, contacts between the different actors in Iparralde were maintained, given that the pro-Basque institution dynamic had preceded events in Hegoalde.[58]

The general political opportunity structure thus was vital in influencing the tactical shift that took place in 1999. And events in this period were also crucial in leading the principal actors to a greater unity of action, a tactic for which AB had already prepared.

The Climax of the First Protest Cycle

Despite the huge demonstration in Baiona in late 1999, practical results were scarcely forthcoming, because ultimately, the French government clearly opposed any notion of territorial modification. This, in turn, provoked a tactical transformation on the part of the pro-*département* movement toward a campaign of civil disobedience, although this campaign was not, as AB had planned in the third of its predicted stages, carried out by the party itself. Instead, a new social movement now took the initiative. Named Demo (an abbreviation for Demokrazia Euskal Herriarentzat, Democracy for the Basque Country), this collective was founded in 2000, and while distinct from AB, its strategy fit perfectly with the notion of generating wide social repercussions concerning the lack of French support for the institutional demands, because, in the ideologically broad nature of the call of October 9, there was an implicit recognition that some acts of civil disobedience would probably be the next step in the face of a negative decision by the French authorities even to consider the issue. Moreover, a growing sympathy for such activity by the population of Iparralde also legitimated the shift to civil disobedience and allowed the Demo collective to maximize its actions.[59] These actions included stealing twenty-one chairs, corresponding to the number of Basque representatives on the *conseil général* (regional council) of the *département* of the Pyrénées-Atlantiques, "kidnapping" two dozen Mariannes (the national emblem of France, prominent in the form of a sculpture or bust in many French towns), and changing monolingual road signs for bilingual ones.[60] As a result, they were clearly seen as mounting a challenge to state authority, even generating a degree of uncertainty as to the severity of measures that an official response might adopt. This, in turn, though, led to an even greater solidarity among these activists, which I will discuss in more detail below.

By mid-2000, a protest cycle that had begun in the period 1994–97 and that gained new momentum after 1999 came to a certain conclusion. Sidney G. Tarrow defines a protest cycle (or cycle of contention) as "a phase of heightened contention and conflict across the social system that includes: a rapid diffusion of collective action from more mobilized to less mobilized sectors; a quickened pace of innovation in the forms of contention; new or transformed collective action frames; a combination of organized and unorganized participation; and sequences of intensified interaction between challengers and authorities which can end in reform, repression and sometimes revolution."[61] This definition is a useful frame by which to assess the pro-Basque *département* movement between 1994 and 2000. This particular protest cycle began in 1994 with Inchauspé's proposal for establishing a new administrative region. His proposal (although unsuccessful) initiated a new dynamic in which, gradually, other actors participated. Such was the case for the Basque nationalists of AB and the PNB, as well as for the French labor union, the CDFT. The proposal also served to awaken a slower-mobilizing process among other actors, such as the AED, the AND, and the PS. Yet ultimately, Inchauspé was only the catalyst of a sensibility that had much deeper historical roots.[62]

The issue raised by Inchauspé and subsequently taken up by the AED and PS complied with two functions necessary for the continuation of any protest cycle:[63] some kind of demonstration of vulnerability on the part of the authorities when faced with the initial challenge, which, in turn, encourages other actors to participate in the demand (for example, the surprising involvement of the *Biltzar* of mayors in 1996), and the direct questioning of an established elite power group, such as was the case with the questioning of both the powerful traditional elected officials in coastal towns and the French government, whether of the right (until 1997) or the left (from 1997 on).

The first stage in a protest cycle is an intensification of the conflict.[64] This is obvious if we compare the possibilities for demanding institutional recognition in the mid-1990s with those available during the late 1970s. First, Inchauspé's proposal proved to be only the first attempt to break down the grand antidepartmental wall that had been constructed by the great and important elected officials of Iparralde, and various political forces and new discourses added to the momentum of what he began, all culminating in the call of October 9, 1999 and the huge popular demonstrations in favor of the initiative that same year. At root, through the mid and late 1990s, there thus emerged a kind of strategic alliance between political and civil groups in favor of institutional change. Interestingly, the particular evolution of this movement went beyond the traditional urban boundaries of social protest to encompass a full perspective of Iparralde, including its rural heartland. This not only allowed the full integration of Nafarroa Beherea and Zuberoa into the spatial realm of the protest cycle, but also allowed the agricultural union, the ELB, to assume an increasingly important role within the movement as a whole.[65]

However, another key factor in any protest cycle is the proclivity of opposition groups or antagonists to also take part in the collective action.[66] In the case of Iparralde, there was a reaction of this kind, although it would perhaps be more accurate to classify the creation of this countermovement as the creation of a "phantom collective." That is, in both its origins and its makeup, the emergence of a movement against the notion of a single Basque *département* was somewhat artificial and rested principally on the negative response of the Association of Mayors of the Pyrénées-Atlantiques to the 1997 publication of the AED: "Pour quoi un département Pays Basque."

Although they did not form any specific organization to combat the diffusion of the Basque institutional model, two other actors had more developed strategies in their struggle against the idea: In mid-2000, the RPR refused point-blank to entertain any notion that there might one day be a Basque *département*, linking the demand directly with a potential extension of the violence in Hegoalde to Iparralde. On August 31, 2000, the president of the RPR, then mayor of Donibane Lohizune and future minister of defense (2002–) Michèle Alliot-Marie, argued that "the call for the creation of a *département* of the Basque Country is, today, among the first demands of ETA's legal framework; it is absolutely inopportune and dangerous, and it is not, in this sense, prudent to encourage the more radical separatist formations." For this reason, the RPR called on "the inhabitants of this '*pays*' . . . to reject adventurous notions" in the hope that "they might demonstrate their ability to construct, within the framework of the institutions of the Republic, a Basque Country loyal to its identity, its language, its culture, open to others, tolerant, and the site of future projects."[67]

In similar fashion, although with fewer repercussions, at least two Gascon cultural groups—CAP-Vivre Ensemble and ACI! Gascona—responded virulently to the proposal for a Basque *département*; considering that the centrality of the Basque cultural dimension to the debate historically overlooked the original, Gascon culture of coastal Lapurdi, and especially of Baiona—a reaction that might be classified as that of a periphery of a periphery. Authors from Juan J. Linz to Francisco Letamendia have used this framework to address the relationship of Iparralde with both its French and Basque (Hegoalde) centers,[68] but it is equally applicable to Gascon identity, if we understand it as the peripheral culture of another cultural periphery, that of the Basque Country in France. However, this initial hostility declined once the departmental movement (and especially the Basque cultural collectives) began, along with its other objectives, to accord Gascon claims a status within its general strategy.

Yet another factor governing whether there is a protest cycle or not is the degree to which the repertoires of action are amplified. As we have seen, this was quite clearly the case with the pro-*département* movement, given the wide spectrum of groups that came to favor the proposal, from the *Biltzar* of mayors to the Demos. The adherence of these disparate groups took place in two phases: During the period from 1996 to 1999, it was a question of an accumulation of forces around the AED-PS-AB axis, while thereafter, these forces grew ever more diverse and combined conventional and disruptive strategies.

The October 9, 1999 demonstration marked the culmination of the initial phase of the protest cycle, the maximum expression of what mass citizen mobilization could achieve. Yet because it did, indeed, reveal the maximum potential for this type of protest, the principal actors within the movement also saw the need to begin a new phase of action. At the same time, the part of the strategy that attempted to go through official channels—and that successfully gained official recognition of the *Biltzar* as an intermediary in the debate—also reached a certain conclusion, especially when the proposals of this body were rejected outright by the French authorities. Finally, even direct action appeared to have achieved all that it could: The Demos gained widespread public sympathy for their acts of civil disobedience, but were faced, too, with two crucial questions: If they went any further than the peaceful and humorous acts that they had committed up to that point, they ran the risk of losing that public sympathy, as well as the support of other actors in the movement as a whole, and if they were reduced to committing less spectacular acts, they also ran the risk of lessening their impact by demonstrating their own declining ability to pursue the path of civil disobedience. Even disruptive action could become routine and marginal.[69]

Consequently, between 2000 and 2002, the movement for Basque institutions went through a period of reconstruction. Initially, this involved a paradoxical decline in all activity, principally because of the very success of the movement through 1999. Another defining element in any protest cycle is its capacity to generate new frames of reference and ideologies.[70] In the Basque case in Iparralde, through to 1999, a central and founding element of the movement had been economic in origin, yet from 2001 on, the linguistic issue also began to occupy more of the discourse, becoming in effect a parallel claim to that of the need for a specifically Basque institution.

Finally, protest cycles are marked by intensified action between challengers and authorities, a key feature of relations between the pro-*département* activists and the French authorities through 1999 and into early 2000. This coincided, as we have seen, with the period of maximum citizen mobilization in favor of a specifically Basque institution. It also coincided with one of the most important opinion polls taken to gauge the feeling of Basque society on the issue. On August 29, 1999, the newspaper, *Sud-Ouest* published the results of the poll (carried out by the firm CSA). Among the findings of this poll, perhaps the most significant were: Of people polled throughout the *département* of the Pyrénées-Atlantiques, 47 percent were totally or fairly in favor of the creation of two different *départements*, one in the Basque Country and the other in Béarn; 37 percent were totally or fairly against it; and 16 percent did not respond. Answering the same question, but this time within Iparralde, 57 percent were favorable to the idea, 29 percent were against, and 14 percent did not respond, while in Béarn, 39 percent were in favor and 43 percent against. Sixty-four percent of those polled in Iparralde were against the idea that "the creation of two *départements* is an attack on the unity of the republic," while the profile of the citizen most likely to favor the change (within the *département* of the Pyrénées-Atlantiques as a whole) was male (58 percent), between twenty-five and thirty-four years old (61 percent), working class (58 percent), and voted for the Greens (59 percent). Also at the departmental level, as regarded a favorable stance by party political affiliation, after the Greens, the next highest level of support came from sympathizers of the RPR (54 percent) and the PS (46 percent), while supporters of the UDF were least in favor (31 percent) of the idea. Finally, there was little difference in the kind of physical environment that those favorable came from, with 57 percent of people from urban areas and 55 percent of people from rural areas supporting the notion.

One year later, in September 2000, an even more detailed poll was published, this time after the first, great wave of protest had ended and when the pro-*département* initiative was in the phase of reconstruction. This time, the results were perhaps even more telling. In fact, far from declining, support for the original notion posed a year earlier had grown, with the backing of 66 percent of those polled in Iparralde and 57 percent in Béarn. According to this poll at least, 56 percent of the total population of the *département* of the Pyrénées-Atlantiques now was in favor of creating two new institutions.

The period from 1994 to 1999 thus witnessed a mobilizing cycle based on several premises that had not previously existed in any movement defending some form of Basque particularity. Chief among these innovations was the unity of action among a wide spectrum of actors who ultimately had different conceptions of the territory they inhabited, but shared the belief that it would be best administered by one specific institutional framework. In short, the economic vision (based on the belief that a single *département* would guarantee greater development) incorporated a cultural element (based on the notion that a single *département* would guarantee the protection and development of the Basque language and culture) and a political dimension (rooted in the notion that a single *département* would guarantee greater contact between the citizenry and the political process).

I have already noted that, to a certain extent at least, this movement was a victim of its own success, in that the initial phase culminated in 1999 with a level of public activity that could hardly be surpassed. In turn, from within the movement there emerged the need to reconfigure a strategy for the new millennium. Yet faced with such success, the French state did not remain a passive bystander. Indeed, in the wake of this success, at the end of 2000, the state began to fight back and attempt to recover the initiative after its initial outright refusal to entertain any notion of a Basque institution. Consequently, it improved its public-development policies and signed an agreement to aid the financial development the three most important coastal towns, Baiona, Angelu, and Biarritz. In total, 400 million euros were designated for seventy projects, most of them approved in the general blueprint for development.[71] And there was an administrative change when the state allocated the subprefecture of Baiona greater powers.

The Reconfiguration Phase, 2000–2002

Between 2000 and 2002, the departmental movement went through a phase of reconfiguration, not just as the result of the fact that the first, mobilizing phase had come to an end, but partly because of the fact that groups within the movement were having to confront a number of internal contradictions. One of the most noteworthy of these confrontations took place within AB itself.

In 2000, Euskal Herritarrok (EH), the successor party to HB in Hegoalde, announced the beginning of an internal process to culminate in the formation of a new party that would be based in both Hegoalde and Iparralde.[72] As a result, some militants within AB also took part in EH's internal debate, although most members signed a statement calling for the Hegoalde party to suspend its processes in Iparralde. EH refused to do this, however, and after a general meeting, AB likewise refused the EH proposal to integrate in the new formation: Batasuna. This led to AB losing 20 percent of its members, who decided to join the new party's branch in Iparralde. In turn, AB agreed a new position on the use of violence—something that until that time it had refused to condemn—demanding of ETA an immediate ceasefire.[73]

From this moment on, then, although AB had lost a significant part of its membership, it was actually internally reinforced by the fact that it could now definitively overcome the controversial issue of where it stood on the question of violence, and as such, it was free once more to take the initiative in leading the pro-*département* movement. Thus, taking advantage of another round of general debate over the question of decentralization at the close of 2002, people from different political backgrounds created the

Batera platform as a means of focusing on four key issues: the *département*, official status for Euskara, a specific university for Iparralde, and an agricultural chamber. In order to understand the specific strategy of the Batera platform, one must first look at events in the period from 2000 to 2002, because although the kind of public mobilization seen through 1999 waned, there were important developments in the pro-Basque institution movement that, from late 2002 on, heralded the beginning of another cycle of activism.

As noted, the previous cycle, culminating in the call of October 9, 1999, centered its strategy on conventional action. Yet in 2000, the baton of protest was taken up by another, more clearly Basque nationalist group, Demo, which began a new phase of more disruptive (though peaceful) activity. Between 2000 and 2003, the Demos maximized the full potential that a campaign of civil disobedience can bring,[74] challenging the authorities with their three demands: the transfer of Basque political prisoners to jails nearer or in the Basque Country, the creation of Basque institutions, and the addition of a specific linguistic plan to the general blueprint for development. With these objectives in mind, as we have seen, the Demos carried out a number of sometimes spectacular acts of civil disobedience. And in these three years, Basque society came to accept a more confrontational or radical (although still peaceful) approach than previous conventional methods for achieving some objectives. As a result, actors who until 1999 had been content to follow more conventional approaches—meetings, demonstrations, and popular mobilizations—began gradually to assume this different logic—that is, the possibility that a more radical strategy might force the authorities at least to negotiate their demands. This was clearly the case with the agricultural union, the ELB, which soon began to adopt these new methods, such as staging sit-ins in public buildings and which even came to enjoy the symbolic support for its actions of the well-known member of the antiglobalization movement and spokesperson for the Via Campesina movement, José Bové.

One of the problems of the previous strategy, culminating in the call of October 9, 1999, was that while many important people, including a number of elected officials, from Iparralde, were involved in the movement, they were not obliged to confront their own political party structures. Therefore, for those individuals who were members of French political parties, their involvement with the movement ultimately had a limit: They could take part up to the point that they did not come into any confrontation with the party of which they were a member. Consequently, it came as no real surprise to see that after 1999, such popular mobilization declined when elections were soon to be held to choose local elected officials. However, the hinges of this party-centered system were loosened in the September 2001 elections to the French senate when a cross-party pro-*département* slate ran, with individuals competing against people from their own party.[75] Thus, despite the fact that popular mobilization had waned, running of this slate demonstrated that the resolve of some politicians had not. And although they were ultimately unsuccessful in their attempt to gain some presence in the lower house, with the support of almost two hundred elected officials in the departmental electoral college, it was the most-voted list in Iparralde. Moreover, despite the symbolic success of the slate, it was also important in that—Basque nationalists apart—the remaining figures actually broke with their respective party lines (PS, RPR, the Greens, and UDF) in lining up against their "official" candidates, a sign that, perhaps for the first time, the issue of a single Basque *département* was actually more important than party politics.

Encouraged by the symbolic success of these elections and aware of the need to reorganize, the original framers of the call of October 9 met once again toward the end of 2001. The result of this meeting was the creation of a new platform designed to overcome the previous personality-based or party-based logic that had dominated the movement. Accordingly, in January, 2002, the Association pour le Département Pays Basque (ADPB, Association for a *Département* of the Basque Country) was established as an autonomous movement with its own distinct internal organization, independent of all other political collectives and formations, structured around local, pro-*départemental* platforms, and with a general strategy based on two goals: the creation of a Basque *département* and gaining official status for both Euskara and Gascon.[76] Thereafter, the ADPB was active in both the presidential and legislative elections of May and June 2002, attempting to get every candidate taking part to take a stance on their twin platform, and toward the end of the year, it began to organize another campaign of mass mobilization. Ultimately, this was never realized, because the ADPB went through a process of change to become Batera.

Between 2000 and 2002, the foundations thus were laid for the beginning of a new protest cycle on the following bases: the use of more radical strategies involving civil disobedience; overcoming party-based logic (and this, in turn, was a key element for accepting the previous point); structuring the movement as a conventional social organization, rather than as the previous personality-based movement, which had lacked a strong social and organizational base; and the addition of other demands—specifically, the linguistic issue—to the previously economically based argument.

The New Strategy and a New Cycle of Mobilization, 2002–

Despite good results for pro-Basque *département* interests at the 2001 cantonal elections, there was a more disappointing outcome at the legislative elections of 2002, with none of the three representatives elected favoring specific institutional recognition for Iparralde. Moreover, while Jospin's PS government (1997–2002) had publicly stated that it would look favorably on the creation of a single *département* if a majority of elected officials called for it, Raffarin's UMP government (2002–2004) and President Jacques Chirac were both hostile to the proposal.[77]

Despite Raffarin's objection to any notion of a single Basque institution, his government was still keen on a reform of the French administrative system. To this end, toward the end of 2002, he introduced a set of new proposals concerning decentralization in France,[78] and this once more awakened expectations among the pro-*département* actors in Iparralde.[79] Raffarin's plan was to test the policy of decentralization by ceding some powers to certain local territorial collectivities. As a prelude to this, plans were made for officials to meet with government representatives and local dignitaries in each territory. Consequently, in November 2002, the CEPB prepared a document to be read before the officials from Paris, a document that for the first time alluded to an explicit demand for some kind of institutional recognition on the part of an elected body. The president of the CEPB, Alain Lamassoure, in front of several ministers of state, spoke of the need to let France know about "a special experience of local government grounded in a differentiated political, cultural, and identity-based personality that demands recognition."[80]

The CEPB thus called for some kind of official response to an issue that had been developing for decades at the local level. More importantly still, the CEPB had openly expressed a thesis that had previously been the reserve of Basque nationalists alone. For example, the CEPB also demanded of the French authorities some kind of response to the question of establishing a separate agricultural chamber for Iparralde, the granting of an official status for Euskara, and the possible creation of a public body to oversee changes in higher education in Iparralde. This shift toward an official debate among elected bodies and representatives of the state, together with the clear support for the pro-*département* movement's basic demands, undoubtedly encouraged the creation of the Batera platform, a platform designed, ultimately, to add component of public mobilization to the labors of the elected officials.

The response of the French government was a clear "No" to any notion of a separate *département* and to any possibility of modifying Article 2 of the French Constitution concerning French as the only official language of the state in order to protect Euskara. The government thereafter turned its back on the elected officials of Iparralde, a move that, in turn, resulted in a radical shift in Batera. Indeed, in October 2003, Batera called for what it termed its "last" conventional mobilization. On October 5, 2003, at a press conference before a plethora of journalists, Jean-Noël "Txetx" Etxeberri announced that Batera was calling for a demonstration on October 11 in order to "begin a new cycle" of activism in Iparralde. And on Saturday, October 11 of that year, eighty-seven hundred people marched through the streets of Baiona in support of Batera's four basic demands. In the closing speech of the demonstration, Etxeberri highlighted the fact that it had been more numerous than other, similar public manifestations regarding, for example, the reform of public pensions. Etxeberri was responding to PS criticism that same week, especially to criticism by the *conseiller général* Jean Espilondo and the sociologist Pierre Bidart that the demands of Batera were of no interest to the population of Iparralde, a curious denial of the social reality of Iparralde, as emphasized most obviously by the attendance at the demonstration of a dozen elected officials (among them the odd Basque nationalist) wearing the official *tricolore* symbol of France, thereby quashing any notion that this was merely a Basque nationalist protest.

Throughout the demonstration, a leaflet was handed to out to the participants asking them for their opinion on which direction the movement should follow thereafter. The document presented various options and was open to suggestions by any interested individuals or collectives. The following December, Batera attempted to accommodate this variety of opinion in a coherent strategy. The group rejected any possibility of creating an electoral platform, which indirectly encouraged the electoral aspirations of another recently formed collective, Elgar-Ensemble. The latter, as previously mentioned, shared many of the goals of Batera, but distanced itself from any association with Basque nationalism, demanding the right to be Basque in France and French in Iparralde. As we will see, Elgar-Ensemble took part in the 2004 cantonal elections, obtaining encouraging results. As a distinct political option compared with the nationalism of AB, for example, Elgar-Ensemble presented a pro-Basque program that was appealing to traditional Christian Democrat sectors in Iparralde while at the same time enjoying the support of many notables who imbued it with a strong mobilizing capacity. Yet its very existence as a political party—as opposed to previous conservative pro-Basque cultural platforms—also demonstrated the transformation that pro-Basque sentiments had gone through compared with the attitudes prevalent in previous decades, the result, mainly, of (successful) Basque nationalist activity to put formerly "cultural" issues on the "political" agenda.

The strategy decided on by Batera at the end of 2003 rested on three basic goals: the creation of a Basque agricultural chamber by 2005, holding a referendum on the question of a separate Basque *département* by 2005, and the creation of a Basque *conseil général* by 2007, although at the same time, the platform did not rule out using the strategy of civil disobedience, particularly spectacular acts that would be useful to publicize their agenda. However, once again, events beyond the borders of Iparralde forced Batera to rethink the latter suggestion. For example, a mysterious terrorist group emerged in France that specialized in planting bombs on railroad lines. Then, especially, the Madrid bombings by groups associated with Al-Qaeda on March 11, 2004 forced any plans for civil disobedience to be put on hold.

Toward a New Contravailing Power

We have seen how new economic development policies encouraged a greater awareness of territory as a central reference point and a potential space for political activity in Iparralde. Together with a growing realization that government networks were ultimately incapable of implementing these new policies, there emerged a consensus among ideologically different actors—at the center of which emerged AB—to work together in favor of creating a Basque institutional framework.

By 1999, a wide range of actors had come to shape this movement: Basque nationalists, socialists, and conservatives from the political world, together with economic interests representing the CCI of Baiona and most of the major collectives in the Basque cultural world, as well as official bodies such as the *Biltzar* of mayors and the CEPB. That year, a multitudinous demonstration and opinion polls indicating widespread support for the initiative only strengthened the movement in the face of repeated official hostility to the proposal from Paris. Thereafter, encouraged in part by the successful strategy of civil disobedience pursued by the Demos, between 2000 and 2003, the movement went through a process of reconstruction, leading to the presentation of a pro-*département* slate at the 2000 elections to the French senate and ultimately to the creation of the more socially based ADPB in 2002, the latter, transforming into the Batera platform later that same year.

Yet an even greater impulse to this reconfiguration (and regeneration) of the movement favoring some form of distinct Basque institution came, ironically, in late 2002 with the anti-Basque *département* Raffarin administration's cautious sounding out of various local bodies on the question of a possible decentralization of the French administrative system. This was the spark that ignited support for the Batera platform—a more united, coherent, and socially well-organized collective than previous incarnations. The clear nature of Batera's demands, together with the cautious alliance of an elected body—the CEPB—with the movement, marked a significant shift toward a new phase in the protest cycle.

By 2003, a clear picture had emerged: The state was clearly opposed to any form of major structural change (whether it be the creation of an agricultural chamber, or a university for Iparralde, or the protection of Euskara). Batera, meanwhile, concentrated its efforts on a twofold strategy. On the one hand, it continued to pursue a policy of raising awareness through public demonstrations. At the same time, it also moved toward the possibility of a more confrontational strategy, based in part on the success of the Demo movement. For example, fourteen members of the executive committee of the CDPB went on strike, an event that raised alarm bells in official circles as a potential threat to the successful implementation of development policies in Iparralde. Finally, Batera announced that in 2004, it would abandon its conventional strategy and would thereafter pursue other means, including civil disobedience.

Gradually, pro-*département* actors abandoned what we might classify as a defensive or reactive ideology—that is, registering their discontent at the actual system by way of gradually demanding certain changes—instead, ultimately embracing a more offensive and aggressive strategy, the first example of which was the creation of their own agricultural chamber. In January 2005, the Euskal Herriko Laborantza Ganbara (Agricultural Chamber of the Basque Country) was formed in Monjolose (Mongelos), Nafarroa Beherea, an unofficial institution that, it should be observed, lacked any kind of support from the French institutional structure, but that, at a personal or individual level, was applauded by several elected officials (including Socialists, Greens, and Christian Democrats), as well as by the president of the *Biltzar* of mayors. The support of the latter institution was especially telling, for in the 1980s, the *Biltzar* had been a conduit for boss-client relations between the French authorities and the elected officials of Iparralde. However, the sociopolitical transformation of that place through the 1990s saw this same institution first support the basic demand for some form of Basque institutional recognition and then gradually back these new strategies of countervailing power.

Ultimately, then, we are witnesses to a complex political picture in Iparralde, marked by the internal contradictions of many local actors, divided at root over whether they support or reject the notion of specific Basque institutional representation.[81] As a result, a new kind of political space has emerged, defined by a strong Basque identity and enjoying the obvious support of Basque nationalists while at the same time being opposed by bastions of French nationalism as represented by important notables and the French authorities.

Therefore, although the new dynamic of local-development policies initiated in 1992 attempted to achieve consensus among a variety of actors with the goal of fostering local development and without questioning the administrative status quo, the results were quite different. Strategies aimed at achieving greater participation broke down the disjointed ideological divisions between many groups, and thereafter, from a policy of coordination based on recognizing differences there gradually emerged a greater consensus of action based on prioritizing the needs of Iparralde. Moreover, this clarification of expectations clashed with a basic reality;–the state's lack of resources to implement the originally agreed-on policies. Unsurprisingly, then, many actors stopped thinking "how" to lead Iparralde into the future and began to consider "who" might do so. And a wide ideological spectrum of different actors with an important nationalist presence began to conceive of a different strategy based on emphasizing the importance of Basque identity as an important regenerating factor in any potential local development. Yet the consistent refusal of the French authorities to entertain any notion of change led to a decline in popular mobilization and a radical turn in efforts to demand specifically Basque institutions.

The result of this was that Basque collectives no longer looked to Paris to initiate reform. Instead, they saw as their only alternative a confluence of forces at the local level and were influenced in part by the successful trail of civil disobedience as a form of symbolic protest left by the Demos. Both Batera and the ELB thus initiated a new phase: from symbolic actions to practical measures–most obviously, the creation of a Basque agricultural chamber in 2005. Perhaps the best evidence that this strategy of countervailing power was working was the angry response of the prefect, Marc Cabane, to the new agricultural chamber and the French authorities' reinforcement, economically and materially, of the official agricultural chamber in Pau so that it might act more efficiently on specific questions relating to Iparralde. Finally, during this period of tremendous identity-based or territorial transformation involving increasing numbers of people learning Euskara, growing relations with Hegoalde, and a greater structuring of various bodies within the recognized spatial boundaries of Iparralde, there were also important social changes. Actors in Iparralde are now basically divided between, on the one hand, their allegiance to the French authorities, and on the other, by either pro-Basque or Basque nationalist sympathies.

The beginning of a participative development strategy in Iparralde (and its limitations) allowed the notion of territory to become very real for the actors involved. It allowed this territory to recover its local culture and identity, helped the actors to believe in the differential nature of the territory, and, faced with the absolute refusal of the French authorities to entertain any possibility of change, it motivated these same actors to redefine their tactics in terms of a locally based strategy of countervailing power. In Iparralde, they discovered, participation and power thus go hand in hand.

Taking account of all this, it should come as no surprise that in November 2005, these same actors began to explore the legal measures necessary to carry out a referendum on the question of a specifically Basque *département*—a petition that would require 46,000 signatures in favor of holding such a vote, an initiative supported by the *Biltzar*, whose members approved the idea by a 60 percent majority. Such a move, should it come about, would obviously mark a new stage in the development of Basque nationalism in Iparralde.

CHAPTER THIRTEEN

The Emergence of the Territory

To argue that a new, intermediary identity has emerged in Iparralde—that is, that another identity exists between the two poles that have traditionally defined the conflict of feeling or belonging—is not without risk. That would be the case with regard to most societies where there is a center-periphery conflict. However, one of the central arguments of the present work has been that beyond the bipolar opposition that historically has characterized the clash of Basque and French identities in a kind of zero-sum game, after 1990, another identity emerged—the identity of Iparralde as the "Pays Basque." Initially, this new identity served as a kind of buffer in reducing the conflict between the two nationalisms that had previously generated so much discord.

Typically, identity-based conflict in societies where nationalisms compete is characterized by two features. The conflict involves, first, a movement that imbues cultural, ethnic, or any other differentiating features (such as language, historical memory, symbolism, or connection to a territory) with political content, thereby allowing it to develop politico-territorial demands—the root objective of all peripheral nationalisms—out of ethnocultural claims. It also involves a state administrative structure and its legitimating framework that emphasize the key elements of state identity and a feeling of belonging among the subordinate population through real, existing institutions that allow the "imagined community"[1] to be imbued with practical content, a structure that gradually acquires validity, in a banal or prosaic manner,[2] through its conspicuous presence in the affective lives of its population.

The first of these—a movement of peripheral nationalism—emerges and operates fundamentally in the realm of symbolic and in some cases, regional-administrative objectification. The second—the opposing force of state nationalism—functions in a sphere of more complete objectification: that of institutional power, with the state understood in Weberian terms as exercising a "monopoly on the legitimate use of physical force within a given territory." These differences do not, however, alter the basic facts that one of the basic reasons for adhering to a peripheral nationalism (or to any identity) continues to be its objectification, and that any objectified (or still to be objectified) identity continues to need a legitimating symbolism.

There are various levels of social objectification in the definition of a group: mutual recognition among the actors who define themselves as a group, recognition of the group by others, and politico-administrative objectification.[3] The task of objectification is obvious in the case of the competing nationalisms that have structured Basque, French, and Spanish identities in the Basque Country. Yet objectification is also crucial, as we will see, in explaining the rise of the ill-defined organizational force behind the articulation of a Pays Basque identity in Iparralde, an identity rationalized by this organizational force in order to pursue the goal of a single Basque *département*.

Besides political objectification,[4] symbolic objectification is also important as a prior condition necessary for the former and as a guarantee for the continuation and/or success of its political counterpart. The first phase in the development of a collective identity in Iparralde—that of mutual recognition—was achieved with the transformation of "being" (*izan*, in Basque) to "naming" (*izen*), a process mirroring the popular Basque refrain that defends the existence of mythological beings according to the maxim "Izena duena bada" (Everything that has a name exists).[5] In other words, the definition of this territory from 1992 on by local elites and the population at large as the Pays Basque contained a clear performative dimension.[6] As Alfonso Pérez-Agote puts it, "when social actors define a collective or group reality, their behavior is predicative in that they configure something—that is, they say something about something. But it is also performative in the sense that they do something, since they generate the same reality that they define."[7] Later, I will explore more thoroughly both the symbolic-performative and the objective-institutional dimensions of Basque identity in the Pays Basque.

Not all identity-based conflict rooted in peripheral-state nationalist opposition is based on an ideal bipolar opposition, however. Identity is a changeable or situational apparatus, the result of specific conditions that individuals face, and no bipolar opposition can prevent individuals from going against what they are expected to be. Although the Manichean (bipolar) dialectic is more ideal than real, it nevertheless remains a useful tool with which to analyze interaction between the opposing poles.

At the same time, the ability of actors to define clearly the contours of identity between each pole fixes the degree to which the symbolic boundaries between one actor and another are either blurred or clearly demarcated. And to the extent that elites framing the discourse of identity are able to reshape both the symbolic and the practical elements of their reference model as fully as possible,[8] the possibilities of a zero-sum game appearing between the two are greater. Yet, such "identity closure" also requires social plausibility—that is such definitions must make sense for actors, citizens, and institutions.[9] Both dimensions—discourse and plausibility—combined in Iparralde from the time of the French Revolution until comparatively recently, allowing the transmission of French identity in a way that Spanish elites were unable to achieve among large sections of the population in what today is the Basque Autonomous Community. This was the form that identity conflict took in Iparralde: based until recently on a zero-sum game where a feeling of Basque belonging had been subsumed by its French counterpart.

Consequently, the case of Iparralde appears paradigmatic of a zero-sum game between two identities: an increasingly institutionalized (French) identity constructed within the powerful framework of a nation-state and grounded in state (or French) nationalism and a Basque identity that, historically, had neither the time nor the opportunity to transform its cultural claims into political demands. Due to the absence of organized Basque nationalism until 1963, the contours of Basque identity in Iparralde gradually took shape between 1790 and 1950 within the logic of the two *patries*.

That said, the Basque feeling of belonging—or, more specifically, the (premodern) bond with the territory—was greater during the initial years of the French Revolution, as evinced by the difficult dissemination of the French republican message throughout the Basque provinces during this time, as well as by the reticence of the popular classes to meet the demands of the new administrative authorities because they remained under the influence of a church that resisted the secular impulses of the new state. This connection to the territory appeared strong through the first half of the nineteenth century, with figures such as Garat and Chaho representing sentimental, inter-Basque fraternal feeling, as well as a sentiment of difference from other areas of France. This difference, however, was never represented as a challenge to the official institutional framework, so that any pro-Basque sentiment that emerged did so based on the logic of the two *patries*.

From the mid-nineteenth century on, however, and especially at the turn of the twentieth century, French identity absorbed its Basque counterpart, the latter proving incapable of finding articulation without the support of appropriate elites to imbue it with political content—(among other reasons, because of the peripheral economic importance of Iparralde. French identity, on the other hand, was backed by a French nationalism served by a consolidated and clearly demarcated state apparatus. Moreover, the state oversaw an effective strategy, based on education and a system of territorial control and local authority (the subprefectures), with local notables acting as mediators between center and periphery. Finally, changes associated with the modernizing of society in Iparralde through the twentieth century broke the historical pattern of socialization in the region, altering the local environment to the extent that it became increasingly difficult (if not impossible) to encourage not just any form of Basque nationalism, but Basque traditions in general—that is, a feeling of belonging to the older community.

The territorial contours of Iparralde were clearly demarcated through 1790, thanks to the prerevolutionary institutions of the French state, while the dominant feeling of belonging there was defined by the Basque language, culture, and tradition. In contrast to this feeling of belonging, which was shared by a majority of the population in Iparralde, a new, French identity emerged that was embraced by a fresh generation of elites (some of them from Iparralde, others from elsewhere) who soon took over from older elites tied to the Basque church. At this point, Basques in Iparralde were incapable of offering an organized political response, as was the case in Hegoalde, to this new identity and to the feeling of injustice felt during the initial stages of French state construction.

After 1789, Iparralde ceased to exist in an institutional sense, giving way to a new frame of reference: the *département*. Consequently, lacking any structure of plausibility and without any nationalist articulation, Basque identity gradually declined. And thus began the zero-sum game so wonderfully and dramatically portrayed by Pierre Loti. A multiple form of identity emerged, but not because a Basque feeling of belonging grew. Rather, it was subsumed by a French identity that allowed Basque identity to remain on purely cultural terms. In effect, the very strength of French identity conditioned the development of Basque identity around the logic of two *patries*. And given the growing crisis for the Basque language and culture, pro-Basque circles reacted through cultural activity alone. Despite the efforts of advocates for Basque culture, this crisis reached a moment when the facts spoke for themselves: The *maskaradak* had disappeared, the transmission of Euskara from parents to children had diminished, and so on. Against a local identity lacking any (nationalist or regionalist) political expression, a durable French nationalism reinforced French identity in Iparralde and the institutional structure in the territory.

In the early 1960s, however, Basque nationalism emerged for the first time in Iparralde.[10] Among other influences, it was based on the third great historical wave of nationalism, this time progressive in form, on the emergence and consolidation of Basque nationalism and the cultural renaissance that had taken place in Hegoalde, and on the dissemination of federalist and anti-internal-colonialist discourse in France. Despite outlining a specific goal—the demand for institutional recognition as mentioned in the Itsasu Charter—this Basque nationalism needed to reconfigure the foundations on which it was based before it could entertain hopes of pursuing a political program: institutional objectification or the effective objectification of this identity—a Basque *département* as the first step toward autonomy and as a prelude to independence.

Thus, the initial activity of this new Basque nationalism that was most important was not its political trajectory—which consisted of the repeated electoral failure of Enbata and EHAS—but rather its work in the cultural realm (salvaging the Basque language, dances, and traditions) and the economic sphere (the rise of the cooperatives). Gradually, a Basque movement emerged in Iparralde, based to a large extent on a frame of reference defined in Hegoalde.[11] As such, two identities were now apparent: a Basque one, still in a minority compared with its French counterpart, but strengthened by the rise of organized Basque nationalism, and a French one, still hegemonic, that reacted virulently against any political expression by its Basque counterpart. The clearest examples of this increasingly bipolar opposition occurred with the emergence of IK in 1973 and the banning of Enbata in 1974.

Finally, Basque nationalism in Iparralde was aided by a Basque identity that had been consolidated and well articulated (from an organizational perspective) in Hegoalde. This aid actually reached the point of (temporary) unification between the Basque nationalism of the North and of the South with the union of EAS and HAS in 1974, all this the result, among other factors, of a wave of political refugees from Hegoalde who had settled in Iparralde in the 1960s an 1970s, influencing the changing discourse of

Basque nationalism there. The result of these events was that by this time, the former logic of the two *patries* had been altered, with the small (Basque) *patrie* claimed by Basque nationalists. From this moment on, pro-Basque sentiment and Basque nationalism began to diverge, with Michel Labéguerie's exit from Enbata the clearest example of this.

In the 1980s, these growing divisions were consolidated and therefore underscored in Iparralde. Slowly, a distinct Basque identity began to grow, thanks mainly to the activity of Basque nationalists. At the same time, French identity also underwent a transformation as the result of structural changes (greater decentralization after 1982) deriving from the need to reform the welfare state. As a result, French nationalism became increasingly blurred, although it did not disappear, an example of which was the rise of socialism in France, with its uncertain policy of decentralization and flag-waving cultural renovation as the central focus of its discourse.[12] Socialists thus supported the call for Basque institutions and the official protection of Euskara in Iparralde, thereby gaining the support of some nationalist sectors and of modernizing elites, which allowed PS representation for Iparralde for the first time in its history. Consequently, the reality of Iparralde came more into focus before the eyes of the population as a whole: After decades of dreaming, a debate emerged over the Basque "being" (*izan*) that would eventually develop into one of identifying or "naming" the territory (*izen*).[13]

Meanwhile, for its part, Basque nationalism in Iparralde began seeking its own space after decades of internal division deriving from the extent to which guidelines framed in Hegoalde should influence the movement in the North. Thus, while Basque identity was maintained and even reinforced in its links between North and South, its political expression was increasingly determined by the specific context of Iparralde.[14]

In the 1990s, however, these two dynamics—one favoring a specific development strategy and the other calling for specific institutional representation—fused, and, timidly at first, but gradually gaining in strength, a new logic emerged that broke the previous bipolar and excluding logic of two identities, Basque and French, articulated by the two nationalisms. The *Basque Country 2010 Report* counted on the support of a cross-section of interests in Iparralde, including, ultimately, both the principal representative of the French state in Iparralde, the subprefect of Baiona (Christian Sapède) and radical Basque nationalists.

A number of conclusions were drawn in this report that alluded to the emergence of a new identity in Iparralde: that of the Pays Basque. This new development dynamic objectified the territory (as the Pays Basque), despite the fact that it did not argue for any distinct institutionalization. In other words, there was general consensus on the recognition of the territory of the Pays Basque—especially from the French authorities and the important elected officials—as long as this was grounded in cultural and economic demands, rather than institutional ones. However, a distinct and clear frame of reference, and therefore a frame of reference that could serve as the basis for political intervention and public policy, had been agreed on, even though this territorial space lacked its own specific institutional representation. Thus, if collective identity indeed has a "performative" dimension—in other words, if actors "do something" to generate the same reality that they define—here was a clear case of generating a specific reality through the territorialization of public policy within the framework of Iparralde.[15]

Moreover, if the social effectiveness of any idea is to be judged by its capacity for mutual recognition and use among a group, thereby generating a sense of belonging, in the emergent notion of a Pays Basque, a new and effective identity emerged in Iparralde.

Furthermore, not only was this definition of the Pays Basque acknowledged by local actors themselves in Iparralde, but also, importantly, the state itself had begun a dynamic by which social objectification mechanisms of group definition were established. Important steps were taken, from self-recognition to external recognition, with, respectively, official approval of the findings of the *Basque Country 2010 Report*, the creation of the CEPB and the CDPB, the establishing of a blueprint for development, and finally, official funding through the signing of agreements in 1997, 2000, and 2001.

In 1995, the dual structure of a civil (CDPB) and political (CEPB) body was established to define the bases on which a development strategy would be implemented in Iparralde. Curiously, the proposed bases resembled many Basque nationalist demands during previous decades as a means of regaining a specific Basque identity—for example, a coherent policy for the coastal and interior regions of Iparralde and closer ties with Hegoalde. Moreover, during this time, demands for a single Basque *département* were temporarily put to one side in favor of demonstrating gradually, through the structure established to oversee local development, a greater sense of belonging to the politico-administrative territory under construction.

Beyond the institutional dimension, however, there is evidence from other areas that a distinct Pays Basque identity emerged during this period: in the reinforcing of Basque cultural expressions; in the changing attitude of the population regarding the teaching of Euskara in schools; in the evolution of demands for Iparralde's own communications sector, as reflected by the creation of *Le Semaine du Pays Basque*, increasing calls to incorporate news from Zuberoa into the Basque edition of the hegemonic *Sud-Ouest*, and the creation of Radio France Pays Basque; in the territorial structuring of key actors and organizations such as the CCI of Baiona, the ELB, the CFDT Pays Basque, and the PS Pays Basque; in the structuring of intercommunal bodies such as the *Biltzar* of mayors; in the strictly economic sphere, with associations such as Hemen and Herrikoa promoting business within the Basque Country and with businesses such as Euskal Herriko Kola Alternatiboa (cola), IparLait (milk) and the Akerbeltz brewery (beer), all producing and distributing their products in Iparralde; and even in the realm of popular culture, with an increasingly Basque identity for the likes of the Biarritz Olympique—the Pays Basque rugby team.

Further still, one can understand the increasingly positive attitude of important and influential local elected officials—such as Michel Inchauspé, Alain Lamassoure, and Jean Grenet (mayor of Baiona)—toward issues such as a single Basque *département*, an official status for Euskara, and making Baiona the capital of this new Basque space only by pointing to the emergence of a Pays Basque identity.[16]

Between 1990 and 1997, then, a new identity emerged in Iparralde out of the conscious and unconscious activity of the principal actors involved in the new politics of development. This new form of self-definition transcended the formerly dominant bipolar logic in which the Basque and French identity clashed and broke open the model of the zero-sum game that had characterized relations between the Basque and French identities since the French Revolution. Only by understanding the transformation in this way can we explain the logic behind the widespread agreement over the *Basque Country 2010 Report* (1993) and the blueprint for development (1997). Thus, a new space opened up between the Basque and French identities, a hybrid sense of belonging that united both without denying each one's separate existence: an unstructured identity that was shared among the population of Iparralde as a whole, but that was stronger among the elites and that ultimately replaced the excluding logic that had defined previous identity struggles.

This hybrid identity, as we have seen, has been latent throughout the modern history of Iparralde: from Garat to Labéguerie, by way of elected officials tied to Catholic sectors that, without denying their belonging to France, supported the promotion of Basque traditions and culture. Indeed, this dual identity served certain notables, such as Jean Etcheverry-Ainchart and Jean Errecart, as a way to cement their hegemony in their respective cantons. However, with the implementation of the Fifth Republic in 1958 and the triumph of Gaullism and French nationalism, on the one hand, and the rise of Basque nationalism after 1963 on the other, any political expression of such a hybrid identity was difficult, if not impossible. Yet in the 1990s, the new politics of local development and the debate over the institutionalization of Basque difference—both of which visualized a specifically delineated local space—saw the reemergence of this hybrid identity, this time with an additional, political element.

That said, from each of the political spectrum there were still repeated attempts to tip the balance in favor of either the central state or Basque nationalism. In this context, it was easier for Basque nationalists to influence developments, because, although they had a minimal electoral presence, they were prominent in the economic and cultural spheres, which, in turn, resulted in their importance in the CDPB. By contrast, the French state authorities and some local elected officials—that is, the principal representatives of French nationalism—fell behind in the race to seize the initiative within this new emergent structure, the CDPB and the CEPB. And because Basque nationalists, temporarily putting to one side their demands for a separate *département*, were playing by the established rules, there was little room to maneuver on the part of the French nationalists. In short, they were forced to accept the proposals of the CDPB if they did not want to appear before society as a stumbling block to new development proposals.

French nationalists were interested in cultivating this new Pays Basque identity, based on the notion that conceding some degree of quasi-institutional status for Iparralde (the CDPB and the CEPB) might lessen the political message of an electorally weak, but more socially and culturally rooted Basque nationalism. During the same period, the articulation of Basque nationalist principles was vaguer than the expression given to their French counterparts. However, they were better defined than in previous eras, mainly as the result of the emergence of AB. Moreover, there was a greater interplay between Basque identity and that of the Pays Basque than, for example, between the Pays Basque identity and a French feeling of belonging, the result, most obviously, of greater common interests. At the same time, there was less direct conflict between Basque and French identities, due to the growth of this Pays Basque feeling of belonging. Of note, too, during this time, was the virtual disappearance of the *département* of the Pyrénées Atlantiques as a space of political activity for these actors, even though Iparralde still did not have specific political recognition and even though the Pays Basque identity lacked any politico-institutional articulation (that is, as a separate *département*).

The very lack of any politico-institutional framework, however, was the spark that ignited a transformation of the political map of Iparralde in the late 1990s. Specifically, the refusal of the French authorities between 1997 and 2000 to fund in any meaningful way any of the proposals that had been presented in the wake of the structural changes in the developmental politics of Iparralde led to a reaction by local actors there: the revival of what had been latent demands for a specific Basque *département*. Moves to reactivate this movement were, of course, aided by increasingly encouraging signs resulting from the development of a Pays Basque identity, signs read by some pro-*département* activists as potentially aiding calls to change the administrative status quo. These signs might be read, in retrospect, as a shift in various sectors—in the economic sphere, and including certain elected officials—from evincing a predominantly French identity to gradually adopting an outlook conditioned more by their allegiance to the Pays Basque. Gradually, then, a pro-*département* movement emerged composed of people with different political perspectives, but united in their conviction that some form of unification was necessary.

This growing structure of plausibility derived from the crisis in the new development policy was strengthened by the emergence of a single discourse out of three different (economic, cultural, and political) visions of the territory on which departmental demands were based. Opportunities for this decidedly more political turn were increased by the refusal once again of the French authorities to respond sufficiently to the new public policy initiatives, by the wide variety and ability of people involved in the pro-*département* movement, and by a division among the elites. As we have seen, the opening up of such opportunities at the local level, contrasted with the closing down of possibilities from the official state structure, only helped promote a carefully designed and widely agreed-on strategy that was principally organized by Basque nationalists,[17] a strategy based on the realization that the time had come to take a step forward from cultural and associative demands to political and elective ones.

At the same time, the emerging Pays Basque identity needed an objective framework that, effectively, could be formed only by the territorial limits of the space that was its foundation. Even the French state seemed to recognize this, creating the *pays* of the Pays

Basque in 1997, a purely administrative unit that lacked any decision-making power, but that did reveal (in however subdued form) some kind of official recognition of Basque difference. However, this did not appease advocates for specifically Basque institutions, for whom a single *département* was the only solution. Consequently, mutual points of reference grew between Basque nationalists and those who embraced the Pays Basque identity through both a general rise in the nationalist vote and an increasing identification between the latter and a nationalist movement at the heart of the pro-*département* movement. At the same time, the Pays Basque identity was also reinforced by an increasing support for these institutional demands, especially after 1999.

Three basic concerns were crucial in developing this Pays Basque identity around the pro-*département* movement—in the area of identity itself, in the realm of economic development, and in the political arena. On the one hand, certain elected officials from both the French right and the French left defined their identity as lying somewhere between that of France and the Pays Basque, a fact that did not stop them from adhering in principle to the pro-*département* movement. On the other, those actors who made up the nucleus of a more solidly French identity faced two options: a position that agreed, as a maximum concession, with the denomination of Iparralde as a *pays*, and another posture that, while publicly rejecting calls to create a single *département*, privately had no problem with it and may even have supported the initiative. The responses open to those faced with accommodating a French and Pays Basque identity thus were considerably reduced, compared with the options available in previous eras. However, those who were not attracted by this new Pays Basque identity reinforced the French aspect of their primary feeling of belonging and therefore their French nationalism. These positions were characterized most vociferously by the anti-Basque-*département* stance of, among others, Michèle Alliot-Marie of the RPR (and later the UMP) and Jean Espilondo of the PS.

In the economic realm as well, for the most part, many supported calls for Basque institutions to give some form of political content to the Pays Basque identity. These included individuals with ties to some elected officials on the right, most of those on the left (the PS), and Basque nationalists. Both the call of October 9 and the Batera platform were created on the basis of this alliance structure. Of special importance, too, was the situation of the CDPB. Under pressure from the pro-Basque-institution lobby, the CDPB had little choice from 1999 on but to come out in favor of a separate *département*. This went against the logic of consensus that had underpinned its founding and its own mission statement, which declared it could pronounce on development matters but not on political issues. The CDPB formed an increasingly close network with both nationalist sectors and economic interests. And ultimately, this network of actors assumed a central position within the organizational and political center of the Pays Basque identity. Meanwhile, the CEPB remained outside the debate, close to pro-Basque-institution elected officials, but within a space dominated by those sectors emphasizing a predominantly French identity.

Finally, if we compare this period to its predecessor, we see an important transformation in both Basque identity and Basque nationalism. Basque nationalism grew, even outside those limits previously defined by pro-Basque cultural and identity sectors, as well as by their left-wing credentials. During this time, Basque identity shifted to the right, so that it increasingly came to share some space with that of the Pays Basque. At the same time, and faced with growing institutional demands, as well as an increasing harmony between Basque and Pays Basque identities, proponents of a French identity were forced to respond in some way. Consequently, after 1999, the bipolar clash of French and Basque identities (together with their respective nationalisms) once again began to resurface, albeit hesitantly at first. This was conditioned by an increasingly more organized movement that witnessed a noticeable growth in the correlation of forces favoring some kind of institutional reform, from the positioning of the *Biltzar* of mayors behind such calls in 1996, through the growing support of elected officials and the CDPB, to the support of 66 percent of the population for reform in a 1999 poll, culminating, as noted, in the call of October 9, 1999 and the large demonstration in favor of the demand for a separate Basque *département*.

After the success of this movement, as exemplified in the demonstration, the French authorities were forced to respond in some way. This they did in 2000 by finally signing agreements to finance local projects outlined in the blueprint for development. At the same time, there was local administrative reform, whereby the subprefecture in Baiona was accorded more power. These were measures obviously designed to deactivate one of the pro-*département* movement's most effective arguments: that the state was incapable of financially guaranteeing the implementation of such development projects. And thereafter, the pro-*département* movement declined as it entered a new period of organizational self-reflection. Yet the spirit of the movement remained, to reemerge in 2002 amid a new set of opportunities for action. In the meantime, by taking these measures, the French authorities also hoped to seize the initiative regarding the cultivation of the new Pays Basque identity. In this regard, one important sector—the one that tacitly supported some modification of the system without calling for a dramatic change in the status quo—were pleased with the results.

However, from 2000 on, the root problems that the core local network (the CDPB and the CEPB) encountered in implementing the agreed-on proposals forced them to create a complex strategy involving putting apparently simple policies into practice by coordinating agreements between an extremely wide variety of actors. As a result, the process became long and difficult, a fact used by pro-*département* sectors to call once again for more substantial change. And with the Raffarin government's tentative decentralizing proposals of 2002, the movement was once again revitalized.

That said, one cannot say that the Pays Basque identity was exclusively the preserve of pro-Basque institutions sectors, or Basque nationalists during this period (2000–2002). The emergence of the Pays Basque identity closed a cycle of confrontation between Basque and French identity that had initially developed in the interwar period and that had lasted until 1990. And from 1990 on, there were a number of connecting spaces between Basque, French, and the Pays Basque identities. For example, as the French authorities blocked the implementation of development policies, so (nonnationalist) Pays Basque sectors allied with their (nationalist) Basque identity counterparts, a strategy that was appealing to Basque nationalists in search of a wider social base. Yet there were also connecting points between French and Pays Basque identities. For example, the new development strategies approved in the early 1990s had been overseen by French nationalist elites, thereby aiding the emergence of the Pays Basque identity, and during the period of "calm" (2000–2002), there was a relative growth in the number of people embracing the Pays Basque identity, including those more disposed to feeling a French identity, not at the expense of other identities, but rather via their integration.

As noted, the two extremes of the identity framework resurfaced during the period after 1999, although poor results for Basque nationalism in the 2001 legislative elections somewhat hindered this expansion, while at the same time, the Pays Basque identity continued to grow. At the same time, as well, while the CDPB adopted an increasingly pro-institutional approach, the CEPB–free of outside pressure because of the financial concessions by the French government after 2000–gradually developed a Pays Basque identity.

However, a definitive change occurred with the opening up of new possibilities in 2002: Raffarin's decentralization proposals. As a response, the Batera platform was created to pursue once again a set of demands around greater institutional recognition for Iparralde. Compared with the previous movement, Batera was much better organized internally and was structured with a clear set of demands regarding a *département*, a university, an agricultural chamber, and official status for Euskara. In many ways, these demands went beyond the earlier movement's demand for territorial reform. Moreover, through the influence of Basque nationalists, there was a merger of the Pays Basque and Basque identities via the demands for a *département*, a university, and an agricultural chamber, on the one side, and for official recognition of Euskara, on the other, to the extent that the movement was both strengthened and better organized than it had been in 1999. Gradually, during this period, the Pays Basque and Basque identities thus began to merge like a matryoshka doll, layer upon layer. This was especially evident when Alain Lamassoure, as president of the CEPB, before a meeting of French ministers, called for some degree of official status for Euskara and recognition of the Basque Country in any potential decentralization process proposed by the Raffarin administration.

Thus, a third phase of identity objectification began. Following the mutual recognition among actors who defined themselves as a group supporting the findings of the *Basque Country 2010 Report*, as a consequence, there had been an acknowledgement of their existence (as a group) by others–by the state. However, politico-administrative structuring–the third phase in the process of social objectification of a defined group– was only partial through 2002. That is, it was accepted by a majority of the population and elected officials in Iparralde, but not by everyone, which explains the more muted position of the CEPB regarding institutional demands between 1997 and 2002. However, when Lamassoure, as head of the CEPB, confronted the French ministers over the status of Euskara and recognition for the Basque Country in 2002, this new phase had begun. Thereafter, albeit for a brief period, all the principal actors in Iparralde seemingly favored the creation of a Basque *département*.

In the face of the issues raised by Lamassoure, there was a temporary stalemate. French nationalists in Iparralde awaited the official response to these united calls for a Basque institution, and the conflict between Basque and French identity was put on hold while those favoring a Pays Basque identity looked toward the center, where French nationalism had taken refuge, and while Paris consulted with representatives of French identity in Iparralde over a response. At the beginning of 2003, however, there was still no official response on the part of the French authorities. This hesitation was in part conditioned elsewhere, by the French government's failed attempts to placate Corsican nationalist demands, a failure that forced the state ultimately to abandon any bold attempts at reform in Iparralde.[18] At the same time, any official status for Euskara was rejected out of hand in the National Assembly.

The twofold response of the pro-*département* movement to these developments was clear and convincing. On the one hand, Batera began organizing another (conventional) campaign aimed at informing the population of Iparralde about the issues and at mobilizing them in protest over the lack of an adequate response by the authorities. However, because the response of the French authorities appeared quite conclusive, Batera also conceived of a more confrontational strategy (following the path charted by the Demos) that ultimately involved members of the CDPB going on strike. Additionally, Batera– a collective composed of people of all political sympathies, but with a strong Basque nationalist core–entered into a process of reflection as to what the next step should be, deciding, definitively, that from 2004 on, it would adopt a single policy of civil disobedience, together with the more conventional goals of calling a referendum on the *département* issue (planned for 2005) and establishing an administrative *conseil général* for Iparralde (planned for 2007).

We come, then, to a crossroads in the history of Basque identity in Iparralde. On the one hand, French nationalism regained some of the dynamic that it had seemingly lost in previous years, as evinced by the opposition of figures such as Espilondo of the PS and the sociologist, Pierre Bidart, to a specifically Basque *département*, a position supported by the French ministry of the interior, which linked the demand for a separate *département* to violence. However, the identity component of this strategy remained weak, without backing by any significant numbers of local elites in the center. By contrast, Basque identity had ultimately all but merged with the Pays Basque identity, forming a strong central nucleus, a development aided mainly by the effective organizational capacity of Basque nationalists.

The Pays Basque identity, meanwhile, expanded throughout this time to occupy most of the space within the movement for specifically Basque institutions. Furthermore, it received specific political expression with the creation of a new party, Elgar-Ensemble, in 2002. As such, there were still common points of union between a Pays Basque sensibility and French identity, although given the response of the French authorities to demands for reform, the logic was, typically, more one of confrontation. Indeed, there was even a direct altercation between the two in the heated exchange between the president of the *Biltzar* of mayors and the prefect after the ELB had created its own agricultural chamber for Iparralde in 2005. For their part, the CEPB and the CDPB steered clear of the debate, refraining from making any explicit statements on the departmental question until Batera and/or the French government had clarified their own tactical positions.

As we have seen, Batera signaled its intentions, the first step of which was the creation of the (unofficial) agricultural chamber. At the same time, pro-Basque sentiment found political expression in Elgar-Ensemble, a new political formation encouraged by initial electoral forays that resulted in it achieving as much as 10 percent of the vote in some of the cantons where its candidates ran during the 2004 cantonal elections. Further, the demonstration that nonnationalists in Elgar-Ensemble were perfectly willing to work with the nationalist-dominated Batera seemed to reveal the political maturation of a society that had overcome completely the traditional logic of two *patries*. In fact, this new Basque movement was grounded in the same principles as Basque nationalism: local recognition.

CHAPTER FOURTEEN

Toward a New Horizon

As we have seen, the strategies that stirred Basque nationalists into renewed activity in the 1990s—stemming from new development initiatives and the growing demand for institutional representation—had two main effects. On the one hand, people in Iparralde "appropriated" the notion of territory. That is, most of the territory's inhabitants began to feel a sense of local difference that encouraged the growth of a Pays Basque identity in tandem with a Basque identity constructed principally by Basque nationalists. Yet beyond this transformation in Basque identity (discussed in more detail below), the role of Basque nationalists in these strategies propelled them to the center stage of local politics and a new unprecedented importance. This was a position that might even improve, given several significant developments from the 1990s on: the reworking of Basque nationalism into three tendencies—one radical, led by Batasuna, one moderate, formed around the PNB and EA, and finally, the most important nationalist formation and the only one to center its activity in Iparralde, AB. The transformation of Basque nationalist activity also had seen a shift away from the use of violence toward the tactic of civil disobedience, a shift in local politics in which the French left had emerged as a significant force, a series of developments that pointed to a crisis in the system of notables, and, finally, the emergence of a new party to capitalize on the Pays Basque identity—Elgar-Ensemble.

The Reworking of Basque Nationalism

From 1997 on, the main Basque nationalist party in Iparralde, AB, attempted to clarify its central discourse around some basic principles: its self-definition as an independent cross-class party, support for a Basque *département* as the first step toward achieving greater degrees of sovereignty (a statute of autonomy and ultimately independence), support for Basque nationalist unity throughout the Basque Country (on both sides of the border) in a context of unprecedented armed and civil confrontation in Hegoalde between 1998 and 1999 and again between 2000 and 2001, and an ambiguous position in relation to the use of violence. However, this fragile consensus, which was based on the basic common denominators uniting the Basque nationalist left in Iparralde, did not please any of AB's different wings, and only the goal of political progress maintained a degree of internal unity within the party.

As a result, despite a certain weakness regarding internal unity, the political scenario was promising. AB had come to occupy a central position in the pro-Basque-*département* movement, which was supported by an overwhelming majority of the population, elected officials, and socioeconomic representatives. Moreover, for the first time since its founding, AB had won significant representative positions: on the *conseil général* (the regional council) of the *département* of the Pyrénées-Atlantiques (for the canton of Baigorri) and the mayorship of one of the few towns with more than 3,500 inhabitants (Hiriburu).[1] AB also managed to unite all Basque nationalist parties in the 1998 Aberri Eguna celebration, the first step in a new political process that culminated in the signing of the Lizarra-Garazi agreement, which recognized the nationalist movement as political in nature and favored dialogue over armed struggle and which was followed by the subsequent ETA ceasefire, the first time in decades that one sensed light at the end of the tunnel in the long struggle for peace and sovereignty.

As a result of these developments, a tide of optimism spread through Basque nationalist circles in Iparralde at the close of the 1990s. However, the breakdown of the Lizarra-Garazi agreement after ETA called off its ceasefire in late 1999 brought serious consequences for AB. The debate over political violence once more came to occupy an important space in the politics of Iparralde, although this time, talk centered on ETA, rather than IK. AB was once more faced with a serious internal conflict, because a part of its membership implicitly supported the use of violence, while another sector that previously saw ETA's tactics as justified now openly opposed the armed group. In its September 2000 general assembly, an attempt was made to resolve the issue, but ultimately, no specific pronouncement was made one way or the other, this despite a motion (known as the motion "of the forty-six") introduced by Jakes Abeberry, and supported by several key figures within the party, which called for AB to reject the use of violence.

The AB-Batasuna Split

The breakdown of the Lizarra-Garazi process intensified a number of issues that had been developing for years. For example, Iparralde suddenly became an important site of contest for Basque nationalist parties in Hegoalde. High-ranking members of the PNV visited the "lost brother" in the North, new branches of these parties were opened in Iparralde, and the principal nationalist labor unions in the South also began to take an interest in establishing some form of representation there.[2] Finally, the Izquierda Abertzale also began a process to unify its organization on both sides of the border.

This idea was not a problem for various youth groups in Iparralde, such as Gazteriak, because for years they had maintained close relations with similar groups in the South. However, despite the fact that AB maintained privileged relations with HB (and later EH)–relations that included economic aid from the South to help finance electoral campaigns in the North–the Izquierda Abertzale's proposal to create one cross-border party (to be known as Batasuna—Unity—and intended to replace EH) threatened to break definitively the fragile internal unity of AB.

From this moment on, four different groups emerged within AB, which split into two factions: Batasuna, most of whose members were in Segi, a new cross-border radical nationalist youth group formed by the fusion of Gazteriak in Iparralde and Haika in Hegoalde, agreed to the idea of a cross-border party fully, yet the other three groups—Burujabe (Self-governing), Matalaz (named after the priest Matalas, who had led a seventeenth-century revolt in Zuberoa), and "the forty-six"—rejected the call at such a key moment for AB. However, none of these three other groups rejected the idea in principle, with at least two calling for some kind of cross-border leftist nationalist party to be established in the future. Common to all three, though, was the belief that such plans should not be implemented for the moment, until conditions in Iparralde had improved and would facilitate such a transition more smoothly.

However, the debate was not postponed, and at the November 2001 meeting, it became apparent that the party, created out of the need for Basque nationalist unity in Iparralde, was beginning to split apart. As a result, many of AB's best and most active members abandoned the group to join Batasuna, while those who opted to stay accepted by majority vote a motion to configure AB as a specifically political organization (thereby effectively and definitively sealing the disappearance of EB, EMA, and HA) and endorsed a strategy based on resurrecting the Lizarra-Garazi process and, therefore, on a call on ETA to declare another ceasefire.

As in similar cases, there were obviously traumatic effects of the split, yet one result was also to reinforce progressive nationalism in Iparralde. The exodus of activists to Batasuna allowed AB to agree on a new broad consensus that appeased the remaining groups within the organization. The policy of resurrecting the Lizarra-Garazi initiative—that is, a nonviolent campaign in favor of full Basque sovereignty—was accepted by a majority of AB's members, while the call on ETA to declare another ceasefire appeased the traditional nationalists within the group and also, in reality, expressed an opinion that, while not publicly stated up to that point, was shared by most of AB's sympathizers. This call did not include a condemnation of the use of violence. Rather, it called on ETA to consider the possibilities of using other means that, until that time, had been little explored and ultimately not allowed enough time to mature:the Lizarra-Garazi process. As a result, AB reinforced its own internal unity while at the same time sending out a clear message to the electorate of Iparralde, a message that would, in turn, reach new progressive sectors that up to that time had guarded a certain distance from the party.

Batasuna, meanwhile, had at its disposal an already experienced organizational structure and members and began to disseminate its call for full independence throughout Iparralde. Indeed, its mere presence in the North raised alarm bells among French centralists, with the neo-Jacobin Jean-Pierre Chevènement arguing that a Pandora's box had been opened.[3] Indeed, the threat posed by such positions was very real, for Batasuna offered the possibility of a creating a strong and united cross-border movement that rejected waiting for the state to effect change.

As a consequence, because both AB and Batasuna continued to share a degree of political terrain, they increasingly competed with one another for control of this space. This resulted in an angry clash of words between them over the issue of the 2002 French legislative elections and the Aberri Eguna celebration that same year. Prior to the elections, AB decided not to share a slate with Batasuna. In turn, Batasuna called for its supporters to vote by spoiled ballot, an initiative ultimately seconded by around one thousand people in Iparralde. Ultimately, the tension between AB and Batasuna led to increasing confusion among the nationalist electorate in Iparralde. At the 2002 legislative lections, for example, there were eight different nationalist options. Despite these complications, though, AB consolidated its position as the leading nationalist party in Iparralde, while the "vote" for Batasuna demonstrated its measured emergence, and the PNB and EA lost up to 50 percent of their electoral base.

However, there were more serious differences between AB and Batasuna over plans to commemorate the Aberri Eguna that same year. AB made plans to celebrate a united Aberri Eguna—emphasizing the goal of independence through nonviolent means—in Donibane Garazi, a call that, in turn, attracted support from and the sending of delegations by various nationalist groups in Hegoalde. After much debate, Batasuna decided to organize its own celebration in Donibane Lohizune, although it also sent a delegation to the AB-sponsored event. The sending of various delegations to the AB-sponsored celebration by progressive and leftist groups in Hegoalde (such as EA, Zutik, Batzarre,[4] and Aralar) provoked later, though moderate, criticism by the Izquierda Abertzale. And this was followed by a furious, disproportionate, and intransigent communiqué by ETA labeling AB's attitude traitorous to its original principles.

Yet to put this polemic in context, it should be recalled that AB's platform, agreed to by 80 percent of its membership (after the breakaway of Batasuna sympathizers) had resulted in three broad developments. Initially, AB consolidated its position as the leading Basque nationalist party in Iparralde. Despite losing 20 percent of its members—predominantly youths and the more active or dynamic members—AB retained sufficient strength to consolidate this position. At the same time, leading nationalists such as Jakes Abeberry, Jean Michel Galant, and Alain Iriart chose to remain within the party.[5] Furthermore, the agreed line of AB—that is, a nonviolent path toward independence by reactivating the Lizarra-Garazi process—obviously implied breaking all historical or symbolic links with ETA. In turn, AB freed itself of such ties and thereby guaranteed its own independence vis-à-vis favoring a political over a military strategy. Finally, given this new context, AB was able to reach out to other sectors beyond the traditional base of Basque nationalism in Iparralde, incorporating a part of both the progressive and pro-Basque vote.

In response, Batasuna intensified its efforts in Iparralde to define its own strategy, an intensification that was marked by the reinforcing of its activism by the creation of Segi, but also by the criminalization of the party in Hegoalde by the Spanish authorities.

For the most part, its strategy coincided with that of AB, but it also sought to extend cross-border links. For example, Batasuna was prominent in the Zuberoa 2010 Project, a campaign designed by Udalbiltza, the Assembly of Basque Municipalities, to raise one million euros to help kick-start a number of development projects in the province. In this sense, Batasuna played an important pedagogical role in raising awareness of issues in Iparralde among its sympathizers in Hegoalde. However, the criminalization of Udalbiltza in 2003 by the Audiencia Nacional (Spain's specialist high court, dealing only with serious crime and terrorism) resulted in the freezing of its assets and in the eventual appropriation by the Spanish judicial authorities of the 400,000 euros raised to help Zuberoa, part of the authorities' paranoid crusade against the Izquierda Abertzale and, by extension, Basque culture in general.

Despite the ground shared by AB and Batasuna, though, a new line had been drawn between leftist nationalists in Iparralde. And even though AB had gained greater internal cohesion as a result of the decisions adopted at its 2001 general assembly (especially regarding the use of violence), its members continued to differ over certain key issues. For example, AB decided to present the candidacy of Gorka Torre (formerly one of the most public faces of the Demo movement) on the Green slate for the 2004 European elections, a list shared with Gérard Onesta, the vice president of the European parliament. This decision, however, was not well received among certain sectors of AB who were still skeptical of the possibilities that a Europe "of capital" could offer and who viewed the Greens as an essentially "French" political party. AB made the decision for both tactical and strategic reasons. For the nationalists, it was a tactical means of reinforcing ties with other parties in the French political system, while at the same time, the Greens, by endorsing Torre's candidacy, (indirectly) approved of his previous role at the head of a civil-disobedience movement. Strategically, meanwhile, the agreement cemented a pro-European strand that had been present within Basque nationalism in Iparralde since its founding.

The reaction of the anti-European faction within the party, though, was immediate in condemning the decision. Thereafter, to clarify its subsequent position on Europe, AB initiated an internal debate as a prelude to the impending 2005 referendum in France over the European Constitution, with the decision made not to embrace publicly any policy that did not have the backing of at least 70 percent of its members. Because no single policy achieved this level of approval, Batasuna remained the single public voice against the European Constitution among Basque nationalists in Iparralde during the 2004 European election campaign. Consequently, many AB sympathizers supported the Batasuna line, and the vote, with Batasuna presenting a symbolic candidacy, produced a surprising result in the similar levels of support gained by both AB and Batasuna.

It should also be mentioned, however, that these years were also marked, from 2003 onwards, by the absence of serious ETA violence—that is, the absence of any fatalities as a result of ETA actions. Indeed, ETA's inactivity in this regard actually led to an improvement of relations between AB and Batasuna. Similarly, the absence of ETA violence during this period also led to the reemergence of the Demo movement, this time with increased support from sectors outside the Basque nationalist world.

The Nonviolent Alternative

Parallel to the nonviolent, prosovereignty line favored by certain left-wing Basque nationalists in Iparralde, another collective emerged after 2000: the Demos (see Chapter 12). The Demo movement based its activity—a series of spectacular acts of civil disobedience designed to draw attention to their demands—on the recommendations agreed to by the officially sanctioned CEPB and CDPB. In other words, Demo activity was grounded in widely agreed-upon proposals (agreed upon by elected officials, together with representatives of the social, economic, and cultural sectors) to protect and encourage the use of Euskara: for example, the implementation of bilingual road signs and the promotion of Basque in public services. The refusal of the French authorities to implement the measures proposed by the CEPB and the CDPB provoked the Demos into taking matters into their own hands. And between 2001 and 2003, their acts became more spectacular as they graduated from changing road signs to occupying the railroad station in Baiona and even staging a sit-in on the railroad tracks themselves.

Regarding calls for separate Basque institutional representation, as we've seen, they stole the representatives' seats for Iparralde from the *conseil général* and the busts of Marianne to highlight their demands. Furthermore, they were also involved in stealing the historical minutes of the prerevolutionary *Biltzar* in Lapurdi from 1790, in which a demand was made for a distinct Basque *département*; an act carried out in the departmental archives in Pau with the aim of highlighting the need for a Basque historical archive in Iparralde.

Through such symbolic activity, the Demos revealed their capacity to challenge the French authorities by mocking the most prestigious local institutions. They also generated a sense of solidarity among wider sections of society. For example, at a press conference to support those being tried for the robbery of the historical minutes, they produced a petition of support for their actions signed by twenty-four prominent public figures: lawyers, notaries, and professors at French universities. Finally, such activity, in a society used to thirty years of activity by IK, also generated a certain degree of nervousness about whether this civil disobedience might descend into more openly violent acts if the French authorities continued to ignore the demands shared by many in Iparralde.[6] As Sidney G. Tarrow observes, such activities may "empower movements by their capacity to engage citizens in disruptive confrontations with authorities while offering the latter no valid pretext for repression. When they are repressed despite their peaceful face, the result is often an expansion of conflict to broader publics, empowered by a sense of outrage and indignation." However, one of the principal consequences of such disruptive activities is that "they can dissolve into violence or become conventional."[7]

Nonviolent protest can become more violent direct confrontation, especially when the response of the authorities to the original activity is overly repressive or out of proportion to the original action itself. However, in the case of the Demos, their activity was based on minimal demands that had been socially legitimated and even backed by official bodies composed of elected officials. This, in turn, generated a widespread social sympathy for their actions that, likewise, served to protect them against repressive measures. Despite such widespread social sympathy,[8] however, the authorities actually dealt more and more harshly with the Demos, from arrests and fines at first, to trials, and, eventually, to imprisonment. This culminated in late 2002 when, at a trial in Baiona of several Demos, friends and sympathizers present (including respectable public figures such as renowned academics and members of the Academy of the Basque Language) were dispersed outside the court by overly heavy-handed police tactics, including the use of tear gas to disperse the small group.

As noted, the more repressive the tactics of the authorities in response to civil disobedience of this type, the more likelihood there is of an escalation of violence. Indeed, this was the case in Iparralde during the 1970s. However, in sharp contrast to the growing militancy of IK (and others) at that time, the Demos were acutely aware of the limitations implied by a recourse to armed activity. In effect, these were different times, in a world marked by the September 11, 2001 attacks in New York and Washington, D.C., and by the damaging effects of a new antinationalist political discourse that sought to link terrorism and nationalism. In many ways, the Demos thus sought to show radical Basque nationalists that there was an alternative route in which to channel social and political activity.

The practical dimension of the Demos' actions was based on the fact that their demands were more than accessible. There was majority support for a specifically Basque institution in Iparralde, and a pro-Euskara policy had been backed by both elected officials and representatives of civil society. Therefore, when the French authorities did not respond to these popular social, political, and cultural demands, the Demos saw the tactical possibility of exposing the limits of democracy in Iparralde, reinforcing their argument by carrying out nonviolent and sometimes humorous protests. If they fell into the trap of using more violent methods, they believed this would delegitimate both their basic demands and Basque nationalism in general. Consequently, their response to the challenge of organizing a successful nonviolent strategy was based on a threefold approach: imagination, disruption, and solidarity.

The Demos made imaginative use of the collective historical memory of Iparralde. Yet they did not just base their activity and objectives on the Basque cultural imagination, as would have been the norm for a nationalist movement, but rather, they extended their discourse to incorporate French symbolism. For example, making the most of the full spectrum of references available,[9] not only did they steal the busts of Marianne, in subsequent communications by the Demos, they introduced the stolen Mariannes, who spoke in favor of their liberators, because they considered themselves "kidnapped in institutions that merely prostituted the democratic principles that they had seen born."[10] Expanding the frame of reference to encompass such an intrinsically French symbol enabled the Demos to get their message to a wider audience in a highly imaginative way and maybe even to people who, beyond any differences of identity, might have felt sympathy for the sentiments expressed.

No symbol was beyond appropriation by this civil-disobedience movement. The courts were labeled "frames of injustice," and the Demos incorporated traditionally Basque recreational pursuits—such as the card game *mus*—into methods of seeking disruption, such as when they held *mus* championships while staging a sit-in on the railroad lines, thereby halting all trains on the coastal line of Iparralde. Similarly, they dressed up as Olentzero, a mythical Basque figure who grants children's wishes at Christmas, to reclaim a greater presence for Euskara in public life, and they put up banners alongside roads throughout Iparralde to publicize the demand. These actions formed a recourse to both Basque and French collective memory and symbolism.

They even resurrected the figure of Garat to further their demands. In October 2000, on the occasion of the meeting of the *Biltzar* of Lapurdi in Uztaritze, there was a parade to celebrate the event. Participants in the parade from the surrounding villages and towns were expected to parody everyday situations as a prelude to a communal lunch afterward. Everything was taking place, as it had done on thirty previous occasions, without incident, when a strange figure emerged from the crowd to exclaim:

> I beg your pardon, ladies and gentlemen; the talk has not finished yet . . . You do not know me; or, rather, you do not know my voice, because I am not of your world, from your era. It was a century and half ago that I died, and my name is Dominique-Joseph Garat.
>
> This is why I am among you today: to celebrate the *Biltzar* of Lapurdi. Here homage is paid to the official site expressing the will of this people [recall that in 1789 the *Biltzar* demanded a specifically Basque *département*], the site today denied us. In this regard, most people have demanded a *département* for some time now. From heaven, I saw twelve thousand people in the streets of Baiona on October 9 . . .
>
> I am proud of how you express yourselves against those who deny your wishes. Two hundred years ago, I pointed out clearly and loudly to the little lords in Paris: My province protests! It does not agree! . . .
>
> For that reason, to all those of you gathered here in this *Biltzar* of Lapurdi, and to all Basques, I urge you to organize yourselves and fight the lack of democracy, as I did in 1789. I urge you to participate in actions like that carried out last March with the help of the Demos, thanks to which we managed to recover for the Basque Country the minutes book of the *Biltzar*. Let us disobey the authorities who do not respect our wishes; it is our right, or more still, our obligation.
>
> Put the yellow T-shirt on [the Demos all wore yellow T-shirts] and make yourselves count!
>
> As I did![11]

Every social movement needs to elaborate a discourse that makes "sense," that is, that is grounded in the reality of the environment in which it operates. Further still, many social movements specifically orient their strategies to the cultural, historical, and mythological context of the people they wish to convince. As Mayer N. Zald observes, "activists in movements and countermovements have a stake in developing metaphors, images, and definitions of the situation that support alternative programs."[12] In the case of Iparralde and claims for a specific Basque *département*, there was no better historical figure to invoke than Garat. Consequently, the reworking of historical and cultural symbols such as the figure of Garat or the bust of Marianne served not only to advance the claims of the Demos, but also to define these claims within a new frame of injustice, an injustice highlighted even more by such a potent symbol of the French Republic as Marianne.

Finally, these imaginative strategies were also designed to convince those sectors of the population that remained undecided about their position on the issues and to motivate them into action against the authorities, not as part of a specifically Basque nationalist campaign, but as part of a wider social movement that played on French identity, too. In one press conference, the Demos even subverted the violent imagery of the militant Corsican nationalist group, the FLNC,[13] appearing like members of this organization, but undermining its armed symbolism by bearing weathercocks instead of guns and a flag with the number 64 inscribed on it (the official number of the *département* of the Pyrénées Atlantiques), thereby visualizing the differences between peaceful subversion and armed resistance, demanding their legitimate right to protest, and also, in passing, emphasizing the fact that IK no longer operated in Iparralde.

As regards disruption, a key element of Demo activity was momentum—that is, resistance to the threat of internal despondency within the movement at the lack of progress. Their first response to this was to outline a series of objectives and make every action clearly relevant (however symbolically) to that objective. Therefore, if the French authorities would not create Basque institutions, the Demos took it upon themselves to physically take the seats corresponding to the Basque representation in Pau and create their own symbolic Basque representative space. Whether they had achieved their specific objective or not, at least it was an act that symbolically represented their goal, kept their members' spirits up, and potentially attracted support.

Principally, however, the Demos decided to concentrate their peaceful disruptive tactics in one area: Between 2001 and 2005, they carried out dozens of acts in railroad stations in Iparralde as a means of highlighting the lack of any signs or services in Euskara. They had (correctly) identified the French national railroad service, SNCF, as the most centralized and Jacobin public service in France. If they could effect change there, other public institutions would be easier to convince. Ultimately, their demands for bilingual services were the same as those agreed to by elected officials and representatives of civil society (many of them not Basque nationalists) and outlined in the blueprint for development agreed to by the French authorities themselves.

In terms of generating solidarity, the repression suffered by the Demos through 2003 was ample evidence of their success. From an original base of fifteen members in 2000,[14] their number grew to two hundred central activists three years later, together with a wider support group of some six hundred people—a not insignificant number when one considers the modest population of Iparralde. This numerical progress was mirrored in the response of the French authorities: Three people were charged during the first trial against them, four in the second, fifteen in the third, and sixty-five in the fourth. In fact, this steady increase in the number of those going to trial served only to generate more sympathy and support, and at present, the Demo movement enjoys the public support of the principal labor unions in Hegoalde, the Academy of the Basque Language, and Kontseilua, a pro-Euskara platform composed of more than two hundred different organizations. In short, jail terms for individual Demos only raised more awareness of their demands and of the injustice to which they referred, and thus they gained wider support.[15]

In general, nonviolent civil disobedience in Iparralde thus appeared to generate widespread social support, in contrast with the failure of violence to achieve such levels of sympathy and solidarity, a fact emphasized still further by the different course of events in Hegoalde during the 1990s. Thus, beyond the ethical questions associated with the use of violence, the Demos demonstrated that it was actually tactically viable and more successful to pursue nonviolent strategies for a number of reasons.

For example, acts of violence that had taken part up to that point in the Basque Country had been carried out secretly, whereas the acts of civil disobedience were very public—and consciously so.[16] Moreover, and linked to this first point, those who carry out violent acts must necessarily be organized into small, well-organized groups. That is, for their own safety and to avoid infiltration, they must operate within a restricted space. The Demos, however, by definition, sought to be as large a group as possible. Indeed, their ideal was to create a mass civil-disobedience movement. Further, all things being equal, the Demos not only wanted to form a mass movement but were in a much better position to do so than the antisystem radical nationalist movement in Hegoalde. There, the Izquierda Abertzale was incapable of contesting the criminalization of Batasuna in 2002, and therefore its main security buffer, allowing it links to other organizations, was gradually eroded. The repression of the Izquierda Abertzale by the Spanish authorities in Hegoalde undoubtedly contributed to the weakening of ETA, whereas in Iparralde, repression of the Demos generated more support for the movement and contributed to its overall success in advancing its cause. Perhaps most importantly of all, however, the use of violence as a means of securing nationalist objectives had been tried unsuccessfully in Iparralde, and many of those involved in those struggles of the 1970s and 1980s were increasingly aware, especially after ETA broke its ceasefire in 1999, that nonviolent civil disobedience might actually attract more sympathizers than three decades of armed struggle in Iparralde had done.

Indeed, radical Basque nationalism in Iparralde, at a moment when it began to suggest that the only outlet for the frustration of future generations was to adopt violent methods, demonstrated great intelligence in considering another form of militancy—a method that was equally capable of demonstrating the determination of the movement's adherents and their capacity to ridicule the official state structure, but one that nobody had dared to exploit to that point. At the same time, the option of nonviolent civil disobedience subverted authority and, while acceptable to wide sections of society, also challenged the status quo. With the Demos, the parricidal tendencies of radical Basque nationalism in Iparralde thus had been overcome. In short, an alternative emerged in Iparralde to challenge the all too familiar model of violent resistance that had left its sanguinary imprint on Basque society for decades. The Demos had effectively provided another strategic model capable of challenging both violent insurrection and insipid attractions of institutional politics.

The Implosion of the Electoral System and the Flowering of the Pro-Basque Movement

Things were indeed changing in Iparralde. As we have seen, beneath the apparently calm and stable surface of political life, there flowed a series of complex and at times contradictory, but always dynamic currents of debate. A basic contradiction emerged from these debates between the lack of any specific institutional recognition for a society that repeatedly had demanded it, all this in a scenario where power fluctuated between the great notables, the traditional mediators between center and periphery, and a new, rising elite with strong links to the territory. These political tensions, moreover, developed in a context of growing pro-Basque sentiment confronted by a still all-powerful state structure that based its principles on a strong sense of French identity, as expressed most clearly by the consistent refusal of the French authorities to respond adequately to the situation of Euskara.[17]

In other words, a debate has been raging for decades in Iparralde over the issue of continuity versus change—that is, over the continuity of a political system dominated by the French right versus change marked by the rise of the French left,[18] Basque nationalism, and pro-Basque sentiment. Under this broad rubric, disputes have proliferated over the lack of political, administrative, and institutional recognition, driven by a widespread social movement that broke down traditional political differences with its call for a Basque *département* and that advocated for official recognition of Euskara on behalf of a population that increasingly wanted to learn and use it. In the process, the two nationalisms—French and Basque—have each been forced to adapt and change, a process marked in Iparralde by vacillation between hope and frustration.[19]

It would appear, however, that as the twenty-first century has advanced, Iparralde has been moving out of this transitory context. A new stage has been marked out by the definitive victory of hope over frustration, the best example of which, to date, were the 2004 cantonal election results. That election (held in ten of the twenty–one Basque cantons) made manifest four phenomena: the beginnings of a crisis in the system of notables, the destruction of conservative illusions concerning a lasting political hegemony in Iparralde, the consolidation of Basque nationalism, and the continued rise of pro-Basque sentiment as represented by Elgar-Ensemble.

As we have seen, through the history of Iparralde, the notable was more than just a powerful local elected official. He acted as intermediary between the center and the periphery, a cultural bridge between Paris and Iparralde who, thanks to this twin access, personified the maximum development potential for his particular local district. And this was, of course, a family concern. For example, the Grenet family–Henri (1959–95) and Jean (1995–)–governed Baiona as successive mayors, while Michèle Alliot-Marie, who served in the city hall of Ziburu and Biarritz, as well as being mayor of Donibane Lohizune, was the daughter of the former deputy mayor of Biarritz, Bernard Marie. And one should not forget the almost ever-present Inchauspé family in Nafarroa Beherea: Michel served as both a deputy for the *département* and as a *conseiller général*, while his father, Louis, was likewise a *conseiller général* and president of the *conseil général*. However, results from the first round of elections in 2004 pointed to a possible transformation of the apparently rigid political stability of the system of notables in Iparralde. For example, after thirty years of winning by absolute majorities in Hazparne (Lapurdi), Jacques Coumet (UDF-UMP) lost 30 percent of his former vote during the first round and withdrew from the elections for fear of more damage to his personal pride.[20] One of the principal bastions of the notable system had fallen, and all eyes looked to the site of the bitterest struggle in the contest: Garazi in Nafarroa Beherea, the fiefdom of the Inchauspé family for more than five decades.

Here, after the first round, the PS candidate, Frantxoa Maitia, was running neck and neck with Inchauspé's chosen successor, Alphonse Iriart (UDF-UMP) after the first round, enough to challenge even further this most well known of notable power bases. However, to take power, Maitia needed the support of AB and its candidate, Peio Iralur. This AB gave when Iralur withdrew from the second round (despite gaining sufficient support in the first to have continued on), and the PS won one of the most bitter electoral battles in the history of Iparralde. With this victory, one of the region's most elaborate patronage systems was dismantled (Michel Inchauspé had retired some months earlier, but his appointed successor, Iriart, had been groomed to take over this dynasty). Importantly, the PS won the canton with the aid of Basque nationalists, a decision made easier by the fact that Maitia was in favor of Basque institutions–unlike, for example, Jean Espilondo, the neo-Jacobin PS candidate in Angelu.

Elsewhere, the majority voting system that had so favored the great notables in the past now led to their downfall in other districts. In Baiona-West for instance, after the second round, the PS candidate, Monique Larran-Lange, won by 83 votes over her UDF-UMP opponent, Jean-Louis Domergue. In similar fashion, another of the important elected officials of Iparralde, Christian Millet-Barbe (UDF-UMP), was defeated in Baiona-North, where the left-wing vote that had seen the candidate of the PCF (Parti Communiste Française, the French Communist Party), Maurice Garcia, win the first round, but give way in the second for the PS candidate, Christophe Martin, to triumph. Finally, to confirm the leftist swing (which had swept France as a whole), in Baiona-East, the PS candidate, Jérôme Agerre, defeated another major elected official, Jean-René Etchegaray (UDF-UMP). Even in Biarritz-West, where Max Brisson was reelected on the UDF-UMP slate, the PS vote grew from 22 percent in the first round to 40 percent in the second.

This major transformation should be viewed in the political context of an apparently conservative society where progressive ideas had traditionally had little place, shattering the illusion that a lasting hegemony of conservative forces always would frustrate hopes for the realization of Basque nationalist aspirations in Iparralde. Yet, more importantly, perhaps, its should also be assessed within the framework of the French majority voting system that, as its name suggests, is designed to consolidate ample and powerful majorities and where the winner (however slight the margin of victory) literally takes all. Indeed, this system probably contributed to a view that political loyalties in Iparralde were overwhelmingly conservative (when they were not) and masked the tensions and divisions within Basque society.

Another key feature of these 2004 cantonal elections was the role of Basque nationalists, especially in the shift of nationalist sympathizers to the PS in the second round of voting, even when some of the UDF-UMP candidates might have been members of the Batera platform. Basque nationalist sympathizers voted for a progressive ticket, and a new political picture began to emerge in Iparralde. Indeed, the PS (with the support of Basque nationalists) began to visualize the prospect of taking Baiona in the next municipal elections in 2008, thereby ending the long saga of the Grenet family's control of the city. Both French Socialists and the remaining notables realized that the nationalists were now an important swing vote. With this in mind, and with the campaign to gain signatures in favor of holding a referendum on the issue,[21] the question of a Basque *département* once again came to the fore. Similarly, linguistic and local development policies might potentially become key electoral issues.

To emphasize the complex nature of politics in Iparralde, these same 2004 cantonal elections demonstrated divisions within Basque nationalism, but also a growth of the nationalist/pro-Basque vote. AB was still the principal nationalist force, without losing too much ground to either the radical nationalism of Batasuna (a legally recognized party in France, although banned in Spain) or the pro-Basque Elgar-Ensemble. Elsewhere, moderate Basque nationalism all but disappeared from the political scene, with the PNB not taking part and EA achieving only 200 votes. It is worth mentioning, however, that Batasuna achieved a stable figure of 1200 votes.

Yet despite these divisions, there may be an emerging belief in the need for unity of action among Basque nationalists. Indeed, all the nationalist formations met in an attempt to establish an agreement prior to the 2004 regional elections, although ultimately this agreement was not ratified by AB. The meeting did, however, demonstrate the will of Batasuna and AB to work together in presenting a nationalist alternative for regional elections that, by their very organizational model, discriminated against minority formations. Ultimately, nationalists used this occasion to call for voters to use the ballots in these elections to write a plea for the repatriation of Basque political prisoners to jails in or near the Basque Country, a call that was met with two thousand people filling out their ballots this way. Through 2004, moreover, representatives of AB, Batasuna, and

EA met regularly in an attempt to agree on a common strategy in favor of demanding Basque institutional representation.

Finally, regarding the watershed 2004 cantonal elections, there was an impressive debut showing of Elgar-Ensemble, the result of this party attracting many sympathizers who had previously voted for statewide parties. Created in 2002 and led by Peyo Labéguerie (son of Michel), it was designed to combine an interest in the Basque language and culture with a strong identification with French republican ideals. It also revived a traditional connection between pro-Basque-culture Christian Democrats in Iparralde with apparent success. Such individuals had voted principally—to that date, at least—for parties such the UDF, yet now they had a new political option, a party that stressed being "Basque in France and French in the Basque Country." While this slogan was dismissed by Basque nationalists as nothing new, it did, in subtle fashion, redress the previous imbalance implied by the hegemony of French identity over its Basque counterpart— that is, it interrupted the zero-sum game deriving from the strength of the state-building process. The political articulation of a dual identity, of belonging to two nations, at least marked the end of the former dominance of French identity. Yet more than this, Elgar-Ensemble's platform was unequivocally pro-Basque and demanded some degree of political recognition for Iparralde. At the same time, the party was tied closely to the Batera platform advocating civil disobedience in the search for Basque institutions. One might even contend that at this moment, at least, Elgar-Ensemble prioritized pro-Basque ideals over French republican ones. In sum, support for Elgar-Ensemble was not nationalist, but had much more in common with nationalism than with Christian Democracy. It is too early to say what effect Elgar-Ensemble might have, but, given its relatively short life as a political party—formed, we should remember, in early 2004—it certainly made an impressive start, achieving 9 percent of the vote in the four cantons where its candidates ran during the 2004 cantonal elections.

One might speculate that Elgar-Ensemble, should it continue to function as a party, might take on more of leading role in the politics of Iparralde at the expense of nationalist formations such as AB, Batasuna, EA, or the PNB, these latter parties having maintained a unanimous position as regards the basic demands of the Batera platform. If this is the case, the role of the nationalist parties in the movement for Basque institutions might diminish. However, independent of this potential conjunctional transformation, the emergence of Elgar-Ensemble has been positive for both Basque nationalism and, more generally, for Basque culture in Iparralde. Forty years ago, the Mouvement Démocratique Basque (MDB) attempted to follow a similar path to that of Elgar-Ensemble, but ultimately this was unsuccessful. Nowadays, a pro-Basque alternative tied to Christian Democratic ideals has found its place in the political spectrum of Iparralde.

What, then, has changed? Why has Elgar-Ensemble succeeded, albeit initially, where the MDB did not? The answer lies somewhere in the changing nature of identity in Iparralde. Where once French identity triumphed in the zero-sum game, now there is a sufficiently strong identity associated with the notion of the Pays Basque among the population of Iparralde, and this despite the lack of any specific institutional representation. While the French authorities continue to deny any administrative powers to Iparralde, it seems like the Pays Basque identity will continue to be politicized in alliance with the Basque identity of nationalism.

The Current State of Identity

The "inside-outside" relationship refers unapologetically to a dichotomy on which all identity games are played out: Humans against the natural world, "my" group against the "others," or "me" against the "others" in my group are the three levels on which a feeling of belonging is constructed. This is always a polar model based on inclusion and exclusion (inside-outside) that is built on a paradox: the factual basis of this model is both objective and arbitrary.[22]

Collective identities need something material that they can use to visualize the difference on which their group originality is founded. There are many fibers from which identities are woven. Gender might be the base of sexual identity, skin color may sustain racial identity, and the material conditions of life could shape class identity. Music, cooking, respect for nature, and religion are objective facts—the elements on which heavy-metal, vegetarian, ecologist, and Tibetan identities might be based. However, I referred to the arbitrary quality of identity, and I did so because I said that gender or religion or the material conditions of life "might" generate their respective identities, while at the same time, they might not. To be sure, history has demonstrated that the "objective fact–identity" relationship (worker = working class identity, for example) is logical. However, it is also unforeseeable. I do not think, as Marx did, that one can envisage the creation of a group on the basis of a specific feature, such as the relationship between "worker" and "class identity." That is, the conditions of an industrial worker might allow for the development of consciousness that leads to this individual getting involved in a progressive working-class organization, but equally, this same worker might be more convinced by the discourse of bourgeois elites and the capitalist system, or even of fascism.[23]

A Necessary Indicator: The Basque Language

Euskara is an objective fact, yet the existence, or more specifically, the use of a language does not necessarily imply that a specific sense of differential identity will emerge from this. Thus, knowledge and use of Euskara in Iparralde does not necessarily mean one should feel a member of the Basque community. For example, many of the most fervent Jacobins, such as the notable Jean Ybarnégaray, developed a discourse of belonging to France in their maternal language—Euskara. At the same time, many others who do not possess the objective fact (Euskara), such as one of Enbata's founders, Jakes Abeberry, have been central to the emergence and development of a consciousness of belonging to a Basque community.

This arbitrary component within identities explains the paradox that the same people with the same differential element (Euskara) evolve in different ways. Specifically, in the case of Iparralde, some people began to conceive of a Basque national consciousness at the beginning of the twentieth century, whereas others joined in the discourse emanating from the (French) center. However, the relationship between identity and language has been, in part, contradictory. Thus, while it is true that the survival of Euskara in the Third Republic did not encourage the development of a politicized expression of a Basque sense of belonging, it is equally the case that the subsequent crisis of the language resulted in a crisis of Basque identity. And now it would appear that the reverse is happening. That is, there seems to be taking place in Iparralde a reevaluation of Euskara that might be regarded as an indicator of a reawakening of Basque identity.

Therefore, by way of conclusion, I would like to address a series of variables that, taken together, led to a renewed sense of hope in Iparralde throughout the 1990s. Despite the linguistic crisis, there emerged a clear will in favor of Euskara on the part of the population as a whole, a favorable position that was subsequently responded to in kind by the public authorities.

There has clearly been a more conscious appreciation of the linguistic situation in Iparralde. Three general sociolinguistic surveys (1991, 1996, and 2001), another undertaken among thirteen-year-olds and fourteen-year-olds in 1999, and the 1999 census all confirmed the dramatic plight of Euskara and led to a new awareness of the problem on the part of the public authorities. According to these surveys, there was still a significant Basque-speaking population (29 percent) in Iparralde, but knowledge of the language fell dramatically among young people (11 percent) and more still among adolescents (9 percent). However, in the Basque Autonomous Community, the situation was the reverse, with a 33 percent Basque-speaking population among adults and 62 percent among young people. The contradiction between these two regions led many to conclude that the cause must be related to the lack of a linguistic policy for Iparralde. And in turn, there was a general movement to facilitate the creation of such a policy, leading to the establishment of a public office for Euskara headed by the UMP's Max Brisson, as well as more general public mobilizations in civil society to promote the position of Euskara in public life and to encourage its transition in families.

The desire to learn Euskara, moreover, has become more evident. All the surveys revealed young people's positive attitude toward the language. Indeed, the number of passively bilingual people has risen significantly, especially in the demographically important Baiona-Angelu-Biarritz (BAB) conurbation, rising from 3.9 percent in 1996 to 8.3 percent in 2001. This can be explained by the more widespread teaching of Euskara in the school system. For instance, those pupils in immersion (Euskara-only) or bilingual classes within the primary school system grew from 3,300 (14 percent) in 1995 to 5,400 (22 percent) in 2002. Similarly, since 1993, there has been a steady growth in the number of pupils learning Euskara as a subject in school: by more than 41 percent in the primary system between 1993 and 1999, by 24 percent in the secondary system since 1995, and by 23 percent in the *lycées* since 1996. That said, one should be cautious about such statistics, because they do not reflect the quality of teaching. Parallel to these efforts, one should also note the important work undertaken in the field of adult learning of Euskara by organizations such as AEK. The reorganization of private Basque-language media (such as the Euskal Irratiak project in radio) was also an important factor in encouraging a greater awareness of Euskara. Finally, to confirm this positive tendency regarding Euskara, a survey commissioned by the department of national education and the BAB regional authority in 2003 demonstrated that 52 percent of parents with children up to two years old in the BAB wanted their offspring to learn Euskara during their school years.

In line with these developments, a mechanism has been put in place to encourage a linguistic policy supporting Euskara. In 2000, the CDPB noted the almost total lack of any measures taken to facilitate such a linguistic policy, underscoring the "absence of a general directive policy for regional languages." It continued that "the effort of the associations has been noteworthy . . . but results have not met the objectives outlined in the territorial project [blueprint for development]."[24] However, shortly afterward, an agreement was reached between the local development networks and regional, departmental, and national authorities to create the bases of an organization capable of defining and implementing a pro-Euskara linguistic policy. Among other instruments, the creation of a Maîtrise d'Ouvrage Publique (MOP, Master of Public Works) as a distinct decision-making authority was important. Created in 2001, the MOP served as a conduit for the work of all the relevant authorities (from the national to the local level) with a mission to create and implement the necessary measures to aid Euskara. Parallel to this, another organization was created in 2001 that served as a kind of watchdog to coordinate linguistic matters and make proposals: Hizkuntza Kontseilua, the Council of the (Basque) Language. This was a body in which representatives of unofficial associations and official institutions came together with experts to formulate proposals and recommendations to the MOP, as well as to oversee and evaluate linguistic matters in the blueprint for development. Further, several other associations and public bodies were in charge, together with the MOP, of actually putting into practice these linguistic strategies: for example, AEK, Euskaltzaindia (the Academy of the Basque Language), Euskal Haziak, Euskal Irratiak (the Association of Basque-language Radio Stations in Iparralde), Ikas, Ikas-bi (the Association for the Promotion of Bilingual Education in public schools in Iparralde), and Uda Leku (the Association for the Promotion of Euskara among children and adolescents in Iparralde). And finally, the state also created a new body, the Groupement d'Interes Public (Public Interest Group), with administrative and regulatory powers to respond to proposals from the above-mentioned groups.

In sum, with the turn of the new millennium, Euskara was increasingly important for the population of Iparralde, and in turn, this made a critical reevaluation of the notion of belonging paramount.

The Evolution of Identity

The state of the language in Iparralde today cannot be removed from the question of feelings of belonging. In this regard, the weak situation of Euskara, or, more specifically, the decline in Basque speakers between the 1880s and the 1990s, was a reflection of the identity crisis experienced by Iparralde during its transition to modernity. Similarly, the more recent change of attitude and nascent realignment of the population in Iparralde toward looking favorably on Euskara can be interpreted as a transformation of many people's sense of identity, ending the previous zero-sum game.

As we saw, the foundation of the modern French state after 1790 was based on the eradication of all vestiges of the *ancien régime* and especially of organizational models such as the *Biltzarrak* deemed to be antirevolutionary. Gradually, a sense of belonging was cultivated that was open to all individuals living within the delineated boundaries of the nation-state, where everyone was equal before the law. Individual freedoms were thus linked to strong central authority and, precisely because of the doctrine of popular sovereignty, any form of collective action that did not pass through the framework of the state was considered illegitimate. In this sense, the Rousseauean tradition bequeathed French nationalism a high level of civic content, in that it tended to emphasize the importance of the individual in constructing the nation, but at the same time, it left no intermediary space between the two poles of state and individual. Thus, democracy meant national unity, centralization, and uniformity. And for this reason, the Basque territories were joined with others of a different language and culture (Occitanian-Gascon) in the same *département*.

Yet no state construction emerges out of nothing. That is, the state must create something on which it can develop. This "something" is created out of a series of symbols, identities, and languages chosen and organized by dominant elites in the center, who, in turn, force their choices on geographical, cultural, and linguistic peripheries. This explains why, for all the emphasis on individual rights, there was an equal denial of any notion of group or collective rights. Indeed, the word "denial" might be too lenient a choice, for in the example of the 1784 Grégoire Report, the revolutionary authorities actually spoke of "destroying" substate group identities. This was, in effect, a policy of extermination for languages other than French, a language that, even by the time of the Third Republic in the late nineteenth and early twentieth centuries, was spoken only by a third of the population as a whole, and as little as 20 percent in rural areas.

In Iparralde, however, a union of interests between the popular Basque-speaking classes and a Catholic elite opposed to the secular tendencies of the new state, coupled with the fundamentally rural nature of the territory, allowed Euskara and the Basque culture to survive in stronger fashion than one might have predicted at the time, given the general force of French state construction. However, between the time of the Third Republic and through the first half of the twentieth century, the Basque language and Basque culture experienced a severe crisis as a result of a number of factors: the loss of the religious elites' influence and their gradual replacement by notables who assumed the national discourse of the French state; the consequences of an industrialization process that undermined the predominantly rural society of Iparralde; the consequences of the mandatory teaching of French in schools; the psychological effects of young people's participation in two world wars, in which they killed and were killed in the name of a nation that they were just getting to know; and the dissemination of Gaullist values—an authentically populist national movement. Taken together, these factors created a new sense of French belonging among the population of Iparralde, tied closely to the idea of embracing modern values. This new French identity, in turn, came into confrontation with its older Basque counterpart, defined by the language and cultural practices that were increasingly associated with the past and tradition, viewed in a negative sense.

This Basque identity found political expression for the first time in 1945—perhaps the nadir of this growing crisis in a Basque sense of belonging—when Jean Etcheverry-Ainchart presented a proposal before the French National Assembly to create a statute of autonomy for Iparralde. From that time on, and especially after the 1960s, Basque identity began to assume a more political dimension, because it was organized and articulated by Basque nationalists. Consequently, and because of various local and universal factors, as well as for structural and conjunctional reasons, gradually, the unitary French model of belonging underwent a transformation as a result of the series of changes described in qualitative fashion above. Yet what of the quantitative dimension of these transformations?

The first conclusion that emerges from the evidence we have regarding identity in Iparralde is that the number of people defining themselves as Basque alone rose continually between 1979 (6 percent) and 2001 (10 percent). Similarly, the percentage of people defining themselves as either more Basque than French or equally Basque and French also rose during the same period—a reflection of the emerging hybrid Pays Basque identity in Iparralde. Conversely, the number of people defining themselves as French alone declined by 5.3 percent during the 1980s and 1990s. Yet while the number of people claiming dual identity generally grew during the same period, it actually suffered a slight decline between 1996 and 2001.

Table 1: Feeling of Belonging in Iparralde

	1979		1996		2001	
Basque	6%		7.3%		9.7%	
More Basque than French	6%	52%	6.8%	59.4%	6.8%	54.1%
Equally French and Basque	28%		33.4%		30.8%	
More French than Basque	18%		19.2%		16.5%	
French	37%		31.7%		31.7%	
Don't Know/No Response	–		4.4%		4.4%	

Source: Juan J. Linz, *Conflicto en Euskadi* (Madrid: Espasa-Calpe, 1986), 375; Eustat [Basque Statistics Office] and INSEE [French National Institute for Statistics and Economic Studies], *Encuesta socio-lingüística de Euskal Herria* (Vitoria-Gasteiz: Eustat, 1996); Eustat and EKE [Basque Culture Institute], *Encuesta socio-lingüística de Euskal Herria*, (Vitoria-Gasteiz: Eustat, 2001).

If we compare the data from 1996 for the Foral Community of Navarre (FCN) and the Basque Autonomous Community (BAC), however, we see that the Basque feeling of belonging is much weaker and attachment to the state much stronger in Iparralde than Hegoalde. Yet that dual feeling of belonging is higher in Iparralde than in Hegoalde (8 percent more than in the BAC and 26 percent more than in the FCN). This is important, because while in Hegoalde such dual belonging tends more to lean toward feeling Spanish, in Iparralde, the reverse is true, and a Basque feeling of belonging tends to outweigh its French counterpart.

If we analyze the data by territory, however, we see that a Basque feeling of belonging decreased in the BAB conurbation between 1996 and 2001, with percentage levels in both cases so small as to be almost insignificant. At the same time, the BAB conurbation also demonstrated the highest levels of a French sense of belonging in the whole of Iparralde. On the other hand, in the remaining areas of Lapurdi and the interior provinces, the percentage of those who defined themselves as exclusively Basque was higher than the average as a whole for Iparralde and increased continually between 1996 and 2001. (The 1979 survey was not taken by specific areas, so we cannot compare data from that time.) Finally, while a dual sense of belonging maintained a constant level in the BAB, it declined in the interior of Lapurdi, Nafarroa Beherea, and Zuberoa, most likely as the result of a polarization of identities in these areas.

Table 2: Evolution of Feeling of Belonging by Area

	Basque		Equally Basque and French/Spanish		French or Spanish	
	1996	2001	1996	2001	1996	2001
Iparralde	7%	9.7%	59%	54.1%	30%	31.7%
BAB	4%	3%	50%	49%	45%	43%
Interior Lapurdi	10%	14%	64%	56%	21%	26%
Low Navarre and Zuberoa	12%	17%	74%	65%	12%	14%
BAC	32%	38.4%	51%	48.6%	8%	5.7%
FCN	23%	19.5%	33%	30.2%	35%	39.7%

Source: Eustat and INSEE, *Encuesta socio-lingüística de Euskal Herria*; Eustat and EKE, *Encuesta socio-lingüística de Euskal Herria*.

As one would expect, in 1996, most of those who felt just Basque were native inhabitants of Iparralde (12 percent) and/or bilingual in Basque and French (22 percent). By contrast, half of all immigrants to Iparralde declared themselves to be just French, and monolingual French speakers were divided between feeling a dual sense of identity (52 percent) or just French (43 percent).

Table 3: Sense of Belonging by Origin (1996)

Origin	Basque	Basque and French	French
Iparralde	12%	75%	11%
One or Both Parents an Immigrant	6%	57%	33%
Immigrants	–	42%	51%

Source: Eustat and INSEE, *Encuesta socio-lingüística de Euskal Herria*.

Table 4: Sense of Belonging by Linguistic Competence (1996) (as a percentage)

Linguistic Competence	Basque	Basque and French	French
Bilingual	22%	72%	–
Passive Bilingual	9%	75%	11%
Monolingual	–	52%	43%

Source: Eustat and INSEE, *Encuesta socio-lingüística de Euskal Herria*.

Unfortunately, we do not have any data that might allow us to assess the evolution of identity based on these criteria. We can therefore deduce only a series of partial (although not insignificant) conclusions. For example, in 1979, eight out of ten monolingual French speakers regarded themselves as French alone (82 percent), and only one in ten felt equally Basque and French (9 percent).[25] However, at present, this dual sense of belonging has grown considerably among this sector of the population by 43 percent, while among the same sector, a single French identity has fallen by 39 percent. Similarly, in 1979, 25 percent of Basque speakers felt French alone, 51 percent equally Basque and French, and 23 percent just Basque.[26] By 1996, those who felt just French among Basque speakers were nonexistent, those who felt a dual identity had grown by 24 percent, and those that felt just Basque remained at about the same level (1 percent less than in 1979).

Regarding the interplay between identity and origin, any comparison between contemporary times and 1979 requires caution, because the 1979 data specify the differences in outside birthplace (Béarn, other areas of France, and abroad, for example), while the data from 1996 and 2001 do not. Generally speaking, though, we can observe that, in 1979,[27] 73 percent of those born in Béarn, 79 percent of those born in other *départements*, and 57 percent of those born outside France felt French, yet in 1996, the total immigrant population feeling just French fell to 51 percent. Meanwhile, in 1979,[28] a dual identity in the same groups mentioned above was felt by 22 percent, 10 percent, and 11 percent respectively, while in 1996, 42 percent of all immigrants felt both Basque and French.

In 2000, the French public-opinion research company CSA carried out a survey throughout the *département* that incorporated questions relating to people's identity. In this case, those polled had five options from which to choose as a response to the question "Personally, in the first instance do you consider yourself French, Basque, an inhabitant of your commune, European, or Aquitanian?" Although the subsequent data cannot be directly compared with the above-mentioned information—due to the different nature of the question and, crucially, the lack of a category for embracing a dual identity—there is still much to be gained from analyzing the findings.

For example, 49 percent of those surveyed considered themselves French, 22 percent Basque, 15 percent as an inhabitant of their commune (municipality), and 13 percent European. At first glance, it appeared significant that the percentage of those who felt just French was actually higher in Iparralde than it was in Béarn (by 5 percent), while those who defined themselves as just Basque was 8 percent lower than those who defined themselves as just Béarnais. This may have been the result of a kind of localist reaction on the part of many Béarnais people to the successful development strategies achieved by Iparralde through the 1990s, strategies that, it should be stressed, were never extended to Béarn. However, any political connotations that may have accompanied these declarations of Béarnais identity were muted by contrast with those who declared themselves just Basque, because such an expression of Basque identity alone, unlike its Béarnais counterpart, was intimately connected to a well-organized and well-articulated nationalist discourse. At most, such an expression of Béarnais identity may have had certain cultural connotations, but it did not challenge the structure of the French Republic politically, as was the case in Iparralde with Basque identity.

Furthermore, because of the fact that in the CSA survey there was no option to state one's dual identity, it seems as if 20 percent of those polled opted to choose a French identity over a Basque one, with 12 percent choosing a Basque over a French identity. Consequently, too, more people defined themselves as Basque in the CSA survey than in the previous polls had defined themselves as Basque or more Basque than French.

Taking as a base figure those 22 percent of people who defined themselves as Basque in the CSA survey, one can draw a number of conclusions. First, young people between eighteen and twenty-four years of age constituted the highest percentage (35 percent) by age group of those feeling Basque, followed by those between twenty-five and thirty-four (26 percent) and then those between fifty-five and sixty-four. By contrast, people between forty-five and fifty-four years of age, precisely those who had been socialized during the period of maximum identity crisis in Iparralde, were the age group that least identified itself as Basque (7 percent) and that identified itsself most as French (60 percent). Further, by territory, the CSA survey revealed that feeling Basque was more typical in rural areas (32 percent) than in urban ones (18 percent). Similarly, by profession, those people who felt more Basque were most likely to come from intermediary positions (30 percent). Finally, the 49 percent of those surveyed who defined themselves as French appear to represent a more homogeneous bloc. That is, people over sixty-five years of age predominated (58 percent), together with the forty-five to fifty-four age group. Moreover, those defining themselves as French were predominantly urban dwellers, while by political leaning they were to be found mainly among sympathizers of the UDF (80 percent) and the PS (66 percent).

The proportion of people in Iparralde who defined a Basque feeling of belonging as stemming from knowledge of Euskara or as having Basque forebears was significantly higher than in Hegoalde, despite the fact that it declined between 1996 and 2001. This information leads observers such as Juan J. Linz to classify Basque identity in Iparralde as primordial or cultural, in that it excludes "from the nation those who do not speak the language, do not descend from a native family, or who were not born in the region, while a nationalist identity [that of Hegoalde], whose ultimate goal is a territorial nation-state, is obliged to include in the nation all those who live in its territory in a process of assimilation of foreign elements."[29] If this is the case, it would explain the difficulty in recovering the Basque language and identity in Iparralde, together with the unlikely consolidation of Basque nationalism as a major political movement there. Even in 2006, when faced with the question of what conditions might lead one to feeling Basque, 53 percent of people in Iparralde responded by stating that being born in the Basque Country was important, as opposed to an average of 39 percent for the Basque Country as a whole; 40 percent of people in Iparralde responded that speaking Euskara was important, as opposed to 17 percent overall; and 31 percent of people in Iparralde believed that having Basque forebears was important, as opposed to an average of 9 percent throughout the Basque

Country. By contrast, in response to the same question, the most popular answers from the Basque Country as a whole were "wanting to be Basque" (41 percent) and "living and working in the Basque Country" (40 percent), while these answers were favored by only 14 and 24 percent of the population in Iparralde.[30]

Although the results of this 2006 qualitative study demonstrate a certain stability in the evolution of a Basque feeling of belonging, with 17 percent of the population in Iparralde feeling predominantly Basque, 24 percent equally Basque and French, and 53 percent feeling French, a number of its conclusions also demonstrate a social awareness of changing patterns of identity. Although the general results hardly changed between 1996 and 2006, only 6 percent more of the population considered themselves "more French than ten years ago," 76 percent considered themselves as just French, but 15 percent defined themselves as "more Basque than ten years ago." Further still, asked how they might feel in a decade's time, only 3 percent responded that they would feel more French, while 9 percent believed they would feel more Basque.[31]

In sum, the conclusions of this latest study are quite revealing for offering an insight into how Basque identity might develop in the future in Iparralde. According to the 2006 study:

> In Iparralde, a change seems to be taking place, although slowly: After many years when one could live easily apart from Basque culture and identity, it seems as if attitudes are changing, little by little, and currently, young people connect with a cultural and identity-based universe of anything Basque that is adapting to modern values, [something that] happens more and more. Taking into consideration the words expressed throughout this study, one might say that, to a certain extent, anything Basque is fashionable among young people in Iparralde (even if it is only symbolic, because more and more young people wear *ikurriñas* [Basque flags] on their clothes or things, or they try to say a few words in Euskara, despite not knowing a lot).[32]

Further still, not only young people, but also some immigrants in Iparralde are changing their attitudes in this regard: "Basque culture represents one of the few examples of resistance to the process of French institutionalization, [a process] that practically finished off most local cultures, leaving in its wake a huge cultural void. In Iparralde, Basque culture has been transformed into an example of resistance and has acquired an important seductive role for the rest of the population in the French state."[33]

In short, the development strategies of the 1990s, the articulation of a social movement that began to demand local representation, and the role of Basque nationalists in both dynamics combined to create a notion of Basqueness that was defined more on territorial and instrumental grounds than on the cultural foundations highlighted by Linz. This idea, of course, fits in with the data pointing to a growing Basque sense of belonging in Iparralde, with the rising number of votes for Basque nationalists, and with the forecasts contained in the qualitative analyses under discussion here.

Conclusion

We are currently witness to a major struggle in Iparralde between different identities over the fundamental need for objectification. In diagram form:

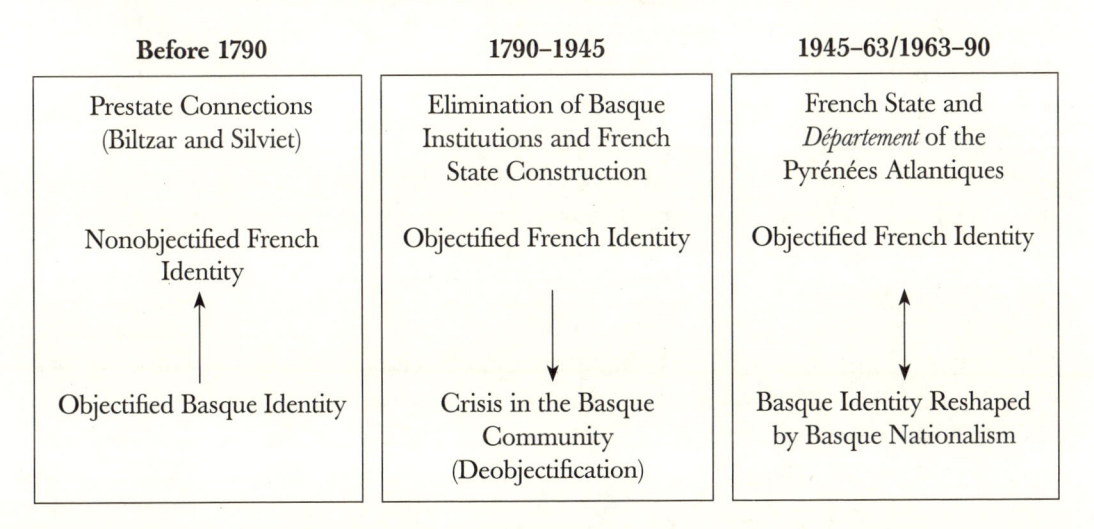

Before 1790	1790–1945	1945–63/1963–90
Prestate Connections (Biltzar and Silviet)	Elimination of Basque Institutions and French State Construction	French State and *Département* of the Pyrénées Atlantiques
Nonobjectified French Identity ↑	Objectified French Identity ↓	Objectified French Identity ↕
Objectified Basque Identity	Crisis in the Basque Community (Deobjectification)	Basque Identity Reshaped by Basque Nationalism

In the prerevolutionary period, a loose form of Basque identity existed that was incapable of challenging the strategy of state construction designed in Paris after 1790. Thereafter, this Basque identity (shared by most of the population in Iparralde) went through a period of crisis as it was gradually absorbed by a stronger feeling of belonging to France. However, pro-Basque feeling survived and was expressed in two ways: in certain contexts (as exemplified by Pierre Lafitte), it emerged as a way of overcoming or exorcizing that identity crisis—that is, it joined an "emotional" Basque nationalist discourse with a minimal form of regionalism that was acceptable among the population as a whole. Similarly, on other occasions, this attitude adapted to the system of notables, who exercised so much local power, a system whereby important elected officials developed strategies within the French political system while defending Basque identity and values within the framework of cultural socialization alone. In both cases—Basque regionalism and the notables' support for Basque culture—the same contradiction was maintained: that of two *patries*, one large (France), the other, small (the Basque Country).

This all changed in the early 1960s, when a Basque nationalist movement emerged, taking advantage of the symbolic capital that remained among the popular classes. Consequently, the rise of Basque nationalism clashed with these previous forms of pro-Basque sentiment, resulting in, on the one hand, a gradual shift of the pro-Basque notable sector to more French positions with the creation of the Fifth Republic in 1958 and the gradual alliance of regionalist Basques with supporters of Basque nationalist positions. Despite these changes, Basque nationalist parties were incapable of achieving significant electoral success, and the cultivation of Basque identity therefore took refuge in the cultural and economic spheres. That said, a new conflict of identity had taken root:

| BASQUE IDENTITY | → ← | FRENCH IDENTITY |

In the 1990s, yet another transformation took place in the objectification of Iparralde, a territory that had officially disappeared after its union with Béarn to create a new *département* after 1790. It resurfaced as a distinct space within which local development policies were designed, while at the same time a new movement emerged to demand some form of Basque institutional representation. With the subsequent retreat of the French authorities from their promises to back these local development strategies financially, the campaign for Basque institutions adopted a more vigorous strategy of popular mobilization in favor of Basque identity, a strategy that ultimately activated several elements within this symbolic universe.

When traditional (French) republican values were applied to the local status of Iparralde, a new identity then emerged: that of the Pays Basque. Thereafter, this new identity came to occupy an intermediary position between the two competing extremes of Basque and French identity, extremes that had opposed one another violently in the 1970s.

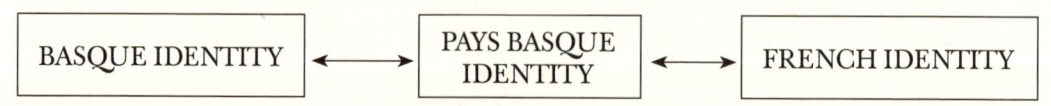

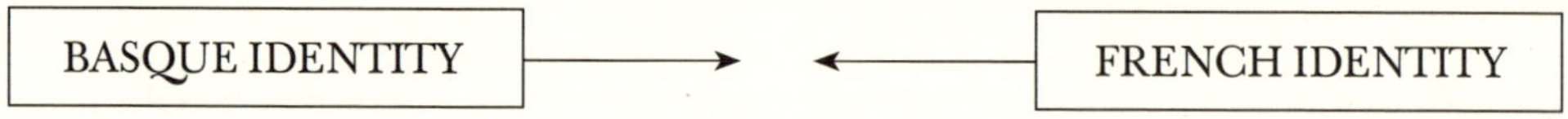

| BASQUE IDENTITY | ↔ | PAYS BASQUE IDENTITY | ↔ | FRENCH IDENTITY |

This new identity, in turn, required some form of objectification. Conscious of this need and of the need to instrumentalize Basque identity in a hostile official French environment, Basque nationalists embraced the call for a specific Basque *département*, thereby abandoning the more radical demand for autonomy favored by IK. Basque nationalists thus came to oversee the cultivation of a specifically Basque identity, that of the Pays Basque. And through this alliance between Basque nationalists and other supporters of Basque interests, the French authorities were forced to respond financially by fulfilling their word on a local development strategy that they themselves began.

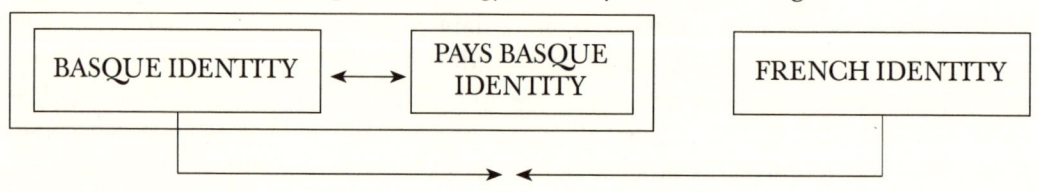

| BASQUE IDENTITY | ↔ | PAYS BASQUE IDENTITY | | FRENCH IDENTITY |

Yet the response of the French authorities—the 1997 development agreement and the 2000 agreement to finance the proposals—remained insufficient in that it did not address the foundation on which all claims to identity are based: some kind of objectification. Moreover, those pro-Basque sectors seeking some degree of institutional expression of their Pays Basque identity felt free to radicalize their positions, because these demands were based on clearly republican ideals (the desire for a separate *département*), rather than on more overtly politicized claims (autonomy). Thus, instead of playing complementary roles, these sectors once more found themselves in opposition, and it seemed as if a bipolar model was once again emerging, although it was uncertain what role the Pays Basque identity might play in the future.

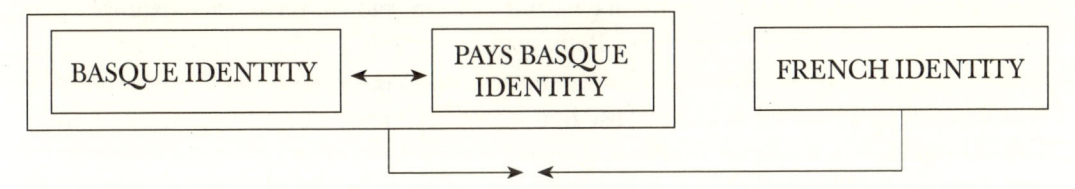

```
[ BASQUE IDENTITY ] <—> [ PAYS BASQUE IDENTITY ]     [ FRENCH IDENTITY ]
                            └─────> <─────┘
```

By early 2006, there appeared to be three potential future scenarios, all of whose features were actually already present. The historical conflict of identity in Iparralde had arrived at a crossroads.

One potential exit from this scenario envisaged the gradual fusion of Basque (nationalist) and pro-Basque identities on the foundation of the former, but with a toning down of its ethnic and political dimensions. Such a position was already evident in the political line of AB, a line that diverged from the Izquierda Abertzale in Hegoalde (for example, AB's demand for a ceasefire from ETA), but that also differed significantly from the governing moderate Basque nationalism of the Basque Autonomous Community. According to this hypothesis, Basque nationalism in Iparralde (as represented by AB) will continue to grow, but also will gradually temper its identity-based, cultural, and ethnic and elements. Indeed, AB may embark on a reworking of what it means to be Basque nationalist in Iparralde, charting a less exclusivist course than that of Hegoalde and breaking the logic uniting the feeling of a Basque identity with being a Basque nationalist. This model envisages a more voluntarist than essentialist form of nationalism and would, in turn, force French nationalists either to withdraw or to react virulently against this new (hypothetical) blend of Basque nationalism and pro-Basque sentiment, which would be on the way to achieving (at least potentially) a hegemonic position in Iparralde. In short, such a route would demonstrate that Basque nationalism in Iparralde definitively opted for deciding its own course, a course different from that already mapped out previously in Hegoalde.

A second hypothesis envisages the implosion of the Pays Basque identity into multiple feelings of belonging without any central quality, attracted at the same time by both polar identities and reshaping its own principles, but also reinforcing a general level of conflict. This potential development, although obviously at odds with the previous scenario, is also partly evident now. There has been increasing tension between the two extremes, as exemplified by the progressively more militant position of radical Basque nationalist sectors that, in 2007, abandoned their adherence to calls for a *département* and once more began to demand autonomy and, at the other end of the spectrum, an increasingly obstructionist stance by the French authorities as they try to free themselves of previous agreements and neutralize the potential differentiating effects of encouraging a Pays Basque identity—principally by adopting a macro *pays* policy throughout France, thereby dissolving any notion of difference in the uniformity of national legislation. Should the situation continue like this, the CDPB would lose its momentum and the Pays Basque identity its raison d'être. Moreover, its eventual implosion would reinforce the two poles, and the resulting conflict would be played out in more radical terms. For example, the civil disobedience of the Demos and Batera might be delegitimated as they undertake new, more audacious, radical, and clandestine activity in response to their former actions becoming routine, as well as in response to the absence of any official response or to official repression. Finally, those sectors whose maximum demand is a *département* may leave the movement for fear of sharing ground with an increasingly radicalized nationalism led by Batasuna. It would therefore come as no surprise, in this scenario, to see frustration give way to violence, and even ETA might feel legitimized to carry out assassinations on French soil for the first time in its history.

A third potential future situation sees a reinforcing of the Pays Basque identity. That is, it would remain closely tied to (but also different from) Basque (nationalist) identity, yet it would relegate its more politicized aspects to a position below its own symbolic dimension. This Pays Basque identity would develop a different discourse from that of local elites—elites that, while they may share the idea of extracting the maximum powers possible from central authority, would never contemplate breaking the basic ties of French republicanism. An example of this strengthened Pays Basque identity was the 2002 document published by the CEPB calling for a separate agricultural chamber to be established for Iparralde, together with an official status for Euskara and the creation of a public body to organize and oversee higher education. Another clear example of this was the creation of Elgar-Ensemble, also in 2002, with its equally pro-Basque and French outlook. Such a scenario would allow the Pays Basque identity to form a foundation on which to build cross-border ties with Hegoalde—thanks mainly to overcoming overly culturalist or politicized dimensions on the issue of such cooperation that have previously aroused suspicion. In this scenario, the two polar nationalisms would remain in place, but any conflict would be lessened, because it would be filtered through this new, reinforced Pays Basque position. However, for this hypothesis to work, without any doubt, the demands of the CEPB would have to be met. That is, Iparralde would have to be recognized in some clear institutional way—whether through the creation of a *département* or through some other constitutional rearrangement (something that, as I write, seems highly unlikely). Finally, it is too early to tell whether the political movement taking shape around the Pays Basque identity (Elgar-Ensemble) will continue to develop at the same rate. Its existence alone, however, is testament to the complex game of identities described above.

Although the three alternative scenarios that emerged in the period 2002–7 all lead to different potential future scenarios, possibly one future scenario will embrace elements of all three. Whatever the case, and beyond the speculation associated with these three hypotheses, it would seem that the buffering effect associated with the rise of the Pays Basque identity between 1992 and 1997 has given rise to a new form of bipolar conflict in which everything would indicate that Basque identity has been strengthened to the detriment of its French counterpart. As a result, the zero-sum game has been transformed into a complex system of multiple identities. However, the future is open to any kind of transformation, and I would not rule out the possibility that the dynamic I have described here may even be reversed.

By this I mean that it is impossible to know whether, on the one hand, this emergent Pays Basque identity is an ephemeral (weak) feeling of belonging that will either dissolve into Basque (nationalist) identity as a result of the oppositional strategy into which it has been introduced or flourish as a consequence of this same strategy, thereby redefining the Basque-French identity conflict. On the other hand, the Pays Basque identity may be a stable (strong) feeling of belonging that constructs a new identity framework by which society in Iparralde can be defined as both different from and complementary to both the rest of France and the rest of the Basque Country before entering another phase in which, if it were necessary, it would resolve the identity question in Iparralde.

Without the existence of this new hybrid Pays Basque identity—which both leans toward and therefore reinforces Basque identity in general—it is impossible to understand the optimistic outlook currently to be witnessed in Iparralde, as reflected by the creation of the Euskal Herriko Laborantza Ganbara (the agricultural chamber of the Basque Country) in 2005 and the widespread support for a referendum on the question of a separate *département*. What seemed impossible in the 1980s might, soon, become reality.

That said, it would seem as if these tendencies will develop further in a place that, from being in a nonexistent or invisible state, has begun to undertake a process of objectification, defined first by the self-recognition of its own inhabitants, then by a degree of external recognition, and that, finally, has arrived at the doors of a third stage: institutional objectification. This dynamic has imparted a previously nonexistent or dormant territorial reality to the collective memory of its inhabitants. And gradually, this dynamic recreates reality, breaking the logic of external or localist development. Iparralde has emerged with a symbolic reality and is itself capable of reaffirming a feeling of Basque and pro-Basque belonging, both of which have undone decades of hegemony by a one-dimensional French identity.

Finally, territory has become the focus of a feeling of belonging in Iparralde. Consequently, doors have been opened to a reworking of the ideas associated with belonging to the Basque community, making this feeling of belonging more open, flexible, porous, and integrating. This issue, tied to the necessary recuperation of the Basque language and culture (the raw material of national consciousness) and the inescapable question of retrieving a historical memory (the connection between past and present on the basis of an unsettled grievance) leads me to speculate that Basque nationalism in Iparralde is about to enter a new stage.

If, until now, the most important point of the quest for identity in Iparralde has been local structuring on the triple foundation of self-recognition, external recognition, and institutional recognition, a corollary of this process has been to move away from a need for uniformity (as a consequence of the crisis of Basque identity and adhesion to a French one) to the necessity of differentiating the local. And this recognition of difference is the first step toward another form of objectification, defined not so much by the object itself—the territory—but by the decision-making subject: the people and their essence, political sovereignty. This, however, will be another story.

For now, and to recapitulate the current situation, I would use the metaphor of judging how full a glass is. For some, the glass of Basque identity is half full, while for less optimistic others it is half empty. However, aside from subjective views, the important thing is not so much the content, as the container. In other words, now the glass is at least in one piece, or at any rate in the process of being mended. Previously, it was riddled with cracks and leaked the contributions of people and organizations from Lafitte, to Legasse, to Labéguerie and from Enbata, to EMA, to Euskal Batasuna. Now, whether half full or half empty, at least it will begin to fill up definitively.

Finally, speaking from Hegoalde, and aware of the profound popular crisis and political conflict around me in this particular part of the Basque Country, I ask whether we in the South can learn anything from the identity games in Iparralde, so that we might redefine Basque identity in more plural or diverse terms, based on the gradual transformation of nationalism in the North and on the hope that this may be paralleled in the South. Undoubtedly, reaching the end of the tunnel of violence would only help, as, in fact, it did in Iparralde. The "little brother" has now been giving its older sibling lessons for some years. Perhaps we should now start learning.

Above all, we in the South should learn not to repeat history and not use our "little brother" in the North to further our own interests, sacrificing the development of Basque identity in Iparralde in pursuit of feeling a superiority that is no longer sustainable. And this implies that whoever defends the interests of the whole Basque Country does not succumb to the temptation of extending to the North the violence that has done so much damage to our country, as well as so much harm to a nonviolent, proindependence nationalism that seeks to situate the Basque community on the international stage with equal rights—no more, no less—with the other peoples and nations of this world.

Afterword

There were important electoral developments following the watershed 2004 cantonal elections (in ten of the twenty-one Basque cantons). After the encouraging results of 2004, AB instigated negotiations with Batasuna, EA and the PNB to form an electoral alliance of all Basque nationalist forces. These negotiations were ongoing, although the PNB pulled out of the proposed alliance after the December 2006 Madrid airport bombings by ETA, the unsatisfactory response to the incident by Batasuna as the reason for its withdrawal. However, the remaining parties did reach an agreement to take part jointly in the 2007 legislative elections.

At these legislative elections, the Euskal Herria Bai (EHBai, The Basque Country, Yes) coalition—AB, Batasuna, and EA—obtained 10,781 votes or 7.99 percent of the total vote during the first round of polling, a modest improvement on the 2002 performance of the combined Basque nationalist forces. While EHBai might have hoped for a better showing, the results were good enough to maintain the coalition intact in order to prepare for the 2008 cantonal elections.

The March 2008 cantonal elections (in the remaining eleven of the twenty-one Basque cantons) confirmed the growth and consolidation of Basque nationalism in Iparralde. Between them, EHBai and the PNB achieved 15.86 percent of the vote (just over 14,000 votes), compared to the 12.13 percent achieved by the different Basque nationalist parties in the same cantons during the 2001 cantonal elections. Importantly, for the first time, the overall vote for Basque nationalist parties broke the 15 percent barrier, meaning that Basque nationalism had become the clear third force in the politics of Iparralde.

The excellent results achieved by the EHBai coalition would appear to indicate a promising outlook regarding the importance of Basque nationalism in future elections. The fact that this coalition held, despite ETA breaking its ceasefire in 2007, would seem to point to its residual strength and the probability of it continuing in the future. That said, however, such continuity will depend on the evolution of relations between Batasuna and AB. As noted in the current study, these are two key formations that, despite sharing similar strategies, maintain significantly different positions on tactical questions such as territorial recognition and a response to the question of political violence.

It is worth mentioning, in more general terms, that Basque nationalism in Iparralde continued to chart its own course in a different way from that of the South. The dominant nationalist group there, AB, remained clearly opposed to the use of violence, in contrast to the ambiguous position of radical Basque nationalists close to Batasuna. Yet Basque nationalism in Iparralde was also differentiated from so-called moderate Basque nationalism in Hegoalde through its grassroots emphasis on citizen participation and mobilization. While attempts were made in the South to follow a similar course—especially through the proposal of the *lehendakari* of the Basque Autonomous Community, Juan Jose Ibarretxe, to consult Basque citizens directly about a negotiated end to ETA violence and the question of self-determination—this was very much a "top-down" model of activism, as contrasted with the by now well established "bottom-up" model in Iparralde. In the case of Iparralde, then, any change resulting from this model will always be slower than that in Hegoalde, but at the same time it will in all likelihood be firmer and more widely agreed on.

Returning to the 2008 results, the traditional power of notables continued to be a feature of political life, too, with victories in the municipal elections for both Jean Grenet (UMP) in Baiona (continuing the Grenet family control of the city since 1959), and Didier Borotra (UDF/MoDem, see below for a discussion of MoDem) in Biarritz. Both, however, were forced into a second round of voting in 2008 after support for them decreased significantly in the first round, compared with their performances in the 2001 elections: from 57 percent to 44 percent in the case of Grenet, and from 54 percent to 41 percent in the case of Borotra. This would appear to indicate that the power of notables continues to be on the wane, although, obviously, such influence will not disappear overnight.

Elgar-Ensemble did not capitalize fully on its impressive electoral debut in 2004, leading me to revise my possibly over generous conclusions regarding its future potential. Indeed, the formation did not even present candidatures for the cantonal elections in 2008. This does not, however, necessarily invalidate the notion that it has a place in Iparralde as the political expression of nonnationalist pro-Basque sentiment. In fact, one might say that the important increase in the Basque nationalist vote in 2008, both for EHBai and the PNB, reveals the growing importance of pro-Basque sentiment in general.

The PS enjoyed mixed results in the 2008 cantonal elections. Its overall vote declined by 1 percent in the first round, a decline explained by PS leaders as stemming from a lower turnout of potential Socialist voters, with the party thereby suffering from increased abstention. Indeed, this was the case for Jean Espilondo who, despite appearing to be the most successful PS candidate (winning the mayorship of Angelu after a long period of UDF control), actually achieved significantly less votes than during the previous elections.

Elsewhere, there was victory in the 2008 elections for Jean Jacques Lasserre (MoDem), who obtained an overwhelming 75 percent of the vote in Bidaxune, Nafarroa Beherea; an increase on the equally impressive 69.41 percent he achieved in 2001. Meanwhile, the French right, represented by the DVD (Divers Droite, Miscellaneous Right-Wing) coalition, also enjoyed clear victories. For example, both Jean-Pierre Mirande and Barthélémy

Aguerre achieved 60 percent of the vote in the first round in the cantons of Maule-Lextarre (Mauléon-Licharre), Zuberoa, and Donapaleu, Nafarroa Beherea, respectively. Elsewhere, Alain Iriart, a well-known member of AB, actually ran as an independent against EHBai for the canton of Hiriburu (where he remained mayor) and won in the first round with a 65 percent share of the vote.

Of the eleven cantons where elections were held in 2008, four changed hands. As mentioned, in the first round of voting the Basque nationalist Iriart (running as an independent) replaced Jean-Pierre Destrade, who had represented the PS in the canton but who had also stood as an independent in 2001, and who did not stand for re-election in 2008. The remaining three changes all took place during the second round of voting. In Baigorri, Jean Michel Galant (EHBai), despite actually improving on the vote he achieved in 2001 and leading after the first round of voting, lost in the second round to an alliance of the center and right around the candidature of Jean-Baptiste Lambert (UMP). Elsewhere, the PS defeated the center-right in Angelu South, with Guy Mondorge's victory over the incumbent Beñat Gimenez (MoDem), and in Hendaia. Here, curiously, Kotte Écénarro of the PS lost the mayorship of the town to Jean-Baptiste Sallaberry of the right-wing DVD coalition, but won the canton from the incumbent Daniel Poulou (UMP).

In 2008, the electoral discourse of the PS was less ambiguous than on recent occasions when it had attempted to seduce pro-Basque sections of the population in Iparralde with apparently positive (or at least less outrightly negative) comments on the question, for example, of a single Basque *département*. In 2008, however, the PS line was unequivocal: it favored no change in the administrative status quo with the exception of issues relating to Euskara. This change can be explained by the declining power of pro-Basque notables within or close to the PS (such as Frantxoa Maitia), together with the growing electoral strength of Basque nationalism itself. That is, the very success of the EHBai coalition—now a potential rival for the PS—complicated any potential rapprochement between pro-Basque and Socialist positions.

François Bayrou created the Mouvement Démocratique (MoDem, the Democratic Movement) party in 2007 to replace the UDF and to run in the French presidential elections of that year. Despite encouraging early results, and especially its spectacular showing in the first round of presidential voting in 2007, it did not fare so well at the 2008 elections throughout France. In Iparralde, however, it maintained its position by connecting with historically important Christian Democratic sectors of the population there. This would explain, for example, Lasserre's impressive victory in Bidaxune, together with victories for the party in Biarritz East (Juliette Séguéla) and Uztaritze (Bernard Auroy). At the same time, however, MoDem's attempts to consolidate the center ground were hampered by a more general trend toward the polarization of political opinion between left and right; to such an extent, in fact, that some of its candidates even shifted to the right and appeared on tickets supporting the new French president, Nicolas Sarkozy.

Notes

Notes, Introduction

1. Iparralde is a name given to is the geographical area comprising the historical provinces of Lapurdi (Labourd, in French), Nafarroa Beherea (Basse-Navarre, in French), and Zuberoa (Soule, in French). The southern or Spanish Basque Country is known as Hegoalde, and comprises the historical provinces of Araba (Álava, in Spanish), Bizkaia (Vizcaya, in Spanish), Gipuzkoa (Guipúzcoa, in Spanish), and Nafarroa (Navarra, in Spanish) or Navarre (I will employ the latter term in the present work). Today, Araba, Bizkaia, and Gipuzkoa form the Basque Autonomous Community (also known as Euskadi), while Navarre is an autonomous community in its own right (the Foral Community of Navarre).

2. At times throughout the work, I will refer back to these original premises.

3. Ricardo de la Encina y Pérez de Onraita, *Poder y comunidad: Una sociología del nacionalismo* (Iruña: Pamiela, 2004), 327. Here and in all subsequent citations, translations of Spanish texts are by Cameron J. Watson.

4. Pedro Ibarra, *Nacionalismo: Razón y pasión* (Barcelona: Ariel, 2005), 25.

5. Ibid.

6. Anthony D. Smith, *Nationalism: Theory, Ideology, History* (Cambridge: Polity Press, 2001), 6.

7. Following Alfonso Pérez-Agote, *La reproducción del nacionalismo: El caso vasco* (Madrid: CIS; Siglo XXI, 1984), English trans. as *The Social Roots of Basque Nationalism*, trans. Cameron Watson and William A. Douglass, foreword by William A. Douglass (Reno: University of Nevada Press, 2006), and Walker Connor, *Ethnonationalism: The Quest for Understanding* (Princeton: Princeton University Press, 1994), who also extend their analysis to the concept of the nation.

8. Benjamín Tejerina, *Nacionalismo y lengua: Los procesos de cambio lingüístico en el País Vasco* (Madrid: CIS; Siglo XXI, 1992), 38–45.

9. Connor, *Ethnonationalism*, 75.

10. Walter Sulzbach, *National Consciousness* (Washington, D.C.: American Council on Public Affairs, 1943), 14, quoted in Connor, *Ethnonationalism*, 86 n. 22.

11. Translator's note: a play on words in reference to the concept of a *bucle melancólico* or ever-decreasing circle as applied by Jon Juaristi, *El bucle melancólico: Historias de nacionalistas vascos* (Madrid: Espasa, 1997; 2nd ed. 2000) (citations are to the 1st ed.).

12. Smith, *Nationalism*, 6.

Notes, Chapter One

1. Louis de Fourcaud, "Discours prononcé a Saint-Jean-de-Luz a l'occasion de l'ouverture du congrès de la tradition basque" (1897), in Pierre Lafitte, *La tradition au pays Basque: Ethnographie, folklore, art populaire, histoire, hagiographie* (1899;Donostia: Elkar, 1998), 6.

2. Sabino Arana was the founder of (firstly Bizkaian and later) Basque nationalism in Bilbao during the last decade of the nineteenth century. Defeat in the Second Carlist War (1873–76) led to the abolition of the *fueros*, or charters, that had granted the Basque provinces a degree of political autonomy in premodern Spain. Subsequently, Bilbao (and later Bizkaia and Gipuzkoa) underwent a profound economic and social transformation that led to rapid industrial development and large-scale immigration from other parts of Spain. The impact of these changes led Arana to conceive Basque nationalism as a defensive and reactionary response to the political, economic, and social changes taking place in Hegoalde.

3. Fourcaud, "Discours prononcé a Saint-Jean-de-Luz," 4–5.

4. "Sociologists of religion would not consider beginning their research asking themselves if a particular religious belief is true or false; rather, they would ask how beliefs were produced and reproduced, and how they shaped the actors' behavior." Alfonso Pérez-Agote, *The Social Roots of Basque Nationalism*, trans. Cameron Watson and William A. Douglass, foreword by William A. Douglass (Reno: University of Nevada Press, 2006), xiv.

5. To paraphrase James E. Jacob, *Hills of Conflict: Basque Nationalism in France* (Reno: University of Nevada Press, 1994), 390.

6. On these ideas, see Pedro Ibarra, *Nacionalismo: Razón y pasión* (Barcelona: Ariel, 2005), 19–20.

7. See Francisco Letamendia, *Game of Mirrors: Centre-Periphery National Conflicts* (Aldershot, UK: Ashgate, 2000), 6.

8. See Benedict Anderson, *Imagined Communities. Reflections on the Origin and Spread of Nationalism*, rev. ed. (London: Verso, 1991), 6.

9. Hastings Donnan and Thomas M. Wilson, *Borders: Frontiers of Identity, Nation and State* (Oxford: Berg, 1999), 9.

10. See Maïté Lafourcade, "La frontière franco-espagnol, lieu de conflits interétatiques et de collaboration interrégionale," in *La frontière franco-espagnol, lieu de conflits interétatiques et de collaboration interrégionale: Actes de la journée d'études du 16 novembre 1996, Biarritz*, ed. Maïté Lafourcade (Bordeaux: Presses Universitaires de Bordeaux, 1998), 2.

11. Ibid., 12–14.

12. Txomin Peillen, "Frontières et mentalités en Pays Basque," in *La frontière franco-espagnol, lieu de conflits interétatiques et de collaboration interrégionale*, ed. Lafourcade, 112.

13. Ibid., 109.

14. Zoe Bray, "Boundaries and Identities on the Franco-Spanish Frontier," CIBR Working Papers in Border Studies CIBR/WP02-2 (2002), available on-line at http://www.qub.ac.uk/cibr/WPpdffiles/CIBRwp2002_2_rev.pdf (last accessed, January 4, 2008).

15. See Jean François Bayart, "L'imaginaire dans l'affirmation identitaire," in *L'identité, l'individu, le groupe, la societé*, ed. Jean Claude Ruano Borbalan (Auxerre: Éditions Sciences Humaines, 1998), 338–39.

16. Ludger Mees, Santiago de Pablo, and José Antonio Rodríguez, *El Péndulo patriótico: Historia del Partido Nacionalista Vasco*, 2nd. ed. (1999; Barcelona: Crítica, 2005), 20 (page citations are to the first ed).

17. See Letamendia, *Game of Mirrors*, 52–56.

18. See Ernest Gellner, *Nations and Nationalism* (Oxford: Blackwell, 1983), esp. chs. 3 and 9.

19. See Juan J. Linz, *Conflicto en Euskadi* (Madrid: Espasa-Calpe, 1986), Mees, de Pablo, and Rodríguez, *El Péndulo patriótico*, and Javier Corcuera, *Orígenes, ideología y organización del nacionalismo vasco (1876–1904)* (Madrid: Siglo XXI, 1979), available in English as *The Origins, Ideology, and Organization of Basque Nationalism, 1876–1903*, trans. Albert Bork and Cameron J. Watson (Reno: Center for Basque Studies, University of Nevada, Reno, 2007).

20. Francis Jauréguiberry, "Europe, langue basque et modernité en Pays Basque français," in *Le Pays Basque et l'Europe*, ed. Pierre Bidart (Baigorri: Izpegi, 1994), 49–52.

21. Peio Etcheverry, "Le siècle de l'âge industriel: La mise en place du pluralisme basque," in Manex Goyhenetche, et al., *Histoire général du Pays Basque*, vol. 5, *Le XIXe siècle, 1804–1914* (Donostia and Baiona: Elkar, 2005), 174.

22. In the case under discussion here, a common language and common traditions, differing from those of France and Spain, existed. Such differences were also apparent in some institutions, based on the foral system, on both sides of the border during the *ancien régime*. The *foral* system was based on a series of consuetudinary medieval charters or legal codes known as *fueros* in Spanish or *fors* in French. For a general introduction to the foral system in Hegoalde, see Gregorio Monreal Zia, *The Old Law of Bizkaia (1452): Introductory Study and Critical Edition*, trans. William A. Douglass and Linda White, preface by William A. Douglass, Basque Classic Series No. 1 (Reno: Center for Basque Studies, University of Nevada, Reno, 2005). For a brief description of the *fors* in Iparralde, see James Jacob, "The French Revolution and the Basques of France," in *Basque Politics: A Case Study in Ethnic Nationalism*, ed. William A. Douglass, Occasional Papers Series No. 2 (Reno: Associated Faculty Press and Basque Studies Program, 1985), 53–56, and *Hills of Conflict*, 3–4.

23. See Andrés de Blas, *Nacionalismo e ideologías políticas contemporáneas* (Madrid: Espasa-Calpe, 1984).

24. Walker Connor, *Ethnonationalism: The Quest for Understanding* (Princeton, NJ: Princeton University Press, 1994), 4.

25. See Jacob, "The French Revolution and the Basques of France," 83–86 and *Hills of Conflict*, 34–35, 38; Jean Baptiste Orpustan, "Rôle et pouvoirs de l'Eglise," in *La nouvelle société basque: Ruptures et changements*, ed. Pierre Bidart (Paris: L'Harmattan, 1980), 139; and Xabier Itçaina, "Les politisations plurielles de la société basque à la fin du XIXe siècle," in Goyhenetche, *Histoire général du Pays Basque*, vol. 5, *Le XIXe siècle, 1804–1914*, 227–32.

26. Willfried Spohn, "Multiple Modernity, Nationalism and Religion: A Global Perspective," *Current Sociology* 51, nos. 3–4 (May–July 2003): 270–71.

27. See Barbara Ann Rieffer, "Religion and Nationalism: Understanding the Consequences of a Complex Relationship," *Ethnicities* 3, no. 2 (2003): 215–42.

28. Jacob, *Hills of Conflict*, 42.

29. In Lapurdi, the legitimacy of specifically Basque traditions were based on the principle of "custom," supported by a *Biltzar* with certain management powers (common land, taxes, communications, and so on), that was composed of parish delegates (with no aristocratic representation) who formed a kind of Third Estate without either legislative or judicial power, the latter belonging to the king and the Bordeaux Parliament, respectively. Similarly, Zuberoa was also guided by the principle of tradition. There, the Third Estate was configured through the *Silviet* (the equivalent to the *Biltzar* in Lapurdi), made up of representatives from different electoral districts and burgs, while the nobility and clergy met at the Orda Assembly, thereby generating a number of conflicts between the two bodies that, ultimately, hastened the downfall of this institutional model. Finally, Nafarroa Beherea retained previous governmental structures, organized around the Assemblies of Navarre (or Estates General), which was recognized as a governmental authority with legislative capacity until 1748. This Estates General, in contrast to those in the other two provinces, drew together representatives of the clergy, nobility, and the Third Estate. For a general introduction to this system, see Manex Goyhenetche, *Historia general del País Vasco*, vol. 1, *Prehistoria, Época Romana, Edad Media* (Donostia: Ttarttalo, 1999), trans. of *Histoire générale du Pays Basque*, vol. 1, *Préhistoire, époque romain, Moyen Age* (Donostia and Baiona: Elkar, 1998).

30. See Jacob, *Hills of Conflict*, 36–38, 39–53.

31. Ibid., 40.

32. One should not underestimate the politicization process underway in rural areas from the Third Republic on, however. See, for example, Itçaina, "Les politisations plurielles de la société basque à la fin du XIXe siècle," 223–37, and Maurice Agulhon, *La République au village: Les populations du Var de la Révolution a la IIe République* (Paris: Seuil, 1979), available in English as *The Republic in the Village: The People of the Var from the French Revolution to the Second Republic*, trans. Janet Lloyd (Cambridge: Cambridge University Press; Paris: Éditions de la Maison des Sciences, 1982).

33. This really dated from the concordat with the church signed by Napoleon I and Pope Pius VII (1801), whereby the state allocated funds from which to pay the clergy's salaries. As a result, from this time on, the state had a say in the appointment of regents for each diocese.

34. Xipri Arbelbide, *Enbata: Abertzalegoaren historioa Iparraldean* (Donostia: Kutxa Fundazioa, 1996), 32–35.

35. Itçaina, "Les politisations plurielles de la société basque à la fin du XIXe siècle," 227.

36. Arbelbide, *Enbata*, 62.

37. Ibid., 34.

38. Itçaina, "Les politisations plurielles de la société basque à la fin du XIXe siècle," 228.

39. See François Fourquet, *Planification et développement local au Pays Basque* (Bayonne: Commissariat Général au Plan, Group de Recherche Sociale Ikerka, 1988).

40. Jauréguiberry, "Europe, langue basque et modernité en Pays Basque français," 46.

41. Battitta Larzabal, "Survol d'un siècle de vie politique au Pays Basque Nord," in Goyhenetche, *Histoire général du Pays Basque*, vol. 5, *Le XIXe siècle*, 240.

42. Jean Marie Izquierdo, *Le Pays Basque de France: La difficile maturation d'un sentiment nationaliste basque*, preface by Daniel-Louis Seiler (1998; Paris: L'Harmattan, 2001), 91, 154.

43. Pierre Bidart, "Revolución francesa y socialización del Estado-Nación," in *Ilustración y revolución francesa en el País Vasco*, ed. Xabier Palacios (Vitoria: Instituto de Estudios sobre Nacionalismos Comparados, 1991), 42.

44. Ibid., 45–48.

45. Jauréguiberry, "Europe, langue basque et modernité en Pays Basque français," 49–52.

46. See Michael Keating, *Nations against the State: The New Politics of Nationalism in Quebec, Catalonia, and Scotland*, 2nd ed. (Houndmills, UK: Palgrave, 2001), ch. 2, esp. 45–48.

47. Letamendia, *Game of Mirrors*, 21–22.

48. Eduardo Bello, "J. J. Rousseau y la Revolución francesa," in *Ilustración y revolución francesa en el País Vasco*, ed. Palacios, 136–39.

49. Keating, *Nations against the State*, 32.

50. Cécile Laborde, "The Culture(s) of the Republic: Nationalism and Multiculturalism in French Republican Thought," *Political Theory* 29, no. 5 (October 2001), 718.

51. Ibid., 718–19. Laborde cites Katherine Kintzler, *La république en questions* (Paris: Minerve, 1996), 29–33.

52. Ibid., 719.

53. Ibid. Laborde cites Dominique Schnapper, *La communauté des citoyens: Sur l'idée moderne de nation* (Paris: Gallimard, 1994), 106.

54. See Manex Goyhenetche, *Histoire générale du Pays Basque*, vol. 2, *Évolution politique et institutionnelle du XVIe au XVIII siècle* (Donostia and Baiona: Elkar, 1999), 160–81.

55. Cited by Wolfgang Geiger, "La Revolución francesa: El concepto de soberanía nacional y las naciones sin estado," in Joseba Goñi Alzuela et al., *Derechos humanos individuales, derechos de los estados, derechos de los pueblos: II Congreso sobre Derechos Humanos Individuales y Colectivos* (Bilbao: Herria 2000 Eliza, 1990), 147. For this reason, the principle used to draw up these new institutional structures—the *départements*—remained within this supposedly objective logic, in that only the then existing communication routes were used to demarcate their boundaries. These limits were drawn so that it would be no more than a day's journey on horseback for any individual to travel between anywhere in the *département* and the principal town. See John Loughlin, *La democracia regional y local en la Unión Europea* (Luxembourg: The Office for Official Publications of the European Communities; Brussels: Committee of the Regions, 1999), 115–16.

56. In 1997, the Basque Country was named a *pays* (literally, "country" but more closely resembling an officially recognized region), the first official recognition by the French Republic. However, as with other *pays* in France, the new title did not bring with it any specific powers. For this reason, this change went mostly unnoticed in Iparralde.

57. Izquierdo, *Le Pays Basque de France*, 49.

58. Bertrand Barère de Vieuzac, quoted in Jacob, *Hills of Conflict*, 32.

59. Pierre Bidart, "La Révolution Française et la question linguistique," in *1789 et les Basques: Histoire, langue et littérature*, ed. Jean Baptiste Orpustan (Bordeaux: Presses Universitaires de Bordeaux, 1991), 150.

60. From this, Pierre Bidart contends that while Euskara was linked to fanaticism, it was not necessarily connected to counterrevolutionary activities or hatred for the Republic. "La Révolution Française et la question linguistique," 149–50. The same point is made by Beñat Oyharçabal, "Les documents recueillis lors des enquêtes linguistiques en Pays Basque durant la période révolutionnaire et le Premier Empire," in *La Révolution française dans l'histoire et la littérature basques du XIXe siècle: Actes du colloque international de l'URA 1055 du C.N.R.S.*, ed. Jean Baptiste Orpustan (Baigorri: Izpegi, 1994), 65.

61. Interestingly, these same contradictory strategies and swings between the one and the other also appeared during the Third Republic. See Patrick Castoreo, "Langue basque et enseignement primaire publique des années 1880 à 1914," in *Pierre Haristoy: Historia jardunaldia, journée d'histoire* (Donostia: Eusko Ikaskuntza, 2005), 137–52.

62. Baiona, for example, came to be known briefly as Port de la Montagne, while Saint-Esprit was renamed Jean-Jacques Rousseau, Donibane Lohizune became Chauvin-Dragon, Sara became La Palombière, Arrosa (Saint-Martin-d'Arrossa) was renamed Grand-Port, Baigorri became Grande-Redoute, and Kanbo became La-Montagne. See Mayi Castaings-Beretervide, *La Révolution en Pays Basque* (Donibane Lohizune: Ikuska, 1994), 37.

63. Jacob, *Hills of Conflict*, 39–40.

64. See Miren Mateo and Xabier Aizpurua, "Euskararen bilakaera soziolinguistikoa," *Euskonews & Media* 201 (February 28–March 7, 2003), available on-line at http://www.euskonews.com/0201zbk/gaia20107eu.html (last accessed January 5, 2008). Oyharçabal, following a survey conducted by Charles-Etienne Coquebert de Montbret in 1808, cites the figure of 108,000 Basque speakers which, if accurate, would account for two-thirds of the population at that time. In his opinion, this same survey distinguished between six different Basque-speaking areas (a decision Oyharçabal attributes to the prefect) in an initial finding that anticipated the later and more well-known research of Louis Lucien Bonaparte (1863) and Paul Broca (1874). See "Les documents recueillis lors des enquêtes linguistiques en Pays Basque," in *La Révolution française dans l'histoire et la littérature basques du XIXe siècle: Actes du colloque international de l'URA 1055 du C.N.R.S.*, ed. Orpustan, 81.

65. Eugen Weber, *Peasants into Frenchmen: The Modernization of Rural France* (Stanford: Stanford University Press, 1976), 5.

66. Pierre Bourdieu, *Language and Symbolic Power*, ed. and intro. John B. Thompson, trans. Gino Raymond and Matthew Adamson (Cambridge: Polity Press, 1991), 50–51.

67. Ibid., 53.

68. Ibid., 48.

69. Ibid., 50–51.

70. Patri Urkizu, "Iraultza frantsesaren garaiko euskal bertsoak (1789–1799)," in *1789 et les Basques: Histoire, langue et littérature*, ed. Orpustan, 231. Some of the specific texts of these pastorals can be found in Txomin Peillen, "Euskaraz idatziak eta beste, Zuberoan, Iraultza garaian," in *1789 et les Basques: Histoire, langue et littérature*, ed. Orpustan, 206.

71. Bourdieu, *Language and Symbolic Power*, 145.

72. Ibid., 59–60.

73. Anthony D. Smith, *Nationalism and Modernism: A Critical Survey of Recent Theories of Nations and Nationalism* (New York: Routledge, 1998), 41.

74. Cited by Joan Mari Torrealdai in *El libro negro del Euskera* (Donostia: Ttarttalo, 2003), 29.

75. See Ernest Gellner, *Nationalism* (London: Phoenix, 1998), 51–52.

76. Eric Savarèse, "Ecole et pouvoir colonial: Retour sur la légitimation de la colonisation," available on-line at http://www.la-science-politique.com/revue/revue2/papier1.htm, *Dialogues Politiques* 2 (January 2003), article 1, (last accessed January 6, 2008).

77. Ibid. Here, Savarèse cites Pierre Nora, "L'histoire de France de Lavisse," in *Les Lieux de mémoire II: La nation*, vol. 1, *Héritage, historiographie, paysages*, ed. Pierre Nora (Paris: Gallimard, 1984), 317–75.

78. Cited by Izquierdo, *Le Pays Basque de France*, 52.

79. Ernest Lavisse, *Histoire de France: Cours moyen* (Paris: Armand Colin, 1920), 266–67, quoted in Savarèse, "Ecole et pouvoir colonial."

80. Savarèse, "Ecole et pouvoir colonial."

81. Ernest Lavisse, *Histoire de France: Cours moyen*, 270–71.

82. See Bérénice Chalot, "Ernest Lavisse: 'Instituteur national,'" history lecture, December 12, 2001, available on-line at http://perso.wanadoo.fr/david.colon/Sciences-Po/lavisse.pdf (last accessed January 6, 2008), 7.

83. See, for example, Xipri Arbelbide, *Iraultza Heletan: Errepublikarentzat hil behorrari* (Donostia: Etor, 1994).

84. A typical Basque surname meaning "new house" and demonstrating the importance of the concept of *etxe* (house) in Basque culture.

85. Rogers Brubaker, *Citizenship and Nationhood in France and Germany* (Cambridge, MA: Harvard University Press, 1992), 8.

86. Francisco Letamendia, "La Revolución Francesa: El liberalismo pensado desde el Estado-Nación," in *Ilustración y revolución francesa en el País Vasco*, ed. Palacios, 154–61.

87. Xipri Arbelbide believes that in World War I, hundreds of conscripted Basques fought more *against* the enemy than *for* France, because they felt themselves to be primarily Basque (although not nationalist) and only secondarily French. For example, in Donibane Garazi, of the 1,314 young men who joined the armed forces, 1,359 deserted, while the numbers for Baigorri were 594 and 347, respectively. It is not surprising, then, that the prefect for Pau (the administrative capital of the *département* in which Iparralde was situated) rhetorically questioned the commitment of some citizens within his prefecture: "Can their deplorable decision [to desert] be explained better still by that special mentality that surfaces among many Basques to make them believe they have no other *patrie* than that corner of the Earth in which they were born?" Quoted in Arbelbide, *Enbata*, 18.

88. See Jean-Claude Larronde, *Mouvement Eskualerriste (1932–1937): Naissance du mouvement nationaliste basque en Iparralde/Eskualerri-Zaleen Biltzarra (1932–1937): Eskualerrizaleen mugimendu abertzalearen sortzea Iparraldean/El movimiento Eskualerrista (1932–1937): Nacimiento del movimiento nacionalista vasco en Iparralde* (Bilbao: Sabino Arana Kultur Elkargoa, 1994), 48–51.

89. Arbelbide, *Enbata*, 20.

90. Jean Paul Malherbe, "Le nationalisme basque en France (1933–1976)," Ph.D. diss., University of Toulouse I, 1977, 33.

91. Michael Billig argues that even the "civic" nationalisms of liberal Western democratic states encourage certain mundane symbols in daily life and discourse, as a means of reinforcing national identity. Indeed, he points out that, all too frequently and erroneously, "liberal Western academics today find it easier to recognize nationalism in 'others' than in themselves," yet nationalism, "is also the ideology that permits [their] states . . . to exist." *Banal Nationalism* (London: Sage Publications, 1995), 15.

92. Arbelbide, *Enbata*, 21.

93. Fourcaud, "Discours prononcé a Saint-Jean-de-Luz a l'occasion de l'ouverture du congrès de la tradition basque," 6.

94. See Robert Lafont, *La révolution régionaliste* (Paris: Gallimard, 1967). The Spanish version is *La revolución regionalista*, trans. Francisco Fernández Buey (Barcelona: Ariel, 1971).

95. Lafont's conclusions are quite clear: "Centralist authoritarianism, internal colonialism [and] ethnic imperialism were, together with external colonialism, the essential characteristics of bourgeois power in France, a power used by [different] state forms and nationalist ideologies to deceive a large part of the popular opinion, including the extreme left." Lafont, *La revolución regionalista*, 170–71.

96. Ibid., 177.

97. Pierre Loti, "La danza de las espadas" (1897), in Pierre Loti, *El País Vasco, la visión de un mundo que terminó en el XIX* (Zarautz: Bibliomanías, 2000), 46.

98. Jon Juaristi, *El bucle melancólico: Historias de nacionalistas vascos*, 2nd ed. (Madrid: Espasa-Calpe, 2000), 46–47.

99. Ibid., 47.

100. Bourdieu, *Language and Symbolic Power*, 45–47.

101. See Letamendia, *Game of Mirrors*, 54–56.

102. Carlism was a complex nineteenth-century political and dynastic movement in Spain that was especially important in Hegoalde. It sought to preserve the political system of the *ancien régime* in the country, based on the *fueros*, or charters granting a degree of autonomy to the regions.

103. Fourcaud, "Discours prononcé a Saint-Jean-de-Luz a l'occasion de l'ouverture du congrès de la tradition basque," 7.

104. See Fourquet, *Planification et développement local au Pays Basque*.

105. Jauréguiberry, "Europe, langue basque et modernité en Pays Basque français," 47.

106. Pierre Bourdieu, cited by Loïc J. D. Wacquant, "Towards a Reflexive Sociology: A Workshop with Pierre Bourdieu," *Sociological Theory* 7, no. 1 (Spring 1989), 40.

Notes, Chapter Two

1. This general historical debate over the worth of the Basque language is captured in Juan Madariaga Orbea, *Anthology of Apologists and Detractors of the Basque Language*, trans. Frederick H. Fornoff, María Cristina Saavedra, Amaia Gabantxo, and Cameron J. Watson (Reno: Center for Basque Studies, University of Nevada, Reno, 2006).

2. Arturo Campión, "La langue basque," in *La tradition au pays Basque: Ethnographie, folklore, art populaire, histoire, hagiographie*, ed. Pierre Lafitte, (1899; Donostia: Elkar, 1998), 458–59.

3. Sabino Arana, quoted in Jean-Claude Larronde, *Mouvement Eskualerriste (1932–1937): Naissance du mouvement nationaliste basque en Iparralde/Eskualerri-Zaleen Biltzarra (1932–1937): Eskualerrizaleen mugimendu abertzalearen sortzea Iparraldean/El movimiento Eskualerrista (1932–1937): Nacimiento del movimiento nacionalista vasco en Iparralde* (Bilbao: Sabino Arana Kultur Elkargoa, 1994), 33.

4. Hastings Donnan and Thomas M. Wilson, *Borders: Frontiers of Identity, Nation and State* (Oxford: Berg, 1999), 10.

5. Pierre Loti, *Ramuntcho*, trans. Henri Pene du Bois, Project Gutenberg EBook, #12, available on-line at http://www.gutenberg.org/author/Pierre_Loti (last accessed January 8, 2008).

6. Pierre Loti, *El País Vasco: La visión de un mundo que terminó en el XIX* (Zarautz: Bibliomanías, 2000).

7. Dominique Haran, "Références historiques des rencontres entre les deux territoires: Synthèse de la journée," in *Baiona-Donostia Euskal Eurohiriori buruzko gogoeta jardunaldiak: Jornadas de reflexión sobre la Eurociudad Vasca Bayona-San Sebastián/Journées de réflexion sur la Eurocité Basque Bayonne-Saint Sébastien*, ed. Jon Basterra et al., *Azkoaga: Cuadernos de ciencias sociales y económicas* (Donostia: Eusko Ikaskuntza, 2001), 264.

8. Carlos Fernández de Casavedante Romani, *La frontera hispano-francesa y las relaciones de vecindad: Especial referencia al sector fronterizo del País Vasco* (Leioa: Servicio Editorial de la Universidad del País Vasco, 1985), 15. For more information on the legal basis of this cross-border cooperation, see, in addition to the cited work, the same author's "El marco jurídico de la cooperación transfronteriza: Su concreción en el ámbito hispano-francés," in *Baiona-Donostia Euskal Eurohiriori buruzko gogoeta jardunaldiak: Jornadas de reflexión sobre la Eurociudad Vasca Bayona-San Sebastián/Journées de réflexion sur la Eurocité Basque Bayonne-Saint Sébastien*, 269–94.

9. Fermín Rubiralta, "El espacio pirenaico y la construcción europea: Fundamento histórico y revitalización de un área transfronteriza," in *La construcción del espacio vasco-aquitano: Un estudio multidisciplinar*, ed. Antón Borja, Francisco Letamendia, and Kepa Sodupe (Leioa: Servicio Editorial de la Universidad del País Vasco, 1998), 30.

10. Javier Fernández Sebastián and Paloma Miranda de Lage-Damon, "Exiliados españoles en Bayona en tiempo de la Revolución (1789–1793)," in *1789 et les Basques: Histoire, langue et littérature*, ed. Jean Baptiste Orpustan (Bordeaux: Presses Universitaires de Bordeaux, 1991), 63.

11. Ibid., 67.

12. See, in general, Jean-Claude.Larronde, *Mouvement Eskualerriste (1932–1937): Naissance du mouvement nationaliste basque en Iparralde/Eskualerri-Zaleen Biltzarra (1932–1937): Eskualerrizaleen mugimendu abertzalearen sortzea Iparraldean/El movimiento Eskualerrista(1932–1937): Nacimiento del movimiento nacionalista vasco en Iparralde* (Bilbao: Sabino Arana Kultur Elkargoa, 1994), esp. 15 and 61–66.

13. Specifically, these ideas flowed from Garat, to Chaho, to Antoine d'Abaddie, to Arana up to 1890 and, from the beginning of the twentieth century on, from Arana to Lafitte or later, from ETA to Enbata.

14. See Alfonso Pérez-Agote, *The Social Roots of Basque Nationalism*, trans. Cameron Watson and William A. Douglass, foreword by William A. Douglass (Reno: University of Nevada Press, 2006), xiv–xv.

15. Ibid., xv.

16. Translator's note: Here and throughout the text, a variety of terms (most typically "pro-Basque") are used to convey the concept of *basquisme* (*vasquismo* in Spanish), that is, pro-Basque (language, culture and so on) but not necessarily Basque nationalist sympathies.

17. Pérez-Agote, *The Social Roots of Basque Nationalism*, xv.

18. For a brief biography, see Madariaga Orbea, *Anthology of Apologists and Detractors of the Basque Language*, 596–98.

19. For a thorough account of Arana's nationalism, see Javier Corcuera, *Orígenes, ideología y organización del nacionalismo vasco (1876–1904)* (Madrid: Siglo XXI, 1979), available in English as *The Origins, Ideology, and Organization of Basque Nationalism, 1876–1903*, trans. Albert Bork and Cameron J. Watson (Reno: Center for Basque Studies, University of Nevada, Reno, 2007) esp. ch.3.

20. For a survey of different modernist interpretations of nationalism, see Anthony D. Smith, *Nationalism and Modernism: A Critical Survey of Recent Theories of Nations and Nationalism* (New York: Routledge, 1998).

21. See Mancur Olson, *The Logic of Collective Action: Public Goods and the Theory of Groups* (Cambridge, MA: Harvard University Press, 1965).

22. John Breuilly, *Nationalism and the State*, 2nd ed. (Manchester: Manchester University Press; New York: St. Martin's Press, 1993), 402.

23. See Elie Kedourie, *Nationalism*, 4th ed. (Oxford; Blackwell Press, 1993).

24. Juaristi remarks that many of the early Basque nationalists came from "the urban middle classes, obliged to compete with the sons of country bumpkins," and later speaks of the movement being composed of an "army of office workers, bookkeepers, and clerks." Jon Juaristi *El bucle melancólico: Historias de nacionalistas vascos*, 2nd ed (Madrid: Espasa-Calpe, 2000), 151, 231.

25. Walker Connor, *Ethnonationalism: The Quest for Understanding* (Princeton, NJ: Princeton University Press, 1994), 73–75.

26. Ibid., 197.

27. Ibid., 76. Of the previously cited authors, only Kedourie explores the role of elites in creating a civil religion that is later integrated by the people. As such, he reduces the "absolute" manipulative role of elites while at the same time empowering the people—to be freely manipulated. Kedourie maintains, for example, that Enlightenment thinkers advocated a notion whereby, "the cohesion of the state, and loyalty to it, depend on its capacity to ensure the welfare of the individual, and in him, love of the fatherland is a function of benefits received." See *Nationalism*, 4.

28. As his biography states in, for example, *The Columbia Encyclopedia*, 6th ed. (2001–2005), available on-line at http://www.bartleby.com/65/ga/Garat-Do.html (last accessed May 25, 2007).

29. This is the thesis of Michel Duhart, *Dominique Joseph Garat, 1749–1833*, 2 vols. (Bayonne: Estrait du Bulletin de la Société des Sciences, Lettres et Arts de Bayonne, 1993–94).

30. Jon Juaristi, *El linaje de Aitor: La invención de la tradición vasca* (Madrid: Taurus, 1987), 83–84, 102.

31. This is the opinión of Joseph Zabalo, *Xaho, el genio de Zuberoa* (Tafalla: Txalaparta, 2004), trans. from French, *Augustin Chaho ou l'Irrintzina du matin basque* (Biarritz: Atlantica, 1999).

32. Eugène Goyheneche, "Un ancêtre du nationalisme basque: Augustin Chaho et la guerre carliste," in *Euskal Herria (1789–1850): Actes du Colloque International d'Etudes Basques (Bordeaux 3–5 mai 1973)* (Bayonne: Société des Amis du Musée Basque, 1978), 229–59; rpt. in Gustave Lambert et al., eds., *Augustin Chaho* (Hélette: Editions Harriet, 1996).

33. Antonio Elorza, *Ideologías del nacionalismo vasco 1876–1937 (De los "euskaros" a Jagi Jagi)* (San Sebastián: Aramburu, 1979), 127–28.

34. Iñigo Urkullu, ed., *Nacionalismo vasco: Un proyecto de futuro con 100 años de historia*, vol. 1 (Bilbao: Sabino Arana Kultur Elkargoa-Fundación Sabino Arana, 1998); Martín de Ugalde, *Biografía de tres figuras nacionales vascas: Arana-Goiri, Agirre, Leizaola* (Donostia: Sendoa, 1985), 15; Jesús Insausti, "Introduction," in Mauro Elizondo, *Sabino Arana: El hombre y su trayectoria* (Bilbao: Fundación Sabino Arana, 1992), 9; and Mauro Elizondo, *Sabino Arana: El hombre y su trayectoria*, 21.

35. A reference to the romantic hero of Alphonse Daudet's novels, who is forced to come to the reality of a more prosaic world than he expected, supplied by Juaristi, *El bucle melancólico*, 144. Specifically, Juaristi observes that "Tartarin is a melancholic figure who grows weary under the Provençal sun; like Don Quixote, he would have died of boredom in his corner of La Mancha had he not got involved in some adventure. . . . The adventure of the chase or chivalric adventure. Sometimes, political adventure is not a bad substitute for aforementioned. Arana, too, would arrive at this point after having tried other, frankly Tartarinesque adventures."

36. Anthony D. Smith, *Nationalism: Theory, Ideology, History* (Cambridge: Polity Press, 2001), 9.

37. Ibid., 25.

38. Ibid., 26.

39. Ibid., 27.

40. Ibid., 29.

41. Ibid.

42. Ibid., 30.

43. See Francisco Letamendia, *Game of Mirrors: Centre-Periphery National Conflicts* (Aldershot, UK: Ashgate, 2000).

44. Smith, *Nationalism*, 31.

45. See Elorza, *Ideologías del nacionalismo vasco 1876-1937*, ch.3; Manex Goyhenetche, *Histoire générale du Pays Basque*, vol. 5, *Le XIXe siècle, 1804-1914* (Donostia and Baiona: Elkar, 2005), 119–22.

Notes, Chapter Three

1. Jean Goyhenetche, "Les Etats de Navarre en 1789: La crise du foralisme provincialiste," in *1789 et les Basques: Histoire, langue et littérature*, ed. Jean Baptiste Orpustan (Bordeaux: Presses Universitaires de Bordeaux, 1991), 11.

2. On this topic, see, for example, Manex Goyhenetche, "L'historiographie ecclésiastique dominante du XIXe siècle," in *Pierre Haristoy: Historia Jardunaldia. Journée d'Histoire* (Donostia: Eusko Ikaskuntza, 2005), 53–59; Pascal Goñi, "L'Abbé Haristoy (1833–1901): Le père d'historiographie conservatrice basque sur la Révolution," in *Pierre Haristoy: Historia Jardunaldia. Journée d'Histoire*, 167–80; and Yvette Cardaillac-Hermosilla, "Les minorités religieuses au Pays Basque d'auprès les documents de P. Haristoy," in *Pierre Haristoy: Historia Jardunaldia. Journée d'Histoire*, 119–36.

3. Jean Goyhenetche, "Les Etats de Navarre en 1789," 11.

4. Ibid., 12. For a more detailed account of this conflict, see Jean Goyhenetche, *Les basques et leur histoire: Mythes et réalités* (Donostia and Baiona: Elkar, 1992).

5. Eugène Goyhenetche, *Le Pays Basque: Soule, Labourd, Basse-Navarre* (Pau: Société nouvelle d'éditions régionales et diffusion, 1979).

6. Jean-Louis Davant, *Histoire du peuple basque*, 8th ed. (1970; Donostia: Elkarlanean, 2000).

7. Jean Goyhenetche, "Les Etats de Navarre en 1789," 12.

8. When I began my research into Iparralde, I was moved and cheered to read an item in the Basque newspaper *Gara* of news that I still recall today. In the report, Manex Goyhenetche spoke enthusiastically about beginning an extensive work on the history of the Basque Country (both Iparralde and Hegoalde) that he intended to publish in the three languages spoken by its people. Thereafter, I forgot about the news item entirely until one day, while in the Mattin Megadenda bookstore in Baiona, I came across the first volume of that work. Today, as I write these words, with his complete works before me, I cannot help but recall the sad day in 2004 when I found out that Manex had died in a hiking accident and think how poor life will be without his erudite and assiduous insight. Agur eta ohore, Manex!

9. As regards this point, Eugen Weber makes the interesting argument that, during the nineteenth century, from the postrevolutionary period through to the Third Republic, there clearly existed two "different" Frances that were intrinsically "hostile" to one another: rural and urban France. Proof of this lay in the contempt felt by urban elites toward the peasantry, which was reflected not only in administrative deliberations and regulations, but also in a literary trend that,

from Zola to Balzac, regarded rural people as dark, ignorant, mysterious, and incompetent. See Eugen Weber, *Peasants into Frenchmen: The Modernization of Rural France* (Stanford: Stanford University Press, 1976). Thus, continual quarrels emerged between Baiona and the rural areas of Lapurdi, a conflict heightened by the important presence of Gascon culture in Baiona, thereby rendering the differences more than those of just competitions for power within the province.

10. Manex Goyhenetche, *Histoire générale du Pays Basque*, vol. 4, *La Révolution de 1789* (Donostia and Baiona: Elkar, 2002), 111–15.

11. Ibid., 117.

12. Ibid., 147.

13. The Physiocratic school of thought was very popular in late eighteenth-century France and advocated that the land is the only source of wealth for a nation. Physiocrats, therefore, believed that the land should form the basis for the majority of tax revenue and that there should be no restrictions on the trade or circulation of products deriving from agricultural production.

14. Manex Goyhenetche, *Histoire générale du Pays Basque*, vol. 4, *La Révolution de 1789*, 151–52.

15. Ibid., 155. These positions echo the role of Garat, whose "logic and system of ideas were coherent and the best expression of eighteenth-century rationalist bourgeois culture, an enemy of *ancien régime* structures. . . . His denunciation of the *ancien régime*'s social structure was faultless; he did not allow for any exceptions." Jean Goyhenetche, "Dominique Garat: Un représentant de l'Esprit des Lumières en Labourd au XVIIIe siècle," in *1789 et les Basques*, ed. Orpustan, 54, 57.

16. Although one should also point out that there still remained references to the natural hereditary principle of the nobility that had little in common with, for example, Rousseau's notion of the citizenry.

17. Manex Goyhenetche, *Histoire générale du Pays Basque*, vol. 4, *La Révolution de 1789*, 178.

18. Pierre-Eustache D'Hiriart was named the *syndic* (a powerful local notable charged with administering a particular district) for Uztaritze in September 1789. Daguerressar was a notary and clerk of the court in Mugerre, Lapurdi. In May 1789, they both formed part of the committee overseeing the correspondence of the *Biltzar* of Lapurdi with its deputies to the Estates General. They later also took part in translating pro-revolutionary proclamations into Basque.

19. As a member of the National Assembly, Barère de Vieuzac closed a speech with the famous sentence "The tree of liberty could not grow were it not watered with the blood of tyrants."

20. Manex Goyhenetche, *Histoire générale du Pays Basque*, vol. 4, *La Révolution de 1789*, 119.

21. Ibid., 126.

22. Ibid., 159.

23. Ibid., 160

24. Ibid.

25. Jean Goyhenetche, "Les Etats de Navarre en 1789: La crise du foralisme provincialiste," in *1789 et les Basques: Histoire, langue et littérature*, ed. Orpustan, 26–29.

26. Ibid., 29.

27. Manex Goyhenetche, *Histoire générale du Pays Basque*, vol. 4, *La Révolution de 1789*, 162.

28. Ibid., 153–54.

29. Ibid., 185.

30. Ibid., 185–86.

31. Ibid., 186. For information about this "English model" of social and political modernization, Goyhenetche cites Pierre Rosanvallon, *L'Etat en France de 1789 à nos jours* (Paris: Seuil, 1990), 97.

32. Manex Goyhenetche, *Histoire générale du Pays Basque*, vol. 4, *La Révolution de 1789*, 183.

33. I have already touched briefly on this evolution, and will discuss it in more detail below. I must, though, by way of introducing the topic, mention an essay (probably published around 1845) by Chaho. In the piece, Chaho ridicules, in almost grotesque fashion, some inhabitants of Iparralde who attempted to celebrate their belonging to France and ended up drunkenly dancing, led by a proconstitutional priest who became the laughingstock of his neighbors.

34. Manex Goyhenetche, *Histoire générale du Pays Basque*, vol. 4, *La Révolution de 1789*, 183.

35. Ibid., 187.

36. As a result, "Navarrese or French feelings of belonging must be analyzed in terms of proximity to political power [and] the attainment of economic prosperity. Ideology was relegated to a secondary level, [always] supposing that it could be autonomous." Ibid., 192.

37. Ibid., 247.

38. In Juan Antonio Moguel's Basque-language novel *El doctor Peru Abarca* (1802), one of the characters, Joanis, is a deserter from Revolutionary France's war with Spain. According to Joanis, "Prantziara ez nuen joan nai, gerlara eramana izan ez nindin" (I didn't want to go to France, so as not to be taken off to war). Cited in Jean Baptiste Orpustan, "De l'histoire a la littérature: L'épisode de Joanis et le chant de soldats de Baïgorri dans le Peru Abarca (1802) de Juan Antonio Moguel," in *La Révolution française dans l'histoire et la littérature basques du XIXe siècle: Actes du colloque international de l'URA 1055 du C.N.R.S.*, ed. Jean Baptiste Orpustan, (Baigorri: Izpegi, 1994), 29. On Moguel, see Madariaga Orbea, *Anthology of Apologists and Detractors of the Basque Language*, trans. Frederick H. Fornoff, María Cristina Saavedra, Amaia Gabantxo, and Cameron J. Watson (Reno: Center for Basque Studies, University of Nevada, Reno, 2006), 391–401. Manex Goyhenetche details the inability of the local authorities in Iparralde to comply with the *levée en masse* decree. See *Histoire générale du Pays Basque*, vol. 4, *La Révolution de 1789*, 266–73. Similarly, Eugen Weber observes that throughout rural France, dissatisfaction with and desertion from the army was commonplace prior to the Third Republic. See *Peasants into Frenchmen*, 292–302.

39. When, for example, 1,175 men from the *département* were called up by the military authorities for the Napoleonic Wars in 1806, only 335 individuals answered the call. Arbelbide, *Enbata*, 24.

40. Arbelbide estimates as many as 100,000, *Enbata*, 23. Manex Goyhenetche calculates figures of 8,000 in April 1793 and 70,000 by July 1794, *Histoire générale du Pays Basque*, vol. 4, *La Révolution de 1789*, 290.

41. For example, in early 1794, the Municipal Council of Donibane Garazi in Nafarroa Beherea recorded the fact that "the lack of timber has reached its limits . . . this municipality has complied, up to now, with its obligation, but at present finds itself totally short of wood within its land." Manex Goyhenetche, *Histoire générale du Pays Basque*, vol. 4, *La Révolution de 1789*, 275.

42. Ibid., 281.

43. For an economic explanation of this situation grounded in the class relations of the time, see Jean Goyhenetche, "Deux cas historiographiques des guerres de la Convention: L'évacuation des communes du Labourd et l'exécution de Madeleine Larralde," in *La Révolution française dans l'histoire et la littérature basques du XIXe siècle*, ed. Orpustan, 177, 185. For a fictionalized account of these events, see Toti Martinez de Lezea, *La cadena rota* (Donostia: Erein, 2005). One of the main characters in this historical novel is Madeleine Larralde, who (as we will see) became one of the martyrlike symbols of the Revolution for the church. However, in the novel, Martinez de Lezea portrays her in a political, rather than religious role.

44. The Popular Society of Baiona asked in October 1793 that "different members be named . . . patriots who speak the language of the land [Euskara] perfectly, in order to [undertake] the apostolic mission of the revolution and everything that tends toward attachment to the *patrie*." Manex Goyhenetche, *Histoire générale du Pays Basque*, vol. 4, *La Révolution de 1789*, 293.

45. Ibid., 295–96.

46. See Joseba Agirreazkuenaga, "La constitución político foral de los vascos," in *Historia de Euskal Herria/Historia general de los vascos*, vol. 5, *Vasconia (1876–1937): Entre la tradición y la modernidad.*, ed. Joseba Agirreazkuenaga (Donostia: Lur, 2005), 40.

47. Manex Goyhenetche, *Histoire générale du Pays Basque*, vol. 4, *La Révolution de 1789*, 298.

48. Ibid., 297.

49. Urkizu records several popular expressions of discontent on this question, such as that reflected in the *astolasterrak* (a form of charivari) of Zuberoa and the verses of the poet and rebel priest Salvat Moho. See "Iraultza frantsesaren garaiko euskal bertsoak (1789–1799)," in *1789 et les Basques: Histoire, langue et littérature*, ed. Orpustan, 226. Orpustan also analyzes the work of Moho, concluding that his poems reflect the sharp about-face of the people at this time (and an even more radical transformation in Moho's case, given that he was a priest): from an effusive greeting from the poet for the role that Garat might have played to classifying him as a "monster" for his part in the execution of Louis XVI, all this within the general tone of a tough and scathing critique of constitutional priests and the civil constitution of the clergy. Thus, from being a realist and reformist poet, Moho became a bitter critic and one of the chief exponents of counterrevolutionary thought. See "Un poète basque au temps de la Révolution: Salvat Moho," in *1789 et les Basques: Histoire, langue et littérature*, ed. Orpustan, 239–55. Similarly, Orpustan analyzes the fictional character from Iparralde, Joanis, in Moguel's *El doctor Peru Abarca* (1802), highlighting his importance in fulfilling the mythically important role for the collective imagination of *euskal-*

dun-fededun (the Basque believer, that is, to be truly Basque, one must have spiritual faith). This was an identity marker that extended throughout both Hegoalde and Iparralde. See "De l'histoire a la littérature : L'épisode de Joanis,", 13–35.

50. Arbelbide, *Enbata*, 23.

51. Manex Goyhenetche, *Histoire générale du Pays Basque*, vol. 4, *La Révolution de 1789*, 314–15.

52. As Arbelbide recalls, "In 1967 . . . a journalist from [the regional French newspaper] *Sud-Ouest* was shocked by what happened in Senpere [Saint-Pée-sur-Nivelle] on July 14 [France's national day]: 'The National Holiday' is a holiday of the French nation. We Basques call it 'the day of the Republic.' At the moment of saluting the flag, in front of city hall, only the mayor and two others gather: the chief of police and a border guard. The journalist carried out his research. He interviewed the hairdresser, tobacconist, and other inhabitants of Senpere: 'At city hall? I didn't know anything was going on!' The mayor himself confessed that, fourteen years earlier, when he assumed office, no one took part in the ceremony. As in most villages! The inhabitants of Senpere explained later to the journalist that the Revolution raised bad memories for them. One hundred and fifty years had gone by, but they still had not forgotten!" Arbelbide, *Enbata*, 27.

53. Agirreazkuenaga, "La constitución político foral de los vascos,"38.

54. On this subject, see Alain Destrée, *La Basse Navarre et ces institutions de 1620 à la Révolution* (Zaragoza: Universidad de Zaragoza, 1955).

55. Michel Duhart, *Dominique Joseph Garat, 1749–1833*, 2 vols (Bayonne: Estrait du Bulletin de la Société des Sciences, Lettres et Arts de Bayonne, 1993–94), 1:162. This is reprinted in Spanish in Michel Duhart, *Yo, Domingo José Garat* (San Sebastián: Txertoa, 1997), 36.

56. Duhart, *Dominique Joseph Garat, 1749–1833*, 1:162.

57. Ibid., 166.

58. Ibid., Duhart, *Yo, Domingo José Garat*, 38.

59. Agirreazkuenaga, "La constitución político foral de los vascos," 39.

60. In effect, these conditions were the result of a combination of ills that only added to the already existing misery and harsh living conditions in the French countryside. The latter are described vividly by Eugen Weber in *Peasants into Frenchmen*.

61. Agirreazkuenaga, "La constitución político foral de los vascos," 47.

62. Ironically, these accusations had a familiar sound to them, in that they paralleled the French Jacobin assertions about the suspect loyalty of Lapurdi at the same time, although, of course, the ideological charges were the reverse in each of these two bordering Basque provinces.

63. Julio Caro Baroja remarks that this suspicion fuelled a feeling of revenge on the part of the Spanish authorities, which may have led to the subsequent abolition of the *fueros* in Hegoalde in 1876. See *El laberinto vasco* (San Sebastián: Txertoa, 1989), 29. Similarly, Javier Fernández Sebastián contends that this episode did, indeed, change the opinion of Spanish liberals who had, until this time, accepted the foral system: "The rhetoric about 'perfect harmony' between the ancestral spirit of liberty in the Gipuzkoan *fueros* and the French Convention might have made certain influential sectors within Spanish politics start to question the traditional arrangement of the exempt [foral] provinces." See "Marchena y el País Vasco," in *1789 et les Basques: Histoire, langue et littérature*, ed. Orpustan, 108.

64. Duhart, *Dominique Joseph Garat, 1749–1833*, 2:107–25.

65. Iñaki Aguirre Zabala, "Nacionalismo vasco y relaciones transnacionales en el contexto de la frontera hispano-francesa: Cuatro modelos históricos," in *Las relaciones de vecindad*, ed. Celestino del Arenal (Leioa: Servicio Editorial, Universidad del País Vasco, 1987), 84.

66. Duhart, *Dominique Joseph Garat, 1749–1833*, 2:221.

67. See Anthony D. Smith, *Nationalism: Theory, Ideology, History* (Cambridge: Polity Press, 2001), 29–32.

68. Duhart, *Dominique Joseph Garat, 1749–1833*, 1:117.

69. Ibid., 2:112. This would explain why Garat's proposal for a unified Basque Country took the name New Phoenicia.

70. Ibid., 2:108.

71. Ibid., 2:109.

72. Ibid., 2:110.

73. Ibid., 2:123.

74. Duhart, *Yo, Domingo José Garat*, 19.

75. Duhart, *Dominique Joseph Garat, 1749–1833*, 1:119.

76. Ibid., 2:110.

77. Smith, *Nationalism*, 24–28.

78. Duhart, *Dominique Joseph Garat, 1749–1833*, 2:116.

79. Ibid., 2:121.

80. Ibid.

81. See EugenWeber, *Peasants into Frenchmen*.

82. See Jean Daniel Chaussier, *Quel territoire pour le Pays Basque? Les cartes de l'identité* (Paris: L'Harmattan, 1997), esp. 23–25.

83. Orpustan, "Un poète basque aux temps de la Révolution: Salvat Moho (1749–1821)," in *1789 et les basques*, ed. Orpustan, 249.

84. Igor Ahedo, *El movimiento Demo y la nueva cocina vasca (desobediente)* (Irun: Alberdania, 2004), 132.

Notes, Chapter Four

1. On Chaho as the first Basque nationalist, see Eugène Goyheneche, "Un ancêtre du nationalisme basque: Augustin Chaho et la guerre carliste," in *Euskal Herria (1789–1850): Actes du Colloque international d'Etudes Basques (Bordeaux 3–5 mai 1973)* (Bayonne: Société des Amis du Musée Basque, 1978), 229–59, rpt. in Gustave Lambert et al., *Augustin Chaho* (Hélette: Editions Harriet, 1996), 21; and Jean-Claude Larronde, *Mouvement Eskualerriste (1932–1937): Naissance du mouvement nationaliste basque en Iparralde/Eskualerri-Zaleen Biltzarra (1932-1937): Eskualerrizaleen mugimendu abertzalearen sortzea Iparraldean/El movimiento Eskualerrista (1932–1937): Nacimiento del movimiento nacionalista vasco en Iparralde* (Bilbao: Sabino Arana Kultur Elkargoa, 1994), 19–28. On Chaho as a separatist, see Éric Dupré-Moretti, "Esquisses biographique et bibliographique d'Augustin Xaho," *Ikuska* 10 (1995): 1–33, reprinted in Gustave Lambert, et al., *Augustin Chaho*, 153 (page citations are to rpt. ed.).

2. Not for nothing was he considered among the leaders of the clairvoyance movement and opposed to "Christian believers."

3. Joseph Zabalo, *Xaho, el genio de Zuberoa* (Tafalla: Txalaparta, 2004), 39. Translation from the French, *Augustin Chaho ou l'Irrintzina du matin basque* (Biarritz: Atlantica, 1999).

4. Smith, *Nationalism: Theory, Ideology, History* (Cambridge: Polity Press, 2001), 30.

5. Zabalo, *Xaho, el genio de Zuberoa*, 50; Jean-Claude Drouin, "L'ésotérisme d'Augustin Chaho: Cosmologie, histoire et politique au XIXe siècle," *Bulletin de la Société des Sciences, Lettres, Arts et Études Régionales de Bayonne* (1973): 265–77, rpt. in Gustave Lambert et al., *Augustin Chaho*, 58 (page citations are to rpt. ed.); and Jean-Claude Drouin, "La place de la Philosophie des Révélations de Chaho (1835) dans l'histoire des idées au XIXe siècle," *Bulletin de la Société des Sciences, Lettres, Arts et Études Régionales de Bayonne* (1981–82): 389–99, rpt. in Gustave Lambert et al., *Augustin Chaho*, 90 (page citations are to rpt. ed.).

6. Augustin Chaho and Vicente de Arana, *Las leyendas de Aitor* (Donostia–San Sebastián: Roger, 2000), 17–19.

7. Ibid., 20–21.

8. Ibid., 21.

9. J. Augustin Chaho, *Viaje a Navarra durante la insurrección de los vascos (1830–1835)* (Donostia: Auñamendi, 1976), 45. Trans. of *Voyage en Navarre pendant l'insurrection des Basques (1830–1835)* (Paris: A Bertrand, 1836).

10. See Drouin, "L'ésotérisme d'Augustin Chaho," and "La place de la Philosophie des Révélations de Chaho."

11. Augustin Chaho, *Philosophie des révélations*, 1, quoted in Zabalo, *Xaho, el genio de Zuberoa*, 79.

12. Zabalo, *Xaho, el genio de Zuberoa*, 79.

13. Augustin Chaho, *Philosophie des religions comparées*, vol. 2, 305, quoted in Zabalo, *Xaho, el genio de Zuberoa*, 79.

14. Jon Juaristi, *El Linaje de Aitor: La invención de la tradición vasca* (Madrid: Taurus, 1987), 80–82.

15. Chaho, *Viaje a Navarra durante la insurrección de los vascos*, 96.

16. Chaho and Arana, *Las leyendas de Aitor*, 76–77.

17. Jon Juaristi, *El bucle melancólico: Historias de nacionalistas vascos*, 2nd ed. (Madrid: Espasa-Calpe, 2000), 81. Chaho had a complex theory associated with the letters "JAO," forming the first part of the word "God" in Euskara (*jaungoiko* in

modern unified Basque). He believed the "j" (sometimes also referred to as an "i") to be the most acute or high-pitched letter, while in contrast the "a" was the lowest and most resonant, and the "o" fell somewhere in between the two. Therefore, for Chaho, the "j" expressed life, the "a" expressed God incarnate, and the "o" the holy spirit: three in one, a primitive trinity. See Zabalo, *Xaho, el genio de Zuberoa*, 79–80.

18. Juaristi, *El bucle melancólico*, 84.

19. Drouin, "La place de la Philosophie des Révélations de Chaho," 93.

20. Jean Baptiste Orpustan, "Une tentative ambitieuse d'Augustin Chaho: La philosophie des religions comparées," *Bulletin du Musée Basque* 93 (1981): 127–42. Rpt. in Lambert et al., *Augustin Chaho*, 83 (page citations are to rpt. ed.).

21. Zabalo, *Xaho, el genio de Zuberoa*, 101.

22. Drouin, "L'ésotérisme d'Augustin Chaho," 57–63.

23. Juaristi, *El bucle melancólico*, 102.

24. Eugène Goyheneche, "Un ancêtre du nationalisme basque," 33.

25. Zabalo, *Xaho, el genio de Zuberoa*, 110.

26. Fermin Arkotxa, "Augustin Chaho, un républicain basque de la monarchie de juillet au second empire," in Manex Goyhenetche, *Histoire général du Pays Basque*, vol. 5, *Le XIXe siècle, 1804–1914* (Donostia and Baiona: Elkar, 2005), 311–12.

27. Ibid., 313.

28. Letter marked "confidential," from Jules Cambacérès, Prefect of the Basses-Pyrénées, to the minister of the interior, May 6, 1849, Archives Nationales (France) F1/bII/19, quoted in Arkotxa, "Augustin Chaho, un républicain basque de la monarchie de juillet au second empire," 314.

29. See Jean Crouzet, "Chaho franc-maçon et la Révolution bayonnaise," in Lambert et al., *Augustin Chaho*, 120; Dupré-Moretti, "Esquisses biographique et bibliographique d'Augustin Xaho," 144; and Larzabal, "Survol d'un siècle de vie politique au Pays Basque Nord," in Manex Goyhenetche, *Histoire général du Pays Basque*, vol. 5, 247–48.

30. Arkotxa, "Augustin Chaho, un républicain basque de la monarchie de juillet au second empire," 303–6.

31. Zabalo, *Xaho, el genio de Zuberoa*, 138.

32. Arkotxa, "Augustin Chaho, un républicain basque de la monarchie de juillet au second empire," 313.

33. See, for example, Pierre Bidart, "Preface," in Joseph Augustin Chaho, *Voyage en Navarre durant l'insurrection des basques (1830–1835); L'agonie du Parti Révolutionnaire en France: Lettre a Monsieur Jacques Laffitte* (1836, 1838; Hélette: Harriet, and Marseille: Laffitte Reprints, 1979).

34. Joseph Augustin Chaho, *Ariel: Républicain de Vasconie* 819 (December 23, 1849), quoted in Zabalo, *Xaho, el genio de Zuberoa*, 140–41.

35. Agosti Xaho [Chaho], *Bizkaiko baten eleak:Palabras de un Bizkaino a la Reina Cristina* (Bilbao: Likiniano, 1999), 58.

36. Chaho, *Viaje a Navarra durante la insurrección de los vascos*, 46. See also an observation, in the same work, that "the Basques have never been conquered. They are invincible in their country," 65.

37. Ibid., 42.

38. See Smith, *Nationalism*, 27–29.

39. The following quotations are taken from Chaho, *Viaje a Navarra durante la insurrección de los vascos* (page numbers in parenthesis): "the long hair still worn by the highlanders has been attributed to their nobility and a sign of free men" (12); "nothing equals the mobility of the Basques' physiognomy; the most contrasting movements change their soul at the speed of lightening" (13); "Basques refer to themselves by the name Euskaldun, the only national name that is a historical mystery" (27); "the power of the forehead, the darkness of the well-curved eyebrows . . . would give him a tough appearance, if the regularity of the nose, the beauty of the facial angle, and the thin beard did not impart his whole physiognomy an overriding feeling of nobility, openness, and even joviality" (35); "you should know that I am a Basque of good stock . . . who obeys the law and does not avail himself of that traitorous liquid whose excess depraves man, shortening his life. I never drink wine" (37); "it is amazing how the Basque language, with its harmonious roots, with its compound words, admirable for the richness of its images and the transparency of its idealism, favors the development of the spirit" (59); "the Basque . . . grows to honor his virility with the most noble virtues. Freedom, law, and justice are the three natural ideas that are deeply embodied in him" (60).

40. Chaho, *Viaje a Navarra durante la insurrección de los vascos*, 177.

41. Ibid., 15.

42. Ibid., 31.

43. Ibid., 93.

44. Joseph Augustin Chaho, "Profession de la foi," *Ariel: Courier de Vasconie* (April 1846), quoted in Zabalo, *Xaho, el genio de Zuberoa*, 68.

45. Joseph Augustin Chaho, *Paroles d'un Biscaïen aux libéraux de la reine Christine*, vol. 2, 9–10, quoted in Zabalo, *Xaho, el genio de Zuberoa*, 60.

46. Xaho [Chaho], *Bizkaiko baten eleak*, 26; also quoted in Larronde, *Mouvement Eskualerriste (1932–1937)*, 18.

47. Xaho [Chaho], *Bizkaiko baten eleak*, 34.

48. Eugène Goyheneche, "Un ancêtre du nationalisme basque," 31.

49. Ibid., 29.

50. Ibid.

51. Karl Marx, *New York Daily Tribune*, cited by Patxi Isaba, *Euzkadi Socialista* (Paris: Du Cercle, 1971), 152, quoted in Goyheneche "Un ancêtre du nationalisme basque," 30.

52. Dupré-Moretti, "Esquisses biographique et bibliographique d'Augustin Xaho," 152.

53. Ibid., 153.

54. Ibid., 151.

55. Ibid., 154.

56. Ibid., 147.

57. An idea substantiated by Arkotxa, "Augustin Chaho, un républicain basque de la monarchie de juillet au second empire," 309.

58. Zabalo, *Xaho, el genio de Zuberoa*, 61–62. Both Dupré-Moretti, "Esquisses biographique et bibliographique d'Augustin Xaho," 147, and Arkotxa, "Augustin Chaho, un républicain basque de la monarchie de juillet au second empire," 306–7, concur with Zabalo on this last point.

59. "The lancers hurried over the roadside. Zumalacárregui unleashed his proud horse and began to gallop, followed by his staff, like Sancho the Strong [the king of Navarre] before his knights." Chaho, *Viaje a Navarra durante la insurrección de los vascos*, 87.

60. Juaristi, *El bucle melancólico*, 106.

61. Ibid., 87.

62. Ibid., 100.

63. Drouin, "La place de la Philosophie des Révélations de Chaho (1835) dans l'histoire des idées au XIXe siècle," 95.

64. Joseph Augustin Chaho, *Ariel: Républicain de Vasconie* 391 (May 16, 1848), quoted in Zabalo, *Xaho, el genio de Zuberoa*, 123.

65. Joseph Augustin Chaho, *Ariel: Républicain de Vasconie* 488 (October 20, 1848), quoted in Zabalo, *Xaho, el genio de Zuberoa*, 139.

66. Joseph Augustin Chaho, interview in *La Sentinelle*, April 18, 1848, quoted in Crouzet, "Chaho franc-maçon et la Révolution bayonnaise," 116, and Arkotxa, "Augustin Chaho, un républicain basque de la monarchie de juillet au second empire," 310. Dupré-Moretti sees no contradiction in these words with Chaho's prenationalist thought. That is, it fit in with his reading of the relative strength of the potentially competing political forces in Iparralde at the time. See "Esquisses biographique et bibliographique d'Augustin Xaho," 146–56.

67. Chaho, *Viaje a Navarra durante la insurrección de los vascos*, 18.

68. "Doubtlessly, you will not have forgotten that Lapurdi, until [17]89, was one of the republics in the Basque federation." Chaho, *Viaje a Navarra durante la insurrección de los vascos*, 46.

69. Chaho, *Viaje a Navarra durante la insurrección de los vascos*, 40.

70. Joseph Augustin Chaho, *Ariel: Républicain de Vasconie* 764 (October 19, 1849), quoted in Zabalo, *Xaho, el genio de Zuberoa*, 72.

71. Joseph Augustin Chaho, *Lettre à l'auteur des Personnalités, au sujet de MM. Desnoyers et Altaroch du Charivari de Agosti Xaho de Navarre, Paris*, ms. (1840), quoted in Zabalo, *Xaho, el genio de Zuberoa*, 111.

72. This would explain Chaho's leading role in promoting Euskara, for example through editing the first entirely Basque-language periodical, *Ariel: Uskal-errico gaseta*, in 1848, or favoring the teaching of Basque in public schools. See Larzabal, "Survol d'un siècle de vie politique au Pays Basque Nord," 246.

73. See, for example, Ander Gurrutxaga, *La mirada difusa: Dilemas del nacionalismo* (Irun: Alberdania, 2002).

74. On Garibay, see Juan Madariaga Orbea, *Anthology of Apologists and Detractors of the Basque Language*, trans. Frederick H. Fornoff, María Cristina Saavedra, Amaia Gabantxo, and Cameron J. Watson (Reno: Center for Basque Studies, University of Nevada, Reno, 2006). 187–94.

75. Antonio Elorza, *Ideologías del nacionalismo vasco 1876–1937 (De los "euskaros" a Jagi Jagi)* (San Sebastián: Aramburu, 1979), 53.

76. Ibid., 54.

77. Ibid., 61.

78. Juaristi, *El bucle melancólico*, 201.

79. Elorza, *Ideologías del nacionalismo vasco 1876–1937*, 63.

80. Juaristi, *El bucle melancólico*, 16.

81. The speech was given on September 21, 2004, and in it, Aznar attributed the roots of the March 11, 2004, train bombings in Madrid to the invasion of the Moors in 711. See Cynthia R. Rush, "For Spain, Zapatero Opposes Aznar's Crusade with Dialogue," *Executive Intelligence Review* (October 8, 2004), available on-line at http://www.larouchepub.com/other/2004/3139aznar_v_zapat.html (accessed March 7, 2008).

82. Elorza, *Ideologías del nacionalismo vasco 1876–1937*, 54.

83. Juan Venancio de Araquistain, "Remitido," *Semanario Católico Vasco-Navarro* (April 4, 1867), 221, quoted in Elorza, *Ideologías del nacionalismo vasco 1876–1937*, 55.

84. Pedro Ibarra, *Nacionalismo: Razón y pasión* (Barcelona: Ariel, 2005), 23.

85. Ibid., 22 n. 3. Ibarra addresses here Benedict Anderson's influential "imagined community" argument in *Imagined Communities. Reflections on the Origin and Spread of Nationalism*, rev. ed. (London: Verso, 1991). Anthony D. Smith, too, critiques Anderson's overly cognitive interpretation. For Smith, nations are "as much communities of emotion or will, as of imagination and cognition," and Anderson "fails to develop [the imagined political community's] affective, let alone its moral, potential," *Nationalism*, 80, 82.

86. See *Peasants into Frenchmen: The Modernisation of Rural France, 1870–1914* (Stanford, CA: Stanford University Press, 1976). Weber's argument rests on the relatively muted effect of state symbols prior to 1870, symbols such as the state's official money, its judicial system, its official communication network, and, of course, its language–French.

87. On the concept of a structure of social plausibility, see Alfonso Pérez-Agote, *The Social Roots of Basque Nationalism*, trans. Cameron Watson and William A. Douglass, foreword by William A. Douglass (Reno: University of Nevada Press, 2006) , xv. Originally published as *La reproducción del nacionalismo: El caso vasco* (Madrid: CIS; Siglo XXI, 1984).

88. Ibarra, *Nacionalismo: Razón y pasión*, 25.

Notes, Chapter Five

1. Javier Corcuera, *The Origins, Ideology, and Organization of Basque Nationalism, 1876–1903*, trans. Albert Bork and Cameron J. Watson (Reno: Center for Basque Studies, University of Nevada, Reno, 2007), 41.

2. Ibid., 40. In this work, Corcuera follows a line of inquiry that parallels my own search for clues to the nature of Basque identity through the liberal-Carlist confrontation, although in his case, this search focuses on Hegoalde. In his own words, "I would emphasize the possibility that, during the first war, Carlists might have come to conceive of their confrontation with liberals as one between Basques and Spaniards; or at least, that this notion might have been suggested. . . . [Yet] the real importance of such a suggestion does not appear to have been too great. . . . It would not be too contentious, however, to point out that if the First Carlist War did not convert Basques into a nation . . . it did at least strengthen their wish to constitute a differentiated community in conflict with Spain." Ibid., 41.

3. Antonio Elorza, *Ideologías del nacionalismo vasco 1876–1937 (De los "euskaros" a Jagi Jagi)* (San Sebastián: Aramburu, 1979), 47.

4. Benjamín Tejerina, *Nacionalismo y lengua: Los procesos de cambio lingüístico en el País Vasco* (Madrid: CIS; Siglo XXI, 1992), 89.

5. See Elorza, *Ideologías del nacionalismo vasco 1876–1937*, 38–44. Similarly, Vicente Arana organized the Basque Festival of Bizkaia in 1883. See Jon Juaristi, *El bucle melancólico: Historias de nacionalistas vascos*, 2nd ed. (Madrid: Espasa-Calpe, 2000), 75.

6. On Arrese Beitia, see Juan Madariaga Orbea, *Anthology of Apologists and Detractors of the Basque Language*, trans. Frederick H. Fornoff, María Cristina Saavedra, Amaia Gabantxo, and Cameron J. Watson (Reno: Center for Basque Studies, University of Nevada, Reno, 2006), 637–42.

7. Felipe de Arrese y Beitia, "Chomiñ eta Premiñ trabenan bersoetan," in *Ama Euskeriaren liburu*, 413, quoted in Elorza, *Ideologías del nacionalismo vasco 1876–1937*, 75.

8. An English-language translation of this poem appears in Madariaga Orbea, *Anthology of Apologists and Detractors of the Basque Language*, 638–42.

9. On d'Abbadie, see Madariaga Orbea, *Anthology of Apologists and Detractors of the Basque Language*, 581–87.

10. According to Beñat Oyharçabal, the letters "M.D.-A." that appear in the margins of Eugène Coquebert de Montbret's work Basque (continuing that of his father, Charles-Etienne) and that call for the need of a Basque writer to help him complete his work refer to d'Abbadie. See "Les documents recueillis lors des enquêtes linguistiques en Pays Basque durant la période révolutionnaire et le Premier Empire," in *La Révolution française dans l'histoire et la littérature basques du XIXe siècle: Actes du colloque international de l'URA 1055 du C.N.R.S.*, ed. Jean Baptiste Orpustan (Baigorri: Izpegi, 1994). 107.

11. They jointly published *Études grammaticales sur la langue euskarienne* (Paris: Arthur Bertrand, 1836), in which they spoke of the originality, purity, simplicity, and richness of Basque. In the bibliography at the end of the work, d'Abbadie listed some seventy books on the topic of Euskara. For an English-language translation of part of this book, see Madariaga Orbea, *Anthology of Apologists and Detractors of the Basque Language*, 583–87.

12. Joseba Agirreazkuenaga, "La renovación de los imaginarios culturales de la vasquidad y la difusión de los nuevos conocimientos científicos," in *Historia de Euskal Herria/Historia general de los vascos*, vol. 5, *Vasconia (1876–1937): Entre la tradición y la modernidad*, ed. Joseba Agirreazkuenaga, (Donostia: Lur, 2005), 273.

13. Manex Goyhenetche, *Histoire Générale du Pays Basque*, vol. 4, *La Révolution de 1789* (Donostia and Baiona: Elkar, 2002), 302–7.

14. Agirreazkuenaga, "La renovación de los imaginarios culturales de la vasquidad y la difusión de los nuevos conocimientos científicos," 273.

15. Joseba Gabilondo, following Juaristi's methodological approach to the nostalgic dimension of nationalism, explores the figure of d'Abbadie in "On the Postcolonial and Queer Origins of Modern Basque Literature: Rethinking *Lore Jokoak* and Anton Abbadie's Contribution," a paper presented at Session Three of the First International Symposium on Basque Cultural Studies, June 29–July 2, 2000. Specifically, he focuses on d'Abbadie after his return from Africa and especially on the subsequent disappearance of a young Ethiopian servant. Gabilondo argues that the logic of colonialism–stemming from d'Abbadie's ethnographic fieldwork in Ethiopia–served to underpin much of d'Abbadie's work, and his search for a new anthropological paradise would lead him, as a result, to focus his hopes and imperialist nostalgia in another direction: the Basque Country. Following Joseba Zulaika in *Del Cromañon al Carnaval: Los vascos como museo antropológico* (Donostia: Erein, 1996), Gabilondo concludes that the invention of the Basque nation in the work of anthropologists such as d'Abbadie may have precluded the development of a Basque nationalism, to the extent that numerous nineteenth-century figures like him were seeking in Europe the remains of primitive "lost" peoples, peoples they ultimately found in existing nations.

16. In Arana's own words, "the elements or characteristics of nationality are fivefold: 1st, Race; 2nd, Language; 3rd, Government and Laws; 4th, Characteristics and Customs; 5th, Historical Personality." Quoted in Iñaki Aguirre Zabala, "Nacionalismo vasco y relaciones transnacionales en el contexto de la frontera hispano-francesa: Cuatro modelos históricos," in *Las relaciones de vecindad*, ed. Celestino del Arenal (Leioa: Servicio Editorial, Universidad del País Vasco, 1987), 87.

17. Sabino Arana, "La patria: A un euskerafilo (1897)," quoted in Aguirre, "Nacionalismo vasco y relaciones transnacionales en el contexto de la frontera hispano-francesa," 91.

18. The arguments range from Juaristi's claim in *El bucle melancólico* that it has persisted throughout the history of the movement to José María Lorenzo Espinosa's contention in *Historia de Euskal Herria*, vol. 3, *El nacimiento de una nación* (Tafalla: Txalaparta, 1997) that race was quickly replaced as the key aspect of Basque nationalism by first language and subsequently the general will.

19. Juan J. Linz, *Conflicto en Euskadi* (Madrid: Espasa-Calpe, 1986), 30.

20. A thesis defended by Linz in *Conflicto en Euskadi*, by Corchera in *The Origins, Ideology, and Organization of Basque Nationalism, 1876–1903*, by Ludger Mees, Santiago de Pablo, and José Antonio Rodríguez, *El péndulo patriótico: Historia del Partido Nacionalista Vasco*, 2nd ed. (Barcelona: Crítica, 2005), and Ander Gurrutxaga Abad, *La mirada difusa: Dilemas del nacionalismo* (Irun: Alberdania, 2002).

21. For an appreciation of this, see Mees, de Pablo, and Rodríguez, *El péndulo patriótico*, esp. chs. 2, 3, and 4, and Santiago Pérez-Nievas, "Partidos y procesos de cambio político: La organización y el desarrollo estratégico del PNV en la transición democrática en España," Working Paper 21/2004, Working Papers On-Line Series, Seminario de Investigación de Ciencia Política, Departamento de Ciencia Política y Relaciones Internacionales, Facultad de Derecho, Universidad Autónoma de Madrid, 2004, available on-line at www.uam.es/centros/derecho/cpolitica/papers.html under *Investigación* and *Publicaciones* (last accessed March 10, 2008), 12–14.

22. Jean-Claude Larronde, *El nacionalismo vasco: Su origen y su ideología en la obra de Sabino Arana-Goiri*, trans. Lola Valverde (San Sebastián: Txertoa, 1977), 154.

23. Sabino Arana, "Euskeldun Batzokija," *Bizkaitarra* 10 (May 24, 1894), quoted in Corcuera, *The Origins, Ideology, and Organization of Basque Nationalism, 1876–1903*, 217–18 and Aguirre, "Nacionalismo vasco y relaciones transnacionales en el contexto de la frontera hispano-francesa," 87.

24. Jean-Claude Larronde, *Mouvement Eskualerriste (1932–1937): Naissance du mouvement nationaliste basque en Iparralde/ Eskualerri-Zaleen Biltzarra (1932–1937): Eskualerrizaleen mugimendu abertzalearen sortzea Iparraldean/El movimiento Eskualerrista (1932–1937): Nacimiento del movimiento nacionalista vasco en Iparralde* (Bilbao: Sabino Arana Kultur Elkargoa, 1994), 31.

25. Ibid., 32.

26. Sabino Arana, *El Partido Carlista y los Fueros Vasko-Nabarros* (1897), quoted in Aguirre, "Nacionalismo vasco y relaciones transnacionales en el contexto de la frontera hispano-francesa," 88.

27. Corcuera, *The Origins, Ideology, and Organization of Basque Nationalism, 1876–1903*, 217.

28. Ibid.

29. James E. Jacob, *Hills of Conflict: Basque Nationalism in France* (Reno: University of Nevada Press, 1994), 57–61.

30. Larronde, *Mouvement Eskualerriste (1932–1937)*, 43.

31. Sabino Arana, *El Partido Carlista y los Fueros Vasko-Nabarros* (1897), quoted in Corcuera, *The Origins, Ideology, and Organization of Basque Nationalism, 1876–1903*, 219, and in Aguirre, "Nacionalismo vasco y relaciones transnacionales en el contexto de la frontera hispano-francesa," 88.

32. Corcuera, *The Origins, Ideology, and Organization of Basque Nationalism, 1876–1903*, 219.

33. Larronde, *El nacionalismo vasco*, 155.

34. Sabino Arana, "La unión (1897)," quoted in Aguirre, "Nacionalismo vasco y relaciones transnacionales en el contexto de la frontera hispano-francesa," 89.

35. Ibid.

Notes, Chapter Six

1. These basic differences in the social, economic, and political framework of European society are examined by Stein Rokkan, *Citizens, Elections, Parties: Approaches to the Comparative Study of the Processes of Development* (Oslo: Universitetsforlaget; New York: McKay, 1970), Daniel-Louis Seiler, *Partis et familles politiques* (Paris: Presses Universitaires de France, 1980) and *Sur les parties autonomistes dans la CEE* (Barcelona: Institut de Ciènces Polítiques i Socials, 1990), and Francisco Letamendia, *Game of Mirrors: Centre-Periphery National Conflicts* (Aldershot, UK: Ashgate, 2000).

2. Cameron Watson, *Modern Basque History: Eighteenth Century to the Present* (Reno: Center for Basque Studies, University of Nevada, Reno, 2003), 84; Manex Goyhenetche, *Histoire général du Pays Basque*, vol. 5, *Le XIXe siècle, 1804–1914* (Donostia and Baiona: Elkar, 2005), 5.

3. On this, see, for example, Susana Serrano Abad, "Industrialización en Vasconia," in *Historia de Euskal Herria: Historia general de los vascos*, vol. 5, *Vasconia (1876–1937): Entre la tradición y la modernidad*, ed. Joseba Agirreazkuenaga (Donostia: Lur, 2005), 75–95.

4. Eugen Weber, *Peasants into Frenchmen: The Modernization of Rural France* (Stanford: Stanford University Press, 1976), 42, 205–6.

5. On this subject, see two works by Xipri Arbelbide, *Iraultza Heletan: Errepublikarentzat hil behorrari* (Donostia: Etor, 1994), and *Enbata: Abertzalegoaren historioa Iparraldean* (Donostia: Kutxa Fundazioa, 1996).

6. James E. Jacob, *Hills of Conflict: Basque Nationalism in France* (Reno: University of Nevada Press, 1994), 54.

7. Xabier Itçaina, "Les politisations plurielles de la société basque à la fin du XIXe siècle," in Goyhenetche, *Histoire général du Pays Basque*, vol. 5, *Le XIXe siècle, 1804–1914*, 229.

8. See Francis Jauréguiberry, "Europe, langue basque et modernité en Pays Basque français," in *Le Pays Basque et l'Europe*, ed. Pierre Bidart (Baigorri : Izpegi, 1994), 45, and Eugen Weber, *Peasants into Frenchmen*, chs. 6 and 18.

9. Jacob, *Hills of Conflict*, 56; Pierre Bidart, "Langue et idéologie dans la culture basque," in *La nouvelle société basque: Ruptures et changements*, ed. Pierre Bidart (Paris: L'Harmattan, 1980), 159–81.

10. Beñat Oyharçabal, "Les documents recueillis lors des enquêtes linguistiques en Pays Basque durant la période révolutionnaire et le Premier Empire," in *La Révolution française dans l'histoire et la littérature basques du XIXe siècle: Actes du colloque international de l'URA 1055 du C.N.R.S.*, ed. Jean Baptiste Orpustan (Baigorri: Izpegi, 1994), 67.

11. Herman Lebovics, "Creating the Authentic France: Struggles over French Identity in the First Half of the Twentieth Century," in *Commemorations: The Politics of National Identity*, ed. John R. Gillis (Princeton, NJ: Princeton University Press, 1994), 241, quoted in Watson, *Modern Basque History*, 215.

12. On this topic, see two works by Mona Ozouf: *L'école, l'église et la République,1871–1914* (Paris: Cana Editions; Jean Offredo, 1982) and *La république des instituteurs* (Paris: Galimard; Le Seuil, 1992).

13. Eric Savarèse, "Ecole et pouvoir colonial: Retour sur la légitimation de la colonisation," available on-line at at http://www.la-science-politique.com/revue/revue2/papier1.htm (last accessed March 14, 2008).

14. Rogers Brubaker, *Citizenship and Nationhood in France and Germany* (Cambridge, MA: Harvard University Press, 1992), 8.

15. Weber, *Peasants into Frenchmen*, 475–78.

16. Davant, *Histoire du peuple basque*, 8th ed., rpt. (1970; Donostia: Elkarlanean, 2000), 94; Arbelbide, *Enbata*, 18.

17. Jacob, *Hills of Conflict*, 45–46.

18. Weber, *Peasants into Frenchmen*, 87, 99.

19. Jacob, *Hills of Conflict*, 55. Eugène Goyheneche estimates that six thousand men–or 4 percent of the population in Iparralde–perished in the conflict. See *Historia de Iparralde: Desde los orígenes a nuestros días* (San Sebastián: Txertoa, 1985), 112. Pierre Laborde calculates that, between 1911 and 1931, the population of Iparralde fell by twenty thousand, or 17 percent. See *Pays Basque: Économie et société en mutation* (Donostia and Baiona: Elkar, 1994), 181–84.

20. Watson, *Modern Basque History*, 210; Mikel Urquijo Goitia, "De una guerra a otra: Política e instituciones en un largo camino a la democracia," in *Historia de Euskal Herria: Historia general de los vascos*, vol. 6, *Dictadura, democracia y autogobierno: La nueva sociedad vasca, 1937–2004*, ed. Joseba Agirreazkuenaga (Donostia: Lur, 2005), 304.

21. See Martin Reynaud, "Nationalisme et antisémitisme en France (vers 1880–1914)," paper delivered in the series La modernisation politique et sociale de la France de la fin du XVIIIe siècle a la Première guerre mondiale (2001–2), Sciences-Po, Institut d'Études Politiques de Paris, December 19, 2001, available on-line at http://perso.orange.fr/david.colon/Sciences-Po/nationalisme.pdf (last accessed March 14, 2008).

22. As an example of the socially deep-rooted nature of these ideas, Edouard Drumont's clearly anti-Semitic *La France juive* [Jewish France] (1886) had, by 1914, been reprinted some two hundred times.

23. For example, by the municipal law of April 5, 1884, peasants could participate more directly in political life by having more opportunities to take part as candidates in local elections. The result was that, by 1913, 46 percent of all mayors in France came from peasant backgrounds. See, in general, Weber, *Peasants into Frenchmen*, ch. 7.

24. Watson, *Modern Basque History*, 219–20.

25. Suzanne Citron, "Ecole, histoire de France: Construction d'une mémoire nationale, crise de l'identité nationale," Actes du Colloque de Carpentras, "Ecole, pouvoir(s), identité(s)," Lycée Victor Hugo, April 29, 2001, in *Dialogues Politiques* 2 (January 2003), available on-line at http://www.la-science-politique.com/revue/revue2/papier2.htm (last accessed March 14, 2008).

26. Suzanne Citron, "Recomposer le passé," *Le Monde*, November 5, 2003.

27. Arbelbide, *Enbata*, 45; Piarres Charritton, *Euskalzaleen Biltzarra-ren historia laburra (1901–2003)* (Baiona: Euskalzaleen Biltzarra, 2003), 6–7; Javier Díaz Noci and Nuria Moret Llosas, "La cultura en Vasconia: Entre la tradición y la modernidad," in *Historia de Euskal Herria: Historia general de los vascos*, vol. 5, *Vasconia (1876–1937): Entre la tradición y la modernidad*, ed. Agirreazkuenaga, 328.

28. Quoted by Jean Marie Izquierdo, *Le Pays Basque de France: La difficile maturation d'un sentiment nationaliste basque* (1998; Paris: L'Harmattan, 2001), 114.

29. See Jean-Paul Malherbe, "Le nationalisme basque en France (1933–1976)," Ph.D. diss., University of Toulouse I, 1977, 17, and Jacob, *Hills of Conflict*, 72. Additionally, the group also sponsored the teaching of Basque, extending educational initiatives to some two thousand children. See Arbelbide, *Enbata*, 46.

30. Jacob, *Hills of Conflict*, 72–73.

31. Indeed, the very name "Aintzina," with its Janus-faced meaning, reflected its role: the defense of Basque traditions and religion and the desire of young activists to begin a program of cultural regeneration.

32. Pierre Lafitte, "Programme Eskualerriste," *Eskual-herriaren alde (Pour le Pays Basque: Court commentaire du programme Eskualerriste à l'usage des militants* (Bayonne: Imprimerie La Presse, 1933), 7–8, quoted in Jacob, *Hills of Conflict*, 76–77.

33. Jean-Claude Larronde, *Mouvement Eskualerriste (1932–1937): Naissance du mouvement nationaliste basque en Iparralde/ Eskualerri-Zaleen Biltzarra (1932–1937): Eskualerrizaleen mugimendu abertzalearen sortzea Iparraldean/El movimiento Eskualerrista (1932–1937): Nacimiento del movimiento nacionalista vasco en Iparralde* (Bilbao: Sabino Arana Kultur Elkargoa, 1994), 62.

34. Pierre Lafitte, "Le congrès du Foyer d'Études Fédéralistes," in *La Presse* (1933), 7, quoted in Larronde, *Mouvement Eskualerriste (1932–1937)*, 292–97.

35. "Erroimendi: Propos d'Outre Rhin," *Aintzina* 16 (January 1936), quoted in Larronde, *Mouvement Eskualerriste (1932–1937)*, 63.

36. Pierre Lafitte, "Parlons net," *Aintzina* 17 (February 1936), quoted in Arbelbide, *Enbata*, 48.

37. Pierre Lafitte, "Le congrès du Foyer d'Etudes Fédéralistes," in *La Presse* (1933), 7–8, quoted in Larronde, *Mouvement Eskualerriste (1932–1937)*, 292–97.

38. Juan Carlos Jiménez de Aberásturi, "De la derrota a la esperanza. Euzkadi en la II Guerra Mundial, 1939–1945," Ph.D. diss., University of the Basque Country, 1998, 770.

39. Jacob discusses the more radical direction that Eugène Goyheneche's thinking took, although this remained a private matter. The public face of the Eskualerriste movement, as represented by Lafitte, was much more moderate in tone. See Jacob, *Hills of Conflict*, 78.

40. Jean de Jaureguiberry, "Renaissance Basque," *Gure Herria* 6, vol. 13 (1933), 535–38, quoted in Larronde, *Mouvement Eskualerriste (1932–1937)*, 201.

41. Larronde, *Mouvement Eskualerriste (1932–1937)*, 69; Malherbe, "Le nationalisme basque en France (1933–1976)," 11–32; Jacob, *Hills of Conflict*, 70, 82–85.

42. Larronde, *Mouvement Eskualerriste (1932–1937)*, 78–89.

43. Ibid., 90–94.

44. Lafitte, "Programme Eskualerriste," quoted in Jacob, *Hills of Conflict*, 83.

45. One might date from this time an emergent preoccupation among Basque regionalists and later nationalists with distinguishing development policies for the coast from those of the interior. Indeed, the relative and persistent strength of the interior, rural sector has been obvious from the growing importance of the contemporary agricultural union in Iparralde, the ELB (Euskal Laborariaren Batasuna, the Basque Workers' Union, later renamed the Euskal Herriko Laborarien Batasuna; United Workers of the Basque Country), created in 1982.

46. For example, in December 1935, *Aintzina* "in tune with articles by Michel Elissamburu in the extreme right-wing and later collaborationist [with the Nazi occupation during World War II] newspaper *Eskualduna*, denounced a 'Masonic conspiracy'" within its pages. Jiménez de Aberásturi, "De la derrota a la esperanza. Euzkadi en la II Guerra Mundial, 1939–1945," 768.

47. Commenting on these elections, an editorial in the Eskualerriste journal argued the following: "Listen, my dear reader: If you want France to become a province of the USSR, the sweet colony of a French Ukraine—it does not sound so bad!—vote for the Popular Front. If you do not wish to be enslaved, vote anti-PF 100 percent." J. Beche (pseud.), "Electeur, médite ceci. . . ," *Aintzina* 17 (1936). Larronde thinks this was written by Father Léon Lasalle, one of the most conservative contributors to *Aintzina*. See *Mouvement Eskualerriste (1932–1937)*, 272.

48. Larronde, *Mouvement Eskualerriste (1932–1937)*, 230–31.

49. Ibid., 248–52.

50. Ibid., 248.

51. "Lutte fratricide," *Aintzina* 22 (July 1936), quoted in Larronde, *Mouvement Eskualerriste (1932–1937)*, 249. In Larronde's opinion (275), these were Lafitte's words.

52. Jacob, *Hills of Conflict*, 93.

53. In his own words, "Yes, I am a friend of Franco, and wish with all my heart that he puts down the Bolshevik revolution." Jean Ybarnégaray, in *La Presse de Sud-Ouest*, October 5, 1937, quoted in Larronde, *Mouvement Eskualerriste (1932–1937)*, 236. Larronde reproduces the full text of this article, 298–302.

54. Larronde, *Mouvement Eskualerriste (1932-1937)*, 242; Jacob, *Hills of Conflict*, 93–96.

55. Larronde, *Mouvement Eskualerriste (1932-1937)*, 241.

56. Ibid., 243. The reference is to General Emilio Mola, head of the military uprising in the North and leader of the assault on the Basque Country. Mention of the "sacred tree" is a reference to the oak tree of Gernika, symbol of the Basque *fueros*. By contrast, the left-wing press in France supported the legitimate Spanish government, condemning the Francoist atrocity in Gernika while at the same time criticizing the ambiguous position of the French authorities toward the conflict.

57. Moreover, many of its militants began to give up their regionalism as a result of their experience aiding refugees from Hegoalde.

58. Miguel de Gorostazu, "Basque Nation," *Gure Herria* 6 (1925), quoted in Larronde, *Mouvement Eskualerriste (1932-1937)*, 47.

59. Larronde, *Mouvement Eskualerriste (1932-1937)*, 61; Izquierdo, *Le Pays Basque de France*, 116 n.144.

60. See Jacob, *Hills of Conflict*, 83.

61. Ibid., 76.

62. "Every language marks those who speak it with a particular mentality. . . . Why would anyone want to stop us from forming our ideas according to the original plan developed through an analysis of our ancient Euskara? Freedom of thought should be accompanied by freedom of expression." "Euskal Herriaren Alde" [the Eskualerriste program], quoted in Larronde, *Mouvement Eskualerriste (1932–1937)*, 86. See the full text of the document, 289–91.

63. Pierre Lafitte, interview in *Garaia* 10 (1976), 7, quoted in Larronde, *Mouvement Eskualerriste (1932-1937)*, 65.

64. Larronde, *Mouvement Eskualerriste (1932-1937)*, 183.

65. As we will see, later, this strategy was also adopted by Enbata.

66. These were ostensibly hiking groups (a popular pastime in the Basque Country), but with a specific political vocation in attracting young people to the Basque nationalist cause. During the Spanish Civil War, these groups were in effect transformed into battalions of Euzko Gudarostea, the Basque army formed to fight the military uprising led by Franco.

67. Jacques Mestelan, provisional statutes of the Menditarrak (Article 3), quoted in Larronde, *Mouvement Eskualerriste (1932-1937)*, 153.

68. It should be noted that this remained a theoretical dimension. The group never undertook any military activity.

69. "Each member could take 150 francs. There was a uniform: gray riding breeches; beige gray socks; a gray flannel shirt; belt; green tie (for town); a dark-green woolen sweater (of a leather vest variety) with gold buttons and, on the left, the emblem of the Menditarrak; a mountaineer's backpack." Jacques Mestelan, founder of the group, quoted in Larronde, *Mouvement Eskualerriste (1932-1937)*, 155.

70. The anthem of the Menditarrak—including the words "Menditarrak, we are loyal Basques/Our fiery blood awaits/ If, unfortunately, an enemy seeks to enter/our Basque Country and make off with it"—seems to have been a hybrid of two songs used by the Mendigoizaleak in Hegoalde: that of 1923, which went "Let us go from mountain to mountain, young Basques/onward and up the slopes/the healthy air gives us life/to salute the entire homeland," and that of 1931, the well-known "Eusko Gudariak Gera" that went: "We are Basque warriors/to save the Basque Country/much is the blood/we would spill for it." Reproduced in Jon Juaristi, *El bucle melancólico: Historias de nacionalistas vascos*, 2nd ed. (Madrid: Espasa-Calpe, 2000), 273–74.

71. "After their excursions to the mountains, the Menditarrak would be stronger, more experienced, more prepared for action. . . . We focused our goals, took account of our strength, [and] understood where we were. We were able to act." Menditar [pseud. of Jacques Mestelan, founder of the group], "Chronique des Menditarrar, Se posséder pour agir," *Aintzina* 15 (December 1935), quoted in Larronde, *Mouvement Eskualerriste (1932-1937)*, 155.

72. See Juaristi, *El bucle melancólico*, 253.

73. Larronde, *Mouvement Eskualerriste (1932-1937)*, 162.

74. For a fuller analysis of Madeleine de Jaureguiberry, see Jean Fagoaga et al., *Madeleine de Jauréguiberry. Omenaldia-Hommage* (Donostia: Eusko Ikaskuntza, 2001). For an examination of the current activity of the Begiraleak group in Donibane Lohizune, inspired by the original Jaureguiberry organization, see Joseba Aurkenerena, *Iparraldeko kronikak* (Bilbao: Gero; Mensajero, 2003).

75. Founding statues of one chapter, Gure Etchea, quoted in Larronde, *Mouvement Eskualerriste (1932-1937)*, 163.

Notes, Chapter Seven

1. Juan J. Linz, *Conflicto en Euskadi* (Madrid: Espasa-Calpe, 1986), 370.

2. That said, one cannot speak of "real" center-periphery relations, like those between France and Spain and the Basque territories, given that there is no official link between the Basque Autonomous Community and Iparralde. On the contrary, my discussion here implies a certain degree of subjectivity and is based squarely on symbolic practices and exchanges.

3. James E. Jacob, *Hills of Conflict: Basque Nationalism in France* (Reno: University of Nevada Press, 1994), 99.

4. Paul Sérant, "En France comme en Espagne les Basques restent basques," *Monde et Vie* (February 1968), 32, quoted in Jacob, *Hills of Conflict*, 99.

5. Juan Carlos Jiménez de Aberásturi, *De la derrota a la esperanza: Políticas vascas durante la Segunda Guerra Mundial (1937–1947)* (Oñati: IVAP, 1999), 125.

6. The Autonomous Government of Euzkadi [the Basque Country], *The Basque Country and European Peace: An Analysis of the German Domination of Euzkadi* (London, 1938), quoted in Jacob, *Hills of Conflict*, 99. Similarly, Jiménez de Aberásturi records how Manuel de Irujo of the EBB (the governing committee of the PNV) stated in 1939 that there should be no "allusion in any way to the north Basque Country, for any such allusion could get us before the Quai d'Orsay [the French Ministry of Foreign Affairs], making any further movement impossible." Manuel de Irujo (1939), quoted in Jiménez de Aberasturi, *De la derrota a la esperanza*, 126–28.

7. Actually, two years previously, the PNV journal *Euzko Deya* 119 (1938) produced a map of "Euzkadi" on the first page of the edition in which "the Basque Country as a political entity remained clearly limited to the single, peninsular [i.e. Spanish] part." Jiménez de Aberásturi, *De la derrota a la esperanza*, 126–27.

8. Jan Mansvelt, "Euskal Herria, Imagined Territory," paper presented at the Standing Group on International Relations Fifth Pan-International Relations Conference, "Constructing World Orders," The Hague, September 9–11, 2004.

9. José Mari Garmendia and Alberto Elordi, *La resistencia vasca* (San Sebastián: Haranburu, 1982), 119–20.

10. See Pierre Letamendia, "La vie politique en le Pays Basque français, 1958–1982: Permanence et mutation d'un sous système politique," *Bulletin de la Société des Sciences, Lettres, Arts de Bayonne* 137–138 (1981–1982): 513–27.

11. Ludger Mees, Santiago de Pablo, and José Antonio Rodríguez, *El péndulo patriótico: Historia del Partido Nacionalista Vasco*, 2nd ed. (Barcelona: Crítica, 200), 77. The authors confirm that any PNV activity in Iparralde would be considered part of its foreign relations (280).

12. Emilio Lopez Adan [Beltza, pseud.], *El nacionalismo vasco en el exilio 1937–1960* (San Sebastián: Txertoa, 1977), 45.

13. Ibid., 78.

14. Jacob, *Hills of Conflict*, 100. The ANV was a nondenominational republican Basque nationalist party created in 1930 as an alternative to traditionalist, religious conservatism of the PNV. It remained the minority nationalist option.

15. Ibid., 66–68.

16. Javier Díaz Noci, "Sociedad y medios de comunicación en lengua vasca en el período de entreguerras (1919–1937)," *Revista de Historia Contemporánea de la Universidad de Murcia* (1995), available on-line at http://www.ehu.es/diaz-noci/Arts/a7.pdf (last accessed March 17, 2008); 12 n. 26.

17. Amaia Ereñaga, *Marc Légasse: Un rebelde burlón* (Tafalla: Txalaparta, 1997), 38.

18. Jacob, *Hills of Conflict*, 105.

19. Jiménez de Aberásturi, "De la derrota a la esperanza," 10–40.

20. On this topic, see Jean-Claude Larronde, *El Batallón Gernika: Los combates de la Pointe-de-Grave (Abril de 1945)*, trans. Rafael Aparicio Martin (Bayonne: Bidasoa; Institut d'Histoire Contemporaine, 1995), 29–62.

21. Michel Oronos, *Le Mouvement culturel basque 1951–2001* (Donostia: Elkar, 2002), 24.

22. *Aintzina* (1943), quoted in Xipri Arbelbide, *Enbata: Abertzalegoaren historioa Iparraldean* (Donostia: Kutxa Fundazioa, 1996), 58–59.

23. I refer here to the Demo group, which I will examine in more detail below. For a more comprehensive analysis of this group, see Igor Ahedo Gurrutxaga, *El movimiento Demo y la nueva cocina vasca (desobediente)* (Irun: Alberdania, 2004).

24. See Sydney G. Tarrow, *Power in Movement: Social Movements, Collective Action and Politics*, 2nd ed. (Cambridge: Cambridge University Press, 1998), 107–10.

25. See Arbelbide, *Enbata*, 63.

26. Ibid., 63. The exact denomination of these candidates is disputed. Ereñaga claims that they presented themselves according to the terms described above. *Marc Légasse*, 66. Jacob, however, contends that both Legasse and Darmendrail ran as "Basque Nationalists," while Landaburu used the term "Nationalist Basque" and Ospital was an "Independent." See *Hills of Conflict*, 121. Whatever the case, clearly all four subscribed to a strategy designed by Legasse.

27. Jacob, *Hills of Conflict*, 121.

28. Ereñaga, *Marc Légasse*, 69.

29. Arbelbide, *Enbata*, 64; Ereñaga, *Marc Légasse*, 69. Jacob says that Legasse's arrest as the result of flyers he was putting up calling for abstention in the 1946 legislative elections. See *Hills of Conflict*, 123.

30. Thorez had deserted from the French Army and had fled to the Soviet Union. After the liberation of France, he received a pardon, going on to lead the French Communist Party and take part in coalition governments.

31. Gordon Marshall, ed. *Oxford Dictionary of Sociology*, 2nd ed. (Oxford and New York: Oxford University Press, 1998), s.v. "anomie, anomy."

32. Quoted in Arbelbide, *Enbata*, 65. Curiously, Ereñaga mentions that the signatory of this document, Dr. Behague, director of the Saint Luc asylum, after the intervention of one of Legasse's uncles, had officially offered to send this note to the authorities, thereby absolving him of having to fulfill the jail sentence for which he had been tried, an offer that Legasse declined. See *Marc Légasse*, 70.

33. Ereñaga, *Marc Légasse*, 70.

34. Arbelbide, *Enbata*, 65; Jacob, *Hills of Conflict*, 123.

35. Marc Legasse, *Le statut du pays Basque dans la République Française: Projet du loi* (Saint-Jean-De-Luz: Dargains, 1945?).

36. A term used in the bluffing card game, *mus*, meaning "all or nothing" in the sense of a challenge.

37. Ereñaga, *Marc Légasse*, 64.

38. Jean Etcheverry-Ainchart, interview by Oronos, *Le Mouvement cultural basque 1951–2001*, 28.

39. Indeed, Legasse claimed that Barandiaran shared his separatist views, unlike many leading members of the PNV. See Marc Legasse, *El zortziko de iraeta para arpa y txalaparta* (San Sebastián: Txertoa, 1990), 91–92.

40. Ibid., 95.

41. Marc Legasse, letter to José Antonio Aguirre, March 25, 1946, quoted by Lopez Adan, *El nacionalismo vasco en el exilio 1937–1960*, 112, and Jacob, *Hills of Conflict*, 125–26.

42. Ibid., 113.

43. Ibid., 114.

44. Ibid.

45. Ibid., 114, and Jacob, *Hills of Conflict*, 126.

46. Marc Legasse, letter to José Antonio Aguirre, March 25, 1946, quoted by Lopez Adan, *El nacionalismo vasco en el exilio 1937–1960*, 114–15.

47. Ibid., 115, and Jacob, *Hills of Conflict*, 126.

48. Marc Legasse, letter to José Antonio Aguirre, March 25, 1946, quoted by Lopez Adan, *El nacionalismo vasco en el exilio 1937–1960*, 116.

49. Ibid., 117, and Jacob, *Hills of Conflict*, 126.

50. Marc Legasse, letter to José Antonio Aguirre, March 25, 1946, quoted by Lopez Adan, *El nacionalismo vasco en el exilio 1937–1960*, 117.

51. See Jacob, *Hills of Conflict*, 182–83.

52. See Mees, de Pablo, and Rodríguez, *El péndulo patriótico*, 253–309.

53. Jacob, *Hills of Conflict*, 224–25.

54. See Francisco Letamendia, *Game of Mirrors: Centre-Periphery National Conflicts*, trans. Karen Hatherley (Aldershot, UK: Ashgate, 2000), 55.

55. On this topic, see Ahedo Gurrutxaga. *El movimiento Demo y la nueva cocina vasca (desobediente)*.

Notes, Chapter Eight

1. Jean-Louis Davant, *Histoire du peuple basque*, 8th ed. (Donostia: Elkarlanean, 2000), 130.

2. Jean-Claude Larronde, "Michel Labéguerie: Son cheminement politique," in *Michel Labéguerie: Omenaldia-Hommage*, ed. Laurent Darraidou et al. (Donostia: Eusko Ikaskuntza, 2001), 102.

3. Xipri Arbelbide, *Enbata: Abertzalegoaren historioa Iparraldean* (Donostia: Kutxa Fundazioa, 1996), 75.

4. Xabier Itçaina, "Michel Labeguerie eta dantza," in *Michel Labéguerie: Omenaldia-Hommage*, ed. Laurent Darraidou et al. (Donostia: Eusko Ikaskuntza, 2001), 47. It should also be noted that during World War II, Labéguerie collaborated with both the French Resistance and the espionage services of the Basque government in exile. See Jiménez de Aberásturi, *De la derrota a la esperanza: Políticas vascas durante la Segunda Guerra Mundial (1937–1947)* (Oñati: IVAP, 1999), 441; and Larronde, "Michel Labéguerie: Son cheminement politique," 81.

5. Indeed, by 1944, it counted within the federation over a dozen dance groups, 150 dancers, and choirs in Baiona, Biarritz, Uztaritze, Kanbo, and Baigorri, as well as in Bordeaux and Paris. That same year, the EGB organized its internal structure along the lines of different technical committees: Language and History (headed by Piarres Charritton), Choreography and Instrumental Music (under Labéguerie, Emile Hirigoyen, and Trinidad Ernandorena), Choir Organization (led by Labéguerie, Michel Limonaire, and Abbé Haramburu), and Lectures and Studies (under Eugène Goyheneche and Labéguerie). See Jean-Claude Larronde, "Culture basque sous l'occupation," in *Oihenart: Cuadernos de Lengua y Literatura* 14 (1997), special ed., *Gerra eta literatura 1914–1944*: 223.

6. Larronde, "Michel Labéguerie: Son cheminement politique," 81.

7. Itçaina, "Michel Labeguerie eta dantza," 47.

8. Arbelbide, *Enbata*, 81.

9. These are detailed by Jean-Claude Larronde, "Histoire du VIIème Congrès d'Etudes Basques, Biarritz, 1948," in *VIIème Congrès d'Etudes Basques. Eusko Ikaskuntzaren VII. Kongresua. VII Congreso de Estudios Vascos*, ed. Jean-Claude Larronde (Donostia: Eusko Ikaskuntza, 2005), 17–61.

10. For example, the Instituto Gernika (Gernika Institute) and its journal, *Eusko Jakintza-Estudios Vascos-Études Basques*. The Instituto Gernika, in turn, created Ikuska—the Sociedad Internacional de Estudios Vascos (International Society for Basque Studies). Ibid., 19–24.

11. Ibid., 35–39.

12. Ibid., 26.

13. Quoted in ibid., 32.

14. For an overview of the conclusions of each session at the conference, see ibid., 31–32.

15. Pierre Lafitte, in *Le Courier*, September 25–26, 1948, quoted in ibid., 35.

16. Piarres Charritton, *Euskalzaleen Biltzarra-ren historia laburra (1901–2003)* (Baiona: Eskualzaleen Biltzarra, 2003), 3.

17. Ibid., 8–13.

18. Amelia Hernández Mata, "Pierre Lafitte bere eskutitzen bitartez: Euskalzaletasuna Iparraldean pizteko saiakera bat," *Oihenart: Cuadernos de Lengua y Literatura* 18 (2000): 65.

19. Manex Goyhenetche, "Idéologies culturelles et espace social en Pays Basque de France á la vieille de la première guerre mondial," *La production social des espaces*, CNRS, 85, quoted in Hernández Mata, "Pierre Lafitte bere eskutitzen bitartez," 66.

20. Daniel Landart, "Michel Labeguerie eta Eskualzaleen Biltzarra," in *Michel Labéguerie: Omenaldia-Hommage*, ed. Darraidou et al., 17.

21. Larronde, "Michel Labéguerie: Son cheminement politique," 83.

22. Mixel Itzaina, *Mixel Labéguerie: Kantu berritzaile eta politika gizona* (Donostia: Elkarlanean, 1999), 115.

23. Mikel Zalbide, "Hendai-Hondarribietako biltzarrak: XX. mendeko hizkuntz plangintzaren iturburu," in *Euskaltzaleen Biltzarraren Mendeaurrena* (Bilbao: Fundación Sabino Arana–Sabino Arana Kultur Elkargoa, 2003), 126–28.

24. Quoted in Jean-Claude Larronde, *Mouvement Eskualerriste (1932–1937): Naissance du mouvement nationaliste basque en Iparralde/Eskualerri-Zaleen Biltzarra (1932–1937): Eskualerrizaleen mugimendu abertzalearen sortzea Iparraldean/El movimiento Eskualerrista (1932–1937): Nacimiento del movimiento nacionalista vasco en Iparralde* (Bilbao: Sabino Arana Kultur Elkargoa, 1994), 171.

25. Xipri Arbelbide, *Piarres Lafitte: Bere Bizia* (Donostia: Elkar, 1986), 70–71.

26. *Poisson rouge* (literally "red fish'" means "goldfish," but here it is a wordplay insinuating "Red" or "Communist." James Jacob, *Hills of Conflict*, 63, 420 n. 3. See also Larronde, *Mouvement Eskualerriste (1932-1937)*, 227, and Arbelbide, *Enbata*, 49.

27. Lafitte edited *Herria* from its founding in 1944 to 1967, to be succeeded by Jean Hiriart-Urruty (1967–69), Emile Larre (1969–2003), and Janbattitt Dirassar (2003–present). Currently, it has a circulation of around 3,000.

28. Piarres [Pierre] Lafitte, *Kazetari lan-hautatuak*, ed. Pako Sudupe (Donostia: Elkar, 2002), 91–92.

29. Arbelbide, *Piarres Lafitte*, 82.

30. See the discussion of this in the Introduction of the present work.

31. Piarres Charritton, *De re publica edo politikaz* (Donostia: Elkar, 2003), 86–87.

32. See Arbelbide, *Enbata*, 79–80.

33. Quoted in ibid., 80.

34. Martzel Rekalde, quoted in ibid., 83.

35. William Safran, "The French State and Ethnic Minority Cultures: Policy Dimensions and Problems," in *Ethno-territorial Politics, Policy, and the Western World*, ed. Joseph R. Rudolph, Jr., and Robert J. Thompson (Boulder: L. Rienner Publishers, 1989), 120.

36. Quoted in Michel Oronos, *Le mouvement culturel basque 1951–2001* (Donostia: Elkar, 2002), 37.

37. Safran, "The French State and Ethnic Minority Cultures," 121; Oronos, *Le mouvement culturel basque 1951–2001*, 39–40.

38. Alan Sibé, *Nations dépendantes France métropolitaine* (Pau: J & D Editions, 1988), 108–10.

39. Jacob, *Hills of Conflict*, 131.

40. Ibid., 132.

41. Oronos, *Le mouvement culturel basque 1951–2001*, 45.

42. Mixel Itzaina, "Algeria, 'Eskual Herrian' Alger-en," in *Aljeriako gerla eta Euskal Herria (1954–1962): La guerre d'Algérie et le Pays Basque (1954–1962)*, ed. Xipri Arbelbide et al. (Donostia: Eusko Ikaskuntza, 2005), 60–65.

43. Xipri Arbelbide, "*Herria*n agertu artikuluak, Aljeriako soldadoen igorririk," in *Aljeriako gerla eta Euskal Herria (1954–1962)*, 34.

44. Quoted by Xipri Arbelbide, *Euskaldunak Aljerian, 1954–1962* (Donostia: Elkar, 2003), 51.

45. Arbelbide, "*Herria*n agertu artikuluak, Aljeriako soldadoen igorririk," 23.

46. Quoted by Philippe Mayte, "Eskualdun Gazteria face à la guerre d'Algérie," in *Aljeriako gerla eta Euskal Herria (1954–1962)*, 165.

47. Ibid., 166.

48. Ibid., 168.

49. Jean-Claude Larronde, "Une plainte contre *Herria* au temps de la guerre d'Algérie," in *Aljeriako gerla eta Euskal Herria (1954–1962)*, 99–100.

50. Pierre Lafitte "A nous lecteurs," *Herria* (June 27, 1957), quoted in Larronde, "Une plainte contre *Herria* au temps de la guerre d'Algérie," 101.

51. Jean Garat, "Editorial: Un scandale intolérable," *Côte Basque Soir*, June 12, 1957, quoted in Larronde, "Une plainte contre *Herria* au temps de la guerre d'Algérie," 102.

52. Lafitte "A nous lecteurs," Herria (June 27, 1957), quoted in Larronde, "Une plainte contre *Herria* au temps de la guerre d'Algérie," 103.

53. Jean Garat, "Le séparatisme basque," *Côte Basque Soir*, June 29-30, 1957, quoted in Larronde, "Une plainte contre *Herria* au temps de la guerre d'Algérie," 104.

54. Jean Garat, "Editorial," *Côte Basque Soir*, January 28, 1958, quoted by Larronde, "Une plainte contre *Herria* au temps de la guerre d'Algérie," 106.

55. For an examination of the positions of the different French political parties regarding the Algerian question at this time, see Txomin Peillen, "Algerian jakile," in *Aljeriako gerla eta Euskal Herria (1954–1962)*, 36–40.

56. Quoted by Isabelle de Ajuriaguerra, "Etienne Salaberry et la guerre d'Algérie," in *Aljeriako gerla eta Euskal Herria (1954–1962)*, 207–8, 217.

57. Ibid., 206.

58. Eguzki Urteaga, "La guerre d'Algérie et le militantisme étudiant basque," in *Aljeriako gerla eta Euskal Herria (1954–1962)*, 118.

59. Jakes Abeberry, quoted in ibid., 118.

60. Urteaga, "La guerre d'Algérie et le militantisme étudiant basque," in *Aljeriako gerla eta Euskal Herria (1954–1962)*, 119.

61. Ibid.

62. Robert Lafont, *La revolución regionalista* (Paris: Gallimard, 1967), 5.

63. Ibid., 119. The notion of internal colonialism had already been raised by René Pleven in his *L'avenir de la Bretagne* (Paris: Calmann-Lévy, 1961).

64. This was the argument used by Emilio Lopez Adan [Beltza, pseud.], "Ipar Euskal Herria: 150 urte historiarik gabe (1789–1934)," *Saioak* 2 (1978): 99–135. It also resurfaced in a reply to Lopez Adan's article by Piarres Charritton, "Historiarik gabeko Ipar Euskal Herria?" *Jakin* 9 (1979): 22–26. Similarly, this argument is also used by Manex Goyhenetche in *L'oppression culturelle française au Pays Basque* (Bayonne: Elkar, 1974) and *Histoire de la colonisation française au pays Basque: Les origines du problème basque* (Hendaye: Mugalde, 1975), as well as by Jean-Louis Davant, *Aberri eta klase burruka euskal mugimenduan* (Baiona: Elkar; Hendaye: Mugalde, 1977). Perhaps the most famous exponent of this notion with regard to the Basque case, however, is Jean Paul Sartre in his preface to Gisèle Halimi, *Le procès de Burgos* (Paris: Gallimard, 1971).

65. Fernando Sarrailh de Ihartza [Federico Krutwig, pseud.], *Vasconia: Estudio didáctico de una nacionalidad* (1962; Bayonne: Elkar: 1973) (page citations are to the 1973 edition).

66. The work criticizes the traditional Basque nationalism of the PNV and offers a Marxist perspective of Basque history. In the final part of the book, Krutwig calls for an armed insurrection through urban guerrilla warfare. Although created in 1959, ETA did not definitively decide on prioritizing an armed struggle until the mid-1960s, a decision that was strongly influenced by Krutwig's ideas.

67. Sarrailh de Ihartza, *Vasconia*, 186.

68. Ibid., 167.

69. Conseil du Développement du Pays Basque, *Lurraldea : 10 ans déjà, 10 ans après* (Bayonne: 2003).

70. Sarrailh de Ihartza, *Vasconia*, 166.

71. Ibid., 176.

72. Ibid., 303.

73. Ibid., 302.

74. Ibid., 293.

75. Jacob, *Hills of Conflict*, 132.

76. Ibid.

77. Arbelbide, *Enbata*, 92.

78. Michel Labéguerie, quoted by Larronde, "Michel Labéguerie: Son cheminement politique," 83.

Notes, Chapter Nine

1. See Jean Paul Malherbe, "Le nationalisme basque en France (1933–1976)," Ph.D. diss., University of Toulouse I, 1977, 35–42.

2. Jean Paul Malherbe, "Le nationalisme basque et les transformations sociopolitiques en Pays Basque Nord," in *La nouvelle société basque: Ruptures et changements*, ed. Pierre Bidart (Paris: L'Harmattan, 1980), 55.

3. Jean Marie Izquierdo, *Le Pays Basque de France: La difficile maturation d'un sentiment nationaliste basque* (Bordeaux: Mémoire, IEP, 1998; reprint, Paris: L'Harmattan, 2001), 123.

4. Particularly after the discovery of gas deposits in Lacq, near Pau, the provincial and departmental capital of Béarn. As a result, some figures in Iparralde began to seek new symbolic points of reference in Hegoalde, proposing a different model of economic development based on a cross-border axis between Lacq and Bilbao.

5. This was especially the case in Zuberoa. See Malherbe, "Le nationalisme basque et les transformations sociopolitiques en Pays Basque Nord," 62. The results of this activity would bear fruit two decades later with the creation of the ELB), a rural labor union and lobby.

6. Pierre Lafitte, *Kazetari lan-hautatuak*, ed. Pako Sudupe (Donostia: Elkar, 2002), 88–92.

7. Malherbe, "Le nationalisme basque en France (1933–1976)," 35–50.

8. James E Jacob, *Hills of Conflict: Basque Nationalism in France* (Reno: University of Nevada Press, 1994), ch. 4; Xipri Arbelbide, *Enbata: Abertzalegoaren historioa Iparraldean* (Donostia: Kutxa Fundazioa, 1996), 95; Mixel Itzaina, *Mixel Labéguerie: Kantu berritzaile eta politika gizona* (Donostia: Elkarlanean, 1999), 77 ; and Jean-Claude Larronde, "Michel Labéguerie: Son cheminement politique," in *Michel Labéguerie: Omenaldia-Hommage*, ed. Laurent Darraidou et al. (Donostia: Eusko Ikaskuntza, 2001), 83.

9. See Jacob, *Hills of Conflict*, 137.

10. Ibid.

11. Ibid., 138.

12. Jakes Abeberry, interview by Bixente Vrignon, *Les années oubliées: Jalons pour une histoire du mouvement abertzale au pays Basque Nord, 1968–1978* (Baiona: Gatuzain, 1999), 23.

13. The death of the Basque president in exile, Aguirre, in Iparralde in 1960, marked an important symbolic moment for the gestation of nationalism in Iparralde. Around five thousand people attended his funeral, and his death seemed to mark a critical juncture for many individuals in Iparralde in their own shift toward more avowedly Basque nationalist positions. This was the case for Haran. See Malherbe, "Le nationalisme basque en France (1933–1976)," 54.

14. *Embata* 1 (September 1960), 1, quoted in Jacob, *Hills of Conflict*, 134.

15. Arbelbide, *Enbata*, 99.

16. For example, in response to the "Caracas Manifesto" dating from this time–a Basque nationalist proposal for an independent Basque Country with Iruñea-Pamplona as its capital–Enbata stated that "in the present conditions, this proposal is impossible to carry out . . . its undertaking requires discipline, a heroic effort that Basques are not prepared for." *Enbata* (November 1961), quoted in Arbelbide, *Enbata*, 102.

17. On Mirande, see Gorka Aulestia, *The Basque Poetic Tradition*, trans. Linda White (Reno: University of Nevada Press, 2000), ch. 10, 152–71.

18. Jon Mirande, "Race, peuple et nation," *Enbata* 5 (July 1961).

19. Jean-Louis Davant and Jakes Abeberry in *Enbata* X (1961), quoted in Arbelbide, *Enbata*, 103.

20. "Because they knew a bar there, for no other reason." Arbelbide, *Enbata*, 109.

21. Itzaina, *Mixel Labéguerie*, 79.

22. Arbelbide, *Enbata*, 110.

23. About one thousand people attended. See Larronde, "Michel Labéguerie: Son cheminement politique," 88, and Vrignon, *Les années oubliées*, 26.

24. *Enbata* 16 (July 1962).

25. Jacob, *Hills of Conflict*, 143.

26. Ibid., 144.

27. Jakes Abeberry, quoted in ibid., 144.

28. Ibid., 144.

29. Jakes Abeberry, in *Mouvement Enbata*, "Pourquoi Enbata?" (1964), quoted in ibid., 141.

30. "In January 1963, in the Burucoa home, eight friends–among them, Labéguerie–put the finishing touches on the 'Itsasu Charter.' In the meeting, at Mixel [Labéguerie's] insistence, the demand for a *département* and an official status for Euskara was incorporated." Itzaina, *Mixel Labéguerie*, 81.

31. "Itsasuko ageria," *Enbata* (1963), in *Documentos Y*, vol. 2 (San Sebastián: Hordago, 1979), 449.

32. Ibid.

33. "Calls for self-determination and the creation of a Basque 'nationality' were not accompanied by calls for secession from France, even in appealing for the uniting of the Basques in a new Europe."Jacob, *Hills of Conflict*, 146.

34. Davant, *Histoire du peuple basque*, 132.

35. Ibid., 134.

36. On political parties in Iparralde during this era, see Jean-Claude Larronde, "Bosquejo de un cuadro social y electoral," in *Ser vasco*, ed. Jean Haritschelhar (Bilbao: Mensajero, 1986), 193–221.

37. Referenda were held on a new constitution (1958), a policy of self-determination for Algeria (1961), the Évian accords (1962) putting an end to the Algerian War, and the proposal to elect the French president according to universal suffrage (also in 1962).

38. Izquierdo, *Le Pays Basque de France*, 90.

39. See Malherbe, "Le nationalisme basque et les transformations sociopolitiques en Pays Basque Nord," 57.

40. Jacob, *Hills of Conflict*, 147. In fact, Jacob continues (148), Basques "had found in de Gaulle and his 'certain idea of France' a congenial defender of their traditional and conservatively clerical political culture. De Gaulle's choice between himself and Communist disorder was no choice at all in these mountain villages."

41. In fact, this was a very personal notion, for he had been one of the principal cultural activists of the 1950s and would ultimately become one of the founding members of Enbata.

42. Itzaina, *Mixel Labéguerie*, 31–96.

43. Larronde, "Michel Labéguerie: Son cheminement politique," 85.

44. Jacob, *Hills of Conflict*, 153.

45. Quoted in Larronde, "Michel Labéguerie: Son cheminement politique," 85.

46. The French elections are conducted as two-round or runoff voting. In this system, the voter casts a single vote for his or her favorite candidate. If no candidate receives an absolute majority of votes, then all candidates except the two with the most votes are eliminated, and a second round of voting occurs.

47. Itzaina, *Mixel Labéguerie*, 55.

48. Later, in 1967, it became the Union des Démocrates pour la République (UDR, the Union of Democrats for the Republic).

49. Larronde, "Michel Labéguerie: Son cheminement politique," 87.

50. Jacob, *Hills of Conflict*, 153.

51. Larronde, "Michel Labéguerie: Son cheminement politique," 89.

52. Ibid., 91.

53. Ibid., 92.

54. Arbelbide, *Enbata*, 167.

55. Larronde, "Michel Labéguerie: Son cheminement politique," 93.

56. Ibid., 102.

57. See Itzaina, *Mixel Labéguerie*, 139, and "Michel Labéguerie et M. l'Abbé Pierre Lafitte," in *Michel Labéguerie: Omenaldia-Hommage*, ed. Laurent Darraidou et al. (Donostia: Eusko Ikaskuntza, 2001), 43.

58. Landart, "Michel Labéguerie eta Eskualzaleen Biltzarra," in *Michel* Labéguerie, ed. Laurent Darraidou et al., 21–26.

59. Larronde, "Michel Labéguerie: Son cheminement politique," 102.

60. See, in this regard, Itzaina, *Mixel Labéguerie*.

61. Jean Haritschelhar, "Michel Labéguerie olerki abestua," in *Michel Labéguerie*, ed. Laurent Darraidou et al., 56.

62. "Gazteri berria" (New Youth), for example, highlights youth issues and the cultural rebirth of Iparralde; "Haurtxo haurtxoa" (Little Baby) is a message of hope from a mother to her son as she speaks of his father who has been imprisoned by Franco's police; "Nafarra, oi Nafarra" (Navarre, Oh Navarre) is an homage to the province that he considered the first of the Basque Country; and "Parisen eta Madrilen" (In Paris and in Madrid) is a song in favor of peaceful disobedience, written at a time when any protest against the state was met with particularly harsh measures.

63. Xabier Itzaina [Itçaina], "Michel Labéguerie eta dantza," in *Michel Labéguerie*, ed. Laurent Darraidou et al., 50.

64. These two formations–the CD and the UNR–were, respectively, replaced by the Union pour la Democratie Française (UDF, Union for French Democracy), founded in 1978, and the Rassemblement pour la République (RPR, Rally for the Republic), founded in 1976–the two principal parties representing the center-right of the French political spectrum until recent times.

65. Larronde, "Michel Labéguerie: Son cheminement politique," 98; Izquierdo, *Le Pays Basque de France*, 148–49.

66. Malherbe, "Le nationalisme basque en France (1933–1976)," 194.

67. Izquierdo, *Le Pays Basque de France*, 150.

68. Ibid.

69. However, in contrast to events in the 1960s, in the new millennium, those who profess the new pro-Basque sensibilities, but do not deny their French identity have, on occasion, aligned themselves with Basque nationalists in opposing French central authority. Such has been the case, for example, in demands for a specifically Basque chamber of agriculture and *département*, as well as official status for Euskara.

70. Larronde, "Michel Labéguerie: Son cheminement politique," 100; Arbelbide, *Enbata*, 128. For a detailed account of why Labéguerie did so badly, see Itzaina, *Mixel Labéguerie*. Itzaina stresses both his loss of support among nationalist voters and as the personal endorsement of de Gaulle for Inchauspé.

71. Larronde, "Michel Labéguerie: Son cheminement politique," 99.

72. By the indirect body of electors, rather than by the direct vote of the people.

73. Itzaina, *Mixel Labéguerie*, 71 and "Michel Labéguerie et M. l'Abbé Pierre Lafitte," 39–44.

74. Lafitte, though, did openly support the MRP through to the 1960 elections. However, after the creation of Enbata, he never revealed his political sympathies. See Lafitte, *Kazetari lan-hautatuak*, 89–91.

75. Michel Labéguerie, *Deia* (1979), quoted in Arbelbide, *Enbata*, 131 and Itzaina, *Mixel Labéguerie*, 92–93.

76. Although prior to this, the PNB did not take part in elections, it did publish a journal, *Ager*.

77. Legasse's prophecy, it seemed, was coming true, with one Enbata militant writing that "we are at the center of discussions by all Basques. There isn't a day that goes by in the villages where there aren't questions about Enbata, whether favorable or hostile." Patxi Noblia, "Rapport de la section Enbata de Bordeaux sur la nouvelle orientation nécessaire au mouvement: Rapport pour le 1965 congrès de Enbata" (ca. 1965), quoted in Arbelbide, *Enbata*, 115 and Jacob, *Hills of Conflict*, 156.

78. Quoted by Arbelbide, *Enbata*, 141.

79. Ibid., 220.

80. Jacob, *Hills of Conflict*, 137.

81. A *circonscription* is an electoral district or constituency.

82. See Arbelbide, *Enbata*, 223–25.

83. As Louis de Fourcaud, the French minister of public instruction and fine arts, had done in 1897. In similar fashion, nearly forty years later, in 2004, Dominique de Villepin, the French interior minister, also made a much publicized visit (by helicopter too) to Iparralde.

84. See the note on two-round voting above.

85. Arbelbide, *Enbata*, 212, Malherbe, "Le nationalisme basque en France (1933–1976)," 122, and Jacob, *Hills of Conflict*, 157, concur in suggesting that, in fact, the results obtained by Etxalus might be viewed more positively. In other words, they suggest, her alleged links with ETA actually served to attract a number of young voters to Enbata who might otherwise have been suspicious of a nationalist movement because of the traditional support for pro-Basque positions by bourgeois and conservative sectors.

86. Christiane Etxalus, interview by Vrignon, *Les années oubliées*, 34.

87. See Arbelbide, *Enbata*, 255–62.

88. This generational conflict would bring another young activist to the fore: Andde Galant. See Vrignon, *Les années oubliées*, 37.

89. Arbelbide, *Enbata*, 254.

90. Jakes Abeberry, interview by Vrignon, *Les années oubliées*, 29.

91. Ibid., 29–30.

92. Arbelbide, *Enbata*, 241.

93. Ibid., 136. Based in Venezuela, Paco Miangolarra was the son of a captain in the Spanish Navy who made a fortune through establishing the largest publishing house in Latin America. He often traveled to the Basque Country, and he bankrolled the publication of Krutwig's *Vasconia*.

94. Ibid., 165.

95. Quoted in ibid., 228.

96. Ibid., 231.

97. Ibid., 233.

98. Quoted in ibid., 185. These accusations were, of course, completely false.

99. Ibid., 183.

100. A form of extortion used by ETA to raise funds.

101. In fact, ETA did not carry out its first planned assassination, that of the police chief of Irun (Gipuzkoa), Melitón Manzanas, until 1968.

102. Arbelbide, *Enbata*, 199. Arbelbide later recalled that, in fact, there were 700 cancellations of subscriptions, because the publication had actually gained 350 readers in the preceding period. See ibid., 199. This is confirmed by Vrignon, who states that *Enbata* had also gained readers during same period. See *Les années oubliées*, 28.

103. Arbelbide, *Enbata*, 211–12.

104. Ibid., 212.

105. Quoted in ibid., 260.

106. Jakes Abeberry, interview by Vrignon, *Les années oubliées*, 30–31.

107. Arbelbide, *Enbata*, 265.

108. "Une autre politique?" *Enbata* 84 (October 9, 1968), quoted in Vrignon, *Les années oubliées*, 41.

109. These differences led to the emergence of separate groups within ETA itself: first ETA-V and ETA-VI and later ETA (m) and ETA (pm). In 1974, the dominant group within ETA suggested allowing its two branches—one dedicated strictly to political and social issues (i.e., not to the use of arms), and the other, a military wing—to operate autonomously at the local level, but with ultimate coordinating power residing with the then dominant "political" faction, that is ETA (pm). The minority "military" faction, ETA (m), however, rejected this proposal, instead suggesting a complete separation between two branches. From that moment on, ETA (m) pursued a violent path based on the notion of revolutionary struggle, while ETA (pm), seeing its own internal organizational deficiencies, decided (after the organization's seventh assembly in 1977) to reconstitute itself as a political party, all of this, of course, within the context of Spain slowly becoming a democracy after Franco's death in 1975. From this moment on, the two branches split away from one another completely. ETA (pm) always kept any "military" tendencies subordinate to a "political" leadership, resulting in their complete suspension in 1981 and the transformation of the faction into a political party: Euskadiko Ezkerra (EE, Basque Left), a party that a decade later integrated into the Partido Socialista de Euskadi (PSE, the Socialist Party of the Basque Country) and an affiliate of the PSOE (Partido Socialista Obrero de España, the Spanish Socialist Party). ETA (m), however, reversed this process, with the "military" faction controlling and organizing its "political" subordinate, a host of different political and social groups. For a detailed analysis of these differences, see Francisco Letamendia, *Historia del nacionalismo vasco y de ETA*. 3 vols (San Sebastián: R & B Ediciones, 1994). In English, see Robert P. Clark, *The Basque Insurgents: ETA, 1952–1980* (Madison: University of Wisconsin Press, 1984), esp. chs. 2 and 3.

110. Christiane Etxalus, interview by Vrignon, *Les années oubliées*, 37.

111. Davant, *Histoire du peuple basque*, 134.

112. See Jacob, *Hills of Conflict*, 170–79.

113. Ximun Haran, "Enbata-ETA-réfugiés," *Ager* 103 (January 1, 1988), 4–5, quoted in ibid., 172.

114. *Enbata* 93 (December 11, 1968), quoted in Vrignon, *Les années oubliées*, 45.

115. *Enbata*, 198 (February 11, 1971), quoted in ibid., 47.

116. Davant, *Histoire du peuple basque*, 134.

117. *Enbata* (April 1971), quoted in Vrignon, *Les années oubliées*, 103.

118. Quoted in Vrignon, *Les années oubliées*, 111.

119. Quoted in ibid., 125.

120. Quoted in ibid., 126.

121. Ibid., 58.

122. Ironically, this same strategy was embraced by the Izan collective, a successor group after Enbata was made illegal by the French authorities that tried to become a kind of lobby pressing for the socialization of Iparralde from a Basque nationalist perspective.

123. Mattin Larzabal, interview by Vrignon, *Les années oubliées*, 61.

124. See Jacob, *Hills of Conflict*, 165.

125. Mattin Larzabal, interview by Vrignon, *Les années oubliées*, 60.

126. Jacob, *Hills of Conflict*, 165; Vrignon, *Les années oubliées*, 62.

127. Enbata, internal document, quoted by Vrignon, *Les années oubliées*, 63.

128. Jacob, *Hills of Conflict*, 165–66.

129. *Pindar* 1 (December 1976), quoted in Vrignon, *Les années oubliées*, 83.

130. Alfabetatze eta Euskalduntze Koordinakundea (Coordination of Education and Literacy in Euskara), an adult literacy group specializing in teaching Euskara to adults, most typically through the medium of evening classes.

131. Arnaud Duny Pétré, interview by Vrignon, *Les années oubliées*, 87, 88.

132. In the words of one of the organization's reports: "Mende Berri, since its founding, has always been concerned about . . . informing young people about the current Basque situation. Students, high-school kids, vocational-school students, were barely able to know the history of their civilization. To alleviate this serious educational deficit, Mende Berri . . . created the Clubes Pays Basque in which its members can be assured of receiving a minimum degree of information." "Mende Berri dans les collèges et les lycées," *Mende Berri-Ikasle* 1 (September 13, 1973), 7, quoted in ibid., 84.

133. In general embracing an anticapitalist outlook and the original theories of Krutwig (adopted in full by Enbata from 1971 on) that the economic underdevelopment of Iparralde was due to its colonial status.

134. Jacob, *Hills of Conflict*, 166.

135. Jakes Bortairu, interview by Vrignon, *Les années oubliées*, 85–87.

136. For example, Ezker Berri termed itself the Biltzar Ttipia (Small Assembly) in clear reference to the various "assemblies" that defined the various incarnations of ETA. See ibid., 189.

137. See Jacob, *Hills of Conflict*, 169–70.

138. On this transformation, see Pedro Ibarra, *Manual de sociedad civil y movimientos sociales* (Madrid: Síntesis, 2005).

139. Arnaud Duny Pétré, interview by Vrignon, *Les années oubliées*, 190.

140. Jacob, *Hills of Conflict*, 165.

141. As of 2008, Jean Lissar was a *conseiller régional* for the Aquitaine region, representing the Greens.

142. Jean Lissar, interview by Vrignon, *Les années oubliées*, 75.

143. Quoted in ibid., 182–83.

144. *Enbata* 186 (November 10, 1979), quoted in ibid., 69–70.

145. Trotskyists, for example, organized around the Ligue Communiste Révolutionnaire (Revolutionary Communist League), a group that, together with the Parti Socialiste Unifié (PSU, Unified Socialist Party)—a splinter of the French Socialist Party—enjoyed increasingly close relations with the ETA-VI faction. Elsewhere, Maoists were involved in the Secours Rouge (Red Aid) group and especially the Marxist-Leninist French Communist Party, an illegal party after May 1968 that had to operate clandestinely. Meanwhile, in the more conservative rural interior of Iparralde, leftist activism was linked to Mouvement Rural de Jeunesse Chrétienne (the Young Christians' Rural Movement), a group that served as a framework through which numerous activists emerged.

146. Ibid., 79–80.

147. Ibid., 80.

148. Davant, *Histoire du peuple basque*, 140.

149. Vrignon, *Les années oubliées*, 41.

150. Jakes Bortairu, interview by Vrignon, ibid., 96.

151. Arbelbide, *Enbata*, 267.

Notes, Chapter Ten

1. This was ETA's most high-profile victim. After a radical turn in its strategy during the 1990s, ETA also assassinated one of the commanders in chief of the Spanish armed forces, General Francisco Veguillas, and carried out attempts on the lives of the Spanish prime minister, José María Aznar and King Juan Carlos I.

2. James E. Jacob, *Hills of Conflict: Basque Nationalism in France* (Reno: University of Nevada Press, 1994), 182.

3. See Jean-Louis Davant, *Histoire du peuple basque*, 8th ed. (Donostia: Elkarlanean, 2000), 141–47; Jacob, *Hills of Conflict*, 182.

4. *Enbata* 97 (January 8, 1969), quoted in Bixente Vrignon, *Les années oubliées: Jalons pour une histoire du mouvement abertzale au pays Basque Nord, 1968–1978* (Baiona: Gatuzain, 1999), 43. Melitón Manzanas, the police chief of Irun (Gipuzkoa), was the first specifically targeted victim of ETA, and was assassinated by ETA on August 2, 1968. According to Robert P. Clark, "Manzanas had acquired a reputation as a brutal and sadistic prison official who (it was alleged) especially enjoyed beating and torturing Basque nationalists. He had in all probability been marked for assassination for some time." See *The Basque Insurgents: ETA, 1952–1980* (Madison: The University of Wisconsin Press, 1984), 49. Jacob observes that this was an "event widely understood by ETA and the Spanish government alike as representing an intensification of the Basque struggle with Spain." *Hills of Conflict*, 162.

5. *Euskaldunak* 1 (April 1974), quoted in Vrignon, *Les années oubliées*, 143–44.

6. Some of the HAS/EHAS leadership rejected Leninism, preferring instead to classify the group as Marxist and revolutionary.

7. Jacob, *Hills of Conflict*, 222.

8. "Mohines de lutte révolutionnaire," ch. 3 in "Déclaration sur la lutte contre le colonialisme en Europe," ms. No. B-9005, Musée Basque, Bayonne (ca. 1976), quoted in ibid., 222.

9. EZ (an acronym also meaning "no" in Euskara) claimed responsibility for eleven acts of sabotage between 1977 and 1979. Hordago! represented a greater challenge to IK, and was attributed with fifteen acts of sabotage between 1978 and 1981. See Jacob, *Hills of Conflict*, 249–52.

10. See Sidney G. Tarrow, *Power in Movement: Social Movements, Collective Action and Politics* (Cambridge: Cambridge University Press, 1994), 63–65, and by the same author, "States and Opportunities: The Political Structuring of Social Movements," in *Comparative Perspectives on Social Movements: Political Opportunities, Mobilizing Structures, and Cultural Framings*, ed. Doug McAdam, John D. McCarthy, and Mayer N. Zald (Cambridge: Cambridge University Press, 1996), 75. See also Hanspeter Kriesi, "El contexto político de los nuevos movimientos sociales en Europa," in *Las transformaciones en lo político*, ed. Jorge Benedicto and Fernando Reinares (Madrid: Alianza, 1992), 115–57, and Donatella della Porta, "Social Movements and the State: Thoughts on the Policing of Protest," in *Comparative Perspectives on Social Movements*, ed. McAdam, McCarthy, and Zald, 62–92.

11. As well as more recent rumors speculating about another violent turn in Iparralde as the result of the French state's unwillingness to negotiate certain minimum nationalist demands, such as the creation of a specifically Basque *département*. See Jean-Noël Etcheverry, "Les partis politiques: Abertzaleen Batasuna," in *Pays Basque: Un département? 100 réponses*, ed. Claude Perrotin (Anglet: Atlantica, 2002), 288.

12. Francisco Letamendia, *Game of Mirrors: Centre-Periphery National Conflicts*, trans. Karen Hatherley (Aldershot, UK: Ashgate, 2000), 55.

13. See Jacob, *Hills of Conflict*, 227–29.

14. Jacob, *Hills of Conflict*, 227–28. See also Xipri Arbelbide, *Enbata: Abertzalegoaren historioa Iparraldean* (Donostia: Kutxa Fundazioa, 1996), 237.

15. Jakes Bortairu, interview by Vrignon, *Les années oubliées*, 226.

16. Letamendia, *Game of Mirrors*, 282–85. According to some former IK members, "the urge that young people felt to get involved in social struggles, together with the defense of the refugees and the creation of movements dedicated to challenging tourist-related projects and [property] speculation, encouraged the growth of armed activity." *Egin*, April 13, 1993.

17. Vrignon, *Les années oubliées*, 131; Jacob, *Hills of Conflict*, 231. However, when the group first emerged, both *Enbata* and *Le Monde* translated the name as "those from the North" (a term that would be more accurately recorded in Basque as "ipartarrak"), most likely as a means of distinguishing the new organization from ETA for their readers.

18. Christiane Etxalus, interview by Vrignon, *Les années oubliées*, 128.

19. Andde Galant, interview by Vrignon, *Les années oubliées*, 130. Indeed, if true, this might also explain the previously mentioned role played by Etxalus.

20. Vrignon, *Les années oubliées*, 234–35.

21. "Appel au peuple basque," *Ildo* 6 (March 1981), 26, quoted in Jacob, *Hills of Conflict*, 272.

22. For example, the rupture between ETA and IK would be mirrored by the split between Euskal Batasuna (which acknowledged the legitimacy of ETA violence, but not that of IK) and EMA (which supported the armed struggle in Iparralde).

23. *Ildo* 1 (1974), 3, quoted in Vrignon, *Les années oubliées*, 132.

24. *Ildo* 1 (1974), 4, quoted in ibid.

25. *Ildo* 1 (1974), 4–5, quoted in ibid., 134.

26. In fact, a Basque agricultural labor union was created in 1982: Euskal Laborarien Batasuna (ELB).

27. *Ildo* 2, "Appel au peuple basque, coordonner les groupes de lutte" (Summer 1978), quoted in Vrignon, *Les années oubliées*, 243.

28. Here, I follow the reflections of Eneko Bidegain, "Iparretarrak: Erakunde baten historioa," unpublished ms. (2006).

29. "La participation de H.A.S. au 1er mai," *Euskaldunak* 14 (May 1975), 2, quoted in Jacob, *Hills of Conflict*, 190.

30. Jacob, *Hills of Conflict*, 190–91, Vrignon, *Les années oubliées*, 147.

31. ETA began to use violence in 1968, but its incapacity—and unwillingness—to be involved directly in politics following the Spanish transition to democracy (1975–78), together with the possibilities afforded by such a strategy, led to the emergence of Herri Batasuna (HB, Popular Unity) in 1978. This party, which later changed its name to Euskal Herritarrok (EH, Basque Compatriots) and then Batasuna (Unity), was tied to other social and political groups (for example, organized around the promotion of the Basque language or against the repressive measures of the state) in a wider collective: the Movimiento de Liberación Nacional Vasco (MLNV, the Basque National Liberation Movement), also known as the Izquierda Abertzale or Left-Wing Basque Nationalism. The MLNV in turn created an pyramidlike organizational structure at the top of which remained a reduced number of activists, while the base was formed by these multiple groups and collectives—the Koordinadora Abertzale Sozialista, KAS, the Socialist Nationalist Coordinating Council. As I have already noted and will later expand on, ETA was established as an antistate organization with a concomitant antisystem legitimizing community, which meant that from the outset, a symbolic hierarchy was created that explains the historical incapacity of HB/EH/Batasuna to distance itself from the armed group.

32. For a detailed examination of EAS and EHAS in Hegoalde, see Natxo Arregi, *Memorias de KAS (1975–1978)* (Donostia: Hordago, 1981).

33. Davant, *Histoire du peuple basque*, 149.

34. Euskal Herriko Alderdi Sozialista, "MANIFESTE," 1, quoted in Jacob, *Hills of Conflict*, 194.

35. Jacob, *Hills of Conflict*, 194–95.

36. *Euskaldunak* 37 (May 1977), 3, quoted in ibid., 196.

37. The nucleus of the group that would eventually become Herri Batasuna and play a key role at the center of KAS while at the same time limiting its sphere of activity to Hegoalde. See Francisco Letamendia, *Historia del nacionalismo vasco y de ETA*, 3 vols., vol. 2, *ETA en la Transición (1976–1982)* (San Sebastián: R & B Ediciones, 1994), 65.

38. "Pour la création d'un grand mouvement socialiste basque," *Euskaldunak* 5 (August 1974), quoted in Vrignon, *Les années oubliées*, 147–48.

39. HA was created as a platform for people who felt isolated by the ideological debates between EMA and EB. It was an unstructured antiauthoritarian and antiestablishment movement rejecting much of the dynamics of electoral strategies and party politics and favoring more popular action. HA included in its ranks former members of groups such as Jazar, Amaia, and Mende Berri.

40. As Vrignon remarks, "the arguments ran into personal bitterness and the question of whether it was a question of an exclusively socialist unification process, or of all Basque nationalist groups." *Les années oubliées*, 201.

41. For example, Ezker Berri alleged that EHAS's "entire tactics were based on trying to gain a hegemony over the leftist nationalist movement and the entire spectrum of Basque nationalism in the North. It was the politics of fait accompli as a product of the relationship of forces at the time." Quoted in ibid., 199.

42. Jacob, *Hills of Conflict*, 216.

43. Vrignon, *Les années oubliées*, 202.

44. "Explication de notre position," *Euskaldunak* 2 (May 1974), quoted in ibid., 145.

45. Jacob, *Hills of Conflict*, 203.

46. Indeed, some members of HAS even ended up joining these parties. Vrignon, *Les années oubliées*, 144.

47. Interestingly, in Arhantsusi (Arhansus), Nafarroa Beherea , 97 percent of the electorate (the highest percentage of any district in France) voted for the eventual winner of the French presidential contest, Giscard d'Estaing.

48. Jacob, *Hills of Conflict*, 205.

49. Ibid., 208–9.

50. Ibid., 219–20.

51. Ibid., 223.

52. *Euskaldunak* 81 (May 1981), 2, quoted in ibid., 225–26.

53. Vrignon, *Les années oubliées*, 210.

54. "Entretien avec le comité de soutien," *Enbata* 514 (June 29, 1978), quoted in ibid., 215

55. The first of these were formed in Biarritz, Hiriburu (Saint-Pierre-d'Irube), Donibane Lohizune, Baigorri, Donapaleu, Garazi, and jointly in Ezpeleta-Itsasu-Kanbo. Jacob, *Hills of Conflict*, 240.

56. "Historique de Herri Taldeak," in *Ipar Euskadi Gaur* (ca. 1985), 73, quoted in ibid., 241.

57. "Historique de Herri Taldeak," in *Ipar Euskadi Gaur* (ca. 1985), 74, quoted in ibid., 241.

58. "Herri Taldeak: Première démarche publique," *Enbata* 703 (February 4, 1982), 6, quoted in ibid., 242–43.

59. "Herri Taldeak et la lutté armée," in *Ipar Euskadi Gaur* (1985), 70, quoted in ibid., 243.

60. Letamendia, *Game of Mirrors*, 330–31; Jacob, *Hills of Conflict*, 293–315; Patrick Cassan, *Francia y la cuestión vasca* (Tafalla: Txalaparta, 1998), 221–22; Sagrario Morán Blanco, *ETA Entre España y Francia* (Madrid: Complutense, 1997), 253–63.

61. I use the term "safe haven" cautiously, because ETA refugees had always been subject to strict controls by the French authorities, whose measures included detention and arrest, designation of living areas, expulsion, extradition, and so on. Having said that, most ETA refugees had settled in Iparralde.

62. Iparretarrak, *Ildo* 5, quoted in Cassan, *Francia y la cuestión vasca*, 96.

63. Cassan, *Francia y la cuestión vasca*, 96. Indeed, from this moment on, the French police began to take IK very seriously, instead of just concentrating their efforts on ETA refugees.

64. Bidegain, "Iparretarrak: Erakunde baten historioa."

65. Cassan, *Francia y la cuestión vasca*, 98. The murders were indeed claimed by one such clandestine right-wing group from Spain, the Batallón Vasco-Español (the Spanish Basque Battalion, BVE).

66. See Jacob, *Hills of Conflict*, 256–59.

67. The two men were kidnapped on French soil in June 1983, transported to Spain secretly, and tortured until their deaths there. Their bodies were found twenty years later as part of the ongoing process investigating Spanish government links with the GAL.

68. Cassan, *Francia y la cuestión vasca*, 102.

69. As Bidegain notes, IK undertook another spectacular act during the same time: the kidnapping of the then minister of education and later president of the UMP (Union pour un Mouvement Populaire; Union for a Popular Movement), as well as defense minister, Michèle Alliot-Marie. Bidegain, "Iparretarrak: Erakunde baten historioa."

70. Ibid.

71. On this experience, see Filipe Bidart, *Bakartasunez, bi hitz* (Tafalla: Txalaparta, 2005). Bidart was finally released, although under strict supervision and with an order preventing him from returning to Iparralde for a period of seven years, in February 2007.

72. Bidegain, "Iparretarrak: Erakunde baten historioa."

73. This is how several former members of IK describe the situation: that a renewed movement in favor of such institutional recognition, its support by IK, and favorable voices emanating from Paris would have been strengthened by a ceasefire. However, its leadership vacillated, and a degree of momentum was lost. The potential offer from Paris was never forthcoming. Ibid.

74. Interviewed in February 2006, Bidart spoke of IK in the past tense, and his evaluation of its strategy stopped in 1998. See Jose Mari Pastor, "Parisera beha egon gabe guhaurrek geure egiturak muntatzen hasi behar dugu," *Berria*, February 1, 2006, http://www.berria.info/testua_ikusi.php?saila=euskalherria&data=2006-02-01&orria=008&kont=011

75. IK, *20 ans de lutte: Autonomie et avant projet* (March 31, 1993).

76. *Egunkaria*, April 14, 1993.

77. "Autonomia aurre proiektuaz," *Herria Eginez* 7 (November 1993).

78. "Herri baten eskubidea," *Herria Eginez* 16 (September 1995), 12.

79. *Egin*, September 25, 1995. These were the declarations of an EMA spokesperson during the Iparralde Eguna (Iparralde Day), a mobilization replete with Basque national symbols where one banner read, "Iparretarrak, zurekin herria xuti"– "Iparretarrak, the people stand with you."

80. "Etorkizunerako hautabideak," *Herria Eginez* 42 (January 1997), 22–28.

81. Jean-François Moruzzi and Emmanuel Boulaert, *Iparretarrak: Séparatisme et terrorisme au Pays Basque* (Paris: Plon, 1988), 53, quoted in Cassan, *Francia y la cuestión vasca*, 97.

82. HASI, *HASIko Aparteko Kongresuari irtetzen den Komite Zentralan Informea. Informe del Comité Central Saliente al Congreso Extraordinario de HASI* (December 1988), 36.

83. On the notion of a principal front, see Igor Ahedo Gurrutxaga, *Presente y pasado del nacionalismo en Iparralde* (Bilbao: Manu Robles-Arangiz Institutoa, 2004), 27–28; on the notion of a single front, see Moruzzi and Boulaert, *Iparretarrak: Séparatisme et terrorisme au Pays Basque*, 53–81; Jacob, *Hills of Conflict*, 272–76.

84. IK, "Communiqué du 4 octubre 1981," *Enbata* 685 (October 8, 1981), 8, quoted in Iñaki Egaña, *Diccionario histórico-político de Euskal Herria* (Tafalla: Txalaparta, 1996), 439, and Jacob, *Hills of Conflict*, 274.

85. See Jacob, *Hills of Conflict*, 272–73.

86. Ibid., 272.

87. "Batasuna Borrokan," *Ildo* 9 (April 1984), 2, quoted in ibid.

88. Ibid.

89. "For ETA, the primary terrain of combat remained in Spain, and IK's fledgling violence threatened to disturb ETA's crucial northern sanctuary." Jacob, *Hills of Conflict*, 274.

90. Ibid., 283.

91. Ibid., 339.

92. Richard Irazusta, quoted in ibid., 341.

93. Jacob, *Hills of Conflict*, 341.

94. Ibid.

95. Ibid., 345.

96. Ibid., 348. In an interview with *Berria*, September 14, 2005, Jakes Abeberry, another founding member of EB, recalled that ETA refugees also played a leading role in lobbying to create this new party as a means of challenging IK.

97. Jacob, *Hills of Conflict*, 349.

98. Euskal Batasuna, "Foundational Manifesto" (1986).

99. *Egin*, July 12, 1986.

100. Izquierdo, *Le Pays Basque de France*, 158–66.

101. Ibid., 174–77.

102. Ibid., 167–70.

103. Jacob, *Hills of Conflict*, 359.

Notes, Chapter Eleven

1. On this, see Jean-Baptiste Coyos, *Politique linguistique* (Baiona: Elkar, 2005).

2. Jakes Abeberry, interview by Vrignon, *Les années oubliées: Jalons pour une histoire du mouvement abertzale au pays Basque Nord, 1968–1978* (Baiona: Gatuzain, 1999), 149–50. For more on the themes discussed in this section, see several works by Jean Daniel Chaussier: "L'échec du projet de création d'un département en Pays Basque," *Le Bulletin du Musée Basque* 120 (1988): 57–72; "La Mission Ravail au Pays Basque (1982): Pouvoir du discours identitaire ou discours du pouvoir sur l'identité?," *Le Bulletin du Musée Basque* 138 (1994): 113–44; *Quel territoire pour le Pays Basque?: Les cartes de l'identité* (Paris: L'Harmattan, 1997); "La question territoriale en Pays Basque de France (exception irréductible ou laboratoire du pluralisme?)," in *La construcción del espacio vasco-aquitano*, ed. Antón Borja, Francisco Letamendia, and Kepa Sodupe (Leioa: Servicio Editorial de la Universidad del País Vasco, 1998), 257–74; and "Pays Basque, un département? Une revendication citoyenne dans un cadre républicain," in *Pays Basque: Un département? 100 réponses*, ed. Claude Perrotin (Anglet: Atlantica,

2002), 11–62. See also Igor Ahedo, "Redes de políticas públicas de desarrollo e institucionalización y movimiento social pro-departamento Pays Basque en los territorios vascos de Aquitania." Ph.D. diss., University of the Basque Country (2002) and *Entre la frustración y la esperanza: Políticas de desarrollo e institucionalización* (Oñati: IVAP, 2003); Eguzki Urteaga and Igor Ahedo, *Le nouvelle gouvernance en Pays Basque* (Paris: L'Harmattan, 2004); and Igor Ahedo and Eguzki Urteaga, *Gobernanza y territorio en Iparralde* (Vitoria-Gasteiz: Servicio Central de Publicaciones del Gobierno Vasco, 2005).

3. Chaussier, *Quel territoire pour le Pays Basque?* 23.

4. Ibid., 112–42.

5. In the 2005 consultation, an absolute majority of mayors supported calls for a separate *département*.

6. Chaussier, *Quel territoire pour le Pays Basque?* 163–65.

7. Jakes Abeberry, interview by Vrignon, *Les années oubliées*, 150.

8. The proposal was seconded by, among others, prominent Socialists such as François Mitterand, Jean-Pierre Chevènement, Henri Emmanuelli, Michel Rocard, and Laurent Fabius.

9. Parti Socialiste, *Proposition du Loi n° 2224 portant création d'un département de Pays Basque* (December 1980).

10. Proposition no. 54, for example, promised that, "state decentralization will be a priority. Regional representatives will be elected by direct universal suffrage and the executive led by its president and bureau. Corsica will receive a special statute. A *département* of the Basque Country will be created. The function of the prefects' authority over local administration will be abolished." And proposition no. 56 stated that "the promotion of regional identities will be encouraged, minority languages and cultures respected." See François Mitterand, "110 propositions pour la France" (1981).

11. Chaussier, *Quel territoire pour le Pays Basque?* 96–113, and "La question territoriale en Pays Basque de France (exception irréductible ou laboratoire du pluralisme?)," in *La construcción del espacio vasco-aquitano*, ed. Borja, Letamendia and Sodupe, 257–74.

12. James E. Jacob, *Hills of Conflict: Basque Nationalism in France* (Reno: University of Nevada Press, 1994), 336.

13. On January 9, 1982, the main headline of the newspaper *Sud-Ouest* was "No to the Basque *Département*," in reference to an interview with Gaston Defferre of the PS (the minister of the interior and decentralization in the then Socialist government) in which he questioned the validity of the proposal.

14. Chaussier, *Quel territoire pour le Pays Basque?* 105–8.

15. Jacob, *Hills of Conflict*, 385, 395. As we have seen, for example, Iparretarrak reactivated its armed struggle from the mid-1980s on.

16. Jakes Abeberry, interview by Vrignon, *Les années oubliées*, 149.

17. Xabier Itçaina, "L'Identité au travail: Economie social et solidaire et mouvement identitaire en pays Basque," paper presented at the First European Conference of the International Society for Third-Sector Research (ISTR) and the EMES European Research Network, April 27–29, 2005, Conservatoire National des Arts et Métiers (CNAM), Paris.

18. Ibid.

19. Ibid.

20. As we will see, the 1990s witnessed a structural change in France whereby a binary relationship between civil and elected bodies was established to aid local development. A representative institution of civil society–the Conseil de Développement du Pays Basque (CDPB, the Council for the Development of the Basque Country)–was created to foment ideas that would then be presented to the elected officials represented by the Conseil des Élus du Pays Basque (CEPB).

21. Ahedo, *Entre la frustración y la esperanza*, 84–85; Urteaga and Ahedo, *La nouvelle gouvernance en Pays Basque*, 106

22. Itçaina, "L'Identité au travail: Economie social et solidaire et mouvement identitaire en pays Basque."

23. Ahedo, *Entre la frustración y la esperanza*, 85.

24. Martine Sistiague, *E.L.B.: Ipar Euskal Herriko laborarien oihartzuna* (Baiona: Gatuzain, 2000), 41–49 and 63–72.

25. Ibid., 74.

26. Every *département* and every region in France has an agricultural chamber. The former serve as a source of information and aid for rural workers in their *département*. The latter serve to coordinate planning and stimulate growth, liaising with their respective departmental chambers, within the agricultural sector of the corresponding region. The ELB, then, lobbied for a distinct agricultural chamber to that of the *département* as a whole.

27. Sistiague, *E.L.B.*, 109.

28. Jean Haritschelhar, ed., *Ser vasco* (Bilbao: Mensajero, 1986), 276–77.

29. Some authors distinguish between pastorals based on sacred, hagiographic, and historical themes. See, for example, Beñat Oihartzabal [Oyharçabal], *Zuberoako herri teatroa* (Donostia: Kriselu, 1985). Others differentiate between religious, secular (covering subjects such as ancient Greece and Rome), romantic, and historical pastorals. See, for example, María Arene Garamendi Azcorra, *El teatro popular vasco semiótica de la representación* (Donostia: Diputación Foral de Gipuzkoa, 1991).

30. See Jon Kortazar, *Euskal literaturaren historia txikia* (Zarautz: Erein, 1997). The stage is divided into two worlds: the right-hand side is for the Christians, with a door over which is draped either the flag of Zuberoa or an *ikurriña*, the Basque flag, and the left-hand side for the "Turks," with another door over which is placed a doll symbolizing a pagan idol. Similarly, the costumes also represent the basic divisions of the characters: White is the principal color of heaven, blue is for the Christians, and red is for the Turks and devils. The same differences are also represented by the movements and dances of the characters: the representatives of good parade with order and dignity, while the evil ones roam wildly about the stage making lots of noise, a scene replicated in the music, too.

31. See Garamendi Azcorra, *El teatro popular vasco semiótica de la representación*, 189–90.

32. Ibid., 46–90.

33. Some observers believe these performances are related to marriage rites or the celebration of the coming of a new year. See, for example, the interpretation of the ethnologist Jean-Dominique Lajoux in *Le Semaine du Pays Basque*, February 3, 1994.

34. François Fourquet, "La Mascarade d'Ordiarp," *Bulletin du Musée Basque* 129 (1990): 101–56; Kepa Fernández de Larrinoa, *Nekazal gizartea eta antzerki herrikoia Pirinioetako haran batean*, Cuadernos de sección, Antropología y Etnografía 9 (Donostia: Eusko Ikaskuntza-Sociedad de Estudios Vascos, 1993). For an English-language account of the *maskarada*, see Kepa Fernández de Larrinoa, "The Folk Arts of the *Maskarada* Performance," in *Voicing the Moment: Improvised Oral Poetry and Basque Tradition*, ed. Samuel G. Armistead and Joseba Zulaika, Center for Basque Studies, Conference Papers Series 3 (Reno: Center for Basque Studies, University of Nevada, Reno, 2005), 209–30.

35. Fourquet, "La Mascarade d'Ordiarp," 155.

36. Patri Urkizu, *Historia del teatro vasco* (Donostia: Erein, 1996), 27.

37. Hélène Etchecopar Etchart, *Théâtres basques: Une histoire du théâtre populaire en marche* (Baiona: Gatuzain, 2001), 83.

38. Etchecopar Etchart, *Théâtres basques*, 74–75, Xabier Itzaina and Idoia Ikardo, "Folklore e identidad en el País Vasco: Pistas para una comparación transfronteriza," in *La construcción del espacio vasco-aquitano*, ed. Borja, Letamendia and Sodupe, 138–39.

39. As Jean Michel Guilcher observes, by contrast with other groups in which dance is used as a means of binding the community, in Iparralde, dance "is still a means of social cohesion, but it is so in another way. Its mission . . . consists of not only assimilating everyone into the group, but even more in delegating power to a whole generation, or part of it, who execute the dance perfectly." "La danza tradicional en Euskadi Norte," in *Ser vasco*, ed. Haritschelhar, 438.

40. Itzaina and Ikardo, "Folklore e identidad en el País Vasco," 140.

41. See, for example, Manuel Castells, *End of Millennium*, 2nd ed. (Oxford: Blackwell, 2000).

42. In 1974, the group Xiberuko Zohardia organized a *maskarada* for the whole of Zuberoa, although this remains an isolated case.

43. The subject matter of the pastoral originally dealt with topics such as Matalas (Bernard Goyheneche), a priest who was executed in 1661 for defending common grazing rights for his parishioners in Mitikile (Moncayolle), Zuberoa, and then others who invoked cross-border characters, such as Antxo Handia (Sancho III Garcés, the eleventh-century king of Pamplona-Iruñea), until finally evoking an imaginary unified Basque Country through ideologically important subjects for Basque nationalism such as the Navarrese Carlist leader Tomás Zumalacárregui, the bard José María Iparragirre, and Sabino Arana, the founder of Basque nationalism. Moreover, beyond this evolution of subjects from Zuberoa to the whole Basque Country, the 2004 pastoral even toured in Hegoalde, with performances in Hondarribia (Gipuzkoa) and Amurrio (Araba), the latter in the presence of the *lehendakari* or president of the Basque Autonomous Community, Juan José Ibarretxe. It was no coincidence that this same pastoral was written by the well-known historian, member of the Basque Language Academy, and long-time nationalist Jean-Louis Davant or that it was the one thousandth anniversary of the accession to the throne of the pastoral's subject in question: King Sancho VI, the Wise, the most important Navarrese monarch.

44. See Haritschelhar, ed., *Ser vasco*, 286, and idem., "La Pastoral souletine: Une tradition renouvelée," *Bulletin du Musée Basque* 127 (1990): 57.

45. See Vrignon, *Les années oubliées*, 179–80, and Etchecopar Etchart, *Théâtres basques*, 98.

46. Together with these *toberrak*, some of them held with a village in which they were held surrounded by the French state security forces, there were other similar expressions that were not so politicized. For these other performances, the principal aim was to generate a minimal form of consensus among the people of the village organizing the event. See Itzaina and Ikardo, "Folklore e identidad en el País Vasco," 144–45, and Etchecopar Etchart, *Théâtres basques*, 103–8 and 120–24.

47. For an English-language account of the Korrika, see Teresa del Valle, *Korrika: Basque Ritual for Ethnic Identity*, trans. Linda White (Reno: University of Nevada Press, 1994).

48. Ikas, "Enseignement de la langue basque—Un bilan de misère," quoted in Michel Oronos, *Le mouvement culturel basque 1951–2001* (Donostia: Elkar, 2002), 50.

49. Furthermore, "the Ikas association feels obliged to let public opinion know about such facts and to denounce the total incomprehension and disdain of the national education authorities and the government toward the legitimate demands of the Basque community. We must highlight the refusal of the public authorities to concern themselves seriously with the teaching of Basque, despite numerous projects and motions. The Ikas association warns the public authorities of the consequences of [such] stubbornness in denying the cultural reality of the [Basque] Country." Ibid., 50–51.

50. Quoted in ibid., 59.

51. Ultimately, this idea was adopted by the new political group, Elgar-Ensemble, and in part by the all-party lobby Batera at the turn of the millennium.

52. Parti Socialiste, *Proposition du Loi n° 2269 relative à la place des langues et cultures des peuples de France dans l'enseignement, dans l'éducation permanent, dans les activités culturelles, de jeunesse et de loisir, dans les émissions de la radio et de la télévision, et dans la vie publique* (December 1980).

53. Quoted in Patrick Cassan, *Francia y la cuestión vasca* (Tafalla: Txalaparta, 1998), 68.

54. For example, one measure proposed the creation of a body composed of members of the different communes to defend Basque culture. Yet perhaps the proposal with the most lasting repercussion was that advocating a development council for the Basque Country to be composed of individuals from different social, political, and economic sectors. At the time, this plan was never realized. However, it ultimately began to take shape and subsequently become very influential ten years later.

55. The 1987 budget, for example, allocated only 30 percent of its funds to Basque projects.

56. Formed in 1984, Pizkundea was an initiative that brought together different cultural groups in an effort to lobby in favor of Basque culture from an apolitical position. See Jacob, *Hills of Conflict*, 356–57; Oronos, *Le mouvement culturel basque 1951–2001*, 85–86.

57. For example, in 1991 the EKE began negotiations with the French government over the possibility of legally receiving the Basque-language transmissions of Euskal Telebista (ETB, Basque Television), the public-broadcasting service of the Basque Autonomous Community in Spain, negotiations that involved the Basque government and that finally bore fruit seven years later with the installation of an antenna capable of transmitting Basque-language television in Iparralde.

58. Club de Prospective, *Pays Basque 2010, Diagnostic* (Bayonne, 1993), 39.

59. "The 'let it be' attitude is ultimately a policy of not aiding a language in danger of dying." Ironically, the report noted, "never has there been such a demand to learn this language; and never has it been so little spoken." Ibid., 42.

60. Ahedo, *Entre la frustración y la esperanza*, 91. According to the plan, "there are two ways of looking at the actual state of Euskara: The passive transmission of Euskara has had practically no effect, [and] the efforts undertaken during the last twenty years in the field of education have partly alleviated the effects of this lack of passive transmission. Yet this is not enough. . . . This forces a total rethinking in which four points of intervention can be identified: The teaching of and in Euskara and the [Basque] literacy of adults; signs and place names in Basque; Basque-language media; [and] the presence of Euskara in public services. These priorities allow for the construction of the essential foundations of a linguistic policy favorable to Euskara." Conseil du Développement du Pays Basque, *Schéma d'Aménagement et de Développement du Pays Basque: Orientations Générales* (Bayonne, 1996), 13.

61. Conseil du Développement du Pays Basque, *Schéma d'Aménagement et de Développement du Pays Basque*, 21.

62. Quoted in Oronos, *Le mouvement culturel basque 1951–2001*, 155.

63. Erramun Bachoc, "Etablir un schéma d'aménagement linguistique de manière à donner à l'euskara sa place de langue identitaire du Pays Basque," in *Enbata* 1414 (March 15, 1996), quoted in ibid., 156.

64. Quoted in ibid., 156.

65. François Bayrou, cited in *Enbata* 1448 (October 24, 1996) and *Sud-Ouest*, October 21, 1996, quoted in ibid., 157.

66. However, on taking account of how the money would ultimately be distributed, it could be seen that, in total, 17 million francs (just under $3 million) would be accorded to promoting both Basque and Gascon (an Occitan language spoken by a few people in Biarritz and Angelu) equally in Iparralde for a period of six years.

67. Ahedo, *Entre la frustración y la esperanza*, 128–29.

68. Oronos, *Le mouvement culturel basque 1951–2001*, 168.

69. Urteaga and Ahedo, *La nouvelle gouvernance en Pays Basque*, 167–74.

70. Here it should be noted that the Council of the Language was actually officially a private association, although its members were elected public officials.

71. Namely, the call for a separate agricultural chamber to be established for Iparralde, together with official status for Euskara and the creation of a public body to organize and oversee higher education. See Conseil des Élus du Pays Basque, *Contribution aux assises des libertés locales* (Bayonne, 2002).

72. Batera, "Charte de Batera" (2002).

73. According to the *rapporteur* (a member of the assembly charged with writing a report on a debate), the signing of a charter that recognized collective rights (in reference to the European Charter of Regional and Minority Languages) "would be contrary to the unity of the Republic." Therefore, "to recognize regional languages constitutionally and allow schools where only Breton is spoken would be a very dangerous step to grant." *Le Journal du Pays Basque*, September 22, 2002.

74. During the trial, when sympathizers of those arrested tried to enter the court building, they were forcibly evicted by the police, using tear gas to disperse them. This, in turn, resulted in the Basque section of the French Lawyer's Association denouncing police tactics at the trial.

75. See Batera, "Proposamenak" (2004).

76. Ahedo and Urteaga, *Gobernanza y territorio en Iparralde*, 71.

77. These new contacts almost certainly also reinforced closer ties between the French and Spanish authorities, especially in regard to the status of ETA refugees in Iparralde.

78. HASI, Entrevista mecanografiada a la Dirección de HASI (1989).

79. Ibid.

80. KAS, *Situación organizativa* (1992).

81. *Enbata* 1333 (June 1995).

82. The interview appeared in *Euskaldunon Egunkaria*, September 15, 1996, and the book was written by Iñaki Egaña, *Diccionario histórico-político de Euskal Herria* (Tafalla: Txalaparta, 1996).

83. KAS, *Situación organizativa* (1992).

84. Araiz, "Cómo vamos a recomponer el jarrón roto?" *Herria Eginez* 29 (November 1995), 8.

85. HB, EMA, HA and EB. *Manifiesto de acción política común en Ipar y Hegoalde* (March 24, 1994).

86. Jakes Sarraillet, quoted in *Egin*, March 5, 1994. Similar statements can be seen by other nationalist figures in Iparralde, such as Txetx Etxeberri or Richard Irazusta, in the pages of *Enbata* between 1994 and 1995.

87. HB, EMA, HA and EB. *Manifiesto de acción política común en Ipar y Hegoalde* (March 24, 1994).

88. Ibid.

89. Patxa was a youth group, created in 1986, that blended a subversive, ironic, and quasi-anarchistic discourse through youth cultural forms, such as rock music, in an attempt to mobilize young people. Oldartzen was another initiative, more serious in tone and created in 1989, that remained close to the positions of HB in the South. See Jacob, *Hills of Conflict*, 359–64.

90. Abertzaleen Batasuna, *Biltzar Nagusiaren Ekarpenak* (1995).

91. Abertzaleen Batasuna, *Biltzar Nagusia* (1996).

92. Especially after the strategic shift within the MLNV that included following a line laid down by KAS and HB in the period 1994–95.

93. This question was at the heart of AB's decision to not take part in the referendum on the European Union Treaty referendum in 2005 if either a "yes" or "no" vote was not passed by absolute majority within the party. Neither side won such a majority, and this explains AB's absence from the debate surrounding the 2005 referendum in France and the

centrality assumed by Batasuna as the principal nationalist voice against the treaty. The French public voted against the treaty, although it received a "yes" vote in Iparralde—something for which Batasuna blamed AB.

94. Here, I follow elements of the analysis established by Francisco Letamendia: causal factors, phases of nationalist violence, ideological elements, the role of an armed group in the legitimating community, the organization of the armed group, and the exclusivity of the armed strategy. See *Game of Mirrors: Centre-Periphery National Conflicts*, trans. Karen Hatherley (Aldershot, UK: Ashgate, 2000), chs. 12 and 13.

95. See Ander Gurrutxaga Abad, *Del PNV a ETA: La transformación del nacionalismo vasco* (Donostia–San Sebastián: R& Ediciones, 1996); Gurutz Jáuregui Bereciartu, *Ideología y estrategia política de ETA: Análisis de su evolución entre 1959 y 1968* (Madrid: Siglo XXI, 1981); Alfonso Pérez-Agote, *The Social Roots of Basque Nationalism*, trans. Cameron Watson and William A. Douglass (Reno: University of Nevada Press, 2006); and Francisco Letamendia, *Historia del nacionalismo vasco y de ETA*, 3 vols (San Sebastián: R&B Ediciones, 1994).

96. See José María Lorenzo Espinosa, *Historia de Euskal Herria*, vol. 3, *El nacimiento de una nación* (Tafalla: Txalaparta, 1997).

97. Letamendia, *Game of Mirrors*, 272–73.

98. ETA, "Actas de la V Asamblea" (1968), in *Documentos Y*, vol. 7 (San Sebastián: Hordago, 1980), 56–100.

99. See Benjamín Tejerina, "Ciclo de protesta, violencia política y movimientos sociales en el País Vasco," *Revista Internacional de Sociología* 16 (1997): 7–38, and Letamendia, *Game of Mirrors*, 248–49.

100. Iparretarrak, "Appel au peuple basque: Coordonner les groupes de lutte," *Ildo* 2 (1978).

101. Iparretarrak, "Ce que nous voulons," *Ildo* 2 (1978).

102. KAS. *Alternativa táctica-estratégica de KAS* (1981).

103. Iparretarrak, *20 ans de lutte: Autonomie et avant projet* (March 31, 1993).

104. See José Manuel Mata López, *El nacionalismo vasco radical: Discurso, organización y expresiones* (Bilbao: Servicio Editorial Universidad del País Vasco, 1993); Pedro Ibarra, *La evolución estratégica de ETA: De la "guerra revolucionaria" (1963) hasta después de la tregua (1989)* (Donostia: Kriselu, 1989); and Letamendia, *Historia del nacionalismo vasco y de ETA*.

105. Roland Jacquard, *La longue traque d'Action directe* (Paris: Albin Michel, 1987), quoted in Cassan, *Francia y la cuestión vasca*, 98.

106. Only 5 percent of the activity associated with *kale borroka* in 1996 took place in Iparralde. However, while IK undertook five actions that year, there were twenty-three incidents of *kale borroka* in Iparralde.

107. The first such organization in Iparralde to follow this strategy was Gazteriak. It officially united with its counterpart in Hegoalde, Jarrai, forming, in turn, first Segi and then Haika. In 2002, most of its members abandoned AB to join Batasuna, a political party emerging out of Euskal Herritarrok in the South, itself the successor to HB.

108. See José Antonio Rekondo, *Bietan jarrai: Guerra y paz en las calles de Euskadi* (Bilbao: Arañadle, 1998). See also Tejerina, "Ciclo de protesta, violencia política y movimientos sociales en el País Vasco," 7–38, and Ramón Zallo, *Euskadi o la segunda transición: Nación, cultura, ideologías y paz en un cambio de época* (Donostia: Erein, 1997).

109. See Rekondo, *Bietan jarrai*.

110. The first victim of this new strategy was Gregorio Ordóñez, the leader of the Partido Popular (PP, Popular Party), the Spanish conservative party, in Gipuzkoa. This shift opened up a new era of civil confrontation in the Basque Country.

111. Zutik is a left-wing political party, created in 1991, that has both nationalist and nonnationalist members (including former members of HB). Aralar is a left-wing nationalist political party, created by a breakaway critical sector within HB in 2000. Both parties reject the use of violence by ETA.

Notes, Chapter Twelve

1. Igor Ahedo Gurrutxaga, *Presente y pasado del nacionalismo en Iparralde* (Bilbao: Manu Robles-Arangiz Institutoa, 2004), 25–32.

2. Igor Ahedo Gurrutxaga, *Entre la frustración y la esperanza: Políticas de desarrollo e institucionalización* (Oñati: IVAP, 2003), 169–81, and *Presente y pasado del nacionalismo en Iparralde*, 37–52. For more discussion of this topic, see Eguzki Urteaga and Igor Ahedo Gurrutxaga, *La nouvelle gouvernance en Pays Basque* (Paris: L'Harmattan, 2004) and Igor Ahedo Gurrutxaga and Eguzki Urteaga, *Gobernanza y territorio en Iparralde* (Vitoria-Gasteiz: Servicio Central de Publicaciones del Gobierno Vasco, 2005).

3. In the *département* of the Pyrénées-Atlantiques, there are fifty-two cantons, each represented by a departmental *conseiller* or councilmember; twenty-one of these cantons are in Iparralde and thirty-one in Béarn. Each French *département* elects deputies to the National Assembly (the legislature). The *département* of the Pyrénées-Atlantiques elects five deputies, each representing a *circonscription*, or district. Two of these five represent exclusively Basque districts—on the coast of Lapurdi—while two are in Béarn. The remaining *circonscription* is divided between Basque and Béarnais territory.

4. François Fourquet, *Planification et développement local au Pays Basque* (Bayonne: Commissariat Général au Plan; Group de Recherche Sociale Ikerka, 1988), 15.

5. See Jacint Jordana, "El análisis de los policy networks: ¿Una nueva perspectiva sobre la relación entre las políticas públicas y el Estado?" *Gestión y Análisis de Políticas Públicas* 3 (1995): 77–90, and Charles O. Jones, *An Introduction to the Study of Public Policy*, 3rd ed. (Monterey, CA: Brooks Cole, 1984).

6. These opportunities are discussed by Jean Daniel Chaussier in *Quel territoire pour le Pays Basque?: Les cartes de l'identité* (Paris: L'Harmattan, 1997). 237–49, and Ahedo, *Entre la frustración y la esperanza*, 53–64. Specifically, they emerged out of a slight decentralization in the French political process, previous local strategies that had emerged (especially in Zuberoa), the rise to power of a new dominant class that was a little more responsive to change than the previous local notables had been, and, undoubtedly, the pressure that IK activity exerted on Basque society at the time (1991 marked the most intense period of IK activity than at any time since the arrest of Bidart).

7. Club de Prospective, *Pays Basque 2010, Diagnostic*.

8. Club de Prospective, *Pays Basque 2010, Analyse structurale* (Bayonne, 1993).

9. Club de Prospective, *Pays Basque 2010, Scénarios* (Bayonne, 1993).

10. I use the term "quasi-institutional" because the networks created, lacking the power to implement the proposals they put forward, could not be defined as fully institutional. Consequently, only the creation of a single Basque *département* (or a similar structure with the authority to implement decisions) could guarantee such local institutionalization. Similarly, I speak of public "macro policies," because the general policy of territorial organization that emerged at this time replaced older traditional models, both in terms of the actors taking part in the process (a blend of local, regional, departmental, national, and European figures) and in terms of its broad content (to the more traditional elements making up the former policy of territorial organization were added other features of scope and importance, such as linguistic, cultural, and "quasi-institutional" issues previously absent in similar debates on both sides of the border).

11. For more detail on these conclusions see Ahedo, *Entre la frustración y la esperanza*, 74–78, and esp. Igor Ahedo Gurrutxaga, "Redes de políticas públicas de desarrollo e institucionalización y movimiento social pro-departamento Pays Basque en los territorios vascos de Aquitania," Ph.D. diss., University of the Basque Country, 2002, 256–85.

12. It should also be noted that, according to all those involved, a key figure in beginning this process was the state's representative (the subprefect) in Baiona, Christian Sapède.

13. Club de Prospective, *Pays Basque 2010, Hypothèse* (Bayonne, 1993).

14. Conseil de Développement du Pays Basque, *Statuts, Conseil de Développement du Pays Basque* (Bayonne: Préfecture de Bayonne, 1994); Conseil des Élus du Pays Basque, *Statuts* (Bayonne, 1995). For further information, see also www.lurraldea.net (last accessed April 5, 2008), the official Web site of both the CDPB and the CEPB. *Lurraldea* means "territory" in Basque, indicating the symbolic importance accorded by these bodies to some form of territorial institutional recognition and the irony of advocating public policies for a region that has lacked any such institutional recognition.

15. Indeed, this had been precisely the case in 1984, when the notables rejected a proposal of the Ravail Mission designed to create a CDPB. See Jean Daniel Chaussier, "L'échec du projet de création d'un département en Pays Basque," *Le Bulletin du Musée Basque* 120 (1988), and "La Mission Ravail au Pays Basque (1982): Pouvoir du discours identitaire ou discours du pouvoir sur l'identité?" *Le Bulletin du Musée Basque* 138 (1994).

16. Such consensus, however, was present only at the beginning of the initiative. For example, the leaders of the CDPB soon began to link local development with the call for more local institutional power. This issue, together with internal problems within the Baiona CCI, led to major changes in 1997, changes that resulted in the exit of the PNB's Camblong as president of the CDPB. For an examination of this crisis, see Ahedo, "Redes de políticas públicas de desarrollo e institucionalización y movimiento social pro-departamento Pays Basque en los territorios vascos de Aquitania," 349–59 and *Entre la frustración y la esperanza*, 114–21. From 1997 on, both organs were subject to increasing pressure from within to demand more Basque institutionalization.

17. See Conseil de Développement du Pays Basque, *Schéma d'aménagement et de développement du Pays Basque*.

18. See Ahedo and Urteaga, *Gobernanza y territorio en Iparralde*, 33–62.

19. See Ahedo, *Entre la frustración y la esperanza*, 94–114.

20. Law No. 95-115 (February 4, 1995). For further analysis of this growing notion of territorial unity through official recognition of the Pays Basque, see Ahedo, "Redes de políticas públicas de desarrollo e institucionalización y movimiento social pro-departamento Pays Basque en los territorios vascos de Aquitania," 359–66 and *Entre la frustración y la esperanza*, 27–32; and Ahedo and Urteaga, *Gobernanza y territorio en Iparralde*, 122–27. Legislative development regarding these new units—the *pays*—in France was based on the experience of Iparralde, which served as the principal model for the rest of the state. Yet Iparralde also served as an exception, given that many of the legal agreements on which this new status were based were never fulfilled, a fact that actually led to greater room for maneuver for the CDPB and the CEPB.

21. CDPB, *Convention Spécifique Pays Basque, Bayonne, 22 décembre 2000* (Bayonne, 2001).

22. Conseil de Développement du Pays Basque, *Lurraldea: 10 ans déjà, 10 ans après*.

23. See Igor Ahedo Gurrutxaga, Francisco Letamendia, and Noemi Etxebarria, *Redes transfronterizas intervascas* (Bilbao: Universidad del País Vasco-Euskal Herriko Unibertsitatea, 2004) and Ahedo and Urteaga, *Gobernanza y territorio en Iparralde*, 73–82.

24. See Alfonso Pérez-Agote, *The Social Roots of Basque Nationalism*, trans. Cameron Watson and William A. Douglass (Reno: University of Nevada Press, 2006), originally published as *La reproducción del nacionalismo: El caso vasco* (Madrid: CIS; Siglo XXI, 1984), , xv.

25. See Urteaga and Ahedo, *La nouvelle gouvernance en Pays Basque*, 83–90 and 149–53.

26. See Jones, *An Introduction to the Study of Public Policy*, ch. 2. See also Yves Mény and Jean-Claude Thoenig, *Las políticas públicas* (Barcelona: Ariel, 1992).

27. See, for example, Johan Olsen, Paul G. Roness, and Harald Saetren. "Norway: Still Peaceful Coexistence and Revolution in Slow Motion?" *Policy Styles in Western Europe*, ed. Jeremy Richardson (London: Allen & Unwin, 1982), 47–79.

28. For an examination of the early calls for a Basque *département*, see the cited work by Jean Daniel Chaussier. For an overview of how this demand evolved, in tandem with the new development strategies, see Ahedo, "Redes de políticas públicas de desarrollo e institucionalización y movimiento social pro-departamento Pays Basque en los territorios vascos de Aquitania," and *Entre la frustración y la esperanza*. See also Ahedo and Urteaga, *Gobernanza y territorio en Iparralde*.

29. Chaussier, *Quel territoire pour le Pays Basque?* 25–108.

30. These would include labor unions such as the ELB and CFDT (the Confédération Française Démocratique du Travail, the French Democratic Confederation of Labor), and cultural groups and associations linked to Basque nationalism.

31. See Fourquet, *Planification et développement local au Pays Basque*, 14.

32. For an appreciation of how such rational considerations influence collective political behavior, see Olson, *The Logic of Collective Action*.

33. On this subject, see Klaus Eder, "La institucionalización de la acción colectiva: ¿Hacia una nueva problemática teórica en el análisis de los movimientos sociales?" in *Los movimientos sociales: Transformaciones políticas y cambio cultural*, ed. Pedro Ibarra and Benjamín Tejerina (Madrid: Trotta, 1998), 337–60.

34. Some people found in his personal political evolution a kind of "pro-Basque conversion." See the transcribed interviews in Ahedo, "Redes de políticas públicas de desarrollo e institucionalización y movimiento social pro-departamento Pays Basque en los territorios vascos de Aquitania," 390–99 and *Entre la frustración y la esperanza*, 147–53.

35. See on this point Bruno Labedan, *Jeu de acteurs et institutions: Études des oppositions autour de la revendication départementaliste contemporaine au Pays basque français* (Bordeaux: IEP, 1998), and Sébastien Segas, *Action collective et formulation d'un projet commun: Le cas de l'Association des élus pour un département Pays Basque* (Bordeaux: IEP, 1998).

36. The general meeting of the *Biltzar* on September 21, 1996, attended by 85 of the 159 mayors in Iparralde, approved the idea of holding a vote (by secret ballot) on the question of a separate Basque *département*. On November 30, 1996, another general meeting was held, attended this time by 151 mayors, a figure that added considerable weight to the subsequent ballot. In total, the vote was passed by 93 (61.6 percent) to 53 (35.1 percent), with five abstentions. In other words, the creation of a single Basque *département* was approved by 58.9 percent of all the mayors in Iparralde. However, the ambiguous or even hostile response of mayors from the populous municipalities (Baiona, Angelu, Donibane Lohizune, and Biarritz) aided opponents of the resolution to minimize the results. For this reason, the *Biltzar* then came up with the idea of holding a vote in each municipal council or city hall, the results of which, once more, were favorable to the notion of a separate *département*. For a detailed exploration of these processes, see Ahedo, "Redes de políticas públicas de desarrollo e institucionalización y movimiento social pro-departamento Pays Basque en los territorios vascos de Aquitania," 460–64, and *Entre la frustración y la esperanza*, 185–88.

37. See Labedan, "Jeu de acteurs et institutions."

38. See Segas, "Action collective et formulation d'un projet commun."

39. On this, see William A. Gamson and David S. Meyer, "Framing Political Opportunity," in *Comparative Perspectives on Social Movements: Political Opportunities, Mobilizing Structures, and Cultural Framings*, ed. Doug McAdam, John D. McCarthy, and Mayer N. Zald (Cambridge: Cambridge University Press, 1996), 275–90.

40. See Sidney G. Tarrow, *Power in Movement: Social Movements, Collective Action and Politics* (Cambridge: Cambridge University Press, 1994), 113–14, and Miguel Jerez, "Los grupos de presión," in *Manual de ciencia política*, ed. Rafael del Águila (Madrid: Trotta, 1997), 13–43.

41. Recalling the role placed by Izan in the 1980s. Indeed, Abeberry, a leading member of Izan, was also in the AED.

42. During the 1995 presidential elections, the PS candidate, Lionel Jospin, promised to create a single Basque *département* if a majority of the Basque elected officials called for it, thereby encouraging a favorable response to the idea within the *Biltzar*.

43. See Abertzaleen Batasuna, *Proposition de campagne pour un institution de Pays Basque, maintenant!* (December 14, 1996).

44. On the instrumental-rational dimension, see Letamendia, *Game of Mirrors*, 291–92.

45. Abertzaleen Batasuna, *Proposition de campagne soumise a l'approbation d'Abertzaleen Batasuna (lors de la prochaine assemblée générale de juin)* (1998).

46. Ahedo, *Entre la frustración y la esperanza*, 145–99.

47. On this, see Tarrow, *Power in Movement*, 96–98.

48. These included most of the major political formations (AB, the PNB, EA, UDF, RPR, the PS, and the Ecologists), economic groups (the CCI of Baiona, the cooperative movement, together with labor and agricultural unions), and practically all of the Basque cultural associations.

49. This represented about 5 percent of the total population of Iparralde.

50. CSA, *Sondage exclusif CSA–Sud Ouest*, August 29, 1999 and *Sondage exclusif CSA–La Semaine du Pays Basque*, September 9, 2000.

51. Biltzar, *1790: Créations des départements; 1998: projet de création d'un département* (1998). For a discusión of this document, see Ahedo, "Redes de políticas públicas de desarrollo e institucionalización y movimiento social pro-departamento Pays Basque en los territorios vascos de Aquitania," 461–62, and *Entre la frustración y la esperanza*, 186–87.

52. It should be noted that the local sphere, too, evinced a closing of certain windows of opportunity for maneuver. For example, several notables, specifically, members of the CEPB, attempted on several occasions to counter the arguments in favor of a single *département*. Yet ultimately this also served only to reinvigorate those working in favor of institutional recognition for Iparralde.

53. See Hanspeter Kriesi, "The Organizational Structure of New Social Movements in Relation to their Political Context," in *Comparative Perspectives on Social Movements: Political Opportunities, Mobilizing Structures, and Cultural Framings*, ed. McAdam, McCarthy, and Zald, 152–84.

54. It also made sense for UDF, a party that had supported decentralization, to favor a Basque *département*. And, in fact, this was the case for many of its elected representatives. However, François Bayrou, the UDF leader and also head of the *département* of the Pyrénées-Atlantiques, ultimately vetoed any official UDF support on the grounds that it would mean political suicide for him in his own power base.

55. The text of the 1998 Lizarra-Garazi pact, signed by the PNV, EA, HB, and Ezker Batua (the Basque branch of the Spanish Communists, IU, Izquierda Unida, the United Left), together with a hundred or so labor unions and social movements, recognized the essentially "political" nature of the "Basque conflict" and favored political dialogue aimed at a resolution that could be presented to society as a whole. After the signing of the pact, ETA declared a ceasefire that held for a year and half.

56. Ramón Zallo, *El país de los vascos: Desde los sucesos de Ermua al segundo gobierno de Ibarretxe* (Madrid: Fundamentos, 2001), 99.

57. The pact was initially signed in Lizarra (Estella) in Navarre, Hegoalde, and then, in more extended form, a further agreement was signed, including the incorporation of AB and other social movements, in Donibane Garazi (Nafarroa Beherea) in Iparralde.

58. The Basque PS did ultimately use ETA's breaking of the ceasefire to extricate itself from the pro-*département* movement, given that its involvement up to that time—and especially its conflict with the PS leadership in Paris—had delegitimized it in the eyes of many locals.

59. On these general connections, see Tarrow, *Power in Movement*.

60. By stealing these twenty-one chairs, the Demos intended to contribute the necessary seats for a Basque institution for which the Basque elected officials had voted; by "kidnapping," or, according to the Demos, "liberating" the busts of Marianne, they intended to show that the principles of democracy that the image represented had been kidnapped–thereby also aligning their own discourse with republican values; and, finally, according to the general plan for the newly recognized Pays Basque–approved by all political parties–all road signs should have been bilingual, yet in the face of this agreement not being implemented, the Demos took the initiative and (illegally) did it themselves.

61. Tarrow, *Power in Movement*, 153.

62. As we have seen, these roots were already obvious in the 1970s, but I would also contend that they stretch all the way back to the initial institutional demands of Garat in the first revolutionary National Assembly of 1789.

63. Tarrow, *Power in Movement*, 96–98.

64. Ibid., 155–56. See also Sidney G. Tarrow, "Cycles of Collective Action," in *Repertoires and Cycles of Collective Action*, ed. Mark Traugott (Durham, NC: Duke University Press, 1995), 89–116.

65. This was more evident from 2002 on, when the ELB intensified its campaign for a specifically Basque agricultural chamber.

66. Tarrow, *Power in Movement*, 157.

67. Rassemblement pour la République (RPR), *Communique de presse du 31 août 1999–RPR, Département Pyrénées Atlantiques* (2000).

68. Juan J. Linz, *Conflicto en Euskadi* (Madrid: Espasa-Calpe, 1986), 370; Letamendia, *Game of Mirrors*.

69. See Tarrow, *Power in Movement*, 112.

70. Ibid., 156–57.

71. As part of previous agreements, some public money had been allocated to other development projects in both 1997 and 2000, but not on this scale of investment.

72. We should remember that while many (and not always radical nationalist) cultural groups had always maintained organizational structures on both sides of the border, antisystem collectives formed in Hegoalde withdrew from Iparralde in the 1980s. However, in the late 1990s, they returned and joined established groups there. For example, such was the case with the youth movement Jarrai-Haika-Segi. At the same time, both the PNV and EA also began to reinforce their presence in Iparralde, together with broader nationalist initiatives–such as Udalbiltza (the Assembly of Basque Municipalities), composed of the spectrum of nationalist parties from both sides of the border–that emerged during the ETA ceasefire of 1998–99. Later, Udalbiltza split into two factions, with one controlled by the PNV and EA and the other by HB-EH.

73. Batasuna took part in the 2002 French legislative lections, appealing for its sympathizers to return spoiled ballot papers as a protest against the French electoral system, leading to calculations of between 500 and 1000 "votes" for the party. It maintained this level of support at the 2004 cantonal elections, but, as we will see, during the 2004 European elections, Batasuna received virtually the same number of votes as AB.

74. See Tarrow, *Power in Movement*, 101–3 and Jesús Casquette, "Estructura e identidad: Los nuevos movimientos sociales," *Inguruak* 14 (1996): 143–75

75. In elections to the French senate, an electoral college (composed of general and regional *conseillers*) votes in one *circonscription* or district per *département*.

76. Association pour le Département Pays Basque (ADPB). *Déclaration de la Association pour le Département Pays Basque* (2002).

77. The Union pour un Mouvement Populaire (UMP, Union for a Popular Movement), was founded in 2002 as a center-right bloc. It was created through the alliance of center and right-wing parties, most notably the RPR, but also the conservative DL (Démocratie Libéral, Liberal Democracy) and many members of the centrist UDF.

78. On these proposals, see Igor Ahedo, "El sistema administrativo y político de Iparralde." *Revista Vasca de Administración Pública* 66 (2003): 11–45, and Ahedo and Urteaga, *Gobernanza y territorio en Iparralde*, 110–19.

79. For a more detailed account of this phase, see Ahedo and Urteaga, *Gobernanza y territorio en Iparralde*, 119–34.

80. Conseil des Élus du Pays Basque, *Contribution aux Assisses des Libertés Locales*.

81. Perhaps the clearest case of this is to be found with the PS in Iparralde. While one sector, led by Jean Espilondo, is aggressively opposed to any notion of a Basque *département*, other major figures–such as Frantxoa Maitia, a *conseiller général* and *conseiller régional*–have been integral members of Batera.

Notes, Chapter Thirteen

1. Benedict Anderson, *Imagined Communities: Reflections on the Origin and Spread of Nationalism*, rev. ed. (London: Verso, 1991).

2. Michael Billig, *Banal Nationalism* (London: Routledge, 1995).

3. Alfonso Pérez-Agote, *The Social Roots of Basque Nationalism*, trans. Cameron Watson and William A. Douglass (Reno: University of Nevada Press, 2006), 16.

4. In the case of the conflict between Basque and French or Spanish nationalism, this takes shape in the desire for a distinct state, and in the case of the Pays Basque, the desire for a separate *département*.

5. See Josetxo Beriáin, "Los ídolos de la tribu en el nacionalismo vasco," in *Relatos de la nación: La construcción de las identidades nacionales en el mundo hispánico*, ed. Francisco Colom (Madrid: Biblioteca Nueva; CSIC; Vervuert, 2005).

6. For example, the CDPB used the term in all its documents, and, moreover, referred to Hegoalde as the Pays Basque Sud (Southern Pays Basque).

7. Pérez-Agote, *The Social Roots of Basque Nationalism*, xv.

8. Or as "strongly" as possible, to use the wording of Gabriel Gatti in *Las modalidades débiles de la identidad: Sociología de la identidad en los territorios vacíos de sociedad y de sociología. Los escenarios d aprendizaje de euskera por adultos* (Leioa: Servicio Editorial, Universidad del País Vasco, 2002).

9. For a discussion of social plausibility and its importance, see Pérez-Agote, *The Social Roots of Basque Nationalism*, xv.

10. Although Marc Legasse had articulated an embryonic form of Basque nationalism in the 1940s.

11. See Igor Ahedo Gurrutxaga, *Presente y pasado del nacionalismo en Iparralde* (Bilbao: Manu Robles-Arangiz Institutoa, 2004), 25–32; idem, *Entre la frustración y la esperanza: Políticas de desarrollo e institucionalización* (Oñati: IVAP, 2003), 47, and Bixente Vrignon, *Les années oubliées: Jalons pour une histoire du mouvement abertzale au pays Basque Nord, 1968–1978* (Baiona: Gatuzain, 1999), 89–110.

12. See William Safran, "The French State and Ethnic Minority Cultures: Policy Dimensions and Problems," in *Ethnoterritorial Politics, Policy, and the Western World*, ed. Joseph R. Rudolph, Jr. and Robert J. Thompson (Boulder: L. Rienner Publishers, 1989).

13. In fact, a kind of circular dynamic surrounding the creation of a single Basque *département* began whereby the Socialists originally initiated the debate with a proposal for the institutionalization if Basque difference (*izan*) in 1980. However, a muted social response, combined with pressure on the French government by its Spanish counterpart against the plan and opposition within the PS hierarchy itself resulted in a different strategy. The presentation of the *Basque Country 2010 Report* in 1993 visualized the existence of a single, named territory (*izen*): the Pays Basque. Through the interest generated by this report, a new movement subsequently emerged to reclaim Basque institutionalization (*izan*), and eventually, the French authorities recognized the differential nature of Iparralde (*izen*), although to date without formally arranging for its political expression (*izan*).

14. Resolving the first of these questions (the rapprochement of identities between the North and the South) was aided greatly by the new institutional framework that emerged in Hegoalde–the Basque Autonomous Community and the Foral Community of Navarre–after decades of repression during the Franco regime. As a consequence of these changes, cultural development in Hegoalde became the central reference for Basque identity in Iparralde. However, the emergence and consolidation of AB in the 1990s revealed the desire of many nationalists in the North to develop their own discourse beyond that in which the interests of the various actors in Hegoalde was inscribed. This ultimately led to the emergence of a left-wing Basque nationalism in Iparralde that was autonomous from its southern counterpart, the MLNV.

15. Pérez-Agote, *The Social Roots of Basque Nationalism*, xiv–xv.

16. As noted in Chapter 12, in the 1980s, Inchauspé was one of the principal critics of demands for a Basque *département*, only to do a U-turn in the 1990s and embrace the notion, to the point of self-financing a campaign to promote the idea and continuing to support it, despite setbacks, thereafter. Similarly, Lamassoure had been the driving force behind Article 2 of the French constitution stating that French was the only official language of the republic. Ten years later, however, as president of the CEPB, he called for the amendment of the same article he had originally proposed. Finally, although Grenet has opposed the creation of a single *département*, at the same time, he has continually referred to Baiona as the capital of the Basque Country, which can only mean that, at the very least, the Pays Basque exists for him as a distinct space.

17. See Ahedo, *Entre la frustración y la esperanza*, 212–24.

18. On this question in general, see Ahedo and Urteaga, *Gobernanza y territorio en Iparralde* (Vitoria-Gasteiz: Servicio Central de Publicaciones del Gobierno Vasco, 2005), 102–19.

Notes, Chapter Fourteen

1. Only 10 of the 157 municipalities in Iparralde have a population of more than 3,500 people, although the coastal conglomeration of Angelu, Biarritz, and Baiona is home to 100,000 people in a total population of 267,000.

2. ELA sounded out the possibility, while the radical Basque nationalist Langile Abertzaleen Batzordeak (LAB, Nationalist Workers' Councils) actually established chapters in Iparralde.

3. Chevènement had been a member of the PS, but disagreements over the Jospin administration's concessions to Corsican nationalists led him to found a new movement—the Mouvement Républicain et Citoyen (MRC, the Citizen and Republican Movement)—advocating a neo-Jacobin French nationalist ideology.

4. Batzarre is a left-wing, pro-Basque (although not strictly Basque nationalist) political party in Navarre, founded in 1987. It shares close ties with Zutik.

5. As deputy mayor of Biarritz, Abeberry was responsible for culture in the town, while Galant had been elected as a *conseiller général* representing Baigorri, and Iriart was mayor of Hiriburu (Saint-Pierre-d'Irube).

6. On this activity, see Sidney G. Tarrow, *Power in Movement: Social Movements, Collective Action and Politics* (Cambridge: Cambridge University Press, 1994), 103–5, and Jean Noël Etcheverry, "Les partis politiques: Abertzaleen Batasuna," in *Pays Basque: Un département? 100 réponses*, ed. Claude Perrotin (Anglet: Atlantica, 2002), 288.

7. Tarrow, *Power in Movement*, 109, 110.

8. Sympathy was forthcoming from nonnationalist sectors, as well as from some public officials. See Igor Ahedo Gurrutxaga, *El movimiento Demo y la nueva cocina vasca (desobediente)* (Irun: Alberdania, 2004), 64–66.

9. See David A. Snow and Robert D. Benford, "Master Frames and Cycles of Protest," in *Frontiers in Social Movement Theory*, ed. Aldon D. Morris and Carol McClurg Mueller (New Haven, CT: Yale University Press, 1992), 133–55.

10. Demo, *Demokrazia Euskal Herriarentzat–Démocratie pour le Pays Basque*, 274.

11. Ibid., 162 and Ahedo, *El movimiento Demo y la nueva cocina vasca (desobediente)*, 77–79. When the Demos arranged to steal the minutes book, one of their number, in order to gain access to the archive, signed his name on the official register as "Dominique-Joseph Garat, Notary."

12. Mayer N. Zald, "Culture, Ideology, and Strategic Framing," in *Comparative Perspectives on Social Movements*, ed. Doug McAdam, John D. McCarthy, and Mayer N. Zald (Cambridge: Cambridge University Press, 1996), 265.

13. Fronte di Liberazione Naziunali di a Corsica, the Front for the National Liberation of Corsica, founded in 1976.

14. Demo, *Demokrazia Euskal Herriarentzat–Démocratie pour le Pays Basque*, 33.

15. After 2004, the French authorities changed their own tactics to personalize their repression of individual Demos in such a way as to penalize them heavily financially, a situation that was more difficult for the movement to overcome and more difficult to generate solidarity from than the basic physical repression of the police and judicial authorities.

16. See Jesús Casquette, "Estructura e identidad: Los nuevos movimientos sociales," *Inguruak* 14 (1996): 157–58.

17. See Igor Ahedo Gurrutxaga, *Entre la frustración y la esperanza: Políticas de desarrollo e institucionalización* (Oñati: IVAP, 2003).

18. On this, see Bixente Vrignon, "El voto en Euskal Herria norte en las elecciones legislativas," in *Historia de Euskal Herria. Historia general de los vascos*, vol. 6, *Dictadura, democracia y autogobierno: La nueva sociedad vasca, 1937–2004*, ed. Joseba Agirreazkuenaga (Donostia: Lur, 2005), 178–83.

19. See Ahedo, *Entre la frustración y la esperanza*.

20. Ultimately, an independent right-wing candidate, Beñat Inchauspé, won in Hazparne.

21. As noted previously, 46,000 signatures were required to force such a referendum. By the fall of 2007, 36,000 people had signed the petition.

22. See Alfonso Pérez-Agote, *The Social Roots of Basque Nationalism*, trans. Cameron Watson and William A. Douglass (Reno and Las Vegas: University of Nevada Press, 2006), 26–28.

23. See on this question Erich Fromm, *Escape from Freedom* (1941; New York: H. Holt, 1994).

24. Conseil de Développement du Pays Basque, *Evaluation du schéma d'aménagement et de développement du Pays Basque* (Bayonne, 2000), 23.

25. Juan J. Linz, *Conflicto en Euskadi* (Madrid: Espasa-Calpe, 1986), 376.

26. Ibid.

27. Ibid., 375.

28. Ibid.

29. Ibid., 379. See also Nigel Ross Parton, "Fire and Blood: A Comparison of Basque Nationalism in France and Spain," M.A. thesis, University of Victoria, 125.

30. Eusko Ikaskuntza, Eusko Jaurlaritza-Gobierno Vasco, and EKE, *Identidad colectiva y prácticas culturales en Euskal Herria* (Donostia: Eusko Ikaskuntza, 2007), 41–42.

31. Ibid.

32. Ibid., 57.

33. Ibid., 66.

Bibliography

Abbadie, Antoine d' and [Joseph] Augustin Chaho. *Études grammaticales sur la langue euskarienne*. Paris: Arthur Bertrand, 1836.

Abertzaleen Batasuna (AB). *Biltzar Nagusiaren Ekarpenak* (1995).

———. *Biltzar Nagusia* (1996).

———. *Proposition de campagne pour un institution de Pays Basque, maintenant!* (December 14, 1996).

———. *Proposition de campagne soumise a l'approbation d'Abertzaleen Batasuna (lors de la prochaine assemblée générale de juin)* (1998).

Agirreazkuenaga, Joseba. "La constitución político foral de los vascos." In *Historia de Euskal Herria/Historia general de los vascos*. Volume 5. *Vasconia (1876–1937): Entre la tradición y la modernidad,* edited by Joseba Agirreazkuenaga. Donostia: Lur, 2005.

———. "Historiographie basque des deux derniers siècles concernant les événements issus de la Révolution française." In *1789 et les Basques: Histoire, langue et littérature*, edited by Jean Baptiste Orpustan. Bordeaux: Presses Universitaires de Bordeaux, 1991.

———. "Katalanismo eta euskaltzaletasun politikoen arteko begiradak (1876–1919)." *Argia* 2034 (April 2, 2006), 50–55.

Aguirre Zabala, Iñaki. "Nacionalismo vasco y relaciones transnacionales en el contexto de la frontera hispano-francesa: Cuatro modelos históricos." In *Las relaciones de vecindad*. Edited by Celestino del Arenal. Leioa: Servicio Editorial, Universidad del País Vasco, 1987.

———. "La renovación de los imaginarios culturales de la vasquidad y la difusión de los nuevos conocimientos científicos." In *Historia de Euskal Herria/Historia general de los vascos*. Volume 5. *Vasconia (1876–1937): Entre la tradición y la modernidad,* edited by Joseba Agirreazkuenaga. Donostia: Lur, 2005.

———, ed. *La articulación político-institucional de Vasconia: Actas de las Conferencias firmadas por los representantes de Alava, Bizkaia, Gipuzkoa y eventualmente de Navarra (1775–1936)*. Volume 1. *Colección de textos forales*. Bilbao: Diputaciones de Alava, Bizkaia and Gipuzkoa, 1995.

Agulhon, Maurice. *Marianne au combat : L'imagerie et la symbolique républicaines de 1789 à 1880.* Paris: Flammarion, 1979. Available in English as *Marianne into Battle: Republican Imagery and Symbolism in France, 1789–1880.* Translated by Janet Lloyd. Cambridge: Cambridge University Press, 1981.

———. *Métamorphoses de Marianne: L'imagerie et la symbolique républicaines de 1914 à nos jours*, Paris: Flammarion, 2001.

———. *La République au village: Les populations du Var de la Révolution a la IIe République.* Paris: Seuil, 1979. Available in English as *The Republic in the Village: The People of the Var from the French Revolution to the Second Republic.* Translated by Janet Lloyd. Cambridge: Cambridge University Press; Paris: Editions de la Maison des Sciences, 1982.

Ahedo Gurrutxaga, Igor. *Entre la frustración y la esperanza: Políticas de desarrollo e institucionalización.* Oñati: IVAP, 2003.

———. *El movimiento Demo y la nueva cocina vasca (desobediente).* Irun: Alberdania, 2004.

———. *Presente y pasado del nacionalismo en Iparralde.* Bilbao: Manu Robles-Arangiz Institutoa, 2004.

———. "Redes de políticas públicas de desarrollo e institucionalización y movimiento social pro-departamento Pays Basque en los territorios vascos de Aquitania." Ph.D. diss., University of the Basque Country, 2002.

———. "El sistema administrativo y político de Iparralde." *Revista Vasca de Administración Pública* 66 (2003): 11–45.

———, and Franck Dolosor. "De *Sud-Ouest* al *Euskal Herriko Kazeta*: Territorialidad y sentimiento de pertenencia en los medios de comunicación escritos de Iparralde." *Zer Aldizkaria–Revista de Estudios de la Comunicación* 15 (2003): 99–117.

———, Francisco Letamendia, and Noemi Etxebarria. *Redes transfronterizas intervascas.* Bilbao: Universidad del País Vasco-Euskal Herriko Unibertsitatea, 2004.

———, and Eguzki Urteaga, *Gobernanza y territorio en Iparralde.* Vitoria-Gasteiz: Servicio Central de Publicaciones del Gobierno Vasco, 2005.

Aierbe, Peio. *Lucha armada en Europa: IRA, RAF, Brigadas Rojas, Rote Zora, FLNC, Células Revolucionarias.* San Sebastián: Gakoa, 1989.

Ajuriaguerra, Isabelle de. "Etienne Salaberry et la guerre d'Algérie." In *Aljeriako gerla eta Euskal Herria (1954-1962). La guerre d'Algérie et le Pays Basque (1954–1962)*, edited by Xipri Arbelbide et al., Donostia: Eusko Ikaskuntza, 2005.

Altzibar, Xabier. "'Zazpiak bat' gaia XIX. mendean." In *Antoine d'Abbadie 1897–1997: Congrès International–Ezhoiko Kongresua.* Donostia–San Sebastián: Eusko Ikaskuntza; Euskaltzaindia, 1997.

Amezaga Iribarren, Arantzazu. "Manuel de Irujo y Ollo (Lizarra/Estella 1891–Iruña/Pamplona, 1981): A los veinte años de su muerte." *Euskonews & Media* 141 (October

26–November 2, 2001). Available on-line at http://www.euskonews.com/0141zbk/gaia14104es.html.

Anderson, Benedict. *Imagined Communities: Reflections on the Origin and Spread of Nationalism*. Revised edition. London : Verso, 1991.

Araiz. "Cómo vamos a recomponer el jarrón roto?" *Herria Eginez* 29 (November 1995): 8. Arbelbide, Xipri. *Piarres Lafitte: Bere Bizia*. Donostia: Elkar, 1986.

——. *Enbata: Abertzalegoaren historioa Iparraldean*. Donostia: Kutxa Fundazioa, 1996.

——. *Euskaldunak Aljerian, 1954–1962*. Donostia: Elkar, 2003.

——. "*Herrian* agertu artikuluak, Aljeriako soldadoen igorririk." In *Aljeriako gerla eta Euskal Herria (1954–1962): La guerre d'Algérie et le Pays Basque (1954–1962)*, edited by Xipri Arbelbide et al. Donostia: Eusko Ikaskuntza, 2005.

——. *Iraultza Heletan: Errepublikarentzat hil behorrari*. Donostia: Etor, 1994.

Arcocha, Aurélie. "Sur la traduction en basque des textes officiels de la période révolutionnaire." In *1789 et les Basques: Histoire, langue et littérature*, edited by Jean Baptiste Orpustan. Bordeaux: Presses Universitaires de Bordeaux, 1991.

Arkotxa, Fermin. "Augustin Chaho, un républicain basque de la monarchie de juillet au second empire." In Manex Goyhenetche, et al., *Histoire général du Pays Basque*. Volume 5. *Le XIXe siècle, 1804–1914*. Baiona: Elkar, 2005.

Arregi, Natxo. *Memorias de KAS (1975–1978)*. Donostia: Hordago, 1981.

Arrien, Gregorio. *La generación del exilio: Génesis de las escuelas vascas y las colonias escolares (1932–1940)*. Bilbao: Onura, 1983.

Association pour le Département Pays Basque (ADPB). *Déclaration de la Association pour le département Pays Basque* (2002).

Aulestia, Gorka. *The Basque Poetic Tradition*. Translated by Linda White. Foreword by Linda White. Reno: University of Nevada Press, 2000.

Aurkenerena, Joseba. *Iparraldeko kronikak*. Bilbao: Gero; Mensajero, 2003. Batera. "Charte de Batera" (2002).

——. "Proposamenak" (2004).

Bayart, Jean-François. "L'imaginaire dans l'affirmation identitaire." Interview with Jean-François Bayart in *L'identité, l'individu, le groupe, la société*, edited by Jean Claude Ruano Borbalan. Paris: Éditions Sciences Humaines, 1998.

Bello, Eduardo. "J. J. Rousseau y la Revolución francesa." In *Ilustración y revolución francesa en el País Vasco*. Edited by Xabier Palacios. Vitoria: Instituto de Estudios sobre Nacionalismos Comparados, 1991.

Bénichou, Paul. *Le temps des prophètes*. Paris: Gallimard, 1977.

Berger, Peter L., and Thomas Luckmann. *The Social Construction of Reality: A Treatise in the Sociology of Knowledge*. Garden City, NY: Doubleday, 1966.

Berhokoirigoin, Mixel. "Kontraboterearen sareak Ipar Euskal Herrian." Lecture, Udako Euskal Unibertsitatea (Basque Summer University), Iruñea (Pamplona), July 20, 2005.

Beriáin, Josetxo. "Los ídolos de la tribu en el nacionalismo vasco." In *Relatos de la nación: La construcción de las identidades nacionales en el mundo hispánico*, edited by Francisco Colom. Madrid: Biblioteca Nueva; CSIC; Vervuert, 2005.

Berzaitz, Pierre Paul. *Harizpe Pastorala*. Muskildi, 1991.

Bidart, Filipe. *Bakartasunez, bi hitz*. Tafalla: Txalaparta, 2005.

Bidart, Pierre. "Langue et idéologie dans la culture basque." In *La nouvelle société basque: Ruptures et changements*, edited by Pierre Bidart. Paris: L'Harmattan, 1980.

———. "Preface." In Joseph Augustin Chaho, *Voyage en Navarre durant l'insurrection des basques (1830–1835); L'agonie du Parti Révolutionnaire en France: Lettre a Monsieur Jacques Laffitte*. 1836, 1838; Hélette: Harriet, and Marseille: Laffitte Reprints, 1979.

———. "Revolución francesa y socialización del Estado-Nación." In *Ilustración y revolución francesa en el País Vasco*, edited by Xabier Palacios. Vitoria: Instituto de Estudios sobre Nacionalismos Comparados, 1991.

———. "La Révolution Française et la question linguistique." In *1789 et les Basques: Histoire, langue et littérature*, edited by Jean Baptiste Orpustan. Bordeaux: Presses Universitaires de Bordeaux, 1991.

———, ed. *La nouvelle société basque: Ruptures et changements*. Paris: L'Harmattan, 1980.

———, ed. *Le Pays Basque et l'Europe*. Baigorri: Izpegi, 1994.

Bidegain, Eneko. "Iparretarrak: Erakunde baten historioa," unpublished manuscript (2006).

Billig, Michael. *Banal Nationalism*. London: Routledge, 1995.

Biltzar. *1790: Créations des départements; 1998: projet de création d'un département* (1998).

Blas, Andrés de. *Nacionalismo e ideologías políticas contemporáneas*. Madrid: Espasa-Calpe, 1984.

Borda, Itxaro. *Allegro ma non troppo*. Hondarribia: Hiru, 1996.

Bourdieu, Pierre. *Language and Symbolic Power*. Edited with an introduction by John B. Thompson. Translated by Gino Raymond and Matthew Adamson. Cambridge: Polity Press, 1991.

Bray, Zoe. "Boundaries and Identities on the Franco–Spanish Frontier," CIBR Working Papers in Border Studies CIBR/WP02–2 (2002). Available on-line at http://www.ub.ac.uk/cibr/WPpdffiles/ CIBRwp2002_2_rev.pdf.

Breuilly, John. *Nationalism and the State*. 2nd ed. Manchester: Manchester University Press; New York: St. Martin's Press, 1993.

Brubaker, Rogers. *Citizenship and Nationhood in France and Germany*. Cambridge, MA: Harvard University Press, 1992.

Campión, Arturo. "La langue basque" (1897). In *La tradition au pays Basque: Ethnographie, folklore, art populaire, histoire, hagiographie*, edited by Pierre Lafitte. 1899; Donostia: Elkar, 1998.

Cardaillac-Hermosilla, Yvette. "Les minorités religieuses au Pays Basque d'auprès les documents de P. Haristoy." In *Pierre Haristoy: Historia jardunaldia, journée d'Histoire*. Donostia: Eusko Ikaskuntza, 2005.

Caro Baroja, Julio. *El laberinto vasco*. San Sebastián: Txertoa, 1989.

Casquette, Jesús. "Estructura e identidad: Los nuevos movimientos sociales." *Inguruak* 14 (1996): 143–75.

Cassan, Patrick. *Francia y la cuestión vasca*. Tafalla: Txalaparta, 1998.

Castaings-Beretervide, Mayi. *La Révolution en Pays Basque*. Donibane Lohizune: Ikuska, 1994.

Castells, Manuel. *End of Millennium*. 2nd ed. Oxford: Blackwell, 2000.

Castoreo, Patrick. "Langue basque et enseignement primaire publique des années 1880 à 1914." In *Pierre Haristoy: Historia jardunaldia, journée d'histoire*. Donostia: Eusko Ikaskuntza, 2005.

Chaho, J. Augustin. *Bizkaiko baten eleak: Palabras de un vizcaíno a la reina Cristina*. Bilbao: Likiniano, 1999. Chaho [Xaho], Augustin, and Vicente de Arana. *Las leyendas de Aitor*. Donostia-San Sebastián: Roger, 2000.

———. *Viaje a Navarra durante la insurrección de los vascos (1830–1835)*. Donostia: Auñamendi, 1976. Translation of *Voyage en Navarre pendant l'insurrection des Basques (1830–1835)*. Paris: A Bertrand, 1836.

Chalot, Bérénice. "Ernest Lavisse: 'Instituteur national'," History Lecture, December 12, 2001. Available on-line at http://perso.wanadoo.fr/david.colon/Sciences-Po/lavisse.pdf.

Charritton, Piarres [Pierre]. *De re publica edo politikaz*. Donostia: Elkar, 2003.

———. *Euskalzaleen Biltzarra-ren historia laburra (1901–2003)*. Baiona: Eskualzaleen Biltzarra, 2003.

———. "Historiarik gabeko Ipar Euskal Herria?" *Jakin* 9 (1979): 22–26.

Chaussier, Jean Daniel. "L'échec du projet de création d'un département en Pays Basque." *Le Bulletin du Musée Basque* 120 (1988): 57–72.

———. "La Mission Ravail au Pays Basque (1982): Pouvoir du discours identitaire ou discours du pouvoir sur l'identité?" *Le Bulletin du Musée Basque* 138 (1994): 113–44.

———. "Pays Basque, un département?: Une revendication citoyenne dans un cadre républicain." In *Pays Basque: Un département? 100 réponses*. Edited by Claude Perrotin. Anglet: Atlantica, 2002.

———. *Quel territoire pour le Pays Basque?: Les cartes de l'identité*. Paris: L'Harmattan, 1997.

———. "La question territoriale en Pays Basque de France (exception irréductible ou laboratoire du pluralisme?)." In *La construcción del espacio vasco-aquitano: Un estudio multidisciplinar*, edited by Antón Borja, Francisco Letamendia, and Kepa Sodupe. Leioa: Servicio Editorial de la Universidad del País Vasco, 1998.

Citron, Suzanne. "Ecole, histoire de France: Construction d'une mémoire nationale, crise de l'identité nationale." Actes du Colloque de Carpentras, "Ecole, pouvoir(s), identité(s)," Lycée Victor Hugo, April 29, 2001. In *Dialogues Politiques* 2 (January 2003). Available on-line at http://www.la-science-politique.com/revue/revue2/papier2.htm.

———. "Recomposer le passé." *Le Monde*, November 5, 2003.

Clark, Robert P. *The Basque Insurgents: ETA, 1952–1980*. Madison: University of Wisconsin Press, 984.

Club de Prospective. *Pays Basque 2010, Analyse Structurale*. Bayonne, 1993.

———. *Pays Basque 2010, Diagnostic*. Bayonne, 1993.

———. *Pays Basque 2010, Hypothèse*. Bayonne, 1993.

———. *Pays Basque 2010, Scénarios*. Bayonne, 1993.

Connor, Walker. *Ethnonationalism: The Quest for Understanding*. Princeton: Princeton University Press, 1994.

Conseil de Développement du Pays Basque (CDPB). *Convention spécifique Pays Basque, Bayonne, 22 décembre 2000*. Bayonne, 2001.

———. *Evaluation du schéma d'aménagement et de développement du Pays Basque*. Bayonne, 2000.

———. *Lurraldea: 10 ans déjà, 10 ans après*. Bayonne, 2003.

———. *Schéma daménagement et de développement du Pays Basque: Orientations générales*. Bayonne, 1996.

———. *Statuts, Conseil de Développement du Pays Basque*. Bayonne: Préfecture de Bayonne, 1994.

Conseil des Élus du Pays Basque (CEPB). *Contribution aux Assises des Libertés Locales*. Bayonne, 2002.

———. *Statuts*. Bayonne, 1995.

Corcuera, Javier. *The Origins, Ideology, and Organization of Basque Nationalism, 1876–1903*. Translated by Albert Bork and Cameron J. Watson. Reno: Center for Basque Studies, University of Nevada, Reno, 2007. Originally published as *Orígenes, ideología y organización del nacionalismo vasco (1876–1904)*. Madrid: Siglo XXI, 1979.

Coyos, Jean-Baptiste. *Politique linguistique*. Baiona: Elkar, 2005.

Crouzet, Jean. "Chaho franc-maçon et la Révolution bayonnaise." In *Augustin Chaho*, Edited by Gustave Lambert et al. Hélette: Editions Harriet, 1996.

CSA. *Sondage exclusif CSA–La Semaine du Pays Basque*, September 9, 2000.

———. *Sondage exclusif CSA–Sud Ouest*, August 29, 1999.

Davant, Jean-Louis. *Aberri eta klase burruka euskal mugimenduan*. Baiona: Elkar; Hendaye: Mugalde, 1977.

———. *Histoire du peuple basque*. 8th ed. Reprint. 1970; Donostia: Elkarlanean, 2000. del Valle, Teresa. *Korrika: Basque Ritual for Ethnic Identity*. Translated by Linda White. Reno: University of Nevada Press, 1994.

della Porta, Donatella. "Social Movements and the State: Thoughts on the Policing of Protest." In *Comparative Perspectives on Social Movements: Political Opportunities, Mobilizing Structures, and Cultural Framings*, edited by Doug McAdam, John D. McCarthy, and Mayer N. Zald. Cambridge: Cambridge University Press, 1996.

Demo. *Demokrazia Euskal Herriarentzat–Démocratie pour le Pays Basque*. Baiona: Gatuzain, 2002.

Desplat, Christian. "El clero vasco-francés y la Revolución." In *Ilustración y revolución francesa en el País Vasco*, edited by Xabier Palacios. Vitoria: Instituto de Estudios sobre Nacionalismos Comparados, 1991.

Destrée, Alain. *La Basse Navarre et ces institutions de 1620 à la Révolution*. Zaragoza: Universidad de Zaragoza, 1955.

Díaz Noci, Javier. "Sociedad y medios de comunicación en lengua vasca en el período de entreguerras (1919–1937)." In *Revista de Historia Contemporánea de la Universidad de Murcia* (1995). Available on-line at http://www.ehu.es/diaz-noci/Arts/a7.pdf.

———, and Nuria Moret Llosas. "La cultura en Vasconia. Entre la tradición y la modernidad." In *Historia de Euskal Herria/Historia general de los vascos*, Volume 5. *Vasconia (1876–1937): Entre la tradición y la modernidad*, edited by Joseba Agirreazkuenaga. Donostia: Lur, 2005.

Documentos Y. 10 volumes. San Sebastián: Hordago, 1979–80.

Donnan, Hastings, and Thomas M. Wilson, *Borders: Frontiers of Identity, Nation and State*. Oxford: Berg, 1999.

Douglass, William A. "Crítica de las últimas tendencias en el análisis del nacionalismo." In *Sociología del nacionalismo*, edited by Alfonso Pérez-Agote. Bilbao: Servicio Editorial de la Universidad del País Vasco, 1989.

Drouin, Jean-Claude. "L'ésotérisme d'Augustin Chaho: Cosmologie, histoire et politique au XIXe siècle." *Bulletin de la Société des Sciences, Lettres, Arts et Études Régionales de Bayonne* (1973): 265–77. Reprint in *Augustin Chaho*, edited by Gustave Lambert et al. Hélette: Editions Harriet, 1996.

———. "La place de la Philosophie des Révélations de Chaho (1835) dans l'histoire des idées au XIXe siècle." *Bulletin de la Société des Sciences, Lettres, Arts et Études Régionales de Bayonne* (1981–1982): 389–99. Reprint in Gustave *Augustin Chaho*, edited by Gustave Lambert et al. Hélette: Editions Harriet, 1996.

Dubar, Claude. "Socialisation et construction identitaire." In *L'identité: L'individu, le groupe, la société*, edited by Jean Claude Ruano-Borbalan. Paris: Sciences Humaines, 1998. Duhart, Michel. *Dominique Joseph Garat, 1749–1833*. 2 vols. Bayonne: Estrait du Bulletin de la Société des Sciences, Lettres et Arts de Bayonne, 1993–94.

———. *Yo, Domingo José Garat*. San Sebastián: Txertoa, 1997.

Dupré-Moretti, Éric. "Esquisses biographique et bibliographique d'Augustin Xaho." *Ikuska* 10 (1995): 1–33. Reprint in *Augustin Chaho*, edited by Gustave Lambert et al. Hélette: Editions Harriet, 1996.

Eder, Klaus. "La institucionalización de la acción colectiva: ¿Hacia una nueva problemática teórica en el análisis de los movimientos sociales?" In *Los movimientos sociales: Transformaciones políticas y cambio cultural*, edited by Pedro Ibarra and Benjamín Tejerina. Madrid: Trotta, 1998.

Egaña, Iñaki. *Diccionario histórico-político de Euskal Herria*. Tafalla: Txalaparta, 1996. Elizondo, Mauro. *Sabino Arana: El hombre y su trayectoria*. Bilbao: Fundación Sabino Arana, 1992.

Elorza, Antonio. *Ideologías del nacionalismo vasco 1876–1937 (De los "euskaros" a Jagi Jagi)*. San Sebastián: Aramburu, 1979.

Encina y Pérez de Onraita, Ricardo de la. *Poder y communidad: Una sociología del nacionalismo*. Iruña: Pamiela, 2004.

Ereñaga, Amaia. *Marc Légasse: Un rebelde burlón*. Tafalla: Txalaparta, 1997.

Etchecopar Etchart, Hélène. *Théâtres basques: Une histoire du théâtre populaire en marche*. Baiona: Gatuzain, 2001.

Etcheverry, Jean-Noël. "Les partis politiques: Abertzaleen Batasuna." In *Pays Basque: Un département? 100 réponses*, edited by Claude Perrotin, 285–88. Anglet: Atlantica, 2002.

Etcheverry, Peio. "Le siècle de l'âge industriel: La mise en place du pluralisme basque." In Manex Goyhenetche, et al., *Histoire général du Pays Basque*, Volume 5. *Le XIXe siècle, 1804–1914*. Baiona: Elkar, 2005.

Euskal Batasuna. "Foundational Manifesto" (1986).

Eusko Ikaskuntza, Eusko Jaurlaritza-Gobierno Vasco, and EKE, *Identidad colectiva y prácticas culturales en Euskal Herria*. Donostia: Eusko Ikaskuntza, 2007.

Eustat and EKE. *Encuesta socio-lingüística de Euskal Herria*. Vitoria-Gasteiz: Eustat, 2001.

———, and INSEE. *Encuesta socio-lingüística de Euskal Herria*. Vitoria-Gasteiz: Eustat, 1996. Fagoaga, Jean, et al., eds. *Madeleine de Jauréguiberry: Omenaldia-Hommage*. Donostia: Eusko Ikaskuntza, 2001.

Fernández de Casavedante Romani, Carlos. *La frontera hispano-francesa y las relaciones de vecindad: Especial referencia al sector fronterizo del País Vasco*. Leioa: Servicio Editorial de la Universidad del País Vasco, 1985.

———. "El marco jurídico de la cooperación transfronteriza: Su concreción en el ámbito hispano-francés." In *Baiona-Donostia Euskal Eurohiriori buruzko gogoeta jardunaldiak/Jornadas de reflexión sobre la Eurociudad Vasca Bayona-San Sebastián/Journées de réflexion sur la Eurocité Basque Bayonne-Saint Sébastien*, edited by Jon Basterra et al. *Azkoaga: Cuadernos de Ciencias Sociales y Económicas*. Donostia: Eusko Ikaskuntza, 2001.

Fernández de Larrinoa, Kepa. "The Folk Arts of the *Maskarada* Performance." In *Voicing the Moment: Improvised Oral Poetry and Basque Tradition*, edited by Samuel G. Armistead and Joseba Zulaika, Center for Basque Studies, Conference Papers Series 3. Reno: Center for Basque Studies, University of Nevada, Reno, 2005.

———. *Nekazal gizartea eta antzerki herrikoia Pirinioetako haran batean*. Cuadernos de sección, Antropología y Etnografía 9. Donostia: Eusko Ikaskuntza-Sociedad de Estudios Vascos, 1993.

Fernández Sebastián, Javier. "Marchena y el País Vasco." In *1789 et les Basques: Histoire, langue et littérature*, edited by Jean Baptiste Orpustan. Bordeaux: Presses Universitaires de Bordeaux, 1991.

Fernández Sebastián, Javier, and Paloma Miranda de Lage-Damon, "Exiliados españoles en Bayona en tiempo de la Revolución (1789–1793)." In *1789 et les Basques: Histoire, langue et littérature*, edited by Jean Baptiste Orpustan Bordeaux: Presses Universitaires de Bordeaux, 1991.

Fourcaud, Louis de. "Discours prononcé a Saint-Jean-de-Luz a l'occasion de l'ouverture du congrès de la tradition basque" (1897), in Pierre Lafitte, *La tradition au pays Basque: Ethnographie, folklore, art populaire, histoire, hagiographie*. 1899; Donostia: Elkar, 1998.

Fourquet, François. "La Mascarade d'Ordiarp." *Bulletin du Musée Basque* 129 (1990): 101–56.

Fromm, Erich. *Escape from Freedom*. 1941; New York: H. Holt, 1994.

———. *Planification et développement local au Pays Basque*. Bayonne: Commissariat Général au Plan; Group de Recherche Sociale Ikerka, 1988.

Gabilondo, Joseba. "On the Postcolonial and Queer Origins of Modern Basque Literature: Rethinking *Lore Jokoak* and Anton Abbadie's Contribution." Paper presented at Session Three of the First International Symposium on Basque Cultural Studies, London, June 29–July 2, 2000.

Gamson, William A., and David S. Meyer. "Framing Political Opportunity." In *Comparative Perspectives on Social Movements: Political Opportunities, Mobilizing Structures, and Cultural Framings*, edited by Doug McAdam, John D. McCarthy, and Mayer N. Zald. Cambridge: Cambridge University Press, 1996.

Garamendi Azcorra, María Arene. *El teatro popular vasco semiótica de la representación*. Donostia: Diputación Foral de Gipuzkoa, 1991.

Garmendia, José Mari, and Alberto Elordi. *La resistencia vasca*. San Sebastián: Haranburu, 1982.

Gatti, Gabriel. *Las modalidades débiles de la identidad: Sociología de la identidad en los territorios vacíos de sociedad y de sociología. Los escenarios d aprendizaje de euskera por adultos.* Leioa: Servicio Editorial, Universidad del País Vasco, 2002.

Geiger, Wolfgang. "La Revolución francesa: El concepto de soberanía nacional y las naciones sin estado." In *Derechos humanos individuales, derechos de los estados, derechos de los pueblos: II Congreso sobre Derechos Humanos Individuales y Colectivos*, edited by Joseba Goñi Alzuela et al. Bilbao: Herria 2000 Eliza, 1990.

Gellner, Ernest. *Nationalism.* London: Phoenix, 1998.

———. *Nations and Nationalism.* Oxford: Blackwell, 1983.

Goñi, Joseba M., and Piarres Charritton. "De quelques différences caractéristiques du catholicisme en Iparralde et Hegoalde." In Manex Goyhenetche, et al., *Histoire général du Pays Basque*, Volume 5. *Le XIXe siècle, 1804–1914.* Baiona: Elkar, 2005.

Goñi, Pascal. "L'Abbé Haristoy (1833–1901): Le père d'historiographie conservatrice basque sur la Révolution." In *Pierre Haristoy: Historia Jardunaldia/Journée d'Histoire.* Donostia: Eusko Ikaskuntza, 2005.

Goyheneche, Eugène [Eukeni Goyhenetxe]. "Un ancêtre du nationalisme basque: Augustin Chaho et la guerre carliste." In *Euskal Herria (1789–1850): Actes du Colloque International d'Etudes Basques (Bordeaux 3–5 mai 1973).* Bayonne: Société des Amis du Musée Basque, 1978. Reprinted in *Augustin Chaho*, edited by in Gustave Lambert et al. Hélette: Editions Harriet, 1996.

———. *Historia de Iparralde: Desde los orígenes a nuestros días.* San Sebastián: Txertoa, 1985.

———. *Le Pays Basque: Soule, Labourd, Basse-Navarre.* Pau: Société nouvelle d'éditions régionales et diffusion, 1979.

Goyhenetche, Jean. *Les basques et leur histoire: Mythes et Réalités.* Donostia and Baiona: Elkar, 1992.

———. "Deux cas historiographiques des guerres de la Convention: L'évacuation des comunes du Labourd et l'exécution de Madeleine Larralde." In *La Révolution française dans l'histoire et la littérature basques du XIXe siècle: Actes du colloque international de l'URA 1055 du C.N.R.S.*, edited by Jean Baptiste Orpustan. Baigorri: Izpegi, 1994.

———. "Dominique Garat: Un représentant de l'Esprit des Lumières en Labourd au XVIII$_e$ siècle." In *1789 et les Basques: Histoire, langue et littérature*, edited by Jean Baptiste Orpustan. Bordeaux: Presses Universitaires de Bordeaux, 1991.

———. "Les Etats de Navarre en 1789: La crise du foralisme provincialiste." In *1789 et les Basques: Histoire, langue et littérature*, edited by Jean Baptiste Orpustan. Bordeaux: Presses Universitaires de Bordeaux, 1991.

Goyhenetche, Manex. *Histoire de la colonisation française au pays Basque: Les origines du problème basque.* Hendaye: Mugalde, 1975.

———. *Histoire générale du Pays Basque*. Volume 1. *Préhistoire, époque romain, Moyen Age*. Donostia and Baiona: Elkar, 1998. Translated into Spanish as *Historia general del País Vasco*. Volume 1. *Prehistoria, Época Romana, Edad Media*. Donostia: Ttarttalo, 1999.

———. *Histoire générale du Pays Basque*. Volume 2. *Évolution politique et institutionnelle du XVIe au XVIII siècle*. Donostia and Baiona: Elkar, 1999.

———. *Histoire générale du Pays Basque*. Volume 4. *La Révolution de 1789*. Donostia and Baiona: Elkar, 2002.

———, et al. *Histoire générale du Pays Basque*, Volume 5. *Le XIXe siècle, 1804–1914*. Donostia and Baiona: Elkar, 2005.

———. "L'historiographie ecclésiastique dominante du XIXe siècle." In *Pierre Haristoy. Historia Jardunaldia. Journée d'Histoire*. Donostia: Eusko Ikaskuntza, 2005.

———. *L'oppression culturelle française au Pays Basque*. Bayonne: Elkar, 1974.

Guilcher, Jean Michel. "La danza tradicional en Euskadi Norte." In *Ser vasco*, edited by Jean Haritschelhar. Bilbao: Mensajero, 1986.

Gurrutxaga Abad, Ander. *Del PNV a ETA: La transformación del nacionalismo vasco*. Donostia-San Sebastián: R&B Ediciones, 1996.

———. *La mirada difusa: Dilemas del nacionalismo*. Irun: Alberdania, 2002.

Halimi, Gisèle. *Le procès de Burgos*. Preface by Jean Paul Sartre. Paris: Gallimard, 1971.

Haran, Dominique. "Références historiques des rencontres entre les deux territoires: Synthèse de la Journée." In *Baiona-Donostia Euskal Eurohiriori buruzko gogoeta jardunaldiak/Jornadas de reflexión sobre la Eurociudad Vasca Bayona-San Sebastián/Journées de réflexion sur la Eurocité Basque Bayonne-Saint Sébastien*, edited by Jon Basterra et al., *Azkoaga. Cuadernos de Ciencias Sociales y Económicas*. Donostia: Eusko Ikaskuntza, 2001.

Haritschelhar, Jean, ed. "Le centenaire de la révolution française dans *l'Euskalduna* (1889–1895)." In *La Révolution française dans l'histoire et la littérature basques du XIXe siècle: Actes du colloque international de l'URA 1055 du C.N.R.S.*, edited by Jean Baptiste Orpustan. Baigorri: Izpegi, 1994.

———. "Michel Labéguerie olerki abestua." In *Michel Labéguerie: Omenaldia-Hommage*, edited by Laurent Darraidou et al. Donostia: Eusko Ikaskuntza, 2001.

———. "La Pastoral souletine: Une tradition renouvelée." *Bulletin du Musée Basque* 127 (1990): 1–6.

———. *Ser vasco*. Bilbao: Mensajero, 1986.

HASI. *HASIko Aparteko Kongresuari irtetzen den Komite Zentralan Informea/ Informe del Comité Central Saliente al Congreso Extraordinario de HASI* (December 1988).

———. *Entrevista mecanografiada a la Dirección de HASI* (1989).

HB, EMA, HA and EB. *Manifiesto de acción política común en Ipar y Hegoalde* (March 24, 1994).

Hernández Mata, Amelia. "Pierre Lafitte bere eskutitzen bitartez: Euskalzaletasuna Iparraldean pizteko saiakera bat." *Oihenart: Cuadernos de Lengua y Literatura* 18 (2000): 63–78.

Hunt, Scott, Robert Benford, and David A. Snow, "Identity Fields: Framing Processes and the Social Construction of Movement identities." In *New Social Movements: From Ideology to Identity*, edited by Enrique Laraña, Hank Johnston, and Joseph Gusfield. Philadelphia, PA: Temple University Press, 1994.

Ibarra, Pedro. *La evolución estratégica de ETA: De la "guerra revolucionaria" (1963) hasta después de la tregua (1989)*. Donostia: Kriselu, 1989.

———. *Manual de sociedad civil y movimientos sociales*. Madrid: Síntesis, 2005.

———. *Nacionalismo: Razón y pasión*. Barcelona: Ariel, 2005.

Insausti, Jesús. "Introduction." In Mauro Elizondo, *Sabino Arana: El hombre y su trayectoria*. Bilbao: Fundación Sabino Arana, 1992.

Iparretarrak. *20 ans de lutte: Autonomie et avant projet* (March 31, 1993).

Itçaina [Itzaina], Xabier. "L'Identité au travail: Economie social et solidaire et mouvement identitaire en pays Basque." Paper presented at the First European Conference of the International Society for Third-Sector Research (ISTR) and the EMES European Research Network, April 27–29, 2005, Conservatoire National des Arts et Métiers (CNAM), Paris.

———. "Michel Labéguerie eta dantza." In *Michel Labéguerie: Omenaldia-Hommage*, edited by Laurent Darraidou et al. Donostia: Eusko Ikaskuntza, 2001.

———. "Les politisations plurielles de la société basque à la fin du XIXe siècle." In Manex Goyhenetche, et al., *Histoire général du Pays Basque*. Volume 5. *Le XIXe siècle, 1804–1914*. Baiona: Elkar, 2005.

———, and Idoia Ikardo. "Folklore e identidad en el País Vasco: Pistas para una comparación transfronteriza." In *La construcción del espacio vasco-aquitano: Un estudio multidisciplinar*, edited by Antón Borja, Francisco Letamendia, and Kepa Sodupe. Leioa: Servicio Editorial de la Universidad del País Vasco, 1998.

Itzaina, Mixel. "Algeria, 'Eskual Herrian' Alger-en." In *Aljeriako gerla eta Euskal Herria (1954–1962)/La guerre d'Algérie et le Pays Basque (1954–1962)*, edited by Xipri Arbelbide et al. Donostia: Eusko Ikaskuntza, 2005.

———. "Michel Labéguerie et M. l'Abbé Pierre Lafitte." In Laurent Darraidou et al., *Michel Labéguerie: Omenaldia-Hommage*, edited by Laurent Darraidou et al. Donostia: Eusko Ikaskuntza, 2001.

———. "Michel Labéguerie: Le bertsularisme et la langue basque." *Michel Labéguerie: Omenaldia-Hommage*, edited by Laurent Darraidou et al. Donostia: Eusko Ikaskuntza, 2001.

———. *Mixel Labéguerie: Kantu berritzaile eta politika gizona*. Donostia: Elkarlanean, 1999.

Izquierdo, Jean Marie. *Le Pays Basque de France: La difficile maturation d'un sentiment nationaliste basque.* 1998; Paris: L'Harmattan, 2001.

Jacob, James E. "The French Revolution and the Basques of France." In *Basque Politics: A Case Study in Ethnic Nationalism*, edited by William A. Douglass. Occasional Papers Series No. 2. Reno: Associated Faculty Press and Basque Studies Program, 1985.

———. *Hills of Conflict: Basque Nationalism in France.* Reno: University of Nevada Press, 1994.

Jacquard, Roland. *La longue traque d'Action directe.* Paris: Albin Michel, 1987.

Jáuregui Bereciartu, Gurutz. *Ideología y estrategia política de ETA: Análisis de su evolución entre 1959 y 1968.* Madrid: Siglo XXI, 1981.

Jauréguiberry, Francis. "Europe, langue basque et modernité en Pays Basque français." In *Le Pays Basque et l'Europe*, edited by Pierre Bidart. Baigorri: Izpegi, 1994.

Jerez, Miguel. "Los grupos de presión." In *Manual de Ciencia Política*, edited by Rafael del Águila. Madrid: Trotta, 1997.

Jiménez de Aberásturi, Juan Carlos. "De la derrota a la esperanza. Euskadi en la II Guerra Mundial, 1939–1945." Ph.D. diss., University of the Basque Country, 1998.

———. *De la derrota a la esperanza: Políticas vascas durante la Segunda Guerra Mundial (1937–1947).* Oñati: IVAP, 1999.

Jones, Charles O. *An Introduction to the Study of Public Policy.* 3rd ed. Monterey, CA: Brooks Cole, 1984.

Jordana, Jacint. "El análisis de los policy networks: ¿Una nueva perspectiva sobre la relación entre las políticas públicas y el Estado?" *Gestión y Análisis de Políticas Públicas* 3 (1995): 77–90.

Juaristi, Jon. *El bucle melancólico: Historias de nacionalistas vascos.* 2nd ed. Madrid: Espasa-Calpe, 2000.

———. *El linaje de Aitor: La invención de la tradición vasca.* Madrid: Taurus, 1987.

Juaristi, Patxi. "Relaciones transfronterizas en el ámbito de la cultura y de la lengua vasca en la CAPV, CFN y en el Consejo Regional de Aquitania." In *La construcción del espacio vasco-aquitano: Un estudio multidisciplinar*, edited by Antón Borja, Francisco Letamendia, and Kepa Sodupe. Leioa: Servicio Editorial de la Universidad del País Vasco, 1998.

Kanblong, Ramuntxo. "Iparraldeko Ekonomia." *Jakin* 9 (January–March 1979): 49–61.

KAS. *Alternativa táctica-estratégica de KAS* (1981).

———. *Situación organizativa* (1992).

Keating, Michael. *Nations against the State: The New Politics of Nationalism in Quebec, Catalonia, and Scotland.* 2nd ed. Houndmills, Basingstoke, Hampshire, UK: Palgrave, 2001.

Kedourie, Elie. *Nationalism.* 4th ed. Oxford: Blackwell Press, 1993.

Kortazar, Jon. *Euskal literaturaren historia txikia.* Zarautz: Erein, 1997.

Kriesi, Hanspeter. "El contexto político de los nuevos movimientos sociales en Europa." In *Las transformaciones de lo político*, edited by Jorge Benedicto and Fernando Reinares. Madrid: Alianza, 1992.

———. "The Organizational Structure of New Social Movements in Relation to Their Political Context." In *Comparative Perspectives on Social Movements: Political Opportunities, Mobilizing Structures, and Cultural Framings*, edited by Doug McAdam, John D. McCarthy, and Mayer N. Zald. Cambridge: Cambridge University Press, 1996.

Labedan, Bruno. *Jeu de acteurs et institutions: Études des oppositions autour de la revendication départementaliste contemporaine au Pays Basque français.* Bordeaux: IEP, 1998.

Laborde, Cécile. "The Culture(s) of the Republic: Nationalism and Multiculturalism in French Republican Thought." *Political Theory* 29, no. 5 (October 2001): 716–35.

Laborde, Pierre. *Pays Basque: Économie et société en mutation.* Donostia and Baiona: Elkar, 1994.

Lafitte, Pierre. *Eskual-herriaren alde Pour le Pays Basque: Court commentaire du programme Eskualerriste à l'usage des militants.* Bayonne: Imprimerie La Presse, 1933.

———. *Kazetari lan-hautatuak*, edited by Pako Sudupe. Donostia: Elkar, 2002.

Lafont, Robert. *La revendication occitane.* Paris: Flammarion, 1974.

———. *La révolution régionaliste.* Paris: Gallimard, 1967. Spanish version, *La revolución regionalista*, translated by Francisco Fernández Buey. Barcelona: Ariel, 1971.

———. *Le Sud et le Nord: Dialectique de la France.* Toulouse: Privat, 1971.

Lafourcade, Maïté. "La frontière franco-espagnol, lieu de conflits interétatiques et de collaboration interrégionale." In *La frontière franco-espagnol, lieu de conflits interétatiques et de collaboration interrégionale: Actes de la journée d'études du 16 novembre 1996, Biarritz*, edited by Maïté Lafourcade. Bordeaux: Presses Universitaires de Bordeaux, 1998.

———. "Les relations entre Bayonne et le Guipuzcoa au XIXème siecle." In *Baiona-Donostia Euskal Eurohiriari buruzko gogoeta jardunaldiak/Journées de reflexio sur l'Eurocité Basque Bayonne-Saint Sebastién/Jornadas de reflexión sobre la Eurociudad Vasca Bayona-San Sebastián.* Donostia-San Sebastián: Eusko Ikaskuntza, 2001.

Landart, Daniel. "Michel Labéguerie eta Eskualzaleen Biltzarra." In *Michel Labéguerie: Omenaldia-Hommage*, edited by Laurent Darraidou et al. Donostia: Eusko Ikaskuntza, 2001.

Larronde, Jean-Claude. *El Batallón Gernika. Los combates de la Pointe-de-Grave (Abril de 1945).* Translated from French by Rafael Aparicio Martin. Bayonne: Bidasoa; Institut d'Histoire Contemporaine, 1995.

———. "Bosquejo de un cuadro social y electoral." In *Ser vasco*, edited by Jean Haritschelhar. Bilbao: Mensajero, 1986.

———. "Culture basque sous l'occupation." *Oihenart: Cuadernos de Lengua y Literatura* 14 (1997), special edition, *Gerra eta literatura 1914–1944*: 221–29.

———. "Histoire du VII_{ème} Congrès d'Etudes Basques, Biarritz, 1948." In *VII_{ème} Congrès d'Etudes Basques/ Eusko Ikaskuntzaren VII. Kongresua/ VII Congreso de Estudios Vascos*, edited by Jean-Claude Larronde. Donostia: Eusko Ikaskuntza, 2005.

———. "Michel Labéguerie: Son cheminement politique." In *Michel Labéguerie: Omenaldia-Hommage*, edited by Laurent Darraidou et al. Donostia: Eusko Ikaskuntza, 2001.

———. *Mouvement Eskualerriste (1932–1937): Naissance du mouvement nationaliste basque en Iparralde/Eskualerri-Zaleen Biltzarra (1932–1937): Eskualerrizaleen mugimendu abertzalearen sortzea Iparraldean/El movimiento Eskualerrista (1932–1937): Nacimiento del movimiento nacionalista vasco en Iparralde*. Bilbao: Sabino Arana Kultur Elkargoa, 1994.

———. *El nacionalismo vasco: Su origen y su ideología en la obra de Sabino Arana-Goiri*. Translated by Lola Valverde. San Sebastián: Txertoa, 1977.

———. "Une plainte contre *Herria* au temps de la guerre d'Algérie." In *Aljeriako gerla eta Euskal Herria (1954–1962)/ La guerre d'Algérie et le Pays Basque (1954–1962)*, edited by Xipri Arbelbide et al. Donostia: Eusko Ikaskuntza, 2005.

Larzabal, Battitta. "Survol d'un siècle de vie politique au Pays Basque Nord." In Manex Goyhenetche, et al., *Histoire général du Pays Basque*. Volume 5. *Le XIXe siècle, 1804–1914*. Baiona: Elkar, 2005.

Lavisse, Ernest. *Histoire de France: Cours moyen*. Paris: Armand Colin, 1920.

Legasse, Marc. *Le statut du pays Basque dans la République Française: Projet du loi*. Saint-Jean-de-Luz: Gargains, 1945?

———. *El zortziko de iraeta para arpa y txalaparta*. San Sebastián: Txertoa, 1990.

Letamendia, Francisco. *Game of Mirrors: Centre-Periphery National Conflicts*. Translated by Karen Hatherley. Aldershot, UK: Ashgate, 2000.

———. *Historia del nacionalismo vasco y de ETA*. 3 vols. San Sebastián: R&B Ediciones, 1994.

———. "La Revolución Francesa: El liberalismo pensado desde el Estado-Nación." In *Ilustración y revolución francesa en el País Vasco*, edited by Xabier Palacios. Vitoria: Instituto de Estudios sobre Nacionalismos Comparados, 1991.

Letamendia, Pierre. "La vie politique en le Pays Basque français, 1958–1982: Permanence et mutation d'un sous système politique." In *Bulletin de la Société des Sciences, Lettres, Arts de Bayonne* 137–138 (1981–1982): 513–27.

Linz, Juan J. *Conflicto en Euskadi*. Madrid: Espasa-Calpe, 1986.

Lopez Adan, Emilio [Beltza, pseud.]. "Ipar Euskal Herria: 150 urte historiarik gabe (1789–1934)." In *Saioak* 2 (1978): 99–135.

———. *El nacionalismo vasco en el exilio 1937–1960*. San Sebastián: Txertoa, 1977.

———. *Nacionalismo y clases sociales*. Donostia: Txertoa, 1976.

Lorenzo Espinosa, José María. *Historia de Euskal Herria*. Volume 3. *El nacimiento de una nación*. Tafalla: Txalaparta, 1997.

Loti, Pierre. *El País Vasco: La visión de un mundo que terminó en el XIX*. Zarautz: Bibliomanías, 2000.

———. *Ramuntcho*. Translated by Henri Pene du Bois. Project Gutenberg EBook. Available on-line at http://www.gutenberg.org/author/Pierre_Loti.

Loughlin, John. *La democracia regional y local en la Unión Europea*. Luxembourg: The Office for Official Publications of the European Communities; Brussels: Committee of the Regions, 1999.

Madariaga Orbea, Juan. *Anthology of Apologists and Detractors of the Basque Language*. Translated by Frederick H. Fornoff, María Cristina Saavedra, Amaia Gabantxo, and Cameron J. Watson. Reno: Center for Basque Studies, University of Nevada, Reno, 2006.

Malherbe, Jean Paul. "Le nationalisme basque en France (1933–1976)." PhD diss., University of Toulouse I, 1977.

———. "Le nationalisme basque et les transformations sociopolitiques en Pays Basque Nord." In *La nouvelle société basque: Ruptures et changements*, edited by Pierre Bidart. Paris: L'Harmattan, 1980.

Mansvelt, Jan. "Euskal Herria, Imagined Territory." Paper presented at the European Standing Group on International Relations (SGIR) Fifth Pan International Relations Conference, "Constructing World Orders," The Hague, September 9–11, 2004.

Martinez de Lezea, Toti. *La cadena rota*. Donostia: Erein, 2005.

Marx, Anthony W. *Faith in Nation: Exclusionary Origins of Nationalism*. Oxford: Oxford University Press, 2003.

Mata López, José Manuel. *El nacionalismo vasco radical: Discurso, organización y expresiones*. Bilbao: Servicio Editorial Universidad del País Vasco, 1993.

Mateo, Miren, and Xabier Aizpurua. "Euskararen bilakaera soziolinguistikoa." *Euskonews & Media* 201 (February 28–March 7, 2003). Available on-line at http://www.euskonews.com/0201zbk/gaia20107eu.html.

Mayte, Philippe. "Eskualdun Gazteria face à la guerre d'Algérie." In *Aljeriako gerla eta Euskal Herria (1954–1962)/La guerre d'Algérie et le Pays Basque (1954–1962)*, edited by Xipri Arbelbide et al. Donostia: Eusko Ikaskuntza, 2005.

McAdam, Doug, John D. McCarthy, and Mayer N. Zald, eds. *Comparative Perspectives on Social Movements: Political Opportunities, Mobilizing Structures, and Cultural Framings*. Cambridge: Cambridge University Press, 1996.

Mees, Ludger, Santiago de Pablo, and José Antonio Rodríguez. *El péndulo patriótico: Historia del Partido Nacionalista Vasco*. 2nd ed. Barcelona: Crítica, 2005.

Mény, Yves, and Jean-Claude Thoenig. *Las políticas públicas*. Barcelona: Ariel, 1992. Translated from the French: *Politiques publiques*. Paris: PUF, 1989.

Mitterand, François. "110 propositions pour la France" (1981).

Monreal Zia, Gregorio. *The Old Law of Bizkaia (1452): Introductory Study and Critical Edition*. Translated by William A. Douglass and Linda White. Preface by William A. Douglass. Basque Classic Series No. 1. Reno: Center for Basque Studies, University of Nevada, Reno, 2005.

Morán Blanco, Sagrario. *ETA entre España y Francia*. Madrid: Complutense, 1997.

Moreau, Jacques. *Administration régionale, départementale et municipale*. Paris: Dalloz, 1999.

Moruzzi, Jean-François, and Emmanuel Boulaert. *Iparretarrak: Séparatisme et terrorisme au Pays Basque*. Paris: Plon, 1988.

Olsen, Johan, Paul G. Roness, and Harald Saetren. "Norway: Still Peaceful Coexistence and Revolution in Slow Motion?" In *Policy Styles in Western Europe*, edited by Jeremy Richardson. London: Allen & Unwin, 1982.

Olson, Mancur. *The Logic of Collective Action: Public Goods and the Theory of Groups*. Cambridge, MA: Harvard University Press, 1965.

Oronos, Michel. *Le Mouvement culturel basque 1951–2001*. Donostia: Elkar, 2002.

Orpustan, Jean Baptiste. "De l'histoire a la littérature: L'épisode de Joanis et le chant de soldats de Baïgorri dans le Peru Abarca (1802) de Juan Antonio Moguel." In *La Révolution française dans l'histoire et la littérature basques du XIXe siècle: Actes du colloque international de l'URA 1055 du C.N.R.S.*, edited by Jean Baptiste Orpustan. Baigorri: Izpegi, 1994.

———. "Idéologie prorévolutionnaire et poésie: Le *lehen eta orain* de J. B. Elissamburu (1879)." In *La Révolution française dans l'histoire et la littérature basques du XIXe siècle: Actes du colloque international de l'URA 1055 du C.N.R.S.*, edited by Jean Baptiste Orpustan. Baigorri: Izpegi, 1994.

———. "Un poète basque au temps de la Révolution: Salvat Moho." In *1789 et les Basques: Histoire, langue et littérature*, edited by Jean Baptiste Orpustan. Bordeaux: Presses Universitaires de Bordeaux, 1991.

———. "Rôle et pouvoirs de l'Eglise." In *La nouvelle société basque: Ruptures et changements*, edited by Pierre Bidart. Paris: L'Harmattan, 1980.

———. "Une tentative ambitieuse d'Augustin Chaho: La philosophie des religions comparées." *Bulletin du Musée Basque* 93 (1981): 127–42. Reprint in *Augustin Chaho*, edited by Gustave Lambert et al. Hélette: Editions Harriet, 1996.

Oyharçabal [Oihartzabal], Beñat. "Les documents recueillis lors des enquêtes linguistiques en Pays Basque durant la période révolutionnaire et le Premier Empire." In *La Révolution française dans l'histoire et la littérature basques du XIXe siècle: Actes du colloque international de l'URA 1055 du C.N.R.S.* Edited by Jean Baptiste Orpustan. Baigorri: Izpegi, 1994.

———. *Zuberoako herri teatroa*. Donostia: Kriselu, 1985.

Ozouf, Mona. *L'école, l'église et la République, 1871–1914.* Paris: Cana Editions; Jean Offredo, 1982.

———. *La république des instituteurs.* Paris: Galimard; Le Seuil, 1992.

Parti Socialiste. *Proposition du Loi nº 2224 portant création d'un département de Pays Basque* (December 1980).

———. *Proposition du Loi nº 2269 relative à la place des langues et cultures des peuples de France dans l'enseignement, dans l'éducation permanent, dans les activités culturelles, de jeunesse et de loisir, dans les émissions de la radio et de la télévision, et dans la vie publique* (December 1980).

Parton, Nigel Ross. "Fire and Blood: A Comparison of Basque Nationalism in France and Spain." M.A. Thesis, University of Victoria, 1995.

Peillen, Txomin. "Algerian jakile." In *Aljeriako gerla eta Euskal Herria (1954–1962). La guerre d'Algérie et le Pays Basque (1954–1962)*, edited by Xipri Arbelbide et al. Donostia: Eusko Ikaskuntza, 2005.

———. "Euskaraz idatziak eta beste, Zuberoan, Iraultza garaian." In *1789 et les Basques: Histoire, langue et littérature*, edited by Jean Baptiste Orpustan. Bordeaux: Presses Universitaires de Bordeaux, 1991.

———. "Frontières et mentalités en Pays Basque," in *La frontière franco-espagnol, lieu de conflits interétatiques et de collaboration interrégionale: Actes de la journée d'études du 16 novembre 1996, Biarritz*, edited by Maïté Lafourcade. Bordeaux: Presses Universitaires de Bordeaux, 1998.

Pérez-Agote, Alfonso. *The Social Roots of Basque Nationalism.* Translated by Cameron Watson and William A. Douglass. Foreword by William A. Douglass. Reno and Las Vegas: University of Nevada Press, 2006. Originally published as *La reproducción del nacionalismo: El caso vasco.* Madrid: CIS; Siglo XXI, 1984.

Pérez-Nievas, Santiago. "Partidos y procesos de cambio político: La organización y el desarrollo estratégico del PNV en la transición democrática en España." Working Paper 21/2004, Working Papers On-Line Series, *Seminario de Investigación de Ciencia Política*, Departamento de Ciencia Política y Relaciones Internacionales, Facultad de Derecho, Universidad Autónoma de Madrid, 2004. Available on-line at www.uam.es/centros/derecho/cpolitica/papers.html under Investigación | Publicaciones.

Pleven, René. *L'avenir de la Bretagne.* Paris: Calmann-Lévy, 1961.

Rassemblement pour la République (RPR). *Communique de presse du 31 août 1999–RPR, Département Pyrénées Atlantiques* (2000).

Rekondo, José Antonio. *Bietan jarrai: Guerra y paz en las calles de Euskadi.* Bilbao: Arañadle, 1998.

Reynaud, Martin. "Nationalisme et antisémitisme en France (vers 1880–1914)." Paper delivered in the series "La modernisation politique et sociale de la France de la fin du XVIIIe siècle a la Première guerre mondiale" (2001–2002), Sciences-Po, Institut d'études politiques de Paris, December 19, 2001. Available on-line at http://perso. orange.fr/david.colon/Sciences-Po/nationalisme.pdf.

Rieffer, Barbara Ann. "Religion and Nationalism: Understanding the Consequences of a Complex Relationship." *Ethnicities* 3, no. 2 (2003): 215–42.

Rokkan, Stein. *Citizens, Elections, Parties: Approaches to the Comparative Study of the Processes of Development.* Oslo: Universitetsforlaget; New York: McKay, 1970.

Rubiralta, Fermín. "El espacio pirenaico y la construcción europea: Fundamento histórico y revitalización de un área transfronteriza." In *La construcción del espacio vasco-aquitano: Un estudio multidisciplinar*, edited by Antón Borja, Francisco Letamendia, and Kepa Sodupe. Leioa: Servicio Editorial de la Universidad del País Vasco, 1998.

Rush, Cynthia R. "For Spain, Zapatero Opposes Aznar's Crusade, With Dialogue," *Executive Intelligence Review* (October 8, 2004). Available on-line at http://www.larouchepub.com/other/2004/ 3139aznar_v_zapat.html.

Safran, William. "The French State and Ethnic Minority Cultures: Policy Dimensions and Problems." In *Ethnoterritorial Politics, Policy, and the Western World*, edited by Joseph R. Rudolph, Jr., and Robert J. Thompson. Boulder: L. Rienner Publishers, 1989.

Sarrailh de Ihartza, Fernando [Federico Krutwig, pseud.]. *Vasconia: Estudio didáctico de una nacionalidad.* 1962; Bayonne: Elkar, 1973.

Savarèse, Eric. "Ecole et pouvoir colonial: Retour sur la légitimation de la colonisation." *Dialogues Politiques* 2 (January 2003). Available on-line at http://www.la-science-politique. com/revue/ revue2/papier1.htm.

Schnapper, Dominique. "Existe-t-il une identité française?" In *L'identité, l'individu, le groupe, la société*, edited by Jean Claude Ruano Borbalan. Paris: Sciences Humaines, 1998.

Segas, Sébastien. *Action collective et formulation d'un projet commun: Le cas de l'Association des Élus pour un Département Pays Basque.* Bordeaux: IEP, 1998.

Seiler, Daniel-Louis. *Partis et familles politiques.* Paris: Presses Universitaires de France, 1980.

——. *Sur les parties autonomistes dans la CEE.* Barcelona: Institut de Ciènces Politíques i Socials, 1990.

Serrano Abad, Susana. "Industrialización en Vasconia." In *Historia de Euskal Herria/ Historia general de los vascos.* Volume 5. *Vasconia (1876–1937): Entre la tradición y la modernidad*, edited by Joseba Agirreazkuenaga. Donostia: Lur, 2005.

Sibé, Alan. *Nations dépendantes France métropolitaine.* Pau: J&D Editions, 1988.

Sistiague, Martine. *E.L.B.: Ipar Euskal Herriko laborarien oihartzuna.* Baiona: Gatuzain, 2000.

Smith, Anthony D. *Nationalism and Modernism: A Critical Survey of Recent Theories of Nations and Nationalism.* New York: Routledge, 1998.

——. *Nationalism: Theory, Ideology, History.* Cambridge: Polity Press, 2001.

Snow, David A., and Robert D. Benford. "Master Frames and Cycles of Protest." In *Frontiers in Social Movement Theory*, edited by Aldon D. Morris and Carol McClurg Mueller. New Haven, CT: Yale University Press, 1992.

Spohn, Willfried. "Multiple Modernity, Nationalism and Religion: A Global Perspective." *Current Sociology* 51, nos. 3–4 (May–July 2003): 265–86.

Tarrow, Sidney G. "Cycles of Collective Action." In *Repertoires and Cycles of Collective Action*, edited by Mark Traugott. Durham, NC: Duke University Press, 1995.

———. *Power in Movement: Social Movements, Collective Action and Politics*. Cambridge: Cambridge University Press, 1994.

———. "States and Opportunities: The Poltical Structuring of Social Movements." In *Comparative Perspectives on Social Movements: Political Opportunities, Mobilizing Structures, and Cultural Framings*, edited by Doug McAdam, John D. McCarthy, and Mayer N. Zald. Cambridge: Cambridge University Press, 1996.

Tejerina, Benjamín. "Ciclo de protesta, violencia política y movimientos sociales en el País Vasco." *Revista Internacional de Sociología* 16 (1997): 7–38.

———. *Nacionalismo y lengua: Los procesos de cambio lingüístico en el País Vasco*. Madrid: CIS; Siglo XXI, 1992.

Toqueville, Alexis de. *The Old Regime and the Revolution*. Edited with an introduction and critical apparatus by François Furet and Françoise Mélonio. Translated by Alan S. Kahan. Chicago: University of Chicago Press, 1998.

Torrealdai, Joan Mari. *El libro negro del Euskera*. Donostia: Ttarttalo, 2003.

Touraine, Alain. *The Voice and the Eye: An Analysis of Social Movements*. Cambridge: Cambridge University Press, 1981.

Ugalde, Martín de. *Biografía de 3 figuras nacionales vascas: Arana-Goiri, Agirre, Leizaola*. Donostia: Sendoa, 1985.

Urkizu, Patri. "Euskal idazleen bertsoak bigarren errepublikaren gainean (1848–1851)." In *La Révolution française dans l'histoire et la littérature basques du XIXe siècle: Actes du colloque international de l'URA 1055 du C.N.R.S.*, edited by Jean Baptiste Orpustan. Baigorri: Izpegi, 1994.

———. *Historia del teatro vasco*. Donostia: Erein, 1996.

———. "Iraultza frantsesaren garaiko euskal bertsoak (1789–1799)." In *1789 et les Basques: Histoire, langue et littérature*, edited by Jean Baptiste Orpustan. Bordeaux: Presses Universitaires de Bordeaux, 1991.

Urkullu, Iñigo, ed. *Nacionalismo vasco: Un proyecto de futuro con 100 años de historia*. 12 volumes. Bilbao: Sabino Arana Kultur Elkargoa-Fundación Sabino Arana, 1998.

Urquijo, Mikel. "De una guerra a otra: Política e instituciones en un largo camino a la democracia." In *Historia de Euskal Herria/Historia general de los vascos*. Volume 6. *Dicta-*

dura, democracia y autogobierno: La nueva sociedad vasca, 1937–2004. Edited by Joseba Agirreazkuenaga. Donostia: Lur, 2005.

Urteaga, Eguzki. "La guerre d'Algérie et le militantisme étudiant basque." In *Aljeriako gerla eta Euskal Herria (1954–1962)/La guerre d'Algérie et le Pays Basque (1954–1962)*, edited by Xipri Arbelbide et al. Donostia: Eusko Ikaskuntza, 2005.

——. *La politique linguistique au Pays Basque*. Paris: L'Harmattan, 2004.

Urteaga, Eguzki, and Igor Ahedo Gurrutxaga, *La nouvelle gouvernance en Pays Basque*. Paris: L'Harmattan, 2004.

Vrignon, Bixente. *Les années oubliées: Jalons pour une histoire du mouvement abertzale au pays Basque Nord, 1968–1978*. Baiona: Gatuzain, 1999.

——. "El voto en Euskal Herria norte en las elecciones legislativas." In *Historia de Euskal Herria/Historia general de los vascos*. Volume 6. *Dictadura, democracia y autogobierno: La nueva sociedad vasca, 1937–2004*, edited by Joseba Agirreazkuenaga. Donostia: Lur, 2005.

Waquant, Loïc J. D. "Towards a Reflexive Sociology: A Workshop with Pierre Bourdieu." *Sociological Theory* 7, no. 1 (Spring 1989): 26–63.

Watson, Cameron. *Modern Basque History: Eighteenth Century to the Present*. Reno: Center for Basque Studies, University of Nevada, Reno, 2003.

Weber, Eugen. *Peasants into Frenchmen: The Modernization of Rural France, 1870–1914*. Stanford, CA: Stanford University Press, 1976.

Zabalo, Joseph. *Xaho, el genio de Zuberoa*. Tafalla: Txalaparta, 2004. Translated from the French: *Augustin Chaho ou l'Irrintzina du matin basque*. Biarritz: Atlantica, 1999.

Zalbide, Mikel. "Hendai-Hondarribietako biltzarrak: XX. mendeko hizkuntz plangintzaren iturburu." In *Euskaltzaleen Biltzarraren Mendeaurrena*. Bilbao: Fundación Sabino Arana–Sabino Arana Kultur Elkargoa, 2003.

Zald, Mayer N. "Culture, Ideology, and Strategic Framing." In *Comparative Perspectives on Social Movements: Political Opportunities, Mobilizing Structures, and Cultural Framings*, edited by Doug McAdam, John D. McCarthy, and Mayer N. Zald. Cambridge: Cambridge University Press, 1996.

Zallo, Ramón. *Euskadi o la segunda transición: Nación, cultura, ideologías y paz en un cambio de época*. Donostia: Erein, 1997.

——. *El país de los vascos: Desde los sucesos de Ermua al segundo gobierno de Ibarretxe*. Madrid: Fundamentos, 2001.

Zulaika, Joseba. *Del Cromañon al Carnaval: Los vascos como museo antropológico*. Donostia: Erein, 1996.

Index

AB. *See* Abertzaleen Batasuna
Abeberry, Jakes, 136, 141–42, 205, 213, 295; in AB, 282, 284, 359n5; in EB, 201, 348n96; in Enbata, 149–52, 157, 163–67, 295; in Izan, 190, 208, 212, 356n41
Abertzale Guzien Oldarra, 176
Abertzaleen Batasuna (AB, Nationalist Unity), 226, 245–49, 256, 262, 307, 356n48; differences with radical nationalist left in Hegoalde, 125, 229–38, 250, 258, 282–85, 353n93; differences with IK, 197, 207, 229, 236; electoral performance of, 232, 239, 282, 284, 292–93, 311–13, 357n73; emergence of, 197, 229, 232–34, 274, 358n14; internal differences, 233, 238, 258, 282–83, 353n107; Lizarra-Garazi Pact and, 282–84, 357n57; strategy of, 232–38, 247, 250–58, 281–85, 307; support of for civil disobedience, 120, 125, 254; unifying dynamic of, 207, 229–36, 251–53, 282, 284, 293–94
Acción Nacionalista Vasca (ANV, Basque Nationalist Action), 116, 335n14
Action Française (French Action), 100–1
Adour. *See* Atturi (river)
ADPB. *See* Association pour le Département Pays Basque
AED. *See* Association des Élus pour un Département Pays Basque
AEK. *See* Alfabetatze eta Euskalduntze Koordinakundea
Agerre, Jérôme, 292
Agirreazkuenaga, Joseba, 66, 91
Aguerre, Barthélémy, 312–13
Aguirre, José Antonio, 107, 122–25, 129, 131, 340n13
Ahierra (Ayherre), 205
Ainhoa, 63

Aintzina (group), 16, 18, 48–49, 89, 102–11. *See also* Lafitte, Pierre; Eskualerriste movement
Aintzina (journal), 103–11, 133, 333n31, 333nn46–47; second incarnation (after 1942), 116–21, 128, 145. *See also* Lafitte, Pierre; Eskualerriste movement
Álava. *See* Araba
Alfabetatze eta Euskalduntze Koordinakundea (AEK, Coordination of Education and Literacy in Euskara), 171, 297, 344n130
Algerian War (1954–62), 39–40, 154, 339n55, 341n37; Basque nationalism and, 128, 136–42, 144–45, 153, 234; criticism of, 134, 137–39, 141; experience of Basques in, 134, 137–38, 141–42
Al-Qaeda, 85, 262, 287
Alliot-Marie, Michèle, 240, 255–56, 275, 292, 347n69
Alsace, 39, 99, 155, 222
Alvarez Enparantza, Jose Luis ("Txillardegi"), 157, 164–65, 175
Amaia, 170–72, 201, 346n39
American Revolution, 53, 59
Amikuze (Mixe), 186
Amurrio, 350n43
AND. *See* Association pour un Nouveau Département
Anderson, Benedict, 329n85
Angelu (Anglet), 190, 201, 292, 313, 352n66, 355n36; BAB urban conurbation, 240, 258, 296, 359n1. *See also* Baiona-Angelu-Biarritz urban conurbation
Anglet. *See* Angelu
ANV. *See* Acción Nacionalista Vasca
Aquitaine, 143, 214, 215, 302, 344n141
Araba, 67, 94, 114, 130, 232, 315n1
Aralar, 238, 284, 353n111

Arana, Luis, 95, 122
Arana, Sabino, 21, 47–51, 89–96, 115, 122, 315n2, 350n43; discourse of, 27, 45–49, 54–55, 90–96, 108, 124; impact of on Basque nationalism in Iparralde, 19, 48–51, 103–4, 108–9, 124, 150–53; influences on, 84, 89, 321n13
Arana, Vicente, 330n5
Aranzadi, Telesforo de, 103
Araquistain, Juan Venancio de, 84, 85
Arbelbide, Martxalin, 151
Arbelbide, Xipri, 56, 128, 133, 177, 324n40, 325n52; Algerian War and, 137–38; on church, 29, 64; on effects of World War I, 40, 319n87; on Enbata, 162–63, 166, 343n102
Arcangues. *See* Arrangoitze
Arhansus. *See* Arhantsusi
Arhantsusi (Arhansus), 347n47
Aristimuño, José de ("Aitzol"), 132
Arrambide, Robert, 205
Arrangoitze (Arcangues), 136
Arrese Beitia, Felipe, 91, 330n6
Arribillaga, Charles, 146
Arrosa (Saint-Martin-d'Arrosa), 318n62
Ascain. *See* Azkaine
Asociación Euskara. *See* Euskaros (Asociación Euskara members)
Association des Élus pour un Département Pays Basque (AED, Association of Elected Officials for a *Département* of the Basque Country), 209, 211–12, 247–56, 356n41
Association pour le Département Pays Basque (ADPB, Association for a *Département* of the Basque Country), 260, 263
Association pour un Nouveau Département (AND, Association in Favor of a New *Département*), 209, 211–12, 252, 254
astolasterrak (form of charivari), 218, 324n49
Atharratze, 34, 77, 121, 192, 210, 243
Atturi (river), 47, 79, 210–11
Auriol, Vincent, 129
Aurnague, Jacques, 205
Auroy, Bernard, 313
Ayherre. *See* Ahierra
Azkaine (Ascain), 63, 205
Azkue, Resurrección María de, 103
Aznar, José María, 85, 329n81, 345n1

BAB. *See* Baiona-Angelu-Biarritz urban conurbation
Bachoc, Erramun, 224–25
Baigorri (Saint-Étienne-de-Baïgorry), 34, 318n62, 319n87, 337n5; elections in, 190, 201, 205, 282, 313, 359n5; emigration from, 134; Etcheverry-Ainchart, Jean, notary of, 120, 154, 156, 203; IK activity in, 186, 189, 195, 201, 347n55
Baiona (Bayonne), 47, 158, 161, 221, 359n1; administration in, 223, 240, 243, 273; Basque Museum of, 118, 121, 136; Basque nationalism in, 116, 119, 166, 172, 174–75, 177, 184, 201, 205; Chamber of Commerce and Industry in, 209–13, 226, 240, 244, 247, 262, 272, 354n16, 356n48; convocation of Estates General and, 56, 65; education in, 135–36; 1848 French Revolution in, 49, 73, 77; French Revolution and, 57, 62, 66, 67, 318n62; Gascon culture in, 256, 323n9; left-wing politics in, 174, 190–91; municipal politics in, 292–93, 312, 359n16; political violence in, 180; pro-Euskara initiatives in, 225–27, 286; seminary of, 29, 117; subprefecture of, 34, 123, 244, 258, 271, 276, 354n12; trade and industry in, 35, 98, 99, 140, 209–11, 213, 240, 244, 258. *See also* Baiona-Angelu-Biarritz urban conurbation
Baiona-Angelu-Biarritz urban conurbation (BAB), 240, 296–97, 300–1. *See also* Angelu; Baiona; Biarritz
Banca. *See* Banka
Banka (Banca), 179, 184
Barandiaran, Jose Miguel, 122, 129, 336n39
Barère de Vieuzac, Bertrand, 35, 57, 61, 323n19
Basque Autonomous Community, 114, 202, 268, 300, 315n1, 351n57; Euskara in, 225, 296, 351n57; *lehendakariak* (presidents) of, 160, 312, 350n43; PNV leadership of, 203, 307; relations with Iparralde, 240, 241, 335n2, 358n14
Basque Country 2010 Report (1993), 224, 240–41, 245, 271–73, 277, 358n13
Basque culture, 64, 116, 128–31, 221, 231, 270, 304; as "living museum," 41; Christian Democrats and, 159–60, 294; clergy and,

27–29, 32, 43, 61, 99, 298; crisis in, 32, 43, 270, 298; dance, 218–19; Eskualerristes and, 104–8; festivals, 91; IK and, 186; measures against, 285; notables and, 31, 43, 305; official support for, 131, 204, 222–33, 241, 258, 351n54, 351n56. *See also* Euskara

Basque language. *See* Euskara

Basque nationalism, 49–52, 68, 93, 114–16, 156–58, 176, 182, 192, 214–15; Arana, Sabino, and, 45–47, 51, 87, 90–94, 150, 315n2, 350n43; differences of in Iparralde and Hegoalde, 108, 234, 239, 307, 312; direct action and, 180–81; divisions within, 189, 204, 230, 293; electoral performance of in Iparralde, 119, 164, 201–5, 270, 277, 293, 311–13; emergence of in Hegoalde, 18, 22, 42–43, 87–97; emergence of in Iparralde, 15–19, 96, 104, 111–14, 126–48, 160, 270, 306; growth of, 220, 229, 273–76, 291, 307; importance of Enbata, 147, 163–64, 169; influence of Hegoalde on Iparralde, 47, 87, 90, 96, 108–11, 125, 173, 202–4, 270–71; Itsasu Charter, foundational document of, 151–53, 270; Labéguerie, Michel, and, 160, 271; language, importance of in, 90–91, 220, 270; leftist turn of in Iparralde, 173–75, 189, 192–93, 358n14; Legasse, Marc, and 116–124, 358n10; in 1990s, 281, 291; Oedipal and parricidal nature of in Iparralde, 124–25, 154, 291; in post-Franco Spain, 199; precursors of, 49–52, 68, 72, 78–84, 97, 104, 125, 330n15; race, importance of in, 90, 92–93, 331n18; territoriality and, 118, 208–9; unity of , 204–5, 239, 243; violence and, 125, 164–66, 176, 180, 189, 197, 199, 290. *See also* French nationalism; nationalism; Spanish nationalism

Basse-Navarre. *See* Nafarroa Beherea

Basses-Pyrénées, *département* of, 34, 66, 210

Bassussary. *See* Basusarri

Bastida (Labastide), 156, 192

Basusarri (Bassussary), 53

Batallón Vasco-Español (BVE, Spanish Basque Battalion), 347n65

Batasuna, 125, 281–86, 290, 346n31, 353n93; support for in Iparralde, 238, 258, 283–85, 293–94, 308, 353n107, 357n73. *See also* Euskal Herritarrok; Herri Batasuna

Batera platform, 216, 226–27, 246, 259–64, 275–79, 293–94, 308, 351n51, 358n81

Batzarre, 284, 359n4

batzoki (PNV center), 93–95, 108

Bayonne. *See* Baiona

Bayrou, François, 225, 240, 313, 356n54

Béarn, 77, 210, 247, 257, 302–3, 354n3; administrative unity with Iparralde, 28, 34–35, 55, 61, 66, 72, 208; differences with Iparralde, 82, 148, 216, 257, 302

Begiraleak, 108, 109–10, 334n74

Benito del Valle, Jose Mari, 157, 165, 175

Bera, 79

Biarritz, 116, 129, 292, 337n5, 347n55, 352n66, 355–56n36; BAB urban conurbation, 240, 258, 296, 359n1; elections in, 119, 190, 201, 205, 292, 312–13, 359n5; tourism in, 99, 140. *See also* Baiona-Angelu-Biarritz urban conurbation

Bidart, Filipe, 189, 195–96, 201, 347n71, 348n74, 354n6

Bidart, Pierre, 31, 35, 261, 278, 318n60

Bidasoa River, 24, 46, 47, 94, 143

Bidaxune (Bidache), 156, 312–13

Bidegain, Eneko, 346n28, 347n69

Bilbao, 47, 67, 143, 315n2, 340n4; Basque nationalism in, 89, 93, 147, 315n2

Billig, Michael, 40, 319n91

Biltzar, 28, 305; of Lapurdi, 56–66, 72, 118, 286, 288, 317n29, 323n18; of mayors, 222, 227, 244–65, 272–79, 355n36, 356n42

Biriatou. *See* Biriatu

Biriatu (Biriatou), 63

Bizkaia, 67, 91, 114, 315n1; Basque nationalism in, 21, 26–27, 47, 49, 94–96, 107, 124; dances of, 128, 219; industrialization in, 93, 143, 315n2

Bonaparte, Louis Lucien, 318n64

Bordeaux, 128, 137, 145, 146, 197, 317n29, 337n5

borders, importance of, 23, 46, 114

Borotra, Didier, 312

Bortairu, Jakes, 172, 176, 182–83

Bourdieu, Pierre, 36–37, 42, 43

Bové, José, 215, 259
Bray, Zoe, 24
Breton language, 35, 135, 352n73
Breton nationalism, 142, 145, 151
Brisson, Max, 228, 292, 296
Brittany, 41, 134, 135, 155, 182, 222, 235
Broca, Paul, 318n64
Brubaker, Rogers, 39, 101
Burgos Trial, 174–76, 235
Burucoa, Michel, 146, 149, 157, 163, 340n30
BVE. *See* Batallón Vasco-Español

Cabane, Marc, 264
cahiers de doléances (documents listing provincial grievances), 56, 58–60, 64
Cambacérès, Jules, 77, 327n28
Camblong, Ramuntxo, 149, 204, 215, 242, 354n16
Cambo-les-Bains. *See* Kanbo
Camino, Alexandre, 155–57
Campión, Arturo, 19, 45, 49, 84, 90–91, 103, 130
Cantabria and Cantabrians, 69, 73, 83, 115
Carcopino, Jérôme, 117–18
Carlism, 42, 77, 80–81, 92, 320n102, 329n2. *See also* Zumalacarrégui, Tomás
Carlist Wars (1833–39 and 1873–76), 43, 49, 80–81, 89, 91, 315n2, 329n2. *See also* Zumalacarrégui, Tomás
Carlists, 75, 79, 80–81, 87, 107, 329n2, 350n43. *See also* Zumalacarrégui, Tomás
Caro Baroja, Julio, 325n63
Carrera, Peio, 171
Carrero Blanco, Admiral Luis, 170, 179, 183
Cassan, Patrick, 195–96
Catalan language, 135
Catalonia, 26, 47, 147; nationalist movement in, 151
Catholic Church, 28, 61, 76, 115
CD. *See* Centre Démocratique
CDPB. *See* Conseil du Développement du Pays Basque
Celts, 73, 74, 78
Centre Démocratique (CD, Democratic Center), 159–60, 342n64. *See also* Union pour la Democratie Française

Centre National des Indépendants et Paysans (National Center of Independents and Peasants), 157
CEPB. *See* Conseil des Élus du Pays Basque
CFDT. *See* Confédération Française Démocratique du Travail
Chaban-Delmas, Jacques, 190
Chaho, Agosti, 17–18, 47–59, 73–92, 323n33, 329n72; as precursor of Basque nationalism, 16–19, 21, 47–51, 78–83, 269, 321 n.13, 328n66; Carlism and, 49, 77, 79–81, 89–90; differences with later Basque nationalism, 95, 96; dual national identity of, 16–18, 87–88, 89, 105; esoteric nature of, 49, 73–76, 82; influence of on later Basque nationalism, 83–84, 87, 89–90; religion and, 75–76, 82, 108, 326–27n17; *Voyage en Navarre pendant l'insurrection des Basques* (1836), 49, 75, 78, 79, 83, 84, 327n39
charivari, 217–18, 324n49
Charritton, Piarres, 117, 133–34, 136, 205, 337n5, 339n64
Chaussier, Jean Daniel, 211
Chéraute. *See* Sohüta
Chevènement, Jean-Pierre, 283, 349n8, 359n3
Chirac, Jacques, 226, 260
Christian Democracy, 135, 149, 153–56, 222, 263; in Iparralde, 31, 116, 135, 148–50, 155–60, 168, 313; of Elgar-Ensemble, 127, 262, 294; of Labéguerie, Michel, 127, 135; of Lafitte, Pierre, 139; of MDB, 159, 294; of MRP, 141, 154, 159; of PNV/PNB, 116, 204; of UDF, 31. *See also* Mouvement Démocratique Basque; Mouvement Républicain Populaire; Parti Nationaliste Basque; Partido Nacionalista Vasco; Union pour la Démocratie Française
Church, Catholic (in France), 28–30, 76; in Basque folklore 217, 220; Basque language and culture and, 28, 99–100, 136; break with pro-Basque circles, 126, 149–50; church-state relations, 28–29, 33, 54–55, 97–100, 102, 317n33; education and, 29, 136; French Revolution and, 269, 324n33; in Iparralde, 29–30, 54–65, 131–38, 159, 215, 269; Spanish Civil War and, 107, 115. *See also* Clergy, Basque

Ciboure. *See* Ziburu
Citron, Suzanne, 102
Cize. *See* Garazi
Clark, Robert P., 345n4
clergy, Basque, 27–29, 54–64, 107, 130; Basque culture and, 27–28, 55, 61, 99–100, 218; French Revolution and, 35, 54, 57, 64, 72, 317n29, 324n49; French state and, 28–29, 56, 317n33. *See also* Church, Catholic (in France),
Clubes Pays Basque, 172, 344n132
collective (group) identity, 16–17, 48, 84–87, 268, 271–72, 295. *See also* collective (group) memory; identity; national community
collective memory, 39, 48, 55, 87, 118, 287–88, 309. *See also* collective (group) memory; identity; national consciousness
Comandos Autónomos Anticapitalistas, 237
Committee of Public Safety, 35, 67
Communism, 99, 105, 107, 341n40, 344n145. *See also* Parti Communiste Français
Confédération Française Démocratique du Travail (CFDT, French Democratic Confederation of Labor), 252, 272, 355n30
Confédération National des Syndicats de Travailleurs Paysannes (National Confederation of Rural Workers' Unions), 216
Connor, Walker, 17, 27, 50
Conseil des Élus du Pays Basque (CEPB, Council of Elected Officials of the Basque Country), 215, 224–29, 241–47, 261–63, 272–79, 349n20, 355n20; demands of, 226, 261, 277, 286, 308; members of against Basque *département*, 356n52.
Conseil du Développement du Pays Basque (CDPB, Development Council of the Basque Country), 158, 224, 241–47, 272–79, 286, 308, 349n20, 355n20; institutional policy of, 242–43, 272–77, 354n14, 354n16; linguistic policy of, 297; pro-Basque circles and, 215, 226, 242–46, 263, 273–78, 358n6
Constituent Assembly (French national), 49, 120
Coquebert de Montbret, Charles-Etienne, 318n64
Coquebert de Montbret, Eugène, 330n10

Coral, Bernard de, 107
Corcuera, Javier, 89, 94–95, 329n2
Corsica, 182, 213, 237, 349n10; nationalism in, 142, 235, 278, 289, 359n3, 359n13
Coumet, Jacques, 292
Council of the Basque Language, 224–26, 228, 244

d'Abbadie, Antoine, 21, 49, 90–92, 102–3, 330n11, 330n15
Daguerressar, 57, 323n18
Darmendrail, Joseph, 119, 336n26
Darraidou, Laurent, 146, 165
Dassance, Louis, 129, 131, 132, 136, 160
Davant, Jean-Louis, 54, 127, 136, 153, 350–51n43; in EHAS, 187–88, 201; in Enbata, 149–53, 163, 168–69, 175–76
Deastrade, Jean-Pierre, 313
decolonization, 141, 148, 153, 182
Defferre, Gaston, 349n13
de Gaulle, Charles, 115, 119, 144–45, 165; and Iparralde, 154–55, 159, 162, 341n40, 342n70. *See also* Gaullism
Deixonne, Maurice (Deixonne Law), 135–36, 221
Delbos, Yvon, 129
d'Elissagaray, Renaud, 222
Delzangles, René, 107, 151
Démocratie Libéral (DL, Liberal Democracy), 357n77
Demo movement, 87, 125, 181, 226–29, 254–63, 285–90, 335n23
D'Hiriart, Pierre-Eustache, 57, 323n18
Diharce, Father Jean, 117
Dirassar, Jeanbattitt, 338n27
Divers Droit (Miscellaneous Right) coalition, 312–13
Domergue, Jean-Louis, 292
Donapaleu (Saint-Palais), 34, 59, 156, 313, 347n55
Donibane Garazi (Saint-Jean-Pied-de-Port), 34, 57, 319n87, 324n41, 357n57; Basque nationalism in, 169–70, 177, 284
Donibane Lohizune (Saint-Jean-de-Luz), 21, 57, 62, 63, 92, 103, 318n62, 355n36; Basque nationalism in, 116, 119, 173–77, 284, 334n74, 347n55; elections in, 119, 205

Donnan, Hastings, 23
Drouin, Jean-Claude, 76, 82
Drumont, Edouard, 322n22
Duhart, Michel, 68, 69, 321n29
Duny Pétré, Arnaud, 171–72, 173
Dupré-Moretti, Éric, 80–81, 326n1, 328n66
Dutournier, Paul, 151
"Dreyfus Affair," 100–1
DVD. *See* Divers Droite

EAS. *See* Euskal Alderdi Sozialista
EB. *See* Euskal Batasuna
Écénarro, Kotte, 313
EGB. *See* Eskualdun Gazteen Biltzarra
EH. See Euskal Herritarrok
EHAS. *See* Euskal Herriko Alderdi Sozialista
EHBai (Euskal Herria Bai, Basque Country, Yes), 311–13
Eizaguirre, José de ("Oxobi"), 132
EKE. *See* Euskal Kultur Erakundea
ELA-STV. *See* Eusko Langileen Alkartasuna-Solidaridad de Trabajadores Vascos
ELB. *See* Euskal Laborarien Batasuna
Elgar-Ensemble, 278–79, 281, 291, 293–95, 308–9, 312, 351n51; Christian Democracy of, 160, 204, 262, 294–95
Elissalde, Jean, 130, 132
Elissamburu, Michel, 333n46
Elizondo, 91, 92
Elorza, Antonio, 84–85
Elosegi, Joseba, 158
EMA. *See* Ezkerreko Mugimendu Abertzalea
Embata, 135, 146, 149–50. *See also* Enbata
Emmanuelli, Henri, 349n8
Enbata (group), 104, 120, 137–38, 147–77, 342n77; banning of, 179, 186, 208, 270; electoral performance of, 156, 162–64, 191, 204, 270; emergence of, 15, 18, 128, 135, 138, 149–51, 161; ETA and, 127, 153–69, 203, 342n85; internal differences in, 124–25, 127, 130, 154, 163, 167, 171; leftist turn of, 125, 148, 154, 168–70, 174, 344n133; membership of, 110, 159, 167–68, 341n41; political line of, 19, 135, 143–53, 165–69, 184, 202, 340n16. *See also* Embata
Enbata (journal), 343n102, 345n17, 352n86
England, 60, 67, 71, 133, 323n31
Enlightenment, 28, 58, 60, 321n27

Eppherre, Michel, 149
Eraikitzen collective, 121, 198, 232
Ereñaga, Amaia, 121, 336n26, 336n32
Ernandorena, Trinidad, 337n5
Errecart, Jean, 151, 154–56, 165, 273
Eskual-Herria, 137
Eskualdun Gazteen Biltzarra (EGB, Association of Basque Youth), 117–18, 128, 337n5
Eskualdun Gazteria (Basque Youth), 133–34, 138
Eskualduna, 108, 117, 118, 132, 133
Eskualerriste movement, 48, 89, 97–111, 126, 159, 333n39, 334n62; regionalism of, 96, 104–5. *See also* Aintzina (group); *Aintzina* (journal); Lafitte, Pierre
Eskualzaleen Biltzarra (Association of Basque Studies), 103, 109, 129, 130–32, 136, 167
Espelette. *See* Ezpeleta
Espilondo, Jean, 261, 275, 278, 292, 312, 358n81
ETA. *See* Euskadi ta Askatasuna
ETA-V, 169, 172–73, 343n109. *See also* Euskadi ta Askatasuna
ETA-VI, 172–73, 343n109, 344n145. *See also* Euskadi ta Askatasuna
ETA (m), 169, 188, 235, 236, 343n109. *See also* Euskadi ta Askatasuna
ETA (pm), 188, 235, 237, 343n109. *See also* Euskadi ta Askatasuna
Etchecopar Etchart, Hélène, 218
Etchegaray, Jean-René, 292
Etchemendi, Eñaut, 201
Etcheverry-Ainchart, Jean, 103, 136, 149, 151, 165, 203, 273; Christian Democracy of, 154, 156, 203; proposal for statute of autonomy, 120–21, 299
Etxalus, Christiane, 162–63, 166, 168, 183, 342n85, 346n19
Etxeberri, Jean-Noël "Txetx," 261, 352n86
Etxebeste, Ttotte, 196
Euskadi ta Askatasuna (ETA, Basque Country and Freedom), 142, 145, 153–85, 290, 345n17, 356n55; AB and, 233, 258, 282–84, 307; assassination of Admiral Carrero Blanco, 179, 344n1; decline of violent activity after 2003, 285–86; EB and, 196–97, 233; IK and, 125, 180–85,

194–200, 230, 234–37, 250, 346n22, 348n96; influence on Basque nationalism in Iparralde, 173, 175–77, 182–85; internal differences within, 175, 343n109; KAS and, 189, 235–36, 346n31; links with Enbata, 125, 127, 153–69, 203, 342n85; MLNV and, 193, 234–37, 346n31; refugees of in Iparralde, 96, 132, 157, 165, 176, 183–84, 194–200, 234, 347n61, 347n63, 352n77; return to arms after 1999, 237–38; return to arms after 2006, 311–12; violent turn of (1968), 175, 339n66, 343n101, 345n4, 346n31. *See also* Burgos Trial; ETA-V; ETA-VI; ETA (m); ETA (pm); Iparretarrak

Euskadiko Ezkerra (EE, Basque Left), 343n109

Euskal Alderdi Sozialista (EAS, Basque Socialist Party), 187–88, 270, 346n32. *See also* Euskal Herriko Alderdi Sozialista

Euskal Batasuna (EB, Basque Unity), 125, 192–205, 214, 229–33, 283, 346n39, 348n96

Euskal Gogoa, 172, 176

Euskal Herria Zuzenean, 208, 221

Euskal Herriko Alderdi Sozialista (EHAS, the Socialist Party of the Basque Country), 125, 180–201, 208–14, 270, 345n6, 346n32, 346n41. *See also* Euskal Alderdi Sozialista; Herriko Alderdi Sozialista

Euskal Herriko Laborarien Batasuna. *See* Euskal Laborarien Batasuna

Euskal Herritarrok (EH, Basque Compatriots), 258, 282–83, 346n31, 353n107, 357n72. *See also* Batasuna; Herri Batasuna

Euskal Ikasleen Biltzarra (Association of Basque Students), 103, 109, 135–36, 145–46

Euskal Idazkaritza, 157, 164–65, 167

Euskal Iraultzarako Alderdia (EIA, Basque Revolutionary Party), 188

Euskal Konfederazioa, 225–26

Euskal Kultur Erakundea (EKE, Basque Cultural Institute), 223–25, 228, 351n57

Euskal Laborarien Batasuna (ELB, Basque Workers' Union), 201, 255, 272, 333n45, 355n30; creation of, 216, 340n5, 346n26; demand for Basque agricultural chamber, 216–17, 227–29, 264, 279, 349n26, 357n65; direct action tactics of, 180–81, 216, 227–28, 259

Euskal Telebista (ETB, Basque Television), 114, 351n57

Euskal Zuzentasuna (EZ, Basque Justice), 181, 194, 237, 345n9

Euskaltzaindia (Academy of the Basque Language), 131, 213, 287, 290, 297, 350n43

Euskara (Basque language), 22–28, 35–39, 74–75, 90–91, 286–304, 318n60, 320n1, 330n11, 334n62, 351n60; church and, 28, 99–100, 136; Council of, 224–26, 228, 244; decline of, 90–91, 106, 221, 224, 270, 296, 298; defense of, 103, 118–20, 128–30, 151, 157, 191, 198–208, 224–25, 258; French and, 43, 295–97; French Revolution and, 35, 55; measures against, 100, 131; as national language of the Basques, 121, 145, 188, 209, 250, 269, 295–97, 309–10, 324n44; official status for, 228, 259–61, 271–78, 291, 308, 340n30, 342n69, 352n71; promotion of, 103, 118, 220–33, 287, 297, 329n72, 346n31, 351n60; protection of, 263, 271; teaching of, 128–29, 135–36, 186, 221, 272, 296–97, 334n130, 351n60. *See also* Basque culture

Euskaros (Asociación Euskara members), 84–85, 91, 108

Eusko Alkartasuna (EA, Basque Solidarity), 203–5, 232, 239, 251, 281, 356n48, 357n72; electoral performance of, 204–5, 284, 293–94, 311

Eusko Gaztedi del Interior (EGI, Basque Youth of the Interior), 165

Eusko Ikaskuntza (Society of Basque Studies), 129, 131

Eusko Langileen Alkartasuna-Solidaridad de Trabajadores Vascos (ELA-STV, Basque Workers' Union), 106, 165, 359n2

ex-combatant mentality, 40, 49, 101, 104

EZ. *See* Euskal Zuzentasuna

Ezker Batua (United Left), 356n55

Ezker Berri, 172–73, 176, 184, 189, 192, 344n136, 346n41

Ezkerreko Mugimendu Abertzalea (EMA, Basque Patriotic Movement of the Left), 125, 186, 192–205, 214, 229–33, 283; differences with EB, 194, 198, 200–2,

346n22, 346n39; electoral performance, 201, 204–5; links with IK, 179, 194, 200–1, 236, 348n79. *See also* Herri Taldeak
Ezpeleta, 63, 157, 347n55

Fabius, Laurent, 349n8
Fagoaga, Jean, 146
federalism, 15, 98, 118–19, 148–49, 153, 190, 270; Algeria and, 137, 140–41; as idea during French Revolution, 59, 61; of Enbata, 135, 137, 143, 150, 153, 168; of Eskualerriste movement (Lafitte), 104–5, 133, 153; of Labéguerie, Michel, 127, 153, 159–60
Fédérations Départementales des Syndicats d'Exploitants Agricoles (FDSEA, Departmental Federations of Agricultural Producers' Unions), 216
Fernández de Casavedante Romani, Carlos, 47
Fernández de Larrinoa, Kepa, 217
Fernández Sebastián, Javier, 47, 325n63
Fifth Republic (1958–present), 31, 154–55, 159, 273, 306
Flemish language, 118
Flemish nationalism, 151
FLNC. *See* Fronte di Liberazione Naziunale di a Corsica
Foral Community of Navarre. *See under* Navarre
fors, 42, 49, 58, 59, 67, 82, 316n22. See also *fueros*
Fourcaud, Louis de, 21, 41, 45, 342n83
Fourquet, François, 217, 218
France, 19, 22, 38, 181, 262, 285, 322n9; church-state relations in, 28–29, 33, 54–55, 97–100, 102, 317n33; confrontation with Spain, 24, 39, 55–57, 61–64, 67, 72, 324n38; culture of, 99, 186; decentralization in, 209, 213, 226–27, 246, 258–63, 271, 349n10, 354n6; decolonization and, 141, 148, 182; experience of war, 38–40, 101, 138, 319n87; federalism in, 104–5, 141, 153, 270; as *grand patrie*, 16, 18, 83, 158, 305; "internal colonialism" of, 41, 142, 182, 270, 320n95; legislative lections in, 106, 118; linguistic unification of, 35, 228; May 1968 and, 148, 160, 167–68, 234; modernization of, 26–27, 98–100; Nazi occupation of, 116, 117; political and administrative structures of, 34, 349n20, 349n26; Spanish diplomatic pressure on, 129, 253; state construction in, 23–35, 99–102, 208, 217, 269, 298–99, 305; underdevelopment in, 41, 140–42
Franco, General Francsico, 24, 113–19, 124, 163, 170–75, 203, 333n53; death of, 160, 189, 343n109; repression of, 128, 130, 132, 158, 334n66; uprising of, 107
Franco-Prussian War (1870–71), 38, 99
French culture, 99, 186
French identity, 113, 268–79, 302–3, 305–7, 309, 342n69; dual (with Basque), 208, 246, 273, 276–77; institutionalized nature of, 99–100, 269–70, 291; shaped by war, 22, 40, 43; struggle with Basque identity, 253, 269–70, 273, 278, 289, 294, 299; transformation of in Iparralde, 271, 274–79, 294; weak sense of, 86, 100
French language, 32–37, 42, 75, 100, 104, 147, 301–2; as official language of state, 28, 33, 213, 228, 261–62, 298, 329n86, 358n16; in church, 29; in education, 36–38, 43, 144, 222, 299; in signposting, 224, 227; use of in pro-Basque circles, 151
French nationalism, 64, 99–102, 119–20, 144, 264, 269–78, 307; "banal" nature of, 40, civic dimension of, 33, 298; Gaullist, 166, 273; as a product of war, 39–40, 101, 104; secular nature of, 27–28; of Third Republic, 100–1. *See also* Basque nationalism; nationalism; Spanish nationalism
French Revolution, 23, 24, 54–66, 82–83, 143, 208; Basque identity and, 269, 273; church and, 27–29, 39; effects of in Iparralde, 31–34, 39, 53–66, 69, 86, 220
Frente Revolucionario Antifascista y Patriota (FRAP, Revolutionary Anti-Fascist and Patriotic Front), 174, 183
Fronte di Liberazione Naziunale di a Corsica (FLNC, Front for the National Liberation of Corsica), 289, 359n13
Fuenterrabía. *See* Hondarribia

fueros, 77, 80–82, 92, 316n22, 320n102, 334n56; abolition of, 55, 67, 97, 315n2, 325n63. See also *fors*

Gabilondo, Joseba, 330n15
GAL. *See* Grupos Antiterroristas de Liberación
Galant, Andde, 163, 183, 342n88
Galant, Jean Michel, 284, 313, 359n5
Garaikoetxea, Carlos, 160
Garat, Jean, 138–41
Garat, Dominique-Joseph, 16–19, 36, 53–72, 288–89, 323n15; dual national identity of, 16, 71, 83–89, 96, 160–61, 269, 273; political activity of, 49–50, 53, 57, 59, 65–66, 71–72; as precursor of Basque nationalism, 17, 19, 47–50, 68–71, 86–87; proposals for Basque institutional recognition (New Phoenicia), 42, 49, 53, 66–68, 209, 325n69, 357n62. *See also* New Phoenicia, plan for
Garazi (Cize), 134, 190, 253, 292, 347n55
Garcia, Maurice, 292
Garibay, Esteban de, 83–84, 329n74
Gascon language and culture, 256, 260, 298, 323n9, 352n66. *See also* Occitan language; Occitania
Gaullism, 31, 135, 148, 154–66, 273, 299. *See also* de Gaulle, Charles; Rassemblement du Peuple Français; Rassemblement pour la République; Union pour la Nouvelle République
Gauls, 69, 74, 75, 78, 102
Gazte, 134, 136–38
Gazteriak, 232, 282–83, 353n107. *See also* Haika; Jarrai; Segi
Gellner, Ernest, 38
Germany, 39, 97, 101, 116, 134
Gernika (Guernica), 78, 107, 152, 334n56
Gimenez, Beñat, 313
Gipuzkoa, 67, 91, 94, 114, 124, 130, 232, 315nn1–2; dances of, 128, 219; Euskara of, 70; French occupation of, 24, 67–68
Giscard d'Estaing, Valéry, 190, 222, 347n47
"gorriak" (secular republicans), 98. *See also* "xuriak"
Goths, 69, 78

Goyheneche, Eugène, 109, 130, 132, 337n5; Basque nationalism of, 160, 333n39; in Aintzina (Eskualerristes), 18, 105; in Euskal Ikasleen Biltzarra, 103; Legasse and, 117, 128; on Chaho, 76, 80; on French Revolution, 54; on World War I, 332n19
Goyhenetche, Jean, 54, 58, 323n15
Goyhenetche, Manex, 131, 322n8, 339n64; on French Revolution, 56–60, 64–65, 92, 324n38, 324n40; in EHAS, 125, 191
grande patrie, logic of, 16, 18, 148, 158. *See also petite patrie*, logic of
Grégoire Report (1784), 33, 35, 298
Grenet, Henri, 292
Grenet, Jean, 272, 292, 293, 312, 359n16
Grupos Antiterroristas de Liberación (GAL, Antiterrorist Liberation Groups), 194–95, 347n67
Guernica. *See* Gernika
Guilbeau, Martin, 103
Guilcher, Jean Michel, 350n39
Guipúzcoa. *See* Gipuzkoa
Gure Etchea, 108,
Gure Herria, 105, 108, 109, 117

HA. *See* Herriaren Alde
Haika, 283, 353n107, 357n72. *See also* Gazteriak; Jarrai; Segi
Haramburu, Abbé, 337n5
Haran, Ximun, 136, 146, 203, 340n13; in Enbata, 125, 149, 151, 162–64, 167, 168
Haristoy, Pierre, 54
Haritschelhar, Jean, 136, 158, 213
Harlouchet, Claude, 205
Hazparne (Hasparren), 98, 140, 163, 191, 204, 292, 360n20
HB. *See* Herri Batasuna
Hebrew, 69
Hegoalde, 24, 53, 315n1; administrative relations with Iparralde, 240–41, 264, 272, 308, 358n6; border with Iparralde, 24, 46, 89; French Revolution and, 67–68; influence of Basque nationalist movement in on counterpart in Iparralde, 19, 103, 108–11, 149, 173, 239, 253, 270–71; modernization in, 26–27, 42, 147, 315n2; pro-Basque literature in, 83–84; refugees

from in Iparralde, 96, 104, 107, 115–17, 148, 157–58, 172–79
Hemen, 214, 272
Hendaia (Hendaye), 46, 190, 205, 313
Hendaye. *See* Hendaia
Héraud, Guy, 190
Herri Batasuna (HB, Popular Unity), 234–38, 258, 346n31, 352n89; breakaway groups from, 238, 353n111; KAS and, 189, 230–31, 346n37, 352n92; Lizarra-Garazi process and, 356n55; policy in Iparralde, 198, 229–31; relations with AB, 230, 234, 250, 282, 353n107; relations with EA, 204; relations with EB, 201–2, 229–30; Udalbiltza and, 357n72. *See also* Batasuna; Euskal Herritarrok
Herri Taldeak, 180, 186, 190, 192–94, 197, 200–1, 216. *See also* Ezkerreko Mugimendu Abertzalea
Herri Urrats, 220
Herria, 117, 119, 132–33, 136–39, 141, 161, 163, 338n27
Herriaren Alde (HA, On the Side of the People), 189–93, 198, 202, 214, 229–33, 283, 346n39
Herriko Alderdi Sozialista (HAS, Popular Socialist Party), 179–82, 186–90, 208, 212, 270, 345n6, 347n46. *See also* Euskal Herriko Alderdi Sozialista
Herriko Alderdi Sozialista Iraultzailea (HASI, Popular Revolutionary Socialist Party), 188–89, 199–201, 230
Herrikoa, 214, 272
Herriot, Édouard, 129
Hiriart-Urruty, Jean, 338n27
Hiriburu (Saint-Pierre-d'Irube), 282, 313, 347n55, 359n5
Hirigoyen, Emile, 337n5
Hirigoyen, Robert, 191
Hitler, Adolf, 117
Hizkuntza Kontseilua (Council of the Basque Language), 297
Hondarribia (Fuenterrabía), 46, 103, 350n43
Hordago (journal), 121
Hordago! (group), 181–83, 194, 237, 345n9
Humboldt, Wilhelm Friedrich von, 74

Ibarra, Pedro, 16, 85, 88, 329n85

Ibarretxe, Juan José, 312, 350n43
Iberia (Iberian Peninsula)
identity, 15–18, 41, 43, 124, 219, 244, 267–68, 295–96, 307, 319n91; Béarnais, 302–3; changing nature of in Iparralde, 294, 298–304; cultural, 51, 68; Gascon, 256; local, 35, 240, 241, 243, 270; Pays Basque, 246, 267–81, 294–95, 299, 306–9, 358n16; territory and, 228; war and, 39; zero-sum game of, 17–19, 43, 46, 98, 119–20, 267–70, 273, 294, 298, 309. *See also* Basque identity; collective (group) identity; collective memory; French identity; national community; national consciousness; national society
Iholdi (Iholdy), 34, 192, 205
Iholdy. *See* Iholdi
IK. *See* Iparretarrak
Ikardo, Idoia, 219
Ikas collective, 129, 135–36, 221–22, 297, 351n49
Inchauspé, Beñat, 360n20
Inchauspé, Louis, 292
Inchauspé, Michel, 292; in Euskal Ikasleen Biltzarra, 135, 146; as Gaullist, 135, 160, 162, 342n70; pro-Basque *département* initiatives of, 228, 247–48, 250–55, 272, 359n16
"internal" colonialism, 41–42, 134, 142–46, 182, 270, 320n95, 339n63
Iparralde, 21, 39, 315n1; administrative structure of, 34–36, 61, 66; agriculture in, 119, 134, 148; Basque identity in, 15–22, 32, 47, 52, 102, 111, 269–71, 296–310; civil society in, 223, 240, 248–49, 287–89, 296, 349n20; church and clergy in, 28, 43, 61, 64, 107; cultural crisis in, 42–43; deportation of inhabitants in, 62–65; effects of war with Spain on, 61–63; emigration from, 101, 111, 134; fishing industry in, 67, 119, 183; *fors* of 42, 49, 58, 59, 67, 82, 316n22; French-Basque identity conflict in, 17–18, 207–8, 267–68, 273; French identity in, 22, 32, 48, 83, 86, 101, 269–70, 278, 299–302; French Revolution in, 34, 53–66, 72; industry in, 32, 98, 148, 214–15; modernization in, 26–27, 31–32, 36, 42, 98–101, 155; notable power in, 30,

43, 148, 292; Pays Basque identity in, 268, 271–74, 299, 307–9; peripheral nature of, 32, 40–42, 114; politics in, 31, 97–98, 106–8, 154–60, 190; political violence in, 19, 118, 126, 192, 282, 311; religion in, 27–29, 99; tourism in, 134, 150, 152, 155, 173–74, 191; use of Euskara in, 28, 35–36, 39, 131, 228, 295–98, 303

Iparretarrak (IK), 125, 176, 179–86, 207, 235–36, 250; death of members, 158, 194, 195; differences with ETA, 180, 185, 194–200, 229, 236–37, 346n22, 348n96; EMA and, 200–1, 230, 346n22; emergence of, 179, 181–82, 190, 193, 199, 270; ideology and strategy of, 185–86, 193–201, 229, 236–37, 289, 306, 347n73; influence of ETA on, 183–85, 197, 199, 230–31; 1998 ceasefire of, 197; relations with HAS/EHAS, 180, 186, 192; violence of, 193–200, 224, 237, 282–87, 347n69, 353n106, 354n6. *See also* Euskadi ta Askatasuna

Iralur, Peio, 292
Iraultza, 230, 237
Irazusta, Richard, 200–1, 204–5, 352n86
Iriart, Alain, 284, 313, 359n5
Iriart, Alphonse, 292
Irigaray, Eneko, 157, 165–66, 175
Irujo, Manuel de, 115, 335n6
Irun, 46, 343n101, 345n4
Israel, 76
Italy, 70, 74
Itçaina (Itzaina), Xabier, 29, 99, 160, 214–15, 219
Itsasu (Itxassou), 63, 140–45, 151–53, 191, 202, 347n55
Itsasu Charter, 15, 148, 150–54, 162, 270, 340n30
Itxassou. *See* Itsasu
Itzaina, Mixel, 137
Itzaina, Xabier. *See* Itçaina, Xabier
Izan collective, 190–91, 208–12, 214, 344n122, 356n41
Izquierda Abertzale (Left-Wing Basque Nationalism), 193–202, 207, 229–32, 250, 282–90, 307, 346n31. *See also* Movimiento de Liberación Nacional Vasco
Izquierdo, Jean Marie, 35, 148, 159
Izturitze (Isturits), 134, 205

Jacob, James E., 107, 114, 116, 155, 205, 345n4; on Amaia, 171; on de Gaulle, Charles, 341n40; on Enbata, 151–52, 168, 171, 179; on Euskal Batasuna, 201; on Euskal Ikasleen Biltzarra, 103, 135; on Goyheneche, Eugène, 117, 333n39; on HAS/EHAS, 181, 188, 189, 191–92; on IK, 182, 195, 200; on Legasse, Marc, 336n26, 336n29; on Third Republic, 28;
Jacobinism, 28, 31, 35, 50, 53, 59; centralizing nature of, 122, 131; contemporary, 227, 283, 289, 292, 295, 359n3; suspicion of culture and institutions in Iparralde, 57, 61, 325n62
Jarrai, 357n72, 353n107. *See also* Gazteriak; Haika; Segi
Jaureguiberry, Jean de, 105, 109, 110, 160
Jaureguiberry, Madeleine de, 110, 136, 334n74
Jazar, 174, 176, 189, 192, 193, 201, 346n39
Jiménez de Aberásturi, Juan Carlos, 105, 115, 335n6
Jones, Charles O., 245
Jospin, Lionel, 226, 249, 260, 356n42, 359n3
Juaristi, Jon, 41–42, 85, 322n35; on Basque nationalism, 50, 321n24, 330n15, 330n18; on Chaho, 75–77, 81–82

kale borroka (street violence), 197, 237, 353n106
Kanbo (Cambo-les-Bains), 63, 318n62, 337n5, 347n55
KAS. *See* Koordinadora Abertzale Sozialista
Kedourie, Elie, 50, 321n27
Kontseilua (pro-Euskara platform), 290
Koordinadora Abertzale Sozialista (KAS, Socialist Nationalist Coordinating Council), 187–89, 199, 202, 230–36, 346n31, 346n37, 353n92
Korrika, 351n47
Krutwig, Federico, 140–45, 151–52, 175, 182, 339n66, 342n93, 344n133

LAB. *See* Langile Abertzaleen Batzordeak
Labarrère, André, 213
Labastide. *See* Bastida
Labéguerie, Michel, 127–36, 149–64, 195, 273, 310, 337n4; as Christian Democrat

(founder of MDB), 127, 135, 158–60; as cultural activist, 127–28, 131–33, 136, 146, 158, 219, 337n5; discrepancies with Enbata, 127, 130, 153, 157, 160–64, 167, 271; in Enbata, 125, 149, 340n30; in public office, 127, 151, 153, 156–57, 160–62. *See also* Enbata; Mouvement Démocratique Basque

Labéguerie, Peyo, 127, 160, 294

Laborde, Cécile, 33–34

Laborde, Pierre, 332n19

Labourd. *See* Lapurdi

Lacq, 340n4

Lafitte, Pierre, 48, 59, 97–111, 130–40, 310, 342n74; as editor of *Herria*, 117, 119, 132–33, 136–39, 163–64, 338n27; as head of Aintzina (Eskualerriste) movement, 89, 103, 105, 117, 159–60, 333n39; Basque nationalism and, 89, 108–9, 133, 148, 305; dual national identity of, 88, 105, 133, 305; regionalism of, 104, 153. *See also* Aintzina (group); *Aintzina* (journal); Eskualerriste movement

Lafont, Robert, 41–42, 140, 142, 182, 320n95

Lamassoure, Alain, 228, 240, 261, 272, 277–78, 359n16

Lambert, Jean-Baptiste, 313

La Mennais, Jean-Marie Robert, 82

Landaburu, Pierre, 119–20, 336n26

Landarretche, Martin, 130

Langile Abertzaleen Batzordeak (LAB, Nationalist Workers' Councils), 359n2

language, 26, 36–37, 42, 267, 295–96; as national attribute, 19, 21, 22–23, 26–27; official, 24–25, 27, 35, 42, 298. *See also* Euskara; French language

Lapurdi, 59–63, 70–74, 94, 145, 153, 198, 300–1; administrative and territorial structure of, 315n1, 354n3; Basque-language and culture festivals in, 91; Basque nationalism in, 104, 191; *Biltzar* of, 60, 65–66, 72, 118, 222, 286, 288, 317n29; *cahiers* of, 59, 65–66; clergy in, 57; deportations in, 63; emigration from, 134; *fors* of, 42; French Revolution and, 34, 54–56, 83, 325n62; Gascon culture in, 256, 322–23n9; IK activity in, 186; immigration to, 219; nobility of, 56–57; pre-French Revolution institutions and privileges in, 34, 59, 83, 317n29; rural-urban divisions within, 322–23n9; Spanish incursions into, 24; Third Estate of, 53, 56, 59–60; tourism in, 98–99; trade and industry in, 67

Larraine (Larrau), 191

Larralde, Madeleine, 92, 324n43

Larran-Lange, Monique, 292

Larrau. *See* Larraine

Larre, Emile, 338n27

Larre, Jean-Louis "Popo," 195

Larresoro (Larressore), 29, 63, 191

Larressore. *See* Larresoro

Larronde, Jean-Claude, 104–10, 128, 131, 156–57, 204, 333n47, 333n51

Larzabal, Battitta, 191, 213

Larzabal, Mattin, 170–71

Larzabal, Piarres (Pierre), 117, 122, 133, 138–41, 149

Lasa, José Antonio, 195

Lasarte, José María, 129

Lasserre, Jean Jacques, 312–13

Lavisse, Ernest, 38–39

Ledru-Rollin, Alexandre Auguste, 77

Le Fur, Marc, 227

Legasse, Marc, 16, 18, 111, 113–28, 148, 151, 336n39; as candidate for elected office, 118–19, 122, 336n26; as critic of Basque nationalism centered in Hegoalde, 113–14, 116, 122–25; as proponent of civil disobedience, 113, 118–20, 126, 336n29

Lekorne (Mendionde), 63

Leroux, Pierre, 82

Letamendia, Francisco, 39–40, 52, 234–35, 256, 353n94

Letamendia, Pierre, 115, 159

Ligue Communiste Révolutionnaire (Revolutionary Communist League), 344n145

Likiniano, Félix, 122

Limonaire, Michel, 337n5

Linz, Juan J., 93, 113, 256, 303, 304

Lissar, Jean, 173, 344n141

Lizarra-Garazi Pact (1998), 253, 282–84, 356n55, 357n57

Locke, John, 32, 60

Lopez Adan, Emilio, 116, 339n64

Lorenzo Espinosa, José María, 330n13

Lorraine, 39, 99
Loti, Pierre, 41, 46–47, 132, 270
Louhossoa. *See* Luhuso
Louis XIV, 102, 144
Louis XVI, 53, 56, 72, 324n49
Louis XVIII, 53
Louis Philippe, 82
Luhuso (Louhossoa), 63

Macaye. *See* Makea
Madariaga, Iulen de, 165–66, 175
Madré, Louis, 156
Madrid, 25, 147, 262, 311, 329n81, 341n62
Maitia, Frantxoa, 292, 313, 258n81
Makea (Macaye), 63, 134, 151, 201
Malherbe, Jean Paul, 40, 155, 159, 166, 171
Manzanas, Melitón, 181, 343n101, 345n4
Marguirault, Jean-Claude "Xan," 180, 189, 191, 193
Marianne, symbol of France, 101–2, 254, 286–89, 357n60
Marie, Bernard, 292
Marseillaise, the (French national anthem), 54, 100
Martin, Christophe, 292
Martinez de Lezea, Toti, 324n43
Marx, Karl, 80, 295
Marxism, 159, 173, 187, 202, 339n66, 345n6
Marxist-Leninism, 167, 173, 181, 235, 344n145
maskarada, 217–20, 270, 350n34, 350n42. *See also* charivari; pastoral; *toberrak*
Mathieu, Henri, 146
Maule, 34, 38, 121, 140, 175, 210, 243, 313
Mauléon. *See* Maule
Maurras, Charles, 100–1
Mayte, Philippe, 138
MDB. *See* Mouvement Démocratique Basque
Mees, Ludger, 25, 335n11
Mende Berri, 171–73, 176, 201, 344n132, 346n39
Mendiboure, Jean, 159
Mendigoizaleak, 109, 334n70
Mendionde. *See* Lekorne
Mendisco, Bernard, 159
Menditarrak, 109, 334nn69–71
Mendizabal, Eustakio (Txikia), 169–70, 179
Mény, Yves, 245
Mestelan, Jacques, 334n67, 334n69, 334n71

Miangolarra, Paco, 164, 343n93
Michelet, Jules, 82, 102
Milafranga (Villefranque), 128
Millet-Barbe, Christian, 292
Miranda de Lage-Damon, Paloma, 47
Mirande, Jean-Pierre, 312
Mirande, Jon, 150, 340n17
Mitterand, François, 116, 182, 190–92, 203, 212–14, 222–23, 349n8
Mixe. *See* Amikuze
MLNV. *See* Movimiento de Liberación Nacional Vasco
MoDem. *See* Mouvement Démocratique
Moguel, Juan Antonio, 324n38, 324n49
Moho, Salvat, 71–72, 324n49
Mola, General Emilio, 108, 334n56
Moncey, Bon Adrien Jeannot de, 67–68
Mondorge, Guy, 313
Mondragón cooperative movement, 168, 214
Mongelos. *See* Monjolose
Monjolose (Mongelos), 263
Montesquieu, 57, 58, 60
Monzón, Telesforo de, 122, 129, 133, 149, 151, 173
Moors, 78, 85, 329n81
Mouguerre. *See* Muguerre
Mouvement Démocratique (MoDem, Democratic Movement), 312–13
Mouvement Démocratique Basque (MDB, Basque Democratic Movement), 155, 158–60, 167, 294. *See also* Christian Democracy
Mouvement Républicain et Citoyen (MRC, Citizen and Republican Movement), 359n3
Mouvement Républicain Populaire (MRP, Popular Republican Movement), 121, 141, 154, 159–60. *See also* Christian Democracy
Mouvement Rural de Jeunesse Chrétienne (Young Christians' Rural Movement), 344n145
Movimiento de Liberación Nacional Vasco (MLNV, Basque national Liberation Movement), 193, 199, 229–30, 233–37, 346n31, 353n92, 358n14. *See also* Izquierda Abertzale
MRP. *See* Mouvement Républicain Populaire
Mugerre (Mouguerre), 116, 323n18

Nafarroa. *See* Navarre

Nafarroa Beherea, 94, 240, 315n1; administration in, 34; Basque nationalism in, 104, 120–21, 173, 205; *cahiers* of, 54; emigration from, 134; Estates General of, 57–58, 65, 317n29; French Revolution in, 34, 54, 61, 66; IK activity in, 179, 186; notable politics in, 292; pre-French Revolution institutions and privileges in, 34, 42, 60, 317n29

Napoleon I, 49, 50, 53, 66–69, 71, 83, 86, 102, 317n33

Napoleon III, 120

Napoleonic Wars, 67, 324n39

national community, 23, 25, 26, 52, 99; Basque, 83, 109, 144; French, 27, 32, 33, 35, 99. *See also* collective (group) identity; identity; national consciousness

national consciousness, 16–18, 37, 38, 40, 84–85; Basque, 55, 84–85, 91, 97, 131–48, 171–72, 295–96, 310; French, 100; raising, 176, 181, 219. *See also* collective memory; identity; national community

National Front, French, 205

national society, 23–26, 32, 36, 52. *See also* identity; national community; national consciousness

nationalism, 15–16; "civic," 319n91; elites, role of in, 50; emotional content of, 330n15; goals of, 51; instrumentalist view of, 50; "peripheral," 15–16, 42, 85, 99, 126, 182, 234, 267–68; popular or populist, 42; progressive, 42; reactionary, 42; state, 319n91; theories of, 15–16, 321n20. *See also* Basque nationalism; French nationalism; Spanish nationalism

Navarre, 47, 67, 83, 225, 315n1, 359n4; Basque nationalism in, 18, 84, 91, 114; Carlism in, 77, 80, 81, 107, 350n43; cultural renaissance in, 45, 91; Foral Community of, 202, 241, 300, 315n1, 358n14

Netherlands, the, 53, 60

New Phoenicia, plan for, 49, 53, 66–69, 325n69. *See also* Garat, Dominique-Joseph

Noblia, Argitxu, 136, 163

Noblia, Patxi, 214, 215, 342n77

"notables," 28–32, 99, 130, 134, 155, 223, 269, 291–92; anti-Basque positions of, 31, 144, 167, 223, 264, 298, 306, 354n15; loss of power, 148–49, 155, 158, 281, 291–92, 312–13; political importance of, 30–32, 107, 154, 162, 273, 291, 305, 312; pro-Basque positions of, 31, 148–59, 166, 204, 246–47, 262, 305

Occitan language, 118, 135, 298, 352n66. *See also* Gascon language and culture

Occitania, 28, 41, 182; nationalism in, 142, 151, 182. *See also* Gascon language and culture

Ohiarzabal, Gabi, 171

Oldartzen, 231, 232, 352n89

Olóriz, Hermilio de, 84

Oloron, 34, 210, 243, 244

Olson, Mancur, 50

Onesta, Gérard, 285

Ordóñez, Gregorio, 353n110

Ordre Nouveau, 105, 106

Oronos, Michel, 224

Orpustan, Jean Baptiste, 324n49

Ospital, André, 119–20, 156, 157, 165, 336n26

Ospital, Pantxo, 171

Otaegi, Angel, 174, 183, 188

Oyharçabal, Beñat, 318n60, 318n64, 330n10

Pablo, Santiago de, 25, 335n11

Pagola, Manex, 163, 191

Paredes Manot, Juan ("Txiki"), 174, 183, 188

Paris, as cultural center, 36, 70, 145; Basques in, 103, 116, 137, 146, 337n5; as economic center, 26, 32, 40, 137, 147; events of May 1968 in, 148, 160, 168, 234; IK activity in, 197; as political center, 22, 25–26, 32, 36, 40, 99, 147, 210, 305; as revolutionary center, 57

Parti Communiste Français (PCF, French Communist Party), 119, 154, 157, 205, 253, 292, 336n30

Parti Nationaliste Basque (PNB, Basque Nationalist Party, Iparralde), 161, 203–4, 239, 251–54, 281, 294, 356n48; electoral strategy and performance of, 204, 284, 293, 311–12, 342n76; links with UDF,

160. *See also* Christian Democracy; Partido Nacionalista Vasco
Parti Radical (Radical Party), 135, 139, 154
Parti Socialiste (PS, Socialist Party), 247–57, 303, 313; anti-Basque *département* stance of, 213, 253, 349n13, 356n58, 358n13; electoral performance of, 213, 312–13; in Iparralde, 190–91, 252, 257–61, 271–78, 292–93, 356n58, 357n81; pro-Basque institucional stance of, 209, 212–13, 247–52, 254–55, 260, 356n48; regionalism of, 182, 208, 222–23, 356n42. *See also* Section Française de l'Internationale Ouvrière
Parti Socialiste Unifié (PSU, Unified Socialist Party), 190, 344n145
Partido Nacionalista Vasco (PNV, Basque Nationalist Party, Hegoalde), 93, 103, 107–10, 122–23, 145, 335n14, 356n55; hegemony of, 188; Iparralde and, 97, 114–16, 202–3, 282, 335nn6–7, 335n11, 357n72; relations with Enbata, 165–66; relations with ETA, 142, 165. *See also* Christian Democracy; Parti Nationaliste Basque
Partido Popular (PP, Popular Party), 353n110
Partido Socialista de Euskadi (PSE, Socialist Party of the Basque Country), 343n109
Partido Socialista Obrero Español (PSOE, Spanish Socialist Party), 343n109
pastoral (popular rural theater), 37, 81, 87, 217–20, 319n70, 350n29, 350–51n43
Patxa, 232, 352n89
Pau, 120, 210, 223, 240, 264, 319n87, 340n4; Demo activity in, 286, 289; IK activity in, 196, 197
PCF. *See* Parti Communiste Français
Peillen, Txomin, 24
Pérez-Agote, Alfonso, 48–49, 268,
periphery, notion of, 15–32, 40–42, 98–100, 113–14, 267–69, 298, 335n2
Péry, Nicole, 225, 249
Pétain, Marshal, 105
petite patrie, logic of, 16, 18, 83, 105, 141, 157–58. See also *grande patrie*, logic of
Physiocratic thought, 56–57, 323n13
Pinet, Jacques, 65
Pius VII, Pope, 317n33
Pius XII, Pope, 119

Pizkundea, 223, 351n56
PNB. *See* Parti Nationaliste Basque
PNV. *See* Partido Nacionalista Vasco
Pochelu, Vincent, 151
political violence. *See under* Iparralde
Pompidou, Georges, 162
Popular Front (France), 106, 333n47
Popular Front (Spain), 107
Portugal, 68
Poulou, Daniel, 227, 313
Poulou, Jean, 151, 165
PS. *See* Parti Socialiste

Quebecois nationalism, 151
Quinet, Edgar, 82

Radio Euzkadi-Euzkadi Irratia, 116, 203
Raffarin, Jean-Pierre, 226–27, 246, 260, 263, 276–77
Rassemblement du Peuple Français (RPF, Rally of the French People), 154, 157. *See also* Gaullism
Rassemblement pour la République (RPR, Rally for the Republic), 31, 275, 341n64, 356n48, 357n77; anti-Basque *département* stance of, 248, 253, 255–56, 260, 275; pro-Basque *départment* sentiment within, 247, 257. *See also* Gaullism
Ravail, Jean (Ravail Mission), 223, 354n15
regionalism, 15, 98, 126, 140, 179, 270, 305–6; of EGB, 128; of Eskualerristes, 96–98, 104–7, 111, 133, 148, 334n57; of PNB, 204; of PS, 182, 208
Renan, Ernest, 100
Ripert, Georges, 117–18
Robespierre, 61
Rocard, Michel, 349n8
Rodríguez, José Antonio, 25, 335n11
Romans, 69, 78, 79
Rousseau, Jean-Jacques, 32–34, 58–61, 68, 298, 318n62, 323n16
RPF. *See* Rassemblement du Peuple Français
RPR. *See* Rassemblement pour la République
Rubiralta, Fermín, 47

Saint-Étienne-de-Baïgorry. *See* Baigorri
Saint-Jean-de-Luz. *See* Donibane Lohizune
Saint-Jean-Pied-de-Port. *See* Donibane Garazi

Saint-Martin-d'Arrosa. *See* Arrosa
Saint-Palais. *See* Donapaleu
Saint-Pée-sur-Nivelle. *See* Senpere
Saint Pierre, Jean, 132
Saint-Pierre-d'Irube. *See* Hiriburu
Salaberry, Etienne, 133, 141
Salagoïty, Léon, 156
Sallaberry, Jean-Baptiste, 313
Sapède, Christian, 271, 354n12
Sara (Sare), 63, 65, 79, 151, 318n62
Sare. *See* Sara
Sarkozy, Nicolas, 313
Sarrailh, Jean, 129
Sarraillet, Jakes, 231
Sartre, Jean Paul, 339n64
Savarèse, Eric, 38, 100–1
Schnapper, Dominique, 33
Seaska, 201–2, 225
Second Republic (1848–52), 77
Second Spanish Republic (1931–36), 107
Section Française de l'Internationale Ouvrière (SFIO, Socialist Party), 154. *See also* Parti Socialiste
Segi, 283, 284, 353n107, 357n72. *See also* Gazteriak; Haika; Jarrai
Séguéla, Juliette, 313
self-determination, 33, 119, 124, 153; for Algeria, 141, 341n37; for Basque Country, 141, 152, 197–98, 202, 231–32, 236, 341n33
Senpere (Saint-Pée-sur-Nivelle), 325n52
SFIO. *See* Section Française de l'Internationale Ouvrière
Sièyes, Abbé Emmanuel Joseph, 34, 56, 61
Silviet (foral institution of Zuberoa), 28, 305, 317n29
Sistiague, Martine, 215–16
Smith, Anthony D., 16–17, 18, 37–38, 51–52, 73, 79, 329n85
social plausibility (structure of), 49, 268, 270, 329n87, 358n9; for Basque Country, 26, 87, 90, 268, 270, 274; for French state, 26, 268
social reality, 48, 185, 218, 240, 241, 261
Sohüta (Chéraute), 191
Sota, Manu de la, 129, 166
Sota y MacMahon, Verónica de la, 122
Soule. *See* Zuberoa

Souraïde. *See* Zuraide
sovereignty, 15, 67, 310; AB and, 233, 281–83; as definition of state, 23, 24, 33, 34, 46, 298; as goal of Basque nationalism, 43, 95, 251, 286; Enbata and, 148, 152; Eraikitzen and, 198; HB and, 231; IK and, 197
Spain, 45–46, 68, 78, 80, 86, 115, 147; anti-Basque *department* stance of, 213, 358n13; border with France, 24, 63, 68; Franco regime, 113–14, 174–75, 179, 203; *fueros* in, 315n2, 316n22; isolationism of, 24; transition to democracy, 114, 160, 199, 203, 343n109, 346n31; war with France, 24, 39, 55–57, 61–64, 67, 72, 324n38; weakness of, 25–26. *See also* Spanish Civil War
Spanish Civil War, 22, 106–10, 219, 334n66; refugees from in Iparralde, 96, 104, 107, 114–16, 151, 176, 202–3
Spanish language, 75, 84, 115
Spanish nationalism, 25, 358n4. *See also* Basque nationalism; French nationalism; nationalism
state, the, 15–17, 22–48, 52–54, 268–69, 298, 305, 321n27
statism, 97, 99, 105, 107
Sud-Ouest, 176, 257, 272, 325n52, 349n13
Switzerland, 70, 134

Tardets. *See* Atharratze
Tarrow, Sidney G., 254, 286
Tejerina, Benjamín, 17–18
Terrier, Léon-Albert, 129
territory, as national attribute, 19, 23
terrorism, 85, 262, 285, 287
Third Republic (1870–1940), 86, 317n32, 322–23n9, 324n38; Basque language and culture during, 36, 61, 296, 298, 318n61; educational policies of, 28, 38, 54, 82, 100–1; French nationalism of, 25, 28, 86, 94, 97–102; religious policies of, 29, 36
Thoenig, Jean-Claude, 245
Thorez, Maurice, 119, 336n30
toberrak (form of charivari), 218–20, 351n46
Torre, Gorka, 285
Treaty of the Pyrenees (1679), 23–24
"Txiki." *See* Paredes Manot, Juan
"Txikia." *See* Mendizabal, Eustakio

"Txillardegi." *See* Alvarez Enparantza, Jose Luis

Udalbiltza, 285, 357n72
UDF. *See* Union pour la Démocratie Française
UDR. *See* Union des Démocrates pour la République
UMP. *See* Union pour un Mouvement Populaire
Union des Démocrates pour la République (UDR, Union of Democrats for the Republic), 190, 341n48. *See also* Union pour la Nouvelle République
Union for the Defense of Basque Issues, 158
Union pour la Démocratie Française (UDF, Union for French Democracy), 31, 292–94, 342n64, 356n48, 357n77; pro-Basque nature of, 160, 260, 294, 356n54; pro-French nature of, 248, 257, 303, 356n54. *See also* Centre Démocratique; Christian Democracy
Union pour la Nouvelle République (UNR, Union for the New Republic), 157, 159, 342n64. *See also* Gaullism
Union pour un Mouvement Populaire (UMP, Union for a Popular Movement), 260, 275, 292–93, 312–13, 347n69, 357n77
United States, the, 60
UNR. *See* Union pour la Nouvelle République
Urcuit. *See* Urketa
Urepele (Urepel), 173
Urketa (Urcuit), 191
Urkizu, Patri, 218, 324n49
Urquijo, Julio de, 130
Urruña (Urrugne), 91
Urteaga, Eguzki, 141
Ustaritz. *See* Uztaritze
Uztaritze (Ustaritz), 56, 128, 288, 323n18, 337n5; elections in, 201, 205, 313

Vera de Bidasoa. *See* Bera
Vichy government in France (1940–44), 116, 117
Villefranque. *See* Milafranga
Villepin, Dominique de, 228, 342n83
Vizcaya. *See* Bizkaia
Vrignon, Bixente, 170, 176, 176, 183, 189, 343n102, 346n40

Walloon nationalism, 151
Watson, Cameron, 102
Weber, Eugen, 36, 86, 101–2, 322–23n9, 324n38, 325n60, 329n86
Weber, Max, 46, 267
Wilson, Thomas M., 23
World War I, 39–40, 97–98, 101–2, 319n87; effects of, 18, 97, 101; resulting identity crisis of, 22, 40, 48
World War II, 40, 43, 114, 116, 132, 133, 158; Nazi occupation of France during, 333n46

Xan Committees, 180, 184, 186, 189–93. *See also* Marguirault, Jean-Claude "Xan"
"xuriak" (Catholic conservatives), 92, 98, 101. *See also* "gorriak"

Ybarnégaray, Jean, 101, 107, 116, 132, 334n53; French nationalism of, 40, 111, 295

Zabala, José Ignacio, 195
Zabalo, Joseph, 73, 75, 76, 81, 321n31
Zald, Mayer N., 288–89
"Zazpiak Bat" (The Seven Are One), political slogan, 90, 93–95, 118, 132, 200
zero-sum game of identity. *See under* identity
Ziburu (Ciboure), 57, 151, 174, 292
Zuberoa, 46, 70, 94, 121, 145, 190, 247, 255, 272, 300, 301, 315n1, 324n49, 354n6; Basque nationalism in, 104, 191, 210; *cahiers* of, 57–59; communications in, 240; economic development in, 211, 244, 285, 340n5; French Revolution and, 54, 65–66; IK activity in, 186; industry in, 98–99, 148; festivals (pastoral and *maskarada*) in, 87, 217–20, 350n30, 350nn42–43; peasant revolt led by Matalas in, 77, 293; pre-French Revolution institutions and privileges in, 28, 34–35, 42, 317n29
Zulaika, Joseba, 330n15
Zumalacarrégui, Tomás, 49, 79–81, 84, 89, 328n59, 350n43. *See also* Carlism; Carlist Wars (1833–39 and 1873–76); Carlists; Chaho, Agosti
Zuraide (Souraïde), 63
Zutik, 238, 284, 353n111, 359n4